Finland

Sweden

Norway

Germany

Czech
Republic

enmark

Neth.

Poland

tria

France

nia

Spain  Italy

Croatia

Serbia

Albania

Tunisia

Algeria

Mali

Niger

Nigeria

Benin

Togo

a

roon

r. Rep.

atorial
Guinea

Gabon

o. Congo

Zambia

Namibia

Zimbabwe

South Africa

Botswana

Estonia

Latvia

Lithuania

Belarus

Slovakia

Hungary

Romania

Ukraine

Moldova

Bulgaria

Greece

Turkey

Macedonia   Leb.

Cyprus

Syria

Iraq

Iran

Kuwait

Jordan

Bahrain

Saudi
Arabia

Israel

Egypt

Eritrea

Sudan

Ethiopia

Libya

Chad

Zaire

Angola

Malawi

Mozambique

Swaziland

Lesotho

Georgia

Armenia

Azerbaijan

Kazakhstan

Kyrgystan

Uzbekistan

Tajikistan

Turkmenistan

Afghanistan

Bhutan

Pakistan

Nepal

U.A.E.

Qatar

Oman

Yemen

Djibouti

Somalia

Uganda

Kenya

Rwanda

Burundi

Tanzania

Mauritius

Madagascar

Russia

Mongolia

N. Korea

China

S. Korea

Taiwan

Japan

India

Myanmar

Vietnam

Bangladesh

Laos

Philippines

Cambodia

Malaysia

Thailand

Sri Lanka

Singapore

Papua-
New Guinea

Indonesia

Australia

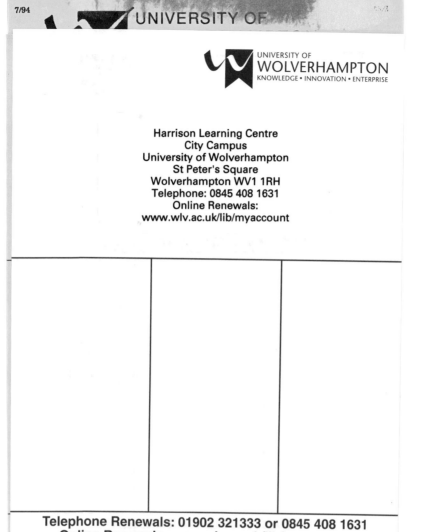

# WORLD POLITICS

# WORLD POLITICS

*THE MENU FOR CHOICE*

*Fifth Edition*

**Bruce Russett**

*Dean Acheson Professor of International Relations and Political Science*

*Yale University*

**Harvey Starr**

*Dag Hammarskjold Professor in International Affairs*

*University of South Carolina*

**W. H. FREEMAN AND COMPANY**
New York

Library of Congress Cataloging-in-Publication Data

Russett, Bruce M.
    World politics : the menu for choice / Bruce Russett, Harvey
Starr. — 5th ed.
        p.   cm.
    Includes bibliographical references and index.
    ISBN 0–7167–2821–4. — ISBN 0–7167–2820–6. (pbk.)
    1. International relations.    I. Starr, Harvey.    II. Title.
JX1391.R88    1995
327—dc20                                                    95-39863
                                                                CIP

Printed in the United States of America

First printing 1996, HP

# CONTENTS

## 6   RELATIONS BETWEEN STATES: BASES AND ANALYSIS OF POWER   115

## 7   RELATIONS BETWEEN STATES: INSTRUMENTS OF INFLUENCE   138

## 8   DOMESTIC CONSTRAINTS: DO COUNTRIES WITH DIFFERENT ECONOMIC, SOCIAL, AND POLITICAL SYSTEMS PRODUCE DIFFERENT FOREIGN POLICIES?   161

# PREFACE

In the three years since we prepared the fourth edition of this book we have witnessed a continuing revolution in world politics. With the end of cold war bipolarity; the resurgence of nationalism in areas formerly under authoritarian rule; and a new focus on democracy, economics, and ecology as global issues; all analysts have had their basic assumptions and theories challenged, and their policy recommendations superseded. The authors of this book are no exceptions, though we think earlier editions did provide readers with some important tools for thinking about these matters. From its first edition, for example, we anticipated the debate about whether the spread of democracy might lead to a more peaceful world and wrote at length about the challenges of promoting greater international cooperation to deal with collective problems, emphasizing the environmental issues that now are moving to the top of the global agenda. Although the fifth edition brings the relationship between democracy, development, and peace into sharper focus, we had addressed these concerns in the first edition, at a time when others focused more narrowly on military security.

No one can hope fully to absorb or to keep pace with such changes. A broad and self-conscious theoretical perspective remains the best resource for comprehending and coping with change. We have reflected the changing currents in world politics through the following:

- We have provided more extensive coverage of the nature and consequences of change in the world system, highlighting the relationship among economic growth, democracy, and peace in an increasingly interdependent world.

- We have highlighted the role and impact of economics in understanding the global system.

- We give stronger emphasis to the politics of a nonbipolar world, reflecting the end of the cold war and the paradox of the United States as the only power with a global military reach but an ever more vulnerable economy.

- We provide more historical background, especially on the origins and nature of the state and the system of sovereign states that has evolved since the Treaty of Westphalia in the mid-seventeenth century; this is crucial given the contemporary challenges to both sovereignty and that system of states.

- We have expanded the discussion of transnational relations and of nonstate actors such as the newly strengthened and relevant United Nations.

- We have clarified important concepts such as democracy and development and provided additional examples of international policy (e.g., in arms control or international trade) to illustrate important theories in action.

- We have maintained and strengthened the contrast among realist, transnationalist, and radical perspectives, showing both the value of the largely dominant realist paradigm and its increasingly evident limitations.

■ We have provided a revised and expanded test bank, available in printed form or on disk for IBM or MAC personal computers. We are also proud to announce the creation of a *World Politics: The Menu for Choice* home page on the Internet (http://www.whfreeman.com/world-politics) with a variety of features designed specifically for this textbook—including syllabi exchanges, current events, maps, and data sets.

During the longer-run changes of recent decades we have also witnessed a revolution in the discipline itself. We have changed the ways we think about the subject: standards of concept formation, of logic, and of evidence are markedly different from what they were. If there has been a revolution in the study of world politics, it can be consolidated only when we have the pedagogical skill and tools to educate the next generation; otherwise, the revolution will experience a well-deserved reaction. The consolidation we have tried for in *World Politics* is inclusive rather than exclusive: we have sought to synthesize the best of the older tradition with newer approaches.

First, we have provided a substantial component of theory, from older and newer sources. Students must learn something about how theory is constructed and tested, and we therefore deal to some degree with scientific method, providing some "how-to" material and standards for recognizing well-executed research. We stress the importance of developing a respect for evidence and learning to recognize a statement for which no evidence can be relevant, and we provide a perspective on "how-to-think-about-it." To survive in a rapidly changing world as active citizens rather than passive objects of historical forces, people must develop a good set of basic concepts and questions, a taste for analysis, a certain degree of skepticism for the "revealed wisdom" of authority, and some tolerance for ambiguity on a subject—the behavior of large human organizations coping with very complex problems—for which the extent of our understanding is, at best, barely adequate.

Second, we have provided a substantial amount of historical and contemporary factual material about the world. One kind of fact is the evidence needed to support or refute major theoretical statements. We have tried to give the student some sense of the volume and quality of evidence relevant to various statements. When we know the evidence to be reasonably solid, we have tried to document it. When we consider the evidence sparse or ambiguous, we have tried to indicate that fact. We have given some references to empirical research, so that students—or instructors—will not have to take our statements on faith, but we have tried not to burden readers with scientific detail or pedantry.

Another kind of essential fact is, simply, information about what it is, and has been, like "out there." History and information about the contemporary system are essential. Therefore, we have also provided material on the characteristics of the major national and nonnational participants in world politics and on the scope and function of major institutions. We have frequently introduced or punctuated our theoretical discussions with detail on how the world works or has worked. The reader will see examples of this not only in the text but also in endpaper maps and the two appendixes: a chronology and a set of comparative data on the characteristics of modern states. In this we have tried to walk a path that will have some appeal to traditionalists as well as to "hard-nosed" scientists.

Any consolidation demands a concern with questions of value: what the world "should" be like as well as what it is like. Sometimes all parties can gain; sometimes one's security is another's insecurity. At times we must choose between equity and security or between peace and justice. Students need guidance on how choices can be made or perhaps avoided, guidance that attends to both the ethical and the empirical dimensions of choice.

Finally, the substance of what is taught today is very different from the substance of courses taught a decade or two ago. In *World Politics* we have tried to convey a more broadly conceived idea of security by combining discussions of military issues with discussions of international political economy and to suggest how the two are related, for example, in the causes and consequences of arms races and in world environmental problems. At the end of the book we show how the needs for growth, equity, political liberty, and peace are inextricably linked.

We have organized the book into two major parts. Part I introduces the student to the modern study of world politics and sets out the six levels of analysis we find useful: the global system, relations between states, the societal level, the governmental level, roles, and the individual actor. The book's subtitle, *The Menu for Choice*, illustrates our perspective that decision makers are in fact limited in their selections by the rather constrained set of options presented by global conditions. (The menu analogy appropriately evokes images of both restaurants and computers.) We discuss and illustrate how influences at various levels affect the process or act of choice.

In Part II we apply these analytical perspectives to particular issues. Topics we consider include arms races, deterrence, and arms control; theories about the economic relations among states, and the pressing dilemma of development facing poor countries; the implications of interdependence among industralized countries (we try to understand why these countries are, almost without precedent or parallel, at peace among themselves); the problems of achieving collective goods in the context of global environmental problems; the role of international organizations; and, finally, an evaluation of demands for continued economic growth in a world of scarce resources and population pressures. We try to communicate a sense that a systematic use of theory is essential to any comprehension of these very pressing contemporary issues.

■ ■ ■

We owe thanks to innumerable colleagues and students over the years as we have worked toward producing this book. Rather than single out some for expressions of gratitude here, we will pass over those who in the past contributed to the formation of our thinking. Many of them, though not all, will find themselves footnoted. We wish to thank all those who have read and commented on parts or all of this book in its journey from the first to the fifth edition: Francis Adams, William Avery, Andrew Bennett, Bruce Bueno de Mesquita, Steven Chan, Claudio Cioffi-Revilla, Major Delane E. Clark, David Clinton, Robert Dorf, Raymond Duvall, Nader Entessar, Michael Francis, John R. Freeman, Scott Sigmund Gartner, F. Gregory Gause, Guy Gosselin, Roger Hamburg, Robert Harkavy, Jeffrey Hart, Terrence Hopmann, Darril Hudson, Patrick James, Robert Jervis, Brian Job, Robert Keohane, Robert Mandel, Zeev Maoz, Douglas Nelson, Rene Peritz, James Ray, J. Rogers, J. David Singer, Randolph Siverson, Patricia Stein Wrightson, Michael Stohl, Richard Stoll, Stuart Thorson, Herbert Tillema, and Dina Zinnes. Thanks also to Susan Finnemore Brennan, Senior Editor at W. H. Freeman and Company, to Shannon Lindsey Blanton who served as research assistant on the fifth edition, and especially to Mike Ward for his creative and diligent efforts to bring about the home page on the Internet. Parts of the book represent research done with the aid of grants from the Ford Foundation, the John D. and Catherine T. MacArthur Foundation, the National Science Foundation, the United States Institute of Peace, and the World Society Foundation (Switzerland). Over the course of five editions our home universities—Yale, Indiana, and South Carolina—have provided truly fine environments for research and reflection. We hope that all these people and institutions will in some degree be pleased with the outcome; any embarrassment with it must be ours alone.

Bruce Russett
Harvey Starr
September 1995

## Analytical Dimensions

*I would rather understand a single cause
than be king of Persia.*
—DEMOCRITUS OF ABDER

# ANALYZING WORLD POLITICS: LEVELS OF ANALYSIS AND CONSTRAINT

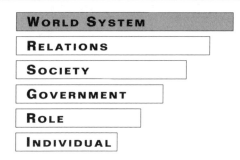

WORLD SYSTEM

RELATIONS

SOCIETY

GOVERNMENT

ROLE

INDIVIDUAL

## THREE FOREIGN POLICY DECISIONS

### Ending the Cold War

In November 1988 Margaret Thatcher, then British prime minister, proclaimed, "The cold war is over." Events since then have dramatically confirmed her judgment. The cold war, which had dominated world politics for more than 40 years, enforcing political domination on hundreds of millions of people and threatening to bring war on billions, was indeed over. The basic values of the West (democratic government and free-market economics) had triumphed—and the end of the cold war was then confirmed, even initiated, by the leader of the "losing" state, Soviet President Mikhail Gorbachev.

The events came in a cascade. First, Gorbachev made limited political and economic reforms in the Soviet Union. Then free elections ousted the communist governments in most of Eastern Europe, and Gorbachev made no move to intervene in their support. In November 1989 the Berlin Wall was breached, and by October 1990 East and West Germany were united. Gorbachev took no military or political action to save what had been the Soviet Union's most important and loyal ally. In response to demands from the new anticommunist governments, Gorbachev withdrew all Soviet military forces from Czechoslovakia and Hungary in 1991 and concluded a major arms reduction agreement with the West. Nearly all the formerly antagonistic NATO and Warsaw Pact countries agreed to reduce their military forces, the Soviets accepting disproportionately deep cuts. Soviet forces assumed a defensive posture, unable to mount any threat of invading Western Europe. Even the Warsaw Pact between the USSR and its former East European satellites—the linchpin of Soviet security and control—was disbanded in 1991, as was the Council for Mutual Economic Assistance (COMECON), which had regulated trade among these countries for over 40 years. Gorbachev announced that Soviet troops would come home, without victory, from the war in Afghanistan, and he insisted that Soviet-dependent governments like that in Nicaragua face the consequences of elections. At home, open dissent and secessionist movements emerged in many Soviet republics; free elections resulted in anticommunist governments in several and brought the end of the communist monopoly on power everywhere. In fact, by the end of 1991, the Soviet Union itself had dissolved as a single entity, ultimately leaving the state of Russia and 14 other successor states of the former Soviet Union (FSU).[1] Gorbachev twisted and turned like an adroit slalom skier, but the slope he was on seemed to be leading ever nearer to drastic economic and political changes. After a reactionary coup against Gorbachev in August 1991 failed, Boris Yeltsin forced even more radical changes.

The end of the cold war, as initiated by Gorbachev's actions, was as astonishing as it was swift. It was one of those world-shaking turns that few theories either clearly anticipate or explain well after the fact. Nevertheless, we have to grope toward an understanding, and in doing so we can at least offer some possible explanations even if we can prove little.

In one clear sense, Gorbachev's own personal characteristics deserve much of the credit. After a series of aging leaders in ill health (his predecessors, Leonid Brezhnev, Yuri Andropov, and Konstantin Chernenko, all died within a three-year period), Gorbachev was only 53 when he came to power. He was vigorous, a skilled politician, and committed to reforming (but not necessarily to revolutionizing) the Soviet system.

---

[1] The collapse of the Soviet Union is recounted by Robert V. Daniels, *The End of the Communist Revolution* (London: Routledge, 1993).

His fresh perspectives, energy, drive, and intelligence were essential to the task. Previous leaders might have seen the need for some reforms but were unable or unwilling to make dramatic changes.[2]

Exclusive attention to Gorbachev's personal qualities, however, leaves much out. He changed Soviet domestic and foreign policies because they hadn't worked even by standards widely accepted among communist leaders. The Soviet economy was stagnant, with per capita income showing essentially no growth since the late 1970s, and the life expectancy of Soviet citizens was dropping. The insular and centrally planned Soviet economy, dependent on heavy industry and collective farms, was increasingly unable to compete in a world market based on innovation driven by high technology and the free flow of goods, capital, and information within and between states. The burden of military spending bore down ever more painfully on Soviet living standards, as did Soviet expenditures to prop up allies in Africa, Asia, and Central America. The USSR had overreached itself globally, acquiring weak clients and eroding its own security. Something had to give—why did it give then, rather than later, or sooner?

Another element was surely the increasingly assertive political and military competition the Soviet Union faced from the United States, which intensified in the decade or so before Gorbachev made his big changes. In the last years of the Carter administration and more dramatically in the Reagan years, the United States and its allies began a spurt of additions to NATO military capabilities, especially by the development and deployment of high-tech weapons that exploited Western scientific advances. American military assistance to opponents of Soviet-backed regimes in Afghanistan, Angola, Cambodia, Nicaragua, and elsewhere raised the costs to the USSR of supporting those governments. Again, the Soviet Union had always been technologically behind the West and had long borne heavy costs. Why could it have not maintained itself longer? In addition, the United States was also feeling the burdens of the cold war and by 1986 was no longer increasing its own military expenditures. American willingness to respond carefully to Soviet overtures, not exploiting Soviet weakness so as to risk "enraging a cornered bear," played an important part in allowing Soviet liberalization to continue.

Yet another influence was the spread of information across international borders, and especially in both directions across what had been known as the Iron Curtain. Citizens of communist countries could know more and more about the prosperity and political liberties enjoyed by their counterparts in the West. By the 1980s most East Germans could regularly watch West German television, and informal personal contacts between Western and Eastern peoples were increasingly difficult to regulate. Under pressure of the human-rights provisions of the wide-ranging Helsinki Accords of 1975, communist governments more and more had to tolerate dissident movements. Western news agencies regularly operated in East European and Soviet cities;

---

[2] For an in-depth look at the personal background and qualities of the man who saw things differently from his predecessors, see Gail Sheehy, *The Man Who Changed the World: The Lives of Mikhail S. Gorbachev* (New York: Harper Collins, 1990).

any violent crackdown on dissent would have been shown immediately on hundreds of millions of television screens around the globe. Technological and cultural changes in the world were making communist efforts to insulate their people from world developments ever more anachronistic, ineffective, and costly. Furthermore, relaxation of the Soviet grip in Eastern Europe interacted with relaxation at home.

All these factors—the nature of the Soviet leadership, domestic political and economic decay, international political competition, global information flows—suggest reasons why the cold war ended. But no single explanation completely dominates the others, nor does it explain why the end came just when it did. If Gorbachev himself was essential to the changes, that still begs the question of why Gorbachev was ready to change, even at enormous personal and national risk. Gorbachev faced opportunities and constraints; he was willing to make certain choices and was given very little latitude to make others. The reasons we list suggest some of the range of influences on world politics that any serious analyst must consider.

## Dropping the Atomic Bomb

Another war—an enormously destructive hot one—ended very differently. On August 6, 1945, the U.S. bomber *Enola Gay* dropped an atomic bomb on the Japanese city of Hiroshima. Coupled with the explosion of another bomb over Nagasaki three days later, this act precipitated the Japanese surrender and the end of World War II. (It also set in place far-reaching influences on the cold war.) Nearly 200,000 people, most of them noncombatant civilians, ultimately died from the explosions. These two bombings represented the first and so far the last time nuclear weapons were used against enemy targets. Exploding a bomb of this magnitude (about 4,000 times more powerful than the biggest conventional World War II explosive) marked an enormous leap in "killing ability." At the same time it brought forth the age of nuclear deterrence, when peace among the great powers was kept, at least in part, by the awesome threat of mutual annihilation. At the time of these bombings, both scientists and statesmen realized that they were engaged in an act that would fundamentally change the future; the nuclear physicist J. Robert Oppenheimer, on watching the first test explosion a month before Hiroshima, quoted to himself the phrase from the Hindu scripture, the *Bhagavad Gita*, "I am become death, destroyer of worlds."

Despite the magnitude of this act and the precedents it set, there was remarkably little discussion within the American government as to whether the bomb should be used in war. Questions of morality were either ignored or quickly stilled with the argument that, overall, use of the bomb would save lives. The only alternative to using the bomb to force Japan's surrender seemed to be an American invasion of the Japanese home islands, in which tens of thousands of Americans and hundreds of thousands of Japanese casualties could be expected. U.S. Secretary of War Henry L. Stimson later wrote, "At no time did I ever hear it suggested by the President, or by other responsible members of the government, that atomic energy should not be used in war." British Prime Minister Winston Churchill reported that "the decision whether or not to use the atomic bomb to compel the surrender of Japan was never even an issue. There was unanimous, automatic, unquestioned agreement."[3] How can we explain this?

Particular characteristics of President Harry Truman may have made some difference. Before President Franklin Roosevelt's death in April 1945 it was assumed that the atomic bomb would be used in combat, although Roosevelt had not entirely ruled out the possibility of first warning the enemy and demonstrating the power of the bomb in a test. But Truman was inexperienced and uninformed about foreign affairs; when he became president he was not even aware of the atomic bomb project. He was therefore in no position to challenge the existing basic assumption about the bomb's intended use or to dissent sharply from the military and foreign policy plans that had been put into effect by the advisers he inherited from Roosevelt. Only one adviser (Admiral William Leahy, whose opinion had already been devalued by his prediction that the bomb would not work at all) did not accept the consensus. There was some disagreement among the nuclear scientists who had produced the bomb, but in the end the prevailing opinion was that since they could "propose no technical demonstration likely to bring an end to the war; we can see no acceptable alternative to direct military use."

Truman was caught up in the near unanimity around him; Roosevelt, although more experienced and politically stronger, probably would not have behaved much differently. Bureaucratic momentum carried matters along, and it would have required either a very unusual president or an exceptionally open structure of decision making to slow that momentum. Furthermore, the alternative seemed technically and politically dangerous. The Japanese could be warned and the bomb tested publicly in some deserted spot, but there was a risk that the bomb would not go off or not look very impressive. The enemy would be uncowed, and, some advisers feared, Congress would be in a political uproar over the fizzled demonstration and consequent American casualties suffered in an invasion. Nowhere—in the executive branch, in Congress, or in the public at large—was there much disagreement over the need to end the war as soon as possible, principally to spare American lives. Consequently, there were few moral restraints on the use of atomic weapons in war. Certainly there had been little objection earlier to the massive conventional bombing of civilian targets in Germany and Japan.

The basic constraints, therefore, stemmed from the international situation: war against a determined opponent in an era when the moral and legal restrictions on warfare were few. Moreover, the international balance of forces likely to emerge after the war reinforced this perspective. The wartime Soviet–American alliance was deteriorating rapidly, especially in the face of severe disagreements about who should control Eastern Europe. Most American decision makers welcomed the atomic bomb as a master card of "atomic diplomacy" to impress the Russians with American power and to encourage them to make concessions to the American view about how the postwar

---

[3] Winston S. Churchill, *Triumph and Tragedy* (Boston: Houghton Mifflin, 1953), p. 639.

world should be organized. Additionally, the Soviet Union had not yet entered the war with Japan. If the atomic bomb could force Japanese surrender before the Russians were to attack Japan (in fact, the surrender came after that attack), it would help to limit Russian intrusion into Japanese-controlled portions of the Far East. American foreign policy decision makers largely agreed on these perceptions, as did most members of Congress and most opinion leaders in the American public.[4]

## Managing a Penetrated Economy

Gorbachev's actions, while heavily influenced by the declining national and international conditions of the Soviet Union, clearly represented a creative choice among the limited opportunities available to him. In contrast, Truman's wartime decision to drop the bomb on Hiroshima seems, with hindsight, to be one that would have been reached by almost any American leader who was president at that time. As we shall see, leaders of underdeveloped countries face different constraints but often not much more latitude.

By 1964 Brazil's economy had stagnated under a democratic government. Inflation was rampant, and government policies had angered the middle class, large landowners, foreign investors, the U.S. government, and the military. The army seized power and instituted a dictatorship that repressed workers and peasants. The new policies were intended to spur economic growth by keeping wages low, attracting foreign investors, and building state- and privately owned domestic industries. The economy grew by almost 10 percent a year, and many people became very prosperous. But others did not; their standards of living improved little if at all and in some cases actually fell, thanks to the government policies that held down wages and forbade strikes. After a while the boom of the "Brazilian miracle" went bust.

Serious trouble came in 1973, when world oil prices began to rise sharply because the Organization of Petroleum Exporting Countries (OPEC) succeeded in restricting petroleum output and in agreeing on the prices member countries would charge for petroleum. Brazil produces little oil, and its economic development depended largely on automobile transport and expensive consumer appliances. The new oil bill put a tremendous burden on Brazil's balance of international payments, a burden made worse by the world economic recession. For a while the Brazilian government coped with the problem by obtaining large loans from foreign banks and international lending organizations. By 1979 Brazil's foreign debts amounted to almost a third of its gross national product (GNP). Brazil continued to accumulate new debts just to meet the interest due on its old loans. By the middle of 1983 Brazil's foreign debt amounted to $90 billion, about four times the value of its annual export earnings. Worse, the

---

[4] A valuable study is Barton J. Bernstein, "The Atomic Bombings Reconsidered," *Foreign Affairs* 41, 1 (January/February 1995), 135–152; for the relevance of diplomacy toward the Soviet Union see, contrastingly, Gar Alperovitz, *Atomic Diplomacy: Hiroshima and Potsdam*, 2nd ed. (London: Penguin, 1985), especially the new introduction, and McGeorge Bundy, *Danger and Survival* (New York: Vintage, 1988), chap. 2.

interest payments alone amounted to about half of all its export earnings. Brazil's per capita income fell 12 percent between 1980 and 1983, and unemployment skyrocketed.

While the military rulers sought to restore support through tentative steps back to democracy, the economic situation became still worse. The inflation rate reached 175 percent, and it became clear that the country could not meet even the interest payments on its foreign debt, let alone repay the principal. Brazil's debt was owed to foreign governments, international agencies like the International Monetary Fund (IMF), and private banks in the United States, Europe, Japan, and elsewhere. The foreign banks, which held 80 percent of the debt, were desperately afraid of a Brazilian default, which would have caused many big American and European commercial banks to fail and possibly set off a worldwide financial crisis. They had little choice but to permit rescheduling of the debt payments, even though that meant delays in receipts and lower interest payments. But they set a stiff price for the rescheduling, forcing the Brazilian government to accept a package of austerity measures, including cuts in government subsidies and controls to keep wage increases far below the inflation rate. These measures made the country more creditworthy but exacted terrible costs from ordinary Brazilians.

After civil unrest and violence, the military ultimately had to yield power to a new president, Jose Sarney. Sarney took power on a wave of hope for democratic rule. He imposed a freeze on prices, economic growth resumed, and his party swept the 1986 congressional and state elections. A price freeze cannot be maintained indefinitely, however, and Sarney lifted his right after the elections. Inflation exploded anew, reaching an annual rate of 545 percent early in 1987. The foreign debt exceeded $108 billion, the trade surplus dwindled, and the economic growth rate was cut in half. Riots again erupted in the streets, and the government had to announce that it was suspending payments on its foreign debt. Negotiations with foreign governments and banks produced some further rescheduling of debt—the payments were postponed—but nothing fundamental was solved. The creditors again prescribed austerity. Sarney was forced to produce a new constitution and permit an unrestricted presidential election.

A new president, Fernando Collor de Mello, took office in 1990. Generally thought to be conservative, he decreed his own set of tough austerity measures, including confiscating savings (his wealthy supporters, who had feared such a move from Collor's leftist opponent, were shocked). But it created no miracle. Brazil's foreign economic position did not improve, with inflation growing at a rate of about 300 percent a year. In 1992 Brazil did get a standby loan from the IMF and renegotiated debt reduction and debt service payments with the commercial banks. However, inflation continued its dramatic rise and remained a barrier to economic progress. After a corruption scandal forced Collor to resign in December 1992, Itamar Franco assumed the presidency. He instituted his own economic austerity plan in 1993, the "Real Plan" (named after the monetary unit, the "real"). Amidst continuing inflation (40 percent a month) and a major congressional corruption scandal, Brazil and a group of 750 creditor banks finalized another restructuring of Brazil's $50 billion of foreign commercial loans.

Overall, the government's international debts prevented it from stimulating the economy or taking any steps to improve the lot of the poor—in a country with one of the most unequal distributions of income in the world. Not only foreign policy actions, but also basic decisions about domestic economic policy, were hostage to the trade and payments deficit.

Brazil's experience in the last two decades was not too different from that of many other underdeveloped countries. Argentina and the Philippines had similar problems with foreign debt. So did Mexico and Nigeria, which had formerly ridden the crest of the oil-price boom (Nigeria's democratic government proved too fragile to handle the economic crisis and was overthrown by the army). All of these countries shared similar vulnerabilities. Their economies were in grave trouble because of global economic conditions, and their problems were compounded by mismanagement, corruption, and overambitious development plans. Their export markets contracted, and they could not pay their ever-mounting debts. These countries had immense natural resources; a fairly large class of technicians, managers, and entrepreneurs; and internal markets that seemed to offer some prospect of self-sufficiency. But they simply could not achieve that self-sufficient state. They were tied too closely to the ups and downs of the world market and to the influence of foreign investors and lenders. Those foreign interests were obliged to protect themselves and to impose political demands on the debtor governments, which had little choice but to accept the demands. Neither the personality of any particular leader nor the form of government made much difference. Military dictators, rightist presidents, and leftist presidents faced similar conditions and made similar decisions. These big and potentially prosperous countries, deeply penetrated by global and political interests, were caught up in events over which they had little control.

We see here a merging of foreign and domestic policy (especially economic policy). Nationalization and regulation of foreign industry, borrowing from abroad, and the devaluing of currency cut across any neat foreign–domestic dividing line. The conduct of elections or the repression of dissent would seem to be domestic policies— except when their execution has clear implications for foreign approval or the ability to meet foreign commitments. Such a merging of foreign and domestic policy could happen in any country, but it is particularly widespread in poor countries—and especially in small poor countries—that are extensively penetrated from abroad.

## LEVELS OF ANALYSIS

The preceding three sketches—the Soviet Union at the end of the cold war, the United States in 1945, and Brazil over three decades—are taken from very different times, treat rich and poor countries, and deal with both military and economic concerns. The quality of evidence for explaining a decision maker's policy choice varies from one case to another, as does the plausibility of our speculations. Political scientists usually find it difficult to predict a single event, such as the American decision to drop the atomic bomb or the revolution in East Germany in 1989. More often we try to understand why certain classes of events occur—for example, why states may engage in acts of violence. Most political scientists see their job as trying to detect comparable preceding events that seem to produce similar types of behavior. The patterns we see often describe what Dina Zinnes has called a puzzle: "pieces of information, the belief that the pieces fit together into a meaningful picture, but the inability to fit the pieces together initially."[5]

How can states and other actors existing within the same environment behave so differently? To address such puzzles we need to describe what international systems look like, how they change over time, and how they affect the behavior of the entities within them. We also need to look at the internal or domestic makeup of states. Doing so helps us understand puzzles about the different behaviors of states at different times or in different circumstances—the conditions in which they will cooperate or coordinate their actions with other international actors, and those in which conflicts will develop, escalate, and even lead to violence. We wish to understand what processes—cooperative or opposing; economic, diplomatic, or military—result in what patterns of outcomes. We wish to understand the causes of the patterns we find.

In our attempts to uncover causes, or significant preceding events, we have found it useful to distinguish between **levels of analysis**—points on an ordered scale of size and complexity. These levels include units whose behavior we attempt to describe, predict, or explain, as well as units whose impact on individual decision makers we examine. That is, a level may refer to the actors themselves, to the states or individuals whose actions we are trying to explain, or (as in our discussions so far) to different kinds of influences on those actors. In our earlier examples, we used influences from various levels of analysis to explain decisions made by national leaders.

## *The International System and the Nation-State*

In a well-known article J. David Singer introduced the idea of levels of analysis, discussing two broad levels: the international system and the nation-state. By so doing, he highlighted a major distinction used in discerning influences on foreign policy: (1) internal or domestic influences, which originate within the boundaries of the nation-state, and (2) external influences, which arise outside the state's boundaries.

The international-system level is the most comprehensive level of analysis, permitting the observer to study international relations as a whole; that is, to look at the *overall* global patterns of behavior among states and the level of interdependence among them. These include the overall distribution of capabilities, resources, and status in world politics. The nation-state level of analysis allows us to use a decision-making approach and to investigate in far more detail the conditions and processes within states that affect foreign policy choices. Thus, although the international-system level provides a more comprehensive picture of patterns and generalizations, the nation-state level provides a picture of greater depth, detail, and intensity. Singer summarizes the level-of-analysis problem with this set of analogies:

---

[5] Dina Zinnes, "Three Puzzles in Search of a Researcher," *International Studies Quarterly* 24, 3 (1980), 315–342.

In any area of scholarly inquiry, there are always several ways in which the phenomena under study may be sorted and arranged for purposes of systematic analysis. Whether in the physical or social sciences, the observer may choose to focus upon the parts or upon the whole, upon the components or upon the system. He may, for example, choose between the flowers or the garden, the rocks or the quarry, the trees or the forest, the houses or the neighborhood, the cars or the traffic jam, the delinquents or the gang, the legislators or the legislature, and so on.[6]

In international relations it is possible to study the flowers/rocks/trees/ houses/ cars/delinquents/legislators, or to shift the level of analysis and study the garden/ quarry/forest/neighborhood/traffic jam/gang/legislature. Thus we may choose to study international phenomena from a "macro" or a "micro" perspective: Is it the international system that accounts for the behavior of its constituent state units, or the states that account for variations in the international system? Do we look at the state or at its societal components—ethnic groups or classes or specific economic interests? Do we look at the government or at the bureaucracies that comprise it? Do we look at bureaucracies or at the individuals that comprise them? Do we look at the system or its constituent parts?[7]

The macro, or inclusive, system forms the environment for its parts. As we will discuss below, the ultimate constituent parts, surrounded by a set of environments, are individuals who act as governmental decision makers. These decision makers in turn constantly try, insofar as possible, to shape and control those environments.

Distinguishing among various levels of analysis helps us to get at different aspects of explanation and understanding. The macro-approach tells one story, explaining what has occurred because of outside factors; the micro approach tells another story, attempting to explain the significance of events from the point of view of people within the units. Using different levels of analysis thus helps us clarify what kinds of questions we want to ask and what kinds of questions might be answered most profitably from which perspective.

The international-system level lets us see under what conditions dropping the atomic bomb would be likely or under what conditions the cold war could end. Analysis at that level is concerned with questions about the impact of the distribution of military power, or about the impact of the changing distribution of wealth in the world economy. Looking at Truman or Gorbachev, their particular situations and characters, gives us a better understanding of how such conditions were perceived and interpreted and leads us to questions about the importance of the individual decision maker in policy choices. In all three cases discussed we can also see how questions are linked across levels. In particular, the various sets of factors involved in

---

[6] J. David Singer, "The Level-of-Analysis Problem in International Relations," in Klaus Knorr and Sidney Verba, eds., *The International System: Theoretical Essays* (Princeton, N.J.: Princeton University Press, 1961), pp. 77–92. However, see critiques by William B. Moul, "The Level of Analysis Problem Revisited," *Canadian Journal of Political Science* 6 (1973), 494–513, and Kenneth Waltz, *Theory of International Politics* (Reading, Mass.: Addison-Wesley, 1979).

[7] This perspective is outlined by Martin Hollis and Steve Smith, *Explaining and Understanding International Relations* (Oxford: Clarendon, 1990). They note, "At each stage the 'unit' of the higher level becomes the 'system' of the lower layer" (p. 8).

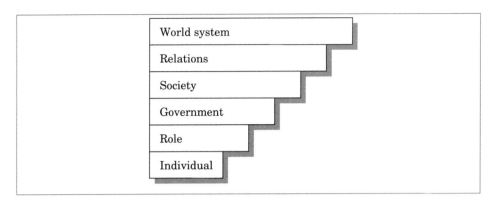

**FIGURE 1.1**   Levels of analysis in world politics.

managing a penetrated economy illustrate how different domestic and international levels blend into one another and link together.

## Six Levels of Analysis

Singer's distinction is valuable, but, as we have already seen, his two levels can be elaborated upon. In later work analysts have found a more useful scheme that identifies six levels.[8] They are: (1) **individual decision makers** and their characteristics, (2) the **roles** occupied by the decision makers, (3) the structure of the **government** within which the decision makers operate, (4) the **society** the decision makers govern and within which they live, (5) the sets of **relations** that exist between the decision makers' nation-state and the other international actors, and (6) the **world system** (see Figure 1.1).

**Individual Decision Makers**   At the micro-level, or most disaggregated level, of analysis we have individual decision makers. In what ways—education and socialization, personality traits, or physical health—does the particular occupant of a major role in making foreign policy differ from other individuals who have held or might have held the position in the past? Explanations at this level must relate differences in the characteristics of decision makers to differences in the decisions they make (for example, what can be explained by contrasting Truman's or Gorbachev's foreign policy inexperience with such experienced predecessors as Franklin Roosevelt or Leonid Brezhnev?).

---

[8] This analytical scheme is adapted from the one presented in James N. Rosenau, *The Scientific Study of Foreign Policy*, rev. ed. (London: Pinter, 1980), chap. 6. The six levels presented in this book, their added complexity, and our use of them also address a number of points in Moul's critique.

**Roles of Decision Makers**   Relations between individual decision makers are heavily affected by the individuals' roles. When acting on behalf of an organization, a decision maker is the focal point of innumerable pressures and constraints. At this level of analysis, the decision maker is seen to act in a particular way because of his or her role in the societal and political system. We would, for example, expect an air force chief of staff, regardless of differences in personality or ideology from other top military officers, to be concerned with protecting the air force as an institution—to see that it receives a fair share of budgets, equipment, and talented personnel and is assigned missions that would improve its operating capabilities but not overtax them in hopeless causes.

Any individual—military or civilian—placed in charge of an institution has a responsibility to look out for the interests of that institution. He or she must also consider the interests of other people and institutions, of course, and not pursue the organization's interests completely to the exclusion of all others. At heart, however, the person in charge knows that if he or she doesn't protect his or her own institution, no one else will. Other institutions are also protected through the pursuit of their own enlightened self-interest and by the existence of institutions at higher levels that include them. Thus the U.S. secretary of defense must arbitrate among the interests of the three military services (and the civilian defense bureaucracy), and the president must somehow reconcile the interests of all competing military and civilian groups. As part of our examination of the individual's role, we must consider the small-group environment (a president and advisers, or a prime minister within the cabinet setting) within which he or she acts and ask how group interaction affects both perceptions and actions.

We must also assume that people tend to acquire other interests and perspectives from their roles in society. For example, corporate executives typically acquire a set of attitudes and perspectives that are not necessarily specific to the particular companies they run but are broadly shared with other executives and distinct from those of labor union officials. Soviet Communist party leaders who had shared common experiences of the Bolshevik Revolution, Marxism, the Western intervention after World War I, and the German invasions of two world wars, as well as of trying to hold together a multiethnic empire, had a set of shared perspectives very different from those of Latin American military officers trying to resolve pressures for political participation and economic development while being buffeted by the world economy (or, indeed, perspectives very different from those of a post–World War II generation of political leaders in Latvia, Lithuania, or Estonia).

**Governmental Structure**   Another set of influences on decisions is determined by the structure of the government—or organization—in which the decision makers operate. Most obviously, a democratic system of government with frequent and truly competitive elections will pose a different set of opportunities and constraints for decision makers than will an authoritarian government. In the former it is probably necessary for a leader to build a wider base of approval for his or her actions, yet he or she is likely to be held accountable for those actions at elections held at regular, specified intervals. In an authoritarian system a leader can work from a narrower political base, repressing opposition, but the fear of a coup or revolt by opponents is always present.

Subtler differences in types of government are also important. Gorbachev attempted in vain to maintain political direction over a Soviet governmental system that was changing from a tightly controlled authoritarian system to a presidential system based on free elections. As the government became more and more open, Gorbachev and other high officials had to operate under ever greater constraints, both from the public and from entrenched interest groups, having opened a Pandora's Box of change in both government and society that ultimately could not be controlled.

**Characteristics of the Society**    Expanding our set of influences still further, we come to nongovernmental characteristics of the society as a whole that affect or condition choices. Governments of rich countries have far more material resources at their disposal than do those of poor countries (see Appendix B and compare the United States and Brazil); they can afford large quantities of modern weapons and can offer economic assistance to other states, while their citizens expect a high and ever-rising standard of living. Again, changing economic conditions in the Soviet Union, through its dissolution and the emergence of the Russian successor state, provide an example of the impact of domestic factors on foreign policy: as the domestic picture worsened, the USSR/Russia moved from its position as an apparently wealthy superpower competitor of the United States to a new role as supplicant for aid and trade from the developed Western states.

Big countries, though they may be relatively poor, still have more resources at their disposal than do small countries. China and India can afford nuclear weapons far more readily than can Laos and Ireland. Small and poor countries are especially likely to be deeply penetrated by other countries or by nonstate actors like multinational corporations. What a leader can do and wants to do is substantially determined by the kind of country he or she represents.

Different forms of economic organization may have foreign policy effects. Various theories treat the requirements and results of capitalism. Are capitalist economies driven by military-industrial complexes? Do they lead to imperialism? Seeking evidence, we might ask whether most capitalist countries have been significantly more prone to war than most socialist countries, and if so, why.

**International Relations**    The actions of states toward each other are affected by the relationship between them, which is determined by the characteristics of the two states. These characteristics help shape the nature of influence between the states—how it is attempted, how successful it is, and what outcomes are produced. A small, weak country will act differently toward a neighboring small, weak country than it will toward a neighboring superpower. Democracies may maintain peaceful relations with each other, but the differences between a democracy and a neighboring dictatorship may bring them into conflict. Rich and poor countries are likely to develop a relationship of dominance or dependence vis-à-vis each other that looks very different depending on the country in which you sit.

**The World System**    Finally, it is essential to consider the wider international, regional, or global system in which a decision maker must operate. A **system** is simply a *set of interacting elements*. A world with two dominant elements—superpowers—

differs in very important ways from a world with four or five powers of essentially equal strength; and both differ from a unipolar world with only one dominant element. A world of two superpowers tends to focus world fears and antagonisms between those two countries; a world of several equal powers produces at least the possibility of shifting alliances or coalitions to balance power without creating permanent antipathies. A unipolar world—as some think has emerged with the dissolution of the Warsaw Pact and the Soviet Union, the continued Russian preoccupation with internal problems, and the demonstration of American military dominance in the 1991 Gulf War—considerably reduces the possibility of effective military alliances (but perhaps not economic ones).

Another aspect of the larger system that makes a difference is the degree of wealth and especially of technological development. As an environment for political decision makers, the contemporary world is a far different place from the world of the eighteenth century. Rapid communication, swift transportation, and techniques of mass destruction have revolutionized the character of warfare and the means of seeking national security. These technologies—and the enormous structure of industry and commerce supported by the wealth of the modern world—also have created a far more interdependent system than existed decades or centuries ago. A cutback in Middle East oil production, the collapse of a major stock market, or atmospheric pollution from a nuclear accident can produce virtually instant and often drastic worldwide repercussions. Thus, as part of the world system, we shall also have to discuss nonstate actors like intergovernmental organizations (for instance, the IMF), as well as nongovernmental organizations (such as religious groups, terrorist bands, and multinational corporations).

It is also essential to bear in mind the extent to which any system is hierarchical. The view from the top is very different from the view from the bottom. For wealthy powers at the top, it is necessary to keep a sharp watch on the poorer debtor states. Militarily, major powers have traditionally kept an eye on the allegiances of small allies and neutrals. Maintaining a balance of power between the top powers in the past has often required intervention in the affairs of small states to keep them in line or to maintain access to bases or resources. The quality of relations between the big powers also matters to those elsewhere in the hierarchy: Will the "end of the cold war" mean less incentive for great powers to intervene in the affairs of small states, or will it mean that each great power feels it has a safer and freer hand to control its own sphere of influence?

## *Actors in World Politics*

These basic levels of analysis will serve as organizing principles for most of this book. In Part I we shall proceed systematically through these various levels, identifying some of the most important ideas or theories about how these levels affect national decision making by providing constraints and opportunities. We shall focus primarily on the policies adopted by the governments of nation-states as influenced by various entities at different levels of analysis within each state's total environment. This focus is typical of the field of study known as international relations or international politics. States usually have control over territory and the people on that territory and a monopoly over the use of military force within that territory. In many ways the state remains the most significant single type of actor in determining conditions of war and peace, as well as the distribution of income and resources.

There are good reasons, nevertheless, to refer to our field of study as *world politics* (rather than as inter*national* relations or inter*national* politics), thus acknowledging the importance of actors other than nation-states. This distinction is observed in the title of this book, and we shall refer many times to nonstate actors. A decision maker typically acts not merely on his or her own behalf but also on behalf of some group or organization. One is the nation-state itself, for which a president or prime minister may act; other organizations relevant to world politics include (1) private organizations operating within a nation-state, such as interest groups and banks; (2) parts of national governments, such as the British ministry of defense or the Republican leadership of the U.S. House of Representatives; and (3) transnational organizations, such as Amnesty International, the International Red Cross, or the Roman Catholic Church.

Within nation-states there also exist numerous *subgroups* based on ethnic, racial, linguistic, religious, cultural, regional, or economic identifications. The process by which subgroupism fragments states and by which subgroups strive for independence as separate international actors (for example, the breakup of the Soviet Union into Russia and 14 other independent units, none of which wished to remain attached to Russia; or the violent fragmentation of what had been Yugoslavia; or the peaceful separation of Czechoslovakia into Slovakia and the Czech Republic) or transnational actors (for example, the Kurds, who are spread across five different nation-states) gives such groups an important place in world politics. James Rosenau includes such subgroups with all the other nonstate actors in his discussion of the rise of a "multicentric" world of politics, which he claims now coexists with the "state-centric" world.[9]

The key point is that *all* these groups are important agents, or actors, in world politics. Although we shall give special attention to the state as actor, we must always remember that it acts within an environment that includes the multicentric world of individuals and group actors of many different types. A careful use of a levels-of-analysis perspective, focusing both on different entities and on different forms of interaction, will identify other major actors important to world politics. Multinational corporations, for instance, need stable and predictable (if not necessarily completely peaceful) relations between major powers if they are to pursue global profits safely. In turn, multinational corporations may create an economic interdependence among states that very seriously inhibits these states from making war, which would sever the bonds of trade and prosperity. Multinational corporations change the relative size and power of social groups and classes where they invest; for example, they increase the labor force in some industries and expand the middle class of technicians and managers. In turn, the political demands of these people, such as attracting more foreign corporations or nationalizing those already in the country, are strengthened. In any case, actors interact across separate levels of analysis.

---

[9] See James N. Rosenau, *Turbulence in World Politics* (Princeton, N.J.: Princeton University Press, 1990).

The complexity of interactions is denoted by the term *system*. When we speak of a global or regional system, we imply that the major elements or influences at different levels of analysis affect one another. We shall see that this **interdependence** is a key element of systems. Nation-states affect multinational corporations or component communal groups, and vice versa; states develop new military technologies and in turn are constrained by the destructive capabilities of those technologies.

It is not too extreme to say that the interdependent interactions of a system mean that everything affects everything else. If you kill a single butterfly, you reduce the stock of genetic material in the next generation of butterflies and therefore change the pattern of evolution for future butterflies—and for predators that feed on butterflies. Over millions of years of evolution you will have an unknowable effect on life and even on the physical environment that life modifies. Probably those effects will be trivial, but they could be very large (chaos theory argues that small changes in initial conditions produce large changes in the ultimate behavior of the system). One mark of a good analyst is the ability to simplify a complex reality in a way that concentrates on the most important relationships and at least temporarily ignores the others. Jacob Bronowski has said:

> I believe that there are no events anywhere in the universe which are not tied to every other event in the universe. . . . But you cannot carry on science on the supposition that you are going to be able to connect every event with every other event. . . . It is, therefore, an essential part of the methodology of science to divide the world for any experiment into what we regard as relevant and what we regard, for purposes of that experiment, as irrelevant.[10]

Any simplification leaves something out. Any level of analysis ignores something important, and another simplification—another level of analysis—will tell us something a little different. In examining the Brazilian crisis we did not look at the specific personality characteristics of the country's leaders; in looking at the atom bomb decision, a role explanation will be different from one based on Truman's personality, and still different from an explanation based on the global power structure or the U.S.–USSR relationship. But we have to start somewhere. Certain questions about national decision makers' behavior are more readily answered from one level than from another. Questions that can be answered from various levels allow different perspectives on the same issue and require different kinds of evidence. Micro-information on the perceptions of individual leaders and their true preferences may, for instance, be very hard to obtain. One may contend that nearly all leaders of poor and weak countries have the same preferences in a given situation; thus detailed information on preferences is not needed so long as one has adequate information at the societal level of analysis and the aim is macro explanation.

---

[10]Jacob Bronowski, *The Origins of Knowledge and Imagination* (New Haven, Conn.: Yale University Press, 1978), p. 58. A related interdependence phenomenon, studied in chaos theory, is known as the Butterfly Effect on weather—"The notion that a butterfly stirring the air today in Peking can transform storm systems next month in New York." See James Gleick, *Chaos: Making a New Science* (New York: Penguin, 1987), p. 8.

The choice of level of analysis is therefore determined by one's theory and by the availability of data, but the choice cannot be capricious. Several different classes of influence (levels of analysis) must be identified and looked for in every analytical instance, as was clearly illustrated by all three of our brief cases. Explanations from different levels need not exclude each other. They may be complementary, each making a contribution to our understanding. To some degree, estimates of the relative weight of each contribution can be compiled through the techniques of data gathering and analysis typical of modern social science. But beyond that point we remain in the realm of speculation, intuition, and informed wisdom.

# THE "MENU" OF WORLD POLITICIANS AND CONSTRAINTS ON DECISION MAKERS

## Opportunity and Willingness

How can we use levels of analysis to help us understand the choices of decision makers who direct international actors? We have noted that at each level we have some sort of system made up of its constituent units. We can study what goes on inside each of these units and the ways in which their behavior is constrained by the surrounding system. As Martin Hollis and Steve Smith put it, "Whatever the unit, its activities can be explained from without or understood from within. Every unit has a decision-making process. Those making the decisions are influenced from outside and from inside."[11] Ultimately, then, we are concerned with the possibilities and constraints that face decision makers (**opportunity**) and with the choices that they make in light of these possibilities and constraints (**willingness**).[12]

The willingness of the decision maker to make certain choices is constrained by her or his own nature (the individual level), as well as by the decision maker's place in the governmental structure (role); the nature and form of the government within which the decision maker operates; the resources, makeup, and politics of the society that houses the decision maker and the government; the web of influence relations that the decision maker's state has with other world actors; and the structure of the world system. Each level affects the opportunities available to decision makers; each level affects the images decision makers hold and how they make choices. Exactly how each of these levels affects opportunity and willingness is developed in Chapters 4 through 11.

---

[11] Hollis and Smith, *Explaining and Understanding International Relations*, p. 42.
[12] These two concepts were originally developed by Harvey Starr and later elaborated in Benjamin A. Most and Harvey Starr, *Inquiry, Logic and International Politics* (Columbia: University of South Carolina Press, 1989), chap. 2.

Using the ideas of opportunity and willingness forces us to engage in both explanation and understanding (in the terms of Hollis and Smith). Opportunity and willingness force us to consider both the world system, or broader environment, and the process of decision making that goes on within that system's constituent units. The various levels of analysis are thus linked by thinking of a decision maker as an entity who must behave within the very complex environment that surrounds him or her. Each level of analysis describes one of the environments within which the decision maker must operate.

**Opportunity**    "Politics is the art of the possible." The environments of decision-making entities provide a structure of opportunities, risks, and potential costs and benefits, constraining decision makers. How are all these elements captured by the concept of opportunity?

First, the environment makes certain opportunities, and not others, *possible*. Here the environment is seen as a set of constraints on what it is actually possible for the entity to do in the environment. Napoleon could not threaten Moscow with nuclear destruction, nor could Franklin Roosevelt coerce the Japanese in 1941 with the atomic bomb—but Truman, with that possibility at hand, had to decide how to use the opportunity it provided. In the eighth century, the Spanish could not draw upon the resources of the New World to repel the initial Islamic invasion of Iberia, because no European knew that there was a New World; the economically besieged countries trying to deal with the Great Depression of the 1930s could not call on the IMF for assistance, because it did not exist. The list is endless.

Possibility includes two dimensions. First, the phenomenon must already exist somewhere in the world system. The phenomenon—be it nuclear weapons, or telecommunications satellites, or Protestantism, or Marxism, or railroads—must have been "invented" so that it is available as a possibility to at least some actors in the system. The second dimension is the distribution of this possibility in the system. Nuclear weapons do exist; however, most states cannot "take advantage" of them because they have neither the wealth nor the expertise to produce their own. The technology needed to place telecommunications satellites in space is known but is not affordable by all. Though a possibility may exist, limits on resources will affect the ability to make use of it.

The unequal distribution of possibilities also makes it *probable* that certain opportunities will be taken. Environmental constraints in any situation make certain behavior more or less likely—there is some normally expected behavior in the situation under consideration. Given that interaction between states is possible, what is the probability they will act in certain ways? For example, what was the probability that the United States and the USSR, the only two superpowers after World War II, would become rivals? Or the probability of interaction between Thailand and Bolivia, small powers in different regions of the world that are separated by thousands of miles? Given the characteristics of the domestic environment (a country's size, wealth, form of government, and ethnic diversity), what is the probability of certain behavior? For example, what was the probability that Britain, Japan, or America would become a naval power? Or that the Swiss would follow a policy of neutrality? Given a terrible war drawing to a close, the impatience of a democratic electorate to end that war, and the existence of a new weapon that could hasten surrender, what is the probability that the weapon will be used?

To summarize, opportunity requires three related conditions: (1) an international environment that permits interaction between states, (2) states that possess adequate resources to be capable of certain kinds of actions, and (3) decision makers who are aware of both the range of interactions and the extent of capabilities available to them. Opportunity can be illustrated with a reference to Lewis Fry Richardson, one of the pioneers of the study of war and peace. Richardson, concerned with "deadly quarrels," drew a parallel between war and murder. Asking why people in one country tended to murder each other more often than they murdered foreigners, he drew the simple conclusion that they had much less opportunity to murder foreigners, since there were far fewer contacts with them.[13] In fact, police records indicate that a person is most likely to be murdered by a close relative or a friend, because constant contact and high levels of interaction provide the opportunity for murder. Similarly, Thailand and Bolivia are *unlikely* to fight each other because their range of interaction is too limited to allow a conflict to develop. Opportunity is the possibility of interaction because of objective conditions that may be perceived in varying ways by decision makers.

**Willingness**   Willingness is concerned with the motivations that lead people to avail themselves of opportunities. Willingness deals with the goals and motivations of decision makers and focuses on why decision makers choose one course over another. Willingness is therefore based on perceptions of the global scene and of domestic political conditions. It derives from calculations of the costs and benefits of alternative courses of action, based not only on objective factors but also on perceptions (for instance, of threat) and emotions (for instance, fear, insecurity, or desire for revenge). Willingness thus depends on *choice* and *perception.* A person reacts according to what she thinks she can do and what others expect her to do.

Decision makers behave on the basis of their perception of the world, a perception that may be very different from what the world is actually like. Such differences may be brought home in many ways when the decision maker attempts to implement a policy in the real world: if someone thinks a glass patio door is open when it is not, the consequences of operating on such a belief can be shattering. Neville Chamberlain, the British prime minister, believed that Adolf Hitler could be appeased and his aggression ended, and so gave in to him at Munich in 1938; the result was further Nazi expansion. History also provides us with the picture of Hitler years later, isolated in his Berlin bunker, moving divisions on a map—lost divisions that were real only to him and that had no impact on the Red Army as it moved inexorably toward the German capital. One argument for dropping the atomic bomb stemmed from the perception that demonstration of its power would restrain the Soviet Union from expansion.

Thus, when we study different environments or levels of analysis, we are also interested in how they affect the image of the world that decision makers hold. Willingness will involve all those factors that affect how decision makers see the world, process information about the world, and make choices.

---

[13] Lewis F. Richardson, *Statistics of Deadly Quarrels* (Chicago: Quadrangle Books, 1961), p. 288.

It is important to understand that *both* opportunity and willingness are required for a given behavior to occur; they are *jointly necessary conditions*. Wishing for something to happen is not enough—the capabilities to act for its fulfillment must be available. Simply being able to do something doesn't mean it will happen unless you have the will to take action. Successful deterrence, for example, requires both appropriate weapons—the opportunity—and the willingness to pay the political and military costs of using the weapons. The development of the atomic bomb made its use a possibility; analysts since 1945 have been studying the willingness to use it.[14]

## *The Menu*

Opportunity, willingness, and the relationships between the decision-making entity and its environment can be summarized and brought together through the analogy of a **menu**. The person (entity or actor) who enters a restaurant is confronted by a gastronomical environment—the menu. The menu provides a number of behavioral opportunities, not determining the diner's choice but constraining what is possible (pizza, lasagna, and linguini are possible in an Italian restaurant, but chicken chow mein and matzo ball soup are not). The menu also affects the probability of the diner's choice through price, portion size, side dishes, specials, and the restaurant's reputation for certain foods. In the Italian restaurant whose menu proclaims that it has served pizza since 1910 and offers over 50 varieties of pizza at low prices today, a diner is most probably going to order a pizza. The restaurant, however, offers other selections as well, and the probabilities they will be ordered are affected by how the diner sees those choices. Though the restaurant is not known for its lasagna, which is extraordinarily expensive, lasagna is still a possibility. A patron who is Russian and unable to read English (and even is unfamiliar with the Latin alphabet) may order the lasagna, believing that he or she is ordering pizza. A patron who is rich and who is obsessed with lasagna of any quality may also make this selection. Thus knowledge of a patron's resources and individual decision-making process in relation to the menu, as well as the diner's perception of it, permits us to analyze his or her restaurant behavior.

The key to the menu analogy is to understand that the opportunities of international actors are constrained in various ways and that these constraints affect the willingness of decision makers to act. Constraints can be external or they can be internal. Most constraint in international relations is self-constraint. For two decades the academic writings of former U.S. Secretary of State Henry Kissinger stressed the domestic and international constraints on the foreign policy decision maker. The true diplomat, Kissinger stressed, understood these constraints and learned to work within them to achieve the desired aims.

---

[14] The joint necessity of having both opportunity and willingness for some action to occur is formally developed by Claudio Cioffi-Revilla and Harvey Starr, "Opportunity, Willingness, and Political Uncertainty: Theoretical Foundations of Politics," *Journal of Theoretical Politics* 7 (forthcoming 1995). The more philosophically adventurous reader might be interested in another version of opportunity and willingness (including the entity–environment relationship and the issue of joint necessity) called the "agent–structure problem." See Alexander E. Wendt, "The Agent–Structure Problem in International Relations Theory," *International Organization* 41, 3 (1987), 337–370.

## PLAN OF THE BOOK

Most of Part I will follow the levels-of-analysis presentation from the preceding pages. First, however, we shall give a brief overview in Chapter 2 of how world politics can be studied; we shall stress a scientific approach. Before moving on to discussions of the different levels of analysis, we shall discuss in Chapter 3 the various actors on the world stage. We shall give much attention to the development of the contemporary nation-state system, nations, and nationalism, and we shall consider how the nation-state compares with other international actors.

The following discussion will begin with the most comprehensive context or environment and work its way down to the most specific. Chapters 4 and 5 will deal with the world system and how the global environment affects the behavior of international actors. Chapters 6 and 7 will look at relations among states and the ways states interact. Chapters 8 and 9 will cover the domestic environment of states and the effects of societal and governmental factors on foreign policy and world politics. Finally, Chapters 10 and 11 will investigate the behavior of decision makers, people who are constrained by their roles and whose individual characteristics affect the way they perceive the world. Part I thus offers an understanding of the complex set of environments within which foreign policy decision makers work; Part II will use the concepts developed to examine major policy issues.

Throughout the book we shall focus on issues of international conflict and cooperation. Although people often think of the international arena as a realm of conflict, there is also a remarkable amount of neutral or cooperative behavior there, especially in the economic sphere. We therefore shall seek not only the causes of conflict and war but also those of cooperative behavior and readiness to address shared problems (many of which are economic and ecological). In doing so we shall summarize the theory and research of many recent efforts. We also shall refer often to historical examples of cooperative and antagonistic behavior, trying to show how current behavior is conditioned by the past experience of world history and how decision makers interpret that experience.

# How Do We Think About World Politics?

## Realists, Transnationalists, and Radicals

World War I left leaders and ordinary people aghast. The balance of power—the relative equality of strength among all the contending major states and the shifting alliances to preserve equilibrium when one state threatened to become dangerous—had provided a very substantial degree of peace in Europe since the end of the Napoleonic Wars in 1815. That system then was violently upset by a war that lasted four years and left 9 million soldiers dead. Many, perhaps foremost among them U.S. president Woodrow Wilson, concluded that the balance-of-power system was fatally flawed and a new world order had to be constructed. These people, many of them political liberals, became known as idealists because they had a vision, or ideal, of how a new and peaceful world order might be constructed. The idealists supported the formation of the League of Nations and other institutions of international law, hoping to build a system of collective security in which democratic nations would be especially peace-loving and in which all nations would band together to defeat unjust aggression. The events leading to World War II, however, disillusioned many of the idealists. Democracy was overthrown in Germany, Italy, Spain, and elsewhere. The United States never joined the League. The United States and members of the League did not band together against the fascists and Nazis until it was almost too late.

After World War II, people once again vowed that global wars must be prevented. Idealists supported the creation of a new organization—the United Nations—to replace the League of Nations. Once again they put their faith in the benefits of collective security, in the rule of law in a global system that limited countries' actions, and in the spread of democracy, partly because they thought democracies would be peaceful. This time the United States would join the international organization, and perhaps the members, having learned a lesson, would cooperate. Some contemporary intellectual descendants of the idealists are often called **transnationalists** because they emphasize the role of institutions and other linkages between nation-states that facilitate and promote cooperation, coordination, and nonviolent modes of conflict resolution. Those linkages may need to be strengthened, but, the transnationalists believe, they are already much more than some distant "ideal."[1]

Others, however—the **realists**—were skeptical. Their insistence that the worst of World War II could have been avoided by earlier resistance to Hitler derived from a "realistic" understanding of conflict and power in international politics. Realists are often, though not always, political conservatives. According to realism—the central approach to the study of international politics for several decades and perhaps even now—people are self-interested and selfish and seek to dominate others. They cannot be depended on to cooperate and will stop cooperating when it is not in their narrow and immediate interest to do so. Realists consider nation-states by far the most important units acting in world politics, with international organizations like the United Nations only as important as their most powerful members wish them to be. Finally, most states are assumed to be rational, unitary actors pursuing essentially the same goals of national interest, regardless of their form of government or type of economic organization. According to realists, a system of competing nation-states is basically an anarchic system, literally a system without a government or ruling authority. States struggle with one another for power, must look out for their own interests, and ultimately depend upon *self-help;* they cannot appeal to some higher authority to enforce international law.

The realist picture is in many ways an accurate description of the world in which we live. But anarchic does not necessarily mean disorderly. On the contrary, there is a great deal of order and predictability in the behavior of nation-states. Usually states

---

[1] For an overview of the basic tenets of idealism and its derivatives (variously called liberal, neo-liberal, transnational, or globalist), and how they flow from Wilson's vision, see Charles W. Kegley, Jr., "The Neoliberal Challenge to Realist Theories of World Politics: An Introduction," in Kegley, ed., *Controversies in International Relations Theory: Realism and the Neoliberal Challenge* (New York: St. Martin's, 1995), pp. 1–24. This entire volume provides a useful presentation of the transnational/neoliberal challenge to the descriptive, explanatory, predictive, and prescriptive adequacy of the realist perspective.

do obey international law, not because they are particularly "good," but because it is in their interest to be law-abiding and to encourage others to obey the law. Nation-states work together in many ways, among them in the peaceful conduct of trade and finance, the movement of people across national borders, the exchange of information, and medical cooperation. Without this cooperation the substantial peace and prosperity we know would be completely impossible. Realism as an approach to international relations helps to explain why states fight or threaten each other, but it is less effective in explaining much of the cooperative behavior we see—the order within the anarchy. It sees any cooperation as stemming only from temporarily converging self-interests. More important, it says little about how more order can be created without imposing some dominating authority, either a world empire or at least one dominant country that can impose its will on others. It is that need to explain order and to seek greater order in a dangerously armed world that compels us to move beyond realism and pay attention to actors other than nation-states (especially international and transnational organizations) and to issues other than the pursuit of military power (such as trade, development, and pollution control).

Both realists and transnationalists possess important but limited truths about the world; each side has a powerful answer to excessive reliance on the other's argument. The world is a dangerous place, we cannot reshape it as we like, and being "good" will not necessarily make a nation safe. Yet moral principles provide goals to strive for, and transnational linkages do moderate the excesses of power politics. As realism was a reaction to the idealist failure to control Nazi Germany, transnationalism was a reaction to the dangers of overemphasizing power politics and the maximization of power in a world of nuclear technology and cold war.

A third philosophical tradition, or worldview, that provides a coherent perspective about how we think things work should be distinguished from both realism and idealism. **Radicals,** whose view often stems from Marxism, share with realists the conviction that people are motivated largely by self-interest and are ready to dominate others, and that those who would oppress must be resisted. Like realists, radicals consider states to be very important actors in world affairs, but they also emphasize the conflicting interests of social classes. Classes (capitalists, workers, peasants) clash for control of state policy within countries, and the government pursues not abstract national interest but the interest of the dominant class or classes. States are not unitary actors. Classes exist across national boundaries; capitalists, for example, may cooperate internationally to maintain a political and economic environment hospitable to investment by multinational corporations. Where realists see anarchy, radicals see a hierarchy of classes and states in which the weak are subordinated to the strong. Like realists, they see individuals as acting from a kind of rationality, but one that is often distorted by false consciousness regarding their interests—for example, by acceptance by the weak of perspectives and values propagated by the strong. Like transnationalists, radicals are dissatisfied with the global status quo and hope to transform the world system so as to make it more equitable and more just. Imperialism and wars, they believe, are caused by capitalists' attempts to maintain their power to exploit other classes, by their acting against the interests both of capitalists in competing states and of noncapitalist states that challenge the system. To have general peace, capitalism must be abolished or at least radically tamed.

Full-blown Marxist radicalism is no longer very popular, chiefly because of the economic and political failures of communism and socialism. Radicals are generally not considered to have a credible model for the organization of society. Nevertheless, as a critique of the excesses of capitalism and power politics, radicalism still has something to say. Whether or not one accepts its basic philosophical premises, it provides an important antidote to complacency about contemporary world conditions. Some non-Marxist critical theorists contend that many of the rules and principles governing international relations have been "constructed" by states and rulers, have changed markedly over the centuries, and could be changed substantially in the future.

These three competing philosophical perspectives offer different predictions and theoretical explanations about world politics. In each case, some of the beliefs are not easily confirmed or refuted by evidence. These perspectives lead their proponents to ask different questions, and they stress different levels of analysis in their explanations. Nevertheless, they often lead to contrasting explanations or predictions that can be tested and found to be more or less correct. At various points in this book we will contrast explanations or predictions derived from the three perspectives; at others you may wish to try to construct and contrast such arguments.[2] To summarize, each of these perspectives, or worldviews, provides a different set of spectacles through which to read the menu. There are other such perspectives, or lenses, that we will note as well. Indeed, two authors have recently written about "gender as a lens on world politics" in presenting a gender-sensitive, or feminist, perspective on how we think about the world and how it works.[3]

For now we turn to a discussion of ways that different explanations or predictions, from whatever perspective, can be evaluated as statements about how the world is.

## A SCIENTIFIC STUDY OF WORLD POLITICS

Just as there have always been different philosophical views about the current or desired nature of world politics, there have also been different views about how world politics should be studied. Some people, especially the realists, with their insistence

---

[2] For treatments contrasting realism (and its variants) with idealism, transnationalism, and radical approaches (as well as their variants), see Kegley, *Controversies in International Relations Theory*; K. J. Holsti, *The Dividing Discipline* (Boston: Allen & Unwin, 1985); and Paul R. Viotti and Mark V. Kauppi, *International Relations Theory: Realism, Pluralism, Globalism*, 2nd ed. (New York: Macmillan, 1993); Alexander Wendt, "Anarchy Is What States Make of It," *International Organization* 46 (Spring 1992), 390–425, discusses how the rules of international order are constructed.

[3] V. Spike Peterson and Anne Sisson Runyan, *Global Gender Issues* (Boulder, Col: Westview, 1993). See also such works as Cynthia Enloe, *Bananas, Beaches and Bases: Making Feminist Sense of International Politics* (Berkeley: University of California Press, 1990), and J. Ann Tickner, *Gender in International Relations: Feminist Perspectives on Achieving Global Security* (New York: Columbia University Press, 1992).

on the overwhelming importance of nation-states as actors, stressed the study of diplomatic history—the study of actions by national governments. Others, especially transnationalists, attended primarily to the study and development of international law. Both approaches were highly descriptive, providing a detailed record of how states *actually* behave. They were also often prescriptive, setting forth ways in which states *should* behave, sometimes with legalistic or moral/ethical arguments.

Another approach—one not primarily associated with any of these philosophical perspectives—was to use relevant results and methods from the behavioral sciences, such as anthropology, economics, psychology, and sociology. This approach was reinforced by the rise of analytical and quantitative research concepts, models, and methods. It made greater use of the comparative study of quantitative data, and in using systematic evidence it remedied the excesses of both the diplomatic-historical (realist) approach and the international law (transnationalist) approach that had dominated earlier studies.[4]

Given the crucial world problems that appeared after 1945, many scholars and analysts felt that only a more systematic understanding would lead to solutions. Problems of war and peace took on new meanings with the advent of nuclear weapons. The interdependence and complexity of the world became greater as the Western colonial empires broke up, scores of new states were created, and political and economic hierarchies around the world were reordered. Older philosophical explanations seemed inadequate.

Historical and legal approaches stressed the description of unique events and sought to explain them. The post–World War II intellectual reaction to these approaches was to seek instead to try to study international relations in a scientific manner, using the procedures and methods of science (as other social sciences, such as economics and psychology, had done previously). Thus the preference was to stress *comparability* rather than uniqueness—to look for patterns of behavior and for probabilities that certain behavior would occur. A social scientific approach assumes that knowledge is possible by investigating patterns of behavior, regularities of actions, and recurring responses in political behavior. These patterns may be investigated cross-nationally (that is, by comparisons of several states at a particular time) or longitudinally (that is, by comparisons of conditions in one or more states at several points in time). Science is concerned with generalizations about classes or types of phenomena. It assumes that over the long run many historic parallels will transcend the specific times, places, and people involved.[5]

In approaching the study of international relations in this way, stress was placed on finding and developing tools for organizing the intellectual complexity of the field: the development of concepts, frameworks, and theories. These tools represent the

---

[4] For overviews of the scientific study of international politics, see two works by Michael Nicholson, *Formal Theories in International Relations* (Cambridge: Cambridge University Press, 1989) and *Rationality and the Analysis of International Conflict* (Cambridge: Cambridge University Press, 1992).

[5] Thus many scholars feel that science, at its core, is about *comparison*. A good treatment of comparative social science is found in Charles C. Ragin, *The Comparative Method* (Berkeley: University of California Press, 1987).

most basic elements of science and help us avoid naive or simplistic scientism. We have already noted that events, situations, or social phenomena *can* be compared. Although in many respects events and people have unique aspects that will never occur again, all of them bear similarities to broader concepts or classes of events. To "think theoretically" we must always be ready to look at some phenomenon and ask: "Of what is this an instance?"[6]

Thus in a very basic way the scientific comparative method distinguishes the study of international relations or politics from the study of international history. Some critics and historians believe that humanity—and international relations especially—is the least promising area for scientific study because events are too complex and singular. Denying the existence of regularities would leave us to study only singular cases or to produce detailed descriptions, with no cumulation of knowledge for the scholar or policymaker. If every historical event is truly unique and thus noncomparable, the gulf between the critic and the scientist is indeed unbridgeable. Some scholars appear to hold this position; however, we don't believe it (and probably neither do they). Everyone has compared two events at some time. By comparing things, we admit the possibility of certain similarities across events. Using a case study to illustrate some concept or phenomenon reveals the same agreement with the principle of comparison and the possibility of patterns. The most basic rationale for the study of social relations and structures—that the past can be used as some sort of guide to the future—must also rest on the similarities of events and the existence of regularities: the possibility of comparison.

Models and concepts also point us to a second basic element of science: a **probabilistic explanation** of human affairs. While science believes that things are comparable and that we should search for explanations that cover many cases, it is a false characterization of science (even the "hard," or physical, sciences) to believe that it promises general laws that explain everything and will predict exactly what will happen. All science is based on models, propositions, or laws that are contingent—that will hold only under certain conditions. As the world approximates such conditions, the probabilities that the events proposed by a model or theory will occur will vary. That the study of international relations does not now and may never look like physics with its apparently "universal laws" does not mean that international relations cannot be scientific. As Rosenau warns us, "To think theoretically one must be tolerant of ambiguity, concerned with probabilities, and distrustful of absolutes." Using probabilistic explanation is what Jacob Bronowski called the "revolution" of thought in modern science, "replacing the concept of the inevitable effect with that of the probable trend. . . . History is neither determined nor random. At any moment it moves forward into an area whose general shape is known, but whose boundaries are uncertain in a calculable way".[7]

---

[6] James N. Rosenau, "Thinking Theory Thoroughly," in Rosenau, ed., *The Scientific Study of Foreign Policy,* rev. ed. (London: Frances Pinter, 1980), pp. 25–26.
[7] Jacob Bronowski, *The Common Sense of Science* (London: Heinemann, 1951), pp. 86–87. See Benjamin A. Most and Harvey Starr, *Inquiry, Logic and International Politics* (Columbia: University of South Carolina Press, 1989), chaps. 1 and 5.

To understand world politics we need to have a high tolerance for uncertainty, the imperfect state of human knowledge, and the whys of human society and politics. The phenomena are extraordinarily complex, and we know far less than we would like. You will doubtless yearn at times for more certainty, more conviction, than the authors of this book can give about the causes and possible solutions of various problems. But knowing what it is that you don't know, why you don't know it, and what you might do to remedy your ignorance is a part of wisdom and maturity.

## THEORY AND EVIDENCE

We have noted that theories, models, and concepts lead to the basic elements of science involving comparison, contingency, and probability. Comparison also implies measurement; to compare two things means we must measure them in some way. How do we measure things? How do we measure things in such a way as to evaluate the relevance and utility of our theories? These two questions identify further basic elements of science.

We must first return to **theory.** A key element in science is the painstaking development of theory. Theory is an intellectual tool that provides us with a way to organize the complexity of the world and order facts into data and that helps us to see how phenomena are interrelated.

> More specifically, a theory is a set of interconnected statements. This set of statements comprises (1) sentences introducing terms that refer to the basic concepts of the theory (theoretical terms); (2) sentences that relate the basic concepts to each other; and (3) sentences that relate some theoretical statements to a set of possible observations.[8]

Theory organizes and simplifies reality, thus helping to separate the important from the trivial by pointing out what we really wish to look at and what is unimportant enough to ignore. This is why theory is so important—it affects not only which answers we come up with, but also what questions we ask in the first place! In what ways would a realist, transnational, or radical theory of the end of the cold war differ? We'll see below.

Theories are used to define, label, and classify the phenomena of world politics carefully. This is part of the *precision* that is basic to science. Scientific theories must be stated in a clear and precise way, so that one knows how to make, and evaluate, the measurements necessary for comparison. **Science** is thus about how to test, evaluate, and compare theories. Again, it is false to think of science as the only way to generate theories. Theories come from all aspects of human experience, and many of the most

---

[8] Garvin McCain and Erwin M. Segal, *The Game of Science,* 2nd ed. (Monterey, Calif.: Brooks/Cole, 1973), p. 99. This book is a clear and helpful introduction to scientific method.

successful scientists, such as Louis Pasteur or Thomas Edison, had a creative knack by which they could look at things differently and draw analogies where others could not. It is important to understand that the questions—where do theories come from? how do we test or evaluate theories?—reflect two very different activities.

Theories tell us what to look at and how the things we look at relate to each other. In so doing, theories provide the basis for *systematic*, or scientific, evidence for our explanations of the world. Because we can argue an opposite and plausible reason, or hypothesis, for almost every aspect of human interaction (for example, "absence makes the heart grow fonder" and "out of sight, out of mind"), we need systematic evidence to test theory. A good theory is one that can be supported or rejected through explicit analysis and the systematic use of data. A theory that cannot be tested—that cannot be disproved in any conceivable way—cannot get us very far. Think, for example, of the proposition, "People always act to advance their own self-interest, no matter how much they delude themselves or others into thinking they are acting in someone else's interest." Since the proponent of such an argument can always support the argument ("The person in question is deluding himself about his motives"), and since that statement cannot be checked against evidence (we cannot get inside the person's mind to look), the self-interest proposition cannot be disproved, or "falsified." It is not a scientific statement because any evidence can be interpreted as agreeing with it. It is also a useless statement, because it does not tell us what the person's specific behavior will be.

We now have two more important observations about science. Despite some current questions about the nature of knowledge and our ability to communicate our understanding about the world (raised by the postmodern, or postpositivist, school of thought[9]), science assumes only that at some point we must be able to match up some aspect of our theories or their predictions with data from the real world. Science assumes that at least some of the patterns we have mentioned can be measured and described. The data that we use to accomplish these purposes must be collected in very specific ways.

Another false characterization of science is that it is value-free, or in some way totally objective. This is not the case. Science is *explicit* in its procedures so that people can judge it, to see if the investigator's values or ideology have slanted the analysis. The evidence used must be objective—the procedures by which it has been collected must be made open to outside observers. Evidence must be collected in such ways as to be relevant to the question at hand. It must be collected in such ways as not to bias the results. Much of scientific endeavor, therefore, requires systematic observation and precise measurement. A careful analyst will insist on a combination of logical deduction and accurate observation—empirical evidence—in evaluating the propositions put forth. Science thus is a systematic way of obtaining information and making generalizations.

---

[9] For a critique of postmodernism that gets at the practical issues important to social scientists, see Pauline M. Rosenau, *Post Modernism and the Social Sciences: Insights, Inroads, and Intrusions* (Princeton, N.J.: Princeton University Press, 1991).

Scientific observation is deliberate search, carried out with care and forethought, as contrasted with the casual and largely passive perceptions of everyday life. It is this deliberateness and control of the process of observation that is distinctive of science, not merely the use of special instruments.[10]

As some experienced social scientists point out, much of what we know about social phenomena is "ordinary knowledge," not derived from systematic scientific endeavors. Ordinary knowledge, or common sense, as it is sometimes called, is "that on which people can agree at a particular time and place."[11] It might include the fact that there are many countries in the world, that there is a war going on somewhere at virtually all times, and that very big states usually have larger armies than do very small states. Yet we must also know when to doubt what passes as ordinary knowledge, when to question it, and how to supplant or supplement it by scientific knowledge when needed. Common sense can be untrue, as were the formerly held beliefs that the world is flat or that light is white. Common sense may be simply the result of changing intellectual fashions, as in the relationship between Isaac Newton's physics and previous knowledge, or Einstein's physics and the earlier Newtonian beliefs. Most important, as pointed out above, common sense is often contradictory. Social science should be directed at key points of inquiry where ordinary knowledge is thus suspect.

## Hypotheses, Laws, and Probability Statements

Theoretical statements that relate to possible observations are called **hypotheses.** The testing of hypotheses—checking their predictions against observation—is a central activity of science. Hypotheses that are confirmed in virtually all the classes of phenomena to which they are applied are often known as *laws*. In the social sciences, interesting laws are quite rare. The phenomena of social science are so complex, with so many different influences or causes acting on a particular event, and our knowledge of these complex phenomena is still so imperfect that few laws have been established. As stressed above, even with much more theory and research, we are likely to have only *probability statements*, statements that most phenomena of a given class will behave in a certain way most of the time. This is why social scientists find it hard to predict how particular events will develop; for example, which Soviet leader, at what specific point in time, would be willing to let the East European states go their independent ways. At best, the social scientist can indicate a probability that a particular action (a threat, a promise, or a concession) will be followed by a specific result.[12]

---

[10] Abraham Kaplan, *The Language of Inquiry* (San Francisco: Chandler, 1964), p. 126. Quoted, with further discussion, in Charles E. Lindblom and David K. Cohen, *Usable Knowledge: Social Science and Social Problem Solving* (New Haven, Conn.: Yale University Press, 1979), pp. 15–16.

[11] See Karl W. Deutsch, "The Limits of Common Sense," in Nelson W. Polsby et al., eds., *Politics and Social Life* (Boston: Houghton Mifflin, 1963), pp. 51–58.

[12] See John Lewis Gaddis, "International Relations Theory and the End of the Cold War," *International Security* 17 (Winter 1992/93), 5–58; James Lee Ray and Bruce Russett, "The Future as Arbiter of Theoretical Controversies: The Scientific Study of Politics and Predictions," *British Journal of Political Science* 25 (forthcoming 1996).

When we say we are hoping to make general statements about phenomena in international relations, we do not necessarily mean generalizations that apply to all countries at all times. Such generalizations may be approximated in physics, but they are hard to make in political science. All states, for instance, may have to react in some way to a shift in the international balance of power. But how they will react depends on other circumstances. They may react in any number of "substitutable" ways—by making war, forming new alliances, building up their national power bases, or making concessions to their opponents. A state's choices depend on its opportunities (whether powerful allies are available and whether in alliance they can conceivably win a war) and on its willingness to act on various possibilities (whether its domestic ideology permits it to ally with a potential partner state; whether its government is strong enough to survive concessions to a foreign enemy).

Such factors create the contingencies useful for "nice laws," statements that cover a group of cases under a specific set of conditions. In different contexts, therefore, the same cause will have different effects. In our discussion above, a generalization about the international system is modified by societal or governmental characteristics. The complex and changing nature of relationships in world politics makes them hard to analyze.[13]

In reviewing ideas or theories about world politics, we shall be considering propositions whose degree of truth varies greatly. Some statements of fact about *empirical reality* will be made with confidence, sometimes because they have been systematically and thoroughly tested by the standard procedures of social science. They represent, in other words, hypotheses that have been widely confirmed. In other cases statements may be made with confidence simply because they are a part of accepted "wisdom." Even though they may not rest on an elaborate basis of scientific examination, they are thought by most observers to be more or less self-evident. Perhaps they can be logically deduced from other statements that are widely accepted or that rest on solid scientific procedure.

If statements have been supported by empirical study, it is also important that they be derived by careful logic from clearly stated assumptions to show us *why* the statement should be correct and how it identifies a *process* or a *causal* relationship. For example, the statement, "young drivers have more traffic accidents than do somewhat older drivers" is an empirically correct statement of fact—a correlation—but it tells us little of interest about causality. Often it is very difficult to uncover the process of causation that underlies a correlation we observe. In this example, is it because younger drivers may be more reckless? less experienced? drive older cars with fewer safety features?

We also have to be very careful about the assumptions we make. It would not be helpful to construct an elaborate logical theory about accidents if one of our assumptions (for instance, "younger drivers have poorer vision") was empirically incorrect. Of course, we sometimes make simplifying assumptions that we know may not be correct or are not fully correct. Such assumptions can be treated as a theory or model, to be judged against their fit to real-world data. Like theories, assumptions must be

---

[13] See Most and Starr, *Inquiry, Logic and International Politics*, especially chap. 5.

relevant to enough cases to make them useful. For example, we can assume that people are rational, that competition in an industry is perfect, or that the speed of a falling body is not slowed by friction with the air. Sometimes these assumptions are close enough to reality that they do not affect our conclusions. Competition among thousands of grain farmers may be nearly perfect; the difference between the weights of iron and lead balls may not produce a significant difference in their speeds when they are dropped from the Leaning Tower of Pisa. In these cases it would take very careful observation to see any differences, and the differences would be so small that in most circumstances we would not care. But if the assumptions were wildly incorrect for a particular set of problems, the results would be irrelevant at best, disastrous at worst. What if we assumed that competition in the international sale of petroleum was perfect? Or that air resistance would make no difference in the speeds of a feather and a lead ball dropped from the tower? By following the precepts of scientific inquiry, a careful analyst will always be alert to the nature of his or her assumptions, to ways in which they may differ from reality, and to the conditions under which the difference may be significant. A careful analyst will want to know what has been simplified and to have some sense of how that simplification may lead his or her predictions to depart from observable reality.

## *Specifying and Testing Hypotheses*

Social scientists often proceed in the following way:

> **1.** Start with some observations or some facts that need explaining.
> **2.** Offer some tentative hypotheses.
> **3.** Evaluate the hypotheses in light of available facts.
> **4.** If these facts do support the hypotheses, look for some implications—general propositions that can be deduced from the first hypotheses and facts.
> **5.** Test such propositions on the first case or on new cases.[14]

Sometimes an analysis along these lines is referred to as a "thinking experiment." It is a purely analytical exercise, unlike clinical or laboratory experiments, in which one varies actual conditions to see what effect the changes have. With citizens and nations, we simply cannot conduct a real-life experiment. Nor are we able for this chapter to gather and document systematically a substantial body of rigorous empirical data on the case we will discuss below. Instead, we shall proceed with a very tentative analysis, proposing hypotheses that would require much more theory and

---

[14] This procedure is nicely presented and illustrated in Charles A. Lave and James G. March, *An Introduction to Models in the Social Sciences* (New York: Harper & Row, 1975), chap. 1.

research but that meanwhile may produce some intriguing suggestions. Still, this exercise highlights another hallmark of science—that propositions must confront evidence and should then be revised or abandoned on that basis. As Rosenau notes, "To think theoretically one must be constantly ready to be proven wrong."

Our example is Gorbachev's decision not to use Soviet troops to suppress the dissidents of East Germany in 1989 and thus save its communist government. This was one of the most dramatic and important decisions that permitted an end to the cold war. The discussion illustrates some approaches to the great guessing game about the sources and stability of Soviet policy up to that point. Different hypotheses can be derived from realist, transnationalist, and radical perspectives.

**Hypothesis 1**  Gorbachev did not use force to support the East German government because he feared a NATO military response, perhaps culminating in World War III. A realist might say that the NATO allies could not have resisted the opportunity to gain a critical power advantage; in this case, to bring all East Germany under their control. A radical might say much the same thing but give as the reason the capitalist world's continuing wish to expand the realm of capitalism and to bring down the competing system of economic and political organization.

*Evaluation*  One problem with either version of this hypothesis is that the NATO countries had passed up similar opportunities in the past. When the Soviet Union crushed the Hungarian revolution in 1956 and the liberalization of Czechoslovakia known as the Prague Spring in 1968, the West did virtually nothing. NATO countries implicitly acknowledged that the Soviet Union had the right to do as it wished within Eastern Europe, its own sphere of influence, and that the risks involved in any NATO military response were much too great. There is little reason to think they would have judged the situation in East Germany differently in 1989.

**Hypothesis 2**  Gorbachev did not use force because he secretly held goals different from those of other Soviet leaders. Perhaps he really was a "closet democrat" who wanted to see noncommunist governments in East Germany and the rest of Eastern Europe (a transnationalist explanation), or perhaps he really was an agent of the CIA whose aim was to betray communism (a radical explanation).

*Evaluation*  There are virtually no facts to support either version of this hypothesis. Gorbachev acted much more like a reformer of communism, with no fully formed goal in mind, than like someone who wanted to do away with the communist system entirely. He came out of much the same set of party and government experiences as did other Soviet leaders, giving no hint of a desire to make a complete break with the past. As for deliberately betraying the system as a Western agent, that belief requires very great faith in the CIA. We find both versions of this hypothesis implausible.

**Hypothesis 3**  Gorbachev feared he could no longer make repression effective and that the effort to do so would only hasten the spread of revolution across Eastern Europe (a transnationalist hypothesis).

*Evaluation*   This hypothesis draws its strength from the increasing growth of transnational communications links that carried new information and ideas into and out of Eastern Europe. It implies that people would rise up in support of those ideas and in support of one another, even in the face of terrible costs. Perhaps the Soviet people, and Soviet troops, would also have rebelled rather than permit wholesale repression. It is true that transnational linkages had grown substantially. Yet comparatively recently, in Czechoslovakia in 1968, they had little effect. While one cannot completely dismiss this hypothesis, it is implausible as a primary explanation.

**Hypothesis 4**   Gorbachev knew that the use of force would alienate the Western countries on whom he was relying for technological and military assistance to rebuild the Soviet economy. No Soviet leader with such a goal could afford to do something that would cut off the possibility of trade with the West (another transnational hypothesis).

*Evaluation*   This hypothesis also has some plausibility, but it does not fit all the facts well. Western responses to previous Soviet crackdowns on dissent had not been very strong. When in December 1981 the communist government of Poland violently repressed the Solidarity movement with Soviet approval and encouragement (but with no Soviet troops), there was only a partial and ineffective Western trade embargo; the same was true in response to the Soviet military intervention in Afghanistan. Gorbachev might have thought that once again the West would accept the Soviet sphere of influence and not enforce severe economic sanctions.

**Hypothesis 5**   Gorbachev did not intervene because Eastern Europe had become not an asset but a serious drain on Soviet resources; he thought that the national interest of the Soviet Union would be better served economically and politically by letting the satellites go (a realist hypothesis).

*Evaluation*   There is a lot of evidence that Eastern Europe had long been an economic drain, receiving many hidden subsidies such as cheap Soviet oil for barter rather than having to purchase it at world market prices for dollars. On the one hand, such considerations had earlier had little effect; on the other hand, we now know that the Soviet economy was in far worse shape than suspected by most analysts. More importantly for the evaluation of theory, national-interest explanations can too easily be created after an event. Almost anything can be described as in the national interest, but the national interest is not something self-evident that all objective observers would agree on.

**Hypothesis 6**   Gorbachev did not intervene because the Soviet Union no longer needed the political and military buffer that Eastern Europe had provided. Gorbachev no longer, if he ever had, feared a NATO attack (another realist hypothesis).

*Evaluation*   Gorbachev might finally have decided that the West did not wish to attack. But it is not clear why Western intentions should have so recently—in the years of tough rhetoric from the Reagan administration about the Soviet "evil empire"—come to seem more benign, or why Gorbachev in particular should have reached that conclusion. Evidence for the realist view may be found in the growing Soviet and American realization that in a world of nuclear parity, nuclear weapons could not be used credibly for anything but the defense of one's homeland, and certainly not to coerce another superpower. Thus as long as the Soviet Union retained a rough nuclear parity with the United States, it could protect itself without allies or the kind of in-depth defense that a shield of sullen East European satellites might provide. After 1986 Gorbachev abandoned most of his previous rhetoric in favor of totally eliminating nuclear weapons from the world, and he may have come to see them as even more necessary than the satellites.

**New Propositions and Possible Tests**   We did not totally reject any of the hypotheses, although the first two seem least compelling. Even the last two, probably the strongest, are expressed in ambiguous terms and cannot be either accepted or rejected confidently. The important part of the exercise, however, is not to make a definitive choice among them but to confront various hypotheses and consider the kind of logic and evidence that would make one more plausible than another. Each stresses different variables and even different levels of analysis. For example, the individuality of Gorbachev is stressed in hypothesis 2 (a micro-explanation based on understanding how a particular individual views the world). Hypothesis 5 emphasizes economic conditions within formerly communist-ruled areas, and hypothesis 6 focuses on superpower military relations in an international system with bipolar nuclear capabilities (these are both macro-explanations based on factors from the global political environment). Making the hypotheses more precise, with sharper definitions of economic burdens or the nuclear balance, would make it clearer how—and whether—they could be tested by confronting systematic evidence from the real world.

They might be tested in several ways. One would be to look more systematically at the several times during the cold war era in which Soviet leaders had to decide whether to use military force to suppress a rebellion. This would have to include not only instances when the Soviet government did use force but also instances when it did not (for example, when Yugoslav president Tito took his country out of the Soviet orbit in 1948). One could compare the different objective conditions and also the different public statements and reasons given for Soviet actions. Public statements may not, however, give real reasons; ultimately, new scholarly access to Soviet government archives may give us a better, but still imperfect, measure of what the real reasons were. Better still would be to treat the hypotheses as general statements about all major military powers and alliance leaders, not just the Soviet Union, to see how widely they may apply. Alternatively, one could look at analyses of the peaceful breakup of the Soviet Union itself for additional evidence (or even hypotheses).

## FACTS AND VALUES

Science can help us in understanding the world. Makers of political decisions take actions every day that affect the lives and happiness of millions of people, but they do not always know what the effects of their acts will be, nor do their advisers. While recognizing that action is necessary, we must retain a sense of humility about the knowledge base of our actions. Similar self-consciousness is needed for statements of *value*. We make such statements all the time: one painting is more beautiful than another; one act is morally right and another wrong. We all make these judgments, with varying degrees of confidence, and we often disagree about them. The systems of thought by which we deduce statements about goodness and beauty may start from very different premises. A Buddhist, a Sunni Muslim, an evangelical Christian, and an atheistic Marxist may well agree that certain elements of life, such as decent living conditions and essential liberties, constitute, in some sense, "basic human rights." But they will differ in how they arrive at that common conclusion, about the specific forms those rights should take, and about the relative importance of each.

Rosenau warns us, "To think theoretically one has to be clear as to whether one aspires to empirical theory or value theory." We need to be concerned with values, because the values held by scholars affect what they study—what questions they ask, using what theories. One of the sources of theory thus may be the questions raised by an analyst's values or ethics. The methods of science cannot establish or compare the validity of different sets of values; these are normative questions. Some cultures value political liberty more highly than do others; poor people may rate decent living conditions as more important than political rights. Religion, ethical systems, other elements of culture, and economic conditions influence people's values and ethical judgments. Science can, however, help us clarify our thinking about values. It can help us understand the consequences of pursuing certain values and help us see to what degree policies or strategies will help us achieve our values. That is, science can help us understand the relationship between our ends and our means.

## THE USES OF A STUDY OF WORLD POLITICS

We can analyze a decision or event from the perspectives of different approaches to world politics and at various levels of analysis. In some of the next chapters we shall be focusing on characteristics of the global system (Chapters 4 and 5), the relations between nation-states (Chapters 6 and 7), and nation-states as actors (Chapters 8 and 9). We shall emphasize the large-scale, highly aggregated units of analysis, working with theories holding that the most important, persistent influences on war and economic distribution are found at the highest levels. This kind of analysis is part of the grand sociological tradition shared in different ways and with different theoretical details by writers such as Émile Durkheim and Karl Marx (and more recently by Kenneth Waltz). The case for this perspective is well argued by Nazli Choucri and Robert North in their analysis of the conditions that brought about World War I:

> The dynamics of national growth and expansion, the conflict of national interests, patterns of growth in military expenditures, alliance-formation, and violence-behavior . . . were not the immediate cause of WWI. The processes set the stage, armed the players, and deployed the forces, but they did not join the antagonists in combat. They created the conditions of an armed camp within which the assassination of the Austrian archduke was sufficient to trigger an international crisis and a major war.[15]

Even if the particular crisis of August 1914 had been resolved by wiser decision makers, from this perspective the underlying international dynamics of national expansion were certain to create further crises, and one or another of them was very likely to escalate out of control. Thus it is important to understand the great forces that regularly produce situations fraught with the threat of war rather than to study the behavior of decision makers alone. Although individuals may be able to extricate themselves from one crisis, they cannot be expected to do so repeatedly in an environment where basic systemic forces continually produce crises.

A scholar pursuing scientific inquiry works at a level of analysis different from that of a policymaker faced with immediate decisions. This difference can be illustrated by comparing the situations of a medical researcher and a practicing physician in relation to coronary illness. Research scientists have established that a number of personal characteristics and environmental conditions contribute to heart disease. They now know that an individual's probability of suffering a heart attack is greater if that person is male and middle-aged or older and if one or both parents suffered heart attacks. Factors that increase the likelihood of heart disease include being overweight, smoking, consuming a diet high in cholesterol-rich fats, and not getting enough exercise. High blood pressure also contributes to this likelihood, as do stress and anxiety in the working or living environment. Finally, some people with aggressive, hard-driving personalities appear especially prone to heart disease. For the scientist, all these influences may seem interesting, providing information that may at some point be important.

For the physician who must treat patients, however, different influences are not of equal interest. Some are beyond the control of the individual patient or doctor: the patient cannot stop growing older, is probably unwilling to change gender, and cannot change biological parents. A patient, to some degree, may be able to change a lifestyle or even quit a stressful job, but most people cannot do much about their basic personality. A doctor may actually increase the danger of heart attack by frightening an already worried or anxious patient.

---

[15] Nazli Choucri and Robert North, *Nations in Conflict: National Growth and International Violence* (San Francisco: Freeman, 1975), p. 9. For Waltz's view of the macro-structure of international politics, see *Man, the State and War* (New York: Columbia University Press, 1959) and *Theory of International Politics* (Boston: Addison-Wesley, 1979).

Other influences, however, can be more readily controlled. High blood pressure or high cholesterol, for instance, can be reduced by medication. A patient can be told to lose weight, stop smoking, change diet, or get more exercise. Controlling just one of these conditions may be enough, especially if two contributing influences interact (if, for example, smoking and obesity together pose a much greater danger than either one alone). In a particular patient, heart disease may be "overdetermined"; that is, *any one* of the several contributing conditions is sufficient to produce a high risk of disease and therefore all must be eliminated. Here, very careful theory, as well as detailed understanding of a particular case, is essential for responsible treatment. Patients who refuse to take any steps to reduce their risks can at least be advised to keep their life insurance paid up—prediction is of some value even without control over the medical events! Finally, some normative considerations may also apply. Suppose a patient also suffers from a painful and terminal cancer. Should that patient be saved from a heart attack only to be faced with a difficult death from cancer shortly thereafter? Neither doctor nor patient can be indifferent to such a question, whatever their answer.

In our concern with world politics, we must take into account many considerations similar to those facing the physician.[16] At times the student of world politics proceeds chiefly with the kind of concern typical of scientists, at times with that typical of policymakers, policy advisers, or citizen activists. A scientist wants to understand the causes of a particular phenomenon; he or she hopes to find those influences or variables that make the greatest difference in the outcome of some dependent variable (in statistical terms, to find the variable or variables that will account for a large proportion of the variation or variance). Practitioners of "pure science" are not so immediately concerned with whether that difference (variance) can actually be controlled in practice, that is, with whether the explanatory variables are themselves readily manipulable by policymakers. Although a good scientist will have theoretically based reasons for expecting a particular variable or level of analysis to be especially powerful, in principle there should be no reason for preferring an explanation in terms of a particular variable or level.

The first step is explanation or understanding and perhaps prediction. Of course, since any scientific endeavor is driven by ethical or value preferences, the social scientist will care about finding practical ways to make a difference (say, in promoting peace). But he or she will neither necessarily expect the immediate application demanded by a policymaker nor need to serve the bureaucratic or political interests that constrain a policymaker's choice of goals and instruments.

The policymaker, by contrast, is concerned with predicting phenomena, especially with an eye toward changing outcomes from what they might otherwise be. Insofar as the concern is with *prediction*, the policymaker, like the scientist, should not in principle care what variable emerges as a good predictor, provided that it is one on which complete and reliable information can be gathered. But to *change* outcomes,

---

[16] Johan Galtung has also argued the parallels between peace research and medical science. See "Twenty-five Years of Peace Research: Ten Challenges and Some Responses," *Journal of Peace Research* 22 (1985), 141–158.

the policymaker must identify not just powerful but also manipulable variables. Explanations that identify something controllable are more interesting to policymakers than those that identify broad historical forces over which the policymaker has little control. Manipulability is of prime interest, prediction next, and simple understanding of little import. In this way the policymaker is likely to be much more interested in explanations about how a crisis can be resolved short of war than in knowing about forces that brought about the crisis. The policymaker may have little control over the latter or may not be willing to exercise much control. The role of pure scientist may not be a popular one.

Suppose we showed that large, bureaucratically unwieldy states are more prone to making war; that great powers with systemwide interests are more likely to be involved in world-endangering crises; that the dynamics of capitalism or communism produce expansionist, aggressive, and war-prone behavior. Would a policymaker for such a government want to take the steps that would reduce the power of the state or fundamentally change its socioeconomic system even if the steps could be identified? An explanation of how decision makers perceive and act under crisis conditions may seem more interesting. The decision maker may in fact have little control over the external environment but may believe that it is possible to exert substantial influence over the decision-making system that obtains in times of crisis and improve it. Even if the perception variable was relatively weak in explanatory power, it would be attractive because of its potential manipulability.

Most people who deal in world politics share elements of the perspectives we have characterized, in extreme form, as those of scientists and policymakers. They want to understand and to effect change. In the long run, even the givens of politics are subject to change: systems decay; powers rise and fall. Sometimes a system may be given a nudge by citizens who care enough. Policymakers may try to change the basic conditions of the international system, as did those Americans and Europeans who, in the decades after World War II, promoted European political and economic integration through the development and implementation of the Marshall Plan and its massive economic aid, or the Europeans who promoted the creation of organizations like the European Coal and Steel Community, which led to the European Economic Community and the present-day European Union.

In this book we are attempting to offer some understanding of world political phenomena without necessarily providing readily manipulable levers to solve problems. We shall address basic questions about war, peace, development, governance, and justice that will be around for many decades and that will require concerted, long-term effort. We shall look at explanations of why wars occur, how crises can be managed to peaceful conclusions, and why crises arise at all. We shall look at arms races and why they can escalate or be restrained, and at problems of economic and political interdependence among the rich industrialized countries of the world and how inflation or depression can spread and constrain national governments. We shall look at relations between rich and poor countries; from one perspective they are seen as questions of access to resources and of promoting growth in national income, and from another as questions of dependence, national autonomy, and internal distribution of economic and political rewards. We shall also look at problems of global resource availability and distribution, population pressures, pollution, and alleged limits to growth. And all of these questions will be considered in light of the global growth of democracy and the effects democracy has on both military and economic relations.

Some of these problems would have been discussed in a textbook written 20 or 30 years ago; others are quite new. Part of the change may be attributed to very important changes in empirical reality in the world around us. Global pollution, for example, certainly is perceived as far more threatening now than it was a few decades ago. Yet pollution has been carried across international borders for centuries, like the industrial pollutants swept down the Rhine River, without being considered a major political issue. Small countries have always been dependent on big ones, but theories about the causes and consequences of that dependence have become widely adopted only with the great increase in the number of politically sovereign states during recent decades. The Soviet Union is gone, and with it the cold war that had dominated international politics since 1945. Yet major powers or empires have come and gone throughout world history. One might argue that democracy has been on the menu of the international system since 1776, but only now, for the first time, could a near-majority of state actors in the system be called democracies.

Thus facts change, values change, problems change, and theories change. At a very basic level, we shall try to teach you *how to think* about political phenomena without referring to particular contemporary problems. Given a set of analytical tools to apply to new problems many years from now, you will have to search for your own manipulable levers—levers appropriate to your circumstances, your political resources, your understanding, and your values.

# International Actors: States and Other Players on the World Stage

## Humans in Groups: Nationalism and the Nation

Now that we have provided some basic conceptions of world politics and how it is studied, one further preliminary issue must be discussed: Exactly what sorts of groups of people are we concerned with? Whose behavior interests us? We must start our discussion of the actors on the world stage at the most basic level. World politics begins with the idea of *relations*, activities between social entities. Thus we must start with the notion of humans forming *groups*.

Perhaps one of the things that makes us human is our need to affiliate into groups. Aristotle observed that people are social animals, a view supported by such disciplines as anthropology and sociology (and ethology, the study of animal behavior). Because our evolutionary heritage provides us with the genetic material most open to the forces and influences of the environment, we also *require a social environment* for the brain to develop and for potential skills like speech and written communication to be realized. Human beings as animals—as physical and physiological creatures—appear to require society and throughout their existence have formed into groups.

The comfort, security, and other advantages that a group provides for its members are central to the study of sociology and psychology. Given the limitations of the human animal, people must form into groups to meet physiological and psychological wants and needs. Thus along with the idea of the group goes the idea of identification. Individuals will identify with groups, give their loyalty to them, and act to maintain their character, security, and survival; the group identity gives individuals a basic sense of "belongingness" and self-esteem. We can say that a group of individuals has developed a group identification and a group loyalty when a certain amount of "we-feeling" exists—when members feel more like "we" than like some other "they." This is reflected in Hobsbawm's notion of "national consciousness"—that any group of people who "regard themselves" as a "nation" should be treated as one.[1]

The group is defined and held together by complex nets of *social communications* among people. Barriers to social communication (because of distance, language, or different belief systems about how the world works based on such things as religion, ideology, or different historical experiences) help create differentiated groups of people. The more easily social communication flows, the greater the probability that such feelings of "we-ness" and identity will develop. These notions of social communication and the development of we-feeling and loyalty underlie group identification from the smallest social organization to the nation-state. In fact, nationalism can be seen as a group consciousness that serves to hold together the largest groupings of people that have ever formed.[2] When people identify with groups, they are cut off from people not in those groups. Much of what occurs in world politics boils down to this separation of "we" and "they." *They* are different; therefore, they are not normal; therefore, they are inferior in some way; and so on. *They* always want something we have. Can *they* be trusted? What do *they* really want?

In discussing the nation-state, we have started with the idea of a **nation,** a people who feel themselves part of some large identity group. The nation results from a complex and lengthy process by which **nationalism** develops. The development of the concept and reality of the state is similarly complex. Historically, as we shall see, state-building occurred in Europe over a period of several hundred years before 1648, when the Treaty of Westphalia was signed, ending the Thirty Years' War. Kings and

---

[1] See E. J. Hobsbawm, *Nations and Nationalism Since 1780* (Cambridge: Cambridge University Press, 1990). For the psychological role that group identity plays for humans, e.g., "belongingness," see Harold Isaacs, *Idols of the Tribe: Group Identity and Political Change* (New York: Harper & Row, 1975), pp. 32–33.
[2] These ideas were developed in Karl Deutsch's classic work, *Nationalism and Social Communication* (Cambridge, Mass.: MIT Press, 1953).

princes extended their central authority over territories that had been a disconnected hodgepodge of feudal fiefdoms. Centralization and consolidation continued throughout Europe until World War I. Each group that identified itself as a people sought to govern and represent itself through the medium of the legal and sovereign entity known as the state—that is, people who identified themselves as a nation sought their own state. State-building could take the form of unification; for example, neither Italy nor Germany was finally united into a nation-state until the latter half of the nineteenth century, when war and diplomatic maneuver were used to forge single units out of many smaller states.

Other European nationalities sought to establish their own states by separating themselves from the larger empires that dominated much of Europe until World War I. These imperial entities included the Turkish Ottoman Empire, which had begun its spread westward into Eastern and Central Europe in the early 1300s and then retreated only slowly after its defeat before the gates of Vienna in 1683. The Austro-Hungarian Empire was the descendant of the Austrian Empire, and before that the Holy Roman Empire of the Hapsburgs. Under Charles V, Holy Roman Emperor from 1519 to 1558, the Hapsburg territories dominated the Continent. When his Hapsburg inheritances were combined with the areas under nominal control of the Empire, Charles's dominions included what is now Spain (and its New World possessions at that time), the Netherlands, Belgium, most of Italy, Austria, and many of the states of Central Europe. A third multiethnic, or multinational, grouping was the Russian Empire. Turkish rule in Europe was ended with the two Balkan wars of 1912–13. The process by which nations separated from larger entities to form their own states culminated, in the aftermath of World War I, with the dissolution of all three of the empires noted above, as well as of Imperial Germany.

The desire of national groups to separate from larger empires and form their own states was the dominant process reflecting nationalism until the end of World War II. Nationalistic separatism has vigorously reemerged over the past decade or so as a crucial issue in world politics, as modern-day "empires" such as the Soviet Union, or multiethnic states such as Yugoslavia, have similarly disintegrated. Other groups with national consciousness but without states, such as the Kurds and the Palestinians, have had important effects on world politics.

It is crucial to note that this process may work in reverse. As we have seen in the post–World War II period of decolonization, it is possible to have governments or states that exist without a nation. This condition is found in areas outside of Europe, especially in Africa, where states have been artificially created out of the Western colonial empires. Thus, in states such as Nigeria or India, the process then becomes one of creating a nation—a we-feeling—to match the already existing state.

So far nationalism has been discussed primarily in terms of we-ness—a condition of mind, a feeling of identification or loyalty to some group of people. This is probably the crucial factor—that people *feel* themselves to be American or German or Canadian or Bulgarian or Cuban. What produces the we-feeling? A number of factors have been identified. One is regionalism, sharing a common territory. People living and interacting in the same area, facing similar problems and challenges, often develop a common feeling and identity. Closely related to regionalism is the effect of common economic activities, of relying on the same resources, engaging in the same types of activities, and having common sets of economic interactions. All these provide people with a similar view of the world and common interests.

A second set of factors is related to cultural similarity. A common language is an extremely important aspect of nationalism. Indeed, in attempting to increase national cohesion, political leaders have reinstituted languages that were dead or had been used only infrequently. The resurrection of the Welsh language by nationalists in Wales is at best only a partially successful attempt to use a language to reinforce or create nationalistic feelings, whereas the use of Hebrew in Israel has been quite successful in drawing together a diverse people.[3] Other common cultural factors that have proven particularly powerful in today's world are a common ethnic background and a common religion. Finally, and maybe most importantly, is the existence of a set of historical experiences and backgrounds perceived as a common history. John Stoessinger defines nationalism as "a people's sense of collective destiny through a common past and the vision of a common future"; Robert Jackman argues that "nationalism entails the invocation of a common historical and political *tradition*."[4]

There is a psychological element that leads a people to desire the territorial and legal aspects of the state. Without this psychological element, any government would have difficulty in ruling a group of people occupying its territory. Many conflicts in contemporary international politics arise from threats (or perceived threats) to group identification and loyalty. Many would explain the Soviet reaction to American pressure in the early 1970s for increased Jewish emigration from the USSR as reaction to a perceived threat to the national identity of Soviet peoples. The critical reaction to Vietnam War resisters in the United States during that conflict stemmed largely from the psychological threat they posed by challenging the solidarity of the national group and appearing disloyal. The swift and often vicious reaction of governments all around the world to regional, tribal, and other movements for autonomy is based on the fear of such disloyalty spreading to other parts of their populations.

States have fought intense civil wars over unity or separation. The Ibo rebellion and the attempt to establish Biafra was defeated by the Nigerian government in a war that lasted from May 1967 to January 1970. In contrast, the Bengali secession from Pakistan was successful. The Bengali population of East Pakistan rose in riots and instituted a general strike in March 1971 after being denied victory at the polls. Though sharing a common religion, East and West Pakistan differed in ethnicity, language, and economic factors and were separated by approximately 1,000 miles of Indian territory. West Pakistani armed attacks on the East Pakistanis led to the December 1971 war between India and Pakistan. The Indian victory permitted the Bengalis to declare their own independent state, Bangladesh. India, a large and diverse country, has itself been wracked by conflict among different linguistic, regional, racial, and religious groups. Violence involving the Sikh religious minority in the Punjab was

---

[3] Protection of group identity is part of the rationale for the European Community's creation, in 1982, of the Bureau for Lesser Used Languages—to help them maintain their existence in the face of unification and the dominance of English, German, and French.

[4] John Stoessinger, *The Might of Nations* (New York: Random House, 1979), p. 10; Robert W. Jackman, *Power Without Force* (Ann Arbor: University of Michigan Press, 1993), p. 102.

responsible for the assassination of Prime Minister Indira Gandhi in 1984 and for increasing separatist violence into the 1990s. The early 1990s also saw the intensification of a Muslim drive for an independent Kashmir and insurgent separatism in the northeast state of Assam. Such communal conflict was intensified by a revival of Hindu fundamentalism, itself a reaction to the long series of challenges to the Hindu domination of India.

Fears of a breakdown in nationalism, however, are not confined to the less developed states or only to those states formed since World War II. Loyalty is based on group interaction. If some part of a group feels it is being exploited or not treated fairly, or that there *no longer exists mutual benefit* from association with the larger group, the loyalty and we-feeling will disintegrate. The *process* of national integration is a continuous one and, unless tended to, is always susceptible to disintegration. The most graphic instance of disintegration is seen in the violent aftermath of the breakup of Yugoslavia; we can also see its effects in the rapid dissolution of the Soviet Union (with its own violence among groups contending for control of territory and governments). Without the authoritarian control of a communist government, the peoples of Czechoslovakia have also separated—peacefully, in this case.

While many new developing countries must worry about diverse ethnic groups that lack strong feelings of national unity, even the older states of Europe must continually work to make ethnic minorities *feel* a nationalist connection to the nation-state as a whole. There are more or less well-organized nationalist movements among the Bretons and Corsicans who are governed by France, the Basques in Spain, and the Welsh and Scots in Britain. In Canada, French-speakers in the province of Quebec have a long tradition of separatist politics. Canada's handling of this problem is a good example of how an established and developed state risks being broken apart and of the dilemmas that a democracy faces in such a situation. Attempts at nation-building included the institutionalization of bilingualism, special constitutional arrangements, and the creation of specifically Canadian images for the national flag and national anthem (the previous flag had incorporated the British Union Jack and the anthem had been "God Save the Queen"). That political crises continue to occur in Canada over the proper constitutional arrangements required to deal with the separatist movement in Quebec and yet satisfy the western provinces indicates the difficulties of building and maintaining a state.

One problem in discussing nationalism is that no single factor seems sufficient by itself to create and maintain the psychological element of we-ness and the individual's supreme loyalty to the national group: language is important, yet several viable nation-states exist with multiple languages (Switzerland, for instance, has four—French, German, Italian, and Romansch); Germany, Nigeria, and the United States have several major religions; other states exhibit regional differences and/or multiple ethnic cultures. Perhaps the closest to a sufficient condition for a we-feeling is the existence of a common history, though it is not always clear why some experiences are perceived as shared by all and others as limited to a subgroup. The sharing of common historical experiences, particularly the anticolonial experience, receives great emphasis in many of the new states that have gained independence since World War II. In the post–World War II system, states with no logic beyond the arbitrary boundary lines drawn on maps by colonial powers are split by diverse tribal, religious, ethnic, and racial groups and are struggling to forge group loyalty from this diversity.

While no one factor appears to be sufficient to account for a group loyalty, it may be that a cleavage along any of these lines is sufficient to bring about group conflict. The pressures toward separatism or fragmentation in the world system are powerful and widespread. Data from 1986 on 166 countries show only a third of these states to be ethnically homogeneous (one group constituting at least 90 percent of the population). In almost half the countries the largest ethnic group accounted for less than 75 percent of the population, and in a quarter of them, less than 50 percent. Kazakhstan is representative of such problems among the former Soviet states—less than 45 percent of the population are Kazakhs, over a third are ethnic Russians, and about 100 other ethnic groups exist in a country that is about four times the size of Texas. Over a third of the countries had major religious cleavages as well. Most modern states "are mosaics of distinct peoples whose identities and aspirations may or may not be accepted and protected by those who hold state power." While noting one estimate by a geographer that perhaps as many as 5,000 distinct communities (communal minorities, or "ethnies") exist with a claim to being a national people, this study by political scientists identifies 233 nonsovereign communal groups—"minorities at risk"—that have been involved in serious conflicts during the post-1945 period.[5]

This research has identified 50 serious ethnopolitical conflicts during 1993–94, conflicts over political independence or control that have followed revolution, the emergence of democracy, or the creation of new states. These conflicts (ranging from war, through low-intensity military conflict, to disputes involving state repression) have caused nearly 4 million deaths and the displacement of almost 27 million refugees. As can be seen from Table 3.1, which lists the 18 ethnopolitical "wars" occurring during 1993–94, fully half are in Africa, and the rest are found in Europe (3), South and Southeast Asia (5), and Latin America (1). The table also indicates that the main issue in these wars is split: half the cases involve "ethnonationalism"—the separatism of large, regionally concentrated groups from the state; half the cases involve communal contention for power—the struggle to control the government.[6]

Nationalism is about "psychological community," or loyalty to a group, and, as we can see, the current system is witnessing a growth of loyalties to nonstate groups where loyalties are based on communal ties of various kinds. The rise of religious fundamentalism is one example of the forces of fragmentation that face the nation-state today. For example, an individual may feel first a Shiite, then a Muslim, and then an Iraqi, in a loyalty chain that finds the state last on the list. One observer sees fragmentation as a major force in world politics that will increase the number of

---

[5] The first set of figures was assembled from John Clements, *Clements' Encyclopedia of World Governments*, vol. 7 (Dallas: Political Research, Inc., 1986); the second set of findings was reported in Ted Robert Gurr and James R. Scarritt, "Minorities at Risk: A Global Survey," *Human Rights Quarterly* 11 (1989), 375–405 and in Ted Robert Gurr, *Minorities at Risk: A Global View of Ethnopolitical Conflicts* (Washington, D.C.: United States Institute of Peace Press, 1993).

[6] These data are from Ted Robert Gurr, "Peoples Against States: Ethnopolitical Conflict and the Changing World System," *International Studies Quarterly* 38 (September 1994), 347–377.

**TABLE 3.1**  Ethnopolitical Wars in the World System, 1993–1994

| Location | Description and Issue | Deaths (1000s) |
| --- | --- | --- |
| Azerbaijan | Armenians seek independence of Nagorno-Karabakh enclave [E] | 15 |
| Georgia | Russian-backed Abkhazians won autonomy in late 1993 [E] | 10 |
| Bosnia | Serbs and Croats seek to partition Bosnia, eliminate Muslims [E] | 200 |
| Burma | Autonomy rebellions by Karen, Shan Kachin, Mon, Arakanese and other hill/tribal peoples [IE] | 130 |
| India | Sikh insurgents fight for independent Khalistan [E] | 20–25 |
| Sri Lanka | Tamil insurgents fight for independent Tamil state [E] | 78–100 |
| India | Pakistan-supported Kashmiris fighting for independence [E] | 250 |
| Afghanistan | Civil war among Pashtun, Tajik, and Uzbek factions [C] | 575–1,000 |
| Angola | Protracted civil war based on Mbundu-Ovimbundu rivalry [C] | 500 |
| Chad | Protracted civil war, currently based on Anakaza vs. Bideyet ethnic conflict [C] | 100 |
| Sudan | Renewed civil war between Muslim government and southern factions; southern interfactional fighting [E] | 1,000–1,500 |
| Burundi | Tutsi–Hutu violence, both tribal and political [C] | 500–800 |
| Somalia | Clans battle in south; Isaaq clan leads independent north [CE] | 350 |
| Liberia | Civil war based on ethnic rivalries [C] | 150 |
| South Africa | ANC vs. Zulu protracted communal war prior to 1994 elections [C] | 14 |
| Rwanda | Exiled Tutsi wars against Hutu regime [C] | 3.5 |
| Djibouti | Afar rebellion against Somali-dominated government [IC] | 1 |
| Peru | Indigenous peoples forced to support leftist Sendero Luminoso guerrillas [IC] | 30 |

Code for issues: C = communal contention for power; E = ethnonationalism; I = indigenous rights.

*Source:* Ted Robert Gurr, "Peoples Against States: Ethnopolitical Conflict and the Changing World System," *International Studies Quarterly* 38 (September 1994), 369–375.

independent actors and shrink the size of many existing states. An example: Having expanded from a small area around Kiev in the ninth century, "Russia" first became the Russian Empire and then expanded further into the USSR; now, it is again Russia (but with only about half the population and three-quarters of the land area of the Soviet Union). Other observers simply note: "Maps which show the world neatly divided into countries, each with its own boundaries and territory, convey a misleading image of people's political identities."[7]

## THE STATE AS INTERNATIONAL ACTOR

Despite a number of trends to the contrary, the **state** (or the nation-state) has been and remains the primary actor in the global system. The number of states in the system has risen steadily since the end of World War II. In the 20 years from 1973 to 1993 the number of states in the international system grew by a full third. Another indicator is the growth in the membership of the United Nations: in 1945 there were 51 charter members of the UN; in 1994 the admission of Palau capped a burst of new members (28 from 1990 to 1994), increasing the membership to 185. Of the 28 new members since 1990, a full two-thirds were the result of the drive for separatism, especially the fragmentation of formerly communist systems. Six other new members were *micro*states such as Andorra, which had long been part of the international system (to be discussed below). The addition of 133 new members exemplifies the continuing desire of groups to achieve statehood in the contemporary system, no matter their size or previous status.

### The Development of the Westphalian State System

There have been large-scale political organizations for 7,000 years, starting with the city-states and empires of the Tigris and Euphrates and the Nile. But the state or nation-state in its present form is relatively new. While many scholars date the modern nation-state from 1648 and the Treaty of Westphalia, the state as it existed in the seventeenth century was the result of a convergence of processes that had been occurring for over 500 years before Westphalia. The 200 years from about 1450 to 1650 mark the transition from one historical epoch to another, when the combination and interaction of political, economic, technological, and religious factors were decisive in bringing about the shift to the modern **Westphalian state system**.[8]

---

[7] Ted Robert Gurr and Barbara Harff, *Ethnic Conflict in World Politics* (Boulder, Col.: Westview, 1994), p. 1. For the discussion of fragmentation, see James N. Rosenau, *Turbulence in World Politics* (Princeton, N.J.: Princeton University Press, 1990).

[8] See Geoffrey Barraclough, *An Introduction to Contemporary History* (New York: Penguin, 1964), for an introduction to these ideas of transition and interaction. Barraclough also reminds us to look for the differences and discontinuities in history.

For hundreds of years before this transition period, Europe consisted of a complex system of feudal entities. With the disintegration of the Roman Empire during the fifth century, the Germanic tribes that conquered the settlements in western Europe remained organized as tribes and had severed their political or economic ties to the Mediterranean region. The Frankish emperor Charlemagne, established in 800, began to create tentatively a realm as large as Europe, but it too was overrun by barbarians. Even after the sacking of Rome the Church maintained a presence and spiritual authority across Europe, and both waves of invaders were assimilated into Christianity. By 1000 a system composed of large numbers of local political entities was in place, based on the feudal relationships between lord and vassal, an agricultural economy, and lack of trade with other parts of the world.

The leaders of these various feudal entities, and their subjects, were enmeshed in a web of multiple loyalties. The various levels and ranks of nobility were both vassals and lords, receiving fealty (loyalty, obedience) from those below them and giving fealty to those above them. In principle such loyalty culminated in two figures: the Holy Roman Emperor, in regard to secular authority and leadership, and the Pope, in regard to spiritual authority and leadership. In stark distinction from the sovereign state that was to develop, no ruler (or people under him) had a monopoly of political authority over any territory.

European history before the rise of states reflected the politics and interactions of cultures, religion, and individual nobles or princes more than of states. As noted, a convergence of political, economic, technological, and religious factors helped to create the state, replacing personal and societal bonds with international relations. All the factors were related in complex **feedback** loops; that is, each affected every other and was in turn affected by the results of earlier processes.[9] Scholars studying the rise of the Western national state focus on two central elements: capital and coercion. As monarchs attempted to expand, centralize, and consolidate their control over territory and people in their struggles against the feudal nobility, they needed wealth and resources (capital) and the means to prosecute war (coercion). These factors provided the opportunities that enabled kings to engage in this process and ultimately to succeed against the nobles.

One key factor was economic: the growth of towns and cities, which starting around A.D. 1000 became centers of trade, manufacturing, and communication. The processes involved in the creation of cities created *wealth*. These included the development of a money economy (to replace the localized barter system that characterized

---

[9] This discussion draws upon Hedley Bull, *The Anarchical Society* (London: Macmillan, 1977); Charles Tilly, "Reflections on the History of European State-Making," in Tilly, ed., *The Formation of National States in Western Europe* (Princeton, N.J.: Princeton University Press, 1975), pp. 3–83; William H. McNeill, *The Pursuit of Power* (Chicago: University of Chicago Press, 1982); Hedley Bull and Adam Watson, eds., *The Expansion of International Society* (Oxford: Clarendon, 1984); Charles Tilly, *Coercion, Capital and European States, A.D. 990–1990* (Oxford: Blackwell, 1990); and Michael Mann, *States, War, and Capitalism* (Oxford: Blackwell, 1988).

feudalism) and a commercial class—the incipient bourgeoisie, or capitalists. Each town or city came to represent a larger regional economy, including surrounding areas of agriculture and trade with those areas. Commercial interests desired continued growth and expansion, including greater trade with the agricultural areas and with other towns and cities. This expansion required security and order: an authority to provide for roads and communication and a centralized bureaucracy to reduce barriers to economic expansion.

At the same time new political and technological developments concerned with coercion helped rulers to create larger, more centralized entities. Kings challenged the theoretical authority of the Holy Roman Emperor and the real military power of the nobles. To engage in such conflict the kings needed to acquire ever more resources—men, arms, and particularly money. They thus needed to draw resources from the towns and the commercial class and to form political coalitions with them. Technological factors were also crucial; military technology, especially gunpowder and cannon, made it possible for an entity with enough wealth to overcome the castle strongholds of knights and other nobility.

The kings thus needed the economic surplus being produced in Europe by the commercial class in order to gain control of the technology and weapons needed to centralize large areas of territory over the opposition of the nobles. Economic surplus was also needed to help create the bureaucracy essential for collecting taxes and to raise and administer armies. And, as victory brought more territory under their control, that territory in turn needed to be administered. Thus there was an important interaction between commerce and bureaucracy. And although they might have taxes imposed upon them by kings, the commercial classes of the cities saw the growing (and potential) power of kings as necessary for the conditions of security and order needed for continued commercial expansion. In an excellent analysis contrasting the experiences of Europe during this period and those of China in earlier times, William Hardy McNeill demonstrates how China lost the advantages of its earlier developments in technology and organization. The Chinese bureaucracy opposed the interactions of commerce and industry with political centralization and with the military applications of technology; these interactions were supported in Europe and eventually transformed it.[10]

Thus one way to begin to define the state is to see it as an entity that expanded to control and govern multiple contiguous regions and their cities. It was the result of activities related to coercion and to the control of goods and services. Coercion included war, to defeat external rivals, and state-making, to defeat internal rivals—the two elements of sovereignty, discussed below.

The interrelationships among commerce, kings, and bureaucracy in Europe promoted the rapid development and use of the military technology that also made possible European expansion to the rest of the globe. In fact, Paul Kennedy attributes

---

[10] McNeill, *The Pursuit of Power,* chap. 3. Such comparative analyses are important in order to move beyond a simple Eurocentric view of history.

the "European miracle," or the rise of Europe rather than areas seemingly more advanced, to the interaction of all these factors. The continual wars and rivalries between kings and nobles, and then among kings, pushed each to find some advantage in arms or wealth and led to rapid technological and scientific innovations (in areas such as weaponry, transportation, navigation, and cartography), as well as innovations in commerce, finance, administration, and bureaucratic structure. The upward spiral occurred not only in arms, wealth, and power, but also and perhaps more importantly in scientific knowledge. All these factors promoted a European expansion that in turn provided another source of wealth for the European states. Tilly has stressed a key relationship: "The state makes war, and war makes the state."[11]

## Sovereignty and the Nature of the State

A final element that created the opportunity for the rise of the state system was religion, which connected all these interrelated elements. Along with the kings' challenge to secular authority, there came, in 1517, Martin Luther's challenge to the spiritual authority of the Pope and the Church of Rome. Luther's challenge was taken up by a number of German princes; Lutheranism spread across much of Central Europe and resulted in a series of increasingly destructive religious wars among the newly forming states and lesser principalities. These wars dominated the history of the sixteenth century and the early seventeenth centuries, culminating in the Thirty Years' War, which ended with the **Treaty of Westphalia** in 1648. They were the last factor in the creation of the sovereign state.

The central principle of the Treaty of Westphalia was apparently simple: the ruler of a territory would determine the religion of that territory. This principle had been articulated as early as the Peace of Augsburg in 1555. Despite its simplicity, this principle had enormous consequences: the major internal issue of the day—religion—was to be determined by the ruler, *not* by an external authority, whether the Holy Roman Emperor or the Pope. No longer was there even the pretense of religious or political unity in Europe. Authority was dispersed to the various kings and princes, and the basis for the sovereign state was established. In each territory there were no longer multiple loyalties and authorities; there was only one: loyalty to the authority of the king or prince. The territory and the people in that territory belonged to the ruler, who did not have to answer to an external authority. Thus the Westphalian state system distinguished itself not only from the feudal principle, but also from the basic imperial or hegemonic principle of the suzerainty of a higher authority that existed elsewhere at that time—in India, China, the Arab Islamic world, and the Mongol–Tatar system.

The key elements of the modern nation-state were now all available: a people, a territory in which they lived, a government with the authority to rule over the people and territory. But this government was also seen as the agent of the *state*, which was a *legal* entity having the special status of **sovereignty.** The very term *state*, which arose in

[11] Paul Kennedy, *The Rise and Fall of the Great Powers* (New York: Random House, 1987), chap. 1; Tilly, *Coercion, Capital and European States*, chap. 1.

the sixteenth century, derived from the Latin *status,* which means the "position" or "standing" of a ruler.

We can now begin to answer the question of why the state was and is the main international actor. The myth of separate secular and spiritual entities disappeared, and the authority that had been vested in both was assumed exclusively by the state. Consequently, the international norms and laws that developed provided the state with a status enjoyed by no other actor. Perhaps the operative word here is *law.* The state is a legal entity; it has been invested with a legal status and a legal equality with all other states that have been denied to other actors on the international or global scene. Like a corporation, the state has no concrete existence; it is a legal abstraction. Through its government and the representatives of that government, the state undertakes legal commitments, both rights and responsibilities: signing treaties, joining organizations, and the like. We should understand, then, that sovereignty can thus act to constrain states as well as give them special status (in Rosenau's terms they are "sovereignty-bound" and in some situations they may have less freedom of action than some "sovereignty-free" nonstate actors).

Sovereignty should be seen as indicating a special, theoretical relationship between each state and all other states. Hedley Bull noted that sovereignty includes "internal sovereignty, which means supremacy over all other authorities within that territory and population," and "external sovereignty, by which is meant not supremacy but independence of outside authorities. The sovereignty of states, both internal and external, may be said to exist both at a normative level and at a factual level."[12] Thus sovereignty has an ideal meaning that in principle gives states an equal legal status. That meaning is that a state has complete control over the people and territory represented by its government. Ideally, it also means that there is external autonomy: *no authority exists to order the state how to act; there is no actor with the legitimate authority to tell a state what to do.* Note that this is the essence of the **"anarchic"** international system.

In principle, this means there is a monopoly over the control of the means of force within the state. No other authority has a right to exercise force or maintain order within the territory of the state. Similarly, through international law, the state has been given a legal monopoly on the use of force in the global arena. Piracy and nonstate terrorism are considered illegal because they entail the use of force and violence by actors other than a state. When implemented by a state, force can be pinpointed, responsibility can be assigned, and other rules of conduct can be invoked. For example, until the creation of the League of Nations, international law was concerned with how states behaved during a special legal condition called war. This condition could exist only between two equal units—equal in the legal sense of being sovereign states. Once this condition existed, belligerents were designated by declarations of war and neutrals by declarations of their neutrality. Each category had rights and responsibilities of behavior toward other states, according to the status they had declared. The various structures of international law were rarely seen to apply to peoples who were

---

[12] Bull, *The Anarchical Society,* p. 8.

outside the system of states, such as aboriginal populations and non-European areas, which were to be conquered, colonized, and dominated by the European nation-states.

In addition to its special legal status, the state has another important characteristic basic to its dominance of the international system: territory. The government of the state represents a group of people who inhabit a piece of territory. Commentators who argue that the state is no longer dominant in the world system must confront the fact that every person lives in territory controlled (at least nominally) by a state. No other form of international actor controls territory. Governments consider territory to be of overriding importance, and the stakes involved in the loss of territory are intimately related to the onset of war.[13]

One problem, as we have seen, is that different states or nations may not coincide *on the same territory*. The separate nationalisms of different ethnic groups may threaten to tear a state apart, as in the former Yugoslavia. Different national identities within a state may tempt another state to intervene on behalf of a minority. Sometimes a feeling of nationality may spill over many states, calling into question the legitimacy of separate states (as in the case of pan-Arab nationalism, or Pan-Arabism). States may therefore suppress minority rights (Bulgaria long prohibited public use of the Turkish language by its Turkish minority); they may force minorities to emigrate (as Vietnam forced the ethnic Chinese boat people to flee) or may even kill them (as Nazi Germany systematically killed Jews).

"Throughout history that unit which affords protection and security to human beings has tended to become the basic political unit."[14] This proposition can be applied to the feudal knight and the protection his castle provided to his villagers. This changed with the advent of gunpowder and the larger military forces developed by kings. The basis of the state was its ability to protect people through its size—its physical territory, which created a "hard shell" around the population in an era of gunpowder and the professional armies of centralized monarchs. Although nuclear weapons and modern delivery systems make the hard shell of the state obsolete, the territoriality of the state still protects the citizens of most states from most conflicts with other states.

While the question of the exact meaning of the state is complex and subject to debate, we can summarize the core of the concept of the nation-state as developed here: the state is a legal abstraction with institutions (the government) to control a territorial area and the people who reside in that territory.[15] In the fully integrated nation-state this control is aided by and dependent on the cement that holds the

---

[13] See Gary Goertz and Paul Diehl, *Territorial Changes and International Conflict* (London: Routledge, 1992), and K. J. Holsti, *Peace and War: Armed Conflicts and International Order 1648–1989* (Cambridge, England: Cambridge University Press, 1991).

[14] See John Herz, "Rise and Demise of the Territorial State," *World Politics* 9 (1957), 473–493, as well as Herz's rethinking of the subject, "The Territorial State Revisited—Reflections on the Future of the Nation-State," *Polity* 1 (1968), 11–34.

[15] For a review of the debate on the meaning of the state and sovereignty, see Joseph A. Camilleri and Jim Falk, *The End of Sovereignty* (London: Elgar, 1992), and Alan James, *Sovereign Statehood* (London: Allen & Unwin, 1986).

people together and gives them a loyalty to that government and state: nationalism. The state's growing control over its people and territory, its freedom from having to answer to any higher external authority, culminated in the development of the concept of sovereignty.

All of these features, but especially sovereignty and territoriality, provide the state with major advantages over nonstate actors in the global arena. The European version of the state expanded throughout the world because it had first won out in the European competition. To survive in Europe, a country needed large amounts of capital, a large population, and significant military forces. European states controlled about 7 percent of the world's territory in 1500, and by 1914 they controlled 84 percent. Tilly summarizes our arguments:

> Because of their advantages in translating national resources into success in international war, large national states superseded tribute-taking empires, federations, city-states, and all their other competitors as the predominant European entities, and as the models for state formation. . . . Those states finally defined the character of the European state system and spearheaded its extension to the entire world.[16]

## The Security Dilemma

The system of sovereign states has other consequences for state behavior that will become clear when we discuss such topics as the world system, power and influence, deterrence and arms control, and a number of global economic and environmental problems. Sovereignty means that states exist in a formally anarchic environment. No legitimate or legal authority is empowered to control, direct, or watch over the behavior of sovereign states (as, for example, the federal government of the United States does over the 50 states of the Union). One consequence of such a system of sovereign states is that each state must in the end look out for its own security, protection, and survival. Remembering that the state in its present form was forged during continual military competition within Europe, we can better understand the origins of a realist perspective.

If there is no legitimate, legal authority to enforce order and punish rule-breakers, then there is no legal or formal recourse if allies or friends fail to assist a state—you cannot sue them to fulfill their alliance contracts! Thus self-help in the international system means that each state must take measures to provide for its own defense. A tragic flaw of the formally anarchic state system is that the requirement for self-help often leads to the **"security dilemma"**: the secure environments of the various states may be mutually exclusive.

> Wherever such anarchic society has existed—and it has existed in most periods of known history on some level—there has arisen what may be called the "security

---

[16] Tilly, *Coercion, Capital and European States,* pp. 183, 160.

dilemma" of men, or groups, or their leaders. Groups or individuals living in such a constellation must be, and usually are, concerned about their security from being attacked, subjected, dominated or annihilated by other groups and individuals. Striving to attain security from such attack, they are driven to acquire more and more power in order to escape the power of others. This, in turn, renders the others more insecure and compels them to prepare for the worst. Since none can ever feel entirely secure in such a world of competing units, power competition ensues, and the vicious circle of security and power accumulation is on.[17]

Thus one state's security may be seen and defined as another state's *insecurity*. The means by which one state prepares to defend its territory and people may be threatening to others—and is thus perceived as offensive, rather than defensive, behavior (what did Israeli activity look like to the Arab countries during most of the post-1948 period?). States may never feel secure, because they never know how much is "enough" for their security. This is particularly so when their own efforts at security spur on the efforts of others.

The formally anarchic system of sovereign states promotes a realist vision of struggle in world politics, through the security dilemma and the concomitant stress on threat, military power, and self-help. The need for military power, and for constant alertness as to its accumulation and use by others, stems directly from the structure of a system of sovereign states (and the realist assumption that human nature is flawed, sinful, and power seeking). The security dilemma is central to many other aspects of interstate relations and will reappear in several different forms later on; for example, in the discussion of arms races and deterrence. How states cope with this condition and create some degree of order out of anarchy will also be addressed throughout this book.

## Beyond the Anarchic Security Dilemma

The anarchic system of states recognized by the Treaty of Westphalia has not survived without challenge. Its initial principle of internal sovereignty incorporated the institution of dynastic succession; that is, the inheritance of royal authority from one generation to another. The ruler embodied that sovereignty. But the French Revolution of 1789 challenged all that. The source of governmental authority, based on the principle of popular sovereignty, was declared to reside in the people, not the monarch. The ideal of internal sovereignty was preserved, but its ideological base was transformed. This "republican" principle proved a powerful organizing and empowering force; it fueled the enthusiasm for enlistment of a huge army of citizens, far larger and displaying more ideological fervor than that shown by previous professional armies serving royal authority. Its strength enabled revolutionary France to turn back the forces of its

---

[17] John Herz, "Idealist Internationalism and the Security Dilemma," *World Politics* 2 (1950), 157. See also Robert Jervis, "Cooperation Under the Security Dilemma," *World Politics* 30 (1978), 167–214.

neighbors, who tried to reinstate the old regime, and then to expand French power by appealing directly to its neighbors' populations.[18]

When Napoleon Bonaparte seized power, he retained much of the republican ideology even as he consolidated his own authority by proclaiming himself emperor. He then compounded that transformation of the basis for internal sovereignty with a direct challenge to the principle of external sovereignty: he sought hegemony. Not content with seeking French security through the balance of power as it had been maintained unevenly since 1648, in his military campaigns he tried to make France the dominant power in Europe. Napoleon absorbed some of his neighbors into France and attempted to reduce the rest to vassals. The Napoleonic Wars were about whether the Westphalian system would survive.

It did, with the victory by a coalition of all the other great powers—Britain, Russia, Prussia, and Austria. Yet the victors recognized their close call. They learned from the failure of the old system and tried to revise it even as they reinstituted it. Their Concert of Europe marked an effort, like the Treaty of Westphalia, to provide an era of peace following a catastrophic period of Europe-wide warfare. They tried to restore dynastic authority, but in a form tempered to the republican spirit that could not be erased from Europeans' consciousness. The great powers allowed France to recover and reenter the system, essentially within its pre-1792 borders, and to participate as an equal partner in great power politics. The Concert of Europe expressed certain normative principles of right behavior: states had a right to security and independence; states should respect one another's legitimacy and should observe international law; differences should be settled by negotiation. To back up these hopes was military power; no state was again to aspire to dominance, nor to be permitted to make the effort. An expansionist state was to be "balanced" (actually, overpowered) by the combination of all others. In this constellation Britain and Russia, as the most powerful states, played key roles. Britain was the world's leading naval and industrial power; Russia was Europe's leading land power, with the largest population and army. Insofar as they pursued expansionist aims, those aims were concentrated outside of Europe. They did not directly threaten other major European powers, and because of their geographic separation they could not substantially threaten each other. As long as Britain and Russia were basically in agreement, no other state could hope to dominate Europe.[19]

This restored but modified Westphalian system worked reasonably well for a full century. A wave of popular and nationalist revolution swept much of Central Europe in 1848, but most of the revolutionary movements were put down by force or tempered in practice. There were only two major wars during the century, neither of them approaching the scope or ferocity of the Napoleonic Wars. Britain and France fought

---

[18] On the evolution of sovereignty in the international system, see Mark Zacher, "The Decaying Pillars of the Westphalian System," in Ernst-Otto Czempiel and James Rosenau, eds., *Governance Without Government: Order and Change in World Politics* (Cambridge, England: Cambridge University Press, 1992).
[19] See Paul Schroeder, *The Transformation of European Politics 1763–1848* (New York: Oxford University Press, 1994), and Adam Watson, *The Evolution of International Society: A Comparative Historical Analysis* (London: Routledge, 1992).

Russia in the C[...] limited goals. More far-reaching in its [...] capped the unification of Germa[ny...] ore, by its territorial settlement—tr[ansferring the provinces] of Alsace and Lorraine [...] m French to German control—it lef[t] a legacy [...] rance. Even so, there was no furth[er] war between major [...] 14. Then everything seemed to co[llapse]. Tensions [...] Alliances [...] military technology appeared to f[avor] the o[ffense] and sharpene[d...] ma; long-term demographic and industrial tr[ends] threatened [...] Russian power to the endangerme[nt] [...] of their neighbors. A Europe-wide w[ar] expandi[ng] to world war, was the result. It reached a level of [...] surpassed [...] apoleonic Wars.

Again t[he] victorious powe[rs...] had failed in its most important p[urpose...] peace and the sovereignty of most of its constituent states. Am[erican] Pres[idents...] Wilson[...] the rights of national groups to s[elf-determination]—internal sovereignty now seemed to mean the right of an ethnica[lly] homogeneous people to govern itself. Some new states in Central Europe ha[d] their boundaries drawn to reflect those principles. But the ethnic map of Europe did not fit neatly into any kind of political map. Peoples were mixed together in ways that defied the creation of any neat or territorially defensible border. Some peoples' aspirations were deliberately submerged to those of more powerful ones. In legitimating an outburst of demands for national self-determination that could not be satisfied, Wilson helped promote a force that would be as disruptive as it was pacifying.[20]

The victorious powers were also looking for a principle of international relations by which to restore order and security. Wilson's vision was of a system of **collective security,** embedded in a League of Nations, by which all members would agree to oppose in common a threat to the security of any of them, from any quarter. But this vision fit badly with the view that the threat to peace stemmed primarily from a few particular states, especially from Germany. This view, expressed most vigorously by France, required cutting territory away from Germany and imposing heavy economic war reparations to weaken it (and initially excluding it from the new League of Nations). In the negotiations for the Treaty of Versailles in 1919, this latter view predominated. Furthermore, the United States Senate—by then representing the world's strongest power, and the one potentially best able to restrain any possible hegemonic aggressor—refused to ratify the treaty, thus precluding American membership in the League. The attempt to institute a new set of rules for the system failed at the outset. Germany recovered its power and nurtured its sense of injustice at the Versailles settlement; eventually Hitler came to power at the head of a totalitarian government determined to impose a new order on Europe and perhaps the world. Britain, France, and the Soviet Union could not agree on how to resist him; the Americans stood aside, while Italy and Japan allied with him. In 1939 began the most dangerous

---

[20] See Daniel Patrick Moynihan, *Pandaemonium: Ethnicity in International Politics* (Oxford: Oxford University Press, 1993).

bid for dominance since Napoleon, driven by an odious ideology of German racial superiority. It ended with 15 million dead in battle and a much greater number of civilian dead.

Yet again, in 1945, the victors met to pick up and rearrange the pieces. The United Nations was to replace the League. This time the United States would join. Again the world organization was founded primarily on the principle of collective security, including the intention of providing the UN with a permanent force of military units earmarked for its use in keeping the peace. By the Charter of the new organization, the Security Council was empowered to authorize and carry out collective military action against anyone it declared to be a threat to international peace. The principal victors—Britain, the Soviet Union, and the United States, with China and France added as something of a courtesy—were declared to be Permanent Members of the Security Council. As such, each was given the power to veto any military or other action against a state. The reasons for giving them this veto power were straightforward. First, the major victors insisted upon it. Second, the founders of the UN were practical; they understood that for the foreseeable future the Permanent Members would be the ones who had to provide most of the military muscle. And if a great power felt a particular proposal for UN action violated its vital interests it would surely oppose such an action whether or not it had a veto. A UN that tried to go ahead with such an action would risk world war anyway. So the veto merely recognized the realities of power. Smaller powers were given no veto. Many of them did not like this two-tiered distinction, but they could not effectively resist it.

In creating the Security Council with its veto power, the founders thus were not being naive, but pragmatic. As it happened, the hope for great-power cooperation did not last long. The cold war was thoroughly underway by 1948, and the Soviet Union had already exercised its veto many times. In effect, the Security Council could act only in those disputes in which the Permanent Members did not have vital interests at stake. No UN military force could be created. The Council did, however, prove able to authorize action in cases where the great powers' vital interests did not conflict, or in cases where their interests would be endangered if the conflict were not contained (as in the Middle East).

Nor was the Security Council all there was of the United Nations. The General Assembly lacked explicit authority to deal with threats to international peace and security, but it had powers to consider a wide range of matters that could well ultimately affect the prospects for peace. Unlike the Security Council, the General Assembly included all member states, large and small, and each had a vote. As the membership of the UN grew, the General Assembly increasingly reflected its members' concerns. Predominantly poor, weak states, from outside Europe and emerging from colonial status to independence only since 1945, they cared deeply about issues of economic development. At the same time, the Western powers who dominated the Security Council increasingly lost their ability to dominate the General Assembly. So both the nature and the topic of debate in the Assembly were often quite different from what went on in the Council. Furthermore, the founders of the UN believed that wars usually had their origin in poverty and injustice. Therefore they established a wide range of specialized agencies concerned with development, human rights, refugee relief, food and emergency assistance, population pressures, environmental dangers, and decolonization. Some of these agencies proved able to operate effectively with limited resources and restricted powers; others were longer on words than on deeds. Yet it is clear by word and deed, in regard to both military security and socioeconomic well-being, that principles of collective "governance" have evolved substantially since the Peace of Westphalia. Both "anarchy" and the "security dilemma" have been tempered by principles of international organization.

The end of the cold war (often dated from the symbolically striking fall of the Berlin Wall in 1989) provided yet another opportunity to revise and strengthen these principles of international organization. The Soviet Union (and its successor state, Russia) cooperated with the Western powers and almost entirely stopped using its veto. China could be persuaded, by a variety of positive and negative means, not to use its veto. Thus it became possible for the Security Council to agree that important events or actions constituted a threat to international peace and security, and to authorize collective action to deal with them. The most spectacular such action was the 1991 war against Iraq to restore the independence of Kuwait, by an international coalition as authorized by the Security Council. But there were many others, usually welcomed by the states involved rather than directed against one of them. Whereas 13 "peace-keeping" operations had been authorized before 1988, 19 new ones were initiated in the six subsequent years. Several of these operations, notably the one in Somalia, expanded the meaning of "threat to peace" to permit military action to support humanitarian assistance when the state's internal authority had broken down. Some of these peacekeeping efforts—as in Cambodia and El Salvador—more or less succeeded; others—in Yugoslavia and Somalia, for example—clearly failed. We can see that the principle of sovereignty itself has evolved, in regard both to internal control and noninterference and external independence from authority—and to a degree that has again worried some small and weak states. Whether the UN's members have the will or the capability to make a new set of rules to bring more order to the anarchic system is an open question, and one as yet unanswered.

## ALL STATES ARE LEGALLY EQUAL (BUT SOME ARE MORE EQUAL THAN OTHERS)

By the principles of sovereignty and international law, all states are juridically equal. But one of the truisms in world politics is that nothing is distributed equally on the face of the globe—not people or their talents, not resources, not climate or geographic features, not technology, not air quality. In fact, many things are distributed in a highly unequal manner. Nation-states are so different from one another in resources, capabilities, available menus, and their ability to exploit and choose from those menus that some observers find it difficult to call all of these units states. In Chapter 6 we shall discuss in detail the concepts of power and influence, the whole range of state capabilities, and the ways in which states attempt to exert their power and influence on others. But here we may simply point out that states range widely in size, from Russia, with 6.6 million square miles (almost 1.8 times the size of the United States), to Nauru, with its 8 square miles; the smallest member of the United Nations is St. Kitts–Nevis, with 101 square miles. Similarly, the People's Republic of China had a 1993 population of almost 1.2 *billion* people, whereas in that year microstates like Nauru and Tuvalu had populations of between 9,600 and 10,000; San Marino, the smallest member of the UN in population, had about 24,000 people.

Sovereignty carries with it only the *principle* of independence from outside authority; it does not ensure equality in capabilities or independence from the outside interference of others. No official authority controls states in the contemporary world system, but many are subject to powerful unofficial forces, pressures, and influences that penetrate the supposed hard shell of the state.

As international law has evolved through the years, and as a corollary of self-help, sovereignty has come to imply that the government of a state has the capacity and ability to carry out the responsibilities of a sovereign state. That is, internally, the government can impose order on its own territory and maintain the government's monopoly over the use of force. Externally, the state can defend its rights under sovereignty and carry out its responsibilities (for example, enforcing its neutrality during a war in which it is not a belligerent). All states are formally sovereign; they have achieved the status of independent states. Most have sought UN membership as a ticket into world society; even the smallest units have resisted pressures to continue as clients, colonies, or satellites of a larger state. As students of the international arena, we are faced with the continued resurgence of nationalism and the state in a world where the hard shell is eroding for many states and can hardly be seen to exist for the smaller members.

The question of the relationship between small and large states has been perennial. Although there are any number of ways to divide states, to categorize and classify them, one division has always existed and been used in the interactions between states: a status hierarchy of size and power. We may always find large and small units, the strong and the weak, the influential and the ineffectual. The largest states of today are *proportionately* neither larger nor smaller than they were 2,000 years ago.[21] Like the debates at the Constitutional Convention in Philadelphia over the representation of states in the U.S. Congress, the major conflicts in setting up the United Nations were over size: "The basic argument in 1944–45 was not between the Russians and the Western Allies, although there were crises in that field too. It was between the big powers and the rest." The small countries "contested very strongly any departure from the principle of one country one vote."[22]

Yet analysts have divided countries into many different categories. For years we simply had the First World (the industrialized Western democracies), the Second World (the communist bloc of Eastern Europe), and the Third World (everyone else); today these terms are of no use to us. Currently the World Bank uses three basic categories of country groups based on economic development: low-income economies

---

[21] Bruce Russett, *Power and Community in World Politics* (New York: Freeman, 1974), chap. 7.
[22] Paul Gore-Booth, *With Great Truth and Respect* (London: Constable, 1974), pp. 133–134.

**TABLE 3.2**    World Bank's Categories of States

| Countries | Total 1992 Population (Millions) | Average Annual Growth in GNP per Capita, 1980–1992 (Percent) | Average 1992 GNP per Capita (Dollars) |
|---|---|---|---|
| Low-income | 3,1291 | 3.9 | 390 |
| Middle-income | 1,419 | –0.1 | 2,490 |
| High-income | 828 | 2.3 | 22,160 |
| Severely indebted middle-income | 505 | –1.0 | 2,470 |

*Source:* World Bank, *World Development Report 1994 (New York: Oxford University Press, 1994).*

(developing countries with a 1992 GNP per capita of $635 or less), middle-income economies (countries with a 1992 GNP per capita over $635 but less than $7,910), and high-income economies (countries with a 1992 GNP per capita over $7,910). The low- and middle-income groups are additionally divided into lower and upper groups. The data for the high-income group reflects primarily the OECD (the developed industrial states of the Organization for Economic Cooperation and Development, known as "the rich people's club"). The World Bank also groups states for analyses on the basis of major export category (manufactures, nonfuel primary products, fuels—mainly oil, services, diversified exporters, and not classified by exports) and the degree of their indebtedness. Some of the characteristics of the income-based groups are presented in Table 3.2.

Additionally, the microstates are the very smallest of contemporary states. There is no agreement on how small a state must be to be called a microstate, but most observers would include the several dozen countries with less than a quarter of a million people and/or areas of only a few hundred square miles. Despite formal sovereignty, these states are most vulnerable to external penetration or intervention; they cannot exercise even substantial control over their boundaries, territory, or population. Nonetheless, they survive. Several scholars have proposed that there has been a growing observance of international norms that outlaw war, especially waged by the strong against the weak.[23] The defense of Kuwait in the Gulf War can

---

[23] See John Mueller, *Retreat from Doomsday: The Obsolescence of Major War* (New York: Basic Books, 1989), and James L. Ray, "The Abolition of Slavery and the End of International War," *International Organization* 43 (1989), 405–439.

be seen as an affirmation of the principle of sovereignty and a rejection of the use of violence to absorb a sovereign state. This was the key normative principle on which virtually all governments of weak states could unite (and which the UN, as an organization of states, not peoples, itself embodies). Small states in the post–World War II period were unusually free from blatant military coercion by larger states. Thus protected, they have proliferated because the potential ruling elites seek the status and prestige of statehood and the chance to have a country of their own to govern.

## NONSTATE ACTORS IN THE CONTEMPORARY SYSTEM

A variety of other, nonstate, actors are increasingly involved in the crucial issues of world politics. These intergovernmental and nongovernmental (or transnational) actors form an important part of the global environment, affecting the possibilities and probabilities of state actions. In viewing world politics, the global system can be seen as a chessboard and the actors as the pieces that move about on it. Or, as did Shakespeare, we can consider the world as a stage; those groups, organizations, and individuals who interact on it are the actors. This is a useful image for several reasons. First, the word **actor** conveys a broad spectrum of interacting entities; it is large enough to encompass all the entities we wish to study. Second, our emphasis is on behavior, and the word helps convey the idea of an entity that is behaving or performing an action. In relation to **nonstate actors,** the term also helps to convey the idea that different actors have different roles, that some occupy center stage and are stars while others are bit players in the chorus. Yet they all interact in creating the finished production.

While a variety of nonstate actors exist in the interdependent global system (as part of what James Rosenau calls the *multicentric* system existing outside state relations), the state is still the dominant international actor on most issues. Thus an entity may be seen as an international actor if it is taken into account in the calculations and strategies of the leaders of states and if its continuing functions have an impact on other actors on the world stage.

Any organized unit that commands the identification, interests, and loyalty of individuals and that affects interstate relations becomes a major competitor of nation-states. As we survey the types of nonstate actors, think of various post–World War II conflicts between international organizations and states: between the United Nations and Iraq or Serbia; between OPEC and the industrialized West; between nonstate groups like the Palestine Liberation Organization (PLO) and Israel, or the Irish Republican Army (IRA) and the United Kingdom; or between a multinational corporation and a state, as in the case of the toxic gas accident at Union Carbide's plant in Bhopal, India. In almost every case the conflict arises when the nonstate actor challenges or tries to reduce the scope of the sovereignty of a nation-state in terms of territory, population, or control over its internal or external politics. The dramatic acts of international terrorism by a wide variety of nonstate groups offer another example of this competition: groups other than states employ force and violence in the global system, directly _____ _____ ____ of force that international law has always granted to state

## Intergove...

Other international actors in the _____ include *international organizations* or intergovernmental organizations (IGOs). This label stresses the fact that such organizations—for example, the United Nations—are composed of states and that the individuals who are sent as representatives to such organizations represent the interests and policies of the governments of their own states. Quite often these organizations have permanent staffs at a permanent home base, so there are also individuals whose primary loyalty is to the IGO, not to their state of origin. Thus the Secretariat of the United Nations is an international civil service of individuals who put the organization ahead of any state. This structure may create an atmosphere of competition between the IGO and the state for the loyalty of individuals.

IGOs may be usefully categorized according to the scope of their memberships and the scope of their purposes. On the one hand, we have universal political organizations such as the old League of Nations and the United Nations, which aim to include as wide an international membership as possible. Such organizations are also general-purpose organizations in that they perform political, economic, developmental, military, sociocultural, and other functions for member states. Other general-purpose organizations have more limited memberships: the North Atlantic Treaty Organization (NATO), the Organization of American States (OAS), the Organization of African Unity (OAU), and several others. The Commonwealth is not regional—its membership is not grouped in any one geographic area—but it is limited to countries with former colonial ties to the British Empire. These organizations, too, perform a variety of functions.

A significantly greater number of organizations, called *functional IGOs* or *limited-purpose IGOS*, perform more specific functions. The total number of IGOs more than tripled from 1945 to 1985, when they hit a post–World War II high of 378; by 1990 their number had declined to around 300 (IGO growth is shown graphically in Figure 3.1). Many of these IGOs are affiliated with the UN or are related to the European Union. Those connected to the UN often have or aim for universal membership. Many more have limited regional membership. Some—such as the Arab League or NATO— stressed military functions in their early days. Others are concerned primarily with economic matters; among them are the various organs of the European Union and organizations like the Central American Common Market and the Association of Southeast Asian Nations (ASEAN). Still others provide various social services—for example, the World Health Organization (WHO) or the International Labor Organization (ILO)—and others, like the International Monetary Fund (IMF) and the World Bank, are involved in monetary matters and economic development. The list becomes almost endless if we include groups with even more specific functional activities: the International Statistical Institute, the International Bureau of Weights and Measures, the International Wool Study Group, or the Desert Locust Control Organization for East Africa.

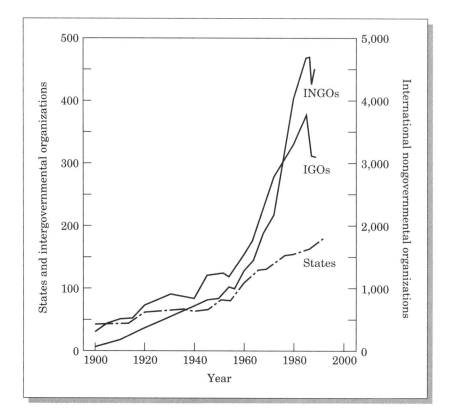

**FIGURE 3.1** Growth of states, IGOs, and NGOs. [*Source:* Barry B. Hughes, *International Futures* (Boulder, Col.: Westview, 1993), p. 45.]

Without going into great detail on the workings of the individual IGOs, let us review them as international actors.[24] First, they have a significant and continuing impact on interstate relations. The international role of many IGOs is clearly institutionalized in that states expect them to act in certain areas. They expect the UN, say, to act in areas of conflict, as it did in 1990 to come to the aid of Kuwait after the Iraqi invasion or in 1993 to bring some semblance of order to Somalia. Regionally, both the European Union and the Organisation on Security and Cooperation in Europe (OSCE) attempted to resolve the violence in Yugoslavia starting in 1991. When a state finds itself in serious economic trouble, it almost automatically looks to the World Bank or the IMF for various kinds of aid. Developing states increasingly find that association with IGOs will help their economic performance. In addition, IGOs are actors in the

[24] See Harold K. Jacobson, William M. Reisinger, and Todd Mathers, "National Entanglements in International Governmental Organizations," *American Political Science Review* 80, 1 (March 1986), pp. 141–159.

sense that they continually affect the foreign policy behavior of their members, to the extent that member states join the organization and value the continuation of membership. Merely sending representatives to an organization, employing resources to maintain IGOs, or interacting with others through IGOs has an impact on the state. Perhaps most importantly, the IGOs may be considered actors because states and leaders *believe* that IGOs are behaving as international actors and must be taken into account in foreign policy deliberations.

IGOs have this effect in several ways. Most clearly seen in the workings of the United Nations, but common to many other IGOs, is the function of acting as a forum in which the member states can meet and communicate. The IGO may act passively, serving only as a line of communication or a meeting place, or actively, as a mediator. IGOs perform a number of regulative functions across such areas as economics, health, communication, and transportation; examples range from the African Postal Union to the International Atomic Energy Agency. Here IGOs, with the consent of member states, regulate how members should interact to function smoothly, efficiently, and beneficially in an area of concern. This management or coordination function is essential to the orderly functioning of day-to-day global relations.

Some IGOs also have distributive functions, dispensing benefits and costs among states. Although organizations such as the World Bank spring most readily to mind, others such as the International Court of Justice, which hands down legal decisions, are equally distributive. States must take into consideration the predispositions and power of the permanent staff of the pertinent IGO, which will decide how to distribute the costs and benefits it has at its disposal.

Taking the distributive function a step further, a very small number of IGOs may be termed **supranational;** these have the power to act separately from the member states and to make decisions that are binding on their members even if some members disagree. These IGOs indeed appear to take aspects of members' sovereignty away from them. In the evolution of the European Union, various organs of that organization have devloped extensive independent powers and are the only true supranational IGOs in existence today.[25]

## Nongovernmental Organizations

IGOs, however, are not the only nonstate actors that have an impact on world politics, forming part of the environment of states and constraining the range of state behavior. While IGOs are organizations composed of states, a large number of organizations are private international actors; they are nonstate, **nongovernmental organizations** (NGOs). The important distinction regards membership: NGOs are organizations that cut across national boundaries and are made up of individuals or national groups, not official representatives of national governments. Many organizations exist below the level of state governments, either within a single country or constituted of international nongovernmental organizations. International NGOs are now very numerous,

---

[25] See Clive Archer, *Organizing Europe: The Institutions of Integration* (London: Arnold, 1994).

having increased from 134 in 1905 to 2,470 in 1972 to more than 4,600 by 1990 (see Figure 3.1).

Like the IGOs, they deal with a great variety of matters. There are religious bodies, professional organizations, sports organizations, trade union groups, and political parties. Their membership may be composed either directly of individuals (the International Political Science Association) or of various national societies that themselves are composed of individuals (as the International Red Cross is composed of the various national Red Cross organizations).

Most often these organizations perform rather low-level, specifically functional tasks, promoting contact across state boundaries on matters of common interest and providing nongovernmental means of communication among individuals of many nations. NGOs help knit the global society together in much the same way that private groups do within a state, although their total membership as a portion of the world's population is only a fraction of the comparable proportion of interest-group members within an economically developed democracy. Sometimes an NGO can function as a pressure group affecting national governments or international organizations. An example is the role of the International Red Cross and the World Council of Churches in mobilizing world concern and aid for African populations facing starvation. A great many NGOs are formally consulted by the international organizations concerned with their problems (health and medical organizations are consulted by the World Health Organization). Some NGOs, such as Amnesty International or the Roman Catholic Church, can exert significant influence on the policies of various states. The political focus of NGOs is usually on national governments, and they are effective through changing government policy rather than through direct action. Much the same is true for purely *subnational* (as contrasted to international) organizations. The role of interest or pressure groups in foreign policy formation hardly needs emphasis, but only in rare instances (the PLO is one) do NGOs act directly, without the intermediary instrument of a national government.

At the most micro-level are individuals. While individuals are important to the operation and impact of transnational organizations and transnational linkages between and among states (in tourism, student exchange, and business and commercial links), individuals are most often powerless in international politics except when they can, through an official or unofficial role, affect the policy of a government. One analyst, however, claims that this is changing and that private individuals are having an ever greater impact on world affairs. Through the growing interdependence of the world system and the growing awareness of individuals of their place in the world through the "microelectronic revolution," individual acts produce significant impacts. Mathias Rust, a West German teenager acting "on behalf of world peace" landed his light plane in Red Square in 1987, exposing the vulnerabilities of Soviet air defenses and leading to the dismissal of the defense minister.[26]

---

[26] See Rosenau, *Turbulence in World Politics*, for these arguments; p. 288 for a discussion of the Rust incident.

## Multinational Corpo

One consistent exception to the ~~~~~ ~tors is the **multi-national corporation** (MNC). The ~~~~~ and ~~~~~ ~~~~~ have grown enormously in recent years. By the ~~~~~ most observers realized ~~~~~ were at least 10,000 firms with business activities in foreign ~~~~~ operating over ~~~~~,000 subsidiaries. In 1960 the value of direct foreign investment ~~~~~ was $?2 billion, rising to $233 billion in 1985 (during the same period ~~~~~ rose from half a billion dollars to $54 billion, and West German investment ~~~~~ less than $1 billion to $60 billion). The Fortune Global 500 corporations (industrial, not financial) had combined sales of over $5.4 trillion in 1993. The United States was home to 159 of these corporations, Japan to 135; the next highest total was 41 in Britain.

Clearly, giant corporations cannot help but affect the policies of many governments and the welfare of many people. The oil companies, for instance, would still have tremendous impact with their pricing and marketing policies even if they did not try to change the policy or personnel of national governments. The MNC has emerged in many ways as one of the major competitors to the nation-state. Whereas nonstate liberation groups (the PLO and IRA) and ethnic groups (the Basques, the Quebecois) have challenged the military and political authority of specific nation-states, the MNC is a much more broadly based and subtle competitor. This is partly because MNCs may become deeply involved in the domestic political processes of host countries—by outright bribery, by support of specific political parties or candidates, or by financing coups.[27] Examples are the actions of the United Fruit Company in the overthrow of the Arbenz government in Guatemala in 1954, of British Petroleum in the removal of the Mossadegh government in Iran in 1953, and the role played by ITT in the coup against the Marxist regime of Salvador Allende of Chile in 1973.

Many multinationals predate the states that have been created since the end of World War II. MNCs also have their own spheres of influence through the division of world markets. They often engage in diplomacy and espionage, traditional tools of state interaction. Most important, MNCs have very large economic resources at their disposal, which gives them an advantage over not only many of the newer and smaller states but also some of the older ones. For example, in 1993 General Motors, listed first in the Fortune Global 500, had gross sales larger than the GNP of Finland or Denmark (and all but 6 of the 173 developing countries so classified by the United Nations Development Programme); Procter & Gamble, listed 34th, had gross sales exceeding the GNP of Chile. Of course, GNP and gross sales are not directly comparable accounting terms; the most accurate comparison would be between GNP and "value added" by the corporation. Nevertheless, the comparison suggests how very large some modern multinational corporations are compared with the often small, underdeveloped states with which they deal.

---

[27] A classic discussion is Raymond Vernon, *Sovereignty at Bay* (New York: Basic Books, 1971); see also Volker Bornschier and Christopher Chase-Dunn, *Transnational Corporations and Underdevelopment* (New York: Praeger, 1985).

## Nation-State Versus Nonstate Loyalty

Although there are competitors to the nation-state, some very formidable in special ways, the state continues to enjoy great advantages over most other international actors. In addition to the legal status of formal sovereignty, the state generally also possesses demographic, economic, military, and geographic capabilities unmatched by other actors. Some IGOs or MNCs command the loyalty of some individuals, but the nation-state commands the loyalty of very large numbers of individuals through nationalism. One clear ramification of the combination of the nation with the state (which is what nonstate actors like the PLO want) is that the state comes to embody the nation and all it stands for through nationalism. That is, the government of the state is seen by the people as representing and protecting cultural values as well as history and tradition. Combined with the idea of sovereignty, this relationship is a powerful force indeed—a force that can rarely be matched by nonstate actors. Before the outbreak of World War I, the socialist parties of Europe, meeting together under the aegis of the Second International, called for loyalty to the proletariat and a refusal by workers anywhere in Europe to take up arms against other workers in the event of war. Here was a direct clash between an NGO and the states of Europe: competition for the loyalty of the workers within the various European countries, especially Germany, France, and Britain. When the war came and choices had to be made, for a variety of reasons the workers rallied to the nationalist standards of their respective states, not to the Red Flag.

Two concluding, if somewhat contradictory, comments are in order. The first is that states possess, in general, a far wider range of capabilities than do nonstate actors and thus have a much larger and more varied menu. Although there has been a tremendous growth in both IGOs and NGOs and the transnational interactions among them (and between them and states), nonstate interactions clearly reflect the structure and distribution of the power of the states in the global system, and the growth of nonstate activity has both mirrored and derived from the expansion of the state system itself in the postwar period. The second point, however, is simply that IGOs and NGOs do exist. And, in a world system characterized by high and growing levels of *interdependence* (which we will discuss in the following chapter), such actors inevitably and consistently affect the menu of constraints and possibilities of states. As components of the global environment, they must be given attention by states and by one another.

# 4

# THE WO‌T
# CONSTR

WORL

RELATIONS

SOCIETY

GOVERNMENT

ROLE

INDIVIDUAL

## THE INTERNATIONAL ENVIRONMENT

Starting our analysis at the level of the international system, we have the most general picture of world politics. The international environment surrounds nation-states and their foreign policy makers; it therefore provides a crucial component to the menu from which states and decision makers choose their behavior. How exactly does the international environment affect the menu? How does it affect what is possible and probable in state behavior?

## The Geopolitical Setting of States

Every nation-state operates within a context shaped by many other states and other international actors. Some of these entities are large and some are small; some possess great military and economic capabilities and others do not; some control important natural resources and others are resource-poor. The arrangement of states includes their political–geographic arrangement as well. First, this means that we care about the physical location of states; for example, China and Russia still share over 2,000 miles of common land border, whereas the United States has a common land border with neither; Britain and Japan are islands, whereas France and Germany border many other states. Some states are distant from the centers of international activity; Australia, for example, is at the periphery of international interaction. Others—Egypt, Israel, and Iraq—are located along historical trade routes or paths of invasion.

The political-geographic arrangement includes not only location but also topographical features. States are concerned with and affected by their neighbors—how many there are, how close or how far, how big or how small—and they are also concerned with the features of land and sea. The menu of a particular power is different if it is an island or a continental power; at the end of a peninsula or at the center of a continental landmass; has long shorelines and good ports or is landlocked; has mountains, deserts, rivers, swamps, or other natural barriers as borders or has its frontiers on open, flat plains. The arrangement of these physical features will limit the possibilities and probabilities of communication and transportation of both economic goods and military capabilities.

The physical arrangement of the international environment also includes less obvious features. Useful natural resources—drinkable water and arable land, as well as forests, animal life, and mineral resources—are unevenly distributed. The definition of "useful" changes over time: states that possessed uranium in the nineteenth century did not gain by it in either wealth or influence. Finally, climate varies across the globe. As parts of the physical arrangement and environment of all states, all these factors affect opportunities for state interaction. Just as the design and structure of a chessboard (or any other gameboard) influence the possibilities and probabilities of movement by the pieces on the board, the international system affects the behavior of states.

Location strongly affects interaction: states tend to get into wars more often with neighbors than with others because they interact more with countries close by than with those far away. Contiguity is one factor that helps to create "dangerous dyads."[1] One view of the relationship between the closeness of states and their opportunities for interaction is that of Kenneth E. Boulding.[2] Boulding developed a principle of viability, whereby any state's power is greatest at home but then declines along a "loss of strength gradient" as the distance from home is increased. This occurs because of the increases in the time and cost of transporting one's power. Because of this, Boulding

---

[1] For evidence of this effect, see Stuart Bremer, "Dangerous Dyads: Conditions Affecting the Likelihood of Interstate War, 1816–1965," *Journal of Conflict Resolution* 36 (June 1992), 309–341.
[2] Kenneth E. Boulding, *Conflict and Defense* (New York: Harper & Row, 1962), chap. 4.

proposes an axiom: "the further the weaker." We see then, that in general, a state should be most concerned with its immediate neighbors and less concerned with those far away. Indeed, except for the interactions of and with some major powers, this is the case.


## Technology

Decision makers of a state are faced with a number of givens: geography, the arrangement of neighbors, and distant states. Another such given is the existing technology in the international system. As we noted when discussing opportunity in Chapter 2, technology plays a major part in determining what is physically possible; in the fourth century B.C. Alexander the Great could not communicate instantaneously with King Darius of Persia, but Nixon could with Brezhnev during the crisis of the 1973 Yom Kippur war.

**Technology** is the application of human skills or techniques to accomplish human purposes.[3] Creative genius has continually led people to develop new technologies to overcome space and time, to generate power for economic and military purposes, to communicate and transport ideas and objects. Obstacles presented by mountains, deserts, or distance are overcome by inventions—the railroad, the automobile, the airplane. Obstacles to the spread of ideas and ideologies have been overcome by the development of radio, television, and communications satellites, all components of Rosenau's concept of the microelectronic revolution. These technologies bring news from all over the world into your home *as* events are happening (for example, the opening of the Berlin Wall in November 1989). Technology also permits us to overcome obstacles posed by disease and age. Advances in medical knowledge and skills have played a large part in the explosive growth of population since World War II by lowering the rate of infant mortality and the death rate in general. New technologies also permit the extraction of resources which had been literally out of reach. The development of synthetics can expand a menu limited by the earth's resources.

In sum, the technology that exists in the system at any time is an important factor for understanding what is possible. Note also that the situation is dynamic: research and development by governments, industry, universities, and individuals are continually changing the technological environment. Such change has become ever more rapid, and it has been taking less and less time for new discoveries to become operational in our world. The gap between Marconi's first radio set and commercial broadcasting was 35 years; but the atomic bomb went from discovery to use in 6 years, and the transistor made the journey in 5 years.

If, as we shall later argue, the menu of a state is intimately tied to its capabilities, influence, and power, then technology affects the basis of a state's power, the scope of that power, and the areas in which the state is interested in using that power. The

---

[3] Harold and Margaret Sprout, *Towards a Politics of the Planet Earth* (New York: Van Nostrand Reinhold, 1971).

menu of any state is limited not only by the technology that exists at any point in time but also by the *distribution* of that technology in the system. Often only the state that originates a new technological innovation possesses it for a period of time, in the way the United States had a monopoly on atomic weapons until the first Soviet atomic explosion in 1949.

## CHARACTERISTICS OF SYSTEMS

We may speak of the structure of a system as the arrangement of various things in that system. In the first chapter we defined a system as a set of elements interacting with each other. A set of billiard balls being broken on a pool table constitutes such a system, for the balls interact with one another. An international system, infinitely more complex, is a set of states and other actors interacting with each other. Sometimes it is useful to treat the states as though they were billiard balls, considering the nation-state as the only type of actor or unit of analysis worth worrying about. Thus we would concentrate on how the state-unit France interacts with other units like Italy and China. But we said that the international system is infinitely more complex than a set of billiard balls. Why is it so?

First, other actors, both within nation-states and among several states, must be taken into account. Also, the kinds of interaction and the number of variables are much more numerous. The billiard balls act on one another only through the expenditure of energy, which can be measured on a single scale. If you know the initial location of the balls on the table, the energy-absorbing capacity of the balls and banks, the degree of level of the table surface, the friction created by the table covering, the amount of energy exerted through the cue, and the initial angles of interaction, it is possible to make a good prediction of where the balls will end up. The prediction requires quite a lot of information, some of it (such as the angles) very hard to obtain, but the number of different aspects or variables at issue is small (about six) and is theoretically manageable. Furthermore, these are the only variables that matter. If you had all the information for them, the effects both of chance and of ignored variables would be quite low. For instance, we can usually forget about the atmospheric pressure of the room (which influences friction). The typical billiard player is not an engineer and will not make the computations but will recognize them as important variables and take them into account from experience and intuition. The player who "knows" the table will also have a good idea of how much force to use on the cue and the angle to try for to get the desired distribution of the balls. Achieving the right shot may not always be possible, but the player knows what to try for.

The analysis of international systems requires, or at least seems to require, information about a great many more variables. We say "seems to require" because we are often not sure which variables exert a great deal of influence and which, like the atmospheric pressure in the billiards room, can be safely ignored without damage to most analyses. Any system is defined by a combination of the attributes of its component units (how many and of what type) and the nature, pattern, and number of interactions among those units. Applying these ideas to the international system, all of the following are important:

**1.** The *number* of state actors.

**2.** The relative *size* of the various state actors. The most relevant measure of size may be population, area, wealth, economic capacity (GNP), military capabilities, some other measure, or some combination of these.

**3.** The numbers and types of *nonstate* actors. In addition to the intergovernmental and nongovernmental organizations mentioned in the previous chapter, we should also include a geographic or political group of states as an actor. Because of institutional bonds or other linkages, such groupings have been called blocs. This is the sense in which many observers commonly used the term "Soviet bloc" during most of the post–World War II period. They assumed that the linkages among these countries were so numerous and strong that the states would act as a unit, often delegating decision-making power to an intergovernmental organization or to one of their number. When such regional groupings, blocs, or alliances act together on a range of issues, they contribute to serious modifications in the structure of an international system that had been a set of states each acting entirely independently. The effect is in some ways analogous to the party organization that molds several fairly cohesive voting groups out of a body of individual legislators in a parliament. Given the concern with capabilities noted in point 2, clearly another type of relevant international actor or organization is the military alliance among several states. As with legislative bodies, there may be two or many such alliances, with great variation possible in their discipline and degree of cohesion. Bilateral alliances typically do not set up formal organizations like NATO, but pairs of states with relatively long-term bonds can nevertheless be included under this heading.

**4.** Linkages or **interactions** among state actors. These include formal government-to-government interactions or other interactions across societies. The latter may take the form of trade, foreign investments, movements of citizens (by tourism, migration, and student exchanges), communications between governments or private citizens (via mail, telephone, telegraph, or now computer), or the mass media (radio and television). These links can be usefully classed together as *transactions,* whether conducted by governments or by private citizens. From the viewpoint of the political analyst, any single event—a particular purchase, a single letter, one student fellowship—is rarely of interest; rather, it is the aggregate number of such acts that is of concern—in other words, whether the total volume of trade or communications is high or low. In addition, there is a class of events that may be of interest either in the aggregate or as a particular event. These events are *acts,* meaning primarily government-to-government interactions. Acts include the signing or denunciation of treaties; visits by heads of state; messages of threat, concern, support, or approval transmitted between governments; and military actions (whether actual international acts of violence or merely the moving and mobilizing of troops) that convey a message to other governments.

**5.** The nature and degree to which interactions link the units of the system together, or *interdependence.*

## INTERDEPENDENCE AND THE INTERNATIONAL SYSTEM

Very simply defined, **interdependence**, in any type of system, is a relationship in which changes or events in any single part of a system will produce some reaction or have some significant consequence in other parts of the system. For example, an infected finger in the system of a human organism will affect the blood system and its white cell defenses; it can cause a fever and speed up the heartbeat. Similarly, by increasing the air in the carburetor of a car, we affect the ignition within the cylinders and the speed and smoothness of the ride. In world politics we can think of the effects within the system of a guerrilla war in a small country in Southeast Asia in the 1960s, of a fundamentalist religious leader coming to power in a strategic, oil-rich Persian Gulf power in 1979, or of a worker in Poland winning the Nobel Peace Prize in 1983. These events all had major effects on many other parts of the global system. The stock market crash of October 19, 1987, when the New York Stock Exchange Dow Jones average dropped more than 500 points, is a perfect illustration. The effects of this event reverberated through markets worldwide, especially in Tokyo, London, and Hong Kong; they affected domestic and foreign policy in almost every noncommunist state. In turn, the resulting rises and declines in these other markets affected the subsequent health of the NYSE.

Interdependence is a quality of a system. In systems, things ramify; more effects than we imagine or expect ripple through the system because of the system's interdependences. Systems thinking emphasizes that everything is related to everything else. By making us think of interdependence, systems thinking makes us aware that the world is much more complex than we might have supposed. This complexity includes the interconnectedness of our problems and our collective well-being. Looking at social systems (such as the international system), Jay Forrester has said, "It is my basic theme that the human mind is not adapted to interpreting how social systems behave. Our social systems belong to the class called multiloop nonlinear feedback systems."[4] For example, a weapon that had been produced by a superpower in order to please one of its armed services is seen as a major threat by the other superpower, which matches this development and then builds more, perhaps leading to an arms race, which then raises tensions that might get out of hand in a crisis.

Similarly, there are surprise effects: when there is a change in the system, be prepared for surprising consequences. Examples include the French Revolution of 1789, the Russian Revolution of 1917, and the October 1973 war of Israel versus Egypt and Syria, which led to the Arab use of oil as a weapon, which led to worldwide economic problems and to conservation efforts that changed the nature of life in advanced industrial countries, and so on. Surprise effects have a number of sources, not simply the major changes that can accompany war or revolution. The interdependent linkages among economic, ecological, political, and social phenomena in the present

---

[4] See Jay Forrester, "Counter-Intuitive Behavior of Social Systems," *Technology Review* 73 (1971), 53–68.

world system are graphically illustrated by the events of 1972. Poor weather in the winter of 1971–72 destroyed one-third of the Russian winter wheat crop. However, the government bureaucracy failed to increase the spring wheat acreage. To meet wheat demands, a massive wheat sale was arranged with the United States in July 1972, doubling the price of wheat in North America and generating public anger. In addition, North American wheat was not available for India (whose food supply had been worsened by monsoon and war) or for China and Africa (both hit by drought), with Africa especially facing conditions of massive starvation. Two analysts note:

> *The most outstanding lesson which can be drawn from these events is a realization of how strong the bonds among nations have become.* A bureaucratic decision in one region, perhaps the action of just one individual—not to increase the spring wheat acreage—resulted in a housewives' strike against soaring food prices in another part of the world and in tragic suffering in yet another part of the world.[5]

International interdependence has two different dimensions. In the first place international actors are **sensitive** to the behavior of other actors or developments in parts of the system. The degree of sensitivity depends on how quickly changes in one actor bring about changes in another and how great the effects are. Second, actors may be **vulnerable** to the effects of those changes. Vulnerability is measured by the costs imposed on a state or other actor by external events, even if that actor tries to avoid those costs in responding to those effects.[6]

A state is sensitive to environmental interdependence if it has to clean beaches blackened by an oil spill that occurred in another state's territorial waters or if a downstream state like the Netherlands must suffer from the river pollution produced by states farther upstream on the Rhine. Such a state is then vulnerable because even after the cleanup its environment may remain impaired and the effects of the damage may be great, perhaps affecting its tourist and fishing industries. In discussing economic interdependence, we may say that if Japan's trade with the United States drops as a result of a recession in America, that trade is sensitive; if Japan also goes into a recession because of the trade drop, it is vulnerable. The United States is certainly not as vulnerable to a recession in, say, Guatemala, as Guatemala is to a U.S. recession. Guatemala may be dependent on the United States; the two are not interdependent as we have defined the term. The vulnerability of the major stock exchanges, as demonstrated in October 1987, is much more even, the New York exchange being perhaps more vulnerable than that of Tokyo, but less so than that of London or Hong Kong.

---

[5] Mihajlo Mesarovic and Eduard Pestel, *Mankind at the Turning Point* (New York: New American Library, 1974), pp. 19–20 (emphasis in original).
[6] See Robert O. Keohane and Joseph S. Nye, *Power and Interdependence*, 2nd ed. (Boston: Scott, Foresman, 1989), for the concepts of sensitivity and vulnerability. See David A. Baldwin, *Paradoxes of Power* (Oxford: Blackwell, 1989), chap. 8, for the relationship between interdependence and power (which we will return to in Chapter 6).

Thus different systems, and different actors within those systems, may be characterized by different levels of sensitivity and vulnerability. If sensitivity reflects the effects of changes in one part of the system on other parts and the speed with which they take place, then the current system, which encompasses the globe and is linked together with modern communications and transportation networks, is more highly sensitive than systems in past eras of international relations. Again, we see that technology affects the international system by affecting the opportunities available and the strength of the interdependent ties among the system's component actors.

## THE EMERGENCE OF A GLOBAL SYSTEM

Interaction and interdependence make a system out of otherwise separate units. Many social, technological, economic, and political factors affect the rate and kind of interaction. Where interaction is much greater among a certain set of actors than between those actors and others outside the set, the interacting set is a subsystem. If the rate of interaction between members of the set and outsiders is extremely low, we may simply refer to the interacting set as a system rather than a subsystem. For example, there has not always been an international system of global scope.

Before the sixteenth century, instead of a global system there were numerous regional systems. European states did not interact at all with the Western Hemisphere, and they interacted in no significant way with Africa south of the Sahara or with East and Southeast Asia. Communication and transportation technologies were too primitive to permit interaction across long distances. With improvements in navigation and sailing technology, Spain, Portugal, Holland, England, and France were able to build huge colonial empires around the globe—the expansion of the European system discussed in the previous chapter. For the first time a worldwide capitalist economic system—production for a global market—emerged. Many peoples and areas were linked to this system only weakly, but many others (slaves producing sugar in the Caribbean, Indians put to work in the silver mines of South America, workers on spice plantations in Southeast Asia, consumers in Europe) found their fortunes linked to, and interdependent with, economic conditions halfway around the world. The world political system still remained fairly fragmented, however. No single state dominated the world, and for a long time it was still possible for many non-European actors to ignore Europe for most purposes. Large parts of Africa and Asia retained substantial independence until the final wave of European colonial acquisition in the second half of the nineteenth century. The United States, with its strength and relative physical isolation, was able to ignore most European political quarrels until World War I.

Figure 4.1 shows what has happened in transportation since the early nineteenth century. Beginning with sailing vessels and the earliest steamships (which moved at about 5 miles per hour), the figure gives the maximum speed of human transportation achievable at various times over intercontinental distances. The graph rises to the speed attained by oceangoing passenger ships in the period between the world wars

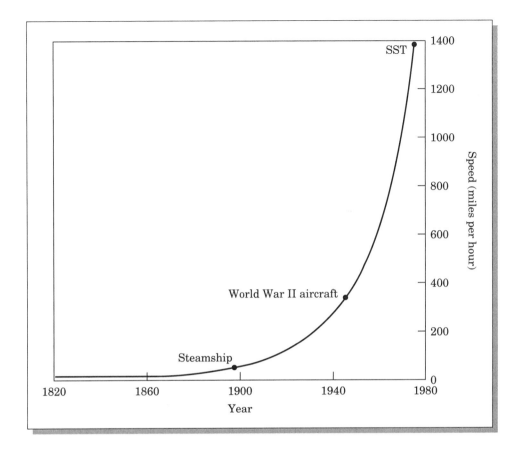

**FIGURE 4.1** A shrinking world: maximum speed attainable for intercontinental travel, 1820–1980.

and then advances rapidly with the long-range jet bombers of the 1960s and the supersonic bombers and SST civil aircraft of the 1970s. Especially with the recent change, the whole world has become irrevocably bound into a closely knit system. America's geographic isolation, which enabled the United States to avoid becoming enmeshed in Europe's wars for more than 100 years, is gone. Indeed, all parts of the world are within 30 minutes' reach of intercontinental missiles from anywhere; all parts of the world are instantaneously connected by satellite communications.

Much the same trend has taken place in the destructive capacity of explosive weapons. Figure 4.2 shows the increase in the radius of destruction of a single weapon, beginning with the artillery shells of the American Civil War and continuing through the guns of the turn of the century, the largest conventional bombs dropped in World War II, and the thermonuclear weapons of the present. The measurements are approximate, but the general picture is clear. The best of the World War II "blockbusters" could seriously damage only those buildings within about 500 feet (one-tenth of a mile), but the Hiroshima atomic bomb (the equivalent of 15,000 tons of

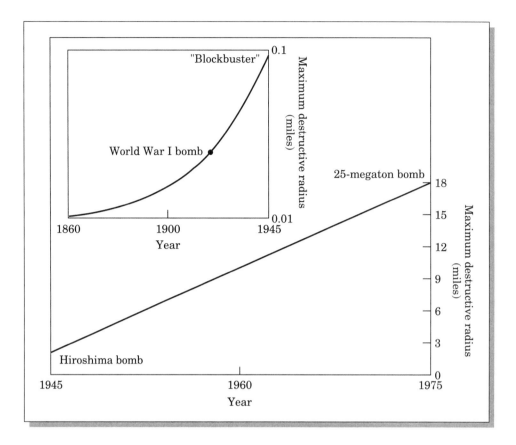

**FIGURE 4.2**   More bang for a bomb: maximum destructive radius of existing weapons, 1860–1975. Destructive radius is defined as sufficient blast overpressure (3 pounds per square inch) to collapse an ordinary frame house. [Calculated from U.S. Atomic Energy Commission, *The Effects of Nuclear Weapons* (Washington, D.C.: U.S. Government Printing Office, 1962), and later data.]

TNT) destroyed most buildings within a mile and a half of the blast. Later scientific developments raised this figure substantially, to about 18 miles for big 25-megaton hydrogen bombs (bombs equivalent to 25 million tons of TNT).[7]

These technological developments have meant that although wars are no more frequent in the international system now than they were 100 years ago, they certainly have become more destructive. Figure 4.3 shows the number of soldiers killed in all

---

[7] The explosive power of weapons has increased at a much higher rate than indicated in Figure 4.2 for destructive radius, since increasing the destructive radius by 67 percent means doubling the power of the bomb. In the years since 1975 much greater accuracy in delivery allowed the superpowers to use smaller bombs—of "only" a megaton or less.

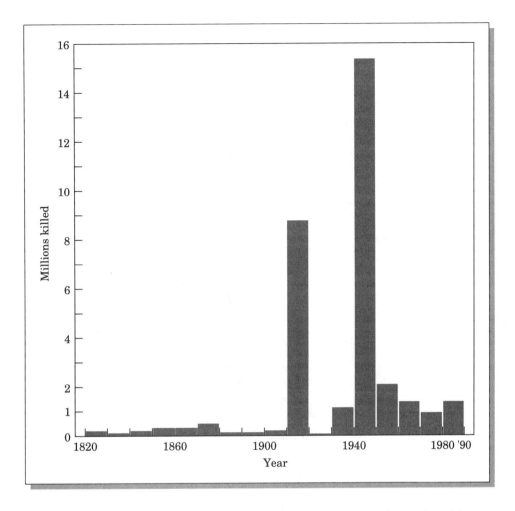

**FIGURE 4.3**   Deaths from international wars, 1815–1990. [Adapted from J. David Singer and Melvin Small, *The Wages of War, 1815–1965: A Statistical Handbook* (New York: Wiley, 1972), and Small and Singer, *Resort to Arms* (Beverly Hills, Calif.: Sage, 1982).]

international wars since 1815. The figures do not include civilian deaths; if they did, the number would be several times higher.

Coupled with the enormous growth in wealth of the industrial powers over the past century, the new technology provides the means for great powers to make their influence felt virtually everywhere and for the entire global system truly to operate as an interacting system. The major powers are particularly involved in interactions with one another. During the cold war era each of the biggest powers had parts of the globe (or regional subsystems) that it dominated and within which it sharply limited the influence of other major powers. The United States was long dominant in Latin America, as was the Soviet Union in Eastern Europe. China has exercised influence in parts of East Asia, competing first with the USSR and now with Japan and Russia. Britain and France once had large spheres of influence in Africa and elsewhere but no longer have as much power, relative either to their former colonies or to the United States, to dominate these regions. At the same time, although certain major powers have clearly predominated over others in particular spheres of influence in certain time periods (for example, Latin America and Eastern Europe), most of the smaller powers within such areas usually maintain significant ties—economic, political, cultural, or military—with other powers as well. Regional subsystems are thus penetrated by the big powers' global activities. Figure 4.4 illustrates several hypothetical international

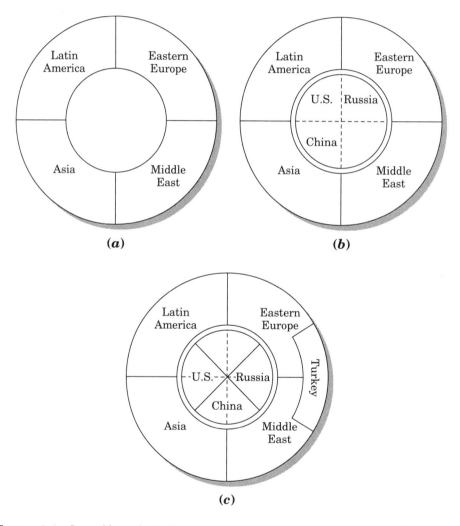

**FIGURE 4.4** Several hypothetical international systems: (a) regional systems; (b) international system with major powers and regional subsystems (spheres of influence); (c) major power penetration across subsystems.

systems: a world with separated regional systems, a global system of major powers and spheres of influence, and major power penetration across subsystems.

# STATUS AND HIERARCHY IN THE INTERNATIONAL SYSTEM

A system is about its component units and their relationships. Both the characteristics of these units and their interactions will indicate how the units, or in our case international actors, *stand in relationship to one another.* Thus we can use the system perspective to stress the degree of **hierarchy** in the international system: who has the most of something (wealth, military capability, prestige, or status), who has the least, who sits in the middle. Hierarchy can also indicate how states are linked together, either essentially as equals or only through the intermediary of one or more great powers. Several writers see a feudal aspect to much of historical and contemporary international politics. They posit a world of several influence spheres, each dominated by a big power that interposes its own facilities between small powers within its spheres (maintaining a lord-and-vassal relationship) and that limits as far as possible the penetration of other major powers into its own spheres. For instance, telephone calls between Senegal and Gabon in West Africa once had to go through Paris; air travel in many parts of the Third World was possible only through London, Paris, or other major cities in the developed world.

## *Spheres of Influence*

The spheres-of-influence perspective tends to emphasize interactions among great powers (or the actions of superpowers as they move to limit each other's influence in their respective spheres) and looks at this process in terms of **balance of power.** The perspective of hierarchy, on the other hand, looks at *structures of dominance* of the weak by the strong and at the possibilities for limited autonomy or independence by those at the bottom, the "underdogs." This is what we meant earlier when we noted that the system could produce constraints on behavior. Smaller states within a feudal system are highly constrained by larger powers, especially if they sit within the sphere of influence of a major power. If, as during the cold war, there are two superpowers competing in an area, each superpower is limited by the other; each restrains its behavior in anticipation (or fear) of the other's response. Having several major powers opens up the menu: the balance-of-power possibilities of coalitions or alliances increase as opportunities for interaction increase. These are just a few of the many possible constraints imposed by the structure of the system. Clearly, those states at the bottom of the international hierarchy have different menus from those at the top.

One way to picture a feudal pattern is illustrated in Figure 4.5, where the lines indicate substantial interactions that states have with one another. Thus *A* and *B*, the "top dogs" or larger powers, interact most with each other and with small powers

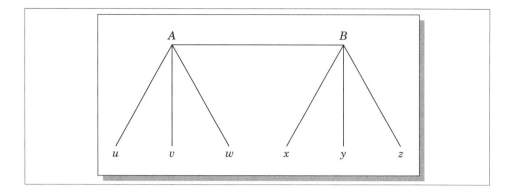

**FIGURE 4.5**  A feudal international system.

in their spheres of influence. The small powers—$u$, $v$, $w$, $x$, $y$, and $z$—interact least, even though they might be in the same geographical region and have many common interests. There are two basic ordering principles of the feudal system: (1) a state that ranks high on one dimension of power is likely to rank high on other dimensions, and (2) interaction tends to be dependent on average power. Thus states that are powerful tend to interact more, powerful and weaker states interact less, and states that are weak interact still less.[8]

Theories about spheres of influence or balance of power typically are "center-oriented" (realist) theories or "views from above," concerned chiefly with relations among the great powers. What goes on among the small powers at the periphery of the world system generally matters little, except that the addition or loss of small states to a big power's alliance or sphere of influence affects the balance of power or the likelihood of war. In effect, the peripheries matter only as pawns in the arena of great-power politics. Indeed, some theorists even praise the advantages of so-called **bipolar systems,** where two major powers or alliance systems confront each other from positions of relative equality. Such theorists sometimes declare that a bipolar system will be stable in large part just because the great powers are able to dominate and control small states.[9]

These perspectives were typical of most U.S. and Soviet theorizing during the cold war era (we shall examine these and other theories about polarity and relative power among big states in Chapter 5). During that period, theorists in Europe and especially in the Third World saw the situation very differently. Their "view from below" was much more concerned with avoiding becoming arenas for superpower conflict and with obtaining some freedom of action for their countries. From below, within spheres of influence, balance of power looks like dominance.

---

[8] Robin Jenkins, *Exploitation* (London: Paladin, 1971), pp. 82–83.
[9] See Kenneth Waltz, *Theory of International Politics* (Reading, Mass.: Addison-Wesley, 1979).

Superpower competition provided benefits as well as costs to some smaller countries by fostering interest by one superpower in areas that might be of importance to the other. Smaller countries found that they could play off the superpowers against each other in competition for economic and military aid. This process halted dramatically in the post–cold war era, when Soviet inability to compete in many areas also promoted American neglect. A similar phenomenon occurred during earlier periods of U.S.–Soviet détente; for example, the volume of American economic assistance to other countries declined from 0.8 percent of GNP to about 0.3 percent from 1962 to 1983 during a period when Soviet–American relations were improving. The "outbreak of peace" in the late 1980s, in areas such as Angola–Namibia, Central America, Cambodia, and between Iran and Iraq, owed much to the end of the cold war and the evolution of a policy of mutual restraint between the United States and the Soviet Union. No longer would the two powers automatically support opposing factions in some local dispute.

Just as big-power theories look chiefly at horizontal relations among approximate equals, theories originating from small powers stress vertical relationships. As noted, some theories characterize international politics as essentially feudal; a related and especially popular kind of theory is concerned with **dependence.** Non-Western and European theorists have examined the effects of big powers' economic, political, and cultural penetration on small powers. The effects at issue in such theories are also different—they are less concerned with war and international political alignments and more concerned with patterns of economic and political development in the developing world.

## *Relative Deprivation and Aggression*

To gain a perspective on hierarchy in international systems, we must examine the distribution of goods and rewards among different states in the system, as well as the linkages between the rich and the poor, the strong and the weak. Top dogs are likely to be feared, rich, and powerful. By looking at the distribution of various desired conditions (wealth, respect, and power) among states in the system, we can find some clues as to which countries' leaders may feel deprived and hence prone to violent, aggressive behavior. Note now that we are specifically talking about how the system structure (or opportunity) affects the perceptions (or willingness) of decision makers within that system.

Theories about status and feelings of deprivation are common in psychology, sociology, and political science. The most important versions assert that aggressive behavior stems from frustration arising out of a feeling of **relative deprivation.** People may act violently or aggressively not because they are poor or deprived in some absolute sense but because they *feel* deprived relative to others or to their expectations of what they should have. Perhaps the best example is pre–World War I Germany's demand for its "place in the sun"; this was a desire for recognition as a great power, especially in comparison to Britain, exacerbated by Kaiser Wilhelm's personal insecurities and jealousies. Similarly, before the Seven Weeks' War in 1866 between Prussia and Austria, Prussia's grievances with Austria had been related to "pride of place"— a demand for equal status with Austria in the German Diet. We shall also find perceptions of comparative status to be important when in the next chapter we look at theories of war involving the periodic rise of challengers against the dominant states in the system.

Feelings of relative deprivation can arise by comparing one's past, present, and expected future condition. Images of this condition are strongly affected by where one (or one's country) sits within the hierarchy of various global or regional systems based on status, prestige, military power, wealth, and so on. Feelings of relative deprivation are likely to arise when a formerly prosperous individual experiences a severe economic setback. Such feelings are widespread during recessions and depressions and often result in severe political unrest. Karl Marx thought that revolutions would occur as the result of the increasing poverty of the working class. Prolonged, severe depression in Germany in the 1930s played a key part in preparing Hitler's rise to power. Some observers fear the parallels between the experience of Weimar Germany and growth of the fascist-like movement supporting Vladimir Zhirinovsky in the economically troubled atmosphere of post–cold war Russia.[10]

On the other hand, in some cases an improvement in people's material conditions can release unrest. Alexis de Tocqueville described the situation before the French Revolution in these terms:

> Thus it was precisely in those parts of Europe where there had been most improvement that popular discontent was highest. . . . Patiently endured so long as it seemed beyond redress, a grievance comes to appear intolerable once the possibility of removing it crosses men's minds.[11]

A more complicated hypothesis combines these two views and asserts that the most dangerous time for social unrest, or for challenges to the status quo in any sort of system, is when a sustained period of improving conditions is followed by a sudden, sharp setback. The period of improvement may lead people to expect continuing improvement; thus, when the setback occurs, it causes more distress than if it had followed a period of unchanged conditions.

Another perspective emphasizes the importance of people's comparisons with one another: "I may be satisfied, even with a bad lot, providing that you do no better. But to the degree I make comparisons with others and find my situation relatively poor, then I am likely to be dissatisfied." Here it is necessary to specify what group or individual is relevant for comparison. For the landless peasant in a traditional society, the condition of the rich landlord may be beyond the peasant's dreams, but the modest prosperity of the middle peasant (the kulak in Russia after the 1917 revolution, for example) may arouse acute feelings of relative deprivation. Generally, such feelings seem more severe for comparisons among people in close contact than for widely separated social groups or strata. Hence, poor whites may feel angrier and

---

[10] For example, see Jacob W. Kipp, "The Zhirinovsky Threat," *Foreign Affairs* 73 (May–June 1994), 72–86.

[11] Alexis de Tocqueville, *The Old Regime and the French Revolution* (Garden City, N.Y.: Doubleday, 1955), pp. 176–177.

more threatened by the gains of blacks than they do about the privileges of rich whites, even though poor whites as well as blacks may be better off than their parents were. Importantly, the microelectronic revolution in communications technology has fostered this phenomenon across continents, cultures, and economic classes.

These two perspectives, emphasizing comparisons across time and across groups, can be usefully combined. The first suggests when serious discontent may arise; the second suggests where in the social system it will be most manifest. Theories of relative deprivation have received a good deal of attention. Part of the reason is that the present day seems to be a period of substantial change in people's status or in their consciousness of differences in status. Feelings of relative deprivation may also arise among those who are excluded from the benefits of improved economic conditions. Many people in the slums and barrios of the developing countries, for instance, may sometimes be better off economically than they had been, but transistor radios, television by satellite, and other forms of modern communications have made them more aware of how well off people in other countries and elites in their own countries really are. This is what is meant by "rising expectations."

We shall return later to aspects of the international system's hierarchy and to some of the consequences of dependence for those at the bottom of that hierarchy. Let us turn now to an important factor in the structure of international systems: how the states near the top of the international hierarchy put together their military alliances in an anarchic system, and how the distribution of power among the leading states or alliances affects the system's stability or the chances that major wars will arise.

## ALLIANCES AND NONALIGNMENT

Alliances tell us much about the political and military structure of the international system: about the geopolitical relationships among states, about the distribution of friendship and enmity, about the distribution of military capability. Like technology, alliances can be used to overcome distance and geographic obstacles, creating new opportunities and risks for the states involved. Alliances can be central to system structure and to the menu presented by any international system; for example, through the distribution of power and the mechanisms of the balance of power.

**Alliances** combine elements of cooperation and conflict. They involve interstate cooperation (between allied states), while addressing an existing or potential conflict with one or more other states.[12] Cooperative behavior can be either formal or

---

[12] A useful overview of alliance studies is Michael D. Ward, *Research Gaps in Alliance Dynamics*, vol. 19, Monograph Series in World Affairs (Denver: University of Denver, 1982), and a recent review of alliance theory is Glenn H. Snyder, "Alliance Theory: A Neorealist First Cut," *Journal of International Affairs* 44 (1990), 103–123. For the geopolitical impact of alliances, see Randolph M. Siverson and Harvey Starr, *The Diffusion of War: A Study of Opportunity and Willingness* (Ann Arbor: University of Michigan Press, 1991).

informal. Informally, two states are in alignment if they act in a similar way toward some third international actor. Again informally, states are said to be in **coalition** if they act cooperatively, displaying common behavior and attitudes toward other actors and issues but without a formal agreement. Alliances are generally defined by at least two special characteristics: they are formalized in written treaties, and they are agreements to cooperate in security or military affairs. The agreements often specify the rights and obligations, the benefits and costs, of the alliance members. In sum, alliances involve the formal collaboration of states, generally for specified and limited periods of time, in regard to some mutually perceived enemy or security problem. The key characteristic of alliances (as well as of alignments and coalitions) is that they reflect a set of *mutual expectations* among members regarding the behavior of the other partners.

## Alliances, Power, and Deterrence

The central issues or calculations in the alliance game involve whether to ally or not; then, what policies to follow in order to maintain the alliance.[13] Throughout history the main reason that states have entered into alliances has been the desire for the *aggregation of power*. Alliances permit states to augment their military capabilities by adding the military capabilities of others. When states $A$ and $C$ are in conflict with each other, they may increase their own power, add the power of other states, or withhold from their competitor the power of other states. Alliance as a foreign policy strategy has been the vital component in the balance of power throughout history (and thus is central to realist views of international relations). The aim of the balance of power is first of all deterrence: to deter some opponent from engaging in some behavior—usually war—because the military capability of the alliance is equal to or outweighs that of the opponent (or will make war too costly to be of benefit).

Deterrence to protect third parties against attack depends on the **credibility** of the deterrent threat. Credibility depends both on capabilities (opportunity) and on the willingness to use them. Alliances strengthen credibility by making international politics more predictable. In terms of capability they make clear that third parties may call on the capabilities of alliance partners. Willingness is communicated in part through such activities as the signing of alliance treaties. A treaty tries to make clear to an opponent, in a formal manner, "This state is my ally; if you attack it, you will have to deal with me also." This notion of "collective defense" was the heart of America's post–World War II alliance system, particularly for the North Atlantic Treaty Organization, which covered much of Europe. Much of American alliance policy was pursued by Secretary of State John Foster Dulles because he felt that the lack of such clear lines was the cause of the North Korean invasion of South Korea in 1950. The logic was that the North Koreans were not deterred from making the attack because it had not been made clear that South Korea was an American ally and would

---

[13] See Glenn H. Snyder, "The Security Dilemma in Alliance Politics," *World Politics* 36 (1984), 461–496.

be protected as such. There is a debate whether an analogous situation occurred with regard to Kuwait and Iraq in the summer of 1990. Clinton's actions in 1994 made it very clear to Saddam Hussein that Kuwait would again be defended if need be.

Alliances, then, are intended to increase an opponent's belief that military aid will be rendered by state $A$ to state $B$ by making it clear that state $A$ identifies its security with that of state $B$. Alliances may thus be seen as indicators of *shared* policy preferences.[14]

If deterrence fails, however, the aggregation of military capabilities permits the alliance to defeat the opponent. The formation of the two alliances before World War I—the Triple Entente of Britain, France, and Russia and the Triple Alliance of Germany, Austria–Hungary, and Italy—illustrates both these aspects of aggregation and balance of power. France and Germany each sought to offset the military capabilities of the other through diplomatic maneuvers that added new alliance partners to its side. In this situation deterrence failed (in part because it was not entirely clear that all the alliance agreements would be kept), and most of the alliances were then used to fight a war.

The addition of the power of others to one's own is not the only reason for alliance and may in some cases be quite secondary. Alliances may also be preemptive, preventing opponents from expanding their own menus. For example, before World War I France and Russia competed with Germany for Romania as an ally. The competition was not so much to add Romania's military might as to prevent its strategic location from falling into the hands of the opponent. The realist view of international relations argues that a state whose national security is threatened should ally with any state that will (1) help offset the power of others or (2) deny its power to the opponent.

The choice of allies, realists argue, should not be affected by nonmilitary considerations, such as ideology, past relationships, or morality. In fact, similarities between states, including bonds of cooperation, ideology, history, and outlook, have had important influences on the alliance behavior of states. When they want to form alliances, states try to aggregate enough military power to win, but in this search states that are ideologically or culturally similar are usually chosen first; this partially accounts for the American predisposition to side with Britain rather than Germany during World War I even before German submarine warfare and diplomacy hardened those predispositions.

As in the case of Romania, a state may be brought into an alliance because of its strategic location. The purpose is to increase one's security and military position

---

[14] Bruce Bueno de Mesquita's expected-utility approach to war, in such work as *The War Trap* (New Haven, Conn.: Yale University Press, 1981), is explicitly based on alliances as indicators of shared policy preferences. This is also central to the study of alliances as a mechanism for the diffusion of war in Siverson and Starr, *The Diffusion of War*. Studies of deterrence for the protection of third parties show that if deterrence fails and the opponent (C) attacks, the protector state (A) is much more likely to fight to defend its protege (B) if a formal alliance exists than if it does not. Potential attackers may be discouraged by strong alliances but may choose weak ones—where the protector's promise to fight is not very credible—as targets. See James Fearon, "Signalling vs. the Balance of Power and Interests: An Empirical Test of a Crisis Bargaining Model," *Journal of Conflict Resolution* 38 (June 1994), 236–269.

through the *projection* of one's own forces to overcome distance and geography, not through the addition of the new ally's military forces. This was one possible reason that Soviet leader Nikita Khrushchev placed missiles in Cuba in 1962. Although it had only a few long-range intercontinental missiles that could reach the United States, the Soviet Union could rapidly have increased its nuclear threat to the United States by placing medium-range missiles in Cuba, only 90 miles from the American mainland, and protected Cuba from the American invasion that it thought was increasingly probable.[15] Projecting forces—sending them to positions in allied states close to the opponent—also makes those forces into "trip wires." The postwar American alliance network allowed the United States to have allies directly on the borders of both the Soviet Union and China, and to have bases and station forces in those allies. Projected forces not only demonstrate the ties between state *A* and its allies but also show state *A*'s resolve to protect its allies. U.S. forces in Europe, for example, were trip-wire forces because a conventional Soviet attack on Europe would have involved an attack on American troops.

## Alliance Policy and the Menus of States

Alliances permit the combining of capabilities, thus adding elements of flexibility to state policy and making more complicated the calculation of relative power among states. Alliances affect the opportunities states have to add to their own capabilities by increasing their own resources or reducing those of an opponent. Alliances also provide interaction opportunities—that is, they serve as conduits by which the conflicts of one or more alliance partners become the conflicts of others; for example, alliances have been found to be factors in the spread, or *diffusion,* of war.

Alliances have been used by large nations to control and dominate smaller alliance partners and by smaller allies to manipulate larger alliance partners. An alliance leader may use alliances to create international *order,* an environment in which the alliance leader is safe, secure, and, indeed, a leader. Order requires organizing relations among the leader's allies—controlling or restraining the behavior of allies. In the post–World War II period both the United States and the Soviet Union used their alliances in this way, particularly in Europe. NATO was officially founded in 1949 as a means to protect Western Europe from Soviet invasion. The Warsaw Pact (formally, the Warsaw Treaty Organization) was established in 1955 as a response to West Germany's entry into NATO. Both alliances served the security interests of the United States and the Soviet Union, protecting their interests in Europe. Ironically, given the unification of Germany in 1991 (and the dissolution of the WTO the same year), both alliances also had been used to keep the lesser allies—especially the two German states—in line. This function of alliances may be more important than it seems. Wars between allies are common, three times commoner than would be

---

[15] See Raymond L. Garthoff, *Reflections on the Cuban Missile Crisis,* rev. ed. (Washington, D.C.: Brookings Institution, 1989).

expected by chance: more than 25 percent of coalition partners eventually go to war against each other. Clearly, alliances are no guarantee of peaceful relations among states.[16]

One danger of alliances is abandonment, having allies renege on alliance commitments. A different danger for the leading member of an alliance is entrapment, being dragged into conflicts by reckless smaller allies. It has been said that commitment is a seamless web: if a state does not honor its commitments to protect others or does not honor its deterrent threats now, similar threats will become much less credible in the future. Small allies have often engaged their larger partners in war by trapping them in positions where the larger partners would either have to support their small allies or back down. Austria–Hungary's aggressive behavior toward Serbia and Russia before World War I illustrates this relationship. Germany felt forced into being a belligerent supporter of Austria–Hungary or losing its Austrian ally by backing down before Russia. According to former President Nixon and former Secretary of State Kissinger, one of the most dangerous moments in U.S.–Soviet relations occurred in 1973, when the Soviet Union threatened to intervene in the October war to prevent its "ally" Egypt (actually an informal coalition partner) from being defeated. This would have forced the United States to intervene on behalf of its client, Israel.

States may also try to go it alone, avoiding alliances by some sort of neutral policy or by attempting to withdraw from the system of states as much as possible. Of course, a state's geopolitical position and the structure of the international system are important in selecting a strategy for security and survival. In the past a strategy of isolation was more useful for large countries that were self-sufficient and could draw inside themselves to develop. Japan was able to do this until the nineteenth century, and the Soviet Union to some degree during the 1920s. However, in the contemporary system, large countries with many economic and political ties and a network of economic, monetary, and resource interdependences find it difficult to withdraw from the international system. It has chiefly been smaller countries on the geographic peripheries of international activity that attempt this strategy. The best examples are Albania and Myanmar (Burma); possibly another is Cambodia after the communist victory in 1975.

Because of economic and political needs, many small states in the contemporary system have opted for a nonaligned foreign policy. The expression **"Third World"** was originally coined to characterize all those less-developed countries that avoided alliance with the First World of the industrialized West or the Second World of the communist East. Choices of alliance or **nonalignment** have been strongly affected by the post–World War II system structure. States had a choice of allying either with the Western bloc in some form or with the Soviet Union. However, the traditional reasons for allying with great powers have been security, stability, and status. In the cold war

---

[16] See Bueno de Mesquita, *The War Trap,* and Harvey Starr, *Coalitions and Future War* (Beverly Hills, Calif.: Sage, 1975). Could these findings be analogous to Lewis Fry Richardson's observation, noted in Chapter 1, about murder victims—that they are people with frequent interaction opportunities with their murderers?

system, allying with one of the great powers often brought just the opposite: fear of threat from the other superpower, internal instability through the clash of Western- and Eastern-oriented political factions (especially if the government chose military links with one side), and a decline in status, becoming a simple satellite or dependent of a superpower. What about alliances with other small powers? Any military combi- nation would have been helpless to challenge either superpower or its military alliance. The Arab League was formed in 1945 and is the only example of a postwar small-power (non-European) military alliance.

So although alliance has been a possibility, the international situation since World War II made a nonaligned strategy attractive to small powers for several reasons. For states that had recently achieved independence from a colonial status, it permitted at least the appearance of an independent foreign policy stance. Nonalignment in the form developed by India and Yugoslavia starting in the 1950s—in other words, not simply fence-sitting but an active and assertive policy directed toward independence, world peace, and justice—also gave smaller states a purposeful policy and a positive diplomatic identity. Nonalignment gave small, non-Western states a way to act as a third force in international organizations.

If, as we have said, a system is a set of elements and their interactions, then alliances have rightly been studied as an important aspect of the international system. They both indicate and affect the distribution of military and political power in the system through the aggregation and projection of military capabilities (note the dramatic impact on world politics produced by the German–Soviet nonaggression treaty of 1939, which surprised and stunned the other great powers). Alliance mem- bership—who is included and who is excluded—indicates policy preferences as well.

# THE WORLD SYSTEM: STRUCTURE, POLARITY, AND WAR

**WORLD SYSTEM**

RELATIONS

SOCIETY

GOVERNMENT

ROLE

INDIVIDUAL

One is one and all alone; "two's company, three's a crowd." In any social system, however small or simple, it makes a difference how many participants there are. Patterns of behavior differ greatly in different-sized groups. Thucydides of ancient Greece, many nineteenth-century European statesmen, and former U.S. Secretary of State Henry Kissinger would all agree that the number of participants in the international system makes a great difference in the way the participants can and must behave, affecting the likelihood of war among them and even their very survival as independent actors. The concern with nation-states, and primarily with the relative strength of the biggest states as actors in the pursuit of power, is typical of realist analysis.

To characterize an international system, we need to know the structure of the system—the opportunities or possibilities it presents—and how the menu provided by the structure affects the international relations within the system. To understand the structure of the system, we need knowledge about the number of state actors, their relative sizes, and the existence of such nonstate actors as alliances built by various bonds or linkages between two or more states.

## MAJOR ACTORS AND THE POLARIZATION OF SYSTEMS

Perhaps the most important theoretical concept for classifying international systems concerns the *number of major actors or* **poles** *in the system.* Each actor can act with significant independence from other major actors; it is its own master, with a wide selection of possible behaviors. A major actor may be either a single nation-state—a major *power*—or a tight and cohesive *alliance* of one or more major powers with other large or small allied powers. Thus the number of poles in a system may or may not be the same as the number of major powers.[1] States may behave quite differently in a system composed of two alliances, each including several major powers, than in a system with only one major power on each side. The various states in an alliance usually retain substantial independence, at least potentially; much negotiation and bargaining may be required for members of an alliance to act together and may result in less than unanimity. The possibility that in important ways the alliance will not behave like a unified actor introduces special instabilities and uncertainties.

At one extreme is the system with only a single major actor, usually a single state, that dominates all the small states. There has never been a *unipolar* *global system*, though a world empire would probably take such a form. Dominated, or hegemonic, systems of less than global extent have been known in the past; China and the Far East of several centuries ago is a good example. In the sense that a major power may be called a "pole" if it possesses a combination of significant military, economic, and political power, some observers have characterized the post–cold war period as unipolar. The United States is seen as the "unchallenged" dominant actor, the "only country with the military, diplomatic, political and economic assets to be a decisive player in any conflict in whatever part of the world it chooses to involve itself."[2] Certainly the global menu changed considerably with end of the cold war bipolarity and the possible

---

[1] Some writers prefer to define polarity only in terms of the number of major states [for example, Kenneth Waltz, *Theory of International Politics* (Boston: Addison-Wesley, 1979)] or the distribution of power among those states, ignoring alliance patterns [for example, Jack S. Levy, "The Polarity of the System and International Stability: An Empirical Analysis," in Alan Ned Sabrosky, ed., *Polarity and War: The Changing Structure of International Conflict* (Boulder, Colo.: Westview, 1985)]. To ignore alliance patterns or the formation of cohesive blocs, however, would be to characterize the international system as multipolar throughout the period from 1700 to 1945 and to ignore, for instance, the way the two opposing alliance systems became solidified and hostile before World War I.

[2] This rather extreme statement of contemporary unipolarity is from Charles Krautheimer, "The Unipolar Moment," *Foreign Affairs* 70, 1 (1991), 23–33, who argues that the United States can support and sustain its unipolar status.

emergence of U.S. unipolarity. Some argue that the apparent problems of American foreign policy under both Bush and Clinton derive from the difficulties of adjusting to a drastically different structural set of opportunities and constraints.

**Multipolar** systems have existed often in the past. During much of the eighteenth to the early twentieth centuries, a precarious multipolar system of many great powers existed in Europe. Occasionally it broke down through the dynamic and aggressive growth of one member (for example, Napoleon's France) or because of rigidities introduced by very close alliances or longstanding and often ideologically based antagonisms. Sometimes large and small states formed into two competing alliances. We can describe a system of two competing alliances as **polarized** between two extremes, as metal filings cluster around the two poles of a magnet. In almost all the international systems we know of, polarization is primarily a phenomenon only of bipolar systems and may not occur even there. The distinction between major powers as relatively independent actors on the one hand, and alliances as actors on the other, is often important. Around 1900 there were several states of similar size and resources: Britain, France, Russia, Germany, Italy, and Austria–Hungary. Because the alliances that existed among them were neither very tight nor permanent, the Europe of the time could be thought of as a multipolar system, one not very polarized.

But just before World War I, in 1914, the great powers became so committed to rival alliance groupings—the Triple Alliance (Germany, Austria-Hungary, and Italy) and the Triple Entente (Britain, France, and Russia)—that it was accurate to speak of a *bipolar and polarized* system in Europe. Polarized bipolar systems are relatively common in world history. A famous one, in ancient Greece, consisted of Athens and Sparta, with their respective allies; another was the United States and the Soviet Union, each with its allies, during a long period after World War II. The possibility that two rival alliances, including more than one major power on one or both sides, will form is common in politics and is an extremely serious source of instability in multipolar systems.

After World War I the basis for a multipolar system was temporarily weakened. The victorious states—Britain, France, Italy, and the United States, with their allies—dominated the system. Austria–Hungary was fragmented into several small countries (Austria, Hungary, Czechoslovakia, and parts of Poland, Yugoslavia, and Romania); Germany was defeated and disarmed; Russia was shattered by defeat and civil war. Nevertheless, the winning alliance quickly broke up. The United States and Japan emerged as major independent powers, and by the 1930s both Germany and Russia had substantially recovered. This worldwide major power system was composed of several states of similar power potential. But by the outbreak of World War II in 1939, it too had become much more polarized, as in 1914. Germany, Italy, and Japan (the Axis powers) allied themselves against France and Britain. Both the United States and Russia remained somewhat aloof from the others until they became drawn into the war on the side of Britain and France. The world was again divided along bipolar lines.

## The U.S.–Soviet Polarized System

When World War II was over, the basis for a multipolar system had been destroyed. Germany, Italy, and Japan were totally defeated. Though France was officially a victor, it too was greatly weakened by its initial defeat and occupation in 1940. Britain was clearly a victor politically but was drained economically and was soon to lose its major colonies. China was poor and in the midst of civil war between the nationalists and the communists: its status as a great power was only nominal. The United States and the Soviet Union were clearly the most powerful states in the world; their superiority was strengthened and dramatized by the fact that for most of the period they were the only two powers with large numbers of hydrogen bombs and the big, sophisticated missile systems necessary to deliver these weapons against a technologically advanced defender. Even today, the United States and Russia still have a very great nuclear advantage over any other state.

The two superpowers quickly formed opposing alliances. Many states in Western Europe and elsewhere sought protection, in alliance with the United States, against the possibility of Soviet expansion. The United States then brought other countries—notably the Federal Republic of Germany (West Germany, the largest part of divided Germany)—into NATO or into other alliances, like the Rio Pact made with most Latin American countries. After installing communist governments in most Eastern European countries, the Soviet Union then incorporated those states into its new alliance, the Warsaw Pact, and formed an alliance with the new communist government of China. Thus the bipolar system became largely polarized; not only were the two superpowers much stronger than anyone else, but each now was additionally strengthened by important allies.

The polarization was never complete, however, because quite a number of Asian and African nations, as well as a few European ones, stayed nonaligned, remaining apart from the rival alliance groupings. To the degree that (1) states stay apart from the two contending blocs, (2) states switch alignment from one bloc to the other, and (3) these states are fairly large with significant bases of power, polarization is somewhat restrained. A combination of processes during the 1970s and 1980s—the weakening of alliance ties; the recovery and growth of China, Germany, and Japan; the development and growth of the European Community; and the declining economic dominance of the United States—somewhat softened the initial U.S.–Soviet confrontation. When the Warsaw Pact collapsed and then the Soviet Union dissolved in 1991, one alliance was gone, and dramatic changes in Russian policy and capability meant that it lacked the resources to compete as a full superpower. The polarized confrontation of a two actor system came to an end.

Of course, in reality international systems never fit abstract models perfectly; for example, the U.S.–Soviet bipolar system was never one of two perfectly matched rivals. The United States and its partners were substantially more powerful than the Soviet bloc. For example, in the 1950s the American economy was three times as large as that of the USSR measured by GNP; the wealth of the Western alliance of NATO plus Japan exceeded that of all the communist states by four to five times.[3] Table 5.1 illustrates these differences between the blocs, whether during the mid-1950s or at a

---

[3] Furthermore, these measures of comparison were fully available at the time and do not depend on later revelations about the weakness and stagnation of communist economies.

**TABLE 5-1** Relative Strength of Major Powers and Alliances, 1955 and 1987–88

| Energy Consumption | | | Military Expenditures | | |
|---|---|---|---|---|---|
| Country or alliance | Million metric tons of coal or equivalent | Percentage of total | Country or alliance | Million of dollars 1988 | Percentage of total |
| 1955 | | | | | |
| U.S. | 1,314 | 53.0 | U.S. | 35.8 | 48.7 |
| USSR | 439 | 17.7 | USSR | 26.4 | 36.0 |
| U.K. | 254 | 10.2 | U.K. | 4.4 | 5.9 |
| West Germany | 175 | 7.1 | France | 3.3 | 4.5 |
| France | 114 | 4.6 | China | 3.1 | 4.2 |
| China | 97 | 3.9 | Japan | 0.4 | 0.6 |
| Japan | 88 | 3.5 | West Germany | 0 | 0 |
| U.S., U.K., West Germany, France & Japan | 1,945 | 78.4 | U.S., U.K., West Germany, France & Japan | 43.9 | 59.8 |
| USSR & China | 536 | 21.6 | USSR & China | 29.5 | 40.2 |
| 1987–88 | | | | | |
| U.S. | 2,366 | 37.5 | U.S. | 307.7 | 40.3 |
| USSR | 1,862 | 29.5 | USSR | 299.8 | 39.3 |
| China | 800 | 12.7 | France | 36.0 | 4.7 |
| Japan | 445 | 7.0 | West Germany | 35.1 | 4.6 |
| West Germany | 341 | 5.4 | U.K. | 34.7 | 4.5 |
| U.K. | 285 | 4.5 | Japan | 28.9 | 3.8 |
| France | 212 | 3.4 | China | 21.3 | 2.8 |
| U.S., U.K., West Germany, France & Japan | 3,649 | 57.8 | U.S., U.K., West Germany, France & Japan | 442.4 | 58.0 |
| USSR | 1,862 | 30.9 | USSR | 299.8 | 39.3 |

*Source:* 1955 data from Bruce Russett and Elizabeth C. Hanson, *Interest and Ideology: The Foreign Policy Beliefs of American Businessmen* (New York: Freeman, 1975), p. 3. 1987 energy data from *U.N. Statistical Yearbook, 1987* (New York: United Nations, 1990), Table 124, 1988 military data from U.S. Arms Control and Disarmament Agency, *World Military Expenditures, 1988* (Washington, D.C.: U.S. Arms Control and Disarmament Agency, 1989). Military data for China and the Soviet Union are subject to error.

point right before the end of the cold war. Here we use another generalized measure of the volume of economic production: energy consumption, though it exaggerates the size of energy-inefficient consumers (the Soviet Union and, to a lesser degree, the

United States) and underplays the size of highly efficient consumers (Japan). Military expenditures provide a very rough indicator of military capabilities. International comparisons are distorted by changing foreign-exchange rates, and Soviet and Chinese military spending was (and is) always very difficult to measure. With these cautions in mind, the data give a useful approximation of capabilities.

The Soviet Union approached equality with the United States on only one dimension—nuclear military capabilities—and even here much of the time the United States possessed an overall military capability superior to the USSR's. That superiority was never so great, however, that the American leadership saw fit to use it directly against the Soviets. Though America between 1945 and the late 1960s could almost surely have inflicted more damage than it received in a general war, the likely damage to the United States would still have posed a prohibitive risk except for the very highest stakes of national survival. Also, the Soviets at virtually all times during the cold war had the ability to destroy America's Western European allies; knowledge of that fact doubtless helped restrain U.S. leaders from using their military superiority casually.

## Limits to Bipolarity

A difficult analytical problem always arises when we try to move from the idealized abstractions of theory to an analysis of real-world conditions. How much of a departure from the theoretical norm of equal size can be tolerated without losing whatever may be the essential characteristics of a bipolar or multipolar system? or the preponderant size for unipolarity? And what are the relevant dimensions of equality or preponderance? Population? Wealth? Military forces? Nuclear and thermonuclear weapons only? In regard to weapons capable of mass destruction, during the cold war only the United States and the Soviet Union could credibly threaten the other or threaten to obliterate any middle-range power. But as it became clear that the nuclear weapons of a superpower were unusable in a quarrel between that state and a smaller one—either from moral restraint or out of fear that such use would only bring in the other superpower on the opposing side—superpower leaders had to think carefully about whether they could subdue distant small states with conventional weapons only. Distances from the great powers' bases, plus the logistical and morale advantages of fighting close to home, nullified many of the superpowers' advantages and contributed to a degree of multipolarity below the level of nuclear force even during the height of East–West confrontation. Additionally, there were many circumstances in which military might was not easily used or threatened—in negotiations, in UN discussions, and in disputes over supplies and prices of raw materials. Such political processes often took on many of the characteristics of a multipolar system.

If one or more of the world's nonaligned states should develop great resources to the point where it could, while remaining nonaligned, rival the one remaining superpower (or Russia as, at best, "half" a superpower), then the system would be clearly be moving in the direction of a multipolar one. The current international system, however, is well below that point. Even though China has some nuclear weapons and a much larger population than any other nation (1.2 billion people as compared with India's 880 million), it is still in the process of economic development, lacking the industrial base even to challenge Russia militarily. China could defend its own territory against virtually any assault, but its army is ill equipped compared with that of the United States and is incapable of much offensive action.

In the 1970s the United States tried to sustain Chinese independence from the Soviet Union (thus weakening the Soviet-led pole) without concluding a full alliance with China (which might have provoked a too-vigorous Soviet response). This policy left China without the power base or allies necessary to become a really strong actor in the system. A power composed of the 15 members of a newly expanded European Union, with a combined population of 370 million and a total GNP of $7 trillion, might be a more convincing rival. But a fully integrated political unit in Europe, with a common defense policy, does not yet exist and is not likely in the near future. Japan has avoided building nuclear weapons or a capacity for military action far from its shores, despite its powerful economy and growing defense expenditures.

The contemporary world cannot be well characterized as bipolar. Strictly in nuclear terms, the United States and Russia remain the only really big powers. But with the Warsaw Pact disbanded and Russian abandonment of other former allies like Iraq, Russia no longer leads a bloc or coalition. It has reduced its own conventional military capabilities and is economically incapable of supporting substantial military activities beyond its borders. Except for its nuclear weapons, Russia is in many respects a less formidable power than Germany or Japan. Thus one might characterize the current system as a situation of U.S. hegemony. The United States is now the only power capable of exerting great military power at great distance (as it did against Iraq in 1991). But its economy is not strong enough to sustain a large-scale global reach; the United States, like Russia, has made some efforts to reduce and share the costs of its military effort. It is an exaggeration, then, to characterize the United States as a hegemon capable of enforcing its will; it cannot fully play the role of a dominating power in a unipolar system. The reality is more complex.

It is theoretically possible that there may someday be a large number of states in the world, none of which is especially more powerful than any of the others, and that no widespread or long-term alliances will form. Economists describe such a market as one of perfect or near-perfect competition, in which no single buyer or seller is big enough to affect the market price of other buyers or sellers. But such a condition has not existed in any of the international political systems or subsystems in recent history, and it is only a possibility to speculate about.

# CHARACTERISTICS OF SYSTEMS: PATTERNS OF BEHAVIOR

Since different systems provide different menus for states, both large and small, we may assume (not much has been proved) that different systems are characterized by different patterns of state behavior. Are there any reasons to prefer one type of system to another, aside from the consideration that most people would probably prefer to live in a powerful and secure country rather than in a weak and vulnerable one? Is there anything about one type of system that makes it preferable—for large states, for small states, or for most of the world's population, regardless of where they live? These questions have become increasingly significant as the world has found itself moving away from bipolarity toward unipolarity on the military dimension and toward multipolarity on the economic and political dimensions.

## Stability and Conflict

In one sense, **stability** means *not being prone to war.* This, however, is a very ambiguous criterion; it might mean simply that wars are infrequent. But if the wars that did occur dragged on for many years, the advantages of infrequency might pale. Thus duration is clearly important. So is severity: one can easily imagine systems where wars are rare but, when they do occur, are savage, include most members of the system, and are fought to the point of unconditional surrender. If "frequency" is the number of wars fought by a given number of states in a particular period, and "duration" is the number of months or years each war lasts, an index of "severity" might be the number of people who are killed.

These are not merely sterile academic distinctions among variables that are closely related in the real world. On the contrary, a survey of all wars between major powers over the past five centuries shows that the correlation between the number of wars begun within various 25-year periods and the number of casualties is moderately negative;[4] in other words, periods with more wars tended to have fewer casualties. Wars may be frequent or severe, depending upon other characteristics of the international system. Bipolar systems, for instance, are marked by the continuing confrontation of two major powers. Many bloody wars would drain the two antagonists of their wealth and resources, either reducing them both to a level so near the second-rank powers that the system would become multipolar, or destroying the weaker one and leaving the way open for a unipolar empire. If a system is to persist, its wars—at least among the major powers—must be either infrequent or not very severe.

The bipolar system that obtained after World War II produced many crises and confrontations. Confrontations, however, do not necessarily produce violent conflicts and military fatalities; on the contrary, in the postwar period there were no acknowledged, direct, violent conflicts between the two superpowers. (Probably some American fliers and Soviet antiaircraft crews killed each other during the Vietnam War, but neither state discussed this publicly.) Both sides feared that, should any such direct conflict begin, it would be very hard to contain it at a low level of intensity and escalation would carry the risk of enormous damage to both sides. Nor were there violent conflicts between any of the major powers, save for a border skirmish between China and the Soviet Union in 1969.

---

[4] Jack S. Levy and T. Clifton Morgan, "The Frequency and Seriousness of War: An Inverse Relationship?" *Journal of Conflict Resolution* 28, 4 (1984), 731–749.

The battlegrounds for almost all the violent conflicts that occurred from the end of World War II until the end of the cold war were in the less developed countries (although there has been an increase in European-based conflict since 1989).[5] Many of the quarrels involved a superpower and a small state. At least thirteen of these conflicts arose between 1945 and 1991, ten involving the United States (North Korea and China from 1950 to 1953, Lebanon in 1958 and 1983, Cuba in 1962, Indochina from 1961 to 1973, the Dominican Republic in 1965, Grenada in 1983, Libya in 1986, Panama in 1989, and Iraq in 1991) and three involving the Soviet Union (Hungary in 1956, Czechoslovakia in 1968, and Afghanistan beginning in 1979). Most of these episodes were quite limited and did not result in heavy casualties. (The Korean, Indochinese, Afghanistan, and Iraqi cases are exceptions: the first three were of long duration, and all four were intense actions involving tens or hundreds of thousands of casualties.) The superpowers, however, proved very successful in restraining conflicts among their own allies. With only a few exceptions—one or two in Central America, between Turkey and Greece over Cyprus, and between Britain and Argentina over the Falkland Islands (known to the Argentines as the Islas Malvinas)—wars between the allies of one superpower were prevented.

## *Stability and Patterns of Interaction*

Another definition of stability is *lack of change in the fundamental pattern of interactions* in the international system. Changes in the number or identity of major actors affect stability only insofar as they affect that pattern.

A unipolar system would be marked by a pattern of dominance by and submission to the major actor. A bipolar system is characterized by competition and conflict between two actors—a pattern of interactions very different from that of the unipolar system. A system with three major actors is marked by shifting patterns of conflict and cooperation, both of which are found on all three sides of the triangle. If an alliance between two of the actors becomes tight and permanent, then it is no longer a three-actor system but a bipolar one, with substantial cooperation between the two formerly autonomous actors, both of which are in conflict with the third.[6]

It may be that in politics, as in love, three-actor systems are almost always unstable, falling too easily into two-against-one alliances that end in the destruction of one of the original parties. The Soviet Union and the United States often feared that an alliance between the other and China might be cemented. The addition of a fourth actor to that three-actor system might have made for a more reliable pattern of shifting conflict and cooperation. But there is always the possibility that the growth of

---

[5] See two articles reporting post–cold war conflict by Peter Wallensteen and Karin Axell: "Armed Conflict at the End of the Cold War, 1989–92," *Journal of Peace Research* 30, 3 (1993), 331–346, and "Conflict Resolution and the End of the Cold War, 1989–1993," *Journal of Peace Research* 31, 3 (1994), 333–349.

[6] For an analysis of tripolar relationships in the postwar system among the United States, the Soviet Union, and China, see Joshua S. Goldstein and John R. Freeman, *Three Way Street: Strategic Reciprocity in World Politics* (Chicago: University of Chicago Press, 1990).

many formal and informal linkages will create a bloc among two or more actors that formerly moved independently. What was once a multipolar system could become a bipolar one; there would still be several major powers, but they would be combined into two opposing alliances.

When there are more than four major actors it is hard to know whether the addition of another would fundamentally change interactions. The difference between a multipolar system with four actors and one with five might be substantial. Beyond that point, as conditions approached those of perfect competition, the pattern of interactions might again be different.

A system that always had four or more major actors within it might be stable even if the identity of the powers changed frequently because of wars, growth, or internal dissension in some states. When the number or identity of major actors (whether national actors or alliance blocs) changes, we say that the system has been transformed to a new system only if the changes seem to produce fundamentally different patterns of interaction.

## CHARACTERISTICS OF SYSTEMS: POLARITY

A lively controversy has raged over which type of system is likely to be less prone to war or to have more stable interactions. Just as in our discussion of war we found it essential to recognize frequency, duration, and severity, to discuss the consequences of various systems we must make some careful distinctions among various meanings of the concept of polarity.

First, as we have seen, we must consider the number of poles, which may be either single countries or alliances. Second, we must recognize the relative capabilities of the various poles, or the *concentration* of power in the system.[7] During the cold war, as noted above, the United States was always stronger than the second-ranking Soviet Union, and those two ranked far above any other powers. Moreover, the Western alliance—including West Germany, France, the United Kingdom, and Japan—as a whole was always much stronger than the Soviet-led alliance, which from about 1960 was further weakened by the defection of China. Thus one could speak of a system that tilted clearly toward the United States and its allies.

Two other system characteristics relevant to many theories are the **tightness** and the *discreteness* of the poles. We call a system *tight* if nearly all members of the pole are bound to one another by alliances or other linkages. It would be as though all the Latin American members of the Rio Pact were formally allied not only with one another and with the United States, but also with the allies of the United States in

---

[7] Edward Mansfield, in *Power, Trade, and War* (Princeton, N.J.: Princeton University Press, 1994), p. 23, notes that, "In contrast to polarity, concentration reflects both the number of major powers and the relative inequality of power among them." He argues that concentration has more to do with the relationship between system structure and war than the simple polarity of the system.

other parts of the world, such as NATO. A system is **discrete** if there are no linkages across poles and the two alliance systems are completely separate. For a long time after the postwar alliance system was fully formed in the mid-1950s there were few changes in formal alliances. A few states (Cuba, Iran, and Pakistan) dropped out of the Western alliance system, and China and Albania broke with the USSR. Spain joined NATO in 1982. But until 1989 neither the tightness nor the discreteness of the European alliance bonds changed greatly.

If we look beyond the legal bonds of alliance to other kinds of linkages among nations, however, there clearly were important changes. Detente, even the limited version of the 1970s, meant the initiation of many linkages of trade, finance, travel, and cultural exchange between Eastern and Western Europe; between Western Europe and the Soviet Union; between Africa and Asia; and, most dramatically, between China and the United States at a time when the links between China and the Soviet Union drastically diminished. A look at those transaction linkages—measured by value of trade or number of travelers, for instance—would show very substantial reductions in both the tightness and the discreteness of the major power groupings.

Then, at the end of the 1980s, changes came in a flood. Popular revolutions in all the Warsaw Pact nations replaced their governments, mostly with anticommunist leaders. They demanded that Soviet troops leave their territories, and the Warsaw Pact collapsed. In 1990 East Germany joined West Germany, and the newly unified country inherited West Germany's membership in NATO and the European Community. Hungary, Poland, Czechoslovakia, and longtime neutrals like Austria and Sweden sought admission to the Community. Barriers to trade, travel, and other exchanges tumbled. Many Soviet/Russian citizens, especially Jews, emigrated. The economically distraught countries of Eastern Europe repudiated central planning, moving toward a capitalist market economy. They, and Russia, and the rest of the new FSU states sought massive inflows of private investment capital and loans from Western governments and international agencies. The Eastern pole dissolved, losing much of its discreteness along with its formal structure. All the defining economic and institutional bonds were gone, beyond reconstruction.

## THE CASE FOR BIPOLAR STABILITY

One common theory argues that bipolar systems will be most successful in avoiding major war, despite the fears and hostilities likely to be built up between the two principal antagonists. In a bipolar system the two major powers are rather evenly matched and neither has a good chance of easy victory. War would be long and costly, and the risks of losing, even for the side that may initially seem stronger, would be substantial.[8]

---

[8] The best-known case for the stability of bipolar systems is that made by Waltz, *Theory of International Politics.*

Consequently, there is always the risk that if a war does break out between the two great antagonists it will be terribly severe; even a low probability of conflict may, in the face of tremendous potential damage, seem unacceptably high. Thus the result is a great emphasis on crisis management and efforts to avoid direct confrontation between the two major antagonists themselves, leaving their local or regional proxies to fight. Even wars that begin only as internal conflicts somewhere on the fringes of a power sphere may potentially be transformed into struggles between blocs and the bloc leaders. After coexisting in the same system for a long time, the leaders of the two sides will have learned what kinds of acts are likely to provoke dangerous reactions from the opponent. This is perhaps especially true for the nuclear bipolar system, but it may also have been true of other pairs in the past.[9]

At the end of the cold war, people began to ask more insistently why there had been such a "long peace"—45 years without war between major powers, an almost unprecedented situation.[10] Bipolarity is one possible explanation. Realists, who think that the structure of the international system very much affects the likelihood of great-power war, began to predict that with the end of the bipolar cold war system we would be entering a period of great uncertainty and risk. Others have argued that different forms of multipolarity, under different conditions of polarization, can produce quite stable multipolar systems. In general, pessimistic analyses of the future of the world system, based on the demise of bipolarity, must be treated with caution.[11]

Some analysts stress that in the post–World War II bipolar system the leaders of each of the two big alliance blocs were very much stronger than any other member of its bloc. These hegemonic leaders, enforcing the order and discipline of hierarchy within each alliance, could reduce the likelihood that their small allies would drag them and others into wars. Opposing bloc members therefore did not face too much uncertainty about possible serious shifts in alliance memberships and the overall power balance. This type of situation was very different from that in 1914, when the inability of great powers to control either their big or small allies contributed greatly to the onset of World War I.[12]

---

[9] Joseph S. Nye, Jr., "Nuclear Learning and U.S.–Soviet Security Regimes," *International Organization* 41, 3 (1987), 371–402, and Alexander George, Philip Farley, and Alexander Dallin, eds., *U.S.–Soviet Security Cooperation: Achievements, Failures, Lessons* (New York: Oxford University Press, 1988).

[10] See John Lewis Gaddis, *The Long Peace: Inquiries into the History of the Cold War* (New York: Oxford University Press, 1987), and Gaddis's chapter in Charles W. Kegley, ed., *The Long Postwar Peace: The Sources of Great Power Stability* (New York: Harper Collins, 1991).

[11] For a statement of the pessimistic view, see John Mearsheimer, "Back to the Future: Instability in Europe after the Cold War," *International Security* 15, 1 (1990), 5–56. Rebuttals to Mearsheimer appear in the "Correspondence" section of the next two issues of *International Security*. A defense of multipolarity may be found in Charles W. Kegley and Gregory A. Raymond, "Must We Fear a Post–Cold War Multipolar System?" *Journal of Conflict Resolution* 36 (September 1992), 573–585. For a more general discussion of the impact of polarity, see Kegley and Raymond, *A Mulipolar Peace? Great Power Politics in the Twenty-First Century* (New York: St. Martin's, 1994).

[12] Manus Midlarsky, "International Structure and the Learning of Cooperation: The Postwar Experience," in Kegley, ed., *The Long Postwar Peace.*

Somewhat related is the view that the U.S. and Soviet blocs could be considered "empires" during much of the cold war and that evidence on historical empires indicates that the core states of competing empires avoid war.[13] Similarly, if the cold war is viewed as an "enduring rivalry" between the United States and the Soviet Union as powerful adversaries—but with the ratio of power always in favor of the United States—we should also expect a low probability of war.

Nuclear weapons themselves, with the particular caution that the mutual vulnerability of the United States and the Soviet Union fostered, may have been an equally important influence. Nuclear weapons made any major-power war seem impossibly costly. Yet World War II, fought with only conventional, nonnuclear weapons until the very end, was also hideously costly in both lives and economic destruction, demonstrating to many that sustained war between developed industrialized states would always be a losing proposition. By this argument, all the chief antagonists of World War II learned that lesson and would have avoided war with each other again even if nuclear weapons had not been a factor. Other analysts have argued that there are "long cycles" in the frequency and severity of wars that may run about 50 or 100 years, and that the cold war just happened to come during a phase in a long cycle that would have been relatively peaceful anyway.[14]

We will consider some of these theoretical arguments later in the book, as well as others about why the post–cold war international system may, like the cold war era, avoid great wars. Some of those theories stress reasons—such as the nature of transnational linkages, the role of international institutions, and whether states are governed democratically or autocratically—that are very different from those emphasized by realist theories. The point to understand here is simply that the absence of all-out war during the cold war era may indeed be attributable to the bipolar international system—or it may just be a coincidence that the system was bipolar and there was no big war. Other factors can, in theory, explain the absence of war, and we cannot rule out any of them by looking only at the single case of the cold war.[15]

---

[13] See Morris Blachman and Donald Puchala, "When Empires Meet: The Long Peace in Long-Term Perspective," in Kegley, ed., *The Long Postwar Peace*.

[14] Kenneth Waltz, in "The Spread of Nuclear Weapons: More May Be Better," *Adelphi Papers*, no. 171 (London: International Institute for Strategic Studies), says that nuclear weapons, as well as bipolarity, contribute to stability. On the excessive cost even of conventional war between developed states see John Mueller, *Retreat from Doomsday: The Obsolescence of Major War* (New York: Basic Books, 1989). A good review of long-cycle theories is Jack S. Levy, "Long Cycles, Hegemonic Transitions, and the Long Peace," in Kegley, ed., *The Long Postwar Peace*.

[15] Benjamin A. Most and Harvey Starr, in *Inquiry, Logic and International Politics* (Columbia: University of South Carolina Press, 1989), chap. 6, demonstrate that different system structures provide sets of behavioral opportunities or possibilities that overlap considerably. Changes in willingness have a greater impact on the onset of war than number of poles or system size. Thus the occurrence (or nonoccurrence) of war behavior will only rarely help us discriminate among systems or show us how systems affect behavior. This is particularly true if we have only one case study—the cold war—to draw upon. A single case study will not permit us to judge among the many possible post hoc explanations for that case; see Bruce Bueno de Mesquita, "Toward a Scientific Understanding of International Conflict: A Personal View," *International Studies Quarterly* 29 (1985), 121–136.

## BALANCE OF POWER IN A MULTIPOLAR SYSTEM

At the other extreme from unipolar and bipolar systems is a system with quite a different menu—many independent centers of power, none of which is strong enough to dominate the others. Perhaps such a system would both be quite stable, maintaining the same pattern of interactions, and have little war. In a system with many states and no permanent polarities, the leaders of one country must maintain proper relations with most of the others. Alignments are likely to shift frequently, as an opponent on one issue today might be needed as an ally on another issue tomorrow. To protect the possibility of future cooperation, it is important that a state not let any temporary antagonisms get out of hand and embitter relations more generally. Multiple and cross-cutting ties of this sort are common in stable democratic politics within states and are important factors in promoting peaceful problem solving. The larger the system, the more numerous the possibilities for coalition forming, and the better the chances for this mechanism to work smoothly. Over a long period, however, there might be wars in which many defeated states would be eliminated; if so, there would be a gradual decrease in the number of actors over time.

Such a many-poled system is hardly in prospect. A more relevant model shows a balance of power among several, but not many, states or groups of states. A balance-of-power system is characterized by a special pattern of state behavior: if several major powers are competing with one another, they will usually group together to prevent any one power or group from becoming dominant. Roughly equivalent capabilities among groups—and especially a willingness to shift alliances or even go to war to keep any one actor from upsetting the balance of power—form the heart of this system. Thus the balance-of-power process is based on deterring potentially dominant states or alliances, along with the willingness to go to war if such deterrence fails.

In 1957 Morton Kaplan listed principles that states should follow if a balance-of-power system is to be stable.[16] These principles are generally consistent with the expectations that realists have about states' behavior.

1. Increase capabilities, but negotiate rather than fight.
2. Fight rather than fail to increase capabilities.
3. Stop fighting rather than eliminate a major power.
4. Oppose any coalition or single nation that tends to become predominant within the system.
5. Oppose any nation that promotes an ideology of subordination of nation-states to some higher authority.
6. Treat all major powers as acceptable partners. Permit a defeated power to reenter the system as an acceptable partner or replace it by strengthening some previously weak power.

---

[16] Morton Kaplan, *System and Process in International Politics* (New York: Wiley, 1957), chap. 2.

If these rules are followed, states will compete with one another and there may even be fairly frequent wars (rule 2). Yet the wars will not be very intense (rule 3), and the system itself will be stable in that the number and even the identity of the major powers are likely to remain quite constant.

With this kind of system, it is likely that rather frequent wars among the major powers could be tolerated without producing major changes in the system. Many such systems may have depended on frequent trials of strength, limited in duration and intensity, to test the balance of power among their members and ensure that no state should grow disproportionately. The virtues of this system are supposedly in the relative restraint with which wars are fought and the stability of the system itself. The frequency of wars nevertheless means that a price is being exacted for the stability. The human and material cost of the total amount of warfare in the system is not necessarily less than in bipolar systems, which presumably have fewer but more intense wars. A preference for either system on this ground must await further theoretical refinement, better evidence for its assertions, and a clarification of the values held by any particular observer. As we have noted, the hypothesized stability of multipolar systems in general cannot be demonstrated by just one or two examples.

It is hard to see how the conditions for successfully maintaining a balance-of-power system could exist in the contemporary world. Kaplan's rules for such a system prescribe how the leaders of nation-states ought to behave rather than describe how they actually do behave. If the rules are ignored or broken, the system will break down. If we examine the rules, we will see how difficult it can be to follow them and thus how fragile a balance-of-power system may be. That examination will also lead us to some more general thoughts about system change.

Especially in an era of democratic politics and mass involvement in decision making, rule 6 ("treat all major powers as acceptable partners") is hard to maintain. In the eighteenth century, with its aristocratic governments and the close family and social ties between the elites of various nations, bitter warfare and harsh peace terms were rare. Since the French Revolution and the rise of nationalism, however, defeat in war can engender such hatred of the victor that the defeated nation is unwilling to ally with its conqueror in the future but instead presses for revenge. This is what happened in the French Third Republic after the 1870–71 Franco-Prussian War. Ideological fervor may inhibit certain alliances; for example, the rapprochement between the United States and China was delayed for several years after it first appeared to be in the two states' interest.

The passions resulting from mobilizing for total war in this century may lead to following rule 2 ("fight rather than fail to increase capabilities") to extremes and to a demand for unconditional surrender, which makes it difficult then to observe rule 3 ("stop fighting rather than eliminate a major power"). Or the experience of fighting an unpopular and unsuccessful war (like the Vietnam conflict) may lead to the loss of the popular support necessary to increase capabilities, if necessary by fighting (rules 1 and 2). If public opinion swings sharply from interventionism to isolationism, it may become difficult for decision makers to effectively oppose a dangerously growing opponent (rules 4 and 5); U.S. domestic politics prior to the Gulf War is instructive here. "Balancing" against a state that is becoming too powerful, or especially against a state that seems threatening and ambitious as well as powerful, is essential to preserving a balance-of-power system. If states are unwilling to form the necessary balance or try to be on the winning side by "bandwagoning" with a potentially hegemonic power, the system could collapse.[17]

Another source of instability arises from changes in states' capabilities that have little to do with the acquisition of new territories or allies (which may be opposed by other members of the system). Scholars concerned with the rise and decline of system leaders and their challengers have focused on the **differential growth of power** among the great powers. This means there can be system change without great war, as occurred with the collapse of the Soviet Union and the movement from bipolarity to the present system. The differential growth of power can come from "imperial overstretch," to use Paul Kennedy's term, or from a variety of domestic conditions affecting economic growth and/or internal stability. High levels of civil conflict, or even revolution, can seriously weaken a state. Especially rapid economic growth can increase a state's capabilities even without a conscious decision by its leaders to increase the state's power in the international system. Technological innovation may occur faster in one state than in another—affecting production, creating new means of exploiting resources, or producing a potent new weapon. Thus economic and military capabilities may shift significantly. A variety of economic, technological, or sociocultural changes may lead to the breakdown of one system and the emergence of another.[18]

Another kind of risk stems directly from both the differential growth of power and the frequent trials of strength that test new power relationships. Such conflicts are an integral part of the balance-of-power system. If wars do occur, sometimes a major power may be eliminated or fatally weakened because of a miscalculation, bitter hatreds among citizens of the victor toward the vanquished, or the lack of internal cohesiveness of the loser. For instance, at the beginning of World War I none of the major enemies of Austria–Hungary expected that empire to break up and utterly disappear from the ranks of major powers. When a major power is eliminated, it may be very hard to find another state capable of filling the gap (rule 6). Some big states will continue to grow bigger despite the efforts of others to restrain them. Thus there are certain elements in any system that tend to eliminate some major powers and to strengthen others, making precarious the maintenance of the sensitive balance required in the long run.

In the contemporary world the spread of nuclear weapons is likely to create a situation quite different from what would exist in the absence of nuclear power but with otherwise similar national power bases. One can imagine a "unit veto" system, where each state in a multipolar system had the power to destroy others without being able to defend itself. The possession of nuclear weapons might instill a sense of caution

---

[17] Stephen Walt, *The Origins of Alliances* (Ithaca, N.Y.: Cornell University Press, 1987).
[18] For discussions of the differential growth of power, power transition, and system change, see Robert Gilpin, *War and Change in World Politics* (Cambridge, England: Cambridge University Press, 1981); Paul Kennedy, *The Rise and Fall of the Great Powers* (New York: Random House, 1988); and Jacek Kugler and A. F. K. Organski, "The Power Transition: A Retrospective and Prospective Evaluation," in Manus Midlarsky, ed., *Handbook of War Studies* (Boston: Unwin Hyman, 1989), pp. 171–194.

and responsibility; the awfulness of nuclear war might restrain leaders from any major exercise of force out of fear that small wars would escalate into big ones. Nevertheless, the existence of nuclear weapons will probably make any war that does occur much more intense. Even if major wars would be somewhat less frequent in a nuclear multipolar system than in a conventional one, the high intensity of such wars would probably cancel out the gains from the reduction in frequency.

## EVIDENCE ON SYSTEMS' PRONENESS TO WAR

Much of the previous discussion is quite theoretical, based on a very limited number of historical experiences. To decide whether it is possible to generalize from these theories or examples with much confidence, it is necessary also to look at a wide variety of international systems at different times in world history and at less-than-global systems in different parts of the world. How, in many different cases, does the structure of the system affect the opportunities for international behavior? Does the formation of alliances lead to war or peace? (Overall, alliances do not seem to make wars more frequent, but they do encourage the expansion of wars to include more states.[19]) What is the relationship between polarity and war, with alliances being one of the key factors in the determination of polarity? By comparing many different kinds of systems over the centuries, for their power distributions and the kind and amount of war they experienced, we might find a more general answer.

Empirical studies of this type, however, have produced conflicting results. The findings are neither entirely clear nor entirely consistent.[20] Part of the problem is simply that the set of cases, or sample, being examined is rather small for statistical analysis (though for the sake of human welfare we can be glad there have not been more wars!). Also, each author has used a somewhat different set of cases, definitions, and analytical or statistical tools. Remember, too, that even though many states have opportunities to go to war, they usually do not have the cause or willingness to do so. Thus, as noted, some systems may produce more opportunities for war without necessarily having more wars. A state may react to an unfavorable power balance by making war, forming a new alliance, building its power base at home, or making concessions to its adversary. Its choice will depend both on its opportunities (whether potential allies are available, for instance) and its willingness (the state of domestic priorities or the predominant ideology). No simple hypothesis provides an adequate explanation.

---

[19] Ido Oren, "The War Proneness of Alliances," *Journal of Conflict Resolution* 34, 2 (1990), 208–233, and Randolph Siverson and Harvey Starr, *The Diffusion of War: A Study of Opportunity and Willingness* (Ann Arbor: University of Michigan Press, 1991).

[20] For summaries of the work on polarity, polarization, and war, see Greg Cashman, *What Causes War?* (New York: Lexington Books, 1993), chap. 8, and John A. Vasquez, *The War Puzzle* (Cambridge, England: Cambridge University Press, 1993), chap. 7.

## CHANGE IN THE INTERNATIONAL SYSTEM AND ITS EFFECTS

We began to speculate about some of the reasons that international systems change. Further discussion of system dynamics—rather than of characteristics of static systems—must address not only the reasons and the ways systems change but also the effects of system change. Most work in this area has been on the relationship between change and the frequency and severity of war. Both some theoretical argumentation and the limited amount of careful empirical study suggest that periods of change may be especially dangerous. George Modelski, arguing long-cycle theory, posits 100-year-long "cycles of global politics." Modelski says that global wars, fought by major powers, result in the establishment of a dominant world power and thus a high concentration of political, military, and economic capabilities. This concentration cannot last forever. Dominant states lose their economic dynamism; they overextend themselves militarily; they may lose their will to dominate. As dominance wanes over a century-long period, the conditions for the next global war are created. More recent work finds global cycles of shorter duration, with periods of economic expansion making it possible for the major powers to sustain big wars.[21]

Studies that have found little systematic relationship between static characteristics of systems and proneness to war have nevertheless found some relationship between change and likelihood of conflict. Rather than polarity, it was **polarization,** or the process by which the distribution of power in the system changed, that had important effects. For example, years when polarity tightened often were followed by war—according to one study, 84 percent of wars in the twentieth century were preceded by years of rising systemic tightness. By contrast, years of decreases in tightness, or of increases in the number of poles, were less likely to be followed by war.[22]

### Change and Rational Calculation

The reason for this may be rooted in the information-processing capacities of decision makers. Decision makers must estimate the relative gains or losses they can expect from various courses of action. A rational decision maker will choose a course of action promising great gain or at least relatively little loss: if you are offered a chance to win $1 million, the attractiveness of the bet depends on whether you think the odds of success are 100 to 1 or 10 million to 1 and whether you must put up $1 or $10,000.

---

[21] George Modelski, ed., *Exploring Long Cycles* (Boulder, Colo.: Rienner, 1987). See also Karen A. Rasler and W. R. Thompson, *War and State Making: The Shaping of the Global Powers* (Boston: Unwin Hyman, 1989), and Joshua S. Goldstein, *Long Cycles in War and Economic Growth* (New Haven, Conn.: Yale University Press, 1988).

[22] Bruce Bueno de Mesquita, "Systemic Polarization and the Occurrence and Duration of War," *Journal of Conflict Resolution* 22, 2 (1978), 241–267, and Frank Whelon Wayman, "Bipolarity and War: The Role of Capability Concentration and Alliance Patterns Among Major Powers, 1816–1965," *Journal of Peace Research* 21, 1 (1984), 25–42.

The estimate of probable gain or loss is composed of two elements, the absolute gain or loss to result if any act succeeds or fails and the probability of success. (This is known as the **expected utility** of a course of action.) Both of these elements—absolute value and probability—are included in the calculations political decision makers must make. The gain from a war fought in order to rule the world might be high if the war should succeed, but most decision makers would consider the probability of success low and the losses in case of failure severe. Most decision makers, therefore, would not undertake such a war.

In making such estimates, a political decision maker has to consider the relative power of his or her own state, enemies, and allies. The probability that one's own allies will help and the probability that the enemy's allies will aid the enemy must be considered. Tightening blocs imply greater clarity of alliance patterns and hence increasingly predictable behavior. Increased tightness may come from upgrading already existing ties or from adding new, highly committed allies. The leader of one alliance may see his or her strength significantly increased and expectations of winning a war improved if the home alliance is tightened but the opposing alliance is not. The leader thus becomes more willing to engage in war.[23] Notice that in this explanation we have interpreted a phenomenon—the tightening or loosening of polarity—at the systemic level of analysis in terms of a characteristic of the states (power) and of a relation between states (alliance). We have then phrased the interpretation in terms of the expected utility calculations by individual decision makers who are more or less in charge of their governments. In any theoretically satisfying explanation of international political phenomena, we have to specify the process by which various levels are linked.

The importance of changes in systems as a cause of war is clear from a careful look at pre–World War I Europe. Between 1900 and 1914 Europe was increasingly polarized, most notably by the addition of previously unallied England to the entente of France and Russia, by increases in the tightness of the opposing alliance, and by a growing shift in military capabilities in favor of the Triple Entente. States that are the furthest apart on measures of power are the least likely to fight each other. Both sides can easily calculate who would win in a military showdown, and the weaker is likely to give in to all but the most extreme demands. Of course, the weaker side does not always give in, as was apparent in the confrontation between the United States and Iraq. Nor does the stronger state always win a war. The United States easily defeated Iraq, but two decades earlier it lost heavily to North Vietnam. As we shall see in Chapter 6, factors such as geographic distance, national morale, and a state's organizational ability make a difference and complicate simple calculations. International violence is more likely among states that are more nearly equal on the measures of power noted in Chapter 3, such as population and GNP, but power relationships are only one of many influences on states' decisions to go to war.

---

[23] Bueno de Mesquita, "Systemic Polarization," p. 263. Bueno de Mesquita further develops these and related propositions in his book *The War Trap* (New Haven: Yale University Press, 1981), and his article "Theories of International Conflict: An Analysis and Appraisal," in Ted Robert Gurr, ed., *Handbook of Political Conflict: Theory and Research* (New York: Free Press, 1980).

## Change During a Period of Near Equality

In a classic statement, A. F. K. Organski argued that "nations are reluctant to fight unless they believe they have a good chance of winning, but this is true for both sides only when the two are fairly evenly matched, or at least they believe they are."[24] Organski focuses on the period of **"power transition,"** when a rising challenger approximates the power of the dominant state: "If great change occurs within a single lifetime, both challenger and dominant nation may find it difficult to estimate their relative power correctly, and may stumble into a war that would never have been fought if both sides had foreseen where the victory would lie." It is the condition of change that affects calculations of relative power. The challenger may start a war because it thinks that now, for the first time, it has a good chance to win. Or the dominant power may foresee its own strength declining and thus calculate that it is better to fight now, while it still has some advantages, than to risk waiting until its position may be significantly worse. By this interpretation it is the fact of change during a period of near equality that makes war likely, not equality itself. Change makes calculations of power and war outcome difficult because the evidence is ambiguous (even though the decision makers may not see the ambiguity). Decision makers may miscalculate, especially when the rate of change is itself changing; that is, when the rate of increase or decrease in relative power slows or speeds up. Miscalculations may then lead to the escalation of small wars, creating a period when major wars are especially likely.[25]

Organski also suggests that "a rapid rise in power . . . produces dissatisfaction in itself," based perhaps in the perceptions of relative deprivation, status, and hierarchy discussed in the previous chapter. This means that the newly powerful state has not yet acquired respect or status as an equal power, so its leaders seek ways to gain respect. Under these changing conditions they may be more willing to risk going to war. Earlier we noted Germany's feeling of deprivation when its rapid economic

---

[24] This and the following quotations are from A. F. K. Organski, *World Politics,* 2nd ed. (New York: Knopf, 1968), pp. 294, 480, 361. Evidence that wars are more common among states nearly equal in power is reviewed by Randolph Siverson and Michael P. Sullivan, "The Distribution of Power and the Onset of War," *Journal of Conflict Resolution* 27, 3 (1983), 473–494. They find some reason to support this idea but term the evidence inconclusive. Thus we do not attribute importance here so much to the power balance as to changes in that balance. J. David Singer reports that although only 13 percent of all militarized disputes between major powers since 1816 escalated to war, the percentage rose to 75 when the parties were approximately equal in military power and there was a rapid military buildup in the three years preceding the dispute. See his "Accounting for International War: The State of the Discipline," *Journal of Peace Research* 18, 1 (1980), 1–18. Work on the likelihood of changes in relative power leading to war includes A. F. K. Organski and Jacek Kugler, *The War Ledger* (Chicago: University of Chicago Press, 1981), chap. 2, and Charles F. Doran, *Systems in Crisis: New Imperatives of High Politics at Century's End* (Cambridge, England: Cambridge University Press, 1991). Gilpin, in *War and Change in World Politics,* makes an important argument, with historical illustrations, supporting this view.

[25] For an evaluation of the power transition and of when in the power transition we should expect war to occur, see Bruce Bueno de Mesquita and David Lalman, *War and Reason* (New Haven: Yale University Press, 1992).

and military growth was not matched by a "place in the sun" with the other great powers. This attitude played a part in Germany's uncritical support of its ally Austria–Hungary, whose attack on Serbia alarmed Russia and brought on the First World War.

What do we make of this information in the current international system? As we saw, for most of the time the post–World War II system was substantially bipolar. But in about 1990 the relative power of the two poles changed drastically. There was no power transition, nor was a power transition even approached. Systemic change occurred, but without general war. In this case the challenger simply faded back. The changes in the relative strength of the poles came first from differing internal rates of economic growth (the failure of Soviet-style command economies compared with market ones) and then from the Soviet Union's loss of allies. With Gorbachev's glasnost of the late 1980s, analysts discovered the extent to which the size and vigor of the Soviet economy had been overestimated. At the same time, the major poles became much looser and less discrete. The immediate result was a widespread feeling of relief. The prospects for war, especially nuclear war, between the major powers seemed dramatically lower.

If we were to take seriously the arguments about why bipolar systems are more stable than multipolar ones, we might fear that the new configuration would become more prone to war—especially if we considered the new system closer to a multipolar one than to a unipolar one. On the other hand, according to the findings of Bueno de Mesquita, recent trends toward a looser system of polarity are encouraging. Thus, so long as polarities continue to loosen, the chances of war do not increase and perhaps even diminish. But other elements—especially the rapid change in the relative power of the leading states—give grounds for concern. What if the current Russian leadership is unable to reform and stimulate the Russian economy, or if Yeltsin is replaced by hard-line nationalist or military leaders, such as the ultra-rightist Zhirinovsky? In that event, the characteristics of the nation-states, and of their leaders, would look more important than the characteristics of the international system.[26]

## SOME POSSIBLE CONSEQUENCES OF POLITICAL CHOICES

At first glance the structure of the international system might seem a given, a non-manipulable element in the calculations of policymakers. Such structure is not, however, entirely outside the long-term control of policymakers in the great powers. The

---

[26] In fact, Bruce Bueno de Mesquita and David Lalman, "Systemic and Dyadic Explanations of War," *World Politics* 41 (October 1988), 1–20, conclude that structural effects produce no significant differences in the likelihood of conflict.

superpowers strove mightily not only to match or surpass each other's military capabilities but also to maintain bipolarity by ensuring that their capabilities far exceeded those of all smaller states. Their policies to prevent nuclear proliferation were also designed, in part, to maintain their own dominance.

Other kinds of decisions also illustrate how policymakers make choices that will ultimately make a huge difference in the kind of international system we inhabit. The question faced by the United States in dealing with China—whether to encourage or inhibit Sino–Russian attempts to heal their rift—had these implications; as do Western choices about whether to extend economic support to Russia. A similar choice was always at issue in U.S. policy toward the European Community, particularly when the United States supported Britain's application for membership in the 1960s. A world with a strongly united Western Europe, including Britain, has a structure far different from one in which Europe remains politically fragmented. During most of the post–World War II years, most Americans regarded European unification as generally a good thing, but not necessarily on the basis of careful consideration of its consequences. The question of whether a united Europe would remain closely allied to the United States or how it would behave if it did not was rarely asked in a rigorous and searching manner. Policy decisions have major implications for what might seem the most intractable and least manipulable of the major influences on international politics: the structure of the international system. The creative, daring, tenacious, and skilled statesman may be able to expand the menu.

In this chapter we found that the nature of the international system depends heavily on the alliances or other linkages between states. It is time, therefore, to shift our focus to a less comprehensive level of analysis to consider the relations among states, especially the questions of what power and influence really mean and how they are exercised in the contemporary world system.

# RELATIONS BETWEEN STATES: BASES AND ANALYSIS OF POWER

| WORLD SYSTEM |
| RELATIONS |
| SOCIETY |
| GOVERNMENT |
| ROLE |
| INDIVIDUAL |

## FOREIGN POLICY AND POWER AS RELATIONSHIPS

**Power** (as well as foreign policy) can be thought of as a relationship. Each takes on meaning only as it affects a state's behavior toward another state or international actor. The menu of any state, then, is constrained or affected not only by its own capabilities, goals, policies, and actions but also by those of the other entity with which it interacts—by the state's attempts to influence others and by the attempts of others to influence it. Relationships between states can be seen in two ways, both of which will be described in our discussion of power. First, we can look at how two states compare on a set of national attributes or characteristics. Second, we can look at the actual set of interactions between pairs of states.

We will be concerned with both *attributes* (or bases) *of power* and *power as a process* of interaction (how states influence the behavior of others). Power bases and influence become meaningful only when compared with the capabilities of others and the goals of influence. In looking at the U.S. decision to drop the atomic bomb, the key elements were the actual existence of the weapon (an attribute, as were the skill, knowledge, and resources that created the bomb) and the arguments about how the bomb could be used to influence the behavior of Japan. Remember also that comparison implies measurement: a key question in international relations is how much power an actor has. In looking at power both as a set of capabilities and as influence, we shall highlight problems of creating indicators to measure power.

## POWER: ONE OR MANY? WHICH METAPHOR TO USE?

Power plays a central role in the study of world politics, but it means many different things to different people. "One or many" here refers to the question of whether we should attempt to find a definition of power that is as general, unified, and multidimensional as possible, or whether we should break down the concept of power into its many forms, deal with each of them, and then drop the word *power* from our vocabulary of analysis. Power has many broad meanings and is conceived of in different ways.[1] To some it is best seen as a set of attributes or capabilities; to others it is an influence process. Still others see it as the ability to *control:* to control resources, to control the behavior of other actors, to control events, and to control the outcomes of interaction (conflictual or cooperative)—even to control the structure of interaction itself, that is, to control the rules of the game. One scholar has even outlined a paradox wherein expanding control over resources might *decrease* a state's ability to obtain the outcomes it desires. The answer to this paradox lies in the balance of power, discussed in the previous chapter: as a state accumulates more resources, at some point it will suddenly appear as a threat to others in the system. To offset the new resources of this state, others will come together in alliances to balance (and thwart) the newly powerful state.[2]

In an era of growing interdependence, power may simply mean the ability to have an impact on the sensitivity and vulnerability of other actors—to affect the menu

---

[1] For two overviews of these various perspectives, see David A. Baldwin, *Paradoxes of Power* (Oxford: Blackwell, 1989),and Karl W. Deutsch, *The Analysis of International Relations,* 3rd ed. (Englewood Cliffs, N.J.: Prentice-Hall, 1988), chaps. 3 and 4.

[2] Zeev Maoz, *Paradoxes of War* (Boston: Unwin Hyman, 1990), chap. 8. See also Emerson Niou, Peter Ordeshook, and Gregory Rose, *The Balance of Power* (New York: Cambridge University Press, 1989), especially chaps. 2 and 3.

of others, even if you are a small and relatively weak actor.[3] Some see power as the ability to reduce uncertainty in the environment. For some it is a means to an end. For others power has come to mean causality, because explaining who has power explains why things happen. Others say power is like money in the sense that it can be saved and spent. Another view is that power is primarily a psychological phenomenon, that you have it if others think you do. The list could go on and on.

As we noted in Chapter 2, realism is a view of international politics that sees people seeking power and desiring to dominate others. Hans Morgenthau, the most widely read exponent of this approach, stated the matter succinctly in his classic textbook, *Politics Among Nations*. The section titled "International Politics as a Struggle for Power" opens with the following words: "International politics, like all politics, is a struggle for power. Whatever the ultimate aims of international politics, power is always the immediate aim." This view of power is centered on struggle among sovereign states within the anarchic international system and is characterized by the use and manipulation of military resources.

Other observers, however, object to the realists' stress on constant struggle and their highly conflictual, coercive, and military interpretation of the concept of power. They argue that although power is central to international politics, it takes many forms. Stressing only the aspects of conflict and struggle distorts how states actually behave and how they attempt to reach their objectives in international politics; power is not exercised only in situations of conflict.[4] More important, what does power mean and how is it to be measured among highly interdependent actors who share a common view of the world, have similar economies, and have excluded military options from their interactions? The realist view of power does not appear to be applicable to just such a group of West European, North American, and other Western industrialized countries (including Japan, Australia, and New Zealand). The weaknesses of the realist view will only be magnified in a post–cold war system in which the military dimension will play a much diminished role in Europe and between the United States and Russia.

So, in our discussion, what will we mean by "power"? Let us start with a very broad definition and then break the concept down into more manageable sections. *Power is the ability to prevail in conflict and overcome obstacles.* This is a useful formulation because it indicates that power is the ability to get what you want, to achieve a desired outcome through control of your environment, both human and nonhuman.

In many areas of social conflict, to prevail does not necessarily mean to engage in struggles involving military threats. States, like people, come into conflict with others every day on a wide variety of issues; we continually find ourselves in situations where there is some form of *incompatibility*. In negotiating with Japan over trade imbalances, in getting permission for military aircraft to fly over French territory, or in dealing with Canada on the effects of acid rain, for a few examples, the set of goals and objectives of the United States is incompatible in some way with the set of goals

---

[3] See Michael Don Ward and Lewis House, "A Theory of the Behavioral Power of Nations," *Journal of Conflict Resolution* 32 (March 1988), 3–36.
[4] See Steven Lukes, *Power: A Radical View* (London: Macmillan, 1974), p. 23.

and objectives of the other state. As long as there are any incompatibilities between these sets of objectives, conflict will arise. But the manner in which these conflicts are resolved and the manner in which the United States attempts to prevail may have little resemblance to the concept of struggle and certainly will not involve military coercion. It will, however, involve some form of *influence*.

## INFLUENCE AND HOW TO GET IT

*Power* means getting one's way. **Influence** is one method by which people and states get their way. In its most general form, influence means getting others to do the things you want them to do. It is the ability to affect the behavior of others (and perhaps to resist others' attempts to affect yours: in most instances in which Jill tries to influence Jack, Jack is also trying to influence Jill). This is the most relational aspect of power. Under this formulation, *influence is a form of power.* If power is the general ability to overcome obstacles and prevail in some situation, influence is one way—in fact, the dominant way—that international actors accomplish this.

Influence itself takes many forms. One involves actually changing the existing policy of another actor: switching voting positions in the United Nations, leaving one alliance and joining another, dropping restrictions on the importation of foreign auto-mobiles. It may mean getting another country to stop an action it is already pursuing in order to compel a result—a policy known in political science as **compellence.** Using the atomic bomb against Japan was aimed at compelling the Japanese to surrender; the Gulf War was directed at compelling Iraq to withdraw from Kuwait. Less success-ful examples include the U.S. attempts, from the early 1960s to 1975, through military, diplomatic, and even economic means, to compel the North Vietnamese to withdraw from South Vietnam or, in 1979, to get Iran to release the American hostages. Because it seeks to reverse an established policy, compellence can be very difficult to achieve.

Influence may also involve encouraging others to continue policies, to maintain current behavior, for example, as trading or alliance partners. In contrast to compel-lence, **deterrence** aims to influence others to continue not to do something. Having the ability to stop others from doing what they may want to do before they do it is a major element of any state's influence. In the contemporary system, nuclear deterrence (which we will discuss in Part II) meant that during the cold war the United States influenced the Soviet Union not to attack it or its allies with nuclear weapons (through fear of retaliation), and vice versa. There are many theories and speculations about deterrence, and in practice it is hard to measure satisfactorily. It is easier (though still difficult) to recognize the actions one has influenced another state to perform than to observe the processes behind something that has not happened. For example, did NATO's strength truly deter a Soviet attack on Western Europe, or did the USSR never want to attack? A desired outcome of influencing another actor by deterrence—an apparent success of the policy—*might have happened anyway.*

Similarly hard to measure, but still very important for understanding world poli-tics, is *potential influence.* Influence is a partly psychological phenomenon, based on the perceptions of the capabilities and intentions of other states. Potential influence is based on other policymakers' perceptions of the influence that one may have in specific situations. If a state has potential influence, other states will not even attempt certain activities because they know that such activities will fail or be very costly. As with deterrence, it is very difficult to measure state $A$'s successful influence when state $B$ removes an option from its menu because it anticipates that it will lose in some way. (How many times in the 1920s and 1930s might Panama have wanted to demand that the United States leave the Canal Zone? We have no idea because we cannot measure how many times the desire occurred and then was suppressed because of fear of American reaction.)

In part this is what we meant earlier when we defined power as control over the structure of the situation, including control over the rules of the game (Who gets to speak first in the meeting? Does a motion require a two-thirds majority to pass?), control over the agenda of issues and potential issues involved (Is it permissible to challenge the free enterprise system in the United States or the dominant role of the Communist party in the People's Republic of China?), and even control (conscious or unconscious) over the ideologies, values, goals, and objectives of the actors one wishes to influence. It is crucial to understand this last aspect of control, for the attempt to change the *will* of another actor is at the heart of the influence process. "Indeed, is it not the supreme exercise of power to get another or others to have the desires you want them to have ... to secure their compliance by controlling their thoughts and desires?"[5]

## METHODS OF INFLUENCE

Some hints to the methods a state might use to get others to behave as it wishes have been provided above. Briefly, a state needs certain capabilities and the willingness to use those capabilities to carry out threats or fulfill promises. The target of the influence attempt must also be vulnerable in some way—that is, have needs or weaknesses. A state's capabilities present that state's decision makers with a more or less restricted menu of what is possible; they also affect those behaviors that the decision makers feel will most probably be successful. The capabilities of a state affect not only its opportunities but also its willingness to exploit those opportunities.

How may those opportunities be used to achieve influence? K. J. Holsti lists six different tactics that might be seen as an influence ladder:[6]

---

[5] Lukes, *Power,* p. 23; Baldwin, *Paradoxes of Power,* p. 107. See also Susan Strange, "What About International Relations?" in Strange, ed., *Paths to International Political Economy* (London: Allen & Unwin, 1984), p. 191, who notes that power includes A's ability "to govern or influence the context or environment within which B has to take domestic or foreign policy decisions."

[6] See K. J. Holsti, *International Politics,* 6th ed. (Englewood Cliffs, N.J.: Prentice-Hall, 1992), chap. 5.

- Use of force
- Infliction of nonviolent punishment
- Threat of punishment (the stick)
- Granting of rewards (the carrot)
- Offer of rewards
- Persuasion

Persuasion here means having another actor behave as desired without the use of promises or threats. Its success depends on the ability to demonstrate to the opponent that a certain behavior is in its interest. Clearly there are many situations in which it is in both parties' interests to behave in certain ways. International politics is not composed entirely of zero-sum games, where if one side wins, the other must lose; in the many situations in which *both* sides can benefit, persuasion means making this clear to the opponent. In getting the Soviet Union to agree to arms-control measures, the United States did not threaten destruction or promise aid; rather, it demonstrated on many occasions that the Soviets would both benefit economically and strengthen their own security by such agreements. Another example was U.S. behavior during the 1960s, which demonstrated to the Soviets that both sides would be more secure if they had safety devices on their strategic weapons to prevent nuclear accidents.

Common interests may be perceived more readily if states share common values. Harold Lasswell and Abraham Kaplan wrote about "bases of influence," things people value that can be used to get them to do other things.[7] They listed four "welfare" values—*well-being, wealth, skill,* and *enlightenment*—and four "deference" values—*power, respect, rectitude,* and *affection.* Persuasion can be successful when one appeals to the values that others hold dear. By demonstrating that one also holds these values, an appeal based on neither promise nor threat can still result in others doing what one wishes. For example, as leader of an ideological movement like anticommunism, pan-Arabism, or religious fundamentalism, you can legitimize your requests to your followers. These values, like all others, are open to social construction through persuasion and discourse as well as through reward and punishment.

## *Bargaining and Leverage: Manipulating Rewards and Punishments*

Persuasion occurs in world politics more often than we think. Realists stress the top of the influence ladder and the application of force as the way to achieve influence in a violence-prone world. However, this crude form of influence is relatively rare in the vast web of daily international interactions. More important for achieving influence,

---

[7] Harold D. Lasswell and Abraham Kaplan, *Power and Society* (New Haven, Conn.: Yale University Press, 1950).

particularly in a world of growing interdependence among like-minded states, is **bargaining**. The bargaining process can include tacit bargaining through behavior and symbolic actions as well as explicit negotiations. Although often used for persuading, bargaining can also be used to *manipulate rewards and punishments* to influence others. Bargaining and **leverage** are core processes in international politics and economics. Leverage refers to whatever means are used by one negotiator to influence, persuade, coerce, or force another negotiator to accept a particular bargain. Leverage can be positive (rewarding, offering the carrot, making side payments) or negative (penalizing, punishing, threatening the stick). Importantly, leverage takes many forms, often economic rather than military.[8]

Punishment, of course, includes the application of force. It may take many other forms, however, such as the withdrawal of some privilege, favor, or mutual contact that already exists. Punishment is intended to hurt the opponent in some way. The potential hurt can be manipulated into deterrent threats—that the punishment will occur whenever an act you dislike is performed and under certain conditions will be escalated. Thus one may simply threaten punishment without applying it, apply punishment to harm the opponent in some specific situation, or apply a lesser punishment as an implicit or explicit threat of further punishment. The emphasis here is on punishment as a means of influence in bargaining, not as brute force intended to eliminate the opponent.

Thus the rationale behind the UN trade embargo on Iraq after its invasion of Kuwait in August 1990 was less to destroy Baghdad's ability to maintain itself in Kuwait or to wage war if it occurred than to demonstrate to Iraq that its occupation of Kuwait (or a possible war) was too costly to justify its goals. The embargo was also intended to convey the threat that unless the Iraqis withdrew, the imposition of punishments could be escalated. In this case the application of the embargo as a punishment and/or a threat of additional punishment did not induce Iraq to withdraw; on the other hand, it was applied for only five months, a very short time in which to expect an embargo to work. A successful example of punishment as a means of influence was the use of two atomic weapons against Japan. The hurt inflicted and the threat of even more damage helped influence Japan to agree to American demands for unconditional surrender.

There are many possible ways to threaten or apply punishment in bargaining situations beyond the use of physical force. More commonly, states look for leverage. A developed country may withhold foreign aid from a poor one; a less-developed state may nationalize the corporate investments of industrialized states or increase the price of its natural resources; trade relations or diplomatic relations may be reduced or cut off entirely; and so on. Notice that in many cases the punishment or threat of punishment consists of withdrawing something that previously had been available; but

---

[8] Robert C. North and Nazli Choucri, "Economic and Political Factors in International Conflict and Integration," *International Studies Quarterly* 27 (December 1983), 446. See also David A. Baldwin, *Economic Statecraft* (Princeton, N.J.: Princeton University Press, 1985), especially chap. 7, for a discussion of "exchange" as a basis of influence.

interference with normal channels of interaction with another country means that both sides in the pair are deprived of possible future instruments of influence over each other's policies.

Thus it may often be useful to establish a positive relationship with another party if only to provide a potential means of leverage or punishment in the future. However, a far more common use of *rewards* in bargaining situations is their immediate potential for influencing the other party: providing the other side with something it wants; demonstrating one's willingness to be of assistance, one's solidarity with the other party, or one's dependability in fulfilling promises; and linking benefits to the desired behavior (positive reinforcement). The would-be influencer must discover what it can do for the other side. Social-psychological research has demonstrated that influence, particularly in bargaining situations, is more often achieved through positive incentives than through punishment. Within countries most people obey laws less out of fear of punishment than out of habit, convenience, an understanding that everyone will be better off, and a conviction that the law is basically just. Too many conceptions of international politics (based on realist assumptions) concentrate on coercion, deterrence, and punishment; even rewards can be perceived negatively if they are seen as bribes. The mutual rewards in trade, economic growth, and security among the industrialized Western countries in the Organization for Economic Cooperation and Development (OECD) and their effects on political and economic integration and peace are discussed in Chapter 14.

## Political Investments

Our reference to mutual benefit and integration leads us to another category of means of influence, one that is closely related to bargaining but deserves separate treatment. Influence may come as a result of *improving one's asset position*, of acquiring new resources and wider options (an expanded menu) in policy-making. The would-be influencer obtains more, in quantity and variety, of the instruments of bargaining; in effect, it *invests* its power in order to increase its influence. The most obvious and perhaps the commonest strategy is a rather straightforward type of material investment: fostering economic growth, encouraging scientific research, or improving the level of education of the population in order to increase available capabilities.

Another kind of political investment is doing favors, thus establishing political credits that can be cashed in later. Or a state may try to see to it that its own citizens or those of its allies occupy key positions in an international organization like the World Bank. This kind of political activity is an important instance of using influence to increase the positions from which one can exert influence—that is, to enlarge one's influence base. But like most investments, there is always a chance of failure. Too obvious an effort to seize key political posts may lead to a counteraction that leaves the would-be influencer weaker than before.

The establishment of trade and aid relations that might later be withdrawn as a form of punishment is a subtler kind of investment. Much the same can be said for various kinds of military assistance or cultural and educational exchanges. A small country might quite deliberately allow a big one to establish a military base on its territory, so that the big power will become dependent on the base and later make concessions—such as large amounts to foreign aid—to the small one in order to retain the base. Turkey, the Philippines, and Spain all engaged in such behavior with the United States during the cold war period. Such examples are very like bargaining; the emphasis here, however, is on creating a situation in which, without overt threats, the other partner comes to realize that the first partner has acquired a more favorable position.

As seen in the OECD countries, another means of influence arises in the **building of a community:** a sense of kinship, of common loyalties and values, and of belonging together. Individuals' perceptions of their self-interest can be greatly broadened so that they are willing to make certain sacrifices whether or not those sacrifices are directly reciprocated. For example, members of a family will make sacrifices for their common welfare or for the welfare of one of them. The identification and affection may be so strong that on some matters a husband or a wife comes to prefer to do what the spouse wants rather than what he or she had originally desired. While observers using a radical perspective can be highly critical of the subtle ways in which common values can shape potential influence, a community-building perspective stresses its positive nature. In part this is because of the tacit agreement—tacit because if stated openly it becomes a very fragile affair—not to coerce others and to limit the scope of bargaining. In effect, one gives up certain bargaining options without having to admit it: within the OECD community, states have substantially given up the use of military force against each other (a circumstance that runs in the face of realist beliefs). As within marriage, each partner bargains. But in a reasonably good relationship the partners recognize their common interest in keeping the bargaining limited and share a desire not to coerce or break up the union.

If you can change the other party's likes and dislikes so that the other will end up wanting the same things you do, then directly persuading the other to do something you want done will not even be necessary. It is for this reason that major powers engage in various kinds of cultural and information programs. The *manipulation of information,* in all its forms, is very important. In the post–World War II period the United States has sponsored the Voice of America, Radio Free Europe, and many cultural activities through the U.S. Information Agency. Advertising by American corporations helps not only to expand the markets for their products but also to promote a pattern of consumption like that in the American free-enterprise economy. The Soviet Union similarly employed Radio Moscow, national "friendship" societies, and inexpensive publications of communist tracts, and it often sent Soviet artistic performers on tour. France continues to spend large sums promoting the French language and French culture. All these activities are intended to help cultivate groups of people who want many of the same things that the Americans, Russians, or French do, who to some extent think like them, and who sympathize with their political goals (". . . to have the desires you want them to have," as Lukes said). Indeed, it is just this kind of influence that people in less developed countries sometimes label "Coca-colonization," or, more generally, cultural imperialism.

# POWER AND INFLUENCE AS ATTRIBUTES: CAPABILITIES AND THEIR MEASUREMENT

National attributes or capabilities greatly influence the menu of activity available to states. What is possible or probable relates to the means at one's disposal. This is especially important in gauging the activity of or reaction toward specific states in specific situations. Capabilities include any physical object, talent, or quality that can be used to affect the behavior of others, including their perceptions of one's state, what one is able to do, and what one is willing to do.

Capabilities, then, are crucial to two different aspects of influence. First, for threats and promises to be useful as instruments of influence, they have to be *credible*. For a threat or promise to be credible, the targeted party has to believe that the other party is *able* to carry out the threat or promise. One debate over using the atomic bomb against Japan concerned demonstrating the capability—the bomb—to the Japanese so that they would believe a threat to use more weapons if they did not surrender. Today the menu of the United States makes it possible for it to threaten to destroy any other state—an option available to few other countries. Credibility, of course, also implies a perceived willingness to carry out such a threat; destruction of another country is a serious step. In 1979 during the Camp David negotiations the American promise to deliver economic aid to Egypt and oil to Israel if they would negotiate a peace treaty was credible because the United States had both the wealth and the oil to deliver on its promises. Most other countries could not make such a promise credible because they lacked the capabilities to carry it out.

Second, if threats and promises do not work, often punishments (political, economic, or military) are carried out. States require capabilities in order to impose the costs or the pain that they feel will coerce others to behave as they wish. By doing so, and by doing so effectively, a state also enhances its reputation by showing that it is willing to carry out threats in a way that gets results. If this occurs, then at some point in the future threats may not have to be carried out; the mere hint of punishment will bring about the desired action. Thus reputation is central to deterrence and potential influence. The actual use of military force in foreign affairs, while a major element of power, may also be seen as a *failure of influence*. The use of the military instrument means that a state has failed to influence another state to do something; it has had to resort to coercive force. The truly powerful state is like the officer in the military: when it expresses a wish to another state, the wish is taken as a command and obeyed.

The ability to get others to do one's bidding will differ with the object of one's influence. Remember that influence (and capability) is relative: what Iraq could do to Kuwait it couldn't do to the United States; what China can get Mongolia to do is much different from what it can get the United States to do. Capabilities by themselves are of no use to our analysis of world politics; they must be studied within the context of the *influence situation*. To repeat, the capabilities of states take on meaning only when they are viewed in relation to the objectives of the state and to the capabilities and objectives of others. For example, India's security objectives in regard to Pakistan are largely achieved; the same capabilities are inadequate, however, if India desires a similar level of security from Chinese military power.

Different types of capabilities and instruments of influence are interchangeable: they can be substituted for one another and converted into other elements of influence. Wealth can be used to obtain military capabilities, knowledge (through research and education), or a healthier population. Conversely, military instruments can be used to acquire wealth. Almost all the bases of influence have some ability to obtain other influence capabilities, but the "exchange rates" can vary a great deal. It is hard, for instance (but maybe not impossible), to buy affection. The problem of substituting one base of influence for another creates many difficulties for realist analyses, where some measure of power is of the essence. One weakness of realism is its assumption that military capabilities are readily converted into other elements of power. This is usually not true. Analysts increasingly seek to measure issue-specific capabilities.[9] Military strength, for instance, may have great value in deterrence but not in stabilizing a country's exchange rate or in dissuading OPEC from raising oil prices.

## ELEMENTS OF A STATE'S CAPABILITIES INVENTORY

Almost all writers concerned with power and influence develop a set of attributes that form the base of a state's power, some sort of power inventory or power potential. It is not really important which specific term or scheme is used. What is important is that the analyst of international politics has some such system for evaluating the universe of possible influence bases; without a systematic and explicit checklist, the analyst is likely to pay far too much attention to certain bases and to forget about others completely. For example, people pay a great deal of attention to the "deference" values of power and respect but often neglect the related values of moral rectitude and affection. This is, in part, a legacy of the realist view of international politics, which ignores the possible effects of bonds of friendship and affection between individual leaders (for example, between Egyptian President Anwar Sadat and Henry Kissinger during the 1970s). Similarly, the moral stature of individuals like Mohandas Gandhi or Pope John Paul II helped them have an impact on international politics.

Other "welfare" values—well-being, skill, and enlightenment—are also often slighted when people concentrate on wealth. International nongovernmental organizations like Amnesty International may, for instance, provide publicity (enlightenment) about alleged violations of human rights (a concern of rectitude). In doing so,

---

[9] See Jeffrey Hart, "Power and Polarity in the International System," In Alan N. Sabrosky, ed., *Power and Polarity* (Boulder, Colo.: Westview, 1985), and Baldwin, *Paradoxes of Power*, for discussions of power, convertibility, and substitution. See also Benjamin A. Most and Harvey Starr, *Inquiry, Logic, and International Politics* (Columbia: University of South Carolina Press, 1989), chap. 5, for a discussion of substituting foreign policy instruments, and Robert O. Keohane, "Theory of World Politics: Structural Realism and Beyond," in Ada W. Finifter, ed., *Political Science: The State of the Discipline* (Washington, D.C.: American Political Science Association, 1983).

they may affect the moral constraints, domestically and globally, within which states must operate. We shall try, in this chapter, to touch on these neglected values.

## Tangible Elements: Size and Capabilities

States are constantly assessed in terms of size—we speak of superpowers, medium powers, small states, microstates. The attributes of population, area, and GNP are central aspects of a state's base of power and size categorization. They constitute a small set of the tangible or measurable elements of a state's power and influence capabilities. Even those scholars who stress the perceptual aspects of smallness or largeness agree that the basic dimensions of power are territorial, demographic, economic, and military—and that a state's self-perception and the ways in which others view it are based to a large extent on its rankings along these dimensions.

Although sheer size or land area by itself is not sufficient to make a state a great power (or, today, a superpower), large size can support a fairly large population, a large industrial base, and large domestic sources of food and natural resources. Size can provide depth for military defense and isolation from neighbors (Russia, China); small countries are much more vulnerable to being overwhelmed by a sudden military attack (Kuwait). Also important are topography (the physical features of the land, especially significant on a state's borders), physical and political location, and climate. Any of these factors may provide advantages or disadvantages, or have no effect.

People have tried to measure economic size and performance by calculating gross national product, or GNP. The wealth and economic growth of a state are also related to the availability of natural resources. Energy sources, such as petroleum, coal, and natural gas, and resources critical to industrial capacity, such as uranium for power and cobalt and chromium for making steel, are particularly important. Not only do abundant natural resources give states the ability to develop and to gain wealth from others through trade, but they may also provide a state with a greater degree of *autarky*, or self-sufficiency. The more self-sufficient a state, the less vulnerable it is to the leverage attempts of other international actors. For much of the post-1945 period, the Soviet Union, China, and the United States were more self-sufficient than most countries, but each steadily became less so (especially Russia in the mid-1990s).

Economic performance controlled for population—GNP per capita—is a good indicator of economic development, showing how well a state has mobilized and used its natural and human resources. Economic performance, both per capita and as total GNP, provides a clue to the state's ability to turn its resources into military capabilities and its ability to exploit its menu in general. At one extreme we find the United States, with a 1993 GNP of $6.4 trillion. By itself, the United States accounts for about one quarter of all the goods and services produced on the earth. Current analyses indicate that the size of the Soviet economy had been overestimated for many years, and substantial steady *declines* in GNP have dropped present-day Russia from the second position given to the USSR during most of the cold war. World Bank figures for 1993 estimate Russian GNP at under $800 billion, less than that of Brazil.

Like large physical size, a large population may be either an asset or a liability, although it seems difficult to be a major power or superpower without one. As well as numbers, we also must look at the age, sex, and spatial distribution of a population and the quality of human resources—the degree to which a people's capabilities have been developed by education or good health care so that they can make a contribution to the state. For example, to understand Israel's military success in the Middle East, we must note the advantages a state gains over its neighbors by having a skilled and healthy population.

One kind of capability is the welfare value Lasswell and Kaplan call enlighten-ment: the extent of higher education and the access to specialized knowledge in sci-ence, engineering, and the professions. Obviously, a state's military strength depends in large part on access to scientific knowledge; building modern weapons requires a body of scientific expertise that is unavailable to small, poor countries and is not uniformly available to big, rich ones. More broadly, a state needs physicians, archi-tects, social scientists, lawyers, and administrators to run a bureaucracy, as well as many others with advanced training and ability. Many possible measures of this capa-bility can be found, among them the number of students in higher education, the number of individuals in all age groups who have completed higher education, the number of scientists, and the number of scientific and technical journals published.

Many aspects of enlightenment are related to wealth and material development: it is expensive to train and equip scientists. The same is somewhat true for a more basic level of knowledge that we can call *skill*. Skill is what it takes to get along in modern life even at a rather low level of sophistication; it may be literacy, familiarity with machinery, or a primary and secondary education. Literacy is especially important because it is required to learn so many other skills and to take advantage of other kinds of enlightenment; widespread literacy is both a resource base for a government and a means whereby the government can communicate information or propaganda quickly to its people. But universal education, even only to produce literacy, is costly and difficult for a poor state to provide. The argument can be turned around; perhaps only a literate and educated state can become rich.

Indeed, the United Nations Development Programme (UNDP) has created a **Human Development Index** (HDI). This is a composite of three basic components of human development—longevity (measured by life expectancy), knowledge (mea-sured by adult literacy and mean years of schooling), and standard of living (mea-sured by GDP per capita adjusted for the local cost of living, or purchasing-power parity).[10] The UNDP idea of human development looks not just at the level of income of a country but at how that income is used; it assumes that improving the quality of life can also improve productivity and economic well-being. It is clear, however, that countries ranking high on the 1992 HDI also tend to rank high on wealth—the 53 countries in the high-HDI group (HDI scores of 0.801 to 0.932) have a GNP per capita average of $13,800; the 54 countries in the low-HDI group (from 0.489 down to 0.191) average $330! Canada ranks first with a score of 0.932; the United States is 8th, at 0.925; Guinea ranks 173rd, and last, at 0.191. The low-HDI group averages 2.0 mean years of schooling, with an adult literacy rate of 47.4 percent; the high-HDI group averages 9.8 years of schooling, with an adult literacy rate of 97.3 percent.

---

[10] See the UNDP, *Human Development Report 1994* (New York: Oxford University Press, 1994), chap. 5.

Another aspect of population quality is the health and well-being of the people. What access do they have to good medical care? How long do they typically live? How free is the country from various contagious diseases that are now, in principle, preventable? Does the state possess really first-class centers of medical treatment where the latest knowledge is available? How evenly distributed is good health throughout the population? Are there substantial minorities whose health facilities are markedly poorer than the average? The health of a state's population is an important base of influence. Since both industrial and military power depend in part on having a healthy population of young people, access to good medical facilities must be available to the entire population, regardless of income. One quite good measure that combines an average with equality of distribution within a population is the infant mortality rate. The infant mortality rate (per 1,000 births) in 1992 for the industrial countries was 13; for the least developed countries, 112; for the low-HDI countries, 98.[11]

## *Military Capabilities*

The military dimension is a central aspect of the capabilities of states and, to most realists, the central indicator. China, Russia, and the United States have millions of their populations under arms; Iceland, Costa Rica, and Mauritius have no armies at all. One might also wish to count specific items in the arsenals of states, such as nuclear delivery systems, bombers, supersonic fighters, and tanks. The sophistication of weapons technology has also become increasingly important. The performance of America's high-tech arms during the 1991 Gulf War caused a number of states to reevaluate their entire military establishment—from strategy, to research and development (R&D), to procurement. Major debates occurred within the Russian and Chinese defense establishments in the aftermath of the Gulf War.

A useful summary measure that takes into account many of these elements of military capability is military expenditure. Again, during the cold war, the Soviet Union and the United States far outdistanced the rest of the world; by 1988 each was spending about $300 billion on its military establishment. Their closest competitors spent only somewhat more than a tenth of that. There are problems, of course, in comparing defense expenditures in different national currencies, in obtaining reasonably accurate data, and in seeing that the same kinds of expenditures are counted in each case. Indeed, Russian defense outlays in the post-Soviet era are very difficult to calculate; one respected source estimates about $47 billion for 1992 Russian defense spending.[12] Yet, in general, the rough overall measure of military expenditure for most countries has great use if employed carefully.

---

[11] See also Appendix B to get a sense of the relationships between GNP per capita on the one hand and the measures of quality of life on the other.

[12] See International Institute for Strategic Studies, *The Military Balance 1993–1994* (London: Brassey's, 1993), p. 98. Most other sources, the 1994 CIA *World Factbook* among them, cannot provide figures for Russian military expenditures.

Since 1945 a key element of military capabilities has been a state's nuclear arsenal. How many bombs and warheads does a state have? What types of delivery systems and in what numbers? How much megatonnage can a state deliver against an opponent? How vulnerable or invulnerable is a state to a first strike? Here, too, the superpower status of the United States and Russia is still evident. In September 1990, before START (Strategic Arms Reduction Treaty), the United States had over 12,500 deliverable strategic warheads/bombs; the Soviet Union/Russia over 10,000. START I reduced these arsenals to 8,500 for the United States and 6,500 for Russia. By 2003, the START II agreement will drop both countries to 3,500 deliverable weapons.[13] In 1990 the other official members of the nuclear club—Britain, France, and China *combined*— had well under 2,000 vehicles (land-based and submarine-based missiles and bombers).

All elements of tangible military capabilities have intangible factors as well: the morale and training of officers and troops, the quality of weapons, and the decline in the effectiveness of military power over distance (the loss-of-strength gradient). And even with nuclear weapons there are questions of accuracy, dependability, the state of computer technology, and the quality of communications for command and control.

## Comparing Capabilities: Indexes of Power

Many people have recognized that power and influence are multifaceted and depend on a combination of capabilities. Attempts have been made to devise indexes based on two or more indicators of national capabilities. We need to take a look at how the various capabilities may be related to one another and at the possible results of using different combinations of indicators.

Table 6.1 is illustrative, showing the relationships of capabilities to one another by presenting the correlations among several indicators of the national capabilities we have discussed. The correlations show the relationship between pairs of indicators (from +1.00 to –1.00). The higher the positive correlation, the more likely it is that when a country's value on that indicator is high, its value on the other will be high. The highest correlation found is that between military expenditures and GNP, suggesting that economically big countries (as measured by GNP) are likely to have large military expenditures. This reinforces the observation that a strong economic base is required for a strong military establishment and that wealth can be turned into military capabilities. Military aid complicates the relationship between a state's wealth and the size of its military: Israel, relatively small, and Egypt, relatively poor, both having large military capabilities, thanks to assistance from the United States. But notice the much lower correlations between area and GNP per capita and military expenditures.

We can note changes across time, and also gain an overview of the relationship among various measures of capabilities, by looking at Table 6.2. Part A shows the top

---

[13] These figures are from Ruth Leger Sivard, *World Military and Social Expenditures 1993*, 15th ed. (Washington, D.C.: World Priorities, 1993), pp. 13–19.

**TABLE 6.1** Correlations Among Some Indicators of a State's Influence Base, 1970

| | Size | | | | Richness of Life | | | Deference |
|---|---|---|---|---|---|---|---|---|
| | GNP | Area | Population | GNP per capita | Science journals | Literacy | Few infant deaths | Diplomats received |
| Size | | | | | | | | |
| Military expenditures | .94 | .38 | .77 | .57 | .81 | .60 | .45 | .86 |
| GNP | | .37 | .81 | .63 | .87 | .60 | .42 | .85 |
| Area | | | .62 | -.14 | .23 | -.26 | -.25 | .43 |
| Population | | | | .05 | .61 | .11 | .05 | .79 |
| Development | | | | | | | | |
| GNP per capita | | | | | .67 | .84 | .73 | .36 |
| Science journals | | | | | | .73 | .53 | .72 |
| Literacy | | | | | | | .78 | .39 |
| Low infant death rate | | | | | | | | .24 |

*Source:* Bruce M. Russett, *Power and Community in World Politics* (San Francisco: Freeman, 1974).

10 states as they ranked in 1965 on area, population, GNP, military expenditures, GNP per capita, literacy, number of scientific journals, and infant mortality rate. The category "diplomats received" is included as a measure of the status, prestige, or respect accorded to a state. Few states have the need or ability to send diplomatic representatives to each of the roughly 190 states in the contemporary system. Thus the decision to send a representative to another state both says something about the perceived importance of that state and may give prestige to any other government having a representative in that capital.

In Part B, the top 10 states are ranked using 1992–93 data. We can now see the changing dimensions of power in the international system. For this more recent set of data, we show the actual figures for each state. Note also that in Part B we are using a different method for calculating GNP and GNP per capita—*purchasing-power parity (PPP) in international dollars.* Conventional methods to calculate GNP are based on international currency exchange rates. Economists are coming to agree that a more sophisticated and valid measure is based on comparing the amount of money it takes to buy a comparable basket of goods: "PPP is defined as the number of units of a country's currency required to buy the same amounts of goods and services in the domestic market as one dollar would in the United States."[14] This measure more accurately captures the economic capabilities of a country. China, which would have been ranked seventh in GNP, now is nearly tied for second; with PPP, India is in fifth place instead of sixteenth. In general, less developed countries demonstrate greater economic power. Indeed, such a measure would have been a better way to gauge Soviet GNP and military spending during the cold war, showing that the USSR looked more like a developing country on important dimensions. Official (controlled) exchange rates actually exaggerated Soviet economic strength—PPP measures would have avoided the exaggeration—and the subsequent astonishment of many at the Soviet collapse.

Looking at Part B, note that Brazil, its production finally reflecting its area and population, now appears in the GNP top 10. Japan's steady but dramatic rise in the international system reflects its growing economic might. Japan's GNP (no matter which measure is used) has jumped from sixth to second, surpassed only by that of the United States. This economic power is also matched by Japan's appearance as one of the major military spenders. But it is also reflected in Japan's use of wealth for the development of human capital. Note Japan's sixth-place ranking in GNP per capita and high rankings on infant mortality and the Human Development Index. Observe that using PPP calculations, China is now only slightly behind Japan in total GNP and that India is also prominently placed.

Except for oil-rich states (United Arab Emirates, Qatar) and Singapore, the states listed on the GNP per capita and infant mortality lists demonstrate the economic strength of the OECD countries; this is especially reflected in the quality-of-life indicator, HDI. The United States ranks second in GNP per capita and retains its overwhelming top position on military expenditures, another category well represented

---

[14] *The World Bank Atlas 1995* (Washington, D.C.: World Bank, 1994), p. 33. The data used in Part B here (and in Appendix B) are taken from this source.

**TABLE 6.2** Ranking of Top States by Capabilities

Part A: 1965 Data

| Rank | Area | Population | GNP | Military expenditure | GNP per capita | Literacy | Scientific journals | Diplomats received | Infant mortality |
|---|---|---|---|---|---|---|---|---|---|
| 1 | USSR | China | U.S. | U.S. | U.S. | Denmark | U.S. | U.S. | Sweden |
| 2 | Canada | India | USSR | USSR | Kuwait | Finland | Japan | Britain | Netherlands |
| 3 | China | USSR | W. Germany | China | Sweden | Iceland | France | W. Germany | Norway |
| 4 | U.S. | U.S. | Britain | Britain | Canada | Norway | W. Germany | USSR | Australia |
| 5 | Brazil | Indonesia | France | France | Iceland | Sweden | USSR | France | Finland |
| 6 | Australia | Pakistan | Japan | W. Germany | Switzerland | Switzerland | Britain | Italy | Japan |
| 7 | India | Japan | China | India | Denmark | Belgium | Italy | Egypt | Switzerland |
| 8 | Argentina | Brazil | Italy | Italy | Australia | Canada | Poland | India | Denmark |
| 9 | Sudan | W. Germany | India | Poland | New Zealand | Czechoslovakia | Sweden | Japan | New Zealand |
| 10 | Algeria | Nigeria | Canada | Canada | Luxembourg | E. Germany | India | Brazil | Britain |

Part B: 1992–93 Data

| Rank | Population (millions) | GNP (billions PPP intl. dollars) | Military expenditures (billions U.S. dollars) | GNP per capita (PPP intl. dollars) | Infant mortality (per 1,000) | HDI scores (1992 UNDP) |
|---|---|---|---|---|---|---|
| 1 | China 1,175 | U.S. 6,387 | U.S. 286.11 | Luxembourg 29,510 | Japan 5 | Canada 0.932 |
| 2 | India 900 | Japan 2,633 | Russia 47.00 | U.S. 24,750 | Ireland 5 | Switzerland 0.931 |
| 3 | U.S. 258 | China 2,492 | Germany 43.96 | Switzerland 23,620 | Sweden 5 | Japan 0.929 |
| 4 | Indonesia 187 | Germany 1,695 | France 42.00 | UAE 23,390 | Singapore 5 | Sweden 0.928 |
| 5 | Brazil 156 | India 1,126 | Britain 36.83 | Qatar 22,910 | Switzerland 6 | Norway 0.928 |
| 6 | Russia 149 | France 1,121 | Japan 33.60 | Japan 21,090 | Finland 6 | France 0.927 |
| 7 | Japan 125 | Italy 1,045 | Italy 24.15 | Germany 20,980 | Iceland 6 | Australia 0.926 |
| 8 | Pakistan 123 | Britain 1,030 | China 18.49 | Singapore 20,470 | Netherlands 6 | U.S. 0.925 |
| 9 | Bangladesh 117 | Brazil 856 | Saudi Arabia 15.20 | Canada 20,410 | Germany 6 | Netherlands 0.923 |
| 10 | Nigeria 105 | Russia 778 | South Korea 10.75 | France 19,440 | Norway 6 | Britain 0.919 |

*Sources:* Part A: Charles Taylor and Michael Hudson, *World Handbook of Political and Social Indicators,* 2nd ed. (New Haven, Conn.: Yale University Press, 1972); Part B: Appendix B, this volume.

by OECD countries. Most striking, of course, is the contrast between 1992–93 Russia and the 1965 USSR. Though smaller, Russia is still the largest country by area (and note that Kazakhstan now also makes the top rankings in area). However, it had dropped from third to sixth in population and from second to tenth in GNP. As estimated above, Russian defense spending is now a distant second, in the same range as that of Germany.

Different analysts have tried to produce composite indexes of national power that combine various elements. Because most of the individual components of any such index are only moderately correlated with one another, the summary ranking will be different with different components, and there is no perfect all-purpose indicator. One study has compared eight different indexes of power, which include anywhere from two to twenty variables combined in very different ways. Roughly, the various indexes include some way of measuring demographic capabilities, industrial capabilities, and military capabilities; many include some indicator of area or territory. The study compared the rank orderings of states produced by these various indexes, finding "no appreciable change in outcome."[15] The lesson is twofold: (1) accurate measurement requires a clear concept and theoretical understanding of the phenomenon one is trying to measure, and (2) with such a theoretical underpinning, indicators of "power" capabilities will give us a generally similar picture.

## A FURTHER WORD ON INTANGIBLES

Any state requires more than the mere existence of the resources that make up capabilities. It must also maintain those political, social, and economic structures that will permit it to *mobilize* for governmental use of the resources that exist within its borders and to *convert* those resources into instruments of foreign policy influence. When looking at the political system of any state, we must ask whether that system efficiently administers the nation-state's resources. What is the quality of political leadership at all levels, especially the highest? Can the leaders motivate the people to support the government's policies, to sacrifice so that the state's resources can be devoted to military capabilities or to heavy industry rather than to consumer goods? Can the leadership achieve and maintain the support of the people and their continued loyalty to the state? In other words, can the resources be converted into the capabilities and willingness needed to support the state's policies?

Such cases as Israel and the Arabs, the Soviet Union during World War II, and Vietnam indicate the importance of the ability of a government to extract and use national resources including the will of its people. Scholars have attempted to measure the national strength of states with an index combining internal and external

---

[15] See Richard L. Merritt and Dina A. Zinnes, "Alternative Indexes of National Power," in Richard J. Stoll and Michael D. Ward, eds., *Power in World Politics* (Boulder, Colo.: Rienner, 1989), quotation from p. 26.

capabilities; one component of the internal capacity is a ratio of the actual extraction of resources compared with the expected extraction. This index has been able to account for the performance of states in war.[16]

These intangibles can be crucial. In sports, a weak team will sometimes beat one much higher up in the rankings. The weaker side does not always lose a war, and the stronger does not always win—as the French learned in Indochina and later in Algeria and as the Americans learned in Vietnam. Intangibles such as leadership, belief in a cause, and especially the cohesion resulting from a threat to survival are important assets for smaller states in unequal, or asymmetric, conflicts. The weaker state, being willing to fight for survival against a larger adversary, increases its war power through its willingness to persevere and to suffer not only the enemy's direct threat but also the sacrifices caused by higher levels of extraction. The larger state, although possessing greater capabilities, often is far from the conflict, is not threatened by the smaller opponent, and is less willing to suffer the costs of war.[17]

For example, much of the debate before the 1991 Gulf War revolved around the level of casualties that would be acceptable to the American people. Willingness to suffer as a dimension of power is particularly acute in democracies, as we have seen in the post-1945 colonial struggles for independence. From the philosopher Immanuel Kant, through Vo Nguyen Giap (North Vietnamese strategist and defense minister), through Saddam Hussein, there has existed the notion that the people in democracies do not wish to bear the costs of war. Because they ultimately do bear these costs, the argument is that people in democracies will not want to fight. Because they also ultimately determine their leaders, the leaders will be less likely to go to war, under the constraint of the wishes of the populace. The costs of war somehow need to be "worth it" to the leaders of democracies. The structure of the political system of a state is thus one aspect of the mobilization of resources.

Other intangibles involve a government's skill in manipulating its resources to influence other states in diplomatic negotiation and bargaining (to be discussed in the next chapter). We must also look at the skill and efficiency of the state's bureaucratic organizations: the size of the bureaucracy; how politicized it is, or how protected it is from political influences; how it is organized and directed; and the quality of the people who staff it in terms of education, training, expertise, and dedication to service (or to corruption) and how overloaded they are.

Finally, we come back to the notion of credibility. The effect of attempts at influence based on promises or threats depends to a large extent not only on a government's ability to carry out the action but also on the perception of its willingness to do so. One major intangible, then, is the reputation that a government (or sometimes a

---

[16] See A. F. K. Organski and Jacek Kugler, *The War Ledger* (Chicago: University of Chicago Press, 1980), chap. 2, and Jacek Kugler and William Domke, "Comparing the Strength of Nations," *Comparative Political Studies* 19 (1986), 39–69.

[17] In short-term confrontations, recklessness and will on the part of the initiator can be more important than physical capabilities. See Zeev Maoz, "Resolve, Capabilities, and Outcomes of Interstate Disputes," *Journal of Conflict Resolution* 27 (1983), 195–229.

people or state) acquires in its international dealings. Our general conclusion about political intangibles is a simple one. If a government—that is, its leadership, its bureaucracy, and the political system within which they both work—is so inadequate or inefficient that it cannot bring the state's capabilities to bear in a particular international situation, then those capabilities remain latent. (Indeed, in such a case a state's claim to sovereignty itself may be called into question if it cannot carry out its responsibilities.) Capabilities that are not mobilized cannot be used to exercise influence in the international arena.

Similar questions can be asked about the economic and social systems of a state. Do the economic system and structure reduce waste and loss? Is it efficient in the use of the state's resources? Does the social system, its values and its structure, promote a unified national effort, or are there major groups that feel alienated from the national society? Is the social system oriented more toward principles of fairness and respect for human rights or toward a system of privilege? The answers to all these questions will affect how thoroughly, rapidly, and efficiently a society will be able to mobilize resources and present a unified front to the world in support of its government's foreign policies. Here some observers would speak of a highly ambiguous concept, related to the willingness to suffer: national morale, a very elusive notion about the state of mind of a nation.

Shifts in national morale occurred in both France and the United States during their involvements in Indochina. In each country, as the war wore on, support for military involvement decreased and general governmental policy was increasingly challenged. Vo Nguyen Giap stated bluntly that the Western powers would lose—that he could make the war go on long enough for their people to tire of the war and its costs. Both the actual outcome and scholarly research have proved his point.[18]

## THE INTANGIBLE OF INTELLIGENCE

A very different aspect of a state's intangible capabilities of power and influence is its ability to collect and analyze information—that is, the quality of its **intelligence**. In *The Nerves of Government*, Karl Deutsch observes that "it might be profitable to look upon government somewhat less as a problem of power and somewhat more as a problem of *steering*."[19] That is, in the uncertainty of the anarchic international system,

---

[18] John Mueller investigated the failure of American policy to drive the North Vietnamese to a breaking point. His findings indicate not so much an American failure as an unprecedented willingness of the North Vietnamese to accept losses much higher than those of previous wars (for instance, battle deaths as a percentage of the prewar population were twice as high as those of the Japanese in World War II). See John Mueller, "The Search for the 'Breaking Point' in Vietnam: The Statistics of a Deadly Quarrel," *International Studies Quarterly* 24 (1980), 497–519.

[19] See Karl W. Deutsch, *The Nerves of Government* (New York: Free Press, 1963), p. xxvii (emphasis added).

any government that knows how to get to where it wants to go has an advantage. Any government that can reduce the uncertainty of the international environment through knowledge of that environment has an advantage. Any government that can reduce the number of times it is surprised—that can provide itself with the time for planning, preparation, and preemption of the actions of other states—has an advantage.

Power may indeed be the ability to steer. To know how to act, how to respond, and whether to continue one's policies or to correct them, a government needs information. To know how to influence other states or international actors, a government needs information on those actors. The information that governments seek falls into three broad categories. Earlier in this chapter we noted that in order to use their capabilities for influence, decision makers have to take into account their own goals and capabilities for influence and the goals and capabilities of others. The first type of information, then, deals with the goals, plans, and intentions of other international actors. We can steer more carefully through the international environment with fore-knowledge of the impending behavior of other states. The many books about World War II intelligence breakthroughs by the Allies indicate that advance warnings of German moves had great payoffs. It is the *failure* of intelligence-gathering organizations to provide warnings that shows the importance of such warnings. Examples include American surprise at the Japanese attack on Pearl Harbor in 1941; Japanese surprise at the Nixon administration's devaluation of the U.S. dollar in 1971; American surprise at the North Korean attack on South Korea in June 1950; the unexpected building of the Berlin Wall in 1961; the apparent failure of Israeli intelligence in the 1973 Yom Kippur war; the inability of U.S. intelligence to estimate accurately the conditions that brought down the shah of Iran in early 1979; Saddam Hussein's invasion of Kuwait in 1990. We cannot know how best to use our tools of influence if we do not know the plans and intentions of others or if we must continuously react to surprising situations.

The same is true if we do not know the capabilities—and vulnerabilities—of others. Thus the second kind of information is knowledge of others' military and economic strength, internal political situation, and domestic unrest. The largest portion of intelligence work is of this sort: the collection of a great deal of information about other states, using readily available sources of information and standard research techniques. The third type of information is feedback. Governments seek information about the effects of their own decisions and actions on the international environment, and steer accordingly. Feedback permits a government either to continue its policies and behavior or to alter them in some way. U.S. policy in Indochina during the 1960s can be seen as a classic case of the failure of information-gathering and -processing activities, as well as the failure of U.S. leaders like Lyndon Johnson to analyze feedback information correctly.

Intelligence involves the collection, analysis, interpretation, and storage of information, as well as the transmission of information to top-level foreign policy decision makers. One reason we consider intelligence capabilities as an intangible is the unreliability of the process. As we shall see, information may be lost or distorted within the government, it may be misunderstood or disbelieved by policymakers, or it may never be collected at all. Nonetheless, governments keep trying. During the cold war the United States and the Soviet Union spent vast sums on intelligence activities, as do countries today with immediate and pressing security problems, such as Israel. (Israeli intelligence, despite its failure to anticipate the 1973 war, has often been touted as the best in the world.)

Even the post–cold war 1992 budget for the group of agencies that make up the U.S. intelligence community was estimated to be over $29 *billion*. The budget of the CIA, the best-known intelligence organization, was over $3 billion, but that amount is only half that of the National Reconnaissance Office, which is responsible for both spy planes and the panoply of U.S. reconnaissance satellites (these are now the single most important source of American intelligence data about the world, as seen during the 1991 Gulf War). The National Security Agency, a code-breaking agency with more than 20,000 employees that monitors foreign communications, also spends more than the CIA. The head of the CIA serves as the director of central intelligence and acts in a broad supervisory role over the entire American intelligence community, including the State Department's Bureau of Intelligence and Research (a very small agency) and the Defense Department's Defense Intelligence Agency (a very large one). In addition, the army, navy, and air force each has a sizable intelligence organization of its own, as do the FBI and the Department of Energy.

Before states can attempt to influence others, then, they must obtain certain information about the world. How well a state collects and handles information will affect the utility of all its other capabilities. How well a state collects and handles information will also affect the goals and objectives of the state and how it seeks to achieve them. Once a set of objectives or goals exists, the foreign policy decision makers of nation-states must try to translate their capabilities into the influence required to achieve their objectives; they must implement their foreign policy decisions. They have a wide range of tools, techniques, and methods with which to deal with other states. In the next chapter we shall look further at some of the methods through which states exercise influence.

# RELATIONS BETWEEN STATES: INSTRUMENTS OF INFLUENCE

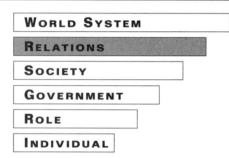

WORLD SYSTEM

RELATIONS

SOCIETY

GOVERNMENT

ROLE

INDIVIDUAL

## DIPLOMACY AND BARGAINING

A British diplomat once said, "Foreign policy is what you do; diplomacy is how you do it."[1] Although this distinction is a good place to start, it is also incomplete—all techniques for the implementation of foreign policy are, or should be, political. However, diplomacy involves direct, government-to-government interactions, acting upon the people in other governments who are able to do the things we want their states to do. Thus **diplomacy** can be considered the central technique of foreign policy

---

[1] Paul Gore-Booth, *With Great Truth and Respect* (London: Constable, 1974), p. 15.

implementation, the only truly direct technique. It is an instrument by which other techniques may realize their fullest potential to influence target states. For example, after a major military victory, it is usually through diplomatic interaction that the defeated party indicates whether it will surrender or modify previously held peace conditions. The military instrument has had an effect on another state, but that effect can be gauged and exploited only through diplomacy. The same may be said for economic activities, such as embargoes and other sanctions that deprive a state of needed commodities.

The central feature of diplomacy is communication. The basis for creating permanent diplomatic missions in the fifteenth century was the desire of kings and princes to have representatives in other courts to carry out continuous and systematic communication with other monarchs. Most of the legal trappings of diplomacy were established to maintain and facilitate communication and to reduce misunderstanding and distortion in interstate communication. The rules of protocol, diplomatic immunity, and noninterference, for example, were established to reduce conflicts over rank and status among diplomats (and thus to permit them to get on with the business of diplomacy), to prevent host governments from interfering with the diplomatic representatives of other states, and to prevent diplomats from interfering in the domestic politics of their hosts. These legal rules codify diplomatic interactions.

Diplomacy has five substantive functions:[2] (1) *conflict management;* (2) *solution of problems* facing two or more governments; (3) the increase and facilitation of cross-cultural *communication* on a wide range of issues; (4) *negotiation* and bargaining on specific issues, treaties, and agreements; and (5) general *program management* of the foreign policy decisions of one country in regard to another. Procedurally, these activities result foremost in communicating the views of one's government and in exchanging information. After such negotiation, diplomacy is often required to implement the agreements reached; lengthy and important talks may be held on exactly how agreements are to be executed. For example, after the Arab–Israeli ceasefire was achieved in 1973, some very hard bargaining was required to separate Egyptian and Israeli forces on the Sinai Peninsula. The resulting Israeli–Egyptian talks on the Kilometer 101 disengagements of 1973 and the implementation of the less-than-precise peace treaty of 1979 are good examples of the importance of postagreement diplomacy.

So far we have discussed diplomacy as a means by which one state directly influences another. But any discussion of the various functions of diplomacy cannot neglect another major function, aimed not at the other party but at third parties observing the diplomatic activities at hand. In this case diplomacy is used less to reach an agreement with the opposing party than to influence other parties through propaganda, undermining the position of the opponent, revealing the opponent's bargaining positions and other confidential information, or taking stances calculated to impress, frighten, or reassure third-party observers. Many of the U.S.–Soviet negotiations over the years were aimed at their various allies, at Third World states, and perhaps especially at China.

[2] Leon P. Poullada, "Diplomacy: The Missing Link in the Study of International Politics," in D. S. McLellan, W. C. Olson, and F. A. Sondermann, eds., *The Theory and Practice of International Relations,* 4th ed. (Englewood Cliffs, N.J.: Prentice-Hall, 1974), pp. 194–202.

Disagreement over how much diplomatic communication should be open and how much secret has been a major issue in the twentieth century. After World War I, there was a reaction to the old diplomacy of the great European powers. In addition to a general feeling that diplomacy was a devious and dishonest business, many people felt that the secret treaties that characterized the pre–World War I period and the formation of opposing alliances were responsible for the outbreak of the war. Idealists like President Woodrow Wilson attacked the immorality of secret treaties that offered territory if states would help others in military offensives. Wilson called for "open covenants . . . openly arrived at." The League of Nations promoted the idea of open treaties by publishing their texts after they were negotiated. Article 102 of the United Nations Charter provides for the compulsory registration of treaties with the UN. If a treaty has not been so registered, it cannot be invoked within the UN system.

Open negotiations almost ended the utility of diplomacy, as propaganda became its central function. Various speeches made in the UN General Assembly and Security Council exemplify how the propaganda function, as opposed to problem solving or conflict resolution, can prevail. After World War II, a hybrid form of diplomacy became prevalent. It combined private negotiations between diplomats with public declarations of what had been achieved—in press conferences, in joint statements, or by the publication of agreements (usually by the United Nations). Former Secretary of State Henry Kissinger was a master of the private conversation and the public spectacle. His techniques were a return to traditional diplomacy: hard bargaining in private; secret trips and agreements (revealed to the public only after their completion); and a style that combined the use of force with the use of words to bring about an agreement every side could live with, but one that required every side to make concessions and compromises.

In the past the bulk of diplomatic communication, as well as most important talks, took place between the regular diplomatic representatives of the foreign services of states. Both day-to-day activity and major talks were handled by the diplomatic personnel of the embassies located in each state's capital. Today much of this activity, especially for smaller and less developed countries, occurs in multilateral forums such as the United Nations. Called *parliamentary diplomacy,* this form of diplomacy includes both the regular meetings of the international body to which permanent representatives are assigned and the informal discussions that occur in a single location where a state's diplomats can meet representatives of many other states. The larger powers, taking advantage of instantaneous communication facilities between governmental leaders, faster transportation, and the willingness to mount summit meetings, have tended to skip over embassy personnel and ambassadors and conduct more and more of their business through the use of special envoys and high-level officials such as foreign ministers or secretaries of state.[3] These activities range from the bilateral summits of U.S. and Soviet leaders to multilateral contexts such as the regular

---

[3] See Henry Kissinger's memoirs, *White House Years* (Boston: Little, Brown, 1979) and *Years of Upheaval* (Boston: Little, Brown, 1982), for details of his high-level negotiations and an understanding of how such a process works. See also his *Diplomacy* (New York: Simon & Schuster, 1994).

meetings of the Group of Seven, a group of the heads of government of the seven major Western industrial countries—the United States, Japan, Germany, France, Italy, Britain, and Canada—that gathers to discuss economic policy.

The modern U.S. secretary of state has regularly engaged in "shuttle diplomacy" of some sort, flying between the capitals of states in conflict to facilitate communication between opposing parties who usually will not sit down together. Kissinger popularized this activity in his work in the Middle East in 1973; Reagan's secretary of state, Alexander Haig, pursued it in trying to settle the Falklands/Malvinas dispute between Britain and Argentina in 1982; and James Baker, Bush's secretary of state, engaged in similar travels in 1991 as he attempted to revive a Middle East peace process following the Gulf War. One problem with high-level diplomacy is that leaders and officials in other countries may come to refuse to deal with lower-level representatives (even ambassadors and undersecretaries of state), especially on crucial issues.

## NEGOTIATION

The first stage of negotiation is based upon the commitment to deal *in good faith*. This means that both parties are negotiating for the purpose of reaching an agreement (as we shall see, there are other purposes). Each party must calculate that the benefits of reaching agreement outweigh the sacrifices that may be necessary in the negotiation. Often this stage requires one party to convince the other that an agreement of some sort would be in the interest of both sides (as was often crucial in Soviet–U.S. arms-control negotiations).

Other reasons for negotiation may include making propaganda, gathering intelligence, and deception. A state may negotiate to gather information about the capabilities, aims, and problems of the other side. Or it may negotiate in order to give the opponent misleading information about its own intentions and capabilities. States may also choose to negotiate simply to maintain contact with the other side, even if chances of an agreement are slim. States may try to substitute diplomacy for the use of force, hoping that as long as both sides are talking neither will resort to armed conflict; some believe that this was an objective of the U.S.–Japanese talks in progress before Pearl Harbor.

Once the first stage of negotiation is achieved, the parties move on to preliminary issues, often as important to both sides as the agreement itself, that must be settled. The *location* of the negotiations must be fixed. States prefer a neutral site when bargaining with an adversary; Paris was the site of the U.S.–North Vietnamese peace talks, and Vienna, Helsinki, and Geneva for the various U.S.–Soviet SALT negotiations. Naming the *parties* to be represented can present a problem, because participation defines who has standing in the issue. In this era of nonstate actors trying to obtain territory or governmental status, simply recognizing their existence is a major substantive concession. Thus, by agreeing to their participation in negotiations, a state has made more than a procedural concession. This was a sticky point for the United States in Paris regarding the Viet Cong and was continually a central issue in the protracted conflicts in Northern Ireland and between Israel and the Arabs. Until the dramatic breakthrough with Egypt in 1977, no Arab state recognized Israel's existence. Israel, in turn, refused to recognize the Palestine Liberation Organization. The historic agreements of 1993 between Israel and the PLO (leading to the Nobel Peace Prize for Yitzak Rabin, Shimon Peres, and Yassir Arafat) could come about only after an array of such nonrecognition barriers fell.

The second stage of negotiation is the *bargaining over the actual terms of the agreement*, that is, defining solutions and working out accords.[4] Because each side has different or conflicting objectives and interests, there is something to bargain over. Much of the interaction involves attempts to find solutions to common problems. Other bargaining interactions are straightforward influence relationships. The objective is to get the opponent to agree with you as much as possible in achieving a solution to the problem. Each side wishes to minimize the costs to itself.

Bargaining takes on features of both *debate* (where "opponents direct their arguments at each other" and "the objective is to convince your opponent, to make him see things as you see them") and *game* (where each party must take into account "the potentialities and evaluations of alternative outcomes; the object in a game is to outwit the opponent").[5] Thus persuasion as well as threats and promises are employed in bargaining, as each side presents its conditions and demands and attempts to convince or coerce the other side to accept as many of these as possible.

The threats and promises must be credible. Each side must try to figure out how far to push demands and how far to push the opponent—when to make concessions and when to dig in and say, "I can't give in any further." In doing all this, states employ specific threats and promises as well as deliberately vague threats and warnings ("We will not stand idly by . . . " and "You must bear the responsibility if . . ."). A state's *bargaining reputation* includes its reputation for bluffing, standing fast, telling the truth, and honoring commitments (or not).

Bargaining involves the complex interactions of mutual influence and expectations, each party both anticipating and reacting to the other. A feeling for the complexity of the bargaining process is given in this quotation from the work of Thomas Schelling, one of the pioneers in the study of international strategy and bargaining:

> Each party's strategy is guided mainly by what he expects the other party to accept or insist on; yet each knows that the other is guided by reciprocal thoughts. The final outcome must be a point from which neither expects the other to retreat; yet the main ingredient of this expectation is what one thinks the other expects the first to expect and so on. Somehow, out of this fluid and indeterminate situation that seemingly provides no logical reason for anyone except what he expects to be expected to expect,

---

[4] The italicized phrases used here come from the chapter titles in the comprehensive treatment by I. William Zartman and Maureen R. Berman, *The Practical Negotiator* (New Haven, Conn.: Yale University Press, 1982). For a good overview of the processes, nature, and theory of negotiation, see Howard Raiffa, *The Art and Science of Negotiation* (Cambridge, Mass: Harvard University Press, 1982); Dean Pruitt and Peter Carnevale, *Negotiation in Social Conflict* (Bemont, Calif.: Brooks/Cole, 1993); and Marc Howard Ross, *The Management of Conflict: Interpretations and Interest in Comparative Perspective* (New Haven, Conn.: Yale University Press, 1993). See also T. Clifton Morgan, *Untying the Knot of War: A Bargaining Theory of International Crises* (Ann Arbor: University of Michigan Press, 1994).

[5] See Anatol Rapoport, *Fights, Games, and Debates* (Ann Arbor: University of Michigan Press, 1960).

a decision is reached. These infinitely reflexive expectations must somehow converge on a single point, at which each expects the other not to expect to be expected to retreat.[6]

## BARGAINING AND THE RESOLUTION OF CONFLICT

A conflict can be resolved in many ways. A test of force—through conquest, forcible submission, or deterrence—is one method. However, conflicts can also be resolved through compromise, third-party mediation or arbitration, or adjudication of some sort (by international courts, multilateral conferences, or international organizations). In these processes, conflict situations are resolved through negotiations.

For successful conflict resolution, the parties involved must be willing to confront the issues in conflict in a rational atmosphere of some mutual respect and open communication. They must try to identify the issues involved in a realistic manner and not act merely to establish favorable conditions for the bargaining process. John Burton has even argued that a bargaining situation must be avoided. His view is that conflicts are based on misunderstandings and that the important thing is to get people sitting down face to face. The largest issues may be set out in the presence of a mediator, who will help the parties see where their misunderstandings exist. Burton argues that once favorable conditions exist for analyzing the misunderstanding that underlies the conflict, the process of solving the conflict is well on its way.

Burton's view that most conflicts are based merely on misunderstandings is extreme, but his emphasis on the need to have the first stage of negotiations carefully approached and worked out is valuable. Our view is that many, if not most, conflicts are indeed concrete. *Objective incompatibilities* do exist in the global arena: the desire to occupy the same territory, to control the same governmental machinery, or to fish the same waters; disagreement over the manner in which certain groups of people (say, coreligionists or people of the same ethnic or linguistic background living within the borders of other states) should be treated. Although most conflicts do have an objective basis, the process of conflict resolution is highly subjective, because of the complex nature of bargaining. Even Roger Fisher, the best-known proponent of this view of conflict bargaining, advocates taking the game element out of conflict resolution bargaining and stressing the debate element.[7]

Fisher stresses trying to understand the opponent's view of the situation and then attempting to figure out what can be done to make the opponent change that view. He

---

[6] Thomas Schelling, *The Strategy of Conflict* (New York: Oxford University Press, 1963), p. 70.
[7] See, for example, John W. Burton, *Conflict: Resolution and Prevention* (New York: St. Martin's, 1990). For presentations of Fisher's general framework for bargaining, see *Getting to Yes*, 2nd ed. (New York: Penguin, 1991), written with William Ury, and *Beyond Machiavelli: Tools for Coping with Conflict* (Cambridge, Mass.: Harvard University Press, 1994), written with Elizabeth Kopelman and Andrea Kupfer Schneider.

specifically notes that "making threats is not enough." How, then, does one try to influence the opponent? First, Fisher argues that one state must be very clear about what it wants the opponent to do. Then, always keeping in mind how the opponent sees the world ("put yourself in their shoes"), the focus should be on *points of choice*; the choices offered the opponent should be made attractive and acceptable. Fisher's concern is that a bargainer's offers and positions appear sensible and legitimate in the eyes of the opponent. This is a hallmark of the debate. He further argues that if making threats is the best you can do, and if punishment must be resorted to, your bargaining influence and your actions will appear to be failures. Coercion is seen to be a failure of influence.

## The Use of International Organizations

In bargaining to resolve conflicts, the least coercive forms of influence are often the most useful, at least initially. Promises of rewards, persuasion, reliance on the legitimacy of claims, and opponents' awareness that you understand their position seem to be better methods of influence than are threats of force. Appealing to values held by the opponent by way of legitimacy is especially helpful. Fisher argues that you should be concerned with precedent and reciprocity in order to make your demands legitimate in the eyes of the opponents—to appear to be consistent with their principles.

A way to do this is to use international law and international organizations. On the whole, no organization was very successful in managing conflicts between members of different cold war blocs. The United Nations was always reasonably effective in non–cold war disputes, however, doing best in the area of resource conflicts (see the discussions in Part II). Regional organizations do well in managing conflicts not involving force, whereas the United Nations has done well with high-intensity conflicts.[8] When the cold war wound down at the end of the 1980s, the UN was able to do things that previously would have been impossible. With the United States and Russia cooperating, the Security Council and the secretary general helped to end a number of civil and international wars (including ones in Namibia and Cambodia). The United Nations also played a key role in bringing the international community together against Iraq after its invasion of Kuwait.

## USE OF THE MILITARY FOR ACHIEVING INTERNATIONAL INFLUENCE

We have already noted that influence may be achieved through the application of force. Throughout history rulers have used war and violence to prevail in conflict and to overcome obstacles. There is no doubt that the use of military capabilities is

---

[8] See Ernst B. Haas, *Why We Still Need the United Nations: The Collective Management of International Conflict, 1945–1984*, Policy Papers in International Affairs, no. 26 (Berkeley: University of California Institute of International Studies, 1986).

generally a coercive or punishment-oriented means of influence. It is also possible, however, to use these capabilities for *rewarding* others. The most obvious rewarding activity is the use of military aid. States, particularly the larger states, may thereby attempt to influence commitment to an alliance, UN voting, or general political orientation. Powers such as the United States, Russia, Britain, and France have the technology, expertise, and capability to produce weapons that most of the world's countries cannot. Non-European countries such as Brazil, Israel, and the two Koreas have also become important suppliers of arms to the developing countries.

Influence gained through providing weapons may be only temporary. Egypt illustrated how a recipient state can turn on its arms supplier when Sadat threw Soviet military advisers and other personnel out of the country in 1971. Although spare parts and maintenance linkages provide supplier states with their primary leverage over recipients, the exchange of aid for influence is far from an automatic equation. U.S. influence on many Israeli policies has been quite variable—from none to some. None of Iraq's arms suppliers, even the Soviet Union, were able to influence Iraqi policy in the six months before the Gulf War broke out. Because there are many possible suppliers of military aid, the ability of powerful states to influence the governments of developing countries is quite limited. Indeed, in the aftermath of the Gulf War, major arms suppliers were forced to recognize the limited influence that arms trade provided, along with the harm that such weapons could inflict within various regions.

Another way to reward states with military capabilities is to promise alliance—adding one's capabilities to theirs. However, a formal treaty is not necessary for state *A* to aid state *B* by either threatening *B*'s enemy or actually using its military forces against *B*'s enemy. The American deterrent umbrella, whether for its allies or for other states that knew they would be protected even without a formal alliance (for example, Austria, Sweden, and Israel), exemplified this form of influence through reward.

Most instances involving the military tool of foreign policy, however, are based on exploiting the use or threat of use of force. Force is coercive; it is the ability to destroy or kill or take away, to occupy and control through violence. Force directly affects the distribution of security, political control, territory, and wealth in the international system. Force is used because decision makers *expect to benefit* from the new distributions that are anticipated after it has been used. States are influenced by the threat of force because they fear what they will lose if others use force. The military technique of influence should be seen as another means to various political ends, not as an end in itself. The objective of using force is the same as that of using any other technique: influence to achieve objectives.[9]

This view of force was most powerfully argued and popularized by the Prussian officer and military historian Karl von Clausewitz, who wrote the classic *On War* after

---

[9] The idea of matching the costs, the benefits, and the probability of alternative outcomes forms the basis of the expected-utility approach to the study of international relations. The classic statement of this perspective is found in Bruce Bueno de Mesquita, *The War Trap* (New Haven, Conn.: Yale University Press, 1981), along with the revised models and expanded applications found in Bueno de Mesquita and David Lalman, *War and Reason* (New Haven, Conn.: Yale University Press, 1992).

his military service against Napoleon. Clausewitz clearly saw the military instrument as a means to an end, as a way to influence the opponent: "War is an act of violence intended to compel our opponent to fulfill our will." Clausewitz also argued that war could not be separated from the political ends of states and indeed must be subordinated to those ends. His famous dictum reads: "War is therefore a continuation of policy by other means. It is not merely a political act but a real political instrument, a continuation, a conduct of political intercourse by other means."

The actual use of force involves *both power and influence.* Brute force overcomes an obstacle simply by destroying it, as the Romans overcame Carthage in the Third Punic War (149–146 B.C.). Rome did not employ force to influence Carthage to engage in desired behavior: there was nothing Rome wanted Carthage to do. Rome simply wanted to wipe Carthage from the face of the earth. The actual use of brute force, then, can entail the destruction of an opponent. In these situations, influence is not the object. In most situations where force is used, however, influence is the aim. The use of force is usually meant to hurt the opponent until the opponent's will to resist further is broken.

Alternatively, one can merely *threaten* to use force, exploiting an opponent's knowledge of one's ability to hurt and inflict costs. Military capabilities are exploited explicitly through diplomatic channels, especially when the aim is deterrence; the deterrer must make clear to the opponent just what actions are forbidden and what will happen to the opponent if those actions are taken. A study investigating the use of American military force short of war as an instrument of influence found that such limited use often had utility: to stabilize a worsening situation, to gain time, and even to defuse domestic American demands for more drastic action. On the other hand, the actual use of military force short of war did not produce long-term benefits. It was best used for deterrence, not compellence, to support existing friendly regimes rather than to change governments or their policies.[10]

Beyond the threat of force, other techniques exist for the use of military capabilities without actually resorting to violence. The aim is to convey to others knowledge of the military capabilities one possesses in order to influence their view of the world and their menu. States often want to be perceived as being militarily powerful, willing to use their capabilities and thus not to be challenged or thwarted ("potential influence" as noted in the last chapter). Such a demonstration may be implicit, or it may be made explicitly through the display of military capabilities—to impress others with one's military strength and to achieve status and prestige as a powerful state. In today's system, nuclear weapons are the most obvious element of military capabilities used for prestige or status. India's nuclear explosion in 1974 was motivated in large part by its search for a means to match the status and prestige of China, both in Asia and in Third World countries around the globe.

Stationing one's forces abroad may serve to influence others in any or all of the ways noted: to reward allies or to threaten opponents, to support deterrence, or to

---

[10] See Barry M. Blechman and Stephen S. Kaplan, *Force Without War: U.S. Armed Forces as a Political Instrument* (Washington, D.C.: Brookings Institution, 1978).

project power and status. Although the end of the cold war has brought about a substantial reduction in foreign-based troops, as recently as 1986 almost 2 million military personnel, from 28 different countries, were stationed in 91 foreign countries on almost 3,000 military bases or installations. More symbolically, states may display their military capabilities to outside observers through a variety of activities: nuclear explosions, war games, military maneuvers, military parades like the May Day parade in Red Square, and by sailing fleets around the world, as in the Falklands war or during the Iran–Iraq war. Mobilizing forces or putting them on high-readiness alerts (as Nixon did during the 1973 Middle East war) can also be used to communicate to an opponent the seriousness of a situation. Here a state is not so much interested in demonstrating its capabilities as it is its willingness to use them in a critical situation.

## The Nonuse of Nuclear Weapons and the Utility of Conventional Ones

Many arguments have been presented to show that in the nuclear age military power has become obsolete—-that nuclear weapons have made Clausewitz's dictum meaningless. With the end of the cold war, these arguments have been strengthened. In this view, the use of nuclear weapons can provide no political utility at all: either the state that used them would also be destroyed by a retaliatory attack, or the devastation would be so great that no territory, wealth, or population would be gained after their use. The costs of a nuclear war would be unprecedented. Given the complex and vital interdependences of modern society because of the importance of cities and their vulnerability to disruption, nuclear weapons would bring a society to a standstill within a few hours. Distance and time, elements that once protected states in war, would do so no longer. In a process that began with the strategic bombing campaigns of World War II, nuclear weapons with their ballistic (and cruise) missile delivery systems have made it totally unnecessary to defeat an opponent's armed forces before being able to destroy its people and its wealth. Also, nuclear weapons have been of no use against guerrilla operations or terrorists, nor could they be used to seize territory or control of a government. The main value of nuclear weapons, once they were created, has rested in their *nonuse:* in deterring their use by other nuclear powers.

There has also been the feeling that any use of force is dangerous because of the risk of escalation—that a war could spread to the nuclear powers. This led some people to proclaim that all war was obsolete. The use of force by Saddam Hussein to take Kuwait and the United Nations response (led by the United States) indicate that this is not the case. The actual use or threat of use of conventional military force against nonnuclear powers, particularly those not located in Europe, and for separatist or revolutionary purposes, has retained value. War has been ubiquitous throughout history, and the use of war as a foreign policy tool continues to the present day.

The legitimacy of force or the threat of force is maintained in several ways. The UN Charter permits states, either individually or collectively in alliances, to use force for self-defense. The collective security function of the United Nations itself is based on the threat to use the collective force of the UN membership against transgressors of international law, as exercised against the North Koreans in 1950 and Iraq in 1991. Such staunch neutrals as Switzerland and Sweden have based their neutrality on strong military establishments. Their military strength is a form of display to deter any would-be aggressor; because of the impression they made, they would argue, they avoided being attacked by Nazi Germany during World War II. Other states have used force when it was convenient or necessary—even India, whose first leaders had been the most outspoken in opposition to violence (in 1961 against Portugal in a dispute over Goa, in 1962 in a border war with China, and in 1947, 1965, and 1971 against Pakistan).

We referred earlier to the work of John Mueller, who argues that norms against the use of force were on the rise even before World War I but were spurred on by that conflict and by World War II.[11] There are, in fact, indications that this is happening. As will be discussed below, democracies only rarely—if ever—fight each other. In addition, there are broader patterns. According to data from the Correlates of War Project, about 15 percent of all "militarized disputes" escalated to war in the period from the Napoleonic Wars to World War II, while only about 3 percent have done so since then.[12] Throughout the cold war the nuclear superpowers, with their adversarial relationship, deterred each other from using nuclear weapons against the other or against other states. They and their allies in Europe refrained from the direct use of force (conventional and nuclear) in Europe. However, they often employed military force elsewhere, as did other states in the system. A look at which states are engaging in conflict, in which parts of the world, suggests that any argument about the obsolescence of the military tool has applied mostly to the superpowers, to East–West relations in Europe, and among the group of OECD countries.

There is little agreement on what exactly constitutes a "war" in the post–World War II international system. With the disappearance of legal trappings such as declarations of war, different scholars have used different criteria to determine what events should be included on their lists of wars or violent conflicts. One study of the period between 1945 and 1992 identifies 149 violent conflicts that qualify as major international and civil wars. Only 7, or 4.7 percent, took place in Europe, with an additional 6 on the territory of the former USSR. Another study counts 68 different countries involved in one of the 115 wars ("an open armed conflict in which regular armed forces are engaged on at least one side, in which the fighters and fighting are organized centrally to some extent and where there is some continuity between armed clashes") occurring between 1980 and 1990. A third study finds 90 armed conflicts to have occurred in the post–cold war period, 1989 to 1993. Of the 47 active armed conflicts in 1993, not one was *interstate*—all were internal. Furthermore, of the 18 armed conflicts in Europe from 1989 to 1993, 15 were on the territory of the former Soviet Union or Yugoslavia. Herbert Tillema's Overt Military Intervention data set, covering the period from 1945 to 1991, identified 690 cases of intervention, only 30 of which took place in Europe. Since World War II, 106 different states have engaged in a foreign overt military intervention at least once. One source estimates over 23 million

[11] John Mueller, *Retreat from Doomsday* (New York: Basic Books, 1989).
[12] See J. David Singer, "Peace in the Global System: Displacement, Interregnum, or Transformation?" in Charles W. Kegley, Jr., ed., *The Long Postwar Peace* (New York: Harper Collins, 1991).

fatalities from the organized use of force from 1945 to 1992 (63 percent of them civilians!). Clearly, policymakers still perceive utility in the use of force.[13]

A central object of violent struggle has been the control of the state. Since World War II almost 150 governments have been created. Because of the multiethnic or multitribal populations of many of these states and the worldwide ideological clash between Western-oriented parties and communist parties, governments have been under constant siege. Force has been used as a principal tool by nonstate actors to challenge established governments for control of a state or a region that hopes to become a state of its own. The use of force by nonstate actors is one of a number of challenges to the nation-state in the contemporary system. As noted, state sovereignty is the legal status that gives the state a monopoly on the internal and external use of force. This monopoly has been and continues to be severely challenged, the largest proportion of the post-1945 conflicts being some form of civil war or internationalized civil war.

The main forms of contemporary nonstate violence have been guerrilla warfare and terrorism. Some observers have called these "new" forms of international violence, but in fact each has a long history. What is new is the changing pattern of international conflict. According to some data, 80 percent of the wars between 1900 and 1941 were of the traditional sort, waged by the armed forces of two or more states. Since 1945 about 80 percent of violent conflict has occurred on the territory of only one state and has been internally oriented. As part of the process of fragmentation and as illustrated by the range of separatist movements in the world, both guerrilla warfare and terrorism are revolutionary activities, challenging the rule and authority of governments. Indeed, a hallmark of both guerrilla warfare and terrorism is the primacy of the political element in the contest between challenger and government. The challenging forces are usually groups from within a state's population, though they often receive support of some kind from outside states.

Internal opposition groups begin in a military position far inferior to that of the established government. Outside parties often try to gain influence through military capabilities by providing aid either to the government or to the guerrilla or terrorist group. Governments may provide support for other governments by supplying equipment, advisers, or expertise in handling the unconventional tactics of the challenger. The Israelis, after their successful commando operation at Uganda's Entebbe airfield in July 1976, provided training to antiterrorist forces of other states.

---

[13] The first data set is found in Ruth Leger Sivard, *World Military and Social Expenditures, 1993* (Washington, D.C.: World Priorities, 1993). The second reference is to Michael Kidron and Dan Smith, *The New State of War and Peace* (New York: Touchstone, 1991). The third study is by Peter Wallensteen and Karin Axell, "Conflict Resolution and the End of the Cold War, 1989–1993," *Journal of Peace Research* 31 (August 1994), 333–349. Herbert Tillema defined overt military intervention as the "the direct combatant or combat preparatory military operations conducted within a foreign territory by a state's regular military units," calling it "the ultimate instrument of forceful foreign policy." See Tillema, "Cold War Alliance and Overt Military Intervention, 1945–1991," *International Interactions* 20, 3 (1994), 249–278. The information on fatalities is from Sivard.

## Terrorism

**Terrorism** is an instrument of influence used by nonstate actors and states alike—a flexible and multipurpose tactic. The principal purpose of terrorism is not the actual destruction produced but its dramatic and psychological effects on populations and governments. Peter Sederberg calls this the publicity objective of terrorism; Brian Jenkins has said, "Terrorism is theater." The objectives of terrorism are to frighten target audiences through the use of dramatic and shocking acts, which include bombings, assassinations, kidnappings, the taking of hostages, and hijackings. Terrorists do this by violating two of the most basic rules of war: the immunity of noncombatants and the ban on indiscriminate use of force.[14]

Terrorism is thus the systematic use of violence for political ends, an ongoing series of acts intended to produce fear that will change attitudes and behavior toward governments. Nonstate actors at various points in time (such as the PLO, the IRA, the Red Brigades, militant Shiite groups, and ethnic and religious separatist groups) wish to undermine governments by making them appear weak, ineffectual, and unable to protect the population. Terrorists wish to gain publicity and attention and to convince the people and government that they are an important political force. Terrorism also weakens governmental support when the government responds indiscriminately with its police and military forces to terrorist acts, "retaliating" on sectors of the population not connected with the terrorists. Thus a government may actually help the antigovernment group by alienating ordinary citizens. Because governments find it so hard to punish those responsible, terrorism can be a frustratingly effective weapon. Over the past decade or so the most prominent examples of terrorist activity by separatist or nationalist groups against governments include the IRA in Northern Ireland, Palestinians in Israel, Basques in Spain, Sikhs in India, and the Tamils in Sri Lanka.

It is important to distinguish dissident terrorism from establishment terrorism, or **state terrorism.** This latter policy takes several forms; one is the support of terrorist groups against the governments of other states. In sponsoring terrorism against other governments, a state pursues the same objective mentioned above: weakening the control of governments of other states by hurting and embarrassing them. In this sense states are using the actions of terrorist groups in surrogate warfare. In the 1980s the Reagan administration labeled Iran, Libya, and Syria as major sources of support to international terrorist groups. A 1993 report by the U.S. State Department cites Iran as still the "most active and dangerous" sponsor of international terrorism, with Iraq another major sponsor.[15]

States also use terror against their own populations to gain or increase control through fear. Tactics include expulsion or exile, failure to protect some citizens from the crimes of others (as in state-tolerated vigilante groups), arbitrary arrest, beatings,

---

[14] Peter C. Sederberg, *Terrorist Myths: Illusion, Rhetoric and Reality* (Englewood Cliffs, N.J.: Prentice Hall, 1989), p. 78; Brian M. Jenkins, *International Terrorism: The Other World War* (Santa Monica, Calif.: Rand, 1985).

[15] For an overview of state terrorism, see Michael Stohl and George A. Lopez, eds., *The State as Terrorist: The Dynamics of Governmental Violence and Repression* (Westport, Conn.: Greenwood, 1984). See also United State Department of State, *Patterns of Global Terrorism 1993* (Washington, D.C.: USGPO, 1994).

kidnappings ("disappearances"), torture, and murder. This use of terror also has a long history. Two famous historical examples of the systematic use of terror by governments against internal opposition are France during the Terror of 1793–1794 and the Soviet Union under Stalin in the 1930s. One scholar has chronicled "democide"—genocide and mass murder—during the twentieth century. From 1900 to 1987 almost 170 million people have been killed by their own governments, far more people than killed in wars. The major "megamurderers" during this period were the most authoritarian states—the Soviet Union, the People's Republic of China, Germany (from 1933 to 1945), and Nationalist China (from 1928 to 1949); the least murderous countries were democracies. One conclusion drawn by the author is that, "Power kills, absolute power kills absolutely."[16]

Note where international terrorist incidents take place. According to State Department statistics, of the 2,853 international terrorist incidents between 1988 and 1993, the areas with the greatest number of incidents were Latin America (32.1 percent) and Western Europe (28.7 percent). While Western Europe was also one of the areas with the least "war," Africa, with a large number of armed conflicts and interventions, accounted for only 6.1 percent of terrorist incidents. Contrasting figures on war and terrorism indicate that terrorism is indeed the weapon of groups that are relatively weak (in comparison to their goals and their opponents) and is used in areas where such groups cannot mount some form of organized military challenge to the government. As with guerrilla war, the instruments of force in terrorism are constantly and consciously directed toward political influence and political ends.

## INFLUENCE BASED ON ECONOMIC RESOURCES

States rely on each other for resources and commodities that enable them to develop and sustain their economies and the well-being of their peoples. This reliance is central to the ideas of leverage and vulnerability described in the previous chapter. Economic resources can be manipulated by those who possess them to influence those who do not. As we stressed earlier, nothing in the international system is equally distributed. This, of course, applies to economic resources as well as to the economic requirements of various states: states that possess a surplus (or a monopoly) of resources may achieve greater economic influence; states that lack the resources and commodities they require are more vulnerable to economic influence. The economic resources of states can be used across the whole range of influence mechanisms.[17] In comparison to diplomacy, however, economic means of influence may be considered

---

[16] See Rudolph J. Rummel, *Death by Government: Genocide and Mass Murder Since 1900* (New Brunswick, N.J.: Transaction, 1994).

[17] For a detailed discussion of resource dependence—what it means and how it can be measured and applied to interstate relations—see Bruce Russett, "Dimensions of Resource Dependence: Some Elements of Rigor in Concept and Policy Analysis," *International Organization* 37 (Summer 1984), 481–499. For a general overview of economic foreign policy tools, see David A. Baldwin, *Economic Statecraft* (Princeton, N.J.: Princeton University Press, 1985).

indirect. Rather than direct interaction with governmental leaders, the objective is to affect some aspect of the state's society—its wealth, production, or well-being. The effect is then taken into account by the state's leaders and so influences their behavior (just as the defeat of an army on the battlefield is taken into account and influences future behavior).

The manipulation of economic resources takes many forms. States can use trade, monetary policy, or international organizations to acquire more economic resources or to deny them to their adversaries. These resources can then be used to generate additional economic and military resources. The wealth from Iraq's oilfields enabled Saddam Hussein to amass the impressive arsenal that he used first to fight Iran and then to seize Kuwait and defy the United Nations. One argument for the use of force against Iraq was that with the wealth generated from Kuwaiti oil, Iraq could buy even more weapons, including sophisticated delivery systems for chemical-biological weapons (and possibly nuclear ones as well). Similarly, from the 1973 Arab–Israeli war until his ouster in early 1979, the shah of Iran continuously pressed for higher oil prices in order to generate the wealth he desired for both his armed forces and his ambitious economic schemes.

The central use of economic techniques for international influence is the exploitation of the **vulnerability** of other states. Few states can even attempt a policy of autarky, because in one way or another all states have economic needs they cannot satisfy. Thus they are vulnerable to the influence of states who have leverage of some kind—what they need. In the past, states like Bangladesh, the Soviet Union, or many African countries have often required more food, especially grain, than they could produce. Most states require petroleum, which is produced on a large scale in only a handful of countries; in this regard Japan and the states of Western Europe are particularly vulnerable. In the 1970s, Henry Kissinger tried to use detente as a way of enmeshing the Soviet Union within a web of world trade in order to make the USSR need more from other states and thereby *become more vulnerable* within the international system. He hoped that the Soviets would thus be "more responsible" world citizens than they would be if they became totally self-sufficient. An autarkic state needs no one to help fill its needs and therefore has a much more open menu; consequently, it is less constrained by its own self-interests.

## *Economic Rewards and Punishments*

As with other types of influence, economic influence may be achieved through the use of rewards or punishments. Table 7.1 shows the variety of specific negative and positive actions that states may take—**economic sanctions.** Negatively, one state may take away, threaten to cut off, or fail to provide another with some economic resource, commodity, or service. The United States used such tactics against the Soviet Union in 1980 after the USSR invaded Afghanistan. The Carter administration renewed a grain embargo to attempt to influence the Soviets. Positively, a state may promise to provide, to continue to provide, or to increase its supply of some resource, good, or service to another state. In fact, however, it is rare for some economic good or service to be cut off completely. More often, punishment and reward deal with the *level* of the good or service being provided or the *price* of that good or service. As we have seen in

### TABLE 7.1    Economic Techniques of Influence

| Negative Sanctions | |
|---|---|
| Trade | Capital |
| Embargo | Freezing assets |
| Boycott | Controls on import or export |
| Tariff increase | Aid suspension |
| Tariff discrimination (unfavorable) | Expropriation |
| Withdrawal of most-favored-nation treatment | Taxation (unfavorable) |
| Blacklist | Withholding dues to international organization |
| Quotas (import or export) | Threats of the above |
| Dumping | |
| Preclusive buying | |
| Threats of the above | |

NOTE:
*Embargo*—prohibition on exports, sometimes used to refer to a ban on all trade.
*Boycott*—prohibition on imports.
*Tariff increase*—increase in taxes on imports from the target state(s).
*Tariff discrimination*—imports from target countries may be treated less favorably than those from other countries.
*Withdrawal of MFN*—ceasing to treat imports from a country as favorably as similar imports from any other country.
*Blacklist*—ban on doing business with firms that trade with the target country.
*Quotas*—quantitative restrictions on particular imports or exports.
*License denial*—refusing permission to import or export particular goods.
*Dumping*—deliberate sale of exports at prices below cost of production; for example, to depress world price of a key export or to gain foothold in a world market to disrupt the economy of the target country.
*Preclusive buying*—purchase of a commodity in order to deny it to the target country.
*Freezing assets*—impounding assets, denying access to bank accounts or other financial assets owned by the target country.
*Controls on import or export of capital*—restrictions on who can transfer how much capital for what purposes into or out of a country.
*Aid suspension*—the reduction, termination, or slow-down of aid transfers.
*Expropriation*—seizing ownership of property belonging to the target state.
*Taxation*—assets of target state may be taxed in a discriminatory manner.
*Withholding dues to international organization*—nonpayment, late payment, or reduced payment of financial obligations agreed to in the past.
*Threats of the above*—making the use of any of the above techniques conditional on certain kinds of behavior by the target.

*(continued)*

**TABLE 7.1**    Economic Techniques of Influence *(continued)*

<table>
<tr><th colspan="2">Positive Sanctions</th></tr>
<tr><th>Trade</th><th>Capital</th></tr>
<tr><td>Tariff discrimination (favorable)</td><td>Providing aid</td></tr>
<tr><td>Granting most-favored-nation treatment</td><td>Investment guarantees</td></tr>
<tr><td>Tariff reduction</td><td>Encouragement of private capital exports or imports</td></tr>
<tr><td>Direct purchase</td><td>Taxation (favorable)</td></tr>
<tr><td>Subsidies to exports or imports</td><td>Promises of the above</td></tr>
<tr><td>Granting licenses (import or export)</td><td></td></tr>
<tr><td>Promises of the above</td><td></td></tr>
</table>

NOTE:
*Tariff discrimination*—import duties favoring imports from the target country.
*Granting MFN treatment*—promising to treat imports from the target country as favorably as imports of similar products from any other source.
*Tariff reduction*—lowering of tariffs in general or on particular products.
*Direct purchase*—payment for service or goods; for example, the purchase of Louisiana Territory by the U.S. government.
*Subsidies to exports or imports*—exports to or imports from the target country may be subsidized; for example, arms sales to Third World countries or above-market prices paid for Cuban sugar by United States before 1960.
*Granting licenses*—permission to import or export particular goods.
*Providing aid*—extension or continuation of aid via bilateral or multilateral channels in the form of grants or loans.
*Investment guarantees*—governmental insurance against some of the risks of private foreign investors.
*Encouragement of private capital exports or imports*—offering incentives to import or export capital.
*Taxation*—especially favorable taxation of foreign capital investment.
*Promises of the above*—making the use of any of the above techniques conditional on certain kinds of behavior by the target country.

*Source:* David A. Baldwin, *Economic Statecraft* (Princeton, N.J.: Princeton University Press, 1985), pp. 41–42.

the industrialized West since 1973, the manipulation of the supply or price of oil can bring clear-cut benefits or costs to the Western states. The Arab states have used this means to affect Western voting patterns in the United Nations, Western treatment of Israel, and Western trade agreements.

Whether an economic good or service is being used to punish or reward another state, the success of the influence attempt and the amount of influence achieved depend on how vulnerable the target is to the manipulation of that economic good or service. The key issue here is **substitutability** and how dependent one state can make another state on the first state's economic goods and services. Discussing why economic sanctions failed in the 1960s and 1970s, Johan Galtung summarized a set of ideal conditions for economic punishment or reward:[18] all relate to the issue of substitutability. The state being punished should already have important economic ties with the punishing state. For example, the countries of Western Europe, faced with the 1973 oil embargo and price rise by the Arab members of OPEC, were strongly affected because they had based their energy policies on the assumption of a continued flow of low-priced oil from the OPEC states, which provided the overwhelming proportion of their supply.

The state being punished must be unable to find a substitute for the sanctioned item, in terms either of goods or of markets. When the United States under President Dwight Eisenhower attempted to punish Cuba by cutting the quota of Cuban sugar, Cuba was able to substitute markets by getting the Soviet Union to purchase the newly available sugar. Similarly, when the United States and Western companies cut off Cuba's oil supplies, Castro was able to substitute Soviet oil. On the other hand, when the Arab oil suppliers decided to embargo oil to the United States, Western Europe, and Japan in 1973, there was some short-term acquiescence by European countries and Japan to Arab demands. The Arab states controlled such a large proportion of the oil supply that most of the target countries found substitution difficult. Nevertheless, one country singled out by the Arabs as "unfriendly"—the Netherlands—soon found that it could meet its oil needs by indirect routes. The chief economic effects were produced by the huge oil price increases rather than by targeting specific countries for embargo. Even then, the effects were largely shifts in target countries' rhetoric (moderated public statements, nearly meaningless votes in the UN), not more substantive shifts. Probably the most important change was simply to increase the prominence of the Arab–Israeli conflict on the agenda of world leaders (especially the United States).[19]

The punishing state, too, must be able to substitute or be able to afford the cutbacks in supply or purchases. If the oil producers had desperately needed every petrodollar garnered from oil sales, then the embargo would not have worked. But there were plenty of other states in the world willing to purchase their oil, and most oil-producing states could easily accept a reduction in oil revenues. In other words, the state doing the punishing must not be as vulnerable to the threatened disruption as the state being punished.

---

[18] Johan Galtung, "On the Effects of Economic Sanctions, with Examples from the Case of Rhodesia," *World Politics* 19 (1967), 378–416.
[19] Roy Licklider, *Political Power and the Arab Oil Weapon* (Berkeley: University of California Press, 1988).

Although these conditions indicate how effective economic influence can be, they also indicate how difficult it is to achieve. A major debate over the necessity and utility of the Gulf War involved whether or not the economic sanctions imposed on Iraq would have forced Iraq to withdraw from Kuwait without war. It is clear that sanctions weakened the country considerably and made living conditions far more difficult. It is not clear, however, whether such effects would have moved Saddam Hussein to comply with the UN resolutions. The continued use of sanctions after the Gulf War has not ousted Hussein from power, but it has prevented Iraq from rebuilding its military forces. Continued sanctions are less for coercion than for prevention.

A similar debate on the effectiveness of sanctions surrounded the moves by the South African government to dismantle the apartheid system in 1991 and the consequent lifting of sanctions by the United States. These cases do show that the greater the number of states complying with sanctions, and the more complete that compliance (more so with Iraq than with South Africa), the greater the impact sanctions will have. They also raise the issue of the indirect nature of economic techniques and which segments of the population are actually punished. Especially in the recent case of Haiti, the argument can be made that the poorest people bear the heaviest costs of sanctions; sanctions affect the governing elites last and least. For sanctions to have an effect on leaders, either the leaders must care about the domestic conditions within their countries, or those deteriorating conditions must have the potential to result in their removal from office.

The success of economic sanctions needs to be measured in terms of the objectives sought through sanctions: compliance, subversion, deterrence, international symbolism, or domestic symbolism. Sanctions usually do not work in achieving compliance; they may be effective in subverting the government of another state only if the state is small and its government already shaky. A study of twentieth-century applications of economic sanctions determined that, overall, sanctions succeeded to a significant degree about a third of the time; when the objective was only modest policy changes, the success rate went up to about 40 percent. Sanctions are also of limited use as a deterrent. However, they can be useful as international and domestic symbols of political support, opposition, or ideology. Not so risky or provocative as the use of military force, they can still provide the public image of "doing something"[20] (while military actions have also occurred, the economic sanctions imposed on parts of the former Yugoslavia give the impression of doing something without really doing much). One study reviewing research on the impact of sanctions concludes simply that their success increases as the target's costs increase and where the target's socioeconomic and political systems are unstable.[21]

---

[20] Gary Hufbauer and Jeffrey Schott, *Economic Sanctions Reconsidered: History and Current Policy* (Washington, D.C.: Institute for International Economics, 1985); James M. Lindsay, "Trade and Economic Sanctions as Policy Instruments: A Reexamination," *International Studies Quarterly* 30 (June 1986), 153–173.

[21] See Peter A.G. van Bergeijk, "Effectivity of Economic Sanctions: Illusion or Reality," *Peace Economics, Peace Science, and Public Policy* 2 (Fall 1994), 24–35.

There are ways to fight back against economic sanctions, to reduce the costs they impose; Galtung mentions several. In 1973 and 1974, seven years after Galtung's article was published, the Nixon administration's energy policy for counteracting the Arab oil "weapon" matched Galtung's recommendations point for point. The major defensive strategy set out is one of self-sufficiency. Nixon announced that the American aim had to be self-sufficiency by 1980. Until self-sufficiency could be reached, he said, people should learn to sacrifice and even learn to like it. One of the first suggestions the Nixon administration made was that thermostats be turned down in homes, adding that cooler temperatures were healthier. The speed limit on American highways was cut to 55 miles per hour, and it was argued that in addition to saving fuel, this speed was also safer. But while the policy matched the prescription, the results did not. It may now be that self-sufficiency is an outmoded strategy in a highly interdependent world (see Chapters 16, 17, and 18).

Galtung also suggested changes in trade with other parties and perhaps even some form of smuggling. Perhaps the clearest example of this strategy was the use Iraq made of its permitted "humanitarian" links with Jordan. Also, at the time of the oil embargo, the United States organized the consumer states into the International Energy Agency as a means of coordinating energy policies, stockpiling, and providing mutual aid if another embargo occurred.

Finally, Galtung suggested that an economy restructure itself to absorb the loss of the embargoed material. The Nixon strategy included not only energy-saving activities by individuals, industry, and government, but also plans for increased mining of coal and more emphasis on nuclear-generated electricity. South Africa attempted to followed similar strategies, but Iraq had neither the time nor the resources to do so. In sum, just as one state aims for influence based on another's vulnerability, the vulnerable state attempts to cut down on the need for specific goods from specific sources.

## Controlling the Flow of Goods

States use various techniques *to control the flow of goods, services, and resources between states* (see Table 7.1). These controls can be used either to punish or to reward, cutting down or expanding the amount of the good being traded or making that good more or less expensive. A state can impose **tariffs** on products entering its borders, that is, taxes levied on imported goods to raise revenue or to regulate the flow of foreign goods into a country. This control is usually related to the protection of the country's domestic industries. If tariffs are raised, then a particular imported item becomes more expensive to purchase and fewer will be sold, particularly in relation to similar domestically produced goods. Low tariffs encourage trade and high ones discourage it. **Quotas** control imports not through prices but through the amount of goods permitted to enter a country from a specific source for a specific time period. The United States, for example, used to impose strict quotas on sugar from Cuba, the Dominican Republic, and other sources. By shifting the quotas around, some countries could be hurt and others helped. This method is particularly effective in dealing with countries that depend heavily on one crop that cannot be stored and thus has to be sold relatively quickly.

States might also grant a special trade status, such as **most-favored-nation (MFN) status,** as a form of influence. MFN status is based on nondiscrimination in trade: any tariff reductions granted to any country will also be extended to the trading partner given MFN status. In 1975 U.S. Senator Henry Jackson and others tried to influence Soviet policy on the emigration of Jews by holding up an agreement to extend MFN treatment to the USSR. The attempt failed. A similar situation arose with China after the brutal repression of the democracy movement in 1989; there was debate in the U.S. government over whether China should be punished by withdrawing MFN status. China has not been sanctioned through the withdrawal of MFN status—a good example of the difficulty of applying economic sanctions to a large economy where the state attempting influence will hurt its own markets as well. In essence, China is too large and important for the United States to effectively apply economic coercion (for instance, needing its cooperation on nuclear proliferation, or in the Security Council).

Other mechanisms for controlling trade include *loans and credits* to stimulate buying by lowering prices, as well as monetary policy to make the goods of one state more or less expensive given the devaluation or revaluation of the state's currency. Additionally, there are devices that can be used strictly to punish other states. These include the **boycott,** in which states cease to buy the goods, resources, or services of another state. Boycotts cut the target state off from its markets. Similarly, an **embargo** entails stopping the sales of economic items to another state. An embargo cuts off the target state's supply of resources and products from the outside.

## Foreign Aid

Finally, there is the matter of economic aid to other states. **Foreign aid** is a major carrot technique. It involves the transfer of economic goods or services from the donor to the recipient. These might be any resource or commodity, money, service, or technical advice. In the economically developing countries, the needs for development capital (money and goods) and for the technical and technological skills to build a modern economy are particularly high. Aid is therefore very useful in dealing with most of the states in the international system today. Giving or withholding aid, attempting to create dependencies through its use, and attempting to substitute aid from one state for that from another are all common strategies for influence (or escape from that influence).

Aid may be used for military assistance, economic development, or relief. The aid may come as outright grants, loans, sales, or technical assistance. In the 1950s and the 1960s grants were the preferred form of aid. More recently, technical assistance and loans have assumed a greater role. Bilateral aid, which is provided by one state directly to another, is particularly susceptible to manipulation. Dependence relationships can be created. Aid may go to states where the donor country wants to strengthen its trading interests or to establish new investments. Donor countries often provide bilateral aid with strings: "tied aid" means that the recipient may be required to buy or trade for goods it does not want or need if it is to receive the aid that it desires. Much of bilateral economic aid goes to countries where the donor expects to gain some clear benefit for its foreign and national security policy. About half of all U.S. bilateral economic assistance, for example, goes to just two countries, Egypt and

Israel. That assistance is provided for obvious political purposes. U.S. aid to Egypt displaced Soviet influence. It was also meant to compensate the Egyptians for the loss of Arab economic aid as a result of the Israeli–Egyptian peace treaty in 1979. Israel has been an important U.S. strategic ally.

Much foreign aid, however, is not given primarily to serve narrow economic interests, as radical theorists might expect, or strategic interests, as realist theorists would predict. Some is provided mainly for immediate humanitarian purposes; for example, to offer relief from earthquakes and famines. To distance themselves from donors' foreign policy aims, recipients typically prefer *multilateral aid,* assistance given through international organizations such as the World Bank, other UN agencies, or regional organizations like the Inter-American Development Bank or the Asian Development Bank. This aid is less subject to donor manipulation, although the United States does have a great deal of influence over World Bank lending decisions. About one-third of all the aid by rich capitalist countries has been channeled through multilateral agencies, so it could not be tied to particular donors. In 1991–92 both Britain and Denmark provided about 45 percent of their foreign aid through multilateral programs (the U.S. figure was 25 percent). U.S. actions are not typical of all aid-giving countries. Those that have given the most aid on a per capita basis—Denmark, the Netherlands, Norway, Sweden—have not directed their aid to where it served evident economic and strategic interests. Those donor countries, with strong welfare states at home, have been primarily motivated by the desire to promote the economic development of poor countries. Overall, about 60 percent of all the economic aid, and over two-thirds of all the multilateral aid, from the wealthy countries has gone to the poorest ones. More abstract concerns for development and justice—not just the donors' immediate national interests—have mattered, as idealists or transnationalists would hope.[22]

## CONCLUSION

In this chapter we have reviewed some of the basic techniques states use to interact and exert influence over one another. We have taken only a brief look at the major diplomatic, military, and economic methods for exercising influence; many related topics have been touched upon only lightly or even skipped entirely. Psychological techniques for exerting influence were mentioned in the previous chapter. The ideological overlay of the cold war prompted heavy use of this indirect technique, whereby states attempt to influence the values, attitudes, and behavior of the people (or specific

---

[22] David H. Lumsdaine, *Ideals and Interests: The Foreign Aid Regime, 1949–1986* (Princeton, N.J.: Princeton University Press, 1992). See also David Cingranelli, *Ethics, American Foreign Policy and the Third World* (New York: St. Martin's, 1993). See Steven Hook, *National Interest and Foreign Aid* (Boulder, Colo.: Rienner, 1995), for comparative analyses contrasting the aid-giving objectives and policies of major donor states.

groups of people) in other countries. Radio and television (such as Voice of America and Radio Free Europe), films, and cultural materials are aimed at the populations of opponents, allies, and neutrals alike. Propaganda is an important tool in attempting to increase other people's respect or improve their images of your rectitude.

A state's menu depends in large part on the array of techniques it possesses to influence other international actors. Its menu is also constrained by the attempts of others to influence that state. The tools for influence that a state possesses very much depend on its capabilities and how those capabilities stand in relation to the capabilities of others. In the next two chapters we shall move within the domestic system of each state and look at the characteristics of the society and government. We have already provided a very general idea of how these domestic factors might influence the foreign policy menu of decision makers, and now we shall study these topics in depth.

# DOMESTIC CONSTRAINTS: DO COUNTRIES WITH DIFFERENT ECONOMIC, SOCIAL, AND POLITICAL SYSTEMS PRODUCE DIFFERENT FOREIGN POLICIES?

WORLD SYSTEM

RELATIONS

SOCIETY

GOVERNMENT

ROLE

INDIVIDUAL

In the past four chapters we discussed elements of constraint and opportunity that originate outside the nation-state. In the next two we shall look at major aspects of the nation-state itself that constrain the possibilities and probabilities open to foreign policy decision makers. According to Henry Kissinger, statesmen are constrained by two sets of influences: politics, power, and actions of other states; and domestic constraints, ranging from public opinion to the attitudes of the government and bureaucracy. The ideal statesman must be able to take both sets into account, deal with them, and master them. Commenting on all the statesmen whom observers claimed (incorrectly) he was trying to emulate, Kissinger said that they had in some way failed to take into account or deal with one of these sets of constraints. A great leader must understand these constraints, master them, and transcend them, bending them to his own will. Contemporary analysts stress the linkages between domestic and international politics, looking at the task of governmental leaders as one of playing simultaneous **two-level games**—dealing with domestic pressures and creating domestic political coalitions at one level, while also trying to deal with other international actors.[1]

We shall begin with some fairly general problems in the comparative analysis of foreign policy, dealing chiefly with *societal* influences but also referring at some points to influences operating from the *governmental* level of analysis. In the second part of this chapter we shall consider a particularly important societal influence on foreign policy: *the economic system of a society.* In Chapter 9 we shall discuss aspects of governmental structure.

These domestic constraints affect both opportunity and willingness, both what is possible and what is probable. What is possible for a set of decision makers is constrained by their capabilities—not only promoting certain kinds of behavior but also ultimately allowing certain kinds of behavior to occur. Decisions to mobilize capabilities—turning them into reality—increase the range of possibilities and probabilities of certain kinds of behavior. An example in the military sphere was the rapid and striking growth of Soviet naval power during the 1960s and 1970s, making the country a global power; growth in South Korea's steel industry has been just as important for that country's menu.

## FOREIGN POLICY: WHAT IT IS AND HOW WE STUDY IT

Foreign policy is the stuff of international relations, but people do not agree on exactly what should be included in the term. Different analysts have been concerned with the policies that states declare, the decisions made within governmental circles, the processes by which governments arrive at policies and decisions, the actions actually taken by governments, and the consequences of the behavior of governments and their official representatives. Foreign policy is the output of the state into the global

---

[1] Kissinger expressed these sentiments in *A World Restored: Metternich, Castlereagh, and the Problems of Peace, 1812–1822* (Boston: Houghton Mifflin, 1957), and "Domestic Structure and Foreign Policy," *Daedalus* 95 (1966), 503–529. See also Robert D. Putnam, "Diplomacy and Domestic Politics: The Logic of Two-Level Games," *International Organization* 42 (Summer 1988), 427–462, and George Tsebelis, *Nested Games* (Berkeley: University of California Press, 1990).

system. Indeed, for some analysts the primary way to study foreign policy is to look only at what has actually happened, at events.[2]

One way to approach the concept of foreign policy is to break it down into its component parts. We can think of policy as a decision or set of decisions or programs that act as a guide to behavior. Policy is a guide to an action or a set of actions intended to realize the goals an organization has set for itself. Policy is rooted in the concept of *choice:* choosing actions (or making decisions) to achieve one's goals. These choices should be reasoned, in the minimal sense of comparing choices to see how well they achieve desired goals.

The ideas of sovereignty and territoriality help us understand what "foreign" means. Sovereignty means control of the territory that exists inside the legal boundaries of the state. Anything beyond those legal boundaries, in areas where the state has no legal authority over people or territory, is foreign. **Foreign policy** is thus a set of guides to choices being made about people, places, and things beyond the boundaries of the state. Although there are different perspectives on the nature of foreign policy, it is possible to uncover several common features.

First, like power, foreign policy—whether we are talking about the process of creating decisions, making decisions, or implementing decisions—is *relational*. The intention of foreign policy is to affect the behavior of other actors, even if only in general terms: how they relate to international organizations, how closely they obey international law, and so on. Because nothing is distributed equally in the global system, every state requires resources, economic goods, military capabilities, political and strategic support, and cooperation and coordination with all other actors. Foreign policy thus concerns behavior toward some other actor for some reason.

Whether the *actual* behavior of a state matches its intentions is another matter. Much of foreign policy analysis is directed toward this question of the links between the intentions of behavior and its consequences. Realist and radical views of foreign policy, which stress the role of power in world politics, claim that foreign policy is based on the idea of continually trying to influence or control other actors, to get them to behave in ways beneficial to one's own state. There are, as we have seen, however, many kinds of goals and many kinds of influence.

Foreign policy, as both process and output, is the link between activities inside a state and the world environment outside it. It puts any state into communication with the external world. As noted by James Rosenau, the analysis of foreign policy is a "bridging discipline" that "takes as its focus of study the bridges that whole systems

---

[2] Both the promise and the problems of events data have received a great deal of scholarly attention. Recent work on events data employ sophisticated computer-based "artificial intelligence" techniques, which attempt to capture not only foreign policy outcomes but also the processes leading to those events. See Richard L. Merritt, Robert G. Muncaster, and Dina A. Zinnes, eds., *International Event-Data Developments* (Ann Arbor: University of Michigan Press, 1993), and Gavan Duffy, ed., special issue, "New Directions in Event Data Analysis," *International Interactions* 20, 1–2 (1994).

called nation-states build to link themselves and their subsystems to even more encompassing international systems of which they are a part."[3]

Rosenau, among others, calls for a comparative approach to the study of foreign policy processes and behavior, looking for patterns of behavior associated with different types of states under different conditions and within different contexts. The key question then becomes *what to compare*. What exactly are we trying to explain? (What is the dependent variable?) What is the explanation? (What is the independent variable?) That is, in trying to explain foreign policy behavior, whether the policy process, policies, decisions, or events, what factors, influences, and characteristics should be investigated?

Any "fact" about the world, or any variable, can be defined along three different dimensions: (1) it is only one of many possible variables (characteristics, types of behavior, relationships, etc.); (2) it is selected from some particular case (a nation-state or some other international actor); and (3) it is drawn from some specific point in time. Thus we can compare the effects of different variables on the foreign policy process or outcome, we can compare states in terms of their processes or behavior, and we can compare processes or behavior across time.

The question of what to compare thus involves very basic decisions about the units involved in the comparisons. For example, does one compare the most different or the most similar units? Should one try to compare many states at one point in time? One state across many time periods? A large number of units across different time periods? Do we compare foreign policies in terms of evaluating their success or failure? Or in terms of normative issues such as whether the foreign policy produces "good" or "bad" outcomes? The answers depend to a great extent on just what research problem we are confronting.

It makes sense to study foreign policy comparatively because regular patterns of variation can be identified and explained. In a classic work on the comparative study of foreign policy, Rosenau presented a "pretheory" of foreign policy. He argued that all influences on foreign policy (independent variables) could be categorized according to level of analysis, and that we needed to determine the relative importance of variables from each of the different levels of analysis (individual, role, societal, etc.) in affecting the foreign policy of states. Rosenau also recognized that there were significant differences among states, so he specified three critical dimensions: size (large or small), economic development (developed or underdeveloped), and the nature of the political system ("open" or "closed"). He then proposed which variables should have what effects on different types of states.[4] Since all comparison involves measurement

---

[3] James N. Rosenau, "Introduction: New Directions and Recurrent Questions in the Comparative Study of Foreign Policy," in Charles F. Hermann, Charles W. Kegley, Jr., and James N. Rosenau, eds., *New Directions in the Study of Foreign Policy* (Boston: Allen & Unwin, 1987), p. 1.

[4] James N. Rosenau, "Pre-Theories and Theories of Foreign Policy," In R. Barry Farrell, ed., *Approaches to Comparative and International Politics* (Evanston, Ill.: Northwestern University Press, 1966), pp. 27–92. For a classic statement of the comparative method, see Adam Przeworski and Henry Teune, *The Logic of Comparative Social Inquiry* (New York: Wiley, 1970); for a more recent overview, see David Collier, "The Comparative Method," in Ada W. Finifter, ed., *Political Science: The State of the Discipline II* (Washington, D.C.: American Political Science Association, 1993), pp. 105–119.

of some sort, many of Rosenau's hypotheses have been tested using quantitative data. One result has been the confirmation that his three dimensions (size, development, nature of government) are indeed central to the explanation of foreign policy.

Most current efforts in the comparative analysis of foreign policy focus on describing and modeling the foreign policy *process:* identifying the important decision units, looking at how individuals and groups perceive foreign policy problems and solutions, describing the dynamics of interaction between groups of decision makers (either within the same government or across state boundaries). Current studies also grapple with the important effects of interdependence. As we shall see in Part II, interdependence among international actors causes us to look much more closely at the influence of economics on foreign policy–making and blurs the traditional distinctions between domestic and foreign policy.

This approach to foreign policy analysis can be translated into a question: Which parts of the environment, or the menu, will be most closely studied by the decision makers of a particular state, under what conditions, and at what stage of the foreign policy–making process? This process begins with the formulation of foreign policy goals and continues as policymakers attempt to adapt these goals to domestic and international environments. This environmental model, which looks at foreign policy as process, output, outcomes, and effects and takes both domestic and external factors into account, is presented in Figure 8.1.

## GOALS AND OBJECTIVES OF FOREIGN POLICY

We can broadly describe foreign policy objectives as those things that leaders of states pursue. The leaders of states have different and changing foreign policy and role orientations. Objectives evolve and there is debate over how those objectives are best pursued; rarely is there national agreement or consensus on what the foreign policy interest should be. Foreign policy decision making "involves the discovery of goals as much as it involves using decisions to achieve particular outcomes."[5]

We may think of a foreign policy objective as an "image of a future state of affairs and future conditions that governments through individual policy makers aspire to bring about by wielding influence abroad and by changing or sustaining the behavior of other states."[6] Objectives may be very concrete: Iraq sought territory in Iran that would give it control over the Shatt al-Arab waterway (and thus precipitated the Iran–Iraq war). Objectives may be much less concrete: creating images or promoting a specific set of values, such as "making the world safe for democracy." Some objectives, often geopolitical ones, remain constant over long periods of time, like the Russian desire for warm-water ports or the British desire for command of the seas. Others are

---

[5] Paul A. Anderson, "What Do Decision Makers Do When They Make a Foreign Policy Decision?" in Hermann, Kegley, and Rosenau, eds., *New Directions*, p. 290.
[6] See K. J. Holsti, *International Politics: A Framework for Analysis*, 5th ed. (Englewood Cliffs, N.J.: Prentice-Hall, 1988), chaps. 4–5. The quotation is from p. 119, citing the words of Snyder, Bruck, and Sapin.

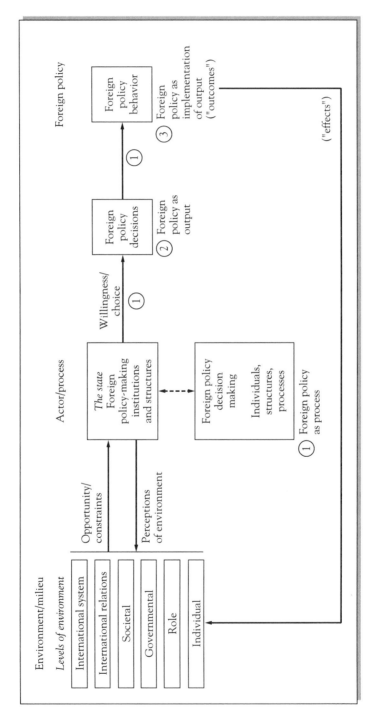

**Figure 8.1** An environmental model for foreign policy analysis. [*Source:* Maria Papadakis and Harvey Starr, "Opportunity, Willingness, and Small States: The Relationship Between Environment and Foreign Policy," in Charles F. Hermann, Charles W. Kegley, and James N. Rosenau, eds., *New Directions in the Study of Foreign Policy* (Boston: Allen & Unwin, 1987), p. 417.]

transitory, perhaps changing from month to month; monetary policy is an example. Some objectives have consequences that affect the whole state; for example, the deterrence of nuclear attack. Still others, mostly economic but sometimes political ones, that aim to keep a particular government in power involve the interests of only a small portion of society. Governments often pursue incompatible objectives. Such was the case when the United States sold huge quantities of wheat to the Soviet Union in 1971 and 1972. The deal would help improve relations with the Soviet Union and might ultimately help the Nixon administration disengage from the American involvement in Vietnam; on the other hand, the administration also wanted to control inflation, keep food prices down, and increase the well-being of the American people. Less societywide objectives were also involved: the 1972 presidential election and profit seeking by certain farm and food transportation groups.

In sum, leaders of states seek a wide range of private and public objectives, some concrete, some quite abstract, and very often in conflict. One factor distinguishing the transnational and radical perspectives from the realist one is the types of objectives that are the focus of their worldviews. Realists stress immediate military/security objectives and downplay economic ones. For transnationalists especially, central foreign policy objectives involve the longer-term economic and social welfare of the state.

## ECONOMIC AND POLITICAL DIFFERENCES

Decision makers act in the names of their states. As we have seen, countries differ in size, income level, and other characteristics that affect both their capabilities and their goals. They also differ in their histories as nations, in the ways their societies and economies are organized, and in the structure of their governments. Compare, for a moment, the United States and Russia.

The United States is a country founded largely by immigrants who came to develop a vast and sparsely populated land and to construct a society in a wilderness. Most people came to the new land to realize hopes that were constrained in their home countries—hopes for political or religious expression or for economic well-being. Their experience in America often offered opportunity and rewarded individual initiative. Especially important for foreign policy, the new land was largely safe from external enemies. Once independence had been won from Britain, the limited transportation technology of the time insulated America from Europe's national wars and provided a security that prevailed for a century and a half.

Russia, by contrast, is inhabited by people who have traditionally lived in insecurity, typified by the wooden stockade fortresses that once dotted the harsh Eurasian plains. Russia was periodically conquered or invaded by Mongols, Poles, Swedes, and Germans, among others. It was ruled by autocratic leaders whose chief virtue was their ability to provide a measure of national unity and strength to ward off attackers. In time the Russian state expanded, ruling its neighbors instead of being threatened by them. As a multinational empire, czarist Russia, and later the Soviet Union, governed or repressed many subordinate nations, whose total population approached that of Russia alone. Economically, czarist Russia was a relatively primitive society, following well behind Europe in the development of industry and the accumulation of capital. When the communists took power in 1917, their ideology seemed a threat to the entire capitalist world as they proclaimed the virtues of world revolution. From 1918 to 1920, European, American, and Japanese forces intervened indecisively on the side of the czarist counterrevolutionaries. The communists ultimately consolidated their power, but only by confirming and deepening the Russian autocratic tradition. They built a modern, centralized, industrial state, one finally capable of providing security from invasion; at the same time, in the inexorable working out of the security dilemma, they became a constant threat to their neighbors.

Thus Americans live with a tradition of security that allows them periodic forays into world politics but protects them from basic threats to national survival. Russians, by contrast, live with a tradition of insecurity and mutually threatening relations with others. Americans live with an economy developed by individual enterprise that provides an unusual measure of opportunity for many (economic development is thought to proceed best when it is least fettered by state interference). Today's Russians live in an economy in which capitalist development began late and was cut short and in which, under the communists, development was controlled and directed by the state bureaucracy. Americans live in a state where the government provided the religious and political liberty so many of its immigrants sought, as well as the freedom for capitalist development. Russians live in a state where people welcomed state control; without control, there could be no unity, no security, and little prosperity.

The experiences of American and Russian citizens—and the selective memories they have of their parents' experiences—help provide the basic structure of belief and ideology through which these citizens view their place in the world and hence the appropriate roles and actions of their governments. These experiences also determine the structure of their economies and governments: capitalist and democratic in the first instance, for a long time socialist and authoritarian in the second.

Furthermore, those individuals, groups, and classes dominant within societies use their power to perpetuate belief systems that will reinforce their power. Americans are taught an ideology that praises freedom and extols capitalism as the engine of prosperity. Russians were taught an ideology that praised the state as provider of individual and collective security. If we exaggerate somewhat, we can say that in America the form of the economy shaped the kind of state that emerged: an economy of relatively decentralized, plural centers of power whose interest was best served by limiting state control. By contrast, during Soviet control, the state—through state ownership of the means of industrial production, collectivization of agriculture, and centralized planning—determined the kind of economy that emerged. An irony is that both nation-states developed under conditions that no longer apply, and their structures therefore seem obsolete. The United States is no longer isolated in the world, the continent is no longer undeveloped, and threats to survival stem largely from the military, economic, and environmental interdependence between Americans and others. The Soviet Union achieved an unprecedented degree of military security; but the state bureaucracy became a burden on individual and national development, directly leading to the predicaments facing present-day Russia.

How much difference do these contrasting histories make for foreign policy? These different pictures may be seen as contrasts in the **cultures** of Americans and

Russians—the broadly accepted sets of norms that guide behavior and the common cognitive maps that pass from generation to generation. It is important to understand culture, cultural differences, and the impact of culture in the formation and implementation of foreign policy, especially when implementation involves bargaining. Some of the strains in Japanese–American relations are attributed to such cultural differences.[7]

Linking these historical and cultural differences to analyses of democracy to be developed later is the question of whether states that are more democratic are also more peaceful and less threatening to their neighbors. It would be reassuring for people who live in democratic countries to believe that their own freedoms made them readier to respect the freedoms of others and desirous only of enjoying their own freedom in peace. Many have thought this true. The American sociologist Seymour Martin Lipset in 1960 dedicated a book to his children in the hope "that they may grow up in a more democratic and, therefore, more peaceful world."[8] Many have feared that autocratic states, because their rulers are less restrained by peace-loving citizens, may indulge their desires for foreign conquest or try to use some imagined foreign threat to unify their peoples.

By contrast, others have feared a crusading spirit in many democracies, inverting Woodrow Wilson's wartime goal, "to make the world safe for democracy," and wondering instead how to make democracy safe for the world. Hypotheses about the effect of different systems of economic organization also abound. These range from propositions about the alleged need of capitalists for world peace and prosperity to statements about the alleged need of capitalists for forcible acquisition of foreign peoples, markets, and resources. Other theories—which we will examine in Chapter 15—insist that the demands of foreign investors and domestic capitalists allied with foreign interests distort the economies, foreign policies, and domestic governments of less developed countries, gravely harming most of their citizens. This range of theories represents the range of worldviews—realist, transnationalist, idealist, and radical.

## NATIONAL INTEREST, PARTICULAR (ECONOMIC) INTERESTS, AND GOVERNMENT STRUCTURE

Realist theory stresses the role of **national interest** in determining states' behavior. Any government, whether democratically controlled or not, will pursue such interests in what power-politics theorists see as the anarchic world of "each against all." In general, realists look at states as "unitary actors," entities with one set of values, preferences, and objectives, which speak with one voice (the "national interest"). In

---

[7] The characterization of culture presented is derived from a broad survey of anthropology; see Milton Singer, "Culture: The Concept of Culture," in David Sills, ed., *International Encyclopedia of the Social Sciences* (New York: Macmillan, 1968), pp. 527–543. For treatments of culture in international politics, see Adda B. Bozeman, *Politics and Culture in International History* (Princeton, N.J.: Princeton University Press, 1960), and Edward W. Said, *Culture and Imperialism* (New York: Random House, 1993).

[8] Seymour Martin Lipset, *Political Man* (Garden City, N.Y.: Doubleday, 1960).

addition, these objectives are determined by the state's power, especially where in the global power-hierarchy the state is located. One difficulty with such theories is that they can easily become mere tautologies, statements that are merely definitions and hence impossible to refute. For example, one can construct arguments to prove that any action, whether initiating a war or keeping the peace, is intended to enhance or preserve the power of the nation-state.

Even when this kind of argument is avoided, however, the fact that different countries have different histories, cultures, and socioeconomic and political structures means that foreign policy preferences or objectives (and thus also foreign policy strategies) derive in large part from the society inside a country, not from its place in the structure of the international system.[9]

We also cannot ignore the fact that within any given nation-state, different individuals, groups, and classes have different interests. Workers share some interests with factory owners (for instance, in seeing that their products can be sold), but they differ sharply on others (such as who gains more from the production of those goods and whether it is better to manufacture goods with high-priced American labor or with cheap labor in a less developed country). Some manufacturers are interested in selling consumer goods in a world at peace; others want to sell armaments that have a market only in a world where states are at war or threatened by war. It then becomes essential to ask, *Whose particular interest is reflected in any particular governmental policy or act?* Which individuals, groups, or classes are most influential in determining government policy? Does this change from time to time or under different international or domestic conditions? Are there some issues on which one group or class has a dominant influence and others on which some other group is dominant? These questions are absolutely unavoidable in any political system where there are several individuals or groups and where each has different wishes or interests. Contrary to the realist assumption, states are not unitary actors with a single purpose. Unless we know how different interests are reconciled into a single decision, we cannot know what particular policy will result. Without more attention to this, our previous discussion of state goals and objectives is necessarily incomplete.

This problem has been well known for a long time and has been elaborated in what is now known as *Arrow's paradox of voting*.[10] Some aspects of the problem can be seen if we imagine that Dick likes peanuts, Jane likes potato chips, and Spot likes dog biscuits. Dick finds a dollar, which will buy only one of the three desired foods. Which do they buy?

---

[9]One study provides a variant of our argument, by analytically distinguishing hawks from doves based on domestic preferences. Doves differ from hawks by preferring to negotiate with rather than coerce an adversary. Additionally, some doves will prefer to capitulate without fighting if attacked, while tough doves will prefer war to capitulation. See Bruce Bueno de Mesquita and David Lalman, *War and Reason* (New Haven, Conn.: Yale University Press, 1992). The point is simple—even formal analyses that encompass many realist assumptions demonstrate the weaknesses of the central realist premises, which ignore domestic factors. See also Bruce Russett, "Processes of Dyadic Choice for War and Peace," *World Politics* 47 (January 1995), 268–282.

[10] Kenneth Arrow, *Social Choice and Individual Values*, 2nd ed. (New York: Wiley, 1963).

It depends. It depends on who is in charge and what his or her preferences are. If Dick is in charge because he found the dollar, and if he chooses to please himself, they will have peanuts. If he chooses to be generous and to please Jane, they will have potato chips. If Jane is in charge (she is older and bigger and takes the dollar), they will have potato chips. If either Dick or Jane chooses to be generous, they may have dog biscuits. (Spot, a member of a weak and inarticulate class, cannot be in charge, so they are not going to have dog biscuits unless the person in charge chooses to be generous to Spot.) In any case, we know what the decision will be only if we know who is in charge and whose taste that person wants to please or what decision rule is used.

If we can imagine Dick, Jane, and Spot in a perfect democracy (dogs and people have equal votes), each holding out for his or her first choice, there is no way to identify a group interest that can be served. Only if we have additional information on preferences or decision making (for example, they may take turns, so Jane gets her way today and Dick tomorrow; or they both hate dog biscuits and Spot likes potato chips almost as much as dog biscuits, and second choices are taken into account) can we begin to make a prediction or identify a way in which their different interests can be combined.

The same is true with much larger social systems like countries: we must know how individual preferences become collective choices—who is in charge, how compromises are reached, how these decision-making procedures differ in different times and circumstances—if we want to talk about what a government may do. That's why it is vital to know what the *structure of the government* of a state is. Whose particular interests will it serve at any particular time? Does the structure of the economy give particular groups or classes (such as finance capitalists or the managers of state-owned enterprises or members of certain tribes, castes, or ethnic groups) particular clout on a particular issue? The realist concept of a national interest may indicate certain core values or goals that most citizens share to some degree (for example, peace, prosperity, and security), but until we break away from the notion of a unitary national decision maker—that is, until we know how different actors' interests are aggregated—we know very little about the *priorities* of the various values or goals or about how they will be pursued in international politics.

# GOVERNMENTAL OPENNESS: DEMOCRACY AND CONFLICT

The ability of a government to control society and the ability of specific interests in society to communicate their needs and demands to government are both related to the openness of government. **Openness** is the extent to which a government is subject to influences from society. This means that a government is accountable: it must satisfy the people of its society or it can be removed from office by regular, agreed-on procedures that are fair by some criterion or other. Being open means that *opposition groups in society can contest groups in government* for the right to control the government through some type of electoral procedures. Being open means that such opposition groups can present their positions and ideologies to the people through a free press and other media, and no group is systematically prevented from acting as an opposition. In the contemporary era, "democracy" denotes a country in which nearly everyone can vote, elections are freely contested, the chief executive is chosen by popular vote or by an elected parliament, and civil rights and civil liberties are substantially guaranteed.[11] (In open societies, the opposition also has responsibilities. Just as the government allows fair procedures that decide who is to run the government, the opposition must also agree to contest for office in a fair manner—that is, if the opposition loses a fair election, it does not run off to start a guerrilla war.)

Realists say that all states must fight when necessary to serve the national interest of power and survival; the type of domestic political organization will make little difference. Liberal transnationalists often claim that democracies are inherently more peaceful than other states. And Marxists and some other radicals regard bourgeois capitalist democracies as inherently aggressive, arguing that socialist or communist states would live peacefully with one another. In this controversy the realists have the best case. There is little evidence to support claims for the superior peacefulness of any particular form of societal, economic, or governmental organization. Studies of large numbers of states, either in the contemporary international system or over the past two centuries, have found no consistent relationship between the frequency of engaging in international war and having a democratic rather than an authoritarian political system or a capitalist rather than a socialist economy. Democracies may not be peaceful in general—we know the history of democracies in colonialism, covert intervention, and other excesses of power. Overall, democracies are nearly as violence-prone in their relations with authoritarian states as authoritarian states are toward each other.

The pioneering peace scientist Lewis Richardson showed that individual states cannot be characterized as inherently warlike or peaceful, as their histories show. Sweden once fought many wars, but since 1815 it has been at peace, as have Germany and Japan since 1945. Many great powers, however, tend to fight many wars as long as they remain great powers. The Correlates of War Project, studying the period between 1816 and 1980, identified 118 large-scale international wars. The top three states in war involvement were France, Britain, and Russia. France was involved in 19 percent of the conflicts and Britain and Russia in 16 percent.[12]

Britain and France, democracies during most of the period, were *not* more peaceful, especially when extrasystemic colonial or imperialist wars and interventions in the internal conflicts of other countries in the post–World War II era are considered.

---

[11] In Appendix B, along with data on population, area, and other societal characteristics, we present a code for political system type or degree of political freedom as those freedoms are known in democracies. The code characterizes states as free, partly free, or not free on the basis of whether free, honest, and competitive elections are held; whether civil liberties (free speech, free assembly, and assurance of a fair trial) are present; and whether political terrorism is largely absent. By these characterizations, 73 of 190 countries (38.4 percent) could be coded as free in 1993; free and partly free countries accounted for 74.7 percent of the international system.

[12] See Lewis F. Richardson, *Statistics of Deadly Quarrels* (Chicago: Quadrangle, 1960); Melvin Small and J. David Singer, *Resort to Arms: International and Civil Wars, 1816–1980* (Beverly Hills, Calif.: Sage, 1982).

However, if the focus is on pairs of countries—do democracies fight against democracies?—then democracies *are* more peaceful.[13]

The relations between stable democracies are qualitatively different. A vision of peace among democratically governed nation-states has long been invoked as part of a configuration of institutions and practices that reduce war. In 1795 Immanuel Kant spoke of perpetual peace based in part on states that shared "republican constitutions."[14] Woodrow Wilson expressed the same conviction in his 1917 war message to Congress when he asserted that "a steadfast concert of peace can never be maintained except by a partnership of democratic nations." This vision once sounded utopian. But now, at the end of the twentieth century, it is newly plausible, indeed figuring in President Clinton's 1994 State of the Union message.

The research of social scientists points to an irrefutable observation: stable democracies are unlikely to engage in militarized disputes with each other or to let any such disputes escalate into war. In fact, they rarely even skirmish. Since 1946 pairs of democratic states have been only one-eighth as likely as other kinds of states to threaten to use force against each other and only one-tenth as likely actually to do so. Established democracies fought no wars against each other during the entire twentieth century. (Although Finland, for example, took the Axis side against the Soviet Union in World War II, it engaged in no combat with the democracies.)

The more democratic each state is, the more peaceful their relations are likely to be. Democracies are more likely to reciprocate each other's behavior, to accept third-party mediation or good offices in settling disputes, and to settle disputes peacefully. Democracies' relatively peaceful relations with each other are not spuriously caused by some other influence such as sharing high levels of wealth, or rapid growth, or ties of alliance or economic interdependence.[15] The phenomenon of peace between democracies is not limited just to the rich industrialized states of the global North. It was not maintained simply by pressure from a common adversary in the cold war, and it has outlasted that threat.

Peace among democracies derives in part from cultural restraints on conflict, primarily from the belief that it would be wrong to fight another democracy. This

---

[13] The literature on democracy and foreign policy, especially the "democratic peace," is expanding rapidly. Much of this section reflects analysis presented in Bruce Russett, *Grasping the Democratic Peace* (Princeton, N.J.: Princeton University Press, 1993). Other good overviews can be found in Bruce Bueno de Mesquita, Robert Jackman, and Randolph Siverson, eds., special issue, "Democracy and Foreign Policy: Community and Constraint," *Journal of Conflict Resolution* 35 (June 1991); "Special Section: Democracy, War and Peace," *Journal of Peace Research* 29 (November 1992); and Steve Chan, ed., special issue, "Democracy and War: Research and Reflections," *International Interactions* 18, 3 (1993).

[14] For a review and application of Kant's thought to international politics, see Michael Doyle, "Kant, Liberal Legacies, and Foreign Affairs," parts 1 and 2, *Philosophy and Public Affairs* 12: 3–4 (1983), 205–235, 323–353; see also, Cecelia Lynch, "Kant, the Republican Peace, and Moral Guidance in International Law," *Ethics and International Affairs* 8 (1994), 49–58.

[15] See Stuart A. Bremer, "Dangerous Dyads: Conditions Affecting the Likelihood of Interstate War, 1816–1965," *Journal of Conflict Resolution* 36 (June 1992), 309–341, and the chapter with Zeev Maoz in Russett, *Grasping the Democratic Peace.*

explanation extends into the international arena the domestic cultural norms of live-and-let-live and peaceful conflict resolution that operate within democracies. The phenomenon of **democratic peace** can also be explained by the role of institutional restraints on democracies' decisions to go to war. It is a complicated procedure to persuade the people, the legislature, and other independent institutions that war is necessary. Consequently, those restraints insure that any state in a conflict of interest with another democracy can expect ample time for conflict-resolution processes to be effective and virtually no risk of incurring surprise attack.

Evidence supports both the cultural and institutional explanations; they reinforce each other. The cultural explanation may be somewhat more powerful, however. A culture of democracy, manifested in the absence of violence in domestic politics and the duration of stable democratic regimes, seems to exert a somewhat stronger influence on peace among democracies than do particular institutional constraints.

Nonindustrial societies, studied by anthropologists, also show restraints on warfare among democratically organized polities that typically lack the institutional constraints of a modern state. Despite that absence, democratically organized units fight each other sigificantly less often than do nondemocratic units. And political stability also proves an important restraint on the resort to violence by these democratically organized units. Finding the relationship between democracy and peace in preindustrial societies shows that the phenomenon of democratic peace is not limited to contemporary Western democracies.[16]

Remember, a democratic peace requires the stability of democracy and involves perceptions of stability. As noted with the concept of culture, "stable" democracy depends in large part on a broadly shared value system that is transmitted across generations. For the near future, at least, that condition is likely to be in short supply in much of the world. If one's neighbor has vast unsolved economic problems, is it politically stable? Has it experienced democracy long enough, with some success in managing its problems—especially an intense or extended period of crisis—to be stable? If it is "democratic" for some, even a majority, of its citizens but forcibly represses its minorities, is it stable? Many of the new states of the old Soviet Union fail these and other tests. Some have not yet had a real democratic transition.

When one looks not at the war-proneness of certain types of political systems in general, but rather at how different types of systems adjust their foreign policies to manage and respond to domestic conflict, domestic factors do make a difference. Characteristics of a society—societal variables—are more influential in affecting foreign policy in truly open or democratic societies than in closed ones. For states where the political process is more authoritarian or closed, it is more useful to look at characteristics of the governments and their structures than at attributes of their societies to explain foreign policy, since in closed societies public opinion and political interests will have less impact.

---

[16] See the chapter written with Carol Ember and Melvin Ember in Russett, *Grasping the Democratic Peace,* and Neta Crawford, "A Security Regime Among Democracies: Cooperation Among Iroquois Nations," *International Organization* 48, 3 (1994), 345–86.

In general, whether a state is confronted with riots, protests, or guerrilla warfare at home tells us little about the likelihood that it will be engaged in conflict with foreign enemies. Many patterns are possible. Internal conflict, as a major type of domestic condition or constraint, may weaken a state and make it an attractive target for another state (this includes all the types of intervention). Sometimes revolution can bring new energy and strength to a country, making it seem a threat to its neighbors and thus also a target for attack (this occurred after the French Revolution). This same vigor and strength might also lead revolutionary states to try to export the revolution; again, the French Revolution, as well as some communist revolutions (Cuba), come to mind.

The initiation of war by governments weakened or threatened by domestic conflict is also the central feature of the "diversionary" theories of war, or theories based on the conflict–cohesion hypothesis. Here, war is used as a means to divert populations from internal violence, domestic grievances, and the like—to refocus energy from internal conflict to an external enemy and promote cohesion through the need to pull together in order to defeat an external enemy. Governments may thus use diplomatic conflict as an excuse to rally their own people behind the government.[17]

A major theme in the study of revolution is that losing a war weakens a government's legitimacy through decreasing its ability to meet society's expectations. A second major theme is that war weakens legitimacy and promotes opposition and dissent because it forces government to extend and deepen its *extraction* of societal resources. As governments seek to take greater resources from society, resistance is generated. Involvement in foreign wars may stimulate domestic protest and dissension. In the United States, the Vietnam War led to domestic turmoil, not vice versa. Democracies, where governments may be unwilling or unable to repress dissent effectively, are especially prone to the problem of foreign conflict leading to domestic unrest. A third theme is based on war's reducing not only the government's ability to meet societal demands (and thus lessening its legitimacy) but also its coercive and repressive capacities. An opposition movement needs to mobilize much fewer resources if the government's ability to control society is destroyed or diminished.

Democracy is also related to the growing phenomenon of ethnic conflict. The assertion of minority rights lies behind the recent explosion of open ethnic conflicts in states formerly ruled by authoritarian regimes. Previously suppressed tensions can now be openly expressed. People who long hated each other in silence now can say how much they hate each other. Minorities long held in a state against their will now can seek independence. Political mobilization can play into the hands of leaders who wish to fan ethnic hatred so as to build separatist power bases. Even minorities who

---

[17] See Jack S. Levy, "The Diversionary Theory of War: A Critique," in Manus I. Midlarsky, ed., *Handbook of War Studies* (Boston: Unwin Hyman, 1989). Levy notes: "The idea that political elites often embark on adventurous foreign policies or even resort to war in order to distract popular attention away from internal social and economic problems and consolidate their own domestic political support is an old theme in the literature on international politics" (p. 259). For a general review of the possible relationships between internal and external conflict, see Harvey Starr, "Revolution and War: Rethinking the Linkage Between Internal and External Conflict," *Political Research Quarterly* 47 (June 1994), 481–507.

might prefer to remain in a multiethnic state fear that new and imperfectly established democratic norms and institutions will provide very imperfect guarantees for the protection of minority rights. Democracy thus may seem to be part of this growing global problem.

Indeed, the *process* of moving, often abruptly, from authoritarian rule to democracy feeds uncertainty and brings fear as well as hope. But democracy itself, once established, is part of the solution. Although some established democracies do exhibit serious tensions among ethnic groups, they typically manage them without major lethal violence. Democracies offer institutionalized protections to minorities, and they provide peaceful procedures and expectations for containing and resolving conflicts. Killings, when they happen, are usually the work of fringe groups representing only a minority within the minority. Full-scale civil war—not uncommon in destabilized authoritarian systems—is virtually unknown in established democracies. True, ethnic conflicts and rival nationalisms may be successfully suppressed for decades by tough and effective authoritarian states. But this is no permanent solution. When the authoritarian rulers of a multiethnic state lose their grip or their nerve, all hell may break loose.

All modern governments are expected to provide peace and prosperity to their people, and democratic governments are under especially great pressure to satisfy the people who elect them. As noted in the last chapter, the most horrendous cases of democide—governments causing the death of their own people—occur in the most authoritarian states. One author has argued that famines always occur in authoritarian states, because they can hide their effects, suppress protest, and resist demands to alleviate them. As in the case of Ethiopia, governments may even use them as techniques of political control.[18]

It is hard to control the economy in a world of rapid movements of investment capital and highly competitive trade relations. Sometimes an economy may be threatened with inflation and unemployment at the same time, and there may be nothing the government can do without angering large blocs of voters. Especially at election times, government leaders may look around for something they can do that will be popular. Belligerent activity toward foreign adversaries may be something acceptable, especially for a great power with some adversaries that are much weaker and thus not too dangerous. The U.S. government, for example, has been somewhat more likely to use military force abroad, or to threaten to do so, in years after the economy has been in a recession or in election years.[19]

Before we can develop carefully stated hypotheses linking particular historical contexts and kinds of systems, we must look at other internal factors. First, let us look at some common theories attributing particular international policies to certain alleged economic causes; then, in Chapter 9, we shall consider the role of public opinion.

---

[18] Amartya Sen, *Poverty and Famine* (New York: Oxford University Press, 1981).

[19] Charles W. Ostrom, Jr., and Brian L. Job, "The President and Political Use of Force," *American Political Science Review* 80, 3 (1986), 541–566. See also Bruce Russett, *Controlling the Sword: The Democratic Governance of National Security* (Cambridge, Mass.: Harvard University Press, 1990).

# IMPERIALISM AND CAPITALISM: ECONOMIC STRUCTURE AND FOREIGN POLICY

Realist theories of world politics assume that it does not matter much how different countries' economic systems are organized: equally rich and powerful countries will have about the same goals, whether they have capitalist or socialist economies. Liberal transnationalist theories, however, say that it does make a difference. Some liberal theorists have believed that capitalists' interests in free trade and prosperous foreign markets would promote world peace: as poor countries developed along capitalist lines they too would contribute to building a more peaceful world order. But other liberals, and especially Marxists and other radicals, have long claimed that capitalist countries are likely to have particularly aggressive foreign policies. This aggression is not limited to acts of war. Capitalism is sometimes considered the cause of a variety of **imperialist** acts, loosely defined as efforts to exert political or economic control over smaller or weaker states. Political and military interventions in less developed countries are of special interest. Other foci of attention include military spending, "militarism," and arms races.

The theories differ substantially as to which particular aspects of capitalism cause imperialism or war. Some radicals cite the alleged needs of the entire capitalist economy, claiming that the capitalist system *as a whole* (or at least the capitalist economy of any major nation-state) is dependent on military spending or on continued access to foreign markets for goods or investment opportunities. Others point to the interests and power of *particular groups or classes*. Foreign investors, the military-industrial complex, or other economically defined groups may have an interest in an aggressive or expansionist foreign policy that can potentially yield great gains for them, even though many other members of the system—capitalists as well as workers—suffer net losses from such a policy. A minority of economic interests, therefore, may successfully maintain a policy that benefits them even though it may be detrimental to the capitalist economy as a whole. Finally, some theories are addressed less to readily definable material interests than to the value structure, that is, the ideology of capitalist systems. According to these theories, this value structure, concerned as much with the desire to preserve the capitalist system as to extend it, produces behavior that is excessively responsive to economic growth and the incentive of material rewards. The resulting foreign policy is thus expansionist and is hostile to socialist states with different value structures whose adoption by major segments within the capitalist system would undermine the privileged place of the capitalists themselves. Contradicting these theories are others that stress the relative unimportance of economic motivations in influencing foreign policy; instead, they emphasize political and cultural ends and other kinds of ideological motivations.

Most of the classical economic interpretations attribute imperialism to demands arising from the organization of production in capitalist economies. The liberal English economist J. A. Hobson argued that the very unequal distribution of income and wealth in capitalist countries, especially England, left the poor unable to consume much. The inadequacy of the domestic market in turn forced capitalists to invest their capital abroad and to compete with others to control foreign markets. The capitalist system of the time was to blame, but according to his theory imperialism was not inherent in capitalism.[20]

Many Marxist writers of the early twentieth century developed extremely influential theories of imperialism. Most famous is the work of Lenin. According to him, surplus capital inevitably arises from the processes of monopolistic capitalist production. Industrial and banking interests combine to gain effective control of the state. Thus the drive to export surplus capital becomes a competition among countries rather than simply a competition among corporations, ultimately leading to war among the capitalist powers.[21] Later Marxist writers drew similar conclusions from capitalist countries' need for market outlets for their products as well as their capital, and their continual need for new sources of raw materials. All these theories came from an effort to explain European colonialism, which divided up the world into competing empires in the decades preceding World War I. These theories, however, have been the subject of intensive criticism, with a number of studies pointing out empirical evidence that contradicts them. For example, most British foreign investment did not go to the African and Asian colonies or other less developed countries; instead, more than three fourths went to the United States, to the predominantly white-settled countries of the British Empire, and to other advanced capitalist countries, which should have been plagued by surplus capital conditions like those supposed to have been occurring in Britain.[22]

Other prominent writers incorporated economic motivations into their analyses of the period, but not in the way of Hobson or the Marxists. Realist theorists have offered primarily political or strategic explanations for imperialism, taking account of economic factors but arguing that the typical situation was one of investments in the service of diplomacy, not vice versa:

> Private investments have usually, in actual practice, been subordinated by governments to factors of general political or military strategy which have a more direct bearing on power. Thus it is that private investors have received strong, even outrageously exaggerated governmental backing where they have been tools and agents of power and prestige politics, while other investors whose projects seemed to run counter to the government's line of political endeavor have experienced official indifference or even active opposition.[23]

Other writers, carefully examining British actions in Africa, declared that their object was political and strategic, not economic.[24] Karl Polanyi concluded that

---

[20] J. A. Hobson, *Imperialism: A Study* (London: Allen & Unwin, 1902).

[21] V. I. Lenin, *Imperialism* (New York: Vanguard, 1929).

[22] Michael Barratt Brown, writing in the Marxist tradition, acknowledges the force of these criticisms in *After Imperialism* (London: Heinemann, 1963).

[23] Eugene Staley, *War and the Private Investor* (Garden City, N.Y.: Doubleday, 1935), pp. 361–362.

[24] R. E. Robinson and John Gallagher, *Africa and the Victorians* (New York: St. Martin's, 1961). But the strategic interests arose for Britain *because* of its existing imperial holdings in India, which leaves open the possibility that the basic motivation was to protect the economic interests there.

"business and finance were responsible for many colonial wars, but also for the fact that a general conflagration was avoided. . . . For every one interest that was furthered by war, there were a dozen that could be adversely affected. . . . Every war, almost, was organized by the financiers; but peace also was organized by them."[25]

Joseph Schumpeter is the best-known theorist to stress noneconomic influences. Although he acknowledged that some monopolists have an interest in the conquest of lands producing raw materials and foodstuffs, he regarded it as a "basic fallacy to describe imperialism as a necessary phase of capitalism, or even to speak of the development of capitalism into imperialism."[26] Some capitalists may gain, but only a small minority. The gains from war for capitalists as a class are more than offset by their losses and burdens. Imperialism is primarily an affair of politicians and military personnel. Basically, imperialism stems from attitudes and behavior patterns among the militarists, a group that evolved historically, in the precapitalist era, to defend the state and establish its security.

In part stimulated by these theories, Nazli Choucri and Robert North examined the great powers' colonial expansionism as a primary cause of World War I. Colonial expansion—especially once the Southern Hemisphere had been just about fully carved up among the imperialist states—led to increasing clashes over colonial borders and spheres of influence. The colonial conflicts increased the incentives of the great powers to maintain large armies and navies so that they could hold and defend their colonies. Moreover, these conflicts, together with the arms races they stimulated, led to increasingly violent relations among the great powers, creating repeated crises of which the last, in August 1914, resulted in World War I. Choucri and North, in examining changes in each country's colonial holdings, military expenditures, and so forth, found substantial evidence for each of the links in this chain. Furthermore, they found that economic pressures, stemming from rising income, population, and trade, produced pressures to obtain foreign markets and raw materials that led to the acquisition of colonies.[27]

This evidence is compatible with many liberal and Marxist theories which assert that imperialism, and ultimately war among imperial powers, had important economic roots. However, this evidence is also fully compatible with the view that individual capitalists did not want large-scale war. A quite different study, for example, has shown a very high correlation between leaders' perceptions of hostility and the outflow of gold from London in the 1914 crisis. Prices on the security markets of all the major powers collapsed at the same time, because financiers were horrified by the impending war.[28] Choucri and North look at the population, technological, and economic pressures that drive a national economy to expand by gaining access to markets and resources. That expansion may generate conflict with other nations' interests.

[25] Karl Polanyi, *The Great Transformation* (Boston: Beacon, 1957), p. 16.
[26] Joseph Schumpeter, *Imperialism and Social Classes* (New York: Meridian, 1955), p. 84.
[27] Nazli Choucri and Robert C. North, *Nations in Conflict: National Growth and International Violence* (San Francisco: Freeman, 1975).
[28] Ole R. Holsti, *Crisis Escalation War* (Montreal: McGill–Queen's University Press, 1972), chap. 3.

If war then looms, although no one may want it, decision makers may find their menu in the crisis so constrained that they must take actions they would prefer to avoid.

## MODERN THEORIES ABOUT THE IMPERATIVES OF CAPITALISM

Few modern theories fully accept the classical Marxist tradition, though several employ major aspects of it. Some argue, for example, that heavy military expenditures serve the capitalist purpose of maintaining prosperity at home. According to them, monopolistic capitalism *does* generate a surplus that must be absorbed. This can only be done by government spending and taxing. Some "welfare state" spending is broadly acceptable, but not to the point of damaging work incentives in the labor market or providing major competition to private enterprise. Consequently, neither private demand nor public spending for civil purposes can sustain the economy. In these circumstances, military spending is entirely acceptable because it does not compete with any vested private interests, and it has the extra advantages of quick obsolescence and effective central control over levels and locations of economic activity.[29]

It is hard to test these ideas satisfactorily. Nearly everyone agrees that rearmament for World War II gave a stimulus to the American economy that brought the country out of the Depression. Since World War II, over a long period of prosperity, U.S. military spending as a proportion of GNP has been at a level unprecedented during peacetime. But other kinds of government spending, taxation, and monetary policy probably deserve more credit as causes of that prosperity. Some other countries—notably Japan and West Germany—have had even more expansive economies, with much less military spending. Nevertheless, political leaders like to increase government spending just before elections to create short bursts of prosperity that will please voters. Spending for weapons is relatively easy to increase and most times is considered a proper function of government.[30]

A different explanation, also with roots in radical theory, states that foreign trade and investments are essential to contemporary industrial capitalism and that the attempt to secure foreign markets or commodities leads to neocolonialism and clashes over spheres of influence with other great powers. However, in terms simply of their proportion of the economy, foreign trade and investment have not been all that important to the United States. Only recently has either come to exceed 12 percent of GNP; and, as with the above example of British investment, two-thirds of this economic involvement is with other industrial countries, not with the less developed countries that were the focus of classical imperialism. The rise of the United States to

---

[29] Paul A. Baran and Paul M. Sweezy, *Monopoly Capital: An Essay on the American Economy and Social Order* (Harmondsworth, England: Pelican, 1968); see especially chaps. 6 and 7.
[30] More general evidence about spending increases before elections is given by Edward Tufte, *Political Control of the Economy* (Princeton, N.J.: Princeton University Press, 1978).

superpower status, in fact, coincided with a period when trade and investment made up a smaller proportion of GNP than earlier in the century. Neither in the heyday of British imperialism nor for the United States after World War II were investments in less developed countries more profitable than those in other industrialized countries.[31] The old arguments about an advanced capitalist economy's dependence on foreign investment or trade to absorb surplus capital are not supported.

Another line of attack is to argue that some foreign economic activities are nonetheless critical to the economy's health. This is consistent with Eugene Staley's general view that the government intervened more often to promote investment or exploration for political or strategic purposes than to act as the subordinate agent of private enterprise. Something like this might surely be going on now, given the substantial and very rapidly growing dependence of the industrialized countries on foreign sources of raw materials, including chromium, nickel, cobalt, bauxite, and tin, as well as oil. Figure 8.2 illustrates the situation that obtained in 1980; American overseas dependence has since been increasing and is expected to continue to increase for each of the materials listed. Any industrial economy, whether capitalist or socialist, would be dependent on these sources, but capitalist ones may be particularly vulnerable because of the high valuation they put on growth (hence requiring more and more resources) and because of their openness to the world economy and need for adequate supplies at low prices.[32]

Surely the possibility of intervention—not only by capitalist states—to ensure access to strategic raw materials is still real. It was one U.S. motive, though hardly the only one, for keeping Kuwait out of the control of Iraq's Saddam Hussein. It will not explain every case of military intervention that has taken place in developing countries, but no single theory should be expected to explain every case. The monetary value of some products may be relatively slight, but the products may be very hard to do without. To capitalists, governments aiming to abolish private ownership and private enterprise may be

> objectionable not only because their actions adversely affect foreign-owned interests and enterprises or because they render future capitalist implantation impossible; in some cases this may be of no great economic consequence. But the objection still remains because the withdrawal of any country from the world system of capitalist enterprise is seen as constituting a weakening of that system and as providing encouragement to further dissidence and withdrawal.[33]

All these theories were put forth at a time when socialism was a lively and threatening alternative to capitalism. Now, with the collapse of socialism as an ideological

---

[31] Data supporting these statements can be found in Chapter 14, Figures 14.2 and 14.3, and in John Oneal and Francis Oneal, "Hegemony, Imperialism, and the Profitability of Foreign Investments," *International Organization* 42 (Spring 1988), 347–374.

[32] Staley, *War and the Private Investor,* p. 76.

[33] Ralph Miliband, *The State in Capitalist Society* (New York: Basic Books, 1969), p. 86.

| | UNITED STATES | |
|---|---|---|
| | Percentage | Major Foreign Sources |

| | | Major Foreign Sources |
|---|---|---|
| Columbium | 100 | Brazil, Canada, Thailand |
| Diamond (industrial stones) | 100 | Ireland, S. Africa, Belgium, Luxembourg, U.K. |
| Graphite (natural) | 100 | Mexico, S. Korea, Madagascar, U.S.S.R. |
| Mica (sheet) | 100 | India, Brazil, Madagascar |
| Strontium | 100 | Mexico |
| Manganese | 98 | S. Africa, Gabon, France, Brazil |
| Bauxite and alumina | 94 | Jamaica, Australia, Guinea, Suriname |
| Cobalt | 91 | Zaire, Belgium, Luxembourg, Zambia, Finland |
| Tantalum | 91 | Thailand, Canada, Malaysia, Brazil |
| Chromium | 90 | S. Africa, Philippines, U.S.S.R., Finland |
| Fluorspar | 85 | Mexico, S. Africa, Spain, Italy |
| Platinum-group metals | 85 | S. Africa, U.S.S.R., U.K. |
| Asbestos | 80 | Canada, S. Africa |
| Tin | 80 | Malaysia, Thailand, Bolivia, Indonesia |
| Nickel | 72 | Canada, Norway, Botswana, Australia |
| Potash | 68 | Canada, Israel |
| Zinc | 67 | Canada, Mexico, Spain, Australia |
| Cadmium | 63 | Canada, Australia, Mexico, Belgium, Luxembourg |
| Tungsten | 52 | Canada, Bolivia, China, Thailand |
| Antimony | 51 | S. Africa, Bolivia, China, Mexico |
| Silver | 50 | Canada, Mexico, Peru, U.K. |
| Selenium | 49 | Canada, Japan, Yugoslavia |
| Barium | 43 | Peru, China, Ireland, Morocco, Chile |
| Titanium | 43 | Australia, Canada, S. Africa |
| Vanadium | 42 | S. Africa, Chile, Canada |
| Mercury | 39 | Spain, Algeria, Japan, Italy |
| Iron ore | 28 | Canada, Venezuela, Brazil, Liberia |
| Iron and steel | 19 | Japan, Europe, Canada |
| Lead | 10 | Canada, Mexico, Peru |
| Gold | 7 | Canada, U.S.S.R., Switzerland |
| Copper | 5 | Chile, Canada, Peru, Zambia |

**FIGURE 8.2**  Percentage of raw materials imported by the United States, the European Community, and Japan, and major exporting countries (1980).

rival, leading capitalist states no longer need worry that important less developed countries will pull themselves out of the world market. And there have been no wars between advanced capitalist states since 1945, despite Lenin's prediction. Will such wars reemerge in the absence of a common threat from communism? Or is the "final stage of capitalism" one of peace?

# THE MILITARY-INDUSTRIAL COMPLEX: SECURITY AND ECONOMICS

In his last public address as president, General Dwight Eisenhower warned about the political influence of a newly powerful "**military-industrial complex**":

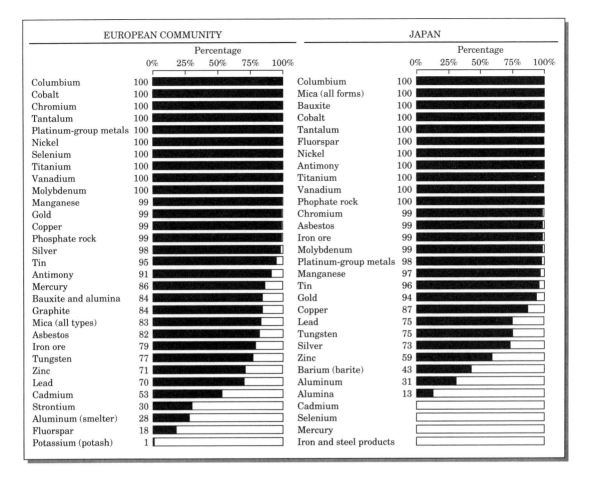

**FIGURE 8.2** *(continued)*

We have been compelled to create a permanent armaments industry of vast proportions. Added to this, three-and-a-half million men and women are directly engaged in the defense establishment. We annually spend on military security alone more than the net income of all United States corporations.

Now this conjunction of an immense military establishment and a large arms industry is new in the American experience. The total influence—economic, political, even spiritual—is felt in every city, every statehouse, every office of the federal government. . . . In the councils of government we must guard against the acquisition of unwarranted influence, whether sought or unsought, by the military-industrial complex. The potential for the disastrous rise of misplaced power exists and will persist.

The phrase "military-industrial complex"—especially if interpreted broadly to include both labor unions and politicians whose districts would benefit directly from military spending—is now a common expression. It represents the understanding that whether or not the entire economic system (usually capitalist, but not necessarily so) benefits from aggressive foreign or military policies, certainly particular interest groups do benefit. Even if the American economy as a whole could prosper without military spending, some industries and some geographic areas would suffer severe short- or medium-term damage from any reduction in military expenditures (as clearly seen in post–cold war closures of domestic military bases). A cutback in military purchases, disrupting production and marketing in these industries and forcing them to make alternative products and find buyers for them, would cause sharp, temporary losses. Defense industry corporations, making use of the technical and political knowledge of former military officers who become defense industry employees (Table 8.1), try hard to maintain their business and to add new contracts. They are helped by government policies that seek to maintain a capacity for ready mobilization in the defense industries, especially the aerospace industry. If a big aircraft manufacturer like McDonnell-Douglas finishes a big contract without getting a new one, the company's experience, skilled labor, and capital equipment will be scattered and lost. Increasingly, the slack is taken up by sales of arms abroad, especially to allies and the less developed countries. Britain, France, and Russia are also heavily dependent on foreign arms sales.

**TABLE 8.1**   Personnel Transfers Between the Department of Defense and Major Military Contractors, 1970–1979

| Company | Total Flow | Flow to Company | | Flow to Department of Defense |
|---|---|---|---|---|
| | | Military | Civilian | |
| Boeing | 388 | 316 | 35 | 37 |
| General Dynamics | 238 | 189 | 17 | 32 |
| Grumman | 88 | 67 | 5 | 16 |
| Lockheed | 304 | 240 | 30 | 34 |
| McDonnell-Douglas | 200 | 159 | 12 | 29 |
| Northrop | 360 | 284 | 50 | 16 |
| Rockwell | 233 | 150 | 26 | 47 |
| United Technologies | 73 | 50 | 11 | 12 |
| Total | 1,874 | 1,455 | 186 | 233 |

*Source:* Adapted from Gordon Adams, *The Iron Triangle: The Politics of Defense Contracting* (New York: Council on Economic Priorities, 1981), p. 84.

Certainly someone stands to gain from every dollar spent on arms; some industries do benefit from military spending and would suffer from its reduction. The important question for theories about the military-industrial-complex is how broad and how deep that suffering would be compared with the benefits to other industries from disarmament. The damage to military industries (and probably to certain regional labor markets as well) would exceed the gains made by any other single sector of industry; that is, although military spending does not necessarily benefit the economy as a whole, the gains from defense spending are greater for a few industries than are the costs to any one sector when spread among all the sectors of the civilian economy. In democracies, pressure groups concentrate their activities on those issues that promise them the greatest gains and will not deeply resist efforts of other groups pursuing their own most important special interests when those efforts involve modest costs (as long as the prospective costs remain modest). Each group seeks to gain something for itself and tolerates similar activities by others. This essentially political explanation would account for the continuing high levels of military spending despite the fact that economic gains are limited to a small segment of the economy.

The end of the cold war has brought renewed debate over the importance of the military-industrial complex. Will there be a "peace dividend" of money, formerly spent on the arms race, to meet the needs of the civilian economy? Does the risk of a renewed threat from Russia (or China, or . . .) require continued expenditure on expensive strategic nuclear weapons? Do American (or British, French, German, and Japanese) economic interests in less developed countries, including access to important raw materials, require continued expenditure on conventional forces that can be employed for global reach? How big a defense-industrial base should be retained in case rearmament is needed? Should arms sales outside of Europe—for example, to areas of continuing rivalries such as the Middle East—be promoted so as to maintain prosperous arms industries in the exporting countries? What factories and military bases, at home and abroad, should be closed despite economic pain to the communities of workers they employ? Real economic interests are at stake in all these decisions, and they exemplify the different interests, foreign policy objectives, and strategies of different groups within a society.

## LEADERSHIP ATTITUDES AND BEHAVIOR

All these different perspectives on economic causes of policies assume that the beliefs, attitudes, and policy preferences of individuals, groups, and classes on matters of foreign and military policy will differ sharply. They will differ according to their *objective interests* and according to their views of those interests. These various actors may also have different views on what is in the *national interest*.

The perspectives, however, lead to quite different predictions and hypotheses. Some suggest that capitalists as a class will have beliefs and attitudes different from those of members of other classes (according to some theories, the capitalists would be more favorable to military spending or to expansionist or imperialist foreign policies; according to others, overseas interests would lead capitalists strenuously to avoid at least those kinds of foreign activities that might lead to war). Other perspectives implicitly or explicitly emphasize differences among different types of capitalists; for example, those whose businesses are entirely domestic versus the leaders of MNCs, or defense industry executives versus other executives. On these matters, there is some good evidence about the beliefs of different American "leadership groups" about foreign policy. Table 8.2 shows the distribution of some of those beliefs, with groups arrayed from most hawkish to most dovish on average over eight different survey questions. (The labels *dove* and *hawk* have value-laden meanings that we do not intend to convey here, but we use the terms as a generally understood shorthand for different sets of beliefs.)

Of all these groups, business leaders were among the more hawkish, although the most hawkish positions were taken, on average, by lawyers. In every instance business leaders were, on average, markedly more hawkish than health-care professionals, media figures (who are found pretty much in the middle), college educators, and high-ranking persons in the clergy, in that order. In previous surveys some other groups were included. For instance, the 1984 national leadership survey by Ole Holsti and James Rosenau found essentially the same ranking, but with Republican party leaders and high military officers even more hawkish than the lawyers, with State Department officials in the middle, and with labor leaders and Democratic party leaders between educators and clergy on the dovish end.

If business executives as a class are toward the hawkish end of the foreign policy spectrum, albeit not at the most extreme end, these results support the arguments of radical theories, but the support is hardly overwhelming. The results are more consistent with broader theories of the military-industrial complex that stress alliances of business leaders with other bureaucratic and political leaders who share a preference for hawkish policies.

An analysis found that, by 1967, prices of shares on the New York Stock Exchange would rise in response to events that gave promise of peace in Vietnam and fall when the war was escalated. Like the evidence about the London gold market in 1914, this would indicate that business and finance generally do not see a major war as furthering their economic interests. In the years before 1967, however, when the Vietnam War was less burdensome to the American society and economy, there was no clear association between war events and stock prices. This suggests that although business interests may abhor large wars, they do not object so overwhelmingly to smaller wars for limited goals.[34]

The differences among capitalists, depending on the nature of their business interests, are more ambiguous. Another survey of business executives, in 1973, provided some information on their firms. Companies surveyed were those selling a large proportion of their product to the Defense Department, those selling or investing substantially abroad, and those with expectations of large markets in the Soviet Union

---

[34] Bruce M. Russett and Elizabeth C. Hanson, *Interest and Ideology: The Foreign Policy Beliefs of American Businessmen* (San Francisco: Freeman, 1975), chap. 5.

**TABLE 8.2** Percentage of Various U.S. Leaders Holding Dovish Positions on Foreign Policy, 1992

| | Leadership Group | | | | | |
|---|---|---|---|---|---|---|
| Issue | Law | Business | Health Care | Media | Education | Clergy |
| 1. Not OK for CIA to overthrow hostile governments | 29 | 41 | 47 | 61 | 67 | 76 |
| 2. US foreign policy relies too much on military advice | 23 | 35 | 51 | 51 | 54 | 63 |
| 3. Military aid brings war | 17 | 34 | 49 | 51 | 53 | 65 |
| 4. Enlist UN to settle disputes | 79 | 87 | 90 | 92 | 92 | 92 |
| 5. No need to maintain high defense spending | 52 | 69 | 76 | 82 | 84 | 84 |
| 6. May not be necessary to use military to stop aggression | 25 | 31 | 41 | 49 | 51 | 61 |
| 7. U.S. does not need SDI | 24 | 35 | 49 | 55 | 61 | 66 |
| 8. U.S. can now dismantle most strategic nuclear weapons | 40 | 41 | 57 | 63 | 65 | 66 |

*Note:* Respondents were asked to agree or disagree with the eight propositions listed below in full. The percentages show which portion of each group agreed strongly or at least somewhat with a dovish position (that is, agreed with propositions 2, 3, 4, and 8, and disagreed with 1, 5, 6, and 7).

1. There is nothing wrong with using the CIA to try to undermine hostile governments.
2. The conduct of American foreign affairs relies excessively on military advice.
3. Military aid programs will eventually draw the United States into unnecessary wars.
4. It is vital to enlist the cooperation of the UN in settling international disputes.
5. Because the future is uncertain, the United States needs to maintain high levels of defense spending.
6. It is necessary to use military force to stop aggression; economic sanctions are not enough.
7. The United States needs to develop SDI to protect against accidental and limited nuclear war.
8. The United States can now dismantle most of its strategic nuclear weapons.

*Source:* Data provided by Shoon Murray of The American University from her Leadership Opinion Project panel study on American opinion leaders. References in the text to data from Ole Holsti and James Rosenau are to materials printed on p. 205 in the fourth (1992) edition of this textbook.

and China. Not surprisingly, executives from firms that sold to the Defense Department were more likely to believe that the level of U.S. defense spending should be raised, but they were not more likely to approve of the Vietnam War or to be more hawkish than other business executives on other foreign policy issues. Nor did other indications of foreign interest on the part of their firms make any systematic difference in the hawkishness or dovishness of their attitudes. Thus hypotheses viewing capitalism either as promoting an aggressive foreign policy or as being a force for peace were unsupported.[35]

These empirical studies neither definitively refute nor strongly support economic-interest theories. However, they do suggest that the interests of particular groups and classes are complex and are not perceived by individuals in any easily predictable manner. Many people who advocate interventionism or national preparedness stand to gain little materially from their views. Individuals' perceptions of their self-interest vary even within groups in which each individual has the same material stake in an outcome. The definition of one's self-interest is a very complex matter, subject to a variety of influences from colleagues, friends, the media, pressure groups, and, of course, one's experiences and political socialization. This is key to understanding how domestic interest groups can affect the foreign policy process and foreign policy–makers.

> A pressure group's job is, in large part, to define the interests of its partisans. Interests may not be self-evident, and a pressure group may define interests in such a way as to gain supporters it would not otherwise have; a firm or businessman may go to either side depending on how the definition is set up for him. . . . Unlike our friends who told us, "Tell me a man's interest and I will tell you his stand," we would say, "Tell us where a man stands and we will tell you what perceptions of his interests will serve to make that stand a self-consistent and stable one." There are perceptions of self-interest available to bolster any stand by any individual.[36]

## IDEOLOGIES AND COHERENT BELIEF SYSTEMS

In the study of American business executives and other leaders, the contribution of identifiable economic interests to predicting foreign policy attitudes proved rather small. A much better predictor is the set of attitudes in matters of domestic policy: civil rights for African-Americans, civil liberties (exemplified by the question of legalizing marijuana or the role of the police and the FBI), and inequality of income. People's views on domestic issues tended to be quite uniform across the entire set; that is, they were consistently either liberal or conservative. More important for our discussion

---

[35] Russett and Hanson, *Interest and Ideology,* chap. 4. Furthermore, in the stock market analysis, stocks of firms oriented toward sales to the Defense Department or to less developed countries behaved on the whole no differently from the general stock index in response to ups and downs in the Vietnam War.

[36] Raymond A. Bauer, Ithiel de Sola Pool, and Anthony Dexter, *American Business and Public Policy: The Politics of Foreign Trade* (New York: Atherton, 1963): quotations from pp. 398 and 142–143.

here is the idea that if we know whether a person is a liberal or conservative on domestic issues, we would have a very good idea about whether that person would be a dove or hawk on foreign policy issues.

That is, the foreign and domestic policy beliefs of American elites share a common structure. The belief dimensions underpinning foreign policy attitudes are not separate from the dimensions that underpin attitudes about domestic politics. Both sets of beliefs are derived from common core values. For example, the never-ending debate on the redistribution of wealth and whether or not to help the needy runs through both domestic and foreign policy. In international affairs, it appears in questions about combating world hunger or giving aid to less developed countries; domestically, it appears in questions of redistributing income from the wealthy to the poor through taxation and subsidies. Another example is in the assessment of the utility and desirability of violence and its use as a deterrent: in foreign policy, this arises in questions about intervention, the use of covert intelligence operations, reliance on military advice, and the benefits of military security; domestically, we see this issue arise in regard to the control of crime and the death penalty.

A coherent and organized set of beliefs—an **ideology**—helps a person to make sense of new pieces of information or to adopt an opinion on a new problem. All of us have ideologies of some sort so that we do not have to deal with each issue on a purely ad hoc, isolated basis. Here we use the term *ideology* in much the same way that Ole Holsti uses **belief system**:

> A set of lenses through which information concerning the physical and social environment is received. It orients the individual to his environment, defining it for him and identifying for him its salient characteristics. . . . In addition to organizing perceptions into a meaningful guide for behavior, the belief system has the function of the establishment of goals and the ordering of preferences.[37]

We shall discuss belief systems in greater detail in Chapter 11. Here, the point is how liberal–dove views and conservative–hawk views are joined across a broad range of domestic and foreign policy issues. Such a joining has been found repeatedly in research on opinions in the United States—for example, in surveys of the general public and in several studies of voting in the U.S. Senate and House of Representatives in the 1960s and 1970s, and most recently in research analyzing 1988–92 data from studies of American foreign policy elites (such as State Department officials, labor officials, foreign policy experts outside government, military officers, and media leaders). This close association of domestic and foreign policy views is strengthened by the belief that money for arms comes at the expense of domestic programs that would benefit minorities and urban areas. Congressional voting studies also show some association of economic interests and foreign policy attitudes. Representatives

---

[37] Ole R. Holsti, "The Belief System and National Images: A Case Study," *Journal of Conflict Resolution* 6 (September 1962), 245.

with military bases or defense industries in their districts will, of course, vote in favor of appropriations that will benefit *their* constituents or fight to prevent base closures in *their* districts. But beyond those very narrow issues, defense-related interests do not affect a representative's voting record very much.[38] Again, views on civil rights and civil liberties are much more closely associated with foreign policy beliefs. We cannot confidently say that one causes the other, but whatever it is—personality, life experience, position in society, or information and acquaintance network—that creates a generally coherent ideological position is a stronger influence than direct economic interest.

Particular policy preferences stem from various motives. Often, as in the case of a conservative former military officer now working for an aerospace corporation, several influences converge, and his or her foreign policy beliefs are said to be over-determined. This happens with liberals as well as with conservatives, and it happens in very different political systems.

Similar interests had been just as powerful in the Soviet Union. Although until recently there were no capitalists in that economy, certainly state industrial managers have had interests in promoting the growth, power, prosperity, and technological preeminence of the arms-manufacturing plants that they control. They, too, shared interests with their clients in the Red Army and the Strategic Rocket Forces and with hawkish ideologues in the Communist party. A cold war—though not necessarily a hot one—had helped to maintain their privileges and central roles in Soviet society. In both countries, therefore, entrenched economic and political interests maintained the momentum of established hard-line policies and resisted change. In a perverse way, the military-industrial complex of each country helped the other. Each embodied the foreign threat that its counterpart in the other country needed to justify its own activities.[39] In the late 1980s Soviet foreign policy did change drastically. Most of the changes were set in motion simultaneously with dramatic shifts toward a free political system domestically; perestroika (domestic restructuring) made glasnost (a foreign policy of openness) more credible. Reformers continually had to struggle with hard-liners, that is, the Soviet military-industrial complex in the military, heavy industry, the government, and Communist party bureaucracies—all of whom vigorously resisted the political changes.

---

[38] On the general public, see Norman Nie, Sidney Verba, and J. R. Petrocik, *The Changing American Voter* (Cambridge, Mass.: Harvard University Press, 1979); for studies of Congress and especially the influence of defense contracts, see James M. Lindsay, *Congress and Nuclear Weapons* (Baltimore: Johns Hopkins University Press, 1991): and Kenneth E. Mayer, *The Politics and Economics of Defense Contracting* (New Haven, Conn.: Yale University Press, 1991).

[39] Two good collections concerning the role of economics and national security policy, including military-industrial complexes, in various countries are Alex Mintz, ed., *The Political Economy of Military Spending in the United States* (London: Unwin Hyman, 1991), and Steve Chan and Alex Mintz, eds., *Defense, Welfare, and Growth* (London: Unwin Hyman, 1991).

## STATE INTERESTS

People often pursue economic interests, and governments pursue the economic interests of some of their citizens. Sometimes, however, government officials act for their own reasons—from personal, ideological, bureaucratic, or strategic considerations. Historically, most states have been formed out of the experience of war; in Tilly's observation, "The state makes war, and war makes the state." States have fought to unify their territory and to bring neighboring peoples under their control; to fight successfully they have had to create centralized, bureaucratic states able to mobilize the economic resources of their people. This is as true of Algerian revolutionaries in their war of independence from France as for France itself over the centuries. In turn, successful wars gave governments the resources to consolidate control over their peoples. Thus states often have developed an interest in sustaining some political tensions with other states.

Government leaders may clothe their foreign policy acts in the language of economic interests to broaden their support, trying to enlist the support of economic interests for policies on which they have already decided for quite other reasons. If we see only the result of policy, it may be impossible to decide what the driving motivation is—who is initiating a policy and who is being used to lend support and legitimacy.

We noted one aspect of this ambiguity in Staley's discussion of the role of private investors in overseas diplomatic intervention. Another appears in a discussion of a famous statement by Assistant Secretary of State Dean Acheson to a congressional committee in 1944. Acheson declared that America must for economic reasons follow a much more internationalist political policy; that is, the economy required expanding markets abroad to absorb its "unlimited creative energy" and to avoid stagnation of the domestic economy. This statement and others like it are frequently referred to by radical and neo-Marxist opponents of American foreign policy. But, to quote Robert W. Tucker,

> Why may we not argue that such statements as the one above [Acheson's] obscure far more than they reveal the true sources of policy, that their purpose is largely to elicit support for a policy that is pursued primarily for quite different reasons?[40]

Realist theories of national or strategic interest attribute the actions of policymakers to their perceptions of security requirements and *Realpolitik*.[41] By this explanation, Western policymakers during the cold war thought in terms of military security, balance of power, containing Soviet expansionism, containing power centers in general,

---

[40] Robert W. Tucker, *The Radical Left and American Foreign Policy* (Baltimore: Johns Hopkins University Press, 1971), p. 61.
[41] See, for example, Stephen Krasner, *In Defense of the National Interest: Raw Materials, Investments and U.S. Foreign Policy* (Princeton, N.J.: Princeton University Press, 1978).

and the importance of honoring commitments to defend one's allies. This perceived need to match, contain, or repress rival world powers stemmed in part from, or at least was reinforced by, the experience of World War II, most especially by the failure of British Prime Minister Neville Chamberlain's hope to appease Hitler successfully at Munich in 1938. By this line of thought, the fact that the Soviet Union was communist was only incidental; that powerful country would have been a threat under any government. Policymakers holding strategically oriented views are basically concerned with containing any rival power center regardless of its ideology or form of domestic organization. An almost perfect example of this line of reasoning is this comment in the *Washington Post* by columnist Joseph Alsop in 1974:

> The choice the British and French made in 1939 was to fight like cornered rats rather than to submit to Adolf Hitler. But with the vast tilt in the power balance that had then occurred, the same choice would have had to be made even if Adolf Hitler had been miraculously replaced by another German leader of undoubted rectitude. The mere presence of overweaning power almost always begets this choice.

Certainly such views are common among American leaders. In the survey of leaders discussed above, the belief in national power and national interests as inevitable causes of conflict was closely associated with hawkish beliefs.

Eventually one encounters the radicals' argument that ideology is a false consciousness, a superstructure manufactured, deliberately or otherwise, to justify international conflict in the interest of particular groups. According to this view, the capitalist economic system in Western industrial countries generates an ideological superstructure of anticommunism that lends political legitimacy and moral energy to the system's foreign policies.[42]

How can we possibly sort out the real motivations from the manufactured ones when both are expressed? Since we cannot get inside a person's head, we cannot know why that person does what he or she does; even the individual may not know, and even psychoanalysts disagree about unconscious motivations. In another sense, however, we can suggest some relevant evidence. If an economic interpretation is to be valid, we should expect that those whose interests are allegedly served by such beliefs will express themselves most frequently or most strongly. That is, if an assertive, aggressive, or vigorously anticommunist foreign policy did indeed serve

---

[42] The classic argument is by Marc Pilisuk and Thomas Hayden: the cold war anticommunist consensus was imposed and manipulated by the elites through their control over education and the mass media; it was a false consciousness made to serve narrow interests. See their "Is There a Military-Industrial Complex Which Prevents Peace?" *Journal of Social Issues* 21 (July 1965), 67–117. A liberal discussion of the power of economic elites to shape society's discussion of policy issues and fundamental economic structures is Charles E. Lindblom, *Politics and Markets* (New York: Basic Books, 1977), chap. 15. The power of elites over opinion is, of course, even greater in authoritarian states, where the government or ruling party directly owns or controls the media of mass communication.

the interests of the capitalist class, then we should expect capitalists to have supported that policy even more than other groups or classes; they did, but only to a limited extent.

Many businesspeople see their economic interests as being served by hawkish policies; many political leaders and military officers must see their bureaucratic and career interests as being served by them, too. This view does not imply that they deliberately subordinate the welfare of their own society or of the world to those interests. They may hold a set of beliefs for reasons quite independent of those interests, and their beliefs about the general welfare may be correct. Some beliefs are, to an important degree, independent of immediate material interests. Yet interests do help to support a broader ideology. At the least, interests provide a reason not to challenge ideological beliefs at times when some of the basic intellectual underpinnings might seem questionable to an objective outside observer. When interests are not the cause of an ideology, they may still, in ways not necessarily traceable to conscious reasoning processes, prevent, delay, or diminish the abandonment of that ideology. We have tried to set out here a suggestion of the range and diversity of interests that exist within any domestic setting, noting especially the various explanations of them based on economic factors.

# DOMESTIC CONSTRAINTS: GOVERNMENTAL STRUCTURE AND THE ROLE OF PUBLIC OPINION

WORLD SYSTEM

RELATIONS

SOCIETY

GOVERNMENT

ROLE

INDIVIDUAL

## CONSTRAINTS AND SUPPORT

In the course of discussing theories about the effects of societal factors, including socioeconomic interests and organization, on foreign policy, we asked whether people with different economic interests tend to have different foreign policy preferences. In discussing theories of the military-industrial complex, we began to ask a second question that may be central to understanding foreign policy in *open* societies: Does public opinion, outside of the opinion of a small set of interest group leaders, really have much influence over policymaking?

What influence does the public have? Public opinions affect foreign policy through their impact on governmental decision makers. People in government have their own interests: to keep or increase their political positions and political power, their wealth and economic position, their position or status within society, as well as to promote their ideological values, beliefs, and ideals. These and other interests lead political leaders to seek societal support—that is, the approval of public opinion—in order to gain control of government, remain in office, and then implement their policies. In order to do this, governments must hear and respond to the demands and needs of society. By meeting societal demands and needs (fixing high tariffs for protection of certain industries, or sending in the Marines to protect foreign investments, or establishing hard-line policies toward Iraqi or Haitian dictators to protect freedom and encourage the spread of democratic government), governmental leaders are just as constrained as they are by the state's capabilities.

Such demands, as we have seen, limit a leader's menu, making some actions simply not acceptable to the populace as a whole or to the elites that control society and government. For example, in the early 1960s President John F. Kennedy expressed the desire to begin friendly relations with Communist China but did not do so, supposedly because his advisers thought the American people would not have accepted such a move. One major societal–governmental relationship that constrains governmental leaders, then, is the desire not to lose office: not to lose an election or a power struggle, or to be overthrown by a revolution. Interests must be attended to. To gain the support of those interests, some policies will not be feasible, and others will be. This requirement for internal support, and the need to attend to domestic politics, is critical for understanding two-level games as introduced in Chapter 8.

Closely related is another major theme, expressed in Robert Dahl's famous question, "Who governs?"[1] One way to see which interests governmental leaders will listen to and which interests they will support is to see who the governmental leaders are. In today's world this question may be phrased in many ways: What tribe are they from? What language do they speak? Of what religion are they? What is the color of their skin? What region of the country are they from? How much money do they have? What family do they belong to? What class or social group do they spring from? What political party are they affiliated with? What ideology do they believe in? By knowing the answers to these sorts of questions, we gain some idea about which section of societal interests will be taken into account in the formulation and implementation of foreign policy.

So far, we have discussed support as it relates to governing officials' efforts to remain in office. We can also examine how societal interests support specific foreign policy positions of the government. Just as society's resources give decision makers the opportunity to act, societal support helps provide their willingness to act. As noted before, neither human power and resources nor economic and military capabilities count for much if a government cannot mobilize them. Governments do not just

---

[1] Robert A. Dahl, *Who Governs? Democracy and Power in an American City* (New Haven, Conn.: Yale University Press, 1961).

passively respond to societal needs and demands; they also try to shape and control them. If a government cannot persuade a people to get behind its policies and use those capabilities to support its policies, the capabilities are useless. If the people are not willing to act militarily, for example, fearing a hopeless, draining involvement, the government itself may be reluctant. Officials in the Reagan administration tried to evade a congressional prohibition of aid to the Nicaraguan Contras in the 1980s with disastrous results. In 1990, President Bush very carefully built up popular, congressional, and international support before going to war with Iraq. Congress may reflect general public unwillingness to get involved, and refuse to support military intervention, as during the war in Bosnia. The governments of Germany and Japan in the 1990s, when asked for military commitments that match their economic status in situations such as the Gulf War, have said that they cannot do so because of popular opposition to military instruments of foreign policy.

An unwilling public affects a country's foreign policy in many ways. When discussing power and deterrence, we noted that to be effective a state has to be able to make credible threats and promises—*any* state, democratic or authoritarian. If societal support is lacking, preventing a government from using certain capabilities, the credibility of that government in the eyes of other states declines. Its ability to influence them shrinks as its reputation as a bluffer grows. Its foreign policy menu will also shrink.

## Societal Resources and Structure: Government and Economics (Again)

The ideology and practice of state ownership, centralized command economies, and communism are now in rapid retreat before a new attitude that stresses the role of private ownership, free markets, and capitalism in promoting sustained development. Much of this new attitude is the result of experience with the inefficiencies of central planning devoid of proper price signals from a free market. It also reflects an understanding of how economic distortions derive from lack of political participation and free expression. A strong and arbitrary government provides little guarantee of private property rights, just as does a weak government that is unable to resist economic predators. In either case, lack of secure property rights discourages investment.[2] Enduring development is hindered by a lack of democracy; reciprocally, democracy cannot flourish under conditions of extreme and highly centralized state ownership.

Non-capitalist states, with command economies and little private ownership of the means of production—like North Korea to this day—are not democratic as that term is used in this book, nor have such states ever been democratic. The key economic condition for democracy seems to be widespread dispersion of wealth and income, which in turn becomes a means for widespread diffusion of political influence. Countries in which the state owns or tightly controls all the major sources of

---

[2] Mancur Olson, "Dictatorship, Democracy, and Development," *American Political Science Review* 87 (September 1993), 567–576.

economic power do not provide the basis for dispersion of political power; rather, political power remains concentrated in the hands of those who occupy powerful positions in state institutions. Political and economic power cannot easily be separated from each other. Programs of democratization without economic deconcentration build on shallow foundations. Conversely, state-directed deconcentration, without the simultaneous creation of working democratic political institutions, involves the risk of replacing a class of state managers with a class of new private monopolists who have highjacked the former state enterprises.

By contrast, capitalist states may be democratic. But they are unlikely to sustain democracy if wealth and income are highly concentrated in the hands of a few individuals, families, or corporations. Historically, democracy usually developed in conjunction with the creation and dispersion of wealth to new groups and classes. In the contemporary world, democracy is usually strongest where that dispersion is wide, and weakest where it is narrow. An economically empowered populace is a politically empowered citizenry. Concentration of economic assets, whether owned by the state or by private actors, deprives political oppositions of the resources needed to sustain criticism of the state or the exposition of alternative policies.

By this understanding, free-wheeling, unrestrained capitalism may not be much more compatible with democracy than is unrestrained state control. Private owners of concentrated wealth are likely to use the state to distort the "free" market, subsidizing or protecting their own enterprises, restraining their competitors, and repressing organized labor. Ownership concentrated in the hands of particular ethnic groups may stimulate hostility and violence from other ethnic groups. Concentrated ownership promotes disillusion both with the distorted process of economic development and with the supposedly democratic institutions that permit it.

In sum, societies affect foreign policy in several ways through their effects on government. First, there are reciprocal relationships among society, economics, and politics. The nature of the society affects the resources available to a government, while the nature of government permits certain forms of economic structures, which in turn affect the amount of resources that can be made available. Clearly, the greater the amount of resources available, the longer the menu. Second, government officials decide how they want to use those resources based on their own background—that is, which societal group or elite they most strongly represent—as well as on their own view of what society wants or should want. Lastly, through interest-group pressures and public opinion, society places political limits on how such resources can be used. How important these limits may be is related to how accountable a government is—in other words, how open or closed it is to societal influences.

## POWER ELITES VERSUS PLURALISM

What determines the degree of public influence over policymaking? Although we will not be able to give any hard-and-fast answers, we can provide some guidance by further considering the content of public opinion and by asking how public opinion is expressed or shaped within different governmental forms. Here we move from the societal level to the governmental level of analysis. For example, in what way does it make sense to say that the foreign policy decisions of a democracy result from public opinion? How can public opinion place constraints on the leadership, and also what opportunities do the leaders have to shape public opinion? What opportunities to shape public opinion are presented to the leadership of a democracy? We shall look especially at ideas and information about the United States, both because a wealth of information is available and because in the United States, a major democracy, we would expect public opinion to have a relatively significant effect. We shall also look at data from Israel, New Zealand, and European democracies. Public opinion matters in authoritarian states, too, but less immediately or directly, and data are usually hard to come by.

A radical perspective starts with the proposition that interests among the leadership groups in American society converge. In this "**power elite**" view, political and major societal leaders fundamentally agree on what the national goals should be. Attitudes among most of the public are thus not even relevant. In the words of C. Wright Mills, the most famous proponent of this view,

> The conception of the power elite and of its unity rests upon the corresponding development and the coincidence of interests among economic, political, and military organizations. It also rests upon the similarity of origins and outlook and the social and personal intermingling of top circles from each of these dominant hierarchies.[3]

In this view, those who occupy the leading positions of power in American society (that is, those who occupy positions of authority in key economic and political institutions) basically agree on the fundamental principles by which American society is organized. Although they may disagree about details or the implementation of particular policies, their commitment to the principles of a market economy, regulated yet also protected by the ruling political structures, provides a basic common denominator. These like-minded individuals are held together by common upper-class origins, educational experience, and social and professional mingling.

The contrasting pluralist view, associated with both liberals and conservatives, is typified in this comment:

> A substantial part of the government in the United States has come under the influence and control of narrowly based and largely autonomous elites. But these elites do not act cohesively with each other on many issues. They do not "rule" in the sense of commanding the entire nation. Quite the contrary, they tend to pursue a policy of non-involvement in the large issues, save where such issues touch their own particular concerns.[4]

Proponents of the pluralist view argue that for every major issue (defense, education, environment, health, and others) there are specialists, and that different groups

---

[3] C. Wright Mills, *The Power Elite* (New York: Oxford University Press, 1956), p. 292.
[4] Grant McConnell, *Private Power and American Democracy* (New York: Knopf, 1966), p. 339. The best-known proponent of the pluralist view is undoubtedly Robert A. Dahl; see especially his *Who Governs?*

fight and win different political battles. Their argument emphasizes the diversity of opinion and the unpredictability of particular political outcomes rather than any fundamental consensus on the form of political and economic order.

In a real sense, the conflict between these two perspectives is irreconcilable. One emphasizes that diversity, unpredictability, and the clash of opinion surely are real (Will the defense budget be increased? Will military bases be closed? Will NAFTA and GATT be supported?). The other dismisses this diversity as trivial and stresses the fact that certain values—liberal democracy, free enterprise, and the support of free enterprise by the government—are common denominators for most people in elite positions in America (or, for that matter, in Japan or Western Europe). Advocacy of alternative forms of economic or political order (extensive socialism or fascism) is clearly outside the mainstream, undertaken only by a small minority and without the sound perspectives essential for those who would be thought responsible in high positions of public trust.

Both views actually are correct. There are important differences within and between elite groups. At the same time, by long-term historic or global standards, the spectrum of "respectable" opinion on major public policy issues in America is not especially wide. There has, however, been some periodic widening of that spectrum. Before World War II, isolationism was widespread; until the Japanese attack on Pearl Harbor, that view had many adherents from both conservative and leftist (socialist and progressive) circles. By the 1950s the number of proponents of this view had shrunk to a small minority, which was held in ill repute by the elite. There was instead a substantial consensus on an internationalist policy of military alliances, a strong defense, some foreign aid (at least to pro-American and procapitalist states), and a generally active involvement of the United States in world affairs. This policy consensus began to break down during the Vietnam War years, as opposition to American military involvement in foreign countries grew. After the Vietnam War was over and the United States seemed to suffer a series of policy reversals with respect to the Soviet Union and its allies in the Third World, opposition to an active American foreign policy again became less common and less respectable. The cycle has reversed once again with the end of the cold war, and there are renewed calls from some circles for American retrenchment from the world scene, especially that the United States avoid the role of world policeman.

The fluctuations in this kind of opinion are illustrated by a public opinion survey question that has been asked repeatedly for more than 50 years. Although the wording of the question has varied slightly, its basic form has been quite stable: "Do you think we are spending too much, too little, or about the right amount for national defense and military purposes?" Figure 9.1 shows the results. The graph shows substantial fluctuation in the early years of the cold war, before a popular and elite consensus was established. Then a long period of stability ensued, during which more people preferred increasing rather than reducing defense spending but the majority of the population was content with the existing level (not indicated in the figure). This consensus was shattered by the antipathy toward the military generated by the Vietnam War; since then, opinions on this matter have proved very changeable. The antimilitary mood of the early 1970s faded and was then abruptly reversed by worsening relations with the Soviets, the Iranian seizure of American diplomats as hostages in 1979, and

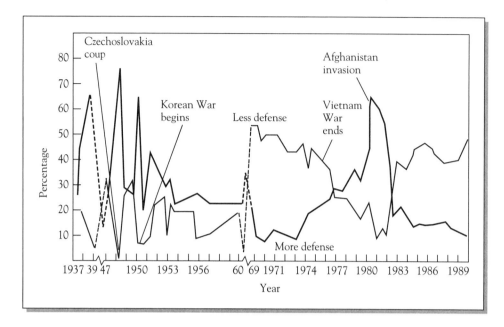

**FIGURE 9.1** Percentage of Americans favoring more or less defense spending, 1937–1990. [*Source:* Bruce Russett, "The Revolt of the Masses: Public Opinion on Military Expenditures," in Russett, ed., *Peace, War and Numbers* (Beverly Hills, Calif.: Sage, 1972), pp. 301–306; later data compiled by Thomas Hartley.]

finally the Soviet invasion of Afghanistan. But by the mid-1980s that mood, too, had passed, leaving almost half the population feeling that the Reagan defense buildup had gone far enough. The Gulf War, reflected in figures for early 1991, showed a dramatic decline in support for more defense cuts; however, this blip was clearly gone by the fall of 1991.

Throughout the cold war, U.S. national security policy, and the public attitudes that supported it, seemed anchored in the great ideological and power rivalry with the Soviet Union. A basic component of that policy, the ups and downs of American military spending, was largely predictable by looking at changes in the level of Soviet military spending and at public preferences, as expressed in opinion surveys, for increases or decreases in American military spending.[5] The end of the cold war

---

[5] For evidence that the largest influence on U.S. defense spending was Soviet military spending, see Charles W. Ostrom and Robin F. Marra, "U.S. Defense Spending and the Soviet Estimate," *American Political Science Review* 80 (September 1986), 819–842, and Thomas Hartley and Bruce Russett, "Public Opinion and the Common Defense: Who Governs Military Spending in the United States?" *American Political Science Review* 86 (December 1992), 905–915.

brought remarkable changes in both policy and attitudes. Rationales for U.S. military spending, for the use of military force abroad, and for international cooperation have likewise changed. As people revised their beliefs about the Soviet Union between 1987 and 1988, attitudes toward some specific policies—such as defense spending—also moved in a dovish direction. Public opinion is the most substantively important influence on the budget that remains after the end of the cold war. In the past it exerted a greater influence on U.S. military spending than did the deficit, and it is likely to continue to play at least as important a role with the end of the Soviet threat.[6]

The swings in American opinion toward the military have been wider than those in other democratic countries. In Britain, for example, the percentage of the public favoring increased military spending varied only between a low of 8 percent and a high of 40 percent, and in West Germany the range was very much smaller (see Figure 9.2). Thomas Risse-Kappen has shown similarly narrow ranges for Japan and France. As he notes, the policy impact of public opinion in liberal democracies seems to depend more on the "domestic structure and coalition building processes" within each country than on specific issues. While public opinion matters (in his study of the United States, Japan, Germany, and France), the effects are indirect in influencing the political coalition-building process along a liberal–conservative continuum.[7]

## Segments of the American Public

In considering public opinion in general and the opinions of leaders in particular, it is important to distinguish carefully among various segments of the population. About 20 percent of the American public, for instance, has little or no interest in or information about foreign affairs, or even about politics in general. They are typically unaware of most international events. For example, in 1986 only about 70 percent of the American people professed to have heard of SALT II, the treaty central to regulating Soviet–American competition in nuclear arms.

Above the 20 percent who are nonpolitical is a "middle mass" of perhaps 75 percent of the populace whose attention moves in and out of politics, depending on the issue and on events. Their attentiveness and knowledge usually are not deep. For example, in the March 1986 survey reported above, only a third of all Americans knew that the United States had not ratified the SALT II treaty. In other surveys barely more were aware of the antiballistic missile (ABM) treaty, and only one-third could define "NATO." That proportion is no less than that for many other issues, however. About the same fraction (though not necessarily the same people) could define "welfare state" and "electoral college." About 25 percent of American adults are somewhat

---

[6] See Bruce Russett, Thomas Hartley, and Shoon Murray, "The End of the Cold War, Attitude Change, and the Politics of Defense Spending," *Political Science and Politics* 27 (March 1994), 17–21. They also note there was a similar sea-change in perceptions of Russian motivations between 1988 and 1992 among American elites. Fully 80 percent of those who had agreed in 1988 that the Soviet Union was generally expansionist in its foreign policy goals did not think the same about Russia by 1992. Likewise, by 1992 an overwhelming majority agreed that defense spending should be cut.

[7] Thomas Risse-Kappen, "Public Opinion, Domestic Structure, and Foreign Policy in Liberal Democracies," *World Politics* 43 (July 1991), 479–512.

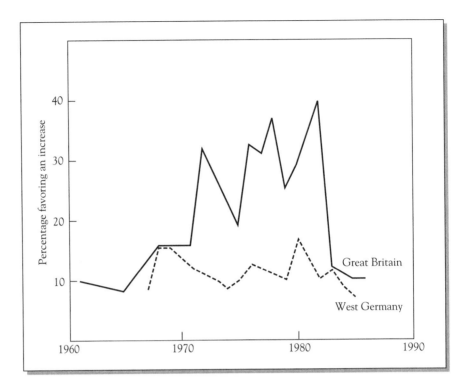

**FIGURE 9.2**    Percentage of Britons and West Germans favoring more defense spending, 1961–1986. [*Source:* Richard Eichenberg, *Public Opinion and National Security in Western Europe: A Study of Public Opinion* (Ithaca, N.Y.: Cornell University Press, 1989).]

knowledgeable about foreign affairs, say they follow news about other countries, and have attitudes that are fairly stable over time. Some of these people talk about foreign affairs with others and discuss their own positions.

But only about 5 percent of the population can be considered politically active. Because of their interest and, to a lesser degree, their social roles (as, for example, teachers, clergy, and active participants in civic affairs), these people are sometimes called opinion leaders. Within this group is a small segment of the population who give money or time to political activities and communicate their opinions beyond their personal acquaintances. Often these people, sometimes called *mobiliz-ables* or, in a weaker sense than in power elite theory, *elites*, write, speak in public, or otherwise reach an extended audience.[8] Constituting no more than 1 or 2 percent of

---

[8] These categories are taken from Barry Hughes, *The Domestic Context of American Foreign Policy* (San Francisco: Freeman, 1978), pp. 23–24, and W. Russell Neuman, *The Paradox of Mass Politics: Knowledge and Opinion in the American Electorate* (Cambridge, Mass.: Harvard University Press, 1986).

the populace, this group primarily includes party politicians, business and labor union executives, senior civil servants, leaders in the mass media, and leaders of economic, ethnic, religious, professional, or other interest groups involved in political activities.

## The Content of Elite Opinion

Not surprisingly, membership in the segment of opinion leaders or mobilizables is closely correlated with education, income, and professional status. People who have a lot of information and who are politically active tend to have reasonably consistent attitudes that form a relatively cohesive ideology. Those who have a sizable amount of accurate information and a high degree of interest will relate various facts and principles to produce a coherent set of beliefs.[9]

Americans of higher social and economic status have tended to support official policy even more strongly than the average American, whatever that policy has happened to be. In the 1950s and early 1960s, when an active foreign policy and a strong defense were popular, highly educated, professional, upper-income Americans were more prodefense and more supportive of foreign aid and the Vietnam War than were people of lower status. When a withdrawal from some overseas commitments and a smaller defense establishment became popular later in the Vietnam period, high-status Americans held those views even more than did the total population. When, in June 1979, SALT II was still fairly popular nationwide and it looked as though it would be ratified by the Senate, higher-status people especially favored it. In the 1980s upper-income and educated people tended to favor foreign aid programs, both economic and military, and were generally more inclined than the average American to favor sending troops or military assistance to U.S. allies if they should be attacked. In Western Europe college-educated people—and also older people—were much more likely to favor their countries' continued membership in NATO than were their less educated or younger fellow citizens, who often endorsed a policy of neutrality toward the two superpowers.

Furthermore, higher-status people are more discriminating in their judgments, as should be expected of individuals with more information at their disposal. For example, when Americans were presented with a list of countries that might be attacked and asked which ones they would be willing to assist with troops, many people in the general populace gave the same answer for every country; on the other hand, American elites were much more likely to pick and choose, supporting principally those countries to which the United States was bound by ties of economic and political interest. Table 9.1 shows these results.

Upper-status Americans did diverge from official government policy in several important areas. They overwhelmingly opposed tariffs and other barriers to international trade and generally were more likely than lower-status people to favor arms-

---

[9] Norman Nie, Sidney Verba, and J. R. Petrocik, *The Changing American Voter* (Cambridge, Mass.: Harvard University Press, 1979).

**Table 9.1**   Support by U.S. Elites and the General Public for Sending U.S. Troops to Help Areas if Invaded by an Adversary, 1994

|  | Elites (Percent) | General Public (Percent) |
|---|---|---|
| Western Europe, by Russia | 91 | 54 |
| Saudi Arabia, by Iraq | 84 | 52 |
| South Korea, by North Korea | 82 | 39 |
| Israel, by Arabs | 72 | 42 |
| Poland, by Russia | 60 | 32 |

*Source:* John Reilly, "The Public Mood at Mid-Decade," *Foreign Policy* 98 (Spring 1995), p. 90.

control agreements, "an immediate, verifiable freeze on testing and production of nuclear weapons," and lower levels of defense spending. Table 9.2 shows some of these results (from 1984 and 1986 polls).

Women at all levels of the population are generally more dovish on foreign policy than are men. For example, in a January 1991 Gallup poll 78 percent of men approved the decision to send U.S. troops to the Persian Gulf, compared with only 54 percent of women. Similarly, 67 percent of men favored going to war to expel Iraq from Kuwait, compared with only 45 percent of women. (In all cases, however, more women said they were "unaware" or gave no opinion; men are more likely at least to say they are interested in foreign affairs, although this aspect of the "gender gap" has been narrowing.)

Faced with this and similar evidence, many scholars believe that the general support for official American foreign policy, both among American opinion leaders and in the populace in general, has been shattered. Some point to a fourfold division of ideology, categorizing people very broadly as "isolationists" versus "international-ists" and as "hard-liners" versus "accommodationists" (in regard to Soviet–U.S. rela-tions). Although internationalists and accommodationists are somewhat more common among the elites than among the general public, all types can be found at all levels. A major project has periodically surveyed top-level American leaders since 1976. The first of these surveys found a fragmentation of opinion among those leaders, which the investigators attributed primarily to the impact of the Vietnam War. About one-sixth of the leaders reported that they wanted to seek a complete military victory both at the beginning and at the end of U.S. involvement in Vietnam. Another sixth tended to favor a complete withdrawal from Vietnam not only at the end but also when the war first became a political issue. Even when surveyed again in the 1980s, these two groups, the extreme hawks and doves, remained large, and opposed each other on a wide range of foreign policy beliefs and attitudes. Within the two-thirds of

**TABLE 9.2** Positions of the U.S. Public on Military Issues, According to Income and Education

| Issue | Annual Income | | Education | |
|---|---|---|---|---|
| | High | Low | High | Low |
| Bilateral nuclear test ban (April 1986) | | | | |
|     For | 65% | 55% | 65% | 50% |
|     Against | 31 | 33 | 31 | 36 |
|     No opinion | 5 | 13 | 4 | 14 |
| Defense spending (March 1986) | | | | |
|     Too much | 47 | 47 | 52 | 44 |
|     Too little | 11 | 13 | 9 | 16 |
|     About right or no opinion | 42 | 40 | 39 | 40 |
| Verifiable freeze (October 1984) | | | | |
|     For | 82 | 74 | 85 | 71 |
|     Against | 15 | 21 | 14 | 21 |
|     No opinion | 3 | 5 | 1 | 8 |

*Note:* "High income" is $30,000 and above in 1984 and $35,000 and above in 1986; "low income" is under $10,000 in 1984 and under $15,000 in 1986. "High education" is having completed college; "low education" is not having completed high school.

*Source: Gallup Report,* various issues.

the leaders who fell in between the two extremes of military victory and withdrawal or who changed their positions in the course of the war, very different conclusions have been drawn about the war, and very different preferences for policy are held today. Although these nonextremists in some sense make up the center of opinion, they show little unity of opinion. They have been divided on arms control and security issues, on whether the United States should intervene militarily abroad, and on policy toward human rights and economic development in less developed countries.

These data suggest that there is no longer any elite consensus on the *means* by which foreign policy should be pursued or even on which *ends* (peace or power, for instance) are most important.[10] It should hardly be surprising, therefore, that similar

---

[10] Eugene Wittkopf, *Faces of Internationalism: Public Opinion and American Foreign Policy* (Durham, N.C.: Duke University Press, 1990); Ole R. Holsti and James N. Rosenau, *American Leadership in World Affairs: Vietnam and the Breakdown of Consensus* (Boston: Allen & Unwin, 1984); Holsti and Rosenau, "Domestic and Foreign Policy Belief Systems Among American Leaders," *Journal of Conflict Resolution* 32, 2 (June 1988), 248–294.

divisions exist among the general public and that broad shifts in policy usually occur whenever a new group of political leaders takes charge of the government after an election.

## Interactions Among the Elite

The power elite perspective also stresses a system of interpersonal relations, past and present, that serves to maintain the unity of opinion among the powerful. For that to happen, elite members would have to interact frequently on a wide scale. They would need a dense network of communication, knowing and seeing one another professionally and socially—on boards of directors, in social clubs, and through civic, private, or professional organizations.

A study by Gwen Moore examined the network of direct personal contacts among people identified in a survey of American leaders. She found that for two-thirds of the leaders, the network of contacts was fragmented into small, relatively isolated groups in which members tended to share interests with one another only on specific issues. The remaining third, however, all were found to be part of a single large cluster of frequently interacting people. In this "central circle," the contacts were broad—not limited to specific issues—and dense, with members having an average of 8.7 different kinds of contacts with one another. In addition, this central circle was connected with many of the small, issue-based circles. Members of the central circle were highly visible and potentially influential. They wrote more, spoke in public more, and were more likely to belong to federal advisory committees or such policy-planning organizations as the Council on Foreign Relations or the Committee for Economic Development. "Wide visibility, as measured by level of communications output, is far higher for members than nonmembers of the central circle in nearly all sectors. This potential influence over public opinion strongly distinguished circle members from nonmembers." These findings suggest that although the allegations that America is ruled by a power elite may well be exaggerated, there does exist a social basis whereby "the central circle directly and indirectly integrates leaders of a wide variety of institutions into a network capable of discussing and resolving issues of national concern."[11]

Whether this potential influence is in fact achieved, especially in foreign policy, we cannot say. We do not have information relating social contacts to specific views among members of the central circle; more important, we do not have information on whether their access to one another is really converted into influence and power. Here is another instance of the problem, discussed in Chapter 6, of trying to infer *effective* influence from *attempts* to influence.

---

[11] Gwen Moore, "The Structure of a National Elite Network," *American Sociological Review* 44 (October 1979), 673–692.

## THE EFFECT OF PUBLIC OPINION ON GOVERNMENT POLICY

We certainly cannot exhaust the topic or provide final answers, but some further observations are worth making, especially concerning American governmental institutions. First, we can ask *how* public opinion, or at least attentive public opinion, affects policy; second, we can ask *when* that effect may be greatest.

### How Public Opinion Affects Policy

1. *By setting broad limits of constraint* and identifying a range of policies within which decision makers must choose if they are not to face retaliation in competitive elections. These constraints—or public opinion "mood"—are clearly quite broad, though they are likely to be felt more intensely as a national election nears. Of course, this still begs the question of how strongly mass opinion is itself merely shaped or controlled by elites who command public attention and the mass media.

2. *By constraining policy execution.* Top decision makers must depend on subordinates, from military officers and high-level civil servants down to foot soldiers and clerks, to carry out their policies. Subordinates have many ways to drag their feet or sabotage policies that they do not like.

3. *By distorting or selectively screening information* given to top decision makers. Top leaders must depend on their subordinates not only to execute policy but also to provide the information on which decisions are to be made. The specific interests or general ideological views of subordinates—perhaps extending quite far down in the information-handling chain—will affect the completeness, nature, and interpretation of information that will be passed upward. An information screen lets some information through and holds other information back; a secretary with the power to screen is a simple but nonetheless potentially powerful example. Screens may be found in organizations within the government—and within individuals' minds as they consider what information to pay attention to and what to ignore.

4. *As part of the climate of opinion,* by eventually shaping the top decision makers themselves. The recruitment base from which future leaders will be drawn is the broad set of today's middle-echelon figures.

### When Public Opinion Affects Policy

1. It matters greatly whether the policy *is important to a specific minority* of citizens or leaders, especially a high-status and thus potentially influential minority. Some issues directly affect important ethnic or religious groups. (Many Mexican-Americans worry about immigration laws, such as the 1994 referendum passed in California; many Jews, as well as other Americans, are strongly committed to Israel's security.) Other issues affect farmers (grain sales to China), auto workers (imports from Japan), arms manufacturers (arms sales abroad), and other economic interest groups (on

broad issues of free trade, including NAFTA or GATT). Others are the focus of groups concerned with protecting the environment (the Sierra Club).

**2.** Not only the specific issue, but *broad classes of issues,* probably make a difference. Most matters of foreign economic policy (for example, trade) are of primary interest only to the kinds of interest groups just noted and are not usually matters of concern to the mass public or to most of the attentive public. In contrast, issues of military or political security (arms control, the Gulf War, U.S. troop missions to Somalia or into the Bosnian situation) are much more likely to capture the attention and concern of broad segments of the public.

**3.** The *time frame* matters. Issues that can or must be resolved quickly, before opinion can be changed or rallied, are not likely to be very constrained by mass public opinion. The longer an issue stays alive, the more public attitudes are likely to matter.

Congress is said to be especially sensitive to the needs and demands of particular, narrow interests. More precisely, particular members of Congress are likely to be especially sensitive to the needs of major interests in their constituencies or other interests that provide them with support at election time. Defense industry executives can expect a favorable hearing from the U.S. representatives in whose districts they employ many workers. Representatives from Iowa will care about foreign grain sales. The representative who chairs the House Merchant Marine Committee is likely to be solicitous of shipowners, shipbuilders, and merchant sailors, wherever those interests are located. They can provide (or withhold) financial and other support at election time.

Sometimes a president can persuade Congress to adopt an important defense or foreign policy measure even if public opinion opposes it. For instance, President Carter in 1978 urged senators to do the "statesmanlike" thing and support the Panama Canal treaties, despite sentiment against the treaties as measured by most polls. Two-thirds of the Senate did support the treaties, and they were ratified. The next year, however, Carter met with failure. SALT II was favored by more people than opposed it, but many either had no opinion or had never heard of the treaty. With such lukewarm approval in the mass public and a worsening international atmosphere, a majority of the Senate remained unconvinced. SALT II was dropped by the Reagan administration when it took office.

A major review of public opinion and government policy changes between 1935 and 1979 found that in two-thirds of all cases (including foreign policy issues) where there was a shift in public opinion and a subsequent change in public policy, the policy change was in the same direction as the public opinion change. Moreover, the government was more likely to shift in the direction of public preferences than vice versa. Studies of the interaction between attitudes toward defense spending and congressional decisions to increase or cut the president's military spending proposals have found a strong relationship between opinion and subsequent policy. Public preferences for higher or lower defense spending are very good predictors of whether actual defense spending will go up or down in the next year. The degree to which their constituencies favored higher defense spending—as measured by public opinion polls—made a great difference in whether individual members of Congress voted for the military expansion during the Reagan years.[12]

This evidence seems to indicate that the American democratic form of government is fairly responsive to the will of the general public. We must nonetheless be cautious with this interpretation, because we do not know *why* public opinion changes. It may well be that public opinion changes because opinion leaders and elites—including government officials—first express a preference and then persuade the attentive public and the mass public to voice that preference. Then Congress, including some of the very people who helped change public opinion, can "respond" to that public change. Certainly this possibility often seems more plausible than the simple notion of Congress merely being obedient to the "voice of the people." The interaction between opinion change and policy change is complex.

## THE CHIEF OF STATE

The chief of state—the president, prime minister, or monarch—embodies the national interest. He or she is at the top of the political pyramid, responsible for bringing together all the separate individual and group interests. Personality, character, experience, and leadership style surely matter in determining what choices a leader makes. So, too, does the relationship he or she has with advisers and subordinates, the people who provide information, help make decisions, and are responsible for carrying out decisions. We shall look intensively at these considerations of individual characteristics and role relationships in the next chapter; here we want to ask another kind of question: How constrained is the top leader by the general structure of mass and elite opinion in the society? Does public opinion matter to the chief? If so, when and how?

### Mass Opinions

According to one view, mass opinions set limits on the range of actions that a political leader may safely take. One version of this view stresses the constraint that ideological anticommunism among the masses imposed on the freedom of action of leaders in the United States.

American policymakers in the 1960s, for example, feared a backlash of militant anticommunism by the general populace in reaction to major foreign policy reverses. They remembered the domestic political costs incurred by the Truman administration

---

[12] The major review is Benjamin Page and Robert Shapiro, "Effects of Public Opinion on Policy," *American Political Science Review* 77, 1 (March 1983), 175–190. The findings on defense spending are reported, with further references, in Bruce Russett, *Controlling the Sword: The Democratic Governance of National Security* (Cambridge, Mass.: Harvard University Press, 1990), Chap. 4, and Larry Bartels, "Constituency Opinion and Congressional Policy Making: The Reagan Defense Buildup," *American Political Science Review* 85, 2 (June 1991), 457–474.

resulting from the trauma of "losing China" and the witch-hunting of the McCarthy era. In the words of former Senator Sam Ervin, "You can't believe the terror that man [Senator Joseph McCarthy] spread among politicians." Thus politicians feared to unleash a popular anticommunism that would punish them for foreign policy defeats and were therefore constrained by popular anticommunism even though they themselves were too sophisticated to accept all its premises.

Consequently, believing that the American people would not tolerate the "loss" of Vietnam, senior officials in Washington resolved that Vietnam would not be lost—at least, not during their terms in office. They would hang on and escalate when necessary to avoid defeat, even though they knew the long-term prospects for holding the country were poor. They could hope to postpone the day of reckoning until a time when they themselves would not be held responsible, perhaps even hoping against all available evidence that events would break favorably so that the ultimate outcome would not be disastrous. According to some analysts, this kind of thinking could be found in every administration from Truman's to Nixon's.[13]

## *Support from the Populace*

A very different point of view, however, maintains that the leader has great potential support among the populace for virtually any kind of foreign policy initiative. A leader can take either hawkish or dovish initiatives and, with the authority and respect he or she commands, still be backed by a substantial portion of the population. For example, the possibilities for leadership even on such a hotly disputed issue as "peace for land" in Israel are shown by responses to a question that asked whether people would "support a peace agreement that involves giving up most of the territories." At first, 45 percent said yes. But when the qualification, "if the government supports it" was added, the proportion of those who would agree rose to 54 percent. Symmetrically, the phrase "if the government is against it" dropped support to 36 percent. In two surveys made in early 1989, the percentage of the Israeli population willing to allow Palestinians to hold local elections jumped by 17 points after the usually hawkish Prime Minister Yitzhak Shamir endorsed a similar plan. An extreme example appeared in answer to the question, "Do you believe it is essential, or not, to support a government during a security crisis, like war, even when one does not agree with what it is doing?" Eighty-eight percent said yes.[14]

---

[13] This is basically the interpretation of Daniel Ellsberg, "The Quagmire Myth and the Stalemate Machine," *Public Policy?* 19, 2 (Spring 1971), 217–274. See also Leslie Gelb and Richard Betts, *Vietnam: The System Worked* (Washington, D.C.: Brookings Institution, 1979). To an important degree, popular anticommunism was built up by policymakers themselves. In 1947, for example, Senator Arthur Vandenberg advised Harry Truman to use the threat of communism to "scare hell out of the country" as a means of getting Congress to approve aid to Greece. Once this force was unleashed, policymakers felt more constrained by it than they wished to be.

[14] See Asher Arian, *National Security Public Opinion in Israel* (Boulder, Colo.: Westview, 1988), and Russett, *Controlling the Sword*, chap. 2.

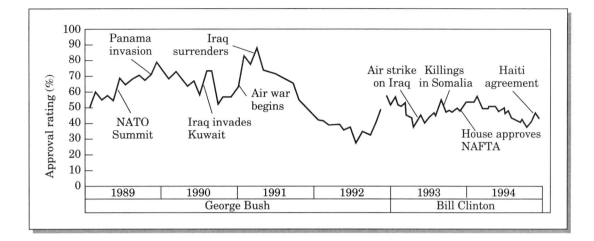

**FIGURE 9.3**  President Bush's and President Clinton's popularity. [*Source:* Gallup poll press release; *New York Times,* September 18, 1994, p. E5; *The Gallup Poll Monthly,* September 1994, pp. 18, 22–23.]

The ability of a nation's leader to gather support for a variety of foreign policy initiatives, so long as the leader is perceived as doing something, has been termed the **rally-'round-the-flag** phenomenon and can be seen in the experience of almost all recent U.S. presidents.[15] Figure 9.3 illustrates trends and fluctuations in a standard Gallup survey question asked about twice every month: "Do you approve or disapprove of the way [name] is handling his job as president?"

Both the trend and the fluctuations are the result of many influences, including domestic events and the state of the economy as well as foreign policy and international events. Every president begins with a "honeymoon" jump in popularity immediately after taking office. And nearly all presidents experience some decline in their popularity over their term in office, as they carry out policies that displease various groups in the population. George Bush and Bill Clinton both have had that experience—and in Bush's case the long-term decline was magnified by his sharp but temporary bursts of popularity associated with major initiatives in the field of national security.

---

[15] The phrase, from a Civil War song, is used in this sense in John E. Mueller, *War, Presidents, and Public Opinion* (New York: Wiley, 1973). A later analysis of data on presidential popularity, refuting some of Mueller's conclusions but confirming most, is Samuel Kernell, "Explaining Presidential Popularity," *American Political Science Review* 72, 2 (June 1978), 506–522.

For example, when in December 1989 he ordered U.S. troops to invade Panama to depose the government of Manuel Noriega, President Bush's popularity rating rose by 9 percentage points. But it then fell fairly sharply until Iraq's invasion of Kuwait in August 1990, and Bush's quick decision to impose an economic embargo and send American troops to defend Saudi Arabia against a possible Iraqi attack. That rally, however, was very short-lived, since people began to fear war with Iraq and the country was deeply divided about the wisdom of war. But in the beginning of 1991, by which time Bush had carefully cultivated national and international support, negotiations failed. Bush's support rose by an extraordinary amount—about 19 percentage points—with the beginning of the air war, went down for a while, and then rose again by 9 points with the short and successful land campaign of Operation Desert Storm. But see from Figure 9.3 that all of these rallies were extremely brief. They usually waned within two or three months, and they did not prevent a long-term decline in Bush's popularity that by mid-1992 brought his ratings nearly as low as Jimmy Carter's had been at the depth of his popularity.

With the end of the cold war and the absence of anything that could be depicted as an immediate threat to vital American interests, President Clinton gained very little benefit from rally effects. As Figure 9.3 shows, he got a short blip of popularity (7 points) in June 1993 by ordering an air strike against Iraq in retaliation for a plot to assassinate Bush, but nothing else helped much. Most popularity changes associated with any Clinton foreign policy action were very small and may have been nothing more than chance variations. There were no jumps accompanying the October 1993 deaths of American peacekeepers in Somalia, for which some people blamed Clinton, or the passage of NAFTA in November 1993. (Each survey takes opinions from a different random sample of Americans, and there is a chance that the percentage expressing an opinion in any poll will differ from that of the preceding survey merely beause of chance differences in the sample. Analysts usually do not treat differences of 3 percent or less between two surveys as statistically significant.)

The best Clinton could do was a 9-point gain in September 1994 when he announced that former President Jimmy Carter had reached an agreement with the Haitian dictatorship for a peaceful turnover of power when American troops went ashore. Half of that gain, however, was gone within a week! The only real popularity winner was Carter; 80 percent of the population approved of the job he had been doing as a foreign policy negotiator.

Leaders of other countries also try to take advantage of a rally-'round-the-flag effect. In the spring of 1982 British Prime Minister Margaret Thatcher gained great personal popularity by her tough response to the Argentine seizure of what Britain calls the Falkland Islands, and she won the next election handily. The Argentine military government also hoped to benefit from a rally. It chose a time when it was politically unpopular, and when the Argentine economy was stagnating, to rekindle the longstanding dispute with Britain and invade the islands. But the effort to make itself popular backfired when it lost the war, and the army government was then overthrown (note that is not the first time in this chapter we have seen the impact of the diversionary logic that was discussed earlier).

## Limits of Leaders' Support

A chief of state cannot do anything he or she likes and expect general public support. There is some evidence that using force or threatening to use force is initially more popular than are conciliatory or cooperative acts toward foreign adversaries: the former seems to produce a rise of 4 or 5 percentage points in the president's popularity; the latter only a 1- or 2-point change, often downward. But people's reaction depends partly on their images of the president. They fear extremes. Presidents perceived by the public as doves, as Carter was, tend to be most approved when they talk or act tough, as Carter did to the Soviet Union when it invaded Afghanistan. President Reagan, generally seen as a hawk, gained especially from more dovish acts. While the public approved his military action in Grenada, they also approved his withdrawal of troops from Lebanon.[16] In 1987, to the consternation of some of his military and hardline political advisers, Reagan signed an agreement with the Russians for nuclear arms control in Europe. One motivation may have been to restore some of his flagging popularity.

As the Israeli survey data showed, people can be led to support either confrontational or conciliatory policies as long as both are in moderation. Strength, toughness, and deterrence all are popular, but so too are negotiation and conciliation. In response to a survey question commonly asked during the cold war, about one fourth of the American population typically chose, "It's clear Russia can't be trusted and we will have to rely on increased military strength to counter them." Another fourth answered, "We should do nothing that is likely to provoke an American–Russian conflict but instead should try to negotiate and reason out our differences." About half essentially combined the two: "We should take a strong position with the Russians now so they won't go any further, but at the same time we should try to reestablish good relations with them."[17] Echoing the truism "negotiate from strength," the last group would emphasize both elements, negotiation and strength. The public thus seems to synthesize realist views of world politics about the importance of power and self-help with transnational/idealist ones about the need for negotiation and cooperation, even with adversaries. Bush's diplomacy before the invasion of Iraq masterfully combined themes appealing to "internationalists" (maintain collective security), "hardliners" (use force against aggressors), and "accommodationists" (start with economic sanctions, and negotiate before fighting). As a result, he was able to amass overwhelming support.

---

[16] Charles W. Ostrom and Dennis Simon, "Promise and Performance: A Dynamic Model of Presidential Popularity," *American Political Science Review* 79, 2 (June 1985), 334–358; Miroslav Nincic, "America's Soviet Policy and the Politics of Opposites," *World Politics* 35, 4 (July 1988), 452–475.

[17] William Schneider, "Rambo and Reality: Having It Both Ways," in Kenneth Oye, Robert Lieber, and Donald Rothchild, eds., *Eagle Resurgent? The Reagan Era in American Foreign Policy* (Boston: Little Brown, 1987), p. 49.

The ability of a leader to shape public opinion and thus to generate support in a crisis usually holds for the short term only. The life of a burst of popular support is four or five months at the most, and more often only about two. By the end of that time, support usually returns to its previous, lower level. The reason is related to the reason for the rally in the first place. In the first week or two after a sudden military action or major diplomatic event, criticism of the president, even by opposition political leaders, is usually muted. The president has the most information about foreign policy and security affairs, especially in fast-breaking crises. Opposition leaders who criticize the president risk being exposed as poorly informed. The absence of criticism looks like bipartisan support to much of the public, and so ordinary people are also reluctant to criticize. But in time, as the chief of state's policy begins to falter or less favorable information about the circumstances becomes available, opposition political leaders become bolder, and their renewed criticism is picked up by the media and then by the general public. The rally effect then decays.[18]

Presidents worry about their popularity with the public. It affects not only their own or their party's prospects for reelection, but also their ability to get support in Congress for their legislative program. Presidents try to preserve and build their popularity by choosing policies and policy instruments that will be popular. Franklin Roosevelt was the first president to use scientific opinion polling extensively; he closely watched public opinion before Pearl Harbor to determine his tactics to move the United States into World War II. He first chose greater military spending and lend-lease—not the draft or direct intervention—because those instruments offered the greatest potential for domestic approval. President Reagan developed an extensive organization to monitor public opinion and used its information in making decisions.

## Are Wars Popular?

The shorter the decision time available to a leader (and short decision time is one element in the definition of a crisis), the less constrained by public opinion he or she is likely to be. The short-term rally effect helps powerfully. This is especially strong in national security affairs, because people tend to feel that the commander in chief has secret information and special competence. We saw this effect after the war with Iraq began. But if a crisis drags on, dissenting voices become more widely heard and constraints built into the political structure become more effective. Bush was careful to make clear to American critics of his policy that the United States had many allies and UN approval for his action. Even so, American strategy was geared to a short war with few American deaths, so as to end the conflict before domestic opposition could build up.

A president who wishes to respond militarily to a foreign adversary can mount an action with existing military forces and without prior approval from Congress. A majority of the public will probably support the action, and if it is successful it may be

---

[18] Richard A. Brody, "International Crises: A Rallying Point for the President?" *Public Opinion* 6, 6 (December 1983/January 1984), 41–43, 60. On Britain, see David Sanders, Hugh Ward, and David March, "Government Popularity and the Falklands War: A Reassessment," *British Journal of Political Science* 17 (July 1987), 281–314.

widely applauded. The year-in, year-out maintenance of military action abroad, however, requires congressional approval and the appropriation of funds in circumstances in which the trade-offs with domestic welfare become much more apparent and politically salient. Domestic constraints may therefore limit the president's menu of choice in a crisis by favoring those forms of military action (bombing, overwhelming force in an invasion, possibly even nuclear weapons) that bring quick results, rather than protracted warfare with heavy American casualties.

In the long run wars are almost always harmful to the political health of those who conduct them. The popularity of Truman, Johnson, and Nixon was damaged by war. After a brief spurt of national unity, wars typically produce a loss of social cohesion and low popular morale, manifested in higher rates of strikes, crime, and violent political protest. Least healthy for a leader is, of course, to lose a major war; every great-power government that lost a major war in the past century was overthrown from within if not by its external enemies.[19] But even leaders, and their parties, who conduct and win costly wars are likely to be punished by the voters. Winston Churchill, the popular British World War II leader, lost the 1945 election to the Labour party by a landslide. Governments lose popularity directly in proportion to the length and cost (in blood and money) of the war. All of America's wars of the past century have shown this pattern, with the president who was in office when the war began and/or his party doing poorly in subsequent elections. (Sometimes they won the elections, but by a smaller margin than would be predicted from the prosperous state of the economy.[20])

Political leaders, especially in a democracy, live a precarious life in which the demands made upon them always exceed the leaders' capacity to satisfy them. They are expected to solve many—and often contradictory—social problems, to provide employment and prosperity without inflation, and, of course, to maintain peace with strength. They know that they will be rewarded or punished at the polls in proportion to the healthiness of the economy. (One of the strongest relationships in political science is that between the change in the rate of economic growth in the year before an election and the share of the vote that will go to the party in power. This is true in almost all industrial democratic societies, including Western Europe, Japan, and Israel.[21]) Knowing this, they try to stimulate the economy so as to raise the necessary popular support. But modern economies are complicated systems, often beyond ready control, and government taxing and spending policies will help some people and hurt others. Thus leaders may be unable to buy electoral popularity by filling their constituents' pocketbooks. If they cannot control the economy, leaders may then turn to foreign policy in order to increase their support.

---

[19] See Bruce Bueno de Mesquita, Randolph Siverson, and Gary Woller, "War and the Fate of Regimes: A Comparative Analysis," *American Political Science Review* 86 (September 1992), 638–657.

[20] Arthur Stein and Bruce Russett, "Evaluating War: Outcomes and Consequences," in Ted Robert Gurr, ed., *Handbook of Political Conflict:Theory and Research* (New York: Free Press, 1980); Timothy Cotton, "War and American Democracy: Voting Trends in the Last Five American Wars," *Journal of Conflict Resolution* 30, 4 (December 1986), 616–635.

[21] The relationship of voting patterns to economic conditions was first well established by Gerald Kramer, "Short-Term Fluctuations in Voting Behavior," *American Political Science Review* 65, 1 (March 1971), 131–143; later work is summarized in Russett, *Controlling the Sword*, chap. 2.

Here is where the rally-'round-the-flag effect may be especially useful. According to one study, a U.S. president is more likely to use or escalate military force if he is seeking reelection during a developing or ongoing war, when he knows that voters will be more concerned than usual about foreign affairs and therefore more likely to hold it against him if the war goes badly (thus, the concern with the proverbial "October surprise" in presidential election years). He is also more likely to win congressional approval on even unrelated international issues in the month following a use of force. Another study showed that over the past century U.S. presidents have been more likely to use or threaten to use military force internationally in years when the economy was doing badly or when there was a national election. However, research indicates constraints on the use of force as well. There is evidence to indicate that the use of force by one democracy against another will result in decreased support and popularity of the leader.[22] This was especially true when poor economic conditions and an election coincided. As an authority on the presidency says, "The desperate search is no longer for the good life but for the effective presentation of appearances. This is a pathology because it escalates the rhetoric at home, ratcheting expectations upward notch by notch, and fuels adventurism abroad."[23]

Leaders of other democratic countries—especially great powers or countries that are a match for regional enemies and that sometimes have control over the timing of when they will engage in international conflict—show similar behavior. A study of Israeli decisions to use force found that, even when controlling for the incidence of aggressive acts by Arab neighbors, the Israeli government was more likely to respond militarily in periods before a national election or when the economy was doing poorly. An example was the raid on the Iraqi nuclear reactor on June 7, 1981. That was just three weeks before Menachem Begin, the incumbent prime minister, was to face voters in a general election. However substantial the military justification for the strike, it could have been postponed for a few months with little harm to Israeli security. As it was, Begin's party benefited greatly from an outpouring of public approval despite severe economic difficulties from inflation. In states without obvious military enemies the rally effect can be dramatic even in the event of major policy conflict with allies. For example, support for a ban on nuclear weapons entering New Zealand almost doubled (from 40 to 76 percent) after the government adopted such a ban and the United States responded with a confrontational policy.[24]

Countries are more likely to engage in international military disputes when periods of domestic political turmoil coincide with opportunities abroad. This does

---

[22] See Alex Mintz and Nehemia Geva, "Why Don't Democracies Fight Each Other? An Experimental Assessment of the 'Political Incentive' Explanation," *Journal of Conflict Resolution* 37 (September 1993), 484–503, for analyses based on experiments run both in the United States and Israel.

[23] Richard J. Stoll, *U.S. National Security Policy and the Soviet Union* (Columbia: University of South Carolina Press, 1990), chap. 3; Charles W. Ostrom and Brian L. Job, "The President and the Political Use of Force," *American Political Science Review* 80, 2 (June 1986), 541–566. The quotation is from Theodore Lowi, *The Personal President* (Ithaca, N.Y.: Cornell University Press, 1985), p. 20.

[24] James W. LeMare, "International Conflict: ANZUS and New Zealand," *Journal of Conflict Resolution* 31, 3 (September 1987), 420–437.

not mean that leaders deliberately involve their countries in war solely to boost their own electoral chances. Sometimes they may actually be taking dramatic steps for peace or arms control, or, more often, they may be tempted to talk tough, make threats, or indulge in small-scale uses of military force to impress the voters or divert voters' attentions from their economic troubles. The risk is that sometimes these acts can get tragically out of hand.

Leaders thus in some sense both respond to and manipulate public opinion. They respond to it by doing what will be popular in the short run when domestic economic and political conditions encourage them to maximize votes. They also may manipulate it by trying to increase their popularity without correcting the underlying causes of mass discontent that endangered their popularity in the first place.

## *Who Governs? Who Cares?*

International and security issues are remote for most people, even those of the upper socioeconomic classes. Only a small proportion of the population directly benefits from military spending; in any given year relatively few travel very far abroad and even fewer obtain much information relevant for evaluating complex foreign policy issues. Foreign policy is thus a prime candidate for what has been termed symbolic politics.[25] In an earlier era people depended heavily on personal contact with opinion leaders, who relayed information and interpreted events. In the electronic era news shows bring information and interpretation directly into American living rooms via television.

People may support a policy for any of three reasons: (1) because doing so satisfies psychological needs, (2) because on the basis of available information they perceive the policy as consistent with certain interests and beliefs, and (3) because the segment of their social environment most meaningful to them reaffirms support. Although high-status people are no more or less likely than others to have particular psychological needs, they are more likely to live in a social environment in which international affairs are considered important. Thus, when cues in their environment change, they are more likely to change their opinions for two interacting reasons. First, new information indicating that a given foreign policy is inconsistent with personal beliefs and interests is especially likely to reach them, thus prompting them to reassess their beliefs. Second, because this likelihood applies to all members of the high-status group, the general support from the social environment for the old beliefs will decrease.

A different kind of perspective emerges when we look at attitudes toward security policy in Western Europe. As noted, support for official NATO defense policy during the cold war was always strongest among the elites there. Lower-status people tended to be less committed to NATO and to specific policies concerning the use of

---

[25] D. O. Sears et al., "Self-Interest vs. Symbolic Politics in Policy Attitudes and Presidential Voting," *American Political Science Review* 74, 3 (September 1980), 670–685.

nuclear weapons. For instance, despite near-solid government support for deployment of new intermediate-range missiles during 1983, the general public was very skeptical. Also, official NATO policy was always that although NATO would never start a war, it would follow a policy of flexible response if the Soviets invaded Western Europe—that is, if the Soviets seemed to be winning, even with a purely conventional (nonnuclear) attack, NATO forces would retain the option of escalating the conflict by a first use of nuclear weapons. But most ordinary Europeans were extremely worried about the consequences of using nuclear weapons in that densely populated region of the world. Fewer than 20 percent of them in the major countries (Britain, France, Italy, and West Germany) said they approved of a first-use policy.[26] What their verbal disapproval really meant in political terms is unclear; they were not necessarily willing, for example, to spend more money to strengthen nonnuclear defense forces. Nevertheless, this longstanding tension between elite and mass attitudes in Europe posed problems for Western security policy and the unity of NATO. It required the pursuit of double-track negotiations: deploying new nuclear forces while simultaneously trying to negotiate—ultimately successfully—a mutual disarmament pact with the Soviet Union.

Overall, our view of the importance of public opinion is complex, depending very much on the kind of *issue, the circumstances, the level of government* at which the decision is made, and other specific features of the political context. Certainly there is no immediate, automatic connection, even in a democracy, between public opinion and foreign policy. Political decision makers are skilled leaders of opinion, with ready access to television, newspapers, and other media; they shape opinion as well as respond to it. Always we are bedeviled by the problems of making inferences about power and of differentiating between the *activity* of people or pressure groups and their *influence*. It is clear, however, that public opinion does matter—whether as an immediate determinant of national willingness, or as a constraint on leaders' search for approval of particular policies and the rhetoric they use to justify their actions. Realist theories that ignore public opinion miss something important.

---

[26] Russett, *Controlling the Sword*, chap. 4.

# INDIVIDUALS AND WORLD POLITICS: ROLE, COMMUNICATION, AND DECISION MAKING

WORLD SYSTEM

RELATIONS

SOCIETY

GOVERNMENT

ROLE

INDIVIDUAL

## SEEING THE MENU AND MAKING CHOICES

Foreign policy decisions are made by people, either as individuals or as part of a group. The individual foreign policy decision maker is surrounded by several layers of environment, external and domestic, which constrain and limit in a number of ways what the decision maker is able or is likely to do. Each layer blends into others that sandwich it. There are connections between systemic and societal factors, between societal and governmental factors, and between governmental and role factors. In this chapter and the next, we shall investigate the individual in world politics as affected by role and idiosyncratic influences. These impinge directly on the individual who plays a part in the development and execution of foreign policy.

By looking at individuals, we have moved from the broadest context, the systemic or the global system, to the narrowest—the individual involved in the foreign policy process. One way in which an entity, here an individual, relates to its environment is through that individual's **perceptions** of the environment. Individuals have images of the world that influence decision making. What is actually "out there" is of less importance than what the decision maker thinks is out there. The possibilities and probabilities provided by the domestic and global environments will affect plans and decisions only as they are perceived and understood by decision makers.

Many constraints on the foreign policy menu of any state thus derive from the perceptions and images of individuals in the government of that state. If the menu cannot be read; if the diner reading the menu sees only what he or she wants to see or later argues with the waiter, insisting that the menu said that wine was served free of charge (when clearly it did not); if the decisions on what to order are made by a group, so that no one really gets his or her preference; or if the individual feels pressured to order something because of the preferences of everyone else—then the range of possibilities and probabilities will be affected. This influence or constraint on behavior comes from within the individual as a pressure to see the world in certain ways. Our concern here is with those things that affect how the individual perceives the world and how the individual makes foreign policy decisions. We are concerned with willingness rather than opportunity.

Moving down our series of levels of analysis, in this chapter we shall discuss the *role factor.* One of the important characteristics of individuals who help make foreign policy is their position within the government. Where a person fits in the government and what duties, responsibilities, and loyalties are connected with that position will affect the individual's images of the world and his or her foreign policy decisions. The heart of decision making, and our attempts to understand and explain it, rests in how information is processed. We must therefore consider the influences that affect how the processing of information takes place. Many such mechanisms exist within organizations and within the government as a whole. It is important to note that where an individual sits within a governmental structure depends on that individual's role. Analogous mechanisms for information processing are found in each individual, as she or he perceives the world and attempts to make sense of those perceptions.

## Governments and Decision Makers as Information Processors

Governments differ in many ways. Most of these differences involve the acquisition, processing, and movement of information. Governments differ in the types and numbers of organizations and institutions within them, the distribution of influence among these organizations and institutions, the numbers and types of personnel in those institutions, and the societal interests they represent. Some governments are large, made up of many organizations and staffed by hundreds of thousands of people; some are small, with few people to staff the few organizations involved. Some governments centralize powers in one institution or group; others distribute governmental power among a number of institutions. Some have strong executives, who make most foreign policy; some have weak executives or executives restricted by other groups. Governments also have different forms of executives. In the United States a president shares foreign policy powers with Congress; Britain's system is a parliamentary system run by a cabinet and a prime minister. In France there is both a president and a prime minister, who are sometimes from different parties. Other systems are ruled by single parties or single individuals, as in communist governments or military dictatorships.

Although scholars have discussed how governments differ and have described those differences, we still have little systematic evidence about how the governmental structure actually affects foreign policy. Some observers argue that closed centralized governments can act more quickly and efficiently, with less public input into the process. Others maintain that more open systems can get the most out of their societies, that although democratic governments work more slowly and less single-mindedly, they produce better foreign policy because they get more diverse and accurate information from society about society's capabilities and about the constraints in both the domestic and foreign environments.

In this sense, open and closed systems differ in the quality of their information processing. Analyzing how well information is collected and employed may be the most useful way we have for comparing governmental structures as producers of effective foreign policies, including how well they "learn" and adapt to the world.[1] In this chapter and the next, we shall also look at information processing in smaller units than whole governments, at how information is handled by individuals, and variously sized groups of individuals, in making decisions.

Information is a vast, ongoing wave of signals, facts, and noise. Like governments, individuals—especially individuals in high-level positions—cannot process, handle, and understand all the available information. They must screen out some of the information directed at them from the environment. Some information is simply ignored; some is altered so as not to upset existing views or beliefs; some is looked at quickly and then either thrown out or buried. Both psychological processes and institutional organizations may be designed specifically for this **screening** process. The use of ideologies or worldviews (such as realist, transnationalist, or radical perspectives on world politics), whose beliefs and values act to filter information, make some things look more important and others less so. An individual's role in an organization—one's "job"—may be used as a way to be involved in some things and not others, to ignore or bias the flow of information. The line between organizational and psychological screening may sometimes be very fine.

Both kinds of factors affect how people make decisions. These are then implemented in some form or other as foreign policy events, which have consequences for the global system. The real world becomes important at this point, because when an

---

[1] See such work as that by Lloyd Etheredge, *Can Governments Learn? American Foreign Policy and Central American Revolutions* (New York: Pergamon, 1985).

action is taken it will become (sometimes painfully) clear how different the real world is from the decision maker's image that produced the decision. The world then provides **feedback** (information on the consequences of the action), giving decision makers a chance to reevaluate their policies, decisions, and images and to change them if necessary. How well this is done is a hallmark of "good" decision-making processes.

## DECISION MAKING: AN OVERVIEW

### Some Definitions and Criteria

Earlier we noted that the foreign policy process is constantly in motion and that all parts of that process involve the decisions and actions of people. Decision making is a process that focuses on the people involved in the foreign policy process and on the part of the process that deals with choosing among alternative courses of action. (Remember, *not choosing* to make a decision is itself a decision.) The study of decision making considers what kind of process decision making is, what factors influence how decisions are made, and what decisions are actually taken.

Many discussions stress the idea that the best decision is the "most rational" one. However, rationality is a very complex concept that carries different connotations for different analysts, and there are ongoing debates about exactly what rationality means. In the simplest formulation, **rational behavior** *is purposive behavior*, and rationality is an ability to relate means to ends. Thus **rationality** assumes that an individual can see relationships among possible alternatives (*A* is preferred to *B*, or *B* is preferred to *A*, or *A* and *B* have exactly the same value) and that some goals are consistently preferred to others. One group of scholars thinks of rationality as doing what you *believe* is in your best interest—a matter of perception.[2] However, exactly how closely means and ends are related, with what certainty they are related, and how closely the actual consequences of behavior match the consequences desired all depend on an understanding of what kind of a process decision making is. There are two distinct views on these questions. One view of rationality assumes "perfect information" that is used to "maximize" the positive outcomes or payoffs of a decision; another view relaxes these conditions and sees rationality as "bounded" by limits on human information processing and calculations, restricting the concept of rationality to the notion of purposive behavior.[3] We shall examine both views.

[2] See, for example, Frank Zagare, "Rationality and Deterrence," *World Politics* 42 (1990), 238–260, and Bruce Bueno de Mesquita, "The Contribution of Expected-Utility Theory to the Study of International Conflict," in Manus Midlarsky, ed., *Handbook of War Studies* (Boston: Unwin Hyman, 1989), pp. 143–169.

[3] See Herbert Simon, "Human Nature in Politics," *American Political Science Review* 79 (June 1985), 293–304, and Zagare, "Rationality and Deterrence."

The first view is an "ideal" picture of decision making, that is, a checklist of "perfect" conditions that would permit "perfect" decisions. No one claims that these conditions can be achieved by policymakers; John Lovell calls his formulation the *"Imaginary* Ideal Machine for Making Policy," and much scholarly work focuses on why they cannot be achieved. However, individuals attempt to approximate these conditions and in so doing are acting under bounded rationality. As our discussion of expected-utility models and models of bounded rationality will show, people can do quite well in matching means to goals.[4]

One version of the ideal maximizing model is as follows. Faced with a *given problem*, the rational decision maker first *clarifies* his or her *values, goals, and objectives* and then *orders* them in some way, usually in a **transitive,** most-to-least desired ranking. (This means that if *A* is preferred to *B* and *B* to *C*, then *A* should be preferred to *C*. This would not be the case, however, if you would prefer a blue car over a yellow one and a yellow car over a white one, but if you had to choose between blue and white, you'd choose white!) Next, the decision maker *lists* all the important possible ways to achieve those goals and then *investigates* all the important consequences of each alternative identified. Now the decision maker *compares the consequences* of the various alternatives. Finally, the decision maker *chooses* the decision or policy alternative with the consequences that most closely match his or her goals.

The decision-making process outlined here demands "perfect information"—a very stringent requirement that is extraordinarily costly in terms of time, energy, and money. We may think of rationality as a preference: people *would like* to act from informed choices that lead them toward their goals. Some scholars argue that it would actually be irrational for people to spend the time and money needed in attempting to get the perfect information required by an ideal model. We thus have models of rational decision making, such as the "vigilant information processing" model or the expected-utility approach, which start from the assumption that people *prefer* to be rational decision makers but *do not assume* the perfect information conditions of ideal models.[5]

Bruce Bueno de Mesquita describes rational choice models as starting from the idea that decision makers do what they believe is in their best interest, although that does not mean that they actually know what that interest might be. Because rational choice models are based on beliefs, they can be very useful in studying decision

---

[4] Thus, though people attempt to meet a perfect ideal, they never really succeed. See John P. Lovell, *The Challenge of American Foreign Policy: Purpose and Adaptation* (New York: Macmillan, 1985), chap. 2.

[5] See Irving Janis and Ralph Mann, *Decision Making* (New York: Free Press, 1977), and Bruce Bueno de Mesquita, "The Contribution of Expected Utility Theory." Janis and Mann's "vigilant problem solving" is based on adequately processing information so that the following problems are avoided: "gross omissions" in surveying alternatives or objectives; poor information search or failure to review the costs and risks of preferred alternatives; failure to reconsider alternatives; and failure to consider implementation problems. See also Gregory M. Herek, Irving L. Janis, and Paul Huth, "Decision Making During International Crises," *Journal of Conflict Resolution* 31 (June 1987), 203–226.

making even under conditions of incomplete information or selective perception.[6] **Expected-utility theory** is based on the idea that decision makers pursue the self-interests of their states and themselves; hence, it has often been associated with realist models of world politics. This association does not have to hold, however: it can be argued that such choice models can be applied to any policymaker, with any goals and values, who acts to achieve them. The core of expected-utility theory, as presented by Bueno de Mesquita, is as follows:

**1.** Individual decision makers are rational in the sense that they can order alternatives in terms of their preferences.

**2.** The order of preferences is transitive.

**3.** Individuals know the intensity of their preferences; that intensity is known as utility.

**4.** Individuals consider alternative means of achieving desirable ends in terms of expected utility (that is, the *utility* associated with those outcomes times the *probability* of achieving alternative outcomes).

**5.** Decision makers always select the strategy that yields the highest expected utility.

These five conditions can be understood as setting out two straightforward conditions. Decision makers' choices among opportunities are constrained by the prospects of success and failure and by the utility or intensity of motivation. Thus structural factors and individual psychology come together to shape choices. So we see that expected-utility models of choice are concerned with opportunity and willingness.

## Problems of Information Search and Processing

Decision makers are not *faced* with problems; they must look out into the world and *identify or perceive* problems. How decision makers see some set of present circumstances depends on what happened previously—"where the players are is strongly influenced by where they have been." Even the most obvious "problems," in retrospect, may have been seen differently at the time. Winston Churchill perceived Hitler as a danger soon after Hitler came to power in 1933, but Neville Chamberlain came to that conclusion only in early 1939.[7] Similarly, at the time of the Cuban missile crisis in 1962, when the Kennedy administration discovered that the Soviet Union had secretly

---

[6] These issues are dealt with in the following chapter. Bueno de Mesquita explicitly incorporates misperception as a factor in his model and explicitly uses expected-utility models with weaker assumptions about information processing. See "The War Trap Revisited," *American Political Science Review* 79 (1985), 157–176, and Bueno de Mesquita and Lalman, *War and Reason* (New Haven, Conn.: Yale University Press, 1992). For a recent overview of rationality, utility, and game theory, see James D. Morrow, *Game Theory for Political Scientists* (Princeton, N.J.: Princeton University Press, 1994).

[7] The quotation is from Robert Jervis, "Realism, Game Theory and Cooperation," *World Politics* 40 (April 1988), p. 320; the example is from Jervis, *Perception and Misperception in International Politics* (Princeton, N.J.: Princeton University Press, 1976), chap. 1.

placed medium-range missiles in Cuba despite assurances that they would not do so, some members of Kennedy's Executive Committee did not think this act important. Different people in different parts of government, or different people occupying the same position—the same role—in government at different times, may not all see the same situation as a problem. Individual, role, ideological, and political factors will all combine to make a person see a problem. Since these factors vary across individuals, not all people, and especially not all relevant foreign policy people, will see the same problem at the same time.

After identifying a problem, the rational decision maker clarifies and orders his or her values and goals. This is not easy. Think of all the competing values and goals in the relatively simple task of purchasing a new automobile: cost, size, comfort, safety, durability, passenger and luggage capacity, gas mileage, as well as more intangible factors, like appearance and status. The decision maker must order these values: which is most important, next important, least important. These values must also be transitive.

If these ordering tasks are difficult for individuals, then they are even more so for governments. Graham T. Allison, in a very important work on different models of decision making, set out three conceptual models for understanding foreign policy activities and decisions.[8] His Model I, or the **"Rational Actor" model,** is the one, he says, that analysts use most of the time. It is a model that rests on a number of the assumptions in the ideal model. Because these assumptions are not satisfied, Allison argues that the Rational Actor model must be supplemented by others. One who uses Allison's Rational Actor model for a nation-state assumes that governments are *monoliths*—that is, they speak with one voice, hold one view, have one set of agreed-on values and one set of agreed-on goals (this is the unitary actor assumption of many realist models). From our very brief discussion of foreign policy goals and governmental influences on foreign policy, we know that this is rarely the case. Allison develops the fact that governments are made up of different organizations and individuals with different views, values, and goals in his two alternative models (Models II and III). In discussing domestic constraints, we used Dick, Jane, and Spot to illustrate the difficulties of finding group interests and acting to achieve them. A non-monolithic government composed of different organizations and individuals presents us with similar problems on a massive scale.

Before making a choice, the rational decision maker must first identify alternatives, list the consequences of those alternatives, and then compare the alternatives with goals to be achieved. However, there are time limits for making decisions, and there are limits on the human resources and money that can be spent on acquiring the

---

[8] See Graham T. Allison, *The Essence of Decision* (Boston: Little, Brown, 1971). While there are a number of commentaries on Allison's recounting of the Cuban missile crisis, for an overview, see David A. Welch, "The Organizational Process and Bureaucratic Politics Paradigms," *International Security* 17 (Fall 1992), 112–146. For an evaluation of the logic of Allison's models, see Jonathan Bendor and Thomas H. Hammond, "Rethinking Allison's Models," *American Political Science Review* 86 (June 1992), 301–322.

information needed. Unlike academic observers, at some point decision makers must act. There will always be a trade-off between the time and resources devoted to gathering more information and the need to take action in the global arena. In the end, one can never be sure that one has all the relevant information. In international relations especially, a great deal of secrecy surrounds a state's capabilities and intentions, as well as uncertainty and just plain ignorance.

Both individuals and organizations set up screens to filter information. In a government broken up into various organizations, each organization will often deliberately pass along only information that is beneficial to itself and not all the information that might be relevant to the situation. In the Bay of Pigs fiasco in 1961, the CIA passed incorrect information to President Kennedy on the probability of success in overthrowing Castro's government. Because of individual psychological screens and organizational screens, decision makers do not have perfect information but only a collection of selected data. The psychological screens are interesting because along with presenting problems in processing information, they may lead decision makers to ignore or fail to grasp the significance of important information they *do* have. A study investigating reasons the U.S. forces at Pearl Harbor were surprised by the Japanese attack in 1941 shows that all the important information needed to indicate an attack was coming was actually in the hands of American decision makers. However, because there was so much "noise"—unimportant or irrelevant pieces of data—the true signals were missed. Those signals that did get through to decision makers, especially those stationed at Pearl Harbor, were dismissed through the working of psychological screens.[9]

Noise is one symptom of information *overload*. Overload forces us to choose what to consider (a major form of screening), obscuring true signals by hiding them in noise. In World War II the Allies' strategy for locating the D-Day landings consciously took advantage of information overload by deluging the Germans with information, much of it false. Under this onslaught of intelligence, it was hoped, the Germans would miscalculate the invasion site, and that was exactly what happened.

The requirements of "perfect" decision making also lead to a paradox. The requirement for perfect information (or at least very large quantifies of information even for minimally complex decisions) conflicts with the fact that as a decision maker is bombarded by more and more information, more and more screens, both bureaucratic and psychological, are used to eliminate information overload. Few individuals or organizations have the ability to process adequately all the information required by an "imaginary ideal" decision machine. Because of information overload, decision makers must reduce the amount of information received so that they can function. Around 190 states in the global system, hundreds of IGOs, and thousands of NGOs each send out information through words and deeds, and hundreds of diplomats as well as intelligence-gathering agencies report on this activity. Decision makers in the

[9] See Roberta Wohlstetter, "Cuba and Pearl Harbor: Hindsight and Foresight," *Foreign Affairs* 43 (1964–1965), 691–707.

contemporary system can be overwhelmed with information. *Overload forces decision makers to decide what to decide.* Paying attention to one issue, situation, or crisis forces one to ignore others. Thus the paradox: in order to function, decision makers must distort their perceptions of the real world. The issue then becomes what degree of distortion is acceptable and how we can recognize and deal with it.

We must also challenge the assumption that decision makers want to go beyond reasoned decision making, that they actually want to make ideal, perfect decisions in which they find the optimal choice or attempt to maximize all their goals and values. The Nobel Prize–winning economist Herbert Simon pointed out years ago in a famous formulation that the decision maker does not maximize but **satisfices.** This means that the rational decision maker searches for an acceptable choice, one that is good enough to meet a minimal set of (expected-utility?) requirements. Instead of reviewing all possible alternatives, the "satisficer" will usually pick the first alternative that meets the minimal set of requirements. Simon argued that people attempt to act rationally but that such rationality is "bounded," or "limited," through the use of a simplified conception of the world.[10]

There are thus a variety of possible objectives for a rational decision maker in addition to maximizing utility: "He may wish to minimize his losses, maximize his gains, minimize his expected losses, or maximize his expected gains. Or he may want to minimize his regret." Or, as noted, simply satisfice. **"Prospect theory,"** an alternative approach to expected-utility theory, argues that the idea of utility for individuals differs in terms of comparable gains or losses—with people being concerned far more with losses than with gains (that is, they are "loss-averse").[11] This model also argues that how a situation is "framed" (is it one that presents a policymaker with losses or gains?) will affect how a decision maker deals with risk.

For example, consider an incumbent president up for reelection at a time when the country has basically been at peace, though without any major foreign policy successes. A voter may consider this record generally acceptable, expecting the incumbent, if returned to office, to continue this policy and record over the next four years. The president's opponent, however, is less known and less predictable, with the possibility either of scoring a great foreign policy success over another country or of beginning a long and costly war. The voter is apt to be risk-averse, playing it safe with the likelihood of more of the acceptable same from the incumbent rather than risking much worse (even though balanced by the chance for big gains) from the challenger. If, however, the situation is framed in a way that is much less flattering to the incumbent (as when the country has for some time been involved in a war), the voter may be more risk-acceptant. Even though the challenger is a risky choice, the voter may well accept the risk of an even worse war for the chance of ending this one, rather than the likelihood of continuing the same unsatisfactory policies by the incumbent.

---

[10] Herbert Simon, *Models of Man* (New York: Wiley, 1957).
[11] Walter Isard, *Understanding Conflict & the Science of Peace* (Cambridge, Mass.: Blackwell, 1992), p. 30. For discussions of prospect theory, see Barbara Farnham, ed., *Avoiding Losses/Taking Risks: Prospect Theory and International Conflict* (Ann Arbor: University of Michigan Press, 1994).

As in the case of screens, we shall find that there are many different ways to simplify the world (again, this is one way to use our realist, transnational, and radical perspectives). A summary comparison of the imaginary perfect process and actual decision making is presented in Table 10.1.

## DECISION MAKING: HOW DO PEOPLE DO IT?

Simon told us that people try to simplify the world through the bounded rationality of satisficing. A related view is that when people make decisions they simplify the world not by looking for grand solutions but by "muddling through." Decision makers often work in an **incremental** manner in order to minimize uncertainty and risk, to rely on the familiar, to reduce the number of alternatives to be examined, and to reduce the complexity of an analysis. That is, instead of contemplating grand decisions that review the total situation as it exists, a decision maker makes small changes that are only slightly different from decisions and actions already taken. This incremental approach is based on taking routine, small steps to reduce the costs of decision making and the costs of making mistakes. Incremental decisions are thus described as (1) remedial (they can be easily reversed or changed if they prove wrong); (2) serial (they build on what has gone before and what is presumably acceptable); and (3) exploratory (one can move into new policy areas to explore new avenues but still pull back if new directions appear to be costly or ineffective). An observer of American foreign policy, who himself was a decision maker in the Kennedy administration, says this about the way foreign policy is made:

> Rather than through grand decisions or grand alternatives, policy changes seem to come through a series of slight modifications of existing policy, with new policy emerging slowly and haltingly by small and usually tentative steps, a process of trial and error in which policy zigs and zags, reverses itself and then moves forward.[12]

The use of incremental decision making can have some clearly negative effects. Precisely because the steps are small and easy to reverse if necessary, it is possible after a time to find oneself deeply embedded in a policy that was never intended. Some have asserted that this was the case with the American involvement in Vietnam: small foreign policy activities led to a massive involvement that was not supposed to have happened. Incremental decision processes can actually be a way of "deciding without really deciding" because policy is not reviewed on a large scale.

Thus we have contrary types of decision-making models. One type has people making decisions based on the large view of the situation, attempting to find the

---

[12] This is Roger Hilsman's observation in *To Move a Nation* (New York: Dell, 1964), p. 5. It is similar to the process described by Charles Lindblom in "The Science of 'Muddling Through,'" *Public Administration Review* 19 (1959), 79–88.

**TABLE 10.1** Decision Making: Imaginary Ideal and Actual

| Task | Capabilities of an Imaginary Ideal Process | Limitations in Practice |
|---|---|---|
| Goal setting | Identification of national needs, interests, and priorities | "National interests" are the object of competing claims; goals are established through political struggle |
| Intelligence | Thorough, rapid, accurate gathering, interpreting, and reporting | Always incomplete; system susceptible to overload; delays and distortions in reporting; biases and ambiguities in interpretation |
| Option formulation | Comprehensive search for options; tallying of probable costs and benefits of each | Limited search for options; comparisons are made in general terms according to predispositions rather than according to specific cost benefit items |
| Plans, programs, decisions | Selection of option most likely to provide optimal ratio of gains to costs | Choices are made in accordance with prevailing mind-sets, influenced by "groupthink" and political considerations |
| Declaratory policy | Effective articulation of policy and rationale, so as to enlist domestic and foreign support | Multiple voices, contradictions and confusion; self-serving concern for personal image and feeding the appetite of the media |
| Execution | Allocation of resources in a manner to ensure effectiveness of each action element and minimize waste; clear coordination and control of all action elements; decisive | Breakdowns in communication; fuzzy lines of authority; organizational parochialism; bureaucratic politics; delays |
| Monitoring and appraisal | Thorough and continuous assessment of the effects of policy actions and commitments; flexibility in correcting for error and adjusting to changing circumstances | Gaps; vague standards; rigidities in adaptation; feedback failures |
| Memory storage and recall | Learning from experience; quick and accurate recall | Spotty and unreliable; "lessons" from experience are remembered selectively and applied imprecisely |

*Source:* John P. Lovell, *The Challenge of American Foreign Policy* (New York: Macmillan, 1985), pp. 27, 32.

optimal or most rational choice and trying to control the situation as much as possible. The other type describes people who make small, marginal choices primarily based on what had previously taken place, a process of "muddling through." In periods of non-crisis, the incremental approach may work adequately. In times of crisis, a wider and more intensive search for alternatives is necessary.

How can scholars come up with two such divergent explanations for the behavior of decision makers, in addition to various intermediate positions of bounded rationality such as expected utility or satisficing? One answer is that there are different forms of the decision-making process. Because there are different processes and different types of decisions to be made, and because each decision is actually a series of decisions, different observers have seen different aspects of foreign policy decision making and have thus come to describe what appear to be very different things.

## Intellectual Processes

Some forms of the rational model, where individuals sit down and work their way through a series of intellectual steps to choose among alternatives, may be called the *intellectual process* of making decisions. We have already seen the sorts of steps the intellectual decision maker takes to come to a decision. Because the decision maker is assumed to be rational, and because we like to think that decisions (especially in foreign policy) are made rationally, Allison argues that the Rational Actor model (Model I) is the most frequently used model for explaining foreign policy. Again, if one is trying to explain why a set of foreign policy decision makers did something, the easiest thing to do is to assume that they are "rational"; then you can try to put yourself in their shoes and see what possible goals they could have had in order to select the actions they did. Assuming that others go through this intellectual process implies that they are purposeful and have thus made their choice because it will further some foreign policy goal. It also implies that the government of the other actor is a monolith and that—most important for the analysis of foreign policy—*important events have important causes.* (The assumptions of both monolithic behavior and chosen, purposive behavior are challenged by Allison's other two models, set out below. Note also that these two assumptions, as well as rational models in general, have been closely linked to realist views of international politics, in which states as unitary actors move rationally to maximize power.) The Rational Actor analysis can be made with little information about the other party because you assume the other party is rational and you can follow the same intellectual steps that party has taken.

## Mechanical and Social Processes

Governments, including those portions involved in the foreign policy process, are made up of many parts—both individuals and organizations. Therefore, decisions are the products of the interaction, adjustment, and politics of people and organizations: social and quasi-mechanical processes.

In a social process there is an active social interaction among several decision makers that results in the decision produced. Roger Hilsman, in his book on the foreign policy of the Kennedy years, notes very simply that "policy making is politics."

Foreign policy emerges from the normal political process, including bargaining, compromise, adjustment, arm twisting, favor trading, and the like. This is the heart of the social process of decision making. Allison's Model III—the **"Governmental Politics"** **model**—presents a picture of decision making very different from that of the Rational Actor. Events are not the result of intellectual choices but the "resultants" of various "bargaining games" among the "players" in the government. Model I may be seen as rational economic man at work; Model III involves a social process in which some market mechanism is at work.

What we have, then, is a process in which each individual player is trying to act in a rational way. Each player—president, prime minister, first secretary, adviser, senator, foreign minister, general, cabinet member—tries to set goals, assess alternatives, and make choices through an intellectual process. Given the costs of and limits on achieving perfect information and perfect decision making, each individual player fails. But this failure is not crucial, because other people are involved in the process. Each brings some information into the process, along with individual goals, alternatives, and calculations of the consequences. With all these people participating, most of what should be considered is put into the process. Each participant or player sees a different facet of the issue under consideration, each has different stakes in the game, and each takes a different stand.

From a social process perspective, the foreign policy behavior of a state is the result of a set of "decision games" followed by "action games." Participants first play bargaining and political games and come out with some resultant, which is government policy. Then there is another set of games by which the decision is implemented: action games. The result of the action games may or may not reflect the decision finally made. Whatever the case, the important event that occurs, such as the construction of a new weapons system (for example, the B-2 bomber or new model of attack submarine), may be far removed from a single, monolithic governmental goal. Some advocates of the "bureaucratic politics" school even argue that most if not all foreign policy is developed with an eye to domestic political problems—keeping special interests happy, balancing off organizations and institutions within the government, keeping a particular administration in power. Social processes of policy making, as reflected in Allison's Model III, very clearly illustrate the domestic side of the two-level games approach introduced earlier.

Decisions are also made through a quasi-mechanical reference to past decisions, precedence, routines, or governmental role—the "standard operating procedures" of organizations. Organizations within governments all have a catalogue of past behavior to draw on. Organizations are conservative, rarely trying anything new; they are happy with incremental changes based on past decisions and behavior. One way to reduce the complexity of the world and to reduce uncertainty is to act as one has acted before. Organizations tend to have rule books, guides, and so on that indicate how things should be done by that organization. Allison's Model II is **"Organizational Process"**: what will happen at time $t + 1$ is best explained by looking at what happened at time $t$. This is a neat summary of the cautious and remedial incremental model. Model II may be summarized by three main points: (1) A government is made up of a "conglomerate of semi-feudal loosely allied organizations"; (2) governmental decisions and behavior should be understood not as rational choice, but as the "outputs of large organizations functioning according to standard patterns of behavior"; (3) each organization, with its standard operating procedures, routines, or programs, will behave today substantially as it behaved yesterday—and will behave tomorrow much as it behaved today. Again, a quasi-mechanical process affects both the decision that is made and the implementation of that decision.[13]

## DECISION UNIT, TYPE OF DECISION, AND DECISION STAGES

Regarding the three different processes or models that focus on different units of analysis—governments personified (Model I), bureaucracies (Model II), and individuals in group interaction (Model III)—it is apparent that how any individual affects a foreign policy decision and its implementation depends on governmental role factors as well as on individual factors. Where each person stands in the government, within which organization, how close to the central decision maker, and what the decision unit is all must be taken into account. The decision unit is particularly important. One group of scholars has defined the "ultimate decision unit" as a group of actors who have both the ability to commit resources and the power and authority to do so. They also identify three broad types of decision units: a predominant leader, a single group, and multiple autonomous groups. There are many examples of predominant leaders, especially in authoritarian systems, among them Hitler, Stalin, and Saddam Hussein. Single groups would include Kennedy's Executive Committee during the Cuban missile crisis, the National Security Council in certain circumstances, the pre-Gorbachev Politburo, and the British cabinet.[14]

How many and what types of people are involved in foreign policy decisions will influence the impact of an individual's role and personality. The size and composition of the decision unit will affect how the social and quasi-mechanical decision processes work. We do not expect the entire State Department to be involved in the Cuban missile crisis decision, nor do we expect the president and his top advisers to be concerned with day-to-day decisions regarding the running of embassies.

The decision unit will change depending on the type of decision being made. A standard typology distinguishes among crisis decisions, general foreign policy decisions, and administrative decisions. The *crisis decision* generally involves a few very

---

[13] For a useful application of organizational process models, see Jack Levy, "Organizational Routines and the Causes of War," *International Studies Quarterly* 30 (1986), 193–222; see also Yaacov Vertzberger's study of Indian policymaking, "Bureaucratic-Organizational Politics and Information Processing in a Developing State," *International Studies Quarterly* 28 (March 1984), 69–95.

[14] See Margaret Hermann and Charles Hermann, "Who Makes Foreign Policy Decisions and How: An Empirical Inquiry," *International Studies Quarterly* 33 (1989), 361–387, and Margaret Hermann, Charles Hermann, and Joe Hagan, "How Decision Units Shape Foreign Policy Behavior," in Charles Hermann, Charles Kegley, and James N. Rosenau, eds., *New Directions in the Study of Foreign Policy* (Boston: Allen & Unwin, 1987).

high-level decision makers. A **crisis** is a special situation with a finite or specified decision time, usually very short. A crisis involves a major threat to the decision makers and their state, or a perception by decision makers of a threat to their values. One prominent student of crisis also adds the element of surprise to the characteristics of crisis (see Figure 10.1 for a representation of crisis based on threat, short or finite decision time, and surprise). Another view of crisis takes out surprise as an important element and adds the notion of crisis as a breakpoint between peace and war that raises the probability of military hostilities.[15]

*General foreign policy decisions* set out future foreign policy, looking at the present and into the near future (and often beyond). The positions of the states of the European Union on potential membership for former Eastern bloc countries, the Japanese stance toward tariffs and trade policy, or the Carter administration's decision to make a commitment to human rights a part of U.S. foreign policy are all examples of general foreign policy decisions. *Administrative decisions* are concerned with very specific situations; they are usually handled by a specific part of the foreign policy bureaucracy. They involve routine situations calling for the application of the expertise and standard operating procedures of foreign policy organizations. The participants in a crisis decision are of the highest level and are relatively few in number. General foreign policy decisions usually involve a large number of medium-level officials interacting with one or two of the high-level foreign policy players. Administrative decisions usually involve low-level officials.

Because of the number of people, the seriousness, and the finite time involved, crisis decisions resemble the intellectual decision-making process more than do other types of decisions. In crisis situations policymakers use an analytic, intellectual, rational model of decision making. Research has also indicated that a crisis context will increase the likelihood of defective decisions. Decision makers try to make decisions as rationally as possible, and when they employ procedures like Janis and Mann's "vigilant problem solving" they will make better decisions, even in crises.[16]

We must keep in mind, however, that some small-group interactions also involve complex social processes and that quasi-mechanical processes can be crucial in determining what information reaches top-level decision makers. General foreign policy decisions, at any rate, are characterized mostly by social processes. Because there is much less time constraint, and because the general direction of foreign policy is of concern to so many sections of the government, these types of decisions generate a high degree of governmental conflict—and thus of bargaining and compromise, as

---

[15] The three-dimensional definition of crisis—short time, high threat, and surprise—is most closely identified with Charles Hermann; see, for example, *International Crises* (New York: Free Press, 1972). Our modifications of the time and surprise elements, and the addition of the hostilities element, derive from the work of Michael Brecher and Jonathan Wilkenfeld; see, for example, Brecher, *Crisis in World Politics: Theory and Reality* (New York: Pergamon, 1993).

[16] See first, Zeev Maoz, "The Decision to Raid Entebbe: Decision Analysis Applied to Crisis Behavior," *Journal of Conflict Resolution* 25 (1981), 677–707; second, Herek, Janis, and Huth, "Decision Making During International Crises."

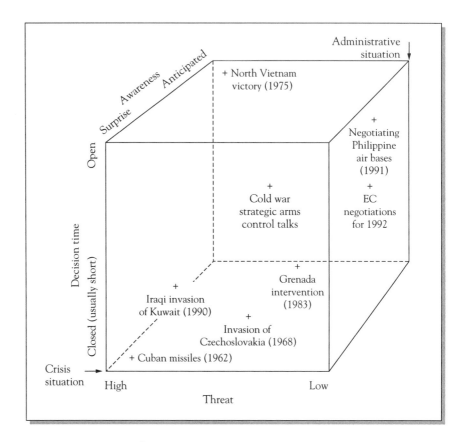

**FIGURE 10.1** A modified "crisis cube." [See also Charles Hermann, "International Crisis as a Situational Variable," in James N. Rosenau, ed., *International Politics and Foreign Policy* (New York: Free Press, 1969).]

competitors try to make policy reflect their personal views or those of the organization they represent. Although the other two processes are also involved, the social processes tend to dominate these general foreign policy decision situations. Finally, administrative decisions are characterized primarily by organizationally generated quasi-mechanical processes.

It should be clear now how various observers come up with different descriptions of how people make decisions. Several different decision processes exist, generally involving different groups of decision makers (or different decision units) as well as different types of foreign policy decisions. In fact, we can make this even more complicated if we look at different *stages* of any particular decision. Decisions may be broken down into a predecisional stage, a formulation stage, and an implementation stage.

The *predecisional* stage involves the collection of information and views and the scanning of the foreign policy horizon for possible problems and issues. The *formulation* stage involves the actual selection of an alternative after evaluating the possibilities. In the *implementation* stage the decision has been translated into some form of action or foreign policy behavior.

Because high-level decisions are usually put into effect by officials at much lower levels in various governmental organizations, the implementation stage (action games) is often affected by bureaucratic screening and the selective action of bureaucrats. The predecisional stage seems to be most important for general foreign policy decisions and administrative decisions; the formulation stage for general foreign policy decisions and crisis decisions; and the implementation stage for crisis decisions and administrative decisions. Again, which decision units one studies may shift even within the process of a single decision. The study of decision makers may reveal several kinds of decision-making processes going on simultaneously within a foreign policy establishment, even for the same decision.

## INDIVIDUALS IN GOVERNMENT: ROLES, DECISION MAKING, AND SCREENS

All the factors discussed above affect the impact an individual has on the foreign policy process. The foreign policy decision maker is embedded within the government and, even more immediately, within the governmental organization or bureaucracy for which he or she works. The individual decision maker is an information-processing system; so is the government as a whole. The information received and passed on will thus be affected by organizational and role influences, as well as by the decision maker's own psychological characteristics.

### Information and Screens

As Karl Deutsch has pointed out, communication is the cement of all social organization; all groups or collectivities are held together by communication. Communications transmit pieces of information and are involved in the control of the flow of information. Social systems, such as societies, governments, and bureaucracies, may be self-controlling systems in that they have goals and are able to respond to stimuli from their environments. For such systems, and particularly for governments, the central metaphor is *steering*. Where are we going? Through which choices? Why, and how? Control of steering, says Deutsch, is the real problem of government. We have seen a similar view in the idea of incremental decision making.[17] Similarly, the work in the area of artificial intelligence is also concerned with representing the structures used by

---

[17] Karl Deutsch's classic, *The Nerves of Government,* 2nd ed. (New York: Free Press, 1966), provides the basis for much of the material presented in this section.

decision makers for ordering information, memory, learning, and adaptation. These questions must be answered in order to best represent knowledge and deal with the question of what intelligence is.[18]

We are now approaching topics that we have already discussed from a slightly different perspective. We can think of organizations, individuals, or any self-controlling system as having to react to the environment—to steer through it by learning. Learning involves feedback, the receipt of information and the use of the information to help us steer. Positive feedback amplifies or reinforces our behavior, encouraging us to continue it. If negative feedback indicates that we are moving away from our goal or missing it by ever greater distances, then our behavior must be changed to bring it back toward the target. How this information gets back to us and how it is screened on the way (by governmental organizations or by individuals) will affect our image of the world and how to behave in it. This is precisely why we are interested in role influence and the effects of the interests of organizations. In the early 1960s, when the United States was becoming involved in Vietnam, in what direction should the United States have steered? Should it have *continued* involvement? Or should it have *changed* course and disengaged? Similar questions concerning steering—of taking small steps that ultimately lead away from one's goals—have been raised about U.S. and NATO policy toward the violence in the former Yugoslavia.

In the case of Vietnam, one important influence on the decision makers in Washington was the information they received about the effectiveness of the American effort. Military and intelligence organizations with an interest in continuing and expanding that effort sent back information supporting a continued increase in military involvement. Individuals with a strong anticommunist ideology and other beliefs that made such involvement seem beneficial also sent back positive feedback. More importantly, information that opposed increasing involvement—negative feedback—was suppressed or eliminated.[19] Such information was screened out at various bureaucratic and individual points. Even when it managed to get through, the information was ignored if individuals did not want to believe it. This example demonstrates why information and images are so important, because it is only through feedback that decision makers are able to steer their states through the troubled waters of the international system.

## Role and Screens: Organizational Process and Decisions

Role is one factor that acts on the systematic omission of information. The word has been used in several ways in this book, but the meaning has always included

---

[18] See Philip A. Schrodt, "Artificial Intelligence and International Relations: An Overview," in Valerie M. Hudson, ed., *Artificial Intelligence and International Politics* (Boulder, Colo.: Westview, 1991), pp. 9–31.

[19] See David Halberstam's account of the Kennedy administration and the Vietnam War, *The Best and the Brightest* (New York: Random House, 1969).

an image of how a state, a government, or an individual *thinks* it should be acting. Role has been defined as those aspects of an actor deriving from the person's policy-making responsibilities and *expected* to characterize *any* person filling the same position. We can think of a role as the interaction between the individual and the political system, the expectations of that system working on the individual. Although the role may constrain what an individual might do, it also has to be perceived and interpreted by the individual in light of that individual's personality and idiosyncracies.

In most cases an individual in a governmental position is in a situation where precedent exists in the behavior of previous individuals who held that office. A strong personality, unafraid to innovate or to shock or to take political risks, may overcome the constraints of precedent. Others may find it comfortable to tread a well-worn path. In Chapter 1 we noted that during his first six months as president, Harry Truman appeared inexperienced, unsure of himself, and strongly bound by the precedents set by Franklin Roosevelt (who had been president from 1933 until his death in April 1945).

An even trickier question involves when an idiosyncratic element becomes a role element. Jawaharlal Nehru, for example, was responsible for Indian foreign policy for many years. Indeed, he was the foreign policy minister for the Indian Congress party for over 20 years before India achieved independence in 1947. Because there had been no one in these positions before him, Nehru had great leeway in stamping his own personality and interpretation on Indian foreign policy. But as the years wore on and he behaved in accordance with his own previous actions, was he acting according to role or to his own idiosyncratic characteristics? Questions may be asked about any individual who was the first to hold a certain position and did so for a long time; Mao Zedong in China is one. In the United States, George Washington was constantly aware that, as the first president, his actions would set precedents for those who followed. Charles Frankel, writing of his experiences in the State Department, noted that "once things have happened, no matter how accidentally, they will be regarded as manifestations of an unchangeable Higher Reason."[20]

Role is also defined by very specific statements of what an individual should be doing, such as legal statutes, constitutions, and job descriptions. These set out an individual's duties and responsibilities, but they are not so important in their constraints as are the expectations of an individual's fellow workers, both superiors and subordinates. Individuals who want to retain their positions or to advance their careers are likely to behave as they think others expect them to behave.

The individual who performs a specific role is often expected to follow the needs and requirements of his or her organizational setting rather than his or her personal convictions. Before World War I, Winston Churchill deplored the naval arms race between Germany and Britain, recognizing that both states were spending large sums of money and raising international tensions in a competition to build more and better

---

[20] See Charles Frankel's account of his experiences, *High on Foggy Bottom* (New York: Harper & Row, 1968).

battleships. He also recognized that when the process was over, both sides would be in approximately the same relationship as before and thus it would all have been futile. However, as first lord of the admiralty he went before Parliament and requested more funds for naval construction. When Caspar Weinberger served as director of the Office of Management and Budget in the Nixon administration, he was known as "Cap the Knife" for his propensity to slash the budget requests of government departments and agencies. But as secretary of defense in the Reagan administration he was constantly asking Congress for more money and oversaw the largest surge in peacetime defense spending in the country's history. When Samuel Hoare was the British secretary of state for air in the 1920s, he fought against naval control of the air forces within the Fleet Air Arm; ten years later, when he became first lord of the admiralty, he argued for exactly the opposite position.

Members of different organizations see different sides of a situation, depending on how that situation affects (and perhaps threatens) their organization. As Allison says, "Where you stand depends on where you sit." An individual's priorities and self-interests are seen to derive in large measure from his or her organization's self-interests. As opposed to a realist's notion that there exists some single "national interest," there is an array of organizations and interests. Of course, each organization (or subgroup) argues that its interests are similar to, or necessary ingredients of, the national interest. In reality there are many separate interests, and, like those of Jane, Dick, and Spot, those interests must be reconciled into policy. Models II and III help us understand how that is achieved.

The parochial nature of organizations is one of the core concepts of the Organizational Process model. Each organization within a government has a narrow range of interests and priorities. The mission of an organization requires capabilities: money and people. To acquire these, the organization needs influence within the government, especially on budget decisions and decisions that distribute new programs and responsibilities to government organizations. Members define the reason for their organization's existence in terms of essence: what missions an organization *should have*. They are deeply concerned with "organizational health," the protection (and often an expansion of the scope) of essence, measured by budget and staffing allocations. The essence of the U.S. Army is a ground combat capability. The U.S. Navy sees its essence as maintaining combat ships to control the seas; the only problem is that people in submarines think this goal should be achieved by subs, air-power proponents support the use of aircraft carriers, and sea-power advocates stress surface combat ships.

Organizational health can also be protected by demonstrating how successful the organization is (or, more commonly, by demonstrating its lack of mistakes). One reason that organizations follow standard operating procedures is to cut down on uncertainty and risk. Organizations behave incrementally for the same reason. But—and this is crucial to the policymaking process—the protection of the organization also entails providing information to top-level decision makers that shows the organization in the best light. This involves withholding information that would embarrass the organization and implementing top-level decisions in a way that meets the best interests of the organization, not necessarily in the spirit of the decision handed down to the organization for implementation. Members of the organization are expected to enhance the organization's health.[21] One advocate of the bureaucratic politics approach summarizes four areas in which organizational parochialism affects policy. All of them call for role occupants to behave in the interests of the organization rather than in the interests of the state as a whole or out of individual conviction. All can have crucial effects on policy formulation or implementation.

**1.** Organizations acquire information to protect their interests, supply others with information that will protect the organization, and get decision makers to see the situation in the way that the organization desires.

**2.** Similarly, when the organization presents options, it attempts to give decision makers a "menu" of options, each of which will support and further the organization's essence.

**3.** The organization will also attempt to prevent top decision makers from selecting options from other organizations that will threaten the organization's interests.

**4.** The organization will implement decisions on the basis of organizational interests—it will delay, alter, and often disobey top-level directives.[22]

Many anecdotes tell of presidents giving up in despair as they tried to get various sections of the bureaucracy to do what was wanted. John Kennedy called the State Department a bowl of jelly; FDR likened the navy to a feather pillow—no matter how hard or long one punched it, it always came out the same. The strength of bureaucratic politics is seen in the way the air force reported bombing results in Vietnam, often using highly unreliable pilots' reports, which exaggerated bomb damage, rather than satellite or reconnaissance photographs; the withholding of crucial information by the CIA in the Bay of Pigs operation; the near breakdown in U.S.–British relations over the Skybolt missile during the Kennedy administration because of intergovernmental miscommunication between bureaucracies.[23] Using Allison's analysis (as well as critiques of his work and new studies), the most closely examined case study of the impact of organizational process has been the Cuban missile crisis. It was only during a reunion of the members of the Executive Committee (ExComm) in 1987, however, that the following powerful example emerged. During the missile crisis (which the call the Caribbean crisis), Kennedy ordered the Strategic Air Command (SAC) to go on full alert. SAC was brought to Defense Condition 2 for the first time ever, involving high-alert status for U.S. missiles and increased numbers of strategic bombers on airborne alert.

---

[21] Model II is not solely an American phenomenon but can be used across many governments. The famous diaries of the British Labour cabinet minister Richard Crossman describe how ministers are trapped, manipulated, ignored, and infuriated by bureaucrats who presume to know what is best for the ministry and hence the government and the country. See Anthony Howard, ed., *The Crossman Diaries, 1965–1970* (London: Methuen, 1979). (Afficionados of television's "Yes, Minister" will quickly recognize Crossman's complaints.)

[22] See Morton H. Halperin, *Bureaucratic Politics and Foreign Policy* (Washington, D.C.: Brookings Institution, 1974), especially chaps. 2–4, 11, and 15.

[23] See, for example, Morton Halperin and Arnold Kanter, eds., *Readings in American Foreign Policy: A Bureaucratic Perspective* (Boston: Little, Brown, 1973).

Most of this activity would have been observed in due course by various means of Soviet information collection. But in this case there was a unique difference: the SAC full-alert process was reported "in the clear" rather than in normal encoded messages. Soviet communications interception personnel must have been shocked suddenly to hear the SAC commander-in-chief address all his senior commanders in an unprecedented message in the clear stressing the seriousness of the situation faced by the nation and assuring them that SAC plans were well prepared and being executed smoothly. Soviet political and military leaders must have been puzzled and alarmed at this flaunting of the American strategic superiority. . . .

Equally extraordinary, and not known in Moscow, was that this remarkable display of American power was unauthorized by and unknown to the president, the secretary of defense, the chairman of the Joint Chiefs, and the ExComm as they so carefully calibrated and controlled action. . . . The decision for bold action was taken by General Thomas Power, commander-in-chief of SAC, on his own initiative. He had been ordered to go on full alert, and he did so. No one had told him *how* to do it, and he decided to "rub it in."[24]

When this story was told at the 1987 conference, the former ExComm members were startled. An observer noted that former Secretary of Defense "McNamara's eyes roll[ed] toward the ceiling in mock exasperation at this military insubordination."[25] This is a good example of the dangers of assuming that governmental decisions flow from a unitary actor or that important events have important causes (in the sense of coming from a considered decision of the top-level decision unit). Rather than these two cornerstones of Model I, this example highlights the importance of implementation and the organizations that control it.

Organizations thus provide individuals with roles and the expectations that are attached to such roles. Before we consider role–individual relationships from the other side in the next chapter, let us look at the conditions under which individuals break out of or reshape their role constraints (expand the menu). The longer a specific role exists, the more precedents are set and the more widely held are the expectations of other government members for people assuming the role. Thus, as an institution becomes older and more complex, it is more difficult for an individual to shape a role in that institution. When Rosenau introduced the idea of role as a pretheoretical factor, he thought that role would be more important in the older, industrialized Western states, those with greater political and economic development. New positions in government provide much more leeway for an individual to shape a role rather than be constrained by it. In addition, the higher the role position is in the governmental hierarchy, the less the role constrains the individual. The higher one goes, the fewer superiors one has and the more likely one is to be confronted with new or unexpected situations. Such situations are also more open to individual influences than those of a role.

---

[24] Raymond Garthoff, *Reflections on the Cuban Missile Crisis*, rev. ed. (Washington, D.C.: Brookings Institution, 1989), pp. 61–62.
[25] J. Anthony Lukas, "Class Reunion: Kennedy's Men Relive the Cuban Missile Crisis," *New York Times Magazine*, August 10, 1987, p. 51.

Whether an individual can modify or shape a role, then, depends on the degree of precedent, the organizational context, and how old the role is. The impact of a role also depends on the individual's personal characteristics and especially on his or her political skills. The Governmental Politics model (Model III) considers the "power and the skill" of the individual players. Much of the power derives from an individual's position in government, or role, but this power can be expanded or reduced depending on the personality and skill of the players involved. Although William Rogers was secretary of state for most of the Nixon years, Henry Kissinger was the unquestioned primary adviser to the president on foreign policy and national security matters. In Kennedy's administration the secretary of defense, Robert McNamara, played a more central part in foreign affairs than did Secretary of State Dean Rusk. Although the office of the secretary of state has not undergone any real role alteration, the strength and skill of its holders has varied, as have their individual relations with the presidents they advised.

## Role and Small-Group Interaction

How an individual behaves within the constraints of his or her role is also affected by the immediate environment of the decision unit. People studying organizations and social psychologists studying small-group behavior have found that being a member of a small group can affect both the perceptions and the behavior of the individual very strongly. More specifically, there are pressures on the individual to conform to the view of the group and not to challenge it. In this process, the perceptions of the individual about both situation and role may be altered to fit the collective views within the group. Here is an example not only of social decision processes (mostly through pressure on members to come to a consensus of some kind) but also of a failure of those processes. One advantage of social decision processes noted earlier was that although each individual has limited information, perceived alternatives, and so on, when that individual interacts with others a wide range of information and alternatives is considered. We shall see that this need not be the case.

Laboratory experiments by psychologists demonstrate the pressures to conform that a small group can have on its members. In one, a group of six to eight people compared visual images—the length of two lines, for example. However, only one member of the group was actually being observed each time this experiment was performed; the others (unknown to the single subject) had been instructed to give false answers. The subject, then, heard the others in this small group say that the shorter line was longer, the smaller cube was larger, and so forth. At first, subjects acted puzzled and upset. Then they began to conform and to describe the stimuli as the others did.[26]

---

[26] See for example, S. E. Asch, "Effects of Group Pressure upon Modification and Distortion of Judgment," in D. Cartwright and A. Zander, eds., *Group Dynamics, Research and Theory* (Evanston, Ill.: Row, Peterson, 1953), pp. 189–200.

A version of the individual's conformity to small-group views has been studied by Irving Janis—a phenomenon he calls **groupthink**. In his study, Janis looked at a number of American foreign policy decisions, such as the Bay of Pigs invasion in 1961, the response to the North Korean invasion of South Korea in 1950, the decision to set up the Marshall Plan, the decisions to escalate the war in Vietnam, the decision making about Pearl Harbor before the attack, and the Cuban missile crisis of 1962. Janis sums up his central theme as follows: "The more amiability and esprit de corps among the members of a policymaking ingroup, the greater is the danger that independent critical thinking will be replaced with groupthink, which is likely to result in irrational and dehumanizing actions directed against outgroups." Groupthink is one important process that generates symptoms of defective decision making, helping analysts identify "low-quality" and "high-quality" decision making.[27]

Two symptoms of groupthink involve self-image. A close and friendly group will produce an *illusion of invulnerability*. This feeling or view of one's group is overly optimistic and encourages risks. Other research has identified the phenomenon of the "risky shift." By themselves, individuals respond to real and hypothetical situations in a more conservative way than when they are in a group. For several reasons, the same individuals are willing to take much riskier positions when asked about the same situations in a group setting, despite individual or role factors.

Similarly, the group tends to have an unquestioned *belief in its own morality*. The group setting leads the individual members to feel that this group of decent people could not be anything but good. This symptom fosters group screening by leading the group members to ignore the ethical or moral consequences of their decisions; the assumption is that the group is moral and that therefore the decisions of the group also will be moral. A third symptom is a stereotyped view of the opponent's leadership as too evil or stupid for negotiations on a good-faith basis.

The groupthink process also leads to a shared illusion of unanimity that often overcomes role influences. Efforts are made to rationalize the group's decisions, to justify them no matter what they might be, screening out warnings or counterinformation that might lead the group to reconsider its decisions. Groupthink also leads to direct pressure on any individual who argues against the stereotypes the group produces, to *self-censorship* of doubts and counterarguments (as in the perception experiment described above).

The conditions that promote groupthink derive from group cohesiveness: how well knit the group is, how well it sticks together. This cohesion is fostered when the group is isolated from outsiders and outside views, as well as from information that might challenge the images of the group. The appearance of a group leader who

---

[27] See Irving Janis, *Groupthink*, 2nd ed. (Boston: Houghton Mifflin, 1982), and *Crucial Decisions: Leadership in Policymaking and Crisis Management* (New York: Free Press, 1989), as well as Janis and Mann, *Decision Making*. For an application, as well as an example of the differences between ideal and bounded rationality, see Gregory M. Herek, Irving Janis, and Paul Huth, "Quality of U.S. Decision Making During the Cuban Missile Crisis: Major Errors in Welch's Reassessment," *Journal of Conflict Resolution* 33 (1989), 446–459.

promotes a preferred solution is another major influence on the creation of group-think. It is not necessary that the others in the group be toadies for this effect to take place. A person becomes a leader because of a number of personal and role character-istics; others in the group will go along with him or her because of shared values or because of the leader's control of promotion decisions.

A good example of this last symptom is the U.S. decision in 1950 to send military aid immediately to South Korea after the administration was informed of the North Korean attack. President Truman walked into the meeting of his advisers and approved the plan presented by Secretary of State Dean Acheson. The rest of the dis-cussion was based on Acheson's view rather than on any other. On the other hand, one of the reasons less groupthink occurred during the Cuban crisis was because John Kennedy consciously removed himself from a number of the sessions of the Executive Committee so that his presence would not inhibit the broadest possible review of options and views (an interesting mixture of the intellectual and social processes at work). Groupthink appears to have been minimized in the Cuban decision because each participant acted as a generalist (not as a representative of a particular role) and was also supposed to be as skeptical and challenging as possible, in an informal atmosphere without a formal agenda or rules of protocol.

A variety of possible remedies for groupthink have been suggested by scholars, from "devil's advocacy"—assigning someone to challenge all assumptions and deci-sions—to multiple advocacy. In the latter, chief executives are advised to ensure that individuals with a range of views are encouraged to advocate those views; executives are to make sure that all views can be heard.[28] Phenomena like groupthink probably cannot be eliminated, but they can be reduced, and decision makers can be alerted to their existence and the effects such phenomena can have on decisions and actions.

## CONCLUSION

Some scholars have combined the Organizational Process model with the Govern-mental Politics model to devise a bureaucratic politics model that takes on the organi-zational and political components of each. The bureaucratic politics model can be summarized in three questions about the foreign policy process: Who plays? What determines each player's stand? How do these different positions merge to yield gov-ernmental decisions and actions? Role is very important in answering the first ques-tion. Both role and idiosyncratic factors are important in answering the second. Both of these in addition to governmental factors (communications channels and struc-tures, the institutional hierarchy, and so on) are important for answering the third.

---

[28] See, for example, Alexander L. George, "The Case for Multiple Advocacy in Making Foreign Policy," *American Political Science Review* 66 (1972), 751–785.

In the bureaucratic politics model, what any government does in some particular situation should be seen largely as the result of bargaining among the players. These players are positioned hierarchically within the government (role factors). The bargaining follows regularized circuits (role and governmental factors). Finally, the bargaining and its results—the decision games and the action games—are affected by a number of constraints, especially the organizational processes (roles) and the individual political skills of the players (idiosyncrasies). This is another indication of the complex and close interaction between an individual's role position and personal idiosyncrasies. The close connection between role and individual factors will be further examined in the next chapter, where we shall look at general statements concerning how individuals perceive the world about them and how idiosyncratic differences affect the foreign policy process.

# INDIVIDUALS AND WORLD POLITICS: PERCEIVING THE WORLD

WORLD SYSTEM

RELATIONS

SOCIETY

GOVERNMENT

ROLE

INDIVIDUAL

## LOOKING AT THE INDIVIDUAL

In a striking section of *The Hero in History*, Sidney Hook tries to imagine "A World without Lenin" in order to demonstrate the historical importance of what he calls the "event-making man." In political science, no less than history, we must also confront the problem with which Hook wrestles. Stated more formally, we are concerned with the impact of personal as well as institutional, cultural, social, and economic factors on the conduct of politics.[1]

---

[1] David J. Finlay, Ole R. Holsti, and Richard R. Fagen, *Enemies in Politics* (Chicago: Rand McNally, 1967), p. 233.

Decision makers hold images of the world; those images are not necessarily accurate representations of the "real" world. The study of the images held by foreign policy decision makers—the *psychological environment* of foreign policy leaders— involves the study of their belief systems and how their images of other peoples, states, leaders, and situations affect their decisions and behavior. Here we recognize that the psychological environment limits the menu just as the other environments do.

We must make several assumptions. The first is that foreign policy is made and implemented by people. Here we are taking a decision-making approach; we do not see states as monolithic, impersonal creatures that somehow behave on their own. The second assumption, the point Hook was making, is that individuals can make a differ- ence in the foreign policy process of a given state, that the governmental structure, as well as the processes of policymaking, permits individuals to have an impact on foreign policy. Presidents, secretaries of state, prime ministers, foreign ministers, revo- lutionary leaders, and dictators can strongly influence the foreign policy process of their own states and of others. Although he never admitted that he could be analyzed either psychologically or psychoanalytically, Henry Kissinger was a firm believer in the importance of the individual statesman in history. As a practicing diplomat, he felt that he had to know and understand the psychological makeup of foreign diplomats and decision makers. In addition to this view (which prompted him to have U.S. intelligence services draw up psychological profiles of the foreign leaders with whom he negotiated), he saw individuals as important to the outcomes of diplomacy and history: "But when you see [history] in practice, you see the differences that the personalities make. The overtures to China would not have worked without Chou En-lai. There would have been no settlement in the Middle East without Sadat and Golda Meir or Dayan."[2] Anyone doubting the impact that single individuals can have on the workings of foreign policy, relations among states, or even the structure of the international system need only examine the consequences of the poli- cies pursued by Mikhail Gorbachev after his accession to power in 1985.[3]

The third assumption derives from the first two. Given that foreign policy is made by people and that individuals can have an impact, we assume the importance of how these people see the world. What affects their perception? The unique characteristics that affect an individual's decision making and behavior include a number of things that are relatively easy to study and some that are quite difficult. An individual's **idiosyncrasies** are made up of values, personality, political style, intellect, and past experience. They work together, creating the individual's set of images about the world—the individual's belief system.

We can address the question of role and individual factors discussed in the previ- ous chapter by looking at the circumstances or conditions under which individual traits are likely to affect decisions. Just as Rosenau proposes that role would be more important in economically developed states, he proposes that idiosyncratic factors

---

[2] Quoted in Hugh Sidey, "An International Natural Resource," *Time* (February 4, 1974), p. 24.
[3] See, for example, Gordon A. Craig and Alexander L. George, *Force and Statecraft,* 2nd ed. (New York: Oxford University Press, 1990), chap. 11.

would be more important in underdeveloped states, societies that are generally new and small and lack established roles or highly structured bureaucracies. He also proposes that idiosyncratic factors would be at work more in closed societies, where the leader is less constrained by the influence of public opinion and interest groups. Idi Amin's rule of terror in Uganda during the 1970s was a good example of how one man and his idiosyncrasies could dominate a new state, small and underdeveloped both economically and politically. Saddam Hussein has thoroughly dominated a larger and more developed society.

Research indicates a number of other circumstances in which idiosyncratic variables have a greater effect on decisions and behavior and where knowledge of these factors is useful. As we noted before, in nonroutine situations such as crises that require more than the quasi-mechanical application of standard operating procedures, the idiosyncrasies of decision makers are more in evidence. Decisions made at the top of a governmental hierarchy, where the individuals are less constrained by pressures for promotion or by superiors, will have more idiosyncratic influences on them. Situations containing uncertainty or ambiguity are also open to individual influences—the subjective guesses of what should be done and a greater reliance on the values of the decision makers. Long-range planning, for example, involves a great deal of uncertainty and questions like "What is important?" and "What is likely?" These decisions are similar to the general foreign policy decisions discussed in Chapter 10 (they also comprise what we called expected utility). As primarily social process decisions, they also call on the individual skill of decision makers, including their political style and ways of dealing with interpersonal relations. Those situations involving very poor or very scarce information will depend a great deal on an individual's existing images and beliefs. At the other extreme, in situations of information overload, images come to the fore as screening mechanisms to deal with such overload. Figure 11.1 indicates how the nature of a situation relates to the decision maker, his or her idiosyncrasies, and his or her place in the government's foreign policy apparatus.

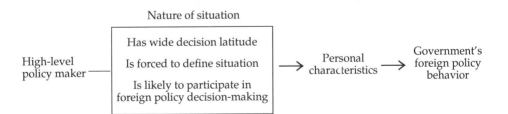

**FIGURE 11.1** The conditions under which individual factors are expected to affect foreign policy behavior. [*Source:* Margaret G. Hermann, "Effects of Personal Characteristics of Political Leaders on Foreign Policy," in Maurice East et al., eds., *Why Nations Act: Theoretical Perspectives for Comparative Foreign Policy Studies* (Sage Focus Editions, vol. 2) copyright © 1978, p. 54, by permission of the publisher, Sage Publications, Inc. (Beverly Hills/London.)]

Some of the data on individual idiosyncrasies may be difficult to obtain, and once obtained may be difficult to interpret. As well as biographical information on decision makers, we want information on their worldviews, their values and opinions, their personalities, and their styles of behavior. In particular, we need to know how these factors are used to form images and how the images work. For foreign policy decision makers, we have a very difficult problem of *access:* How do we get to them while they are embedded within the vast and overlapping governmental structures of the modern state? As one political scientist inquired, "How can we give a Taylor Manifest Anxiety Scale to Khrushchev during the Hungarian Revolt, a Semantic-Differential to Chiang Kai-shek while Quemoy is being shelled, or simply interview Kennedy during the Cuban missile crisis?"[4]

The psychological or *psychohistorical* study of individuals requires imagination and creative research programs. Interviews with the subjects themselves are most useful, but sometimes the best available method is interviewing people close to the subject. There have been psychoanalytic studies of written and spoken materials and the psychoanalysis of biographical and historical details of an individual's life. Access may also be achieved by *content analysis,* a systematic study of the communications produced by an individual that makes inferences from the subject's words. Some studies use content analysis or similar techniques (such as questionnaires) to determine psychological characteristics of an individual and then correlate those characteristics with behavior. Finally, there are a number of *artificial* techniques by which one tries to study the behavior of people in general under certain conditions. This can be done in the psychologist's laboratory or in simulations and gaming activities run by governments, political scientists, or others. These include all-human role-playing games, simulations that combine people with complex computer-generated information, and all-computer simulations. The results of these experiments are then used to form hypotheses about how foreign policy decision makers might behave under similar conditions and to help guide research on decision makers: what we should look at, what we should look for, and how we might explain what we find.[5]

## BELIEF SYSTEMS: IMAGES AND PERCEPTIONS

Before a situation—a problem—exists for the foreign policy decision maker, three things have to occur. First, there has to be a *stimulus* from the environment—a trigger event. Then *perception* of the stimulus must take place, a process by which an individ-

---

[4] Richard Brody, "The Study of International Politics qua Science," in Klaus Knorr and James N. Rosenau, eds., *Contending Approaches to International Politics* (Princeton, N.J.: Princeton University Press, 1969), p. 116.

[5] For a review of the applicability of various content-analysis approaches to the study of foreign policy decision makers as well as a full study that actually employs a variety of these techniques, see Harvey Starr, *Henry Kissinger: Perceptions of International Politics* (Lexington: University Press of Kentucky, 1984). The artificial intelligence approaches noted in Chapter 10 are the newest attempts to gain access to decision-making processes and the cognitive structures of individuals.

ual selects, organizes, and evaluates incoming information about the surrounding world. Finally, there must be an *interpretation* of the perceived stimulus. Both perception and interpretation depend heavily on the images that already exist in the mind of the individual decision maker. In applying social psychology to history, we want to ask: What information are decision makers exposed to? How do they interpret it? How does it affect their beliefs? All this goes back to the differences between how people see the world and how it really is. There are a wide variety of psychological approaches and theories about human behavior. Although we have drawn from a range of these approaches, we have not highlighted the debates among them, such as the one between personality theories and cognitive theories.[6]

An individual's response to a stimulus will be based on his or her perception of that stimulus, not necessarily on the objective nature of the stimulus itself. Decision makers, like other human beings, are subject to all the psychological processes that affect perception—defense mechanisms, reduction of anxiety, rationalization, displacement, and repression—as well as to other characteristics that make up individual personalities.

Our images affect our perceptions in many ways. Initially, a person's values and beliefs help determine the focus of his or her attention—what is selected as a stimulus and what is actually looked at and attended to. Then, on the basis of previous attitudes and images, the stimulus is interpreted. In an *open image* new information, contradictory information, or modifying information is incorporated into existing images, changing them to fit reality. A *closed image* is one that, for various psychological reasons, resists change, ignoring or reshaping contradictory information or selecting only the bits and pieces that might be used to support the image already held. Whether open or closed, *images are screens.* Each of us is attentive to only part of the world around us, and each of us has a different set of images for interpreting incoming information. Perception, based on images already held, is a selective process: "Since we must select, we must be blind to what we have left out."[7]

A **belief system** is the collection of beliefs, images, or models of the world that any individual holds: "The belief system is composed of a more or less integrated set of images which make up the entire relevant universe for the individual. They encompass past, present, and expectations of future reality, and value preferences of 'what ought to be.'"[8] The belief system performs some very important functions for the individual. It helps orient the individual to the environment, organizes perceptions

[6] See Deborah W. Larson, *Origins of Containment: A Psychological Explanation* (Princeton, N.J.: Princeton University Press, 1985), chap. 1; see also Morton Deutsch and Shula Shichman, "Conflict: A Social Psychological Perspective," in Margaret G. Hermann, ed., *Political Psychology* (San Francisco: Jossey-Bass, 1986), pp. 219–250. For a classic statement of the nature and impact of images, see Kenneth Boulding, *The Image* (Ann Arbor: University of Michigan Press, 1956).

[7] Anatol Rapoport, *Fights, Games and Debates* (Ann Arbor: University of Michigan Press, 1960), chap. 16. Note that Rapoport sees the objective of debate as modifying the image the opponent has of the situation and himself.

[8] Ole R. Holsti, "The Belief System and National Images: A Case Study," *Journal of Conflict Resolution* 6 (1962), 244–252.

as a guide to behavior, helps establish goals, and acts as a filter to select relevant information in any given situation. Some foreign policy decision makers did not begin with clear or coherent belief systems. Instead of belief systems influencing behavior, behavior in office helped to shape the belief system.[9] Returning to the rational models discussed in Chapter 10, we see that *even if* we could obtain perfect information about alternatives and consequences, problems of perception make meaningless the notion of an ideal, or perfectly rational, choice among alternatives. From all that information, only some of it will be perceived or selected. The *interpretation* of the information will depend on the individual decision maker's belief system and images. **Misperception** means that, for any number of reasons, the behavior of one state or its decision makers is seen to diverge from what has actually taken place or diverges from the meaning of the act intended by the state or decision makers taking that action. Studies of the European leaders in the weeks immediately preceding the outbreak of World War I strongly support this observation.[10]

## Mechanisms of Selective Perception

In *misperception*, images are screening out important signals—ignoring them completely, interpreting them incorrectly, or changing the information to fit existing images. Images can act as *intervening variables*, mediating between the incoming information and the behavior based on that information. There are a number of psychological processes and mechanisms by which decision makers process information and select it on the basis of held images. These are cognitive distortions, the difficulties that any "careful and logical" individual will have in processing information under conditions of uncertainty.[11]

We must remember that the various information-screening processes that occur in the course of perceiving the world are *normal processes*. They are found widely among people in general, including decision makers, and are not peculiar to "madmen" who distort their images of the world. For decision makers to act at all in a complex world

---

[9] See Larson, *Origins of Containment*, for an extended discussion of this phenomenon. She also notes that policymakers such as Averell Harriman, James Byrnes, and Harry Truman lacked coherent belief systems. Keith L. Shimko, *Images and Arms Control: Perceptions of the Soviet Union in the Reagan Administration* (Ann Arbor: University of Michigan Press, 1991), reports a similar lack of coherence in Reagan's belief system, as well as the development of beliefs by George Shultz and Caspar Weinberger while in office.

[10] For a summary of these pathbreaking studies, see Ole R. Holsti, *Crisis Escalation War* (Montreal: McGill–Queen's University Press, 1972). Jack Levy has also looked at misperceptions of capabilities and intentions in theorizing about the causes of war in "Misperception and the Causes of War: Theoretical Linkages and Analytical Problems," *World Politics* 36, 1 (1983), 76–99.

[11] Another distortion is *affective distortion*, distortion resulting from personal emotions like hostility or insecurity, addressed later in the chapter. For a review of studies on misperception and distortion, see Robert Mandel, "Psychological Approaches to International Relations," in Hermann, ed., *Political Psychology* 1986), p. 253. Perhaps the most inclusive work in the area of misperception is Robert Jervis's classic, *Perception and Misperception in International Politics* (Princeton, N.J.: Princeton University Press, 1976). Much of this section is based on Jervis's study and Mandel's comprehensive review.

of information overload (one filled with tremendous amounts of noise), they must use screens, including perceptual ones.

Like all of us, decision makers perceive the world selectively for different reasons and in different ways. People try to achieve **cognitive consistency:** they want the images they hold not to clash with or contradict each other. Sometimes new information forces an image to change so that it contradicts other images; this often happens when information contradicts a stereotype of a group of people or of an enemy. Rather than change one image and cause a reappraisal of others, a person may simply ignore or reshape the new information, as did John Foster Dulles, Eisenhower's secretary of state, in order to maintain his image of the Soviet Union as aggressive and imperialistic, cooperative only when weak or frightened.

Another mechanism that influences selective perception is the *evoked set.* People perceive and evaluate the world according to what they are concerned with at the moment; this is the "blindness of involvement." The use of often imperfect historical analogies also leads to selective perception: noticing those details of a present episode that look like a past one, while ignoring the important differences. Such analogies are basic to schema theory, which holds that individuals use categories and labels for events and people in order to simplify and organize memories and perceptions. One study argues that simple schemas based on historical analogies were more important than ideology in the development of the American containment policy after World War II.[12] One of the most famous examples of this mechanism is the Munich syndrome. Decision makers in the United States and Britain who had been active during the 1930s, when the Western democracies attempted the appeasement of Hitler (of which the Munich agreement was the main symbol), tended to use this traumatic event as an analogue for postwar events that only partially resembled it. The Suez crisis of 1956 was generated in part by the selective perceptions of British Prime Minister Anthony Eden, who saw Egypt's Nasser as another Hitler and thus as someone who could not be appeased. The historical analogy necessitated selecting certain aspects of the situation and ignoring others. A study of the effect of Reagan's belief system on his dealings with the Soviet Union suggests that he was similarly affected by the Cuban missile crisis, which until the rise of Gorbachev served as Reagan's main historical analogy.[13]

A related process affecting perception is **wishful thinking,** the influence of fears and desires on perception. A content-analysis study of the chief European decision makers in the period immediately before World War I found that Kaiser Wilhelm feared Britain, which had been ruled until recently by an uncle whom he had also feared. Apparently the kaiser believed that the events he feared were actually coming true. Simply hearing that the British felt they still had freedom of action caused the

---

[12] Larson, *Origins of Containment;* Larson, "The Role of Belief Systems and Schemas in Foreign Policy Decision Making," *Political Psychology* 15 (March 1994), 17–33. See also Richard E. Neustadt and Ernest R. May, *Thinking in Time: The Uses of History for Decision Makers* (New York: Free Press, 1986).
[13] See Russell Leng, "Reagan and the Russians: Crisis Bargaining Beliefs and the Historical Record," *American Political Science Review* 78 (June 1984), 338–355.

kaiser to write, "The net has been suddenly thrown over our heads and England sneeringly reaps the most brilliant success of her persistently prosecuted anti-German world policy." Leaders who strongly wanted to see peace thought they saw it in 1938 when Prime Minister Chamberlain returned to Britain from Munich after the carving up of Czechoslovakia, exulting that there was "peace in our time." Wishful thinking is a form of motivated misperception. A leader whose domestic political position is weak may try to build support by initiating conflict with another state (making use of the rally-'round-the-flag effect). Eager to build support in that way, the leader may be motivated to underestimate the strength or determination of the other state and the risks involved in provoking it.

Some common misconceptions recur in foreign policy. First, foreign policy decision makers often underestimate how *unclear* a message, speech, or other communication may be to someone else (in spite of the sender's best efforts). Second, decision makers often do not realize that their behavior may not convey what they *intend* to communicate. They assume that others will understand their actions and behavior much more easily than is the case.

These two observations are directly related to the more substantive misconceptions common in foreign policy. An important one is the tendency for decision makers to see other states, particularly adversaries or competitors, as *more hostile than they are.* Perception leads one to select the information that supports hostility or to interpret behavior as being hostile. Social-psychological research shows that the characteristics and effects of behavior generate similar characteristics and effects. When this involves hostile words, actions, and feelings, a "malignant process" of hostile interaction ensues as

> sane and intelligent people, once they are enmeshed in a pathological social process, engage in actions which seem to them completely rational and necessary but which a detached, objective observer would readily identify as contributing to the perpetuation and intensification of a vicious cycle of interactions.[14]

Because others are seen as more hostile, some of the phenomena related to the **image of an enemy** take place. This type of image leads one to see the behavior of other states as more centralized and coordinated than it really is. One ignores or underestimates the role of chance, mistakes, and particularly the influence of bureaucratic politics when looking at the behavior of other states. This result derives from the use of the Rational Actor model, which assumes that the other state is monolithic, acting in a rational, single-minded way, and that every event has a good reason for occurring. When others act in the way you want, the tendency is to overestimate the influence you had on the opponent's behavior; on the other hand, when the adversary does something undesired, the tendency is to find internal forces in the opposing state to explain the behavior.

---

[14] The phrase and quotation are from Morton Deutsch, *The Resolution of Conflict* (New Haven Conn.: Yale University Press, 1973).

## Psychological Processes Affecting Perception

Seeing others as opponents or enemies is one psychological process central to international relations. Once this happens, the opponent labeled "enemy" takes on certain characteristics, and we then behave toward that state in certain ways. Seeing others as the enemy is a powerful influence on the perceptions and behavior of the leaders of states. Some other, and related, psychological processes that distort reality are **defense mechanisms.** These act to protect the individual from things that would otherwise make him or her uncomfortable and anxious. One defense process is *projection* onto others of the feelings, characteristics, and desires that we cannot admit exist in ourselves.

A major factor in projection is the existence of a **scapegoat.** An enemy acts as a scapegoat when it is accused of the things that one dislikes in oneself. The accusation is used to justify one's own behavior, which is similar to that of the opponent. In foreign relations an enemy is usually seen as aggressive, seeking dominance and conquest, capable of evil and brutality (for example, Dulles saw the Soviet Union as atheistic and evil). Being able to crusade against such an enemy brings great psychological satisfaction. One can ignore one's own behavior and preserve one's self-image, because no matter how badly one is behaving, the object of that behavior is an enemy even more evil. Much of this sort of behavior was observed in the United States during the Vietnam War, when some Americans refused to question various U.S. tactics such as napalm bombing, the torture of prisoners, or the killing of civilians.

Having an enemy allows one the satisfaction of recognizing one's own moral superiority, of having a cause and being needed by that cause to oppose and defeat the enemy; one has as well the satisfaction of being able to hate and kill without being bothered by one's conscience. Having an enemy permits one to see the world in clear-cut distinctions of good and evil, precluding anxiety. A nasty "they" helps to define the "we." During World War II, Japanese and Americans each held strong images of their own racial superiority and the other's barbarism; these images, reinforced in wartime propaganda, then excused the commission of terrible atrocities by both sides.[15] A study of the two world wars and the Vietnam War delineated what has been called a "black–white diabolical enemy image." Included in this is a "virile" and "moral" self-image, a "pro-us" illusion that creates a positive self-image, with no shades of gray. The image of the enemy distorts one's view of the opponent: seeing the opponent as something evil, one lacks empathy and cannot see an opponent's desire for peace, an opponent's fear, or an opponent's anger; one is unable to see the world as the opponent might see it. This inability makes for only a very incomplete view of a situation, and a dangerous one at that: one cannot see how one's "virtuous" behavior may appear to the other party and is unaware of how one's action may worsen a situation. In addition, by seeing another party as an enemy, one often screens out any conciliatory, cooperative, or tension-reducing behavior by the opponent, thus losing

---

[15] John W. Dower, *War Without Mercy: Race and Power in the Pacific War* (New York: Pantheon, 1986).

possibilities for constructive conflict resolution. Ignoring such overtures, one may miss chances to avert a war or to end a war already begun.[16]

This lack of empathy has been discovered in several studies. A major content-analysis study of the European decision makers in the period before the outbreak of World War I indicated that the decision makers of each state perceived, correctly or not, threats of hostile behavior from the states in the other alliance; these perceptions led to hostile behavior toward the opposing states. Stated differently, other states were seen as enemies—they were in opposing military alliances and had engaged in arms races and in competition for colonies. Those who were enemies were then seen as behaving in a hostile manner (whether they were doing so or not). This hostility was then matched by the perceiver's hostility. This type of process, known as a *conflict spiral,* can escalate a minor incident (or, indeed, one that might not have even happened) into a war.

When such images are held by each side in a conflict, there is a **mirror-image situation.** Each side sees the other as an enemy or a devil, and each sees itself as moral, virile, and so on. The term was popularized by research about how ordinary people of the Soviet Union and the United States saw each other early in the cold war—with the other as aggressors, as having a government that exploits and deludes its people, as being a country where the mass of the people do not support their government, as being untrustworthy, and as having a policy that bordered on madness. Mirror images like these may keep a conflict going for a long time and make ending it that much more difficult; it is not surprising they have been found to be influential in such protracted conflicts as the cold war, the Arab–Israeli situation, and in Northern Ireland.

Some writers hope that the analysis of such selective perception or misperception may sensitize decision makers to the dangers that exist and make them more thoughtful about how they communicate to others and interpret others' behavior and how their own behavior appears to an opponent. Decision makers should be made aware that they do not make unbiased analyses but are influenced by the images they hold. Because such images are held, the theories they generate should be made as explicit as possible, so that decision makers and others understand the basis for decisions and actions. Other advice to decision makers has included the suggestion of trying to put oneself in the place of the opponent and see what the situation looks like from the other side—"seeing with the eyes of the other."[17] A related attempt, trying to

---

[16] See Ralph K. White, *Nobody Wanted War: Misperception in Vietnam and Other Wars* (New York: Doubleday, 1970), and Dean G. Pruitt, "Aggressive Behavior in Interpersonal and International Relations," in Paul C. Stern et al., eds., *Perspectives on Deterrence* (New York: Oxford University Press, 1989). See also Arthur E. Gladstone, "The Concept of the Enemy," *Journal of Conflict Resolution* 3 (1959), 132–137. Much of this discussion is based on Gladstone and White.

[17] This advice is from Joseph DeRivera, *The Psychological Dimension of Foreign Policy* (Columbus, Ohio: Merrill, 1968), a pioneering work connecting social psychology to the analysis of foreign policy. See also Irving Janis, *Crucial Decisions: Leadership in Policymaking and Crisis Management* (New York: Free Press, 1989).

understand how things work on the other side and trying to go beyond the Rational Actor model, could help one evaluate decisions from a framework outside one's own images and beliefs or those of a small group of people. Such advice is similar to the suggestions for avoiding the negative consequences of groupthink.

The following excerpt, describing how American decision makers viewed the United States and the Soviet Union during the cold war, is a good description of the pitfalls described above:

> I have heard it argued: "Oh, well, they [the Soviets] know we [the United States] have no aggressive intentions. They know we have no idea of using these arms for an attack on them." To this there are two things to be said. When one attempts to explain to people in the Pentagon and to likeminded civilians that perhaps the Russians are not really eager to attack the West—that they have very good reasons for not planning or wishing to do anything of that sort, one is met with the reply: "Ah, yes, but look at the size of their armaments, and concede that in matters of this sort we cannot be bothered to take into account their intentions—intentions are too uncertain and too hard to determine; we can take into account only capabilities; we must assume the Russians to be desirous, that is, of doing anything bad to us that their capabilities would permit them to do." Now is it our view that [we] should take account only of *their capabilities*, disregarding *their intentions*, but we should expect them to take account only *of our* supposed *intentions*, disregarding *our capabilities?* . . . If we are going to disregard everything but their capabilities, we cannot simultaneously expect them to disregard everything but our intentions.[18]

## AFFECTING THE IMAGE: PERSONALITY AND PERSONAL IDIOSYNCRASIES

There have been many psychological, psychoanalytical, and personality studies of individual foreign policy decision makers, as well as studies of leaders compared on the basis of personality characteristics. One of the classic studies of this type argued that Woodrow Wilson's approach to a number of issues involving power and control over others, including his unwillingness to compromise with political opponents (as in the crucial matter of ratifying the Treaty of Versailles, where the Senate's failure to ratify killed Wilson's dream of American participation in the League of Nations), were consequences of his childhood relationship with his father. Wilson's need to dominate others stemmed from his competition with and aggression toward his father, "political power was for him [Wilson] a compensatory value, a means of

---

[18] George Kennan, *The Cloud of Danger* (Boston: Little, Brown, 1978), pp. 87–88 (emphasis added).

restoring the self-esteem damaged in childhood." Kaiser Wilhelm, the German monarch in 1914, had an analogous insecurity of massive proportions.[19]

Studies of Hitler and Stalin also reveal basic personality disturbances. Stalin's paranoia was matched in the early cold war period in the United States by that of James Forrestal, the first secretary of defense, who committed suicide. Extreme personality disturbances are relatively rare among leaders of large bureaucratized organizations like nation-states, especially under normal conditions, where a potential leader has to work his or her way up through the organization over a long time. People who think or act very peculiarly will be weeded out of positions of leadership or will fail to be promoted. A person with a severe personality disturbance is likely to spend so much energy coping with psychological problems that he or she will be unable to perform at the level required for high achievement in a large organization.

During times of great social and political upheaval, however, a person with very unusual personality characteristics may achieve power when normal people are unable to cope with social problems. Hitler, for instance, came to power in a period of terrible inflation and unemployment in Germany; Stalin, during the upheaval following a revolution and civil war. Moreover, the behavior of such a leader—especially one entrenched for many years in an authoritarian system—may become much more abnormal over time. Both Hitler and Stalin became even more aberrant after 10 years or so in power.

In countries where and at times when the accession to power is more routine, the range of personality types found in office is substantially narrower. Even so, there is enough variation to warrant the use of psychoanalytic techniques to study foreign policy decision makers, sometimes through the use of a categorization system. The most famous of these is a typology created for the study of American "presidential character." The character and style of any president, it is argued, are rooted firmly in his political experiences very early in his career. The experience and style of the individual are molded in the "first independent political success" and go far in determining whether the individual is "active" or "passive" (how much energy is given to the job) and whether the individual is "positive" or "negative" (whether the individual actually enjoys his or her job). An active and confident president who enjoys his job—an active-positive—would be one like Franklin Roosevelt or John Kennedy. The opposite, a president with little liking for the office and low activity and self-confidence, is a passive-negative, for example, Calvin Coolidge. Some of our recent presidents have been active-negatives: almost compulsively active in office but not deriving much pleasure from the job because of low self-esteem and confidence; examples are Lyndon Johnson and Richard Nixon. Reagan was categorized as a

---

[19] See Alexander and Juliet George, *Woodrow Wilson and Colonel House: A Personality Study* (New York: Dover, 1964), p. 320. (For a review of three decades of commentary and debate on the Georges' work, see William Friedman, "Woodrow Wilson and Colonel House and Political Psychology," *Political Psychology* 15 (March 1994), 35–59.) See also Robert G. L. Waite, "Leadership Pathologies: The Kaiser and the Führer and the Decisions for War in 1914 and 1939," in Betty Glad, ed., *Psychological Dimensions of War* (Newbury Park, Calif.: Sage, 1990), pp. 143–168.

"passive-positive"—receptive and compliant, with superficial optimism and a strong need for affection.[20]

Psychobiographical analyses of Henry Kissinger have attempted to link his past experience to his personality and style, which affected his behavior in the foreign policy arena. One observer sees the trauma of Kissinger's boyhood world crumbling about him in Nazi Germany as the main influence on his personality and style. The "inner chaos" that resulted motivated his search for external order, his search for the "strong individual"—even if it is an opponent. Another psychohistorian sees Kissinger's quest for order as the basis for his quest for power.[21] The picture that emerges is of an active-negative, a man of incredible energy and drive who never succeeded in dispelling unease over the chaos that might recur at any time. Perhaps it is not unusual that two active-negatives like Nixon and Kissinger were able to work well as a foreign policy team. Studies of Ronald Reagan indicate that from boyhood he found success through an "energetic attack on obstacles in his path and the avoidance of emotional and intellectual ambiguities." His turn to the political right in the late 1940s "was an adaptation to a personal and political crisis. Anticommunism served certain ego defensive and social adjustment needs for him at a time when his personal and private life had bottomed out."[22]

If we are concerned with the range and variety of personality types that hold office, and how early life experiences can affect both character and style, we cannot overlook the possible impact of gender on decision makers. A number of recent writers argue that investigation of gender roles is necessary for understanding how different gender socialization affects perceptions of power, size, order, and progress (or, indeed, the elements underlying a realist world view). Recent research on post–World War II America, for example, has shown that this gender explanation accounts for differences between American men and women—women have been more opposed to war and less militaristic than men; men are also much more partisan than women. The research indicates that women "learn to put off the use of violence until later in the course of a conflict than do men, to escalate its use more slowly, and to be more emotionally upset by it." There is, in essence, a different underlying structure of attitudes.[23]

---

[20] James D. Barber, *The Presidential Character*, 3rd ed. (Englewood Cliffs, N.J.: Prentice-Hall, 1985).

[21] See Dan Caldwell, ed., *Henry Kissinger: His Personality and Policies* (Durham, N.C.: Duke University Press, 1983), especially the chapter by Dana Ward; Starr, *Henry Kissinger;* and Stephen G. Walker, "The Interface Between Beliefs and Behavior: Henry Kissinger's Operational Code and the Vietnam War," *Journal of Conflict Resolution* 21 (1977), 129–168.

[22] See Betty Glad, "Reagan's Midlife Crisis and the Turn to the Right," *Political Psychology* 10 (1989), 593–624. See also Glad, *Jimmy Carter: In Search of the Great White House* (New York: Norton, 1980); Bruce Mazlish, *In Search of Nixon* (New York: Basic Books, 1972); and the set of psychobiographical studies in Barber, *The Presidential Character*.

[23] This research is presented in Pamela Johnston Conover and Virginia Sapiro, "Gender, Feminist Consciousness, and War," *American Journal of Political Science* 37 (November 1993), 1079–1099 (quotation is from p. 1096).

## *Private Motives and Public Objects*

These various examples of psychological-, personality- and individual-oriented research all hark back to the classic formulation of Harold Lasswell—that there is a displacement of *private* motives onto *public* objects. Just as all people take out their emotions, frustrations, and personality quirks on the world around them (for example, kicking the dog when you are angry with your spouse), decision makers will also displace their private (idiosyncratic) personality drives onto the world around them. In their case, however, private drives can have wide-ranging influence, for the outside world is also the world of diplomacy and foreign policy decision making.

One way to study private motives and public objects is to match indicators of various types of personalities to the behavior most likely to be associated with that personality. For example, scholars have been concerned with the personality attributes associated with the willingness to take risks, to cooperate, or to go to war. Some of these studies have used content analysis of decision makers' statements to isolate personality characteristics such as the need for power, conceptual complexity, trust or distrust of others, need for affiliation, belief in control over events, and nationalism. Such studies have shown that the greater the need for power exhibited by the decision maker, the more aggressive his or her government will tend to be; the more **cognitively complex** (having the ability to see various sides to issues rather than in simple terms of black and white) the decision maker, the more cooperative his or her government will tend to be. In updating research to include Ronald Reagan, these findings were reinforced. Compared with previously studied heads of government, Reagan was highly nationalistic, among the highest in the need for power, and lowest in cognitive complexity; this last finding is consistent with the findings from psychohistorical analyses noted above.[24]

One creative study looked at the cognitive complexity—sometimes called "integrative complexity"—of leaders during crisis. Characteristics such as flexibility, empathy, and the ability to recognize alternatives were considered. The analysis of speeches and other public words showed what we would expect: compared to precrisis measures, the cognitive complexity of foreign policy decision makers *dropped* during the stress and pressure of a crisis. There was one exception. Of the 16 individuals studied, only Andrei Gromyko evidenced an *increase* of integrative complexity during crisis. Perhaps Gromyko's ability to keep his head while all about him were losing theirs was one reason for his amazing longevity in office. Until his death in 1989 he had served with every Soviet leader except Lenin and had dealt with every American administration since Franklin Roosevelt's. Applying the same analysis to successful nineteenth-century foreign policy leaders, similar results emerged for individuals such as

---

[24] See, for example, Margaret G. Hermann: "Leaders' Foreign Policy Orientations and the Quality of Foreign Policy Decisions," in Stephen Walker, ed., *Role Theory and Foreign Policy Analysis* (Durham, N.C.: Duke University Press, 1987); "Assessing Personality at a Distance: A Profile of Ronald Reagan," *Mershon Center Quarterly Report* 7 (1983), 1–8.

Bismarck and Wellington. Even more interesting, such increases in integrative complexity were not a mere function of time in office, but were a function of personality.[25]

Similar studies have also been done on people at lower levels in the foreign policy bureaucracy, such as foreign policy specialists in the U.S. State Department. One found a relationship between personality factors and the willingness to use force. Those who were mistrustful, who had low self-esteem, who liked to compete with others, and who were active and ambitious were more likely than other personality types to advocate the use of force by the United States. Interestingly, however, if people combined ambition with high self-esteem, they were also more likely to advocate the use of force.[26]

One very interesting study shows how scholars can combine historical materials (using history like a math textbook with the answers in the back) and laboratory controls. This study used both content analysis and simulation to study the impact of personality on foreign policy, running two simulations with students playing the roles of decision makers. Each student was set up to match the role of a European leader before the outbreak of World War I, but the situation was masked so that the students did not realize they were participating in a World War I simulation. On the basis of the content-analysis studies done by the group at Stanford who researched the European decision makers in the pre–World War I crisis, the personality characteristics of the actual European decision makers could be outlined. After tests were made on the students, they, too, were classified according to such characteristics as dominance and self-control. In one simulation students were matched to the roles of decision makers on the basis of similar personality characteristics; in the second simulation personalities were not matched. Where personalities were matched, the students' perceptions of the events that occurred correlated quite highly with those of the actual decision makers in 1914. In addition, the events that occurred were quite similar to those of 1914, and the simulation led to the brink of war, with alliance configurations similar to those of 1914. The close fit between events and perceptions did not occur, however, in the simulation where personalities were not matched.[27]

## Belief System, Personality, and Perception: The Case of John Foster Dulles

One of the most famous studies in this field is by Ole Holsti of John Foster Dulles, Eisenhower's secretary of state from 1953 to 1959. Holsti's study addresses many of the issues and factors discussed in this chapter. He studied Dulles's "image of the

---

[25] Michael D. Wallace and Peter Suedfeld, "Leadership Performance in Crisis: The Longevity–Complexity Link," *International Studies Quarterly* 32 (December 1988), 439–451.

[26] Lloyd Etheredge, *A World of Men: The Private Sources of American Foreign Policy* (Cambridge, Mass.: MIT Press, 1978).

[27] Charles F. Hermann and Margaret G. Hermann, "An Attempt to Simulate the Outbreak of World War I," in James N. Rosenau, ed., *International Politics and Foreign Policy*, rev. ed. (New York: Free Press, 1969), pp. 622–639.

enemy"—how Dulles perceived the Soviet Union across time and along several dimensions. His study dealt with some of the basic psychological processes involved in the closed image and the screening of information. One part of the study, for example, clearly demonstrates projection. Holsti used an **"operational code"** approach to analyze Dulles's writings before he became secretary of state. This approach is an informal method of content analysis based on a set of questions used to elicit an individual's belief system. These include philosophical questions such as: "Is the political universe essentially one of harmony or conflict?" "How much control or mastery can one have over historical development?" There are also instrumental questions concerning one's style of behavior in the political world, such as: "What is the best approach for selecting goals or objectives for political action?" "What is the best timing of action to advance one's interests?"[28] Two of Dulles's instrumental beliefs about how one should act in regard to foreign policy were: when one's opponent is strong, one should avoid conflict; when one's opponent is weak, one should be willing to run risks. These beliefs were culled from a number of books written by Dulles on foreign policy. Yet when Dulles later became secretary of state, he asserted that it was the Soviet Union that was cooperative or friendly only when it was weak or afraid. Here is a clear case of an individual projecting his beliefs onto the actions of another.

Holsti's research included a full study of Dulles's belief system and personality and how those factors were related to his perceptions of the Soviet Union. This study is a good example of the effect that psychological variables can have on an individual who is not aberrant, possessing a normal (if strong) personality.

Decision makers, as we have discussed, behave according to their images of a situation and of the other parties involved. If the image or the theory is too tightly held, however, the images become stereotyped and unchanging. Holsti was interested in how this process might be related to the image of the enemy: "Enemies are those who are defined as such, and if one acts upon that interpretation, it is more than likely that the original definition will be confirmed." The thrust of Holsti's presentation is that cognitive processes maintain images of an enemy. Describing Dulles's images of the Soviet Union, he demonstrates that the picture was not only a very negative one but also one that resisted change.

Part of Holsti's study involved a content analysis of all of Dulles's public statements while he was secretary of state. In these documents Holsti searched for Dulles's evaluations of the Soviet Union. He divided these into four groups: evaluations of Soviet capabilities, Soviet success, Soviet hostility, and a general evaluation. Each of the more than 3,500 evaluations was placed into one of these four categories and given a rating (determined by a set of rules) on scales between +3.00 and −3.00, from strength to weakness, success to failure, friendship to hostility, good to bad.

[28] A review of this method for gaining access to decision makers, and its development, may be found in Stephen G. Walker, "The Evolution of Operational Code Analysis," *Political Psychology* 11 (1990), 403–418. The classic statement is Alexander George, "The Operational Code: A Neglected Approach to the Study of Political Decision-Making," *International Studies Quarterly* 13 (1969), 190–222.

Dulles's general view was that the Soviet Union was atheistic, totalitarian, and communist. He held an "inherent bad faith" image of the Soviet Union, believing that it could not be trusted and would only act in a friendly way when weak or afraid. His images included the view that the Russian people were "good," but that the communist leaders were "bad." The Russian national interest was evaluated more positively than were the interests of international communism. He also evaluated the Russian state much more favorably than he did the Communist party.

Although over the years Dulles's view of Soviet capabilities, success, and hostility did change, nothing seemed to change his general evaluation of the Soviet Union. As we can see from Figure 11.2, the other three categories rise and fall, but general evaluation is almost a straight line at the bottom of the graph. The other three categories correlate with each other (for example, when Dulles saw the Soviet Union being less successful or decreasing in capabilities, he saw it as less hostile, and conversely). Dulles's general evaluation, however, did not correlate with any of the others. Holsti uses this as evidence to support the conclusion that Dulles had a closed image of the Soviet Union: "Dulles interpreted the very data that would lead one to change one's model in such a way to preserve that model." Information contrary to Dulles's image

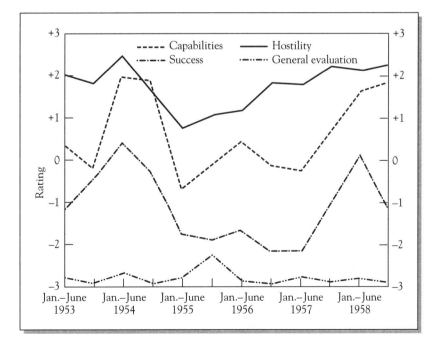

**FIGURE 11.2** John Foster Dulles's perceptions of the Soviet Union, 1953–1958. [*Source:* Ole R. Holsti, "The Belief System and National Images: A Case Study," *Journal of Conflict Resolution* 6 (1962), 245. By permission of the publisher, Sage Publications, Inc.]

was reinterpreted to leave the original image intact: cuts in the size of the Soviet armed forces were attributed to Soviet economic weakness and to bad faith; Dulles believed that the men released from service would be put to work building more lethal weapons. The psychological consequences of admitting that the Soviets could be good or act cooperatively out of any motive other than fear or weakness would have opened up to question other parts of Dulles's belief system.

Not only does the Holsti study illustrate many of the ideas presented in this chapter and demonstrate how several methods might be used to study individuals, it is also part of an example of cumulation in scientific research. We may contrast the findings with those of Harvey Starr's study of Henry Kissinger. The Kissinger study was explicitly modeled on that of Dulles so that the effect of idiosyncratic variables could be systematically compared. If we look at the images that Kissinger held of the Soviet Union, the differences from Dulles's view are striking (Figure 11.3). In addition to making far more positive evaluations, Kissinger had an open and flexible image of the Soviet Union. How good or bad the Soviets were seen to be was related to their behavior: the friendlier Soviet behavior appeared to be to Kissinger, the better his general evaluation of the Soviet Union. Kissinger, who was able not only to negotiate the SALT arms-control agreements with the Soviet Union but also to begin a period of detente, had a more positive and more flexible view of the "enemy." He was able to

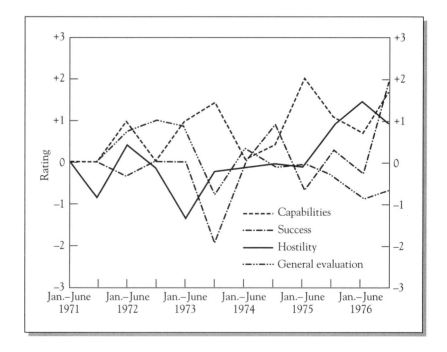

**FIGURE 11.3** Kissinger's perceptions of the Soviet Union, 1971–1976.

modify that view according to the behavior that the opponent exhibited. Although we have to take into account the fact that Dulles was operating in a period of cold war and Kissinger dealt with the USSR during a period of detente, we also know that individuals may have some impact on foreign policy and that they can, if they desire, slow down or accelerate changes in the direction of foreign policy when they take office. Dulles may have had to deal with the Soviets during the cold war, but he was also responsible for helping to continue that state of affairs; Kissinger not only worked within a period of detente but also was largely responsible for continuing and accelerating a trend that existed when he took office.[29]

## AFFECTING THE IMAGE: THE DECISION MAKER AS A PHYSIOLOGICAL ANIMAL

If we look at foreign policy and foreign policy decisions as the product of human behavior, it would be foolish to overlook the fact that decision makers are physical beings, influenced by their physiology and possibly by their genetic heritage. On a very simple level, whether information is received and the degree to which it is understood and interpreted depend on the physical ability of the individual. Thus the physical as well as the mental health of decision makers can affect foreign policy and the decision-making process. The strain of high public office is great: look at before-and-after photographs of almost any U.S. president since World War II. The effect of this strain often breaks down the health of the leader. This is even more important when we remember that many political leaders, particularly the heads of governments and senior ministers, are older individuals and thus even more susceptible to the strains of office. Some, like Mao Zedong (who died at 84), Charles de Gaulle (79), and Leonid Brezhnev (75), remain in office to an advanced age. The former communist countries seemed particularly susceptible to groups of aged leaders. The average age of the Eastern European leaders in 1989, when communism fell, was 76. None of the Chinese communist leaders who were responsible for the Tiananmen Square attack, also in 1989, were under 75.

People today are basically the same physical creatures that evolved as plains hunters tens of thousands of years ago. Human physiology operates so that in a situation provoking fear, anger, or anxiety, the body gears up for "fight or flight." Physiological reactions—increased heartbeat, the release of adrenaline, the movement of blood to the muscles—prepare the body for physical combat or for running away as fast as possible. The stress that builds up in the body is released by one or the other of these physical actions.

---

[29] As further evidence of cumulation, these conclusions were reinforced by a set of comparisons among Dulles, Kissinger, and John F. Kennedy, using operational code and content analyses; see Douglas Stuart and Harvey Starr, "Inherent Bad Faith Reconsidered: Dulles, Kennedy and Kissinger," *Political Psychology* 3 (Fall–Winter 1981–1982), 1–33.

The body chemistry of today's foreign policy decision maker still works that way, but "fight or flight" is only a metaphor. The modern official does not run screaming down the White House lawn but sits in conference or talks on the telephone or broods alone in an office. The internalized stress is not released as intended, and the health of the decision maker is impaired. The stress imposed by a crisis negatively affects performance in information handling and clarity of thought.

A study of the medical histories of twentieth-century political and military leaders indicates an extremely high rate of medical disabilities. These ailments and the drugs and other treatments taken for them have a number of purely physiological effects on the individual that could affect his or her perception of the world and decision-making procedures. Even common psychoactive drugs like alcohol, caffeine, tranquilizers, and sedatives can affect perceptions and mood without an individual's knowing it. For example, alcohol can increase risk-taking and recklessness (what effects might Boris Yeltsin's reputed alcohol problem have on his decision to attack Chechnya?). Tranquilizers can increase hostility. Cocaine can induce feelings of euphoria and increased strength.[30]

Perhaps the best example of these effects is the behavior of British Prime Minister Anthony Eden during the Suez crisis of 1956. From a variety of sources, it was clear that Eden was ill, suffering from hypertension and nervous disorders. Reports claim that he was also taking benzedrine, which imparts a feeling of control and confidence. We know that Eden's decision-making behaviors at that time differed markedly from those he had displayed in other cases. He was much more secretive and consulted only a very small group of colleagues. He suffered a physical breakdown right after the crisis. We have already noted that stress can lead to suicide, as in the case of Forrestal or the attempted suicide of Presidential National Security Adviser Robert McFarlane during the Iran–Contra affair in 1986.

Almost every president and high-level decision maker has had major physical problems. Woodrow Wilson had a stroke during his stressful and unsuccessful campaign for the League of Nations. Some analysts blame the stroke, rather than lifelong psychological problems, for his stubborn, uncompromising, and counterproductive behavior thereafter. Eisenhower's heart attacks weakened his control over policy; his turning over the government to Vice President Nixon partly prompted the adoption in 1967 of the 25th Amendment to the Constitution on presidential disability and succession. The death of top decision makers or their inability to function can bring the decision-making processes of government to a halt or cause great disruption. The ill health of Brezhnev, Andropov, and Chernenko in the early to mid-1980s brought great instability and uncertainty to the analysis—and running—of Soviet foreign policy.

People have always been concerned about human nature, wondering if there is a built-in human instinct for violence, aggression, and domination. The debate over "nature versus nurture" is an old one. What accounts for human actions: innate

---

[30] See, for example, Roy Lubit and Bruce Russett, "The Effects of Drugs on Decision Making," *Journal of Conflict Resolution* 28 (1984), 85–102.

genetic characteristics or the cultural environment? A form of the debate continues between ethology (the study of animal behavior) and anthropology. The most extreme ethologists say that there is a strong biological basis for human behavior and that biological influences on behavior are very powerful. More moderate exponents claim that ethology simply provides us with analogies between mechanisms found in animals and similar mechanisms found in human cultures. Opponents of this view claim that the genetic or biological impact is either extremely small or nonexistent.

For animals higher on the evolutionary ladder, the influence of the environment is greater. Each animal has a "biogram," a program, or template, built into its genes. For the oldest and least complicated forms of life, much if not all behavior is guided by such a program. However, more of the behavior of a higher animal depends on stimuli from its environment—hearing its parents sing the proper bird song or watching a mother lion hunt. Human beings have by far the most open and flexible program of all. Group life itself may be a biological necessity, built into human genes, along with language, but what group one lives with, what culture one is surrounded by, and what language one speaks are all completely undetermined. Anthropologists have demonstrated that just about any conceivable type of behavior, in almost every conceivable combination, can be found in the groups of men and women that live and have lived on earth.

But war, violence, and aggression may not be built into humanity and thus may be prevented. The famous anthropologist Margaret Mead argued that war was simply another human invention; as noted earlier, John Mueller maintains a similar view that war, like slavery and dueling, can be "unlearned." One review, by a psychologist, of the available arguments concludes that humans are *not* inherently violent.[31] Although ethology provides us with some interesting analogies and explanations for human behavior, it cannot explain decisions to go to war or to act cooperatively in international relations. We cannot fall back on "human nature" to explain foreign policy behavior. We are all human, and thus we all share the same human nature—but some societies are much more peaceful than others. The people of modern Scandinavia are widely regarded as peaceful and antiwar; Sweden, for instance, has not fought a war since 1815. Their ancestors, however, were the fierce Vikings who pillaged and looted all around Europe during the Middle Ages.

Under the auspices of the Spanish National Commission of UNESCO a group of leading biologists and social scientists from twelve countries (and five continents) formulated the Seville Statement in 1986. The Statement, adopted by numerous academic and professional organizations in many disciplines and countries, specifically rejects the proposition that arms and war are inevitable because of inherent influences of human nature (Table 11.1). Instead, we should do much better to look at how certain types of situations affect individual perception and individual and group decision making.

---

[31] See Leonard Berkowitz, "Biological Roots: Are Humans Inherently Violent?" in Glad, ed., *Psychological Dimensions of War*, pp. 24–40.

**TABLE 11.1**  The Five Propositions of the Seville Statement on Violence, Seville, May 16, 1986

IT IS SCIENTIFICALLY INCORRECT to say that we have inherited a tendency to make war from our animal ancestors. . . . Warfare is a peculiarly human phenomenon and does not occur in other animals.

IT IS SCIENTIFICALLY INCORRECT to say that war or any other violent behavior is genetically programmed into our human nature. While genes are involved at all levels of nervous system function, they provide a development potential that can be actualized only in conjunction with the ecological and social environment.

IT IS SCIENTIFICALLY INCORRECT to say that in the course of human evolution there has been a selection for aggressive behavior more than for other kinds of behavior. . . . Violence is neither in our evolutionary legacy nor in our genes.

IT IS SCIENTIFICALLY INCORRECT to say that humans have a "violent brain." While we do have the neural apparatus to act violently, it is not automatically activated by internal or external stimuli. . . . There is nothing in our neurophysiology that compels us to react violently.

IT IS SCIENTIFICALLY INCORRECT to say that war is caused by "instinct" or any single motivation.

## AFFECTING THE IMAGE: CRISIS SITUATIONS

One type of situation studied extensively by students of international relations is the *crisis*. We noted that a crisis is characterized as a *high-threat situation* that requires action in a finite, usually short, time. This is exactly the type of situation that places a decision maker under the most stress. The crisis situation in which decisions have to be made will affect the perceptions of decision makers differently from noncrisis situations such as general foreign policy decisions or administrative decisions. The decision processes will also tend to be different, and the constraints, mainly psychological, will also be different. A crisis situation presents a decision maker with a different menu and makes the decision maker see that menu in a special way; it will affect the propensity of any decision maker to act rationally. Decision makers will be most like rational actors, deciding analytically, when stress is neither too high nor too low.[32]

Quite often, because of the time pressure, a crisis is a period of information overload for the decision maker: messages come in from observers on the spot, from aides

---

[32] Exactly how and what decision makers learn from the handling of previous crises is investigated by Russell Leng, *Interstate Crisis Behavior, 1816–1988: Realism vs. Reciprocity* (Cambridge, England: Cambridge University Press), 1993.

who have been asked to find out what is happening, from ambassadors, from others. The combination of stress and information overload will usually lead decision makers to overreact or underreact. Again, screens and the psychological processes that set up those screens are at work. The distorted view of the world will reduce the decision maker's ability to interpret and the quality of the interpretation. (Sometimes inappropriate reaction results when the situation is exactly the opposite, of course—when there is no information about what has happened.)

Studies comparing crises help us understand their impact. We have already discussed the "blindness of involvement"; a crisis caused by a high threat is also a situation of high involvement. One analysis of the pre–World War I period, the Cuban missile crisis, and the Vietnam War examined the intensity of involvement. As the intensity grew, there was a tendency in World War I and the Vietnam War for decision makers to make tangible and specific issues more symbolic. Thinking back to the bargaining analyses of Roger Fisher, we can see that as issues become more intangible and symbolic, they become more difficult to bargain over and resolve. Indeed, in both World War I and Vietnam, war either broke out or escalated. Neither of these things happened in Cuba. Another study that compared the pre–World War I crisis and the 1962 Cuban missile crisis demonstrated other differences. The United States and the Soviet Union perceived each other's behavior far more accurately than did actors in prewar Europe. Somehow the problematic effects of perception in crisis did not happen in the Cuba situation. Why not?

Several possible explanations may be offered. One version of the "advice to decision makers" we discussed earlier in this chapter did occur. John Kennedy had read *The Guns of August*, Barbara Tuchman's history of the period preceding the outbreak of World War I. Although Kennedy did not explicitly state his argument in terms of misperception and conflict spirals, he did recognize that these processes were largely responsible for the onset of war. Memoirs of the missile crisis point out that Kennedy wanted to be careful to avoid such mistakes; he did not want to see a book entitled *The Missiles of October*. A second possible factor was the clear knowledge of the disastrous consequences of failing to control the crisis. In 1914 many decision makers saw the possible war as a replay of the Franco–Prussian War of 1870, a brief war of several sharp encounters. Thus they were not frightened, as they would have been if they had imagined four years of trench warfare, over 9 million battle deaths, and the destruction of the German, Russian, Austrian, and Turkish monarchies. Kennedy and Khrushchev had no illusions about the consequences of losing control of the crisis and engaging in nuclear war. The stakes were so high that extra caution was employed as an antidote to the usual misperception induced by crisis.

In brief, studies of World War I, the Korean War, and the Cuban missile crisis have indicated the following sorts of effects on perception. During a crisis, *communications tend to become shorter and more stereotyped* as stress increases. Stereotypes not only distort but also produce black-and-white images and foster the creation and maintenance of the image of an "enemy." Not surprisingly, then, crisis also can lead to an overperception of the level of hostility and violence of one's opponents or a perception of hostility that might not exist (and through such perceptions, aggravate or create hostilities—a case of the self-fulfilling prophecy). On the other hand, *one underperceives the hostility and violence in one's own actions.*

As we have seen, if a state sees itself as the object of hostility, it will express hostility. We are in a **conflict spiral,** a mirror-image situation between two states that perceive each other as enemies. This fits with psychologist Morton Deutsch's "crude law of social relations": "that the characteristic processes and effects elicited by a given type of social relationship (cooperative or competitive) tend also to elicit that type of social relationship." That is, hostility begets hostility, and cooperation begets cooperation.[33] Perceptions of anxiety or fear are likely to increase in these circumstances; as they do, they may also lead decision makers to ignore perceptions of capabilities. The desire to break the tension through any resolution of the crisis—even war—can lead to ignoring the strength or weakness of oneself, one's allies, and one's opponents. Luckily, this did not happen in the Cuban missile crisis. Neither Kennedy nor Khrushchev called nuclear weapons "paper tigers" (as the Chinese did before they acquired them), nor did they underplay the destructiveness of such weapons. Each went out of his way to stress the consequences of their use. Recent revelations by U.S. and Soviet policymakers involved in the missile crisis highlight the extreme caution in the behavior of both Kennedy and Khrushchev.

The last general point—related to other perceptions of the opponent as a rational monolith—is that as the crisis grows, decision makers increasingly feel that their *own range of alternatives becomes more restricted.* The crisis, therefore, reduces their perceptions of available alternatives. At the same time, decision makers see the *alternatives of their opponents as expanding:* "Although *we* have no choice but to go to war, *they* could avoid war by doing any of a number of things." Crisis situations can produce significant and potentially damaging effects. The study of crisis management becomes very important.[34]

## CONCLUSION

In this and the previous chapter we have investigated individuals and the way they make decisions. The key issues and assumptions raised at this level of analysis can be summarized by what Brian Ripley has called the basic tenets of foreign policy decision making:

**1.** Decision-making elites are the most important actors in international politics.

**2.** In order to interpret patterns of behavior in global politics, we must endeavor to understand the decision maker's own "definition of the situation."

**3.** Foreign policy can best be understood as an unending task of sequential problem-solving by goal-directed elites operating within organizational and cognitive constraints.

**4.** The primary currency of foreign policy is information.

---

[33] Morton Deutsch, *The Resolution of Conflict,* p. 365.

[34] For a comprehensive overview of the effects of crisis on decision making and the consequences for international politics, see Ole R. Holsti, "Crisis Decision Making," in Philip E. Tetlock et al., eds., *Behavior, Society, and Nuclear War,* vol. 1 (New York: Oxford University Press, 1989), pp. 8–84.

**5.** The global system is an arena of politics rather than the major force in international politics.
**6.** Policy prescriptions involve efforts to compensate for individual misperception and organizational pathologies.[35]

In Part I we have looked at a series of environments, contexts, or sources of influence and constraint on the foreign policy–making process. We began with the global system and concluded with a look at the individual and his or her psychological environment. These resources are presented in Table 11.2, which also provides some notion of the degree to which these sources can change over time.

| **TABLE 11.2** | The Sources of Influence or Constraint on Foreign Policy | | |
|---|---|---|---|
| | Time Continuum | | |
| Systemic Aggregation Continuum | Sources that tend to change slowly | | Sources that tend to underg rapid change |
| Systemic sources | | Great power structure | Situational factors: external |
| | | Alliances | Issue areas |
| | | | Crises |
| | Size | Technology | |
| | Geography | | |
| Societal sources | Culture and history | Economic development | Situational factors: internal |
| | | Social structure | |
| | | Moods of opinion | |
| Governmental sources | | Political accountability | |
| | | Governmental structure | |
| Idiosyncratic sources | | | Values, talents, experiences, and personalities of leaders |

*Source:* James N. Rosenau, "The Study of Foreign Policy," in James N. Rosenau, Kenneth Thompson, and Gavin Boyd, eds., *World Politics* (New York: Free Press, 1976), p. 18. Copyright © 1976 by The Free Press, a division of Macmillan Publishing Co., Inc.

---

[35] Brian Ripley, "Psychology, Foreign Policy, and International Relations Theory," *Political Psychology* 14 (1993), 403–416.

The place of the individual and the idiosyncratic factors affecting perception may be highlighted by looking closely at the table. Although the other factors exist in the real world and change slowly, the perceptions of these other factors by a changing set of decision-making individuals can shift very rapidly. We have stressed the existence and significance of the psychological environment. We can then compare that environment with the reality of the other environments and investigate the crucial disparities between the real and the perceived. As we have seen, even in the most normal of decision makers, selective perception is an important influence on policymaking. Decision makers, whether individually or in groups, are human beings whose perceptions of their interests will often vary from what an observer might expect.

# Contemporary and Future
# Problems of World Politics

Our emphasis so far has been on general tools of analysis, offering some wide-ranging theories and abstract statements. Often we have illustrated propositions by referring to particular phenomena of contemporary or recent world politics. Nevertheless, the discussion has been very different from what you might encounter in an issue-oriented study of current events. This has been deliberate—partly because what seemed current when we wrote the book probably would be dated by the time it found its way to a classroom. However, the more important reason for a relatively abstract and theoretical presentation has been to help to establish a set of principles for thinking about world politics. To establish such principles, you need theory rooted in real political problems and political structures. You need historical information and concrete illustrations. You also need to be able to see the utility and the beauty of more general and abstract theoretical inquiry.

We cannot envision in any detail the kinds of problems that we, as citizens of our countries and of the world, will see in our lifetimes. Our crystal ball is almost as clouded about the nature of future problems as it is about solutions. Nevertheless, we do have some ideas about the kinds of problems that will endure.

In Part II we shall examine four kinds of problems, along with an attempt to pull them together for a look toward the future—combining a discussion of historical detail with an evaluation of contemporary theory and research relevant to those problems. In doing so, we shall look at the nature of political, economic, and social conflict and cooperation in the international system.

**1.** *Arms races, deterrence, and arms control*—aspects of the eternal quest for security and the role of force in enhancing or diminishing that security, with special attention to the challenges posed by nuclear weapons, nuclear strategy, and the consequences of nuclear war.

**2.** *Peaceful relations among the industrialized countries*—how the interdependence of industrialized nations has shaped the ability to achieve security without war but has also helped make common problems out of previously individual ones.

**3.** *Dependence of less developed countries on the industrialized world,* especially as that dependence is seen by the developed countries and how it can shape the quest of citizens of less developed nations for decent living conditions and political liberties.

**4.** *The ecology of the world system*—incorporating the pressures and needs for growth with the constraints of resource limits, the pollution-absorbing capacity of the environment, and the political dilemmas of achieving some degree of order in an often anarchic world.

**5.** *Can good things go together? The future of development, democracy, and peace.*

In our examination we shall frequently move from one level of analysis to another, illustrating how understanding these problems requires taking analytical perspectives from virtually all levels. We shall also note the differences in power of various levels of analysis when dealing with different problems. Questions, values, explanations, and proposed solutions are very different for rich and powerful countries and weak countries—and also for rich and powerful people in a given country as opposed to poor and weak ones. For our discussion we have chosen a set of broad problems that are both important and varied.

Thus, in looking at different theories about the causes of war and peace, the relationships between and among rich and poor countries, the ecological challenges facing the world community, and the linkages between economic development, democracy, and peace, we will return to the phenomenon of *interdependence* among actors in the global system and questions of how to manage interdependence.

# CONFLICT AND COOPERATION IN ARMS RACES

International politics, like all social life, involves a mixture of conflict and cooperation. In all our relations, even with friends and family, we both compete and cooperate. Usually in personal affairs the competitive elements are kept under control because it is more important to maintain the cooperative aspect of a relationship. As a result, we occasionally give in to a friend's or relative's interest when it conflicts with ours. With someone we love and with whom we share a sense of identity (a spouse, a parent, a child, or a close friend), it is sometimes a pleasure to give up something for that person. In international politics, however, there is little affection and a limited sense of shared identity. Common interests and the need to maintain a cooperative relationship may seem less immediate; thus we tend to emphasize the elements of competition. But both conflict and cooperation are there, and any effort to achieve our own goals must include both.

We often think of interdependence primarily in positive terms; for example, that economies can grow best when trade and investment capital can flow relatively freely. Actions to reduce positive interdependence, by emphasizing conflictual aspects such as whose economy will grow *more,* may make it harder to achieve mutually desired goals. Some other forms of interdependence, however, start with negative elements, such as the implicit and explicit exchange of threats that characterizes an arms race. In these relationships, interdependence can harm both sides through the security dilemma: I see your armaments as threatening me, and to counter them I acquire arms that you see as threatening you. In addition, arms such as nuclear weapons with ballistic delivery systems produce vulnerabilities for other states—vulnerabilities they *cannot* escape. Here, interdependence produces negative consequences for the actors, who find themselves in an interdependent system. Management of this kind of interdependence requires introducing positive aspects of interdependence (such as an arms-control inspection system that allows each to see that the other's arms are strictly defensive and not excessive). It may also require some limitations on interdependence (building arms that really are defensive and do not pose a threat).

## A BRIEF HISTORY OF THE SOVIET–U.S. ARMS RACE

Let us examine some of the interactions of conflict and cooperation in the cold war arms race between the United States and the Soviet Union. First, we shall outline a brief history of the strategic arms race, using four broad historical periods, and then analyze the interactions, attempting to understand how the world entered, endured, and survived the era of nuclear confrontation.

### 1945–1950: The Period of U.S. Nuclear Monopoly

After World War II, the United States and to a lesser degree the Soviet Union both disarmed from the high levels of global war. The atomic bomb was the central element in America's policy of deterrence. Although the Soviet Union retained large land forces (which could have threatened Western Europe), for all practical purposes the Soviets had no atomic weapons. They exploded their first bomb in 1949, but it was several years before they built up a stockpile adequate for fighting a war, and, in any case, they lacked intercontinental bombers capable of reaching the United States. The Americans could have bombed the Soviet Union, inflicting substantial damage, though the number of American bombs was not large (probably only about 300, even at the end of this period), and they were *fission* (atomic) weapons rather than the much more devastating *fusion* (thermonuclear, or hydrogen) weapons that followed.

### 1951–1957: The Period of U.S. Nuclear Dominance

As the culmination of a series of threatening incidents in the emerging cold war (the communist takeover of Czechoslovakia and the Berlin blockade in 1948, a communist victory in China, and the Soviet atomic bomb explosion in 1949), the Korean War (which began in June 1950) initiated a great American program of rearmament, during which annual U.S. defense expenditures nearly tripled. U.S. Secretary of State John Foster Dulles declared that the United States would respond to any further communist attack on "free world" nations "in a manner and at a place of our own choosing." In other words, in the face of any such "proxy war" the United States would feel free to strike not at the small communist ally but directly at the Soviet Union, in "massive retaliation" with nuclear weapons. Such a threat was credible because the United States had by then built up a very large stockpile of nuclear weapons and an intercontinental bombing force to deliver them, including the hydrogen bomb (first tested by the United States in 1952 and by the Soviets in 1953). The ability to inflict damage was so greatly imbalanced in favor of the United States (which also maintained bases in Europe and Asia quite near the USSR) that we can speak of this era as the period of American strategic dominance. In response the Soviet leaders pursued a very cautious and generally unprovocative foreign policy—and a major rearmament effort. Figure 12.1 illustrates U.S. and Soviet defense expenditures throughout the post–World War II period in constant (inflation-adjusted) 1985 dollars. Recall that the estimates of Soviet military spending are very rough and controversial, since the USSR never published accurate military budget data. These were the best estimates available during the cold war era.

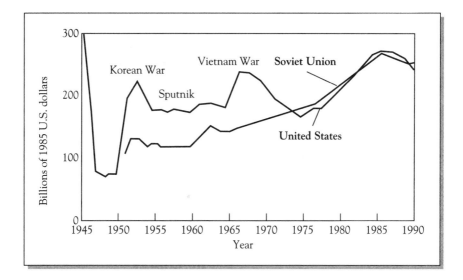

**FIGURE 12.1** Military expenditures of the Soviet Union and the United States, 1945–1990 (billions of 1985 U.S. dollars). Our estimates of Soviet spending are subject to large error.

## 1958–1966: The Period of U.S. Preponderance

American dominance over the Soviet Union decreased from 1958 to 1966, and the new term we use to describe American superiority is simply *preponderance*. Still, it was a period when the United States could at least consider the option of attacking the Soviet Union with nuclear weapons in response to a proxy war started by a Soviet ally. The United States still had something of a **first-strike capability** in that it could hit the Soviet Union first and greatly reduce the Soviet ability to retaliate. Any American temptation to relax was eliminated by the shock of *Sputnik:* in 1957 the USSR became the first country to put a satellite into orbit around the earth, indicating that the USSR had perfected very large rockets that could also be used as intercontinental ballistic missiles (ICBMs)—the delivery vehicles for nuclear and thermonuclear bombs. Behind in this technology, the United States feared a Soviet first-strike capability—that the Soviet Union would build so many ICBMs that they could attack and destroy the bombers on which the United States relied for its deterrent. This led to a new crash program of development and deployment of American land- and sea-based ICBMs (though the "missile gap" never actually materialized). American preponderance was maintained, although the Soviet Union was increasingly developing a capability to do much damage to the United States, in retaliation if not in a first strike. Partly to remedy this imbalance, in 1962 the Soviets put a variety of nuclear-armed missiles and bombers into Cuba, precipitating the Cuban missile crisis of October 1962. During the 10-day crisis, President Kennedy made it clear that the United States was prepared to launch a nuclear first strike against the forces in Cuba and perhaps against the Soviet Union if those forces were not removed. Because the United States had such overall nuclear predominance (as well as local nonnuclear superiority in the Caribbean, an area of vital importance to it), the Soviet leaders believed the American counterthreat and withdrew their missiles and aircraft. However, in reaction to this very public demonstration of their weakness, the Soviet leaders began a new program of strategic armament, revealed in a steadily rising level of Soviet military expenditure after 1965.

## The Period of Essential Equivalence: 1967 to the End of the Cold War

From 1966 until 1975 the United States was deeply involved in another long, painful, and costly land war in Asia, this time in Vietnam, during which American military expenditures climbed to new heights. By 1973, in reaction to the war, American military expenditures dropped below the pre-Vietnam level and remained there until 1977, then resumed a slow climb. Meanwhile, the Soviet Union maintained its military buildup in conventional as well as nuclear arms. By the 1970s it was spending about as much as the United States and thereafter was substantially on a par with the United States in strategic nuclear forces. Most observers characterize this period as one of essential equivalence when all elements of strategic weapons are taken into account. In 1963 the United States maintained a clear quantitative (and qualitative) superiority in all classes of strategic delivery vehicles: ICBMs (land-based missiles, like the Minuteman), SLBMs (missiles, like the Trident, launched from submarines), and

**TABLE 12.1** Chronological Overview of U.S. and Soviet Strategic Forces

|  | 1963 | 1972 | 1981 | 1990 | 1993 | Post–START I |
|---|---|---|---|---|---|---|
| **Total delivery vehicles** | | | | | | |
| U.S. | 1,278 | 2,167 | 1,976 | 1,930 | 1,524 | 1,193 |
| USSR/Russia* | 387 | 2,136 | 2,504 | 2,497 | 2,162 | 1,052 |
| **Total warheads & bombs** | | | | | | |
| U.S. | ? | 5,598 | 9,000 | 13,398 | 9,970 | 5,966 |
| USSR/Russia* | ? | 2,292 | 7,064 | 11,641 | 10,456 | 5,526 |

*For 1993, figures are for Russia, Belarus, Kazakhstan, and Ukraine.

*Sources:* 1963 data from Bruce Russett and Bruce Blair, eds., *Progress in Arms Control? Readings from Scientific American* (New York: Freeman, 1979), pp. 6, 7; 1972–1981 data adapted from Herbert Scoville, Jr., *MX: Prescription for Disaster* (Cambridge, Mass.: MIT Press, 1981), p. 67; 1990 and 1993 data from International Institute for Strategic Studies, *The Military Balance, 1990–91, 1993–94* (London: IISS, 1990, 1993), pp. 212–213, 235–236.

long-range bombers, like the B-52. By the 1970s, however, the Soviet Union had developed very large rockets and warheads and surpassed the United States in numbers of ICBMs; the United States retained advantages in bombers and deliverable warheads from SLBMs. Table 12.1 illustrates, in part, the changing strategic balance.

The result was a situation in which neither side could attack the other without suffering enormous damage from the opponent's retaliation. This gave both sides a **"mutual assured destruction"** capability, sometimes abbreviated as MAD. In other words, each side possessed a **second-strike capability:** the capacity to absorb an enemy attack and have enough weapons remaining to retaliate and inflict unacceptable damage on the opponent. Thus, no matter how the size of nuclear arsenals was measured, for all intents and purposes neither side could win a nuclear war. The logic of the strategic relationship was quite simple. A country with first-strike capability might be tempted to attack by the *belief* that the opponent could not retaliate (and therefore had no effective deterrent threat). In a situation where *both* sides had achieved second-strike capabilities and both were able to retaliate, the deterrent threats of each were believable, and neither was tempted to strike. The situation was thus "stable"—neither country had an incentive to launch an attack and start a war.

With the end of the cold war and the dissolution of the USSR, the strategic rivalry basically collapsed. Even with the substantial mutual reductions negotiated during the START (Strategic Arms Reduction Talks) process (to be discussed below in the section on arms control), the United States has once again assumed a position of strategic preponderance greater than the simple numbers might suggest.

# CONFLICT AND COOPERATION IN THE ARMS RACE

Returning to Figure 12.1, we can see patterns in the military spending of the United States and Russia. The continuing and parallel increase in military spending by both powers is what some people mean by the term "arms race," an image in which the two superpowers compete against each other and react to each other's exertions in an upward spiral. However, the term is not always apt in describing the long history of Soviet–U.S. superpower relations.

The theory of games describes a situation called the **prisoners' dilemma** that illustrates how people—including the leaders of states—can become trapped by self-defeating acts. It stresses the interdependence of each side's choices in the combination of conflict and cooperation found in many social situations. Game theory, if used carefully, can allow us to think in terms of the equivalence of roles: "How would my behavior look if I were in the other person's shoes?" It may at least avoid the perspective that simply says, "We can only be provoked; they must be deterred."

Conflict and cooperation situations can be seen as mixed-motive or non-zero-sum games. These are situations in which the combined value of the outcomes to each of two players totals something other than zero and *both* players may lose or gain. By contrast, in **zero-sum games** one person's gain equals the other's loss; added together, the net change is always zero. In this analysis, we must be able to assume that gains and losses can be measured in some common unit. In many situations that is a serious simplification; in others the simplification is less distorting.

In most of the games we play for sport, such as chess or tennis, winning or losing is not everything. Even when we lose the match, we presumably gain from the exercise and the pleasure of the competition. In international relations, too, it is a *fundamental mistake to think of most conflicts as zero-sum situations*. On the contrary, two countries often gain something by remaining at peace, and both usually incur serious losses by going to war. Peaceful coexistence is precisely such a situation. Each big power continues to compete and to gain or lose power at the expense of the other, but each also has an interest in keeping the competition from becoming militarily or economically destructive to both of them. We shall explore some conditions that may encourage or hinder cooperative behavior, starting with an imaginary example of criminal behavior and then applying it to situations of international politics.

In the basic story of the prisoners' dilemma, two people are arrested. Each is held incommunicado in a police station after an armed robbery and murder have been committed. Each person is presented with a pair of unattractive options, and each is questioned separately and given a choice by the police official: "I'm pretty sure that you two were responsible for the killing, but I don't have quite enough evidence to prove it. If you will confess first and testify against the other prisoner, I will see that you are set free without any penalty, and your accomplice will be sentenced to life imprisonment. On the other hand, I am making the same proposal to your buddy, and if it's accepted, you will be the one to spend life in prison, and the other prisoner will go free. If you both confess on the same day, we will have a little mercy, but you will be badly off, because you will both be sentenced to 20 years in prison for armed robbery. If you both want to be stubborn, we cannot convict you for a major crime, but

**TABLE 12.2**   Prisoners' Dilemma

| | | Red | |
| --- | --- | --- | --- |
| | | Cooperate | Defect |
| Blue | Cooperate | 3,3 (R,R) | 1,4 (S,T) |
| | Defect | 4,1 (T,S) | 2,2 (P,P) |

we can punish you for a small crime you committed in the past—one that carries a one-year prison term. If you want to take a chance that your fellow prisoner will keep quiet, go ahead. But if not—and you know what sort of criminal your pal is—you will do very badly. Think it over."

To analyze these problems, we shall illustrate the dilemma with a simple table (Table 12.2). All possible outcomes for the two players, Red and Blue, are represented. The first number represents the outcome for Red; the second, for Blue. A 4 is the best possible outcome; a 1, the worst. The letters represent the payoffs (again, the first for Red and the second for Blue). *R* is joint reward received; *P* is joint punishment received; *T* is the temptation to defect when the opponent cooperates; and *S* labels the opponent as a sucker (or, if you prefer, a saint).

What will the prisoners do in this situation? Since they cannot communicate with each other, each must make the best possible choice regardless of what the other does. In terms of rational self-interest, according to the theory of games, each should act to achieve the better of the two possible outcomes for each of the opponent's choices. Consider Red's options, for example: If Blue should confess (that is, defect from the partnership with Red), Red will get a 20-year term (a 2) by choosing to defect but life imprisonment (a 1) for keeping quiet (that is, if Red's choice is to cooperate with Blue). In this situation, Red is better off defecting. If, on the contrary, Blue should cooperate, Red receives a one-year sentence (a 3) by choosing to cooperate, but gets off free (a 4) by choosing to defect. Again, Red is better off defecting. In fact, *whatever* Blue does, Red does better by defecting and, by this logic, will confess. Blue—in the same situation—will also confess. Because of their cold-blooded rationality, both will receive 20-year sentences! Acting individually, both will end up much worse off than they might have had they been able to coordinate their strategies and depend on the other to cooperate. This is the prisoners' dilemma.

This style of analysis can be applied to many kinds of problems in international politics, especially arms races and crisis behavior.[1] To do so, however, we must move

---

[1] Good introductions are Avinash Dixit and Barry Nalebuff, *Thinking Strategically: The Competitive Edge in Business, Politics, and Everyday Life* (New York: Norton, 1991), and Steven J. Brams, *Superpower Games: Applying Game Theory to Superpower Conflict* (New Haven, Conn.: Yale University Press, 1985).

from a situation with easily measured outcomes (years of prison sentence) to one with outcomes that are much harder to measure. In war we may speak about billions of dollars of damage done or millions of people killed, but it is hard to combine dollars and people into a single sum. There are other values—such as justice, freedom, the maintenance of a culture or civilization—that dollars and casualties measure very imperfectly, if at all. But despite these difficulties, we generally, to varying degrees, prefer certain outcomes to others. For our purposes, we need only assume that we can say which outcomes are better; we do not have to assume that we can say how much better one is than another.

In applying this analysis to an arms race, the worst outcome usually occurs when the other side has a much stronger capability than one's own—especially a credible first-strike capability. To be at the mercy of such a force is the sucker (S) outcome; to have such an advantage is the temptation (T) outcome. To curtail an arms race and so be able to devote more resources to domestic needs is quite a good outcome, one of reward (R). In a highly competitive and ideologically charged situation, perhaps such a reward seems less desirable than being able to wipe out one's opponent, but it is clearly better than the joint punishment (P) of a mutual arms race carried on at substantial expense.

Thus the payoff situation is just the same as for the hapless prisoners who are asked to confess. Given the conditions laid down for the prisoners' dilemma (that the relative payoffs are as described, that there is no communication, and that this is a one-time, single-play situation), the rational choice for each player acting alone is to take the temptation to defect. That assures him or her of the better outcome, no matter what action the other takes. If the second player also defects, the first gets P, which is bad but still better than S; if the second does not defect, then our first gets T, which is even better than R. There is no effective incentive to cooperate; hence, both prisoners will defect and both will end up with quite a bad outcome (P), though not the very worst that might have happened to either if one cooperated while the other defected (S). Thus in the prisoners' dilemma the players defect whether their motives are aggressive or defensive: the results are the same.

## THE SECURITY DILEMMA (AGAIN)

Given the relative payoffs in a prisoners' dilemma, are two countries in an arms race condemned to the risk and waste of a never-ending, costly arms competition? In 1950 that seemed to be the case. President Truman's scientific advisers told him that they could build a powerful new thermonuclear weapon—the hydrogen bomb—hundreds of times more powerful than the atomic bomb. Some Americans would have liked best to be sole owner of the new bomb (T) but would have settled for a situation in which no country had it (R). But the Soviets had pretty much the same scientific knowledge that the Americans had, and neither power would consider allowing the other to have such a fearsome weapon unless it also had one. It seemed better to go ahead and build the hydrogen bomb if the Soviets were going to build it also (P). Even though building a hydrogen bomb would leave both countries exposed to its dangers, it seemed better than being at the mercy of the Soviets without a counterweapon ($S$). Lacking any prospect of an enforceable agreement that neither would build hydrogen bombs, each side felt forced to build a weapon that it wished did not exist.[2] This is the essence of the security dilemma: one may lose greatly by failing to trust the other, but one risks losing even more if the trust proves misplaced.

But this is not always the outcome. Unlike the prisoners, national governments sometimes find it possible to communicate and to commit themselves to cooperate. A formal agreement, perhaps a treaty, that includes a provision to verify whether the agreement is being kept provides the instrument for commitment. Moreover, unlike the act of defection in prison, which requires only a moment, it takes a long time to build and deploy enough modern weapons to be militarily decisive. With good inspection and verification techniques, a nation can detect betrayal before that betrayal becomes effective; thus, at worst, it ends up with a $P$ payoff rather than with an $S$. Inspection may be agreed on and jointly executed (with inspectors permitted to roam about each other's countries) or unilaterally executed by mutually tolerated means (observation satellites and perhaps spies). But only if each has reliable information about the other's activities and knows that the other has such information can two nations make and keep a commitment.

Not all arms-race situations fit the prisoners' dilemma model, though communication is critical to any effort to cooperate. The previous example assumed that strategic parity at a lower level of armament was a reasonably good solution for both countries, the second-best of four solutions and better than anything except superiority for oneself. But imagine instead that both sides decide that the alleged advantages of strategic superiority are overrated. (In the famous words of Henry Kissinger, "What in the name of God is strategic superiority? . . . What can you do with it?") When both sides have large and secure nuclear retaliatory forces (MAD), the side that happens to have more nuclear weapons than the other may not be able to derive much military or political advantage from its edge. While each might prefer to have more than the other, both might now be tired of the arms race and prefer substantial mutual disarmament, reducing expenditures and risks all around, to trying for that edge. At the same time, each would want to avoid disarming while the other armed. The distribution of payoffs then would look like that in Table 12.3. In that table we label the players US and SU for the United States and Soviet Union toward the end of the cold war; the labels emphasize the symmetries of the situation we are imagining (though, of course, neither the real world nor game theory situations are always symmetrical).

Unlike in the prisoners' dilemma, where the result of both sides "defecting" (confessing, or racing harder) was dominant or "obvious," even though not a good outcome, there is no dominant or obvious solution here. If each side believes that its adversary, like itself, really prefers disarmament best of all, then the two sides might be able to cooperate and reach that outcome jointly. But if they do not believe that, instead thinking that the adversary really prefers strategic superiority as the best outcome, then, as in prisoners' dilemma, they end up racing harder, with the outcome

---

[2] See Richard Rhodes, *Dark Sun: The Making of the Hydrogen Bomb* (New York: Simon and Schuster, 1995).

**TABLE 12.3**   Arms Race Fatigue

|  | | SU | |
| --- | --- | --- | --- |
|  | | Limit arms | Race harder |
| US | Limit arms | 4,4 (R,R) | 1,3 (S,T) |
|  | Race harder | 3,1 (T,S) | 2,2 (P,P) |

in the lower right-hand corner. In other words, even if their true preferences are for disarmament above all, if they think the other's true preferences are the same as in prisoners' dilemma, they probably will end up behaving as though they really are in a prisoners' dilemma and getting a bad outcome (though not the very worst).

Because this situation depends so much on what each side thinks or perceives about the other, it has been called a **perceptual dilemma.** It is easy to believe that the other side has more malign intentions than one's own. If we know that we would like to avoid an arms race but nevertheless find ourselves in one, then it is easy to assume that the other side must be to blame. If it is hard to see what the other side is actually doing, if we have little contact with people from the other side and thus little chance to judge their intentions at first hand, if they speak a language that few of us understand and have a culture and ideology different from ours, then we may readily attribute hostile intentions to them and create the image of the "enemy" (all these conditions will be eased if the other country is a democracy). If we have reasons to doubt their intentions, or are even mistrusting merely because of inadequate contact, then the safest line of action may be to continue defecting and race harder. While the great opportunity for mutual disarmament will be lost, the risk of being in a militarily inferior position will be avoided.[3]

In looking at the winding down of the arms race at the end of cold war, there is an implication that the players' *preferences* changed. They may have changed because of changes in technology (because it became impossible to achieve a meaningful superiority, or because high levels of arms on both sides associated with the effort to gain

---

[3] S. Plous, "Perceptual Illusions and Military Realities: The Nuclear Arms Race," *Journal of Conflict Resolution* 29, 3 (September 1985), 363–388, coined the term "perceptual dilemma" and gave some evidence that it accurately described the perceptions of Soviet and U.S. leaders. Trying to avoid the worst outcome is being "risk-averse"; "risk-acceptant" means trying for the best outcome even at the risk of getting the worst instead.

superiority became too threatening), or because each power decided that military superiority could not bring any politically useful results. In the real world people do change their preferences about what they want, what they may be capable of achieving, and what they are willing to try to achieve.

## PROMOTING COOPERATION

Confrontations between the same parties occur repeatedly in international politics. In such a series, each country's actions in any single round of the game have consequences for the payoffs not only in that round, but in later rounds as well. It is a logical next step, then, to consider what happens when a prisoners' dilemma occurs within what the participants think will be a string of relationships (called "iterated games"). Many experimental psychologists and other experts, including Anatol Rapoport and his colleagues, have examined situations like this under laboratory conditions. Their studies now include thousands of players, each making 50 to several hundred plays. There is a typical sequence that many players adopt.

At the beginning, participants often play cooperatively, with rewards to each partner. After a short while, however, one partner becomes tempted to defect. The victim will usually retaliate after being betrayed once or twice, so both take the punishment outcome. At this point each may try to reestablish cooperation, but without means for overt communication that is difficult to do. A would-be cooperator may well suffer the sucker's penalty. He or she may interpret this as betrayal and so return to defection.

In international politics, too, it may be very hard to change to cooperative behavior. The first initiatives may not be seen as cooperation at all, or if perceived as such they may be interpreted as weakness and thus be exploited. After a good deal of trial and error, however, many players do in fact succeed in cooperating consistently again, but it may be a long, painful time before this favorable pattern is established.

Under these conditions each play is eventually seen not as an end in itself but as a means of communicating one's hope of promoting joint cooperation in later plays. In this way the game resembles the ongoing politics among states, where cooperation breeds expectations of cooperation and defection breeds expectations of defection similar to Morton Deutsch's "crude law of social relations" discussed in Chapter 11. Ultimately, over many plays, it becomes possible to develop trust as the players become increasingly confident that each knows how the other will behave.

Similarly, a country may keep an agreement (such as an arms-control treaty) out of ethics and morality, or out of self-interest, even when in the short run it might seem in its interest to violate the agreement. International law is, of course, violated frequently, but in normal day-to-day procedures such as those concerning transportation, communication, respect for the persons of ambassadors, and travel between states, governments far more often observe the accepted conventions. Especially if their acts can be easily seen by others (here again, communication between states is crucial), nation-states pass up the immediate benefits of seizing a valuable cargo or person because they cannot afford the reprisals and disruption of future traffic that would surely follow. Thus, if the United States can make it in the Russians' interest to observe an agreement, it can trust them to serve that interest. An image of them as necessarily honest or moral is not required.

Other circumstances affect how often players, under experimental conditions, choose cooperative rather than competitive strategies. Of course, it is a long jump from the laboratory to the world of national leaders, but the findings about variations in experimental procedures are nonetheless intriguing. If we want to speculate on the future we will have to look at behavior under other conditions and try to draw analogies where appropriate.[4]

**1.** Competitive strategies are more common where there are no means of communication between the players. Many kinds of information need to be communicated: knowledge of activities, reasons for those activities, intentions, and preferences (that is, payoff structures) matter in varying degrees. Formal government-to-government communication facilities are a key element, and so are trade and various person-to-person contacts, such as tourism and cultural exchange.

**2.** When players do communicate, it is essential that the communication be honest. If one player uses the opportunity to deceive the other, the result is often a longer run of mutual defection and double-crossing than happens when no communication is permitted. For example, President Carter decided to impose economic sanctions on the Soviet Union after its invasion of Afghanistan partly because he was angry that Brezhnev had lied to him. Brezhnev had told Carter that Afghanistan leader Hafizullah Amin had "requested the assistance" of Soviet troops—troops who then supervised Amin's deposition and assassination.

**3.** Some of these principles are employed in a strategy developed by social psychologist Charles Osgood, who called it "Gradual and Reciprocated Initiatives in Tension-reduction," or **GRIT**. By this strategy, one side makes some limited conciliatory gestures unilaterally (such as not building some weapon, or even scrapping an existing one), communicates the fact to the other side, and then looks for a similar move by the other in return. If the other side seems to be taking advantage of one's apparent weakness by escalating, then one retaliates with a step carefully matched to the other side's escalation. One may later try other conciliatory gestures. With this strategy, actions may start off as unilateral, but they are limited and continue only if the other side responds favorably.[5] First Bush, and then Gorbachev, successfully initiated big arms cuts this way in the autumn of 1991.

**4.** It helps to have some experience in doing things together to gain some common reward. The "robbers' cave" experiment, performed by several psychologists in a boys' camp, supports this point. The leaders divided the boys into two groups and deliberately encouraged rivalry between them. After the two groups had become

---

[4] These and other relevant findings are regularly reported in several journals: *Behavioral Science, Journal of Conflict Resolution, Simulation and Games,* and *International Journal of Game Theory.*
[5] Charles Osgood, *An Alternative to War or Surrender* (Urbana: University of Illinois Press, 1962). A rigorous analysis of how repeated conciliatory moves ultimately produced reciprocal behavior is Joshua Goldstein and John Freeman, *Three-Way Street: Strategic Reciprocity in World Politics* (Chicago: University of Chicago Press, 1990).

quite hostile, the leaders sought means of reducing tension. They tried bringing the groups together for enjoyable events, but that did little good. Then they created situations in which the two groups had to cooperate in order to obtain something they both wanted. After reluctantly taking part in these activities, the boys eventually developed a new spirit and antagonisms eased. This experiment suggests that a major cooperative action by a hostile government has an importance that goes far beyond the immediate goal that the government may be trying to reach.[6]

**5.** Players are more likely to cooperate if the stakes in any one round are low and they expect to play many more times—if **"the shadow of the future"** is long. If they don't expect to play again many times, or if the stakes are so high that a single defection by the other player (for example, starting a big war) can destroy oneself, the temptation is to defect oneself as a precaution.

**6.** Players develop reputations. A player who usually defects may develop a reputation for defecting, and when other players meet that player, they are also likely to defect immediately. The player with the reputation for defecting will therefore get the punishment outcome most of the time. Any advantage he or she may get from finding an occasional sucker could be wiped out, overall, by all the punishment outcomes. But a player who develops a reputation for cooperating may get others to cooperate right away when they meet him or her again. If so, the sucker losses the player takes from meeting a few regular defectors may be more than compensated by the rewards from meeting other cooperators.

Robert Axelrod has done some of the most interesting work on how rational people can cooperate in repeated prisoners' dilemma situations. In one experiment he conducted a tournament among 13 social scientists to see whose computerized strategy for playing repeated prisoners' dilemma games would be most successful. Players who defected too often were eliminated. Of all the strategies played, Axelrod found that **tit for tat** (cooperating after the opponent cooperated, defecting after a defection) was most successful, especially when coupled with *optimism* (opening with a cooperative move) and being somewhat *forgiving* (punishing once, then trying again to cooperate). But in analyzing the results carefully, he found that being somewhat more forgiving would have been even more successful; that is, all the social scientists played more competitively than would have been best for their interests.[7] Both GRIT and tit for tat were reflected in the early 1970s, when the leaders of the two superpowers, Nixon and Brezhnev, tried to carry out a policy of *detente* (this French word means "relaxation" or "easing"). Evidence of this can be seen in Figure 12.2.

**7.** It makes a difference how the experimenter describes the purpose of the game to the players before they begin. The object may be presented as (1) each player doing his or her best, regardless of what happens to the other player, (2) each player doing better than the other, or (3) both players doing well. Not surprisingly, people cooperate least often when the experimenter emphasizes doing better than the other; the game description becomes a self-fulfilling prophecy. Similarly, it may matter very

---

[6] Muzafer Sherif et al., *Intergroup Conflict and Cooperation: The Robbers' Cave Experiment* (Norman: University of Oklahoma Press, 1961).

[7] Robert Axelrod, *The Evolution of Cooperation* (New York: Basic Books, 1984).

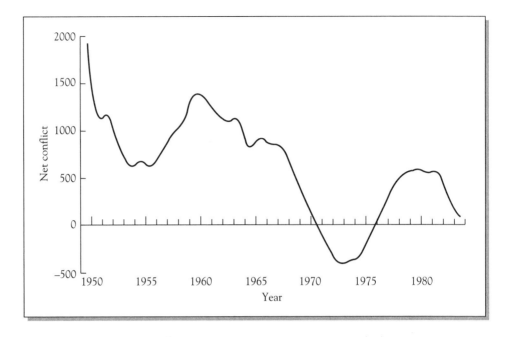

**FIGURE 12.2**  Tension and Detente in U.S.–USSR Relations, 1948–1986. [*Source:* Jan Nijman, *The Geopolitics of Power and Conflict* (London: Belhaven, 1993), p. 25.]

much what preconceptions people bring to the analysis of international politics. People can be taught to think about joint rewards and to care about others. Those who have been taught, informally or in school, to think of the world in stark realist terms, "red in tooth and claw," with the overriding goal being to maximize the national interest of one's own state over all others, will be less ready to cooperate when they choose policies. What should be non-zero-sum situations may be interpreted such that the player's only concern is to maximize his or her own well-being (and result in producing mutual misery).

Thinking back to the prisoners in the police station, imagine how different their situation would have been if one or both of them had held some principle of honor among thieves and possessed a prickly conscience that made it painful to betray the other. Suppose that both were in fact innocent—and moral, at that. Each might well prefer to accept a long prison term rather than unjustly condemn the other to an even longer term. The payoffs thus would not coincide merely with jail terms. In these circumstances (where the pangs of conscience associated with the temptation of defecting make *T* a very undesired outcome) the prisoners would actually get what would be for them the highest possible payoff: both would refuse to defect and thus would receive the very short jail sentence (*R*). In international politics it is often easy to dismiss the effect of morality, since not too many people are prepared to say "Better me than both of us dead" when considering deterrence of a country regarded as an enemy. But such considerations should not be ignored.

For example, even though the detente of the early 1970s itself didn't last, many of its elements (many of the exchanges, the Helsinki accords, some of the arms-control agreements) survived and provided the basis for the dramatic East–West changes of the 1980s. Both sides learned from past mistakes of both misguided trust and excessive suspicion. We must always remember that international politics requires both conflict and cooperation. This is a fundamental argument against excessively realist strategic thinking about cold war problems. The idealists of one side alone cannot make all conflicts go away; yet if we insist on seeing the world as a constant struggle, we indeed make it more so.

## THE CAUSES OF ARMS ACQUISITION

Why do countries arm, and how can an arms race be controlled? The prisoners' dilemma and an action–reaction arms race illustrate realist explanations of states' behavior. Those ideas represent an advance over the ideas prevalent in the early cold war years, when it seemed to many Americans that the action–reaction phenomenon was all one way; that is, that the United States was reacting to Soviet militarism and aggressive behavior. But when the period of isolation under Stalin drew to a close and Soviet and U.S. scientists began to make contact with each other, it became apparent that Soviet citizens typically held the mirror image of that perspective: they saw the Soviet Union as simply reacting to American threats. From this exchange, people developed a more general understanding that in some real sense each side was reacting to the other and that it was extraordinarily difficult to sort out particular causes, especially once the action–reaction process was well under way.

From the end of the Korean War, Soviet and U.S. arms levels were more or less constant for a long time, not showing a clear move upward until the 1960s. An arms race, of course, need not imply an upward spiral. A race does imply competition, but if two long-distance runners maintain a steady pace, the race is progressing just as much as if their speeds were continually increasing. It is the element of *competition*, or *interaction*, that characterizes a race. To some degree, that interaction seemed to be present in Soviet and U.S. behavior. It was not a steady dynamic but moved in fits and starts in response to particular acts that seemed especially provocative. The notion of a race surely does not explain every element of this behavior. It may tell us about the fact of interaction in arms spending but not the level at which that interaction takes place. Moreover, the idea of interaction does not explain what happened in the 1970s. Interaction suggests that the Soviet Union would have moderated its military spending once the Americans slowed down theirs after Vietnam. No such moderation took place; rather, quite the contrary. Something else was going on.

International hostility may help to start and maintain an arms race, but, as seen earlier, various kinds of domestic influences also help to maintain high levels of military spending. To understand further what drives this internal machine, we must move down to some lower levels of analysis typically neglected in realist explanations.

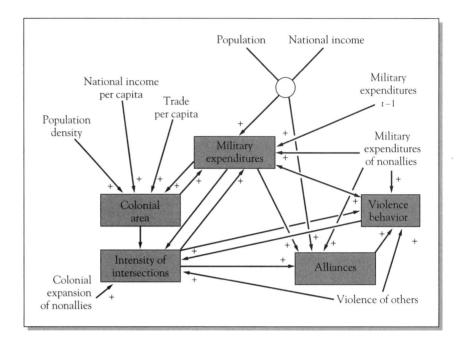

**FIGURE 12.3**　A Model of the Dynamics of International Violence. [*Source:* Nazli Choucri and Robert C. North, *Nations in Conflict: National Growth and International Violence* (New York: Freeman, 1975), p. 168.]

It will be helpful to look at a diagram (Figure 12.3) prepared by Nazli Choucri and Robert North to identify the causes of war; it provides an especially comprehensive framework for the causes of World War I.[8] The authors were not very concerned with explanations at the individual level of analysis. Rather, they were trying to identify the conditions at the governmental, societal, relational, and international-system levels that brought about the crisis. They were looking at the constraints that were imposed on decision makers and trying to understand the causes of those constraints.

The diagram is complex, but international politics is complex; there are few short-cuts to understanding. At one point or another we have discussed most of the influences identified in the diagram. Each of the arrows with a plus sign indicates a causal relationship, in which an increase in one factor or variable helps to produce an

[8] Nazli Choucri and Robert C. North, *Nations in Conflict: National Growth and International Violence* (New York: Freeman, 1975).

increase in the variable to which the arrow points. Changes in some variables, of course, are caused by two or more other variables. Although this diagram includes more variables than are discussed here—it includes the causes of war (what the analysts call "violence behavior"), not just military expenditures—it provides us with many useful points of discussion. It also leads to another question for consideration: Do arms races lead to war?

*Hypothesis 1:* Arms are purchased as a reaction to the arms acquisitions of adversaries.

The box labeled "military expenditures" has six arrows pointing to it. We can treat each arrow as representing a competing hypothesis, not necessarily mutually exclusive with other arrows or hypotheses. One on the right leads from "military expenditures of nonallies." Considering that the Soviet Union and the United States were certainly nonallies, we have a reference to the type of arms race that we have been discussing. Obviously the largest, most important, and most potentially threatening nonallies are the most relevant to military-spending decisions. Buying arms as a counter to what an adversary has acquired is the most common explanation of arms acquisition. The broad term "nonallies" reminds us that many arms races are not purely bilateral phenomena. As we noted, during most of the cold war both the Soviet Union and the United States were concerned also with the power and behavior of China.

*Hypothesis 2:* Arms races are caused by conflicts over spheres of influence.

Two other arrows to the military expenditures box come from the left-hand boxes labeled "colonial area" and "intensity of intersections." Together, these arrows suggest conflicts over international spheres of influence. Choucri and North use the term "intensity of intersections" to refer to what they call the "intensity of violence in specifically colonial conflicts between the actor state and other major powers." In the late twentieth century, there are few colonial territories as such; most areas of the world are composed of formally sovereign states. Yet most major powers clearly do have spheres of influence that include states over which they exert substantial control. The Western Hemisphere (excluding Cuba) is such a sphere for the United States. Most of Eastern Europe, with communist states that were often referred to as satellites of the Soviet Union, was until recently a major Soviet sphere of influence. But the two powers competed sharply with each other in these areas and, especially, in other areas of the world, using economic, political, and military means to further their goals in Africa, the Middle East, and Asia. States sometimes move from one power's sphere of influence to the other's in a process that may include a great deal of military violence. Or one power may repulse an effort to shift a state out of its sphere of influence, often using substantial military force.

The Vietnam War, as well as related conflict in Indochina, was the most vivid example of such a use of force, but there are many others. For example, the United States and the Soviet Union were deeply enmeshed in the Arab–Israeli conflict, sending arms to various and changing allies; in Indochina the Soviet Union helped the Vietnamese, while the United States supported anticommunist rebels in Afghanistan, Angola, Cambodia, Ethiopia, and Nicaragua. In sum, dominant powers—or would-be dominant powers—in the international system require large armed forces, whether to deal with spheres of influence or with the pressures of balance-of-power situations.

In each of three relationships involving military expenditures in Figure 12.3 (with colonial area, intensity of interactions, and violence behavior), two arrows run between the paired boxes, one in each direction. In each case two variables are interacting with each other in a positive way, creating feedback. Military expenditure creates the opportunity for colonial expansion, intense interactions, and violence; each of these in turn creates a need or demand for more arms. With a large, well-trained, well-equipped, and mobile military establishment comes a potential for force and perhaps a temptation to use it. Here, capabilities create an opportunity as well as increase the willingness to take advantage of the opportunity. It is true that local conflicts are made possible by, as well as stimulate, military expenditures.

*Hypothesis 3:* Arms acquisitions are caused by domestic influences.

Look now at the variable at the upper right corner of Figure 12.3, labeled "military expenditures$_{t-1}$." The mathematical expression is a way of referring to a previous time period. Thus the label indicates that the level of military expenditures at any given time depends in part on previous levels of military spending. Pressures to maintain and to increase military expenditures arise within a country in at least three different ways, each of which may be treated as a separate subhypothesis.

The first refers to *bureaucratic pressures* and inertia within the government. As we have seen earlier (in discussions of Allison's organizational process model in Chapter 10), the leader of any large organization must be assumed to be deeply concerned with the interests of his or her organization, especially in maintaining or increasing its budget. Moreover, the leader's own power in the government and in society at large depends heavily on the size of the organization. Just about the best predictor of the size of any organization's current budget is the size of its last budget. Military organizations are by no means exceptions to this observation.[9] Usually, when a major weapons system becomes outmoded or obsolete, the military organization will provide a ready interest group to press either to modernize the weapons or to replace them with something else that will do a similar job and keep the same people and resources employed. For example, as the B-52 bomber became more nearly obsolete, air force generals looked around for a new bomber, and the B-1 was developed to replace it. And because of the air force's organizational interests, air force evaluations of the merits of a proposed new strategic bomber were unlikely to be entirely objective and disinterested.

This argument does not imply that military leaders are corrupt or that their advice to maintain or acquire a weapons system is necessarily mistaken. Their evaluation of the national interest and that of most objective observers might well coincide. But it does imply that the allocation of resources within a government is strongly resistant to reduction or elimination. This year's military budget is a good predictor

---

[9] The most important early work on this topic was Otto Davis, M. A. H. Dempster, and Aaron Wildavsky, "A Theory of the Budgetary Process," *American Political Science Review* 60, 3 (September 1966), 529–547; see also Aaron Wildavsky, *The New Politics of the Budgetary Process* (Boston: Scott, Foresman, 1988). For an application to the Department of Defense, see Arnold Kanter, *Defense Politics: A Budgetary Perspective* (Chicago: University of Chicago Press, 1979).

(along with such external factors as intersections and opponents' spending) of next year's military budget.

The second, and related, subhypothesis, referring to a pressure that arises from the society and economy at large, is the *military-industrial complex.* Many elements of society—labor unions, defense contractors, politicians, and government bureaucrats— have a stake in maintaining and expanding a high level of military spending. This subhypothesis is found especially in radical writings. A balanced version recognizes that although the structure of their economies is different, similar pressures and interests characterize both the United States and the Soviet Union (now Russia). After the 1990 democratic revolution in Czechoslovakia, the government vowed to end all foreign arms sales. But when economic restructuring and nationalist passions hit Slovakia, the government had to keep Slovak tank production lines open by sales to Syria. Arms sales, for any size power, are also useful to help the balance of payments. American and European arms sales to Iran before 1979 and to the Arab states helped to pay the increased cost of oil imports from those same countries; China sells arms for their hard-currency earnings. Nearly all of the current—and still quite large—global trade in arms is pursued for economic reasons, not because of ideology or strategic interests.[10]

The third subhypothesis refers to the pressure of **technological momentum.** Military research and development employs half a million of the best-qualified scientists and engineers worldwide, and absorbs one-third to one-half of the world's human and material resources devoted to research and development. Individuals compete with one another, corporations and military services compete with their counterparts, and, of course, their countries compete. The process, however, takes a long time. Lead times of 10 years or more are typical from conceptualization through design, model production, improvement, repeated testing, evaluation, prototype production, training, and final deployment. Scientific inertia intertwines with bureaucratic inertia to make it very difficult to halt a promising project once it is under way, even when its initial purpose (as with the Reagan administration's SDI, or "Star Wars" defense system) becomes no longer relevant.[11]

These three influences help explain why the lines for military spending shown in Figure 12.1 generally maintained their previous level or rose. Usually a "ratchet effect" occurs from a war; after the level of military effort has been geared up to a high wartime level, bureaucratic and political–economic pressure keeps it from dropping to its prewar level. The new expenditure floor is usually well above the previous level.

---

[10] A still-useful book to read is Andrew J. Pierre, *The Global Politics of Arms Sales* (Princeton, N.J.: Princeton University Press, 1982). See also Michael Brzoska, "Current Trends in Arms Transfers," in S. Deger and R. West, eds., *Defense, Security and Development* (New York: St. Martin's, 1987), pp. 161–179, and Norman A. Graham, ed., *Seeking Security and Development: The Impact of Military Spending and Arms Transfers* (Boulder, Colo.: Lynne Rienner, 1994).

[11] Discussing the process by which MIRV (multiple, independent reentry vehicles) warhead and delivery technology was developed, Herbert York, who observed the process from inside, remarked, "Once the technology was developed MIRV assumed a momentum of its own; the chances of halting it were by then slim." Herbert York, "Multiple Warhead Missiles," *Scientific American* 28, 2 (1973), 16.

This phenomenon appeared in the United States after most of its major wars in the past 90 years (the Spanish–American War, World Wars I and II, and the Korean War—but not the Vietnam War).

*Hypothesis 4:* Arms acquisitions are caused, or at least facilitated, by an expanding economy.

The other arrow leading into the military expenditures box in Figure 12.3 originates in the interaction between "population" and "national income." This factor suggests various domestic societal-level influences; here it chiefly implies that economic and population growth provide the means for a military establishment to expand. A big country can support a big army. In a growing economy more resources can be devoted to military purposes without reducing anyone's share of the expanding pie. By the same token, a stagnating economy may force leaders either to squeeze civilian needs or to cut back their military expansion. Part of Gorbachev's interest in ending the cold war and in arms control stemmed from the snowballing collapse of the Soviet economy from the accumulated strain of decades of military buildup.[12] Indeed, economic troubles for both superpowers may well have been the most important force working to end the arms race.

Together, all the domestic influences seem so strong that some analysts have maintained that military establishments are essentially autistic actors that, like autistic children, shut themselves off almost completely from outside social stimuli and respond only to their own internal psyches. By this characterization, the arms race is not really a race at all, if by race we mean that the runners really care about each other's positions. The governmental and societal leaders in an autistic system maintain a level of military capability almost solely as a result of demands and pressures from within their own countries, not as a result of international incidents or military gains by the other "racer." By this explanation, states race against themselves; international events are irrelevant except as they provide an excuse for societal elites to demand sacrifices for military purposes. The enemy's actions thus become useful domestic propaganda to support policies that leaders desire on other grounds. Such an explanation certainly does not rule out some collusion between the leadership groups of two ostensibly competing countries, each acting aggressively to permit the other to justify its own buildup.

Many countries have military establishments that are ostensibly directed toward external enemies but in reality are chiefly directed toward internal ones as instruments of internal control and repression. This continues to be true in many developing countries.

## Which Influences Are Most Important?

It is one thing to list the various influences that may promote military spending or militarism and quite another to assess the truth of the assertions or their relative

---

[12] The Soviet economic collapse seems not to have been precipitated by pressures from the Reagan defense buildup but had begun earlier. See Fred Chernoff, "Ending the Cold War: The Soviet Retreat and the U.S. Military Buildup," *International Affairs*, 67, 1 (1991), 111–126.

importance. Most of the explanations seem plausible, and there is some evidence for each. Choucri and North report that for most of the major powers in the years before World War I, most of the contributing factors to military expenditures shown in Figure 12.3 were significant. But they see domestic factors as more powerful than international ones:

> The primary importance of domestic factors . . . does not preclude the reality of arms competition. Two countries whose military establishments are expanding largely for domestic reasons can, and indeed almost certainly will, become acutely aware of each other's spending. Thereafter, although spending may continue to be powerfully influenced by domestic factors, deliberate military competition may increase and even take the form of an arms race (although the race may be over specific military features and may be a very small portion of total military spending).[13]

Other research efforts concentrated on the Soviet–U.S. and NATO–Warsaw Pact arms increases. The results do not point unequivocally to the dominance of either domestic or international influences. Rather, it is clear that both matter under conditions that vary at different times and for different participants.

Many problems arise in trying to do a good arms-race analysis. The results are rarely conclusive, and the time to be analyzed is relatively short. The data available are highly aggregated; usually one must deal with total military spending rather than, say, spending for strategic arms, which might be the most relevant figure to an arms-race hypothesis. The quality of the data on Soviet military spending is very poor and subject to rather wide differences in interpretation. The lags in the budgetary process, which may extend over several years, add further difficulties. As a result, any analysis is bound to contain substantial error. Moreover, both the bureaucratic politics and arms-race explanations lead us to expect very similar behavior–namely, steady or gradually increasing expenditures by both sides. Given these problems, as well as the "substitutability" of foreign policy responses we examined in Chapter 6, it is very hard to separate different causes and to document those differences in a convincing way.[14] With the present state of our art and science, we can say only that both domestic and action–reaction influences operate and that these influences, from different levels of analysis, often reinforce each other.

Since the empirical results are not conclusive, and since each of the "independent" or causal influences is itself caused by other factors in the chain, it is hard to identify the most effective ways to reverse an arms race. Further attention to governmental and bureaucratic factors in the momentum behind arms spending is in order. For instance, it might be easier to restrain scientific research and development than to

---

[13] Choucri and North, *Nations in Conflict*, p. 218.

[14] The arms-race literature is reviewed in: Bruce Russett, "International Interactions and Processes: The internal vs. External Debate Revisited," in Ada Finifter, ed., *Political Science: The State of the Discipline* (Washington, D.C.: American Political Science Association, 1983); Randolph M. Siverson and Paul F. Diehl, "Arms Races, the Conflict Spiral and the Onset of War," and Michael D. Intriligator and Dagobert L. Brito, "Richardsonian Arms Race Models," both in Manus I. Midlarsky, ed., *Handbook of War Studies* (Boston: Unwin Hyman, 1989).

head off bureaucratic pressures to deploy newly developed systems. Some people, accepting one version of the autism argument, insist that only a drastic change in domestic economic, social, and political institutions can make a difference. For a long time both the United States and the Soviet Union behaved similarly despite their very different domestic systems. Obviously, shifts in popular or leadership preferences and in the perception of threat can help slow the arms race. That is just what happened when a new leader in the Soviet Union—Gorbachev—initiated massive changes in Soviet foreign policy and the domestic political system. To slow or reverse an arms race, several conclusions must be kept in mind: bureaucratic and domestic interests will have to be satisfied (and thus informal agreements may be easier to reach than formal treaties); there needs to be a major reduction of competition for spheres of influence; and agreements must be adequately verified. The purpose of verification is to see that the adversary cannot cheat in a way and to a degree that will significantly alter the military balance without running an unacceptable risk of having that cheating detected.

## WHAT'S WRONG WITH ARMS RACES, ANYWAY?

We seem to have skipped past a very simple question: Why should we care about arms races at all? Are they really so bad? After all, states are faced with a security dilemma in this anarchic world of each state against all. Perhaps the continuing, competitive acquisition of weapons may be the best way to find a measure of security; arms purchases might provide a necessary and otherwise unobtainable deterrent. As a Roman writer on military affairs in the fourth century put it, "If you would have peace, prepare for war." The case against large-scale arms acquisition rests on three arguments:

**1.** It is wasteful, imposing an enormous financial burden and squandering resources.
**2.** It ensures that if war ever does occur, it will be much more destructive than if such great accumulations of killing power had not been amassed. Conceivably, a thermonuclear war could mean the end of humanity.
**3.** It increases international tension and therefore increases the likelihood of a major war. Arms races are a cause of war.

### Waste

The amount of money the world spends on military purposes in one year alone now exceeds the value of the entire output of the world in 1900 (measured in constant dollars, that is, not counting the effects of inflation). In 1913, immediately before World War I, roughly 3 to 3.5 percent of total world output was devoted to the military; now the proportion is about 5 percent of the world output, measured as the GNP of all countries. Current world military expenditures equal the value of the GNP of all

South Asian and African countries combined, or total worldwide governmental expenditures on education or health. What this means in terms of world opportunities forgone—in misery, ignorance, starvation, and disease—cannot be measured precisely, but it can be imagined. As President Dwight Eisenhower said, "Every gun that is made, every warship launched, every rocket fired signifies, in the final sense, a theft from those who hunger and are not fed, those who are cold and are not clothed. This world in arms is not spending money alone. It is spending the sweat of its laborers, the genius of its scientists, the hopes of its children."

Many people have argued that military spending drains the economy of productive potential; by diverting funds and skilled labor to the dead end of the military establishment, investment and technological innovation in civilian sectors are lost. High-technology enterprises and top-flight scientists who might otherwise produce goods and services that could be sold abroad to compete with foreign industry never get to produce those goods.

It is easy to point to the much lower military expenditures of Germany and Japan (2.8 and 1.0 percent of GDP, respectively, in 1990–91) than of the United States (5.1 percent) and their substantially higher growth rates over a long period of time. Since World War II, the United States has carried a substantially higher military burden (military spending as a percentage of GNP) than any other industrialized capitalist country. Such a long-term absorption of high-technology resources for what are economically unproductive uses must have negative effects.

Many of these arguments seem plausible. Nevertheless, there are some sensible counterarguments: for example, that Japan and West Germany had special advantages in helping their economies to grow (for West Germany, postwar U.S. aid and the stimulus of the European Community; for Japan, some aid and, in the 1950s, special concessions for Japan to establish itself in export markets), or that military spending represents "only" a little over 5 percent of the American economy. For these and other reasons, systematic studies have failed to find any convincing and regular relationships between military spending and economic growth, either within particular countries or by comparing different ones. Because of the complexities, there is no guarantee that a cut in military spending would result in much more investment, in much more money spent on health and education, or in satisfying human needs. Any allocation of a post–cold war peace dividend will depend on economic conditions and especially on conscious political choice.

Sometimes military spending is justified as a way to create employment. The part of military spending that goes primarily for high-technology equipment (electronics, aircraft, and missiles), however, probably produces a net loss of jobs when it substitutes for civilian expenditures. High-technology goods are made by highly skilled and highly paid workers. The salaries are higher, but the number of jobs is smaller. Comparisons for this kind of spending have demonstrated that almost any other kind of spending, either private or public, would create more jobs. Table 12.4 shows, for example, estimates of the number of jobs created by spending for a guided missile or by spending the same sum on various alternative goods. But for other kinds of military spending (uniforms, for instance, or wages and salaries for military and civilian personnel at bases) more jobs may be created. Sweeping general statements should be

**TABLE 12.4** Employment Impact of Alternative Uses of $1 Billion of New Spending (Adapted to 1984 Dollars)

| Alternatives | Direct and Indirect Employment |
| --- | --- |
| Guided missile | 21,392 |
| Railroad equipment | 21,783 |
| Solar energy/energy conservation | 26,145 |
| Public utility construction | 26,459 |
| Housing | 27,583 |
| Mass transit equipment | 31,078 |

*Source:* Adapted from David Gold et al., *Misguided Expenditure, An Analysis of the Proposed MX Missile System* (New York: Council on Economic Priorities, 1981).

avoided, but positive and negative effects on particular industries, labor markets, and areas can easily be found.[15]

## *Destructive Potential*

The destructive potential of modern weapons needs little emphasis. Before World War II, military aircraft had a combat radius of only a few hundred miles and could carry only a ton or so of high-explosive bombs. Today, bombers and missiles are able to reach halfway around the globe, carrying payloads whose explosive power can be nearly 100 million times that of a pre-World War II bomber. Indeed, one Trident submarine can carry weapons equal in firepower to three times that used in all of World War II. Studies of possible full-scale nuclear exchanges between the United States and the Soviet Union during the cold war (using thousands of warheads on urban and industrial targets) indicated the devastating results to both societies. For example, estimates of U.S. deaths within 30 days of such an exchange ranged from one-third to two-thirds of the total American population. Such studies also demonstrated the vulnerability of modern, urban, and technologically based societies. Well over half the American population (as well as over 70 percent of its doctors) lives in its 71 largest urban areas. Certainly, the loss of essential medical facilities would make things even

---

[15] Balanced reports on the effect of military spending are Steve Chan, "Grasping the Peace Dividend: Some Propositions on the Conversion of Swords into Plowshares," *Mershon International Studies Review*, 39, 1 (April 1995), 53–95, and Alex Mintz, *The Political Economy of Military Spending in the United States* (London: Routledge, 1992).

worse; if all major cities were hit, there would not be much "outside" from which help could come. Gas pipelines, oil pipelines, and electricity grids would be fragmented. Without fuel, the entire transportation system would be crippled. Railroad lines would be chopped up. Water supply and sewage facilities would break down everywhere, creating epidemics and further straining the already impossibly overburdened medical facilities. If food were still available in agricultural areas, it could not be processed and shipped, since those facilities are generally in metropolitan areas. No possible level of preparation or civil defense could significantly ease this disaster.

We have not even mentioned long-term ecological results, such as depletion of the ozone layer, the selective destruction of some plants and animals and survival of the hardier forms, cancer from radioactive fallout, etc., etc., etc. Worse yet, a major scientific report in 1983 raised the possibility of **"nuclear winter"** and global climatic catastrophe. Dust and especially soot from fires following nuclear explosions might bring on a period of darkness—much too dark to see, even at midday, for a week—and a temperature drop of 20 degrees Celsius (36 degrees Fahrenheit) in the Northern Hemisphere; the temperature, even in summer, would remain below freezing for three months. An entire growing season for crops might be lost.[16]

## Likelihood of War

If we could be sure that these destructive capabilities would never be used, that the "balance of terror" would be reliably stable, the situation might be tolerable. But there can be no such absolute assurance. Technological change and the spread of nuclear weapons to other countries, along with accidental or unauthorized firings of nuclear weapons by an insubordinate military commander or a terrorist group, could easily make war more likely. Increasing the number of weapons also immensely complicates the problems of command and control. These problems will be more severe as poor countries, unable to spend billions of dollars on good command and control systems, acquire such weapons. Nuclear war can still happen.

Research on the question of whether arms races lead to war has, until recently, been inconclusive. Some people have argued that there is no evidence that arms races typically result in war. On the other hand, Choucri and North concluded that military expenditures played a significant role in promoting international violence in the period before 1914.

More generally, a study of great powers since 1815 found that the vast majority of disputes arising during accelerating arms races did, in fact, end in war, whereas only a small number of serious diplomatic disputes not combined with arms races ended in war. This evidence is basically correlational—that is, it shows that arms races tend to be followed by war—and not persuasively causal. Therefore, it is possible to argue

---

[16] See Arthur M. Katz, *Life After Nuclear War* (Cambridge, Mass.: Ballinger, 1982); Carl Sagan, "Nuclear War and Climatic Catastrophe: Some Policy Implications," *Foreign Affairs* 62 (Winter 1983/84), 256–292; and Stanley Thompson and Stephen Schneider, "Nuclear Winter Reappraised," *Foreign Affairs* 64 (Summer 1986), 981–1005.

that states engaged in arms races were experiencing such conflict and tension that they would have gone to war anyway, whether or not they were engaged in an arms race. By this argument, the pre-1914 arms race was a symptom, not a cause, of the conflict that ended in war. Also, the results depend somewhat on how an arms race is defined: how much interaction, whether one party is far ahead of the other, whether the gap is closing.[17]

We do know enough to say that engaging in an arms race is certainly not a very reliable way of preventing a war. The fears that must inevitably arise during an arms race, fears that the other side will obtain some decisive advantage, must increase tensions that may, especially in periods of crisis, result in the outbreak of violent conflict. Indeed, the problem of instability in crisis, when tensions may cause fear, threats, and violence to spiral rapidly, lies at the heart of many analysts' concern about contemporary deterrence. To understand and evaluate this argument, we must now turn to an extended discussion of deterrence theory.

---

[17] The general study is Michael Wallace, "Arms Races and Escalation: Some New Evidence," *Journal of Conflict Resolution* 23, 1 (March 1979), 3–16. This analysis has been subjected to several critiques that qualify without fully refuting its conclusions. See Paul Diehl, "Arms Races and Escalation: A Closer Look," *Journal of Peace Research* 30, 3 (1983), 205–212.

# 13

## DETERRENCE AND ARMS CONTROL

## CONTEMPORARY ARMS AND STABLE DETERRENCE

The cold war is over. With the dissolution of both the Warsaw Pact and the Soviet Union in 1991, and with Russia entering the Partnership for Peace with NATO in 1994, the cold war ended *without* escalating into a hot, nuclear war. How was this achieved? If one of the costs of arms races was the steady increase in destructive potential, how was this reversed?

In Soviet–U.S. experience, the stability of deterrence in crisis (that is, no sudden escalation to nuclear war) and the relative stability of the arms race (that is, few very sharp increases in spending) had both depended on the fact that neither side possessed a first-strike capability. Because of existing technology, *neither* side's nuclear retaliatory forces became highly vulnerable. If *one* side had been vulnerable, the situation would have been quite different. It also would have been different if *both* sides' forces had been vulnerable; that is, if striking first would have made a significant difference in the outcome of a war. Knowledge of that vulnerability could have been highly dangerous in a crisis and fueled the arms race.

The difference between first- and second-strike capability is crucial to understanding the arms race and deterrence theory. A first-strike capability means that one can attack and destroy the other's retaliatory (second-strike) capability and suffer only minimal damage. It can thus become very tempting to make the attack. Under conditions of stable deterrence, each side has only a second-strike (retaliatory) capability, not a first-strike force. Each has an assured capability to inflict enormous destruction on an attacker; thus neither is tempted to attack the other. To protect their second-strike capabilities, both sides spent many billions of dollars on the research, development, and procurement of advanced weapons. The arms strategies they followed included:

**1.** Producing *large numbers* of delivery vehicles so that an attacker would not be able to destroy all of them.

**2.** *Dispersing* delivery vehicles widely, again to multiply the number of targets an attacker would have to hit, making it impossible for one attacking warhead to wipe out more than one delivery vehicle. For that reason bombers were widely dispersed among many airfields, and ICBM silos were separated.

**3.** *Hardening* the launching sites of delivery vehicles. For example, American missile silos were built to be enclosed in enough steel and concrete to withstand the blast of a near miss. Yet continued technological developments improved missile accuracy, making direct hits possible.

**4.** Making the delivery vehicles *mobile,* since a moving target is hard to track and hit; submarines for launching missiles take advantage of this feature.

**5.** *Concealment* of missile launching sites. Again, submarines, operating hundreds of feet below the surface of the ocean, are well concealed, making the submarines for launching SLBMs the most dependable and secure strategic second-strike force.

**6.** The *active defense* of retaliatory forces, including systems which would intercept bombers and (it was also hoped) missiles.

**7.** A *"launch under attack"* policy. This meant that land-based ICBMs that were vulnerable to a first strike would be launched before they could be struck by incoming missiles. This would have been a desirable policy only if we could be confident of avoiding false alarms (and it might not have been desirable even then).[1]

All these ways to protect nuclear retaliatory forces required intensive and costly efforts to provide secure means of command, control, communication, and intelli-

---

[1] See John Steinbruner, "Launch Under Attack," in Bruce Russett and Fred Chernoff, eds., *Arms Control and the Arms Race: Readings from Scientific American* (New York: Freeman, 1985).

gence—known in government as C³I—from headquarters to the numerous, dispersed, mobile, and well-concealed launching sites. Civilian leaders—in the United States, the president—must be confident that they have secure command and control facilities from which to deal with the military chiefs and that the military people operate only on orders from the civilian commander in chief.

Neither side depended solely on one type of weapons system in its strategic forces. Each side possessed land-based intercontinental missiles, large numbers of bombers capable of attacking the other's home territory (intercontinental bombers and, in the case of the United States, bombers stationed in Europe or on aircraft carriers), and, most important, many SLBMs on submarines. Together, aircraft, land-based missiles, and submarine-based missiles formed a **triad** of different kinds of weapons, each having different capabilities and each protected in different ways. This formed the core of the strategic planning of both sides. Even though one or even two parts of the triad might become vulnerable through technological change, the other element(s) would still be secure. Without major breakthroughs in antisubmarine warfare, the SLBMs were depended upon for retaliation. With them, neither side could have had a complete first-strike capability, and deterrence remained stable.

## DETERRENCE AND CRISIS INSTABILITY

We must now step back from the details of military hardware to consider the theory of deterrence and how it may work in a crisis. The "normal" situation of deterrence is the "balance of terror," using the prisoners' dilemma as a model. The true prisoners' dilemma is probably not a common situation in international politics. Under some circumstances, however, there are grave risks that a previously safe, non-zero-sum situation may turn into a dangerous form of the prisoners' dilemma. Mutual nuclear deterrence always carries this risk to some degree.

Table 13.1 represents the relative values that two nuclear-armed antagonists might have attached to the use of nuclear weapons in a typical noncrisis situation. For

**TABLE 13.1** Noncrisis Decisions About the Use of Nuclear Weapons

|  |  | Alpha | |
|---|---|---|---|
|  |  | Wait | Attack |
| Beta | Wait | 4,4 (R,R) | 1,3 (S,T) |
|  | Attack | 3,1 (T,S) | 2,2 (P,P) |

both participants, the best outcome was that both would wait—that peace would be preserved. Even under the best of conditions, war would have left both parties much worse off than at present. Given the capabilities of each side to retaliate, the first strike was a very unattractive course of action.

Remember that in the prisoners' dilemma one side is better off defecting (in this case, attacking) whether the other side defects or cooperates. In this example, however, although each side is better off attacking if the other intends to attack, each is also clearly better off waiting if the other also waits. Since the payoff for peace (R) greatly exceeds the temptation to hit first (T), this is *not* a case of prisoners' dilemma. Neither side will attack, and peace will be preserved. This is essentially what a situation of stable deterrence looks like. It was also the condition of the world from the mid-1960s until the end of the cold war.

But a policy of restraint was acceptable only so long as neither side had a first-strike capability and so long as each was confident that the other also saw a first strike as poor policy. Stability could have been shaken by several possible developments. A great technological breakthrough for one side, such as an extremely effective ABM (antiballistic missile) and air defense system and very accurate MIRVs, would have raised the gains from a first strike (T); that is, it would have reduced the damage expected from the opponent's retaliation. Even the perception—correct or mistaken— that the adversary was about to achieve such a breakthrough might suddenly have changed the estimates of the country receiving such information. If the adversary seemed about to gain the ability to attack you, a preemptive attack might have seemed the rational thing to do.

Most kinds of technological change by themselves were unlikely to shake deterrence stability so long as both superpowers maintained heavy research and development programs and possessed the triad of weapons. A more plausible set of events that could upset the deterrent balance can be imagined in a crisis—perhaps one something like the Cuban missile crisis of 1962. This would happen if one power violated a principle laid down by Henry Kissinger:

> If crisis management requires cold and even brutal measures to show determination, it also imposes the need to show opponents a way out. Grandstanding is good for the ego but bad for foreign policy. Many wars have started because no line of retreat was left open. Superpowers have a special obligation not to humiliate each other.[2]

As it happened, in 1962 President Kennedy was careful to give Khrushchev an opportunity to withdraw the Soviet missiles with some dignity. Kennedy termed the outcome a victory for peace, not a victory for the United States. But suppose he had dramatized the situation as an American victory and a great loss of prestige for the Soviets, claiming that it proved they were unable to deter any serious American pressure against the communist world. Then suppose Kennedy had followed up with

---

[2] Henry Kissinger, *Years of Upheaval* (Boston: Little, Brown, 1982).

**TABLE 13.2**  Possible (Hypothetical) Crisis Options for the Soviet Union

|  |  | SU | |
|---|---|---|---|
|  |  | Wait | Attack |
| US | Wait | 3 *(R)* | 4 *(T)* |
|  | Attack | 1 *(S)* | 2 *(P)* |

efforts to overthrow the Castro government. In these circumstances, the value of peace (*R*) to the Soviets—and especially to the humiliated Khrushchev, who would have faced immediate ouster—would have dropped sharply. At the same time, Khrushchev might have interpreted Kennedy's actions as indicating that the Americans had much greater confidence in their first-strike capability than he had previously thought. That might have led the Soviets to raise substantially their estimates of the damage the Americans could inflict (*S*) and of the likelihood of a U.S. attack. Thus, even though a Soviet first strike would still have resulted in a bad outcome for them (*T unchanged*), using even a moderate first-strike capability might have looked better to the Soviet Union than continuing to live in humiliation with the Americans. Whether the United States attacked or waited, the situation for the Soviets would have *become* a case of the prisoners' dilemma, and attacking the United States would have been the better of each pair of generally bad outcomes for the Soviet Union (Table 13.2).

Alternatively, suppose that President Kennedy, who in our scenario acted rashly and claimed a victory over the Soviets, then thought the matter over more calmly and realized the risks he was running. He then might have decided that he had prompted the Soviets to make a preemptive attack and felt required to preempt the preemption! In the course of a crisis, previously stable conditions can be suddenly upset.[3]

Many international crises do not resemble the prisoners' dilemma so much as they do the adolescent game of **chicken,** played in the 1950s. Two boys would line up their cars facing each other on a deserted stretch of road. Each car would have its left wheels on the center line, and they would drive toward each other at high speed. Friends of either sex might be riding in the cars; others would stand on the sidelines,

---

[3] This view of anticipation ("He will do this because of what he thinks I will do because of what I think he will do"), as well as many related points about strategic decision making, was developed by Thomas C. Schelling, *The Strategy of Conflict* (Cambridge, Mass.: Harvard University Press, 1960).

**TABLE 13.3**  Diplomatic Crisis as a Game of Chicken (A Cuban Crisis Scenario)

|  |  | SU | |
|---|---|---|---|
|  |  | Give In | Stand Firm |
| US | Give In | 3,3 *(R,R)* | 2,4 *(S,T)* |
|  | Stand Firm | 4,2 *(T,S)* | 1,1 *(P,P)* |

cheering on the contestants. If neither car swerved, they would collide, and the occupants would be badly injured or killed. That was, of course, the worst outcome. But the next worst was to be the driver who swerved first, the humiliated "chicken." An acceptable, if not especially satisfying, outcome was to swerve at exactly the same moment as the adversary. And the best outcome was for the *other* driver to be "chicken," thus allowing the first driver to receive cheers and perhaps other rewards from the adoring crowd. Various strategies were possible. For example, one player might show he had lost control by taking his hands off the steering wheel and jumping into the right-hand seat and therefore could not swerve. The usual result was that one driver would be chicken; less often, both players would pull away simultaneously. No one really intended to kill and be killed. But occasionally there was the sobering result (and a little sobering was in order) when both players miscalculated and neither swerved in time.

Some international crises are "games" of bargaining and brinkmanship, contests of nerve to make the other side give in. Plausibly the Cuban missile crisis was such an instance, in that nuclear war would be the worst result for both countries: there would be no meaningful winner and both would be left worse off than if one had capitulated. The goal was to make the adversary swerve or, if absolutely necessary, be able to swerve oneself at just the last minute before someone (possibly an unauthorized lower-level commander) began using nuclear weapons deliberately or by accident. In such a situation, the game table looked like Table 13.3.

In the Cuban missile crisis it was the Soviet leader, Khrushchev, who swerved. Maybe he swerved because he was less courageous, or less foolhardy; perhaps Soviet military forces were so much weaker than those of the United States that the Soviets' punishment (*P*) would be even worse than the Americans'. (In the chicken analogy, Khrushchev would have been killed while Kennedy would only have suffered broken bones.) Whatever the reason, he did swerve; but Soviet leaders swore they would build up their forces so that the United States could never threaten them that way again. Chicken is a dangerous game. In nuclear diplomacy, it assumes that both sides will be able to control their forces well enough that war will not occur accidentally and that at least one party will be fearful (or sensible) enough to swerve in time. A player once humiliated may be unwilling to swerve in a subsequent crisis.

The scenarios just sketched may seem improbable, but in fact they are not. Kennedy said at the time of the Cuban missile crisis that he thought the chances of nuclear war were about one in three. Perhaps he was mistaken, but such a belief can become a self-fulfilling prophecy. Thinking that war is near can bring it near through pressures for preemption, just as thinking war is near can also bring greater efforts to avoid disaster. The problem of crisis stability is especially serious because human leaders are fallible, and they can easily misunderstand each other's intentions, especially under the enormous pressures of a nuclear crisis.

World War I was a war that most of the leaders of Europe did not want—at least they did not want it then, and they did not want it so big and costly. But World War I happened anyway, in large part because of the rigidities inherent in making and executing decisions in a crisis and because no leader was motivated strongly enough to make a concession. Inflexible military plans were especially responsible. In 1914 Germany had only one really reliable ally (Austria–Hungary) and was flanked by two powerful enemies (France and Russia). The German military high command decided that the only way they had a chance to win a war was to mobilize their forces as soon as war seemed likely, so that they could hold the frontier against Russia in the east while quickly defeating France in the west. The French and Russians understood Germany's situation and therefore had plans to mobilize their own forces immediately. Any country that did not mobilize (shipping troops and equipment up to the borders in rapid, tightly integrated railroad movements) when its adversary did would be unable to defend its borders. Once mobilization was begun, it could not be stopped without leaving the army in chaos. Nor were there any plans for partial mobilization; for example, Russia moving against Austria–Hungary but not against Germany. The German mobilization plans were especially audacious. They called for German forces to cross the border into neutral Belgium to seize favorable positions there in a move guaranteed to bring France and perhaps Britain into war against Germany. The result was that as soon as any country mobilized its forces, all the others would do the same. Russia mobilized to put pressure on Austria–Hungary and Germany. The czar intended his move to deter Austria-Hungary by threat, but in fact he triggered German mobilization and thus war.[4] Similar fears and rigidities could bring war between nuclear powers if leaders put their missile forces on alert to coerce the adversary or to be able to launch on warning of attack if necessary.

Some of the assumptions about decision making that were implicit in our abstract discussion of deterrence in crisis do not necessarily hold in life.

---

[4] For a lively controversy, see Marc Trachtenberg, "The Meaning of Mobilization in 1914," and Jack Levy, "Preferences, Constraints, and Choices in July 1914," *International Security* 15, 3 (Winter 1990–91), 120–86, continued in *International Security* 16, 1 (Summer 1991), 189–203.

**1.** *The assumption of a single event.* In a real crisis, of course, decision makers must consider not just what is happening now but what has happened in the past and, especially, what may happen in the future. How will my opponent, my allies, and third-party observers interpret my behavior if I act reasonably? The specter of Prime Minister Chamberlain's effort to appease Hitler at Munich in 1938 still haunts contemporary leaders. We noted this consideration in our discussion about repeated plays of the prisoners' dilemma and in Chapter 7, where we discussed a state's bargaining reputation.

**2.** *The assumption of symmetry in values.* To simplify matters, we have usually assumed that both parties had the same valuation of the various outcomes. This is, of course, not necessarily true (as we noted when discussing prospect theory). A power favoring the status quo will value peace more than will leaders who feel their country has been deprived of status.

**3.** *The assumption of unitary actors.* We must shift levels of analysis. In a real crisis many decision makers will be involved on each side, giving advice and, in the case of military chiefs, having some direct control over the outcome. Each will be concerned with his or her own personal and organizational interests, as well as his or her perception of the national interest. Elements of group decision making and groupthink determine how those various interests will be used to form one final decision. Even the chief of state is not immune from such considerations. A political leader must worry about being returned to office in the next election. The temptation to take short-term gains or to avoid short-term losses, even at the risk of greater long-term costs to the country at large, may be very strong, especially if the public does not understand the probability of long-term losses. In the Cuban missile crisis, President Kennedy felt that any display of weakness was likely to damage his party badly in the congressional elections only a month away.[5] If, however, he had sensed a great popular fear of war, Kennedy might have grasped at "peace in our time," even at the risk of later war. In any case, different decision makers will have different values for the various outcomes and different attitudes toward risk taking. It matters who is making the decisions (Neville Chamberlain or Margaret Thatcher, Adolf Hitler or Helmut Kohl). An understanding of organizational politics, domestic politics, and psychology is helpful here.

**4.** *The assumption of only two choices.* In a real crisis, a decision maker does not choose only between the two options, attack and no attack. There are several options, if he or she looks carefully, ranging from cooperation to competition. No one can hope to consider all possible alternatives. Even in the best of circumstances a leader must choose within a limited time span and within the limits of human frailty. The quality and scope of a search for options and the definition of the problem differ for different decision makers and for different organizational constraints. (Some determinants of search and problem definition were discussed in Chapter 10.) The options are not picked out of the air at random, but rather reflect the decision maker's search proce-

---

[5] Graham Allison, *Essence of Decision: Explaining the Cuban Missile Crisis* (Boston: Little, Brown, 1971), p. 194.

dures. For instance, in the early stages of the Cuban missile crisis, Kennedy's advisers quickly converged on a choice of two options: an air attack on the Soviet missile emplacements or a landing in Cuba by U.S. troops. Kennedy disliked both choices and insisted that his advisers come up with something else—that "something else" was the blockade.

**5.** *The focus on threats, especially military threats.* Naturally, military leaders will be involved in military decisions. Both they and political decision makers may overemphasize the role of military instruments in solving the problem (a common criticism of a realist view of international politics). Threats of heavy punishments, or punishments carried out, may arouse great fear and stress in decision makers and interfere with their ability to assess probabilities and their own and others' values. By evoking irrational behavior, threats may be counterproductive.[6]

**6.** *The assumption of nonstressful perception and behavior.* The preceding points remind us how hard it is to understand and assess other people's motives and behavior. It is especially hard in cross-cultural assessments, as when capitalist Americans have to try to think like communist Chinese. It becomes even harder in times of crisis. In Chapter 11 we saw how behavior under stress is different from behavior under normal conditions. The rational person in the prisoners' dilemma has a difficult time at best. We nevertheless assume that such a person can clearly perceive the available options, calmly consider the probable actions of an opponent, and carefully weigh the values attached to possible outcomes. Yet great stress is likely to bring procrastination, shifting of responsibility to others, and an exaggeration of possible favorable consequences and a minimization of unfavorable ones. Highly stressed decision makers may react fatalistically and become more prone to anger and despair. In the World War I crisis of 1914, for instance, some tired, tense, and overworked leaders simply stopped searching for further ways to escape an unwanted war.

**7.** *The assumption of control.* It is may not be easy to control the use of nuclear weapons in a crisis, especially with thousands of weapons in planes, on the ground, and at sea. If a state were to be attacked by SLBMs and ICBMs, the decision time between confirmation of an attack and the point at which vulnerable ICBMs could be launched to retaliate would be less than 10 minutes. Perhaps there would be no time at all. It is possible that a government could be "decapitated"; that is, the executive and the other top leadership could be killed by a strike on the capital of the country. During the cold war the U.S. and Soviet governments spent tens of billions of dollars trying (but not succeeding) to solve the problems of $C^3I$ and to provide reliable control. Many national security analysts regard this as the most important focus for arms control.

With the end of the cold war, problems of nuclear crisis stability have seemed less urgent. Severe crisis is less likely as conflicts over spheres of influence abate, with good political relations defusing much of the danger posed by strategic technology.

---

[6] On some of the difficulties with deterrence theory, see Richard Ned Lebow and Janice Gross Stein, "Beyond Deterrence," *Journal of Social Issues* 43, 3 (1987), 5–71, and other contributions to that special issue of the *Journal.*

Nevertheless, future nuclear crises are imaginable; for example, in the volatile Middle East or among some combination of China, India, and Pakistan. Nuclear proliferation poses the risk that a future nuclear crisis would be multilateral—and thus much harder to control than the bilateral crises of the past. The problem of crisis escalation remains a matter of concern.

## Arms-Control Efforts Since World War II

In May of 1994 the United States and Russia officially announced that they had stopped targeting each other's territory with missiles. While perhaps considered unremarkable in the post–cold war atmosphere, such an event was the result of a long process of arms control, both between the two superpowers and in multilateral agreements over various forms of weapons of mass destruction. The major arms-control agreements since 1959 are listed in Table 13.4. The final column indicates whether they were bilateral U.S.–Soviet (or Russian) agreements or multilateral agreements. First, however, look at Figure 13.1 for a picture of U.S.–Soviet treaty activity from 1946 to 1988.

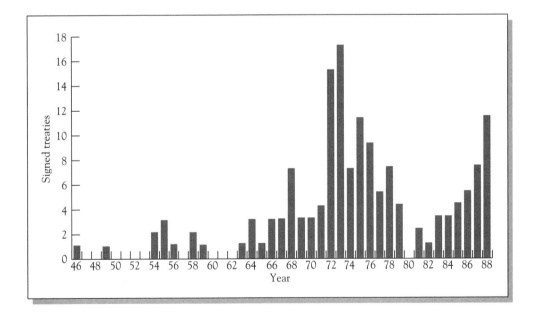

**Figure 13.1**   Bilateral U.S.–Soviet treaties and agreements established per year, 1946–1988. [*Source:* Jan Nijman, *The Geopolitics of Power and Conflict* (London: Belhaven, 1993), p. 26.]

**Table 13.4**  Major Arms-Control Agreements Since 1959

| Year Signed | Agreement | Provisions | Multilateral (M) or Bilateral U.S.–Soviet (B) |
|---|---|---|---|
| 1959 | Antarctic treaty | Prohibits all military activity in Antarctic area. | M |
| 1963 | Partial nuclear test–ban treaty | Prohibits nuclear explosions in the atmosphere, in outer space, and under water. | M |
| 1963 | "Hot-line" agreement | Establishes direct teletype communications between the United States and the Soviet Union for use in emergency. Updated in 1971 and 1974. | B |
| 1967 | Outer space treaty | Prohibits all military activity in outer space, including the moon and other celestial bodies. | M |
| 1967 | Treaty of Tlatelolco | Prohibits nuclear weapons in Latin America. | M |
| 1968 | Nonproliferation treaty | Prohibits acquisition of nuclear weapons by nonnuclear nations. Renewed indefinitely in 1995. | M |
| 1971 | Seabed treaty | Prohibits emplacement of nuclear weapons and other weapons of mass destruction on ocean floor or subsoil thereof. | M |
| 1971 | Nuclear accidents agreement | Institutes various measures to reduce risk of accidental nuclear war between the United States and the Soviet Union. | B |
| 1972 | High seas agreement | Provides for measures to help prevent dangerous incidents on or over the high seas involving ships and aircraft of both parties. | B |
| 1972 | SALT I ABM treaty | Limits deployment of antiballistic missile systems to two sites in each country. Reduced to one site by 1974 agreement. | B |

**TABLE 13.4**　Major Arms-Control Agreements Since 1959 *(continued)*

| Year Signed | Agreement | Provisions | Multilateral (M) or Bilateral U.S.–Soviet (B) |
|---|---|---|---|
| 1972 | SALT I interim offensive arms agreement | Provides for five-year freeze on aggregate number of fixed, land-based ICBMs and also SLBMs on each side. Later extended to 1980. | B |
| 1972 | Biological weapons convention | Prohibits development, production, and stockpiling of bacteriological and toxic weapons and requires destruction of existing biological weapons. | M |
| 1973 | Nuclear war prevention agreement | Institutes various measures to help avert outbreak of nuclear war in crisis situations. | B |
| 1974 | Threshold nuclear test–ban treaty | Prohibits underground tests of nuclear weapons with explosive yields greater than 150 kilotons. | B |
| 1976 | Peaceful nuclear explosions treaty | Bars explosions greater than 150 kilotons for "peaceful purposes," such as excavation or mining. | B |
| 1977 | Environmental modification convention | Prohibits military or other hostile use of environmental modification techniques. | M |
| 1979 | SALT II offensive arms agreement | Limits numbers and types of strategic nuclear delivery vehicles. *Not ratified.* | B |
| 1981 | Inhumane weapons convention | Bans variety of mines and fragmentation, and incendiary weapons. | M |

| Year Signed | Agreement | Provisions | Multilateral (M) or Bilateral U.S.–Soviet (B) |
|---|---|---|---|
| 1985 | South Pacific nuclear-free zone treaty | Bans testing, manufacture, acquisition, stationing of nuclear weapons (Treaty of Rarotonga). | M |
| 1986 | Confidence and security-building measures and disarmament in Europe | Notification of military movements and maneuvers, with observers and inspection. | M |
| 1987 | Intermediate-range nuclear forces (INF) | Eliminates all missiles with range between 500 and 5,500 kilometers. | B |
| 1987 | Crisis reduction centers | Establishes communication centers in Moscow and Washington. | B |
| 1990 | Chemical weapons agreement | Immediate end to chemical weapons production and deep cuts in stocks by 2002. | B |
| 1990 | Underground testing verification | Protocol to 1974 and 1976 treaties delimiting verification procedures. | B |
| 1990 | Troop levels in Central Europe | Limits U.S. and Soviet forces in Central Europe to 195,000 each. | B |
| 1990 | Conventional armed forces in Europe (CFE) | Sets limits to NATO and Warsaw Pact forces in regard to tanks, other armored vehicles, artillery, combat helicopters and aircraft. Updated in 1992. | M |
| 1991 | Strategic Arms Reduction Treaty (START I) (and 1992 Protocol) | Reduces number of U.S. and former Soviet strategic nuclear warheads by approximately one-third; Lisbon Protocol makes Russia, Belarus, Ukraine, and Kazakhstan responsible for carrying out former USSR treaty obligations. | B |

**TABLE 13.4**   Major Arms-Control Agreements Since 1959 (*continued*)

| Year Signed | Agreement | Provisions | Multilateral (M) or Bilateral U.S.–Soviet (B) |
|---|---|---|---|
| 1992 | Open skies treaty | Creates a regime for confidence-building and stability of arms control, by supervising observation flights by unarmed reconnaissance aircraft over signatory states. | M |
| 1993 | START II | Reduces the number of deployed U.S. and Russian strategic nuclear warheads to 3,000–3,500 each by the year 2003; bans multiple-warhead land-based missiles. | B |
| 1993 | Chemical weapons convention | Bans the use, production, development, and stockpiling of chemical weapons. Requires the destruction of all chemical weapons stockpiles within 10–15 years of treaty's entry into force. | M |

In reviewing the arms-control record after World War II, it is important to remember that ***arms control** is not necessarily **disarmament***. Arms control is a process that produces agreements on weapons and the use of weapons—types, deployment, characteristics, safety conditions to prevent accidents, and so forth. Many arms-control agreements are concerned with the creation of stability in the sense that neither side is tempted (as in the *T* of the prisoners' dilemma) to use weapons first. The aim of disarmament is to reduce the numbers of weapons. Thus arms control may be seen as a distraction from the quest for disarmament. Alternatively, some kinds of disarmament could work against stability (for instance, by reducing second-strike capabilities). Similarly, the famous Strategic Defense Initiative (SDI) of the Reagan administration was controversial in terms of what its effects could have been. *If* it could have been built— and *if* it could actually have worked—the system was designed as a perfect defense against attacking strategic missiles. Such a system, however, would have removed one side's second-strike capability deterrent threat and injected a destabilizing element into the strategic relationship. These sorts of possible contradictions created serious conflicts within the ranks of those who wanted to reduce the threat of war.

The limitations on weapons types, characteristics, and deployment that enhance stability can be broken down into several basic categories. Arms control can mean the removal of a geographic area from the arms race by forbidding the deployment of weapons of mass destruction there—as in the Antarctic, outer space, and seabed treaties, or the Treaty of Tlatelolco. Arms control may be aimed at minimizing miscalculation and accidental war, as in the "hot-line" agreement or the nuclear accidents, high seas, and crisis reduction centers agreements. Arms control may deal with limits on the nature of weapons and their characteristics, such as nuclear test–ban treaties, those dealing with biological and chemical weapons, or the environmental modification convention. Arms control may also deal with the growth (or reduction) in the numbers of certain kinds of weapons. This was the most visible focus of American–Soviet arms control, which culminated in the SALT and START agreements. Major reductions of weapons began with INF in 1987 and continued with START. Finally, the arms-control issue of the twenty-first century will be *proliferation*— based around the cornerstone of the 1968 nonproliferation treaty.

## NUCLEAR PROLIFERATION

Generally, multilateral treaties aim to prevent the spread of weapons of mass destruction to areas and countries where they have not already been deployed. Thus treaties regarding the Antarctic, outer space, the seabed, and environmental modification all provide that signatories will continue to refrain from doing something they have not yet done. The biological and chemical weapons agreements called for destroying stocks of weapons, but most analysts of modern warfare agree that both biological and chemical weapons are generally inferior to nuclear ones as weapons of mass destruction; that is, if a state already has large stocks of nuclear weapons, chemical and especially biological weapons are largely superfluous except for small encounters. Thus the most important targets of biological and chemical weapons agreements are the nonnuclear states. For them, such weapons can be "the poor country's atom bomb." The danger becomes much greater as more and more countries are able to build or buy medium-range ballistic missiles. The war with Iraq showed how important it is to control these weapons.

Most observers agree that nuclear proliferation will be the central issue of arms control into the next century. With the end of the cold war and the dissolution of the Soviet Union came the successful negotiation of the START agreements—bringing about a significant reduction in the nuclear arsenals of both the United States and Russia. With the annual dismantling of around 2,000 nuclear warheads by each country, one observer noted, "Far more nuclear weapons are being retired and dismantled in 1993 than are being produced."[7] Thus, by bringing about significant reductions in superpower nuclear arsenals, the START agreements have become an important part of the set of nonproliferation agreements and activities (or "regime"). The original bargain between the superpowers and smaller states in the 1968 **nonproliferation treaty** (**NPT**) was supposed to have been limits on "horizontal" proliferation to new nuclear powers in return for reduction—real disarmament—in the "vertical" proliferation of the superpowers' arsenals. Such "real disarmament" is now occurring.

The NPT was directed toward reducing the risk of nuclear war, both war between nuclear states and "catalytic" war, a war initially involving lesser powers that draws in a superpower. In signing the NPT, states that did not already have nuclear weapons promised not to acquire such weapons, and states that did have nuclear weapons agreed not to transfer them to nonnuclear states. Meeting in New York in May 1995, over 170 signatories of the NPT agreed to extend the original treaty permanently into the future. (Iraq and North Korea did not vote, but are nevertheless legally bound by the extension.) Hard bargaining and intense pressure from the United States persuaded virtually all of the nonnuclear powers to go along; in return, the big nuclear powers pledged to move toward a comprehensive ban on nuclear tests, and to renew their efforts toward the continued reduction and ultimately the complete elimination of nuclear weapons.

The collapse of the Soviet Union has also highlighted two continuing proliferation problems: the ownership and control of nuclear weapons in FSU countries (including Russia itself, and until it completes its nuclear disarmament program, Ukraine); and the spread of nuclear materials and technology.[8] By the 1980s Israel, India, South Africa, and perhaps Pakistan had crossed the threshold to actual possession of a nuclear capability, and other non-NPT states such as Argentina, Brazil, South Korea, and Taiwan were moving in that direction. But since 1992, with the U.S.–Russian arms reduction agreements and the accession of France and China to the NPT, all the sub-threshold states had cancelled their nuclear weapons programs; South Africa destroyed all seven of the bombs it had built, and also signed the NPT. A worrisome development, however, is the emergence of a new group of "renegade" states, parties to the NPT who continue to attempt to acquire nuclear weapons: Iraq, Iran, Algeria (and possibly Libya and Syria). The renegade state attracting perhaps the most attention has been North Korea, with its ever-changing policies towards the NPT, on-site inspection of its nuclear facilities, and negotiations over its compliance to the treaty.

---

[7] Ruth Leger Sivard, *World Military and Social Expenditures 1993* (Washington, D.C.: World Priorities, 1993), p. 17.

[8] For a discussion of both threshold and renegade states, as well as a detailed review of current nonproliferation activities, see John Simpson, "Nuclear Arms Control and an Extended Nonproliferation Regime," in Stockholm International Peace Research Institute, *SIPRI Yearbook 1994* (New York: Oxford University Press, 1994), pp. 605–629. For reviews of the literature on proliferation and its consequences, see Scott D. Sagan, "The Perils of Proliferation," *International Security* 18 (Spring 1994), 66–107; and Barry R. Schneider, "Nuclear Proliferation and Counter-Proliferation: Policy Issues and Debates," *Mershon International Studies Review* (October 1994), 209–234.

There are a number of dangers to proliferation. One is the acquisition by governments of the material and know-how needed to make bombs. New nuclear powers, which would likely include a number of aggressive authoritarian states, will lack the experience of existing nuclear powers in controlling the use of such weapons and will lack the resources to manage the elaborate command and control capabilities required; this is especially true of the less developed countries. Also, many of these governments will be involved in serious local conflicts, a situation that increases pressures to use such weapons in warfare. Such factors as these convince us that a world of many nuclear powers would be a perilous one indeed, despite some arguments that a system in which *everyone* possessed nuclear weapons would be quite stable—due to a megabalance of terror of the MAD of all against all.[9] Just because the "long peace" during the cold war may in some measure have been the result of mutual U.S.–Soviet deterrence does not provide a basis for arguing that proliferating nuclear weapons in the present system would have peacekeeping value.

A second danger is the opportunity it provides for terrorists to gain control of nuclear materials (which may have been acquired by governments for peaceful purposes) or finished weapons. Such terrorists may be based within the countries they wish to harm, or far away, simply taking advantage of opportunities to acquire nuclear materials from governments that are unable to take sufficient security precautions.

To meet the threat of proliferation, several different kinds of incentives for proliferation must be recognized. For some countries, the problem of security against present nuclear powers may be paramount (for example, the case of Pakistan against India). More often, however, security is sought against local powers that are not yet nuclear (for example, by Israel against the Arab countries and South Korea against North Korea). For still other states, military security is not a primary concern; rather, they may wish to obtain big-power prestige or the technological information that can be obtained from the development of peaceful and military nuclear capabilities (as was possibly the case in past Argentine efforts). For still others—India, for example, perhaps all three kinds of incentives are involved.

A note on nonnuclear proliferation is in order. As discussed earlier, the Gulf War heightened interest in the acquisition of advanced-technology weaponry throughout the world, including missile delivery systems. Such interest in turn raised concern among the five permanent members of the UN Security Council: the United States, Russia, China, Britain, and France—the countries responsible for about 80 percent of the global trade in conventional weapons. In an attempt to control the transfer of weapons and technology through the development of guidelines, meetings were held in 1991–92. These efforts were only partially successful, ending in late 1992 when China walked out over U.S. sales of jet fighters to Taiwan.

---

[9] Kenneth Waltz, today's most prominent structural realist, has advanced this argument, which is vigorously rebutted by Scott Sagan. See Sagan and Waltz, *The Spread of Nuclear Weapons: A Debate* (New York: W. W. Norton, 1995). John Mearsheimer has presented arguments similar to Waltz's with regard to the creation of a strong Ukrainian nuclear force; "The Case for a Ukrainian Nuclear Deterrent," *Foreign Affairs* 72 (Summer 1993), 50–66. In the same issue, Steven E. Miller rebuts Mearsheimer in "The Case Against a Ukrainian Nuclear Deterrent," 67–80.

Many people—scholars, citizens, and government leaders—have devoted their energies to reducing the prospects of war and reducing the levels of arms with which wars might be fought. Our review of arms-control and disarmament efforts since World War II leaves us with a mixed picture. There has been progress. The world has not blown up; no nuclear weapon has been exploded in war since 1945. By historical standards, that is a long time without a major war. Despite the common fears voiced in each decade, there has *not* been a steady proliferation of nuclear weapons. Beyond the United States, Russia (noting the negotiations for the disarmament of the other Soviet successor states), Britain, France, and China, only India has exploded a "peaceful nuclear device." (Israel has also had a large number of nuclear weapons for years, and Pakistan is close to having some.) As we have seen, there have been international agreements to ban nuclear weapons from many environments (Antarctica, outer space, and the seabed) as well as to prohibit atmospheric testing and proliferation. Yet such progress must be viewed with caution, given the continued dangers that nuclear weapons pose to humanity. The breathing space humanity has provided itself must not lead to complacency in thinking about arms control and disarmament.

## ETHICS AND WAR

In our discussion of arms races and deterrence, we have concentrated on the historical record, analytical perspectives that illuminate our understanding, and empirical evidence supporting propositions set forth about the causes and consequences of arms races. Occasionally we have alluded to moral and ethical considerations as possible restraints on behavior, but that has been the extent of our discussion of ethics and morality. We have not considered such issues as what actions are moral or ethical or what moral and ethical principles should guide our behavior and the behavior of our leaders both in peacetime and in war.

Moral or ethical propositions concern how people ought to behave rather than how people do behave. Ethical reasoning is essentially deductive reasoning. One starts with a very few given principles and deduces from them a set of propositions. Ethical deductive reasoning can be as rigorous as mathematical or other formal reasoning.

Many social scientists are reluctant to engage in ethical discussions because of the great difficulty we have, in modern industrial societies, in establishing a common frame of reference. Few people live in cultures where a single value system is dominant. Although modern values are heavily influenced by Greek and Judeo-Christian traditions, there is no commonly accepted authority, and only a few propositions are shared across most contemporary religions and other ethical systems. Humanists, Marxists, agnostics, and atheists share some common ground with religious believers, but that ground is not very extensive. Even within many of the major traditions, authority is repudiated and a wide variety of opinions are tolerated.

We cannot, however, completely ignore such issues in a discussion of deterrence and war. Are there circumstances in which nuclear weapons should not be used? Are there targets that should not be attacked, according to widely accepted ethical precepts? Our purpose here is not to insist on answers, but to offer a number of considerations to open up these issues to discussion.

## The Realist Position

At one end of the spectrum of ethical thought about warfare are the views (1) that any act in war is justifiable if it seems to serve the national interest and (2) that rightness depends solely on the ends sought rather than on the methods used to obtain those ends. The first view implies that if the populace as a whole is thought to desire something, leaders should seek to obtain it with whatever means are available. This version of realism takes a very pessimistic view of human nature and the human condition. It holds that regardless of the moral restraints that bind our interpersonal behavior, international politics is so anarchic—a war of each against all—that mere self-preservation requires the abandonment of moral inhibitions. For those who hold to the second view, there are legitimate and illegitimate goals in world politics; but if your goals or ends are just, any means may be employed to reach them.

Although many people may express such viewpoints, it is not clear how many really believe they are guides to action. Most adults come to believe that the law is important; it should be obeyed most of the time; and if it is disobeyed, it should not be disobeyed lightly. Civil disobedience is permissible only if undertaken for some higher moral purpose. International law is generally regarded as one of the least authoritative and least effective forms of law, but even it is given some respect and observance, and not solely out of self-interest. When occupying the Vietnam village of My Lai, Lieutenant William Calley deliberately ordered and supervised the killing of hundreds of innocent, noncombatant civilians. His action may have safeguarded a few U.S. troops from communist Vietcong guerrillas disguised as civilians (though this possibility seems rather far-fetched). Nevertheless, his act violated U.S. Army regulations, international law, and most people's moral sense of what was right and wrong. Calley was tried and convicted by an army court.

Similarly, after World War II many German and Japanese wartime leaders were tried by Allied military tribunals at Nuremberg and Tokyo. They were charged with the deliberate killing of civilians and prisoners of war and with "waging aggressive war." Some of these acts, such as killing prisoners of war, were clearly forbidden by instruments of international law, such as the Geneva Convention. Others, like waging aggressive war, were less clearly outlawed; yet it was widely agreed that the enemy leaders had committed acts that were morally if not legally outrageous. Many of the leaders were convicted and executed. Most people act as though they believe that legal, moral, or ethical restraints are relevant to international behavior.

## The Pacifist Position

The pacifist's view is very different from the realist's "anything goes" position. A completely pacifist position may result from a philosophical and moral predilection for nonviolence, a rejection in principle of the use of force as an instrument of national policy, a belief in the spiritually regenerative effect of a nonviolent response to violence, or an overriding concern for the preservation of human life.

Pacifism has deep roots in a number of secular and religious traditions. It seems to have been the dominant view in the early Christian church before the Roman emperor Constantine converted to Christianity. The Roman Empire was pagan and often persecuted Christians; no Christian could in good conscience serve in the army of such a power. Pacifism is not the dominant tradition in contemporary Christianity, but it is still a common and respected view in many Christian churches. It is a central principle of the Society of Friends (the Quakers) and was practiced by Martin Luther King, Jr., in his program of civil disobedience against racial segregation. Mohandas Gandhi blended part of this Christian pacifist tradition with Hinduism in his resistance to British rule in India, and his example has had great influence worldwide. Plans for nonviolent resistance—a war without weapons against a would-be conqueror—are commonly discussed and sometimes practiced.[10]

## Intermediate Positions

Between these two extreme views are a variety of positions. For those who accept the use of force as a legitimate instrument of state policy in many but not all circumstances, there are two principal moral considerations in determining limitations. One is concerned with the norms that govern the *resort* to war (in international law, *ius ad bellum*), and the second with the norms that govern the *conduct* of war (or, *ius in bello*).

The first limitation, which concentrates on what conditions justify an initial resort to physical violence, is typically less concerned with how the conflict is conducted once it is begun. In the American philosophical tradition, the only just war is one undertaken in self-defense. In this context self-defense includes (1) defense of one's allies in keeping with a formal commitment, (2) assistance to a small power under the principle of collective security when authorized by an international organization, such as the United Nations, even if there is no treaty commitment, or (3) assistance to another government in response to its request for aid. Furthermore, the "self" to be defended is generally defined broadly to include not only the physical territory but also the values and way of life believed to characterize the nation. No other grievances, however severe, would justify the initiation of war; grievances should always be addressed only through negotiation or arbitration, or they should be endured in the hope that they will become more tolerable as circumstances evolve. This position can become a very conservative one politically and is rejected by those who declare that oppression and exploitation must be resisted by force if necessary. Furthermore, once a war in self-defense is undertaken, limits on both the political objectives to be achieved and the means used to pursue them become very hard to establish.

The most common Marxist view holds that a war need not be undertaken in self-defense to be justifiable; war-making is blameless if its purpose is to redress class oppression or national subjugation. In this respect the Marxist approach differs widely from the classical American doctrine. Even for the Marxist, however, a just war must

---

[10] Gene Sharp, *Civilian-Based Defense: A Post-Military Weapons System* (Princeton, N.J.: Princeton University Press, 1990).

not have a reactionary effect. Thus a nuclear war that would annihilate both capitalist and socialist civilizations would not be initiated.

## Analysis of a Just War

Quite a different position, embodied in the **just-war tradition,** stems from Christian moralists. This tradition has its origins in ancient Greek and Roman thought, was developed in the Middle Ages and later refined, and now is the predominant Christian view. It also provides a foundation for very similar positions taken by some non-Christian thinkers today. Just-war thinking was the core of a pastoral letter from Roman Catholic bishops in the United States that attracted much attention in 1983.[11]

Three elements of the just-war tradition are especially important to questions about nuclear war. The first is the requirement of **discrimination,** or observing the principle of noncombatant immunity. Especially in modern warfare, it is often hard to distinguish civilians from combatants. Workers in weapons factories, for instance, are hard to classify, but many others are clearly civilian noncombatants: children, old people, hospital patients, farmers. The requirement of discrimination forbids direct, deliberate attacks on civilians. The bishops wrote, "Under no circumstances may nuclear weapons or other instruments of mass slaughter be used for the purpose of destroying population centers or other predominantly civilian targets. . . . No Christian can rightfully carry out orders or policies deliberately aimed at killing noncombatants." This is a strong statement. It implicitly condemns the bombing of Dresden, a city with no military significance; the firebombing of hundreds of thousands of Japanese civilians in World War II; and the atomic bombing of Hiroshima and Nagasaki, cities that were chosen as civilian, not military, targets. According to this principle, the fact that these bombings may have hastened the end of the war and even may have reduced the total number of civilian casualties from what they might otherwise have been is not sufficient justification. By this principle, the direct killing of civilians as a means to achieving some good end or avoiding some evil is never morally permissible.

Discrimination directly opposes policies adopted by all the nuclear powers. Until 1973 American *declaratory* policy always emphasized "countercity" deterrence; that is, the ability to destroy a large fraction of any enemy's industry and to kill a large fraction of the enemy's population in retaliation for any attack on the United States or its allies. American *operational* policy (what in fact was in the war plans) never concentrated on civilian targets, despite the declaratory policy. A war plan from 1948 (actually known as "Broiler"), for example, called for the use of 34 bombs against targets in 26 cities. The targets of these plans included military sites, "military-related industry," trans-

---

[11] National Conference of Catholic Bishops, *The Challenge of Peace: God's Promise and Our Response* (Washington, D.C.: U.S. Catholic Conference, 1983); its continuing relevance is discussed at length in Charles W. Kegley, Jr., and Kenneth L. Schwab, eds., *After the Cold War: Questioning the Morality of Nuclear Deterrence* (Boulder, Colo.: Westview, 1991). Similar statements, though less prominent and comprehensive, have been made by other religious groups. For an earlier Protestant statement, see Paul Ramsey, *The Just War* (New York: Scribners, 1968); for a secular but closely related view, see Michael Walzer, *Just and Unjust Wars* (New York: Basic Books, 1977).

portation centers, and electricity-producing facilities. Most of these targets were in major population centers, and bombing them would have resulted in a large number of civilian deaths. Some decision makers saw these deaths as unintended but unavoidable; to others they were "bonus effects" that strengthened deterrence.[12]

A second principle of just-war analysis is **proportionality:** the harm done by an act, even unintentionally, may not be disproportionate to the good sought or to the evil to be avoided (the calculation is inevitably subjective and uncertain). The principle of proportionality recognizes that in almost any war, some civilians will unavoidably be killed if military targets are hit, and it accepts some number of civilian deaths as a by-product of striking a military target. But civilians are not to be killed without limit, even unintentionally. Massive civilian casualties would surely occur in any nuclear exchange, even one directed only at military targets. The bishops' letter is filled with references to the interspersing of military facilities and civilian living and working areas, resulting in a "horrendous" number of civilians who would necessarily be killed coincidentally with the hitting of military targets. By the principle of proportionality, discrimination alone—merely targeting a nuclear strike to military targets—is not enough to make a policy morally acceptable.

Many strategists and government officials have maintained that improvements in strategic weaponry are movements in the direction of greater moral acceptability. Some have argued that improvements in accuracy, coupled with the elimination of the very large warheads placed on older missiles, had the effect of limiting damage. On first encounter, it seems hard to argue against smaller weapons with greater accuracy. A reduction in unintended civilian deaths would be consistent with traditional moral principles. But on examination, the problems are immense. As mentioned in Chapter 12, any large-scale nuclear exchange, even of discriminating weapons, would inevitably result in tens of millions of civilian casualties. The combination of immediate casualties from blast and radiation with longer-term casualties from fallout, disruption of the medical, sanitation, transportation, communication, and economic systems, ecological devastation, climatic effects, and so forth would be very great, even if attacks were limited to strictly military targets—imagine, if you will, hundreds of Chernobyls. The effect would hardly be different than if population centers had been specifically targeted. There are not many causes to which such deaths would be proportionate.

One problem is therefore the illusion that any large-scale nuclear exchange could in any real sense be limited in its consequences. The other problem is the expectation that nuclear war could be fought in some precise fashion of strike and counterstrike, that in any major nuclear exchange the war could be restricted to a limited number of strictly military targets. There were (and are) people who imagine that such a war could be waged with acceptable consequences. The majority of analysts, however, have considered the likelihood of such limitation, under wartime conditions of anger, confusion, ignorance, and loss of control, to be extremely small. One of the most

---

[12] David Alan Rosenberg, "The Origins of Overkill: Nuclear Weapons and American Strategy," *International Security* 7, 4 (Spring 1983), 371.

knowledgeable experts on this matter is John Steinbruner, who noted in the early 1980s:

> Once the use of as many as 10 or more nuclear weapons directly against the USSR is seriously contemplated, U.S. strategic commanders will likely insist on attacking the full array of Soviet military targets. . . . If national commanders seriously attempted to implement this strategy (controlled response) in a war with existing and currently projected U.S. forces, the result would not be a finely controlled strategic campaign. The more likely result would be the collapse of U.S. forces into isolated units undertaking retaliation on their own initiative against a wide variety of targets at unpredictable moments.[13]

Limitation of nuclear war thus fails a third principle of the just war: *reasonable chance of success*. To many people the idea of "winning" or "prevailing" in a nuclear war seems only a dangerous fantasy, along with any notion of the viability of the United States and other democracies as free societies after such a conflict.

Many U.S. analysts came to advocate a policy of "no first use" of nuclear weapons as a way of easing both the strategic and moral dilemmas posed by deterrence. By this policy the defense of allies and vital interests against nonnuclear threats would be undertaken predominantly by conventional military forces. Nuclear weapons would have been used only in response to nuclear attack. Readiness to use conventional forces would then be coupled with a doctrine of preparation, of physical capability, and of public declaration that the superpower would not be the first to use nuclear weapons.

So much for what could—or could not—be done in war. Is deterrence, as contrasted to what one actually does in war, different? After all, the purpose of deterrence is to prevent war. The trouble is that, whatever our good intentions, deterrence can fail. If we make plans—build weapons, set up strategic programs, proclaim doctrines, instruct commanders—on the basis of principles that we are not willing to act upon, we may be called to act upon them anyway. Many things happen almost automatically. In the 1914 crisis the powers' competitive mobilization plans worked automatically, making World War I almost unavoidable. Plans we adopt in the name of deterrence could be activated, whatever our desires, when a crisis occurs. If war should come as the result of some uncontrollable crisis or a physical or human accident, plans calling for morally unacceptable acts in the name of deterrence would very likely be implemented—as morally unacceptable acts.

## Was the Gulf War a Just War?

Questions about the morality of warfare resurfaced with Operation Desert Storm against Iraq. The allies, operating as a UN coalition, claimed to have a *just cause;* namely, to restore Kuwait's independence after it had been invaded. In the just-war tradition, self-defense—including collective self-defense and the defense of a weaker

---

[13] John Steinbruner, "Nuclear Decapitation," *Foreign Policy* 45 (Winter 1981–82), 22–23.

state by a strong one—is considered a just cause. Even with the Kuwaiti government's less-than-sterling human-rights record (but far better than Saddam Hussein's), that nation had a right to resist occupation, and others had a right to help it.

Another just-war principle requires that war be declared by a *legitimate authority.* This principle was once meant to exclude private wars, terrorism, and vigilante actions. Now it means that the basic constitutional rules of the state must be followed. In the United States, the president is commander in chief, but Congress must declare war. In the contemporary post–cold war world, certain rules about the use of military force seem to be emerging. As the United States and Russia become able to agree in the UN Security Council (where they, China, Britain, and France have individual veto power), it becomes expected that they should agree and that collective security operations against an aggressor should have UN approval. This expectation of joint response restrains any one big powerful state from unilaterally deciding that it has a just cause in defending someone else. In effect, some powers of legitimate authority are shifting from a national to a supranational level. Understanding that domestic and international support depended on involving Congress and the UN in the decision, President Bush did so (albeit by a lot of persuasion and by cutting some deals).

Yet another just-war principle requires that war be a *last resort*, engaged in only after diplomacy and negotiation have failed. Diplomacy had narrowed the gap between the coalition and Iraq, but serious differences were not settled. Economic sanctions were tried; Bush declared that they had failed and that force was needed to get Iraq out of Kuwait. Reasonable people still disagree—among them, General Colin Powell, then Chairman of the Joint Chiefs of Staff. He thought sanctions should have been given more time; but we will never know whether force was indeed the last resort or sanctions would have been sufficient to achieve the aim.

The military forces of the coalition attempted to observe the principle of *discrimination* by the use of "smart bombs" that made it possible to hit many military targets, even in civilian areas, with relatively few civilian deaths. Attacks were generally confined to military targets, although one civilian bomb shelter was hit, and some targets—transportation networks, telecommunications, and electrical plants—were vital to civilian life as well as being militarily important.

The greatest question from a just-war viewpoint turned on *proportionality.* Even in a just cause, was it worth killing about 100,000 Iraqis (mostly soldiers, but inevitably many civilians, too) during the war itself? Was it worth the many postwar civilian deaths—especially among children and the sick—from diseases arising from the destruction of water, sewage, and health facilities, the devastation of agricultural capacities, and the loss of essential transportation and electricity? Answers to the question of proportionality are inevitably subjective.[14] But maybe it is a good thing that they were asked explicitly in the public debate. The debate affected the way the war was conducted and will affect decisions about whether to fight in the future.

---

[14] In a national survey in February 1991, most Americans described Operation Desert Storm as a just war. When asked to evaluate it by each of the just-war principles, the greatest reservations (but still with large majority support) concerned discrimination and proportionality. *The Gallup Poll Monthly,* February 1991, p. 120

## WHAT KIND OF FUTURE?

Political conditions now are very different from those of the cold war era. The Warsaw Pact has been dissolved. All states have adopted more clearly defensive stances, cutting back on weapons useful in a rapid attack. The CFE agreement has sharply reduced the number of conventional weapons in Europe. At their summit meeting in July 1990, the NATO leaders agreed that they were moving toward a transformed Europe, "making nuclear forces truly weapons of last resort." While not proclaiming a no-first-use policy, they declared they were moving to reduced dependence on nuclear weapons. As part of the package to extend the Nonproliferation Treaty, in 1995 all the big powers supported a UN Security Council resolution agreeing not to use nuclear weapons first against states that did not themselves have nuclear weapons or were not allied to nuclear powers. The present threat to European security is one of long-suppressed but now-surfacing nationalist violence over borders and sovereignty in the countries of Eastern Europe and the former Soviet Union. Political cooperation has much to offer for solving these problems; nuclear deterrence is nearly irrelevant. Nuclear weapons merely compound the problem, raising anew the danger of uncontrolled or inadvertent use.

Did nuclear weapons keep the "long peace" between the superpowers? Only in part. As both sides acquired a second-strike capability, the threat of using nuclear weapons if an ally was attacked conventionally no longer was credible. Nuclear threats could not prevent proxy wars or wars like those in Vietnam and Afghanistan. Nuclear threats can convey a superpower's serious concern if an ally is threatened, and they bring with them the danger that events will spiral out of control. But they still do not make a nuclear-armed adversary think one will use them deliberately.[15] Their second-strike capabilities did, however, give each superpower security against any direct attack on itself. That ultimately may have allowed Gorbachev to acquiesce in the loss of Eastern Europe without feeling that Soviet security had been fatally compromised.

Reliance on conventional rather than nuclear weapons for deterrence fits in well with the kind of analysis outlined above. It avoids the need for quick-reaction, highly accurate, silo-busting, first-strike forces that could endanger stability in a crisis. The risks of first use of nuclear weapons are too great to justify ever beginning a nuclear war. Less dire threats are terrible enough. With the end of the cold war, and no fear of surprise attack (or even inadvertent attack) to deter, nuclear weapons are of very little utility to the large powers. With agreements such as the 1992 open skies treaty, and the combination of increasing political and economic openness, both Russia and China

---

[15] On the limited utility of nuclear first-use threats, see Richard K. Betts, *Nuclear Blackmail and Nuclear Balance* (Washington, D.C.: Brookings Institution, 1987); Barry Blechman, "The Political Utility of Nuclear Weapons: The 1973 Middle East Crisis," *International Security* 7, 1 (1982), 132–156; and Paul Huth, "The Extended Deterrent Value of Nuclear Weapons," *Journal of Conflict Resolution* 34, 2 (1990), 270–290.

are becoming more "transparent," making major cheating on arms-control agreements much less likely. In a situation such as this, we can now begin to contemplate a condition of zero, or at least near-zero, nuclear weapons as a plausible goal of disarmament. At the least, nuclear inventories can be drastically reduced. The United States and Russia have demonstrated an ability and willingness to make significant cutbacks in their nuclear arsenals, more than many developing countries ever thought possible.

Whereas the knowledge of nuclear weapons cannot be unlearned, maybe that very knowledge and the threat to act on it could serve as the necessary deterrent to violation of a comprehensive disarmament program. Permanent acceptance of the realist vision of anarchy and conflict seems, on a centuries-long scale with nuclear weaponry, a recipe for catastrophe. No form of deterrence can provide a perfect solution; every possibility contains moral and practical dangers. We have come this far without nuclear war; in 1945 many people did not expect that much success. The success has not come by accident. It has come because people have puzzled and struggled. Some of those people are scientists, government officials, and military officers. Others are ordinary citizens who, by their votes and their protests, have forced leaders to take their fears seriously. There is no choice but to continue wrestling with the dangers and contradictions of our nuclear dilemmas.

# Causes of Peace Among Industrialized Countries

## The Achievement of Peace and Prosperity

Many of the achievements of the past five decades in the rich industrialized countries of the world are very impressive indeed. Despite periods of recession and/or inflation, these countries have experienced a period of economic well-being unrivaled in history. Despite serious inequalities and remaining pockets of real poverty within many industrialized countries, for the first time in history prosperity has been widespread—benefiting not only the ruling classes, as was the case in most of the great empires of the world.

All this has happened in spite of the enormous loss of life and physical destruction caused by World War II, at the end of which the economies of Japan, Germany, and many other states were in ruin. Moreover, all states—but especially the industrialized countries—are now tightly linked by a network of trade, investment, communications, and travel to a degree also unprecedented. Most citizens of Europe and North America could probably afford an intercontinental trip, and the plane journey is a matter of hours. The prospering national economies are tightly interdependent: growth, inflation, and recession are readily transmitted from one country to another with little control. We have, then, a group of countries that are highly interdependent with—and highly vulnerable to—each other. However, they have *managed* their interdependence to produce positive results for all involved.

Equally important but not noticed so often as the achievement of prosperity is the achievement of peace. Among the developed market economies—the capitalist and industrialized OECD countries of Europe and the United States, Canada, Japan, Australia, and New Zealand—there has been no war or other violent conflict since 1945. Not only has there been no war among them in over 50 years; neither has there been much expectation of or preparation for war among them.[1] The seemingly most permanent hostility, between France and Germany, appears well buried since the 1960s. Individual German and French citizens may not love one another, but neither do they expect the other's state to attack or wish to mount an attack. Europeans, Americans, and Japanese may still fear security threats from outside the OECD; they may continue to use or threaten to use military force against small or poor states to retain their spheres of influence. But among countries within the OECD area, peace and the confident expectation of peace are the norm. When the U.S. government wanted the British and French to withdraw from Suez in 1956, it coerced them with economic sanctions, not with military force. Despite recent U.S.–Japanese trade disagreements, there has been no hint of armed violence.

This is an extraordinary achievement by the standards of recent history. Until 1945, war or the expectation of war among most of these countries was the norm. (There were some localized exceptions—for example, Canada–the United States–Britain, and within Scandinavia.) These countries were the instigators and major combatants of both world wars, which resulted in the deaths of tens of millions of people. The preceding century saw many major wars among these same countries, beginning with the extended Napoleonic Wars among all the major states of Europe (and provoking the War of 1812 between Britain and the United States) and including several wars leading to the unification of Germany in 1870. Even in periods of peace, it was recognized that peace was precarious, depending on constant watchfulness, readiness and ability to fight, and maintenance of a balance of power. Crises and war scares were common; several conflicts threatened to provoke a general European war before one finally did in August 1914.

The vast majority of international wars since 1945, however, have been fought in less developed countries (LDCs), and mostly among LDCs (perhaps with outsiders

---

[1] A marginal exception is the brief, limited conflict between Greece and Turkey over the control of Cyprus in 1974. However, Greece and Turkey are the least wealthy and least industrialized countries of the OECD (an important factor, as we shall see).

supplying one or both sides). No war has been fought on the territory of an OECD country. A partial explanation might be the success of deterrence by the OECD states of communist countries or the logistical inability of LDCs to instigate or sustain an attack on OECD states. But the total lack of war between OECD countries is not so easily explained. This picture would be reinforced if we had included the set of post–World War II civil wars, almost all of which have been fought in LDCs (again, often with intervention by OECD or communist countries).[2]

Peace among the OECD countries is also an extraordinary achievement by the standards of world history. The countries involved contain a total population of over 800 million, spread over a geographic area equal to nearly half the land of the Northern Hemisphere. By both measures it is a larger zone of peace than has ever existed before. These are simple facts, but facts that cry out for explanation—particularly given the expectations of realists and radicals. If we could understand why such a large set of peoples, who only recently fought bitterly and bloodily, now live at peace with one another, we would know something very important.

We have talked often about possible causes of war. Applying the levels-of-analysis scheme, we have discussed power rivalries in the context of different kinds of international systems, threats and bargaining in the relations between states, economic systems as the source of societal pressures for expansion, different incentives for peace and war presented by democratic and authoritarian governments, bureaucratic politics as a source of policies unsuited to the "national interest," and fear and misperception by individual decision makers.[3] But the question "What are the causes of peace?" is not simply the opposite side of the question "What are the causes of war?" If we could find the causes of peace among the OECD countries, we might have a key to promoting peace over a wider area, even the entire globe.

## Peace: Salaam or Sulah?

To some, peace is simply the absence of war, the absence of organized violent conflict. For most of us, however, that is not enough. One cannot, for example, make a wasteland and call it peace. The kind of peace we want is not a world in which every individual or group who could conceivably resort to violent conflict is simply destroyed—that would leave no one but the extreme pacifists. Ideally, we wish to achieve a stable peace, which, among the OECD countries, can be defined as *the absence of preparation for war or the serious expectation of war* with each other. A stronger view of stable peace is that the alternative of war is never considered. Kenneth Boulding calls stable peace "a situation in which the probability of war is so small that it does not really enter into

---

[2] See the discussion in Chapter 7 on the use of military force in the post–World War II system.

[3] Wide-ranging reviews of the literature addressed to the causes of war are: Jack S. Levy, "The Causes of War: A Review of Theories and Evidence," in Philip Tetlock et al., eds., *Behavior, Society, and Nuclear War*, vol. I (New York: Oxford University Press, 1989), pp. 209–333; John A. Vasquez, *The War Puzzle* (Cambridge, England: Cambridge University Press, 1993); and Greg Cashman, *What Causes War?* (New York: Lexington Books, 1993).

the calculations of any of the people involved."[4] If we prepare for or expect violent conflict—or if we repress violent conflict by force—we have what Boulding calls "unstable peace." An unstable peace can be enforced by deterrence, the fear of violent retribution, in which case we continually fear for the continuation of peace under a mutual balance of terror. The causes of peace are not simply the opposite of the causes of war.

If there is no balance—if deterrence is merely a one-way rather than a mutual relationship between two hostile parties—then we talk of repression. By some values and for some people, especially the most privileged, the absence of violent conflict even if achieved by repression and coercion may be better than the outbreak of violent conflict, but it is hardly anyone's ideal. Repressive and coercive relationships can be found between powerful and weak states as well as between powerful and weak groups within states. People may be deprived of political liberties, made materially poor, or allowed to die from sickness or starvation without direct physical violence. Some analysts thus refer to "structural violence"—deprivations enforced by coercive social and political systems—in contrast to the direct or physical violence of war or imprisonment.[5] "Structural violence" is in fact a very slippery and hard-to-define term. Nevertheless, the central distinction between stable peace under conditions that are generally acceptable to both sides and a situation of nonwar maintained only by threats (whether unilateral or reciprocated) is clear enough. It corresponds roughly to the Arabic terms *salaam*, which means an enduring peaceful relationship based on mutual respect, and *sulah*, which means only the end of hostilities or a truce.

One of the most important theorists about the conditions of peace was Karl Deutsch, who characterizes an area where peace is expected as a **security community**:

> A *security community* is a group of people which has become "integrated." By **integration** we mean the attainment, within a territory, of a *"sense of community"* and of institutions and practices strong enough and widespread enough to assure . . . dependable expectations of "peaceful change" among its population. By sense of community we mean a belief . . . that common social problems must and can be resolved by processes of "peaceful change."[6]

Note that in discussing "security community" as the result of a process of social integration, there is an emphasis on peaceful change, an ability and willingness to accommodate new demands and needs, not merely the maintenance of a status quo that may be unjust. It is a situation in which participants have a relationship that is reasonably equal and symmetrical and in which they frequently harmonize their interests,

---

[4] Kenneth Boulding, *Stable Peace* (Austin: University of Texas Press, 1979), p.13.
[5] See Johan Galtung, "Violence, Peace and Peace Research," *Journal of Peace Research* 6, 3 (1969), 167–191.
[6] Karl W. Deutsch et al., *Political Community and the North Atlantic Area* (Princeton, N.J.: Princeton University Press, 1957), p. 5.

compromise their differences, and reap *mutual rewards*. There still may be conflict, but the use or threat of force to resolve conflict is absent.

These conditions have essentially been met within the OECD area. Conditions of injustice, coercion, and repression do exist there. But compared with many other parts of the world, it is fair to say that a security community largely exists both among and within the OECD countries. The greatest exceptions are within rather than between countries. The most significant cases of violent political deaths within the last decade or so have been within the United Kingdom (the continuing conflict in Northern Ireland) and Spain (violence by Basque separatists). In both of these cases the violent acts involve people who do not wish to be subject to their present government and seek either independence (the Basques) or inclusion in another country (the Republic of Ireland). Violence directed at existing governmental institutions by separatists thus is somewhat more of a threat than is violence among OECD governments.[7] This is a point to which we shall return.

## THE MOVEMENT FOR EUROPEAN UNITY: THE POLITICS AND ECONOMICS OF INTEGRATION

Achieving peace by integrating smaller political units into larger ones has long been a goal of political theorists and policymakers. The Roman Empire brought the Pax Romana to much of the world for several centuries. Although there were some revolts within the empire and continuing battles with the barbarians on its borders, the Roman Empire did preside over a remarkable era of peace as well as of prosperity. Of course, it was largely a peace of domination, not the kind of stable peace or security community capable of peaceful change to which we aspire. Writing in the fourteenth century, Dante nevertheless looked back on the Roman Empire as being far better than the situation he knew—almost constant warfare among the Italian city-states. He argued that "in a multitude of rulers there is evil" and hoped for the emergence of a unified Italy under a single crown.

Following the devastation of World War II, the second enormously destructive war in only 30 years, some people adopted the principles of world federalism, the idea that permanent peace could be achieved only by establishing a world government. In Europe many leaders vowed that wars among Europeans had to cease and saw some form of European unification as the means to secure that goal. In May 1950 Robert Schuman, foreign minister of France, announced:

---

[7] In a controversial article, John J. Mearsheimer, "Back to the Future: Instability in Europe After the Cold War," *International Security* 15 (1990), 5–56, argues that a post–cold war Europe will be endangered by expansive "hypernationalism." We disagree. A much more likely source of conflict is the fragmentation or separatism discussed here and in earlier chapters.

The French Government proposes to put the whole of the Franco–German coal and steel production under a joint High Authority, in an organization which is open for the other European countries to enter. . . . It will change the destiny of these regions which for so long have been used for making weapons of war of which they have been most frequently the victims. The solidarity between the two countries established by joint production will show that a war between France and Germany becomes not only unthinkable but materially impossible.

Schuman further declared that his plan would "establish the basis for a European Federation . . . indispensable for the safeguarding of peace." From this initiative the European Coal and Steel Community was born a year later, including not only France and Germany but also Belgium, Luxembourg, the Netherlands, and Italy. This was the first major European supranational institution; that is, an institution with powers to overrule the members' national governments on some issues.

Promoting interdependence among the heavy industry sectors of the European economies seemed a good way to limit the independent war-making ability of individual states. Wider economic union could do so even more effectively. Another French leader, Jean Monnet, wrote:

There will be no peace in Europe if countries build up their strength on a basis of national sovereignty. . . . The countries of Europe are too limited to assure their people the prosperity that modern times afford. . . . Larger markets are needed. Prosperity and vital social development are inconceivable unless the countries of Europe form a federation or a European entity which in turn creates a common economic union.

This kind of thinking led to another major Western European institution, EURATOM, intended to undertake collectively the enormously expensive but promising development of nuclear power. It ultimately led to the signing of the 1957 Treaty of Rome, which established the European Economic Community (EEC), or Common Market, among the same six countries that had formed the Coal and Steel Community and EURATOM. These separate institutions were then merged into the European Community (EC). The new organization had broad powers to abolish tariffs and other restrictions on trade within the community; to regulate working conditions, environmental controls, and marketing practices within the community; to establish a common set of trade restrictions on outside countries; and to provide free movement of persons (particularly workers) and financial capital within the community.

In Monnet's vision, the economies and ultimately the people would be bound inextricably by economic union, making war "unthinkable." Notice, however, that in Monnet's statement another motive appears. In addition to providing peace, European unity would bring prosperity. Europeans had experienced not only war but also the terrible economic destruction and deprivation that followed. Even before World War II, the economies of the separate states suffered from various trade restrictions that severely limited commerce among them and, by dividing the continent into many small markets, made impossible the kind of economies of scale that helped make American enterprise so efficient in the enormous U.S. market. For example, economic disunity contributed to the competitive trade restrictions and currency devaluations that worsened the Great Depression of the 1930s.

True prosperity seemed to require creating a large European market without internal barriers; for such a market to work effectively, a wide range of controls on goods, capital, and labor had to be coordinated. That market has now grown to a remarkable size, and with minimal barriers to the movement of goods, finance, and people. In 1973 the Six became the Nine, with the addition of Britain, Denmark, and Ireland. Greece joined in 1981; Spain and Portugal in 1986. By 1993 the twelve countries of the European Community had a combined population of almost 350 million, a combined GNP approximately the size of that of the United States, and combined exports almost three times as large as that of the United States. In addition, the Maastricht treaty (formally, the "Treaty on European Union"), signed in 1992, came into effect in November 1993. This treaty contains 240 measures designed to create a single market among the twelve countries—a true economic union (with, eventually, a single currency). The Maastricht treaty also transformed the European Community into the European Union (EU), with additional provisions to promote a common foreign policy as well as a common security policy. With governmental and popular approval, in 1995, the Twelve grew to Fifteen with the addition of Austria, Sweden, and Finland. (Norway, however, rejected entry.)[8]

The issue of common security policy returns us to another motive pursued by many Europeans in the movement for European unity in addition to internal peace and prosperity: external security. Big countries have great power, and only big countries are great powers. In a postwar world dominated by the Soviet and U.S. giants, each with several times the population and wealth of any single European state, European nations could have the benefits of great-power status collectively if not individually. Thus Europeans, who retained great concern for their military security from the Soviet Union and who did not trust the United States to observe its NATO commitments indefinitely, wanted to see Europe as a united political and military unit.

This aim largely motivated the attempt to create a European Defense Community (EDC) in 1950. Because of the continued deterioration in relations with the Soviet Union, made still more threatening by the outbreak of the Korean War earlier in 1950, many Europeans and Americans came to the conclusion that the military security of Western Europe could not be guaranteed unless West Germany could be rearmed. Germany at this time was still occupied, by the United States, Britain, and France in the western zone and by the Soviet Union in the eastern zone; it had no army and no control over its foreign policy. Because of their recent Nazi experience, the Germans were still intensely distrusted. The EDC, therefore, was conceived as a way to harness

---

[8] As of early 1995, three other countries had applied for EU membership: Turkey, Malta, and Cyprus. For a full review of the development of the European Union as well as the range of other European institutions created since World War II, see Clive Archer, *Organizing Europe: The Institutions of Integration* (London: Arnold, 1994).

German personnel and industrial strength to the common defense. It also would have controlled German militarism by uniting all the member states' armies under a single commander. The EDC would have had a directly elected European parliament and an executive that could be dismissed by the parliament, making it virtually a "United States of Europe."

In the end the EDC idea was rejected. Not enough Europeans (especially the French) were ready to give up such sweeping powers to a supranational institution. Guided by the Maastricht treaty, the European Union will attempt to fill the major gaps in European unification concerning military security and international politics. Europeans make various efforts to coordinate foreign and military policy and to pursue some common military activities, along with other powers, within such organizations as NATO, the Western European Union, and the OSCE (Organization on Security and Cooperation in Europe). Still, to date, they have no joint military force, common nuclear deterrent, or even common foreign policy in such areas as Bosnia or the Middle East. Of the three goals behind European unification—goals that different Europeans rank differently in importance—unified foreign and military policy remains the most elusive.

## TRYING TO EXPLAIN PEACE

Scholars of world politics have offered several explanations for why there is peace within the OECD area. They are presented below, and alternative hypotheses are evaluated.

**Hypothesis 1: Cohesion in the Face of Outside Threats**    Peace in the OECD area resulted when nations came together in response to a *common threat* by an external enemy—in this case, the Soviet Union.

Most, though not all, citizens of the OECD countries indeed felt a security threat from the Soviet Union for most of the period since World War II. A desire for common defense, the strength that derives from a joint effort, was one of the motivations behind the European unity movement and, of course, behind NATO. The perceived need to act together helped produce a determination to overcome differences within the OECD community and was initially important. The sense of threat was greatest in the early years of NATO, the late 1940s and the 1950s, and may have helped to bring peace within Europe and to spawn NATO. But the threat was not necessary to *sustain* peace among these countries, nor was the threat urgent enough to establish the EDC. During Soviet–U.S. detente in the 1960s and early 1970s, people in the West no longer thought a Soviet invasion of Western Europe or a Soviet attack on the United States was very likely. If the sense of external threat was the principal cement holding the OECD countries together in peaceful relations, we should have seen a decline in stable peace during recent decades. Actually, quite the opposite occurred: people also

became more confident about the maintenance of peace between the traditional enemies among the industrialized countries. Possibly one might claim that the peace
among U.S. allies was enforced by the United States itself, so as not to weaken the
common defense. But except for the conflicts between Greece and Turkey, enforcement simply has not been needed in Western Europe. By contrast, the Soviet Union
repeatedly intervened militarily, as well as threatened to do so, in the affairs of its East
European allies. In general, allies are more likely to fight each other than are unallied
states.[9]

We also find that the OECD case does not very well meet the set of conditions
under which social psychologists have found that an external threat promotes internal
cohesion. These conditions include a sense that there is an ability to counter the threat,
some prior experience in acting as a group, and the view by all parties that the threat
is common, affecting all members of the group equally.[10]

The first of these conditions was met: OECD members knew that if they could act
together, they certainly had the resources—population, wealth, and technological
sophistication—to counter any Soviet threat. The second condition, however—prior
experience as a group—was not met. There was little experience of close cooperation
among OECD countries before World War II, and during World War II the group was
clearly divided. Nor could it be said that the threat affected all members equally.
Some, like Japan and West Germany, were very close to Soviet military power and the
threat of invasion; others, like the United States and Britain, were protected by distance and natural barriers. Peace among these countries, therefore, does not seem the
result of any uniform experience of a common external threat. Indeed, we know that
in some cases an external threat can fracture cohesion. The possibility that the Aus-
tro–Hungarian Empire would be invaded in World War I was seen not always as a
danger but sometimes as an opportunity for some of the subjugated Slavic peoples
(Czechs, Slovaks, Poles, Croatians, and Slovenes) to free themselves from Austrian
and Hungarian domination. Similarly, a perceived common threat from Israel has not
brought peace among all the Arab countries. Clearly, other factors are at work.

**Hypothesis 2: Institution Building**     Peace in the OECD area resulted from the construction of governmental institutions, especially the supranational institutions binding together several countries. The best examples are the political and economic
institutions developed during the evolution of the European Economic Community
into the European Union.

For some theorists, the important aspect of *institutions* is that they can forcibly keep
the peace. They are the wielders of the only legitimate instruments of violence—the

---

[9] See Erich Weede, "Extended Deterrence by Superpower Alliance," *Journal of Conflict Resolution* 27, 2
(1983), 231–254; see also Bruce Bueno de Mesquita, *The War Trap* (New Haven, Conn.: Yale University
Press, 1981).
[10] See Arthur Stein, "Conflict and Cohesion: A Review of the Literature," *Journal of Conflict Resolution*
20, 1 (March 1976), 143–165.

army and police—and as a result can impose order and compel obedience for the common good. For other influential theorists concerned with the processes and outcomes of social integration, specific institutions attending to particular needs or functions of society can create habits of obedience and cooperation. This group of theorists owes much to the **functionalist** ideas of David Mitrany; their views are well expressed in the early work of Ernst Haas on neo-functionalist models of integration.

Perhaps Haas's greatest contribution was to focus attention on the political process of *transferring loyalties to new institutions* rather than simply focusing on institution building alone. Two quotations from his classic study, *The Uniting of Europe*, make this clear. First: "Political community, therefore, is a condition in which specific groups and individuals show more loyalty to their central political institutions than to any other political authority." Second, defining political integration as the process leading to the transfer of loyalties: "[T]he existence of political institutions capable of translating ideologies into law [is] the cornerstone of the definition." For Haas it was particularly the loyalties of elites—those involved in or with the government—that matter, more than the loyalties of the mass public.[11]

Studies have shown that, regardless of the focus of mass loyalties or attention, major political actors, including interest groups, know that the action is to be found at EC (now EU) headquarters in Brussels. For instance, in 1960 the Commission of the EC numbered 1,000 permanent civil servants, and 167 lobbying organizations (producers' and professionals' groups) were registered in Brussels. However, by 1988 those numbers had grown to 15,000 and 435, respectively; by the end of 1994 there were 18,000 Brussels bureaucrats.[12] The Commission can set common standards for the movement of goods, services, workers, and capital across national boundaries. Further harmonization of standards, elimination of nontariff barriers and national regulations, and creation of a European monetary system were included in the Maastricht treaty, which was the fulfillment of the Single European Act sponsored by the Commission's chief, Jacques Delors. The Commission forms the executive branch, complemented by the European Court of Justice as the judiciary branch and the European Parliament as the legislature. The Parliament, however, has few powers over the Commission, leading some people to regard the Commission as a rather undemocratic institution.

For functionalists the important aspect of what happens is the *spillover* of activities from some functions (for example, the coal and steel industry), creating the impetus toward more integration. One analyst defines spillover as

---

[11] Ernst Haas, *The Uniting of Europe* (Stanford, Calif.: Stanford University Press, 1957), pp. 4, 7. Haas later moved away from his earlier concerns with institutions to look at multidimensional patterns of interdependence both within and outside regional groups: see "Turbulent Fields and the Theory of Regional Integration," *International Organization* 30, 2 (Spring 1976), 173–212.

[12] Willem Moelle, *The Economics of European Integration* (Aldershot, England: Dartmouth, 1990), p. 476. See also Edward Nevin, *The Economics of Europe* (London: Macmillan, 1990), and Archer, *Organizing Europe*.

the process whereby members of an integration scheme—agreed on some collective goals for a variety of motives but unequally satisfied with the attainment of these goals—attempt to resolve their dissatisfaction either by resorting to collaboration in another, related sector (expanding the scope of mutual commitment) or by intensifying their commitment to the original sector (increasing the level of mutual commitment) or both.[13]

Thus Robert Schuman could say, "Europe will not be built in a day nor as part of some over-all design. It will be built through practical achievements that first create a sense of common purpose." Many theorists thought that spillover might progress automatically as well as be irreversible, leading inexorably to full European integration. We now can see, however, that the process is more deliberate: "The European Community can best be viewed as a set of complex overlapping networks, in which a supranational style of decision-making, characterized by compromises upgrading common interests, can under favorable conditions lead to the pooling of sovereignty."[14]

It is certainly true that stable peace has been achieved among members of the EU. For countries now so highly interdependent, the EU institutions are essential in solving members' common problems and perhaps in preventing tensions that could endanger the peace. Yet the area of peace includes all the OECD countries, not just the EU. Although there are a variety of important institutions like the Council of Europe, NATO, and the OECD itself, these are not in any significant way coercive organizations. For instance, in peacetime the NATO Supreme Headquarters does not command the troops of the constituent countries. Save for the institutions of the EU, they must work principally by negotiation and consensus among members, not by enforcement.

A national government coerces all of us by requiring us to pay our taxes. We may grumble, but on the whole we accept this coercion as long as it is applied reasonably equally among people. Because we want most of the benefits—health care, education, defense, and so forth—that a modern government provides, we are more or less willing to be coerced to pay our share as long as others are equally required to pay. Most OECD institutions lack this kind of power; rather, they *facilitate* mutual attention and problem solving among the members. This role is very important and probably essential for interdependent countries, but it is a far cry from a common government.

In addition, the only serious expectation or actuality of violent conflict within the OECD area in recent years has been within a few countries, notably Northern Ireland. It is not simply that an institution—the common government—is unable to prevent violence; rather, the fact of common government is a *cause* of the violence. The separatists want to be free of the common government. There have been many cases of civil war or secessionist revolution in history. The revolt of the 13 American colonies

---

[13] Philippe Schmitter, "Three Neo-Functional Hypotheses About International Integration," *International Organization* 24, 1 (Winter 1969), 162.

[14] Robert O. Keohane and Stanley Hoffmann, "Conclusions: Community Politics and Institutional Change," in William Wallace, ed., *The Dynamics of European Integration* (London: Pinter, 1990), p. 276.

and the later unsuccessful secession attempt by the Confederate states well illustrate this fact. One of the most significant contributions of Karl Deutsch's *Political Community and the North Atlantic Area* (1957) was to point out what should have been obvious: people may fight against a common government but then live in peace as separate states. Common institutions are no panacea for peace; thus, neither is any simple prescription of world government. For Deutsch the goal of integration is peace; institution building at best contributes to that kind of integration but is often irrelevant or even destructive to it. A second significant contribution of Deutsch's work has been his reminder that there is always the possibility of *dis*integration. Integration must be thought of as a difficult process that needs continual attention—an "imperfect assembly line" that may fail at any number of points.[15]

**Hypothesis 3: Economic Ties and Social Communication**    Peace in the OECD area resulted from strong *economic ties and links of social communication.*

The importance of economic and communication links is strongly emphasized by Deutsch and others who share his perspective. These links become facilities for attention to one another and for identifying one's interests with those of others. One cannot help to meet the needs of another without knowing what those needs are; that is, without a large, continuous flow of information. There is a social fabric between as well as within nations that is built from such bonds as trade, travel (as migration and as tourism), cultural and educational exchange, and the use of communication facilities like the telephone and television. These ties communicate the needs and perspectives of one group of people to others; they strengthen the sense of a collective identity within the collectivity. In the tradition of sociological theory, these community bonds are part of the *Gemeinschaft*—common loyalties and values, a feeling of belonging together—in contrast to the *Gesellschaft*, which emphasizes competitiveness, contractual arrangements, and institutions. These bonds affect not only the elites but also the attitudes and beliefs at all "politically relevant strata" of the population, which include the mass public in democracies. Deutsch terms the relevant sense of **community**

> a matter of mutual sympathy and loyalties; of "we-feeling," trust, and mutual consideration; of partial identification in terms of self-images and interests; of mutually successful predictions of behavior . . . in short, a matter of a perpetual dynamic process of mutual attention, communication, perception of needs, and responsiveness in the process of decision making.[16]

"Learning during regional integration is a direct result of mutually rewarding actions among regional partners."[17] In Chapter 8 we reviewed some liberal trans-

---

[15] See Karl W. Deutsch, "National Integration: Some Concepts and Research Approaches," *Jerusalem Journal of International Relations* 2 (1977), 1–29.

[16] Deutsch et al., *Political Community and the North Atlantic Area*, p. 36.

[17] Donald Puchala, "The Pattern of Contemporary Regional Integration," *International Studies Quarterly* 22, 1 (March 1968), 51.

nationalist theories about the peace-promoting effect of economic ties. A piece of evidence from the very early days of European integration illustrates the contribution of such ties to predicting each other's behavior and communicating desires accurately. A study of French business leaders and their attitudes toward the (ultimately rejected) EDC found that those who engaged in no foreign trade whatever tended to favor the establishment of the EDC by a margin of two to one, but individuals whose firms did at least half their business in foreign trade favored the EDC by a margin of six to one. The issues at stake went well beyond the direct economic interests of the individuals involved. Economic contacts become general channels of communication, opening up individuals to information and viewpoints they would not otherwise receive.[18] A review of the literature on international exchange and attitude change concluded:

> These are not necessarily changes in general favorableness toward the host country, but rather changes in the cognitive structure—for example in the complexity and differentiation of images of the host country. Such changes are probably more meaningful in the long run than total approval of the country would be; they indicate a greater richness and refinement of images and a greater understanding of the other society in its own terms.[19]

Though they usually seem to bind nations or social groups together, trade, tourism, and migration can also serve as irritants. The most important qualification—a serious one—is that the exchanges must be mutual and on a basis of relative equality. Ties perceived as exploitative or colonial, however strong, do not seem to bring groups together. Contacts that are involuntary for one party (an extreme case being the payment of reparations) are not facilitative, nor are highly status-conscious relations, such as those between employer and employee.

Contacts between very disparate cultures are also as likely to arouse conflict as to bring the cultures together. Tourists from rich countries to poor countries, for instance, may create animosities among their hosts and distress in their own minds. The nature of the contacts in each particular case must be examined before any firm conclusions about their effects are made. However, a very general observation can be made: ties between nations that are culturally similar and perhaps geographically close are more likely to be favorable.

Economic interdependence also gives one party a material stake in the prosperity and stability of the other's economic system. One cannot sell goods or services to others unless the others can afford to buy them. When strong economic links work both ways, each party has an important stake in the other. The trade among the OECD countries, for example, accounts for over 75 percent of their total international trade. The ratio of foreign trade to GNP is another useful indicator of the degree of interdependence—of the importance of foreign commerce to the overall level of economic activity. The total trade of OECD countries is about one third of their GNP. In looking at the pattern of conflict and war throughout the world since 1950, a new

---

[18] Daniel Lerner, "French Business Leaders Look at EDC," *Public Opinion Quarterly* 20, 1 (1956), 220.
[19] Herbert Kelman, ed., *International Behavior* (New York: Holt, Rinehart & Winston, 1965), p. 573.

study has found that economic interdependence—along with influences like wealth, economic growth, and democracy, which we shall discuss shortly—contributed importantly to reducing the likelihood of violence between countries.[20]

The relatively weak economic ties within the industrialized world during the Depression years after 1930 help explain the political tensions that culminated in World War II. The high levels of economic interdependence created among those countries since about 1970 certainly help reinforce the peaceful and basically cooperative relations they now enjoy. But peace among the industrialized countries was well established even before the high levels of economic interdependence were achieved in the 1970s. Economic interdependence therefore should receive some credit, but other forces also must be at work.

**Hypothesis 4: Economic Benefits**   Peace in the OECD area resulted from the achievement and continued expectation of *substantial economic benefits* to all the members.

This hypothesis reflects Deutsch's findings that conditions that promote a security community include superior economic growth, the expectation of joint economic rewards, and a wide range of mutual transactions. Deutsch found these conditions "helpful" to what he called "**pluralistic security communities,**" security communities that include several independent countries *without* a common supranational government. The concept of a pluralistic community is important, because it indicates that a successful integration process can take place without necessarily resulting in a new, unified, or consolidated state. Deutsch, however, suggested that these economic conditions might be essential for a security community in which various peoples were united under a common government. Economic growth provides the resources to compensate people who lose some of their traditional markets or benefits (a significant aspect of the debates about, and adjustments to, the expansion of EU authority and regulation). If the total pie is getting larger, they may be able to find new ones.

Certainly a high level of economic activity and a high rate of economic growth are prominent features of the OECD. Virtually all the OECD countries experienced rapid economic growth after World War II. This was especially true for the defeated states, Germany and Japan, which benefited from various forms of American assistance and by 1960 had totally recovered from their devastation. By contrast, the negative economic growth for most OECD countries during much of the 1920s and 1930s—the time of the Great Depression—was probably a major cause of World War II. Germany's economic difficulties, including rampant inflation followed by mass unemployment, led directly to Hitler's accession to power in 1933. Many of the industrialized countries, in an effort to maintain their own balance of payments, adopted various protectionist measures to restrict imports from other industrial countries. The result was a set of "beggar-thy-neighbor" policies that reduced international trade and led to a further decline in everyone's income. Conflicts over economic poli-

---

[20] John Oneal, Frances Oneal, Zeev Maoz, and Bruce Russett, "The Liberal Peace: Interdependence, Democracy, and International Conflict, 1950–1986," *Journal of Peace Research* 33, 1 (February 1996).

cies were a major cause of international tension and contributed to Japanese expansionist political and military actions. Here we have a good example of low or negative growth severely damaging the prospects for peace.

We must also be aware, however, that in several important theories about the causes of violence, economic growth plays the villain's role. Some of the theories that we shall examine in the next chapter specify that rapid economic growth within LDCs, especially if its benefits are distributed very unequally, leads to serious domestic conflict. If some people are gaining little or actually losing while others are visibly enriching themselves, economic growth may well produce feelings of relative deprivation and make revolutionary movements popular. Thus the distribution of economic rewards is an important element in determining whether growth contributes to peace.

Here we see another of Deutsch's conditions, the need for joint economic reward. On this ground the OECD countries of the past 30 or 40 years fare very well. Except for a couple of oil-rich OPEC countries, the OECD countries are by far the world's richest, with an average GNP per capita of about $21,500 in 1991, when the world average was $4,000. Moreover, these high living standards apply fairly equally among the various developed industrialized countries. Whereas worldwide GNP per capita ranged from under $100 in Mozambique to more than $33,600 in Switzerland, the range within the OECD was narrower: from Switzerland to Turkey's $1,780.[21]

Income is also distributed relatively equally within these countries. Figure 14.1 shows the distribution of income in the United States, which is fairly typical of developed-market economies, and in Brazil, a less developed country. In the developed countries, the poorest 20 percent of households typically receive around 5 percent or more of the income of all households in the country; the richest 10 percent of households typically receive between 20 and 30 percent of all household income. (Many OECD countries in fact have even greater income equality than does the United States.) In LDCs, the poorest of the poor, the lowest 20 percent, may get less than 5 percent of all the income of the country, whereas the richest 10 percent may take in 40 to 50 percent. Certainly there are serious inequalities even within the industrialized countries, particularly among ethnic and racial minorities or in particular geographic regions. But compared with most less developed countries, OECD countries distribute their income quite equitably.

Within the OECD, however, equality is not a sufficient condition for peace. Economic inequalities, while significant, do not constitute the main grievance in Northern Ireland, where conflict is based on religious and cultural differences. The Basques live in one of the most prosperous parts of Spain; again, the conflicts are over cultural and linguistic autonomy rather than over economics. These few exceptions are not enough to indicate that economic equality is irrelevant to peace. It still may matter in important ways. Without equality, a state of "nonwar" is likely to be imposed by the dominance of the rich over the poor. Thus the trade relations between rich and poor

---

[21] These are World Bank figures calculated using standard methods based on exchange rates. Differences are somewhat smaller using PPP-based GNP calculations, where the lowest GNP per capita is estimated at $380 for Mozambique or Ethiopia, and the highest is Luxembourg's $29,510. The gap closes within the OECD as well.

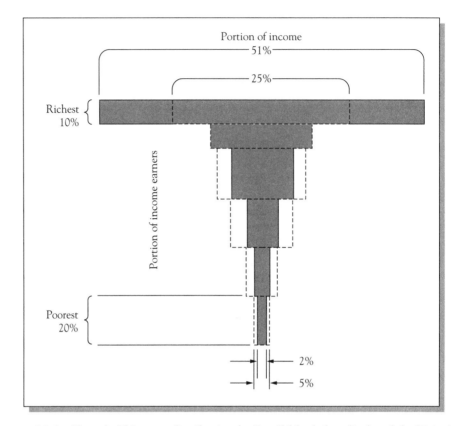

**Figure 14.1** Household income distribution for Brazil (shaded outline) and the United States (dashed outline). [*Source:* Data from World Bank, *World Development Report, 1993* (Washington, D.C.: World Bank, 1993), p. 297.]

countries may be significant, but if they are not seen as producing equivalent rewards on both sides, they will not promote peaceful relations. High levels of wealth and equality do mean that all citizens would have a great deal to lose in a war. The level of destruction from a big war among industrialized countries would be far greater than the gain realized from any victory.

This suggests that perhaps a combination of moderate growth (not so great as to produce rapid social change and dislocation or to stimulate imperialism greatly), equality, and a high level of economic activity constitutes a set of conditions for peace. This makes sense if most decisions to go to war are rational acts; that is, if war is initiated by decision makers who calculate, to the best of their ability, the probable costs and benefits of their acts. Decision makers value many things (honor, prestige, cultural autonomy, their own political positions, and so forth) besides material advantage. Moreover, they often calculate poorly, on the basis of incomplete or erroneous information. What may look like an act that will produce more benefits than costs may turn out to do quite the opposite. Nevertheless, decision makers attempt to make such calculations. In a war among OECD countries, the prospective gains would not be high (existing equalities mean that a conquered rich country would not be so much richer than its poorer conqueror). The costs of such a war, however, would likely be very high: economic growth would be interrupted, many buildings and much capital equipment would be destroyed, and existing wealth would be severely eroded. With such high prospective costs, war with another developed-market economy just does not look cost-effective at all. Any rational wars, with other kinds of countries, will be limited and distant, where the expected losses would be low. Rich countries and economically growing countries are less likely than others to have serious disputes with each other.[22]

Thus we have one plausible hypothesis: stable peace can be maintained under conditions of moderate growth, equity, and a high level of economic activity. Where such conditions do not exist, peace is more likely to be maintained, if at all, only through deterrence, mutual or one-sided. This leaves us with an unanswered question: Why did we not have stable peace (rather than a peace maintained only by deterrence) between the OECD countries and the Soviet Union and Eastern Europe? Perhaps there was not quite enough equity between the two sides. For instance, in 1985 the average GNP per capita in Eastern Europe and the Soviet Union was under $5,000, compared with about $11,500 in the OECD countries. Or perhaps we have reached the limits of arguments about economic conditions as causes of peace or war and must now look for additional explanations.

Deutsch suggests that two additional conditions are essential for achieving a security community: that the major values held by the populations in question be compatible and that a situation of mutual responsiveness exist among these populations. Neither of these conditions, however, sounds like an independent cause. We suggested earlier that mutual responsiveness was likely to arise when there was a high level of communications and transactions between countries; without creation of a community with such links, there is insufficient knowledge about one another to make responsiveness possible. Compatibility of major values sounds like a condition that would contribute to responsiveness and not merely be incidental. Actually, both responsiveness and compatibility appear to arise in large part because of the ties of community. They can then contribute to peace and be firmly established by the condition of peace. But neither seems like an independent factor contributing to peace.

Furthermore, compatibility of major values sounds like a circular argument: if there is no peace, major value differences seem to explain its absence. Without very carefully specifying what constitutes a major value (religion, political system, culture,

---

[22] The theoretical argument is well presented by John Mueller, *Retreat from Doomsday* (New York: Basic Books, 1989). Systematic empirical studies are Stuart Bremer, "Dangerous Dyads: Conditions Affecting the Likelihood of Interstate War, 1816–1965," *Journal of Conflict Resolution* 36, 2 (June 1992); Zeev Maoz and Bruce Russett, "Normative and Structural Causes of Democratic Peace, 1946–1986," *American Political Science Review* 87, 3 (September 1993), 624–638; and Bruce Russett, *Grasping the Democratic Peace* (Princeton: Princeton University Press, 1993).

or type of economic structure), it is too easy to twist facts to make them fit. Thus the OECD countries are very similar in some kinds of values (every OECD country is now a constitutional democracy and has a market economy), but very different in other ways, holding values that in the not-too-distant past were the cause of major wars. In the seventeenth-century European religious wars, Catholics and Protestants slaughtered each other by the millions; consequently, it is not convincing to say that Christianity constitutes a compatible major value. Even more damaging to the significance of a compatible major value are the great cultural differences that still exist between Japan and the rest of the OECD countries, whose cultures are of European origin. This difference is very substantial, yet it does not prevent Japan and the others from living in a condition of stable peace. This situation may nonetheless suggest a value that, if widely held, would contribute to peace: constitutional democracy.

**Hypothesis 5: Democratic Practice and Belief**   Peace in the OECD area resulted from the widespread acceptance in all countries of the values and institutions of *constitutional democracy*.

Since the restoration of democracy in Greece, Portugal, and Spain in the early 1970s, all OECD countries have had democratic forms of government. Their governments are, by worldwide standards, relatively nonrepressive—certainly less repressive than many governments in the less developed world or the former communist regimes of Eastern Europe. In this respect the present OECD governments also differ markedly from many of their governments in the late 1930s, when Germany, Italy, Japan, Spain, and Portugal were all ruled by fascist dictatorships.

Studies of the frequency of war over the past two centuries have shown clearly that although democracies were as likely to be involved in war as were countries with other kinds of government, the experience of democracies did stand out in one respect: democratic countries almost never (or *never,* by some definitions of democracy and war) made war on each other (review the discussion presented in chapter 8). They also were very *unlikely even to have serious militarized disputes,* short of war, with each other. This is true even when controls are made for other variables that also affect the frequency with which countries have conflicts with one another: distance, common alliance membership (Hypothesis 1), economic interdependence (Hypothesis 3), and wealth and economic growth (Hypothesis 4).[23]

It is this particular form of government that seems to matter. If similarity of form of government in general were enough, then we would expect to have seen peace between the Soviet Union and China, between the Soviet Union and its Eastern European neighbors, and between China and Vietnam. Despite important differences in political values and organization among the communist countries, they were much more like one another, especially in values or ideology, than like the democracies or even like right-wing dictatorships. Yet war or the threat of war between these countries was commonplace.

---

[23] See Bremer, "Dangerous Dyads," and Russett, *Grasping the Democratic Peace,* and Oneal et al., "The Liberal Peace."

Several explanations have been offered for this striking phenomenon. One emphasizes perceptions of individual rights, expectations of limited government, shifting coalitions, and toleration of dissent by a presumably loyal opposition. By this explanation, the culture, perceptions, and practices that permit the peaceful resolution of conflicts of interest without the threat of violence within democracies come to apply across national boundaries toward other democratic countries. In short, people within a democracy perceive themselves as autonomous, self-governing people who share norms of live-and-let-live and who respect the rights of others to self-determination, if those others are also perceived as self-governing and hence not easily led into aggressive foreign policies by a self-serving elite. The openness of society and free flow of information that characterize democracies facilitate these perceptions. They also help prevent the development of demonic enemy images, which are often created by elites as necessary to justify war against another people. The same structures and behaviors that are assumed to limit our aggression, both internally and externally, may also be expected to limit similarly governed people in other political units. Even though all these images may involve a significant degree of myth as well as reality, they still operate as powerful restraints on violence between such systems.[24]

By contrast, these restraints do not apply when the two countries are governed according to very different norms and at least one of them is not democratic. The leaders of the nondemocratic state are seen as being in a permanent state of aggression against their own people, and thus also against foreigners. For example, the essence of cold war ideology on both sides was always that the United States (Soviet Union) had no quarrel with the Russian (American) people, but only with the atheistic communist (greedy capitalist) elites who repressed (exploited) them. Such a vision of the other people as not in self-governing control of their own destiny justified the hostile policy on each side.

An alternative explanation argues that institutional constraints—a structure of division of powers, checks and balances—make it hard for democratic leaders to move their countries into war. The argument becomes complex. Foreign policy decision makers develop images of the government and public opinion of other countries. They regard some governments or peoples as reluctant to fight (doves) or as belligerent (hawks). In developing these images, leaders look for cues in other leaders' and countries' past behavior in diplomatic or military disputes and in other countries' forms of government. If leaders generally regard democracies as doves (reluctant to fight, either because of the institutional constraints or because of a general aversion of the people to war), democracies will not fear being attacked by another democracy. Two democratic states—each constrained from going to war and assuming that the other is so inhibited—will be likely to settle their conflicts short of war.

Nondemocracies, however, if they are themselves hawks, may anticipate that democratic countries (doves) will be slow to go to war, and therefore they may be

---

[24] See R. J. Rummel, "Libertarian Propositions on Violence Within and Between Nations," *Journal of Conflict Resolution* 29, 3 (1985) 419–455; Michael W. Doyle, "Liberalism and World Politics," *American Political Science Review* 80, 4 (December 1986), 1151–1169; and Bruce Russett, *Grasping the Democratic Peace*. See also footnotes 14–16 in Chapter 8.

more likely to threaten or bully a democracy to make concessions. That in turn would raise the threshold of "provocation" facing the democracy and perhaps overcome its initial unwillingness to fight. This would account for the fact that the overall frequency of participation in war by democracies is not very different from that of nondemocratic states, and that we might also expect democracies to be aggressive toward nondemocratic hawks.[25]

All the evidence is not in as to whether the perceptual or the structural explanation for democracies' peaceful behavior toward each other is the more powerful. Probably both make a contribution. Something important certainly does.

## POLITICAL AND ECONOMIC CONDITIONS FOR GLOBAL PEACE

When it was specifically applied to the OECD countries, we largely rejected Hypothesis 1, attributing peace to the existence of an external threat. Arguing only for Hypothesis 1 reveals the flaws in realist analyses. One realist scholar has indeed argued that the postwar peace stemmed from the distribution of military capabilities in the anarchic system and that peace in Western Europe stemmed from the Soviet threat. Such a position ignores the theory and actual occurrence of integration; it ignores the positive aspects of interdependence and stresses only the negative aspects. It ignores the effects proposed in Hypotheses 2 through 5.[26]

Hypothesis 2 was not so clearly rejected as Hypothesis 1. Institutions and community ties surely make important contributions to achieving and maintaining OECD peace, but there is peace among OECD countries with low as well as high institutional bonds. Hypothesis 3 certainly provides some explanation, even though there was peace in the OECD area in the 25 years or so before economic interactions reached the high level characterized by the last quarter of a century. The two remaining hypotheses look even more persuasive: Hypothesis 4, which we restated as a requirement for moderate growth, equality, and a high level of economic activity (that is, the achievement and continued expectation of mutual economic rewards), and Hypothesis 5, the acceptance of the values and institutions of constitutional democracy. Both look plausible as applied to the OECD and have a more general base of evidence from other times and places.

We looked at influences operating at all levels of analysis. At the individual level, we noted the important role that people of vision, like Jean Monnet and Robert Schu-

---

[25] Bruce Bueno de Mesquita and David Lalman, *War and Reason* (New Haven, Conn.: Yale University Press, 1992), chap. 5, present this institutional-perceptual hypothesis and some confirming evidence. Harvey Starr supports their arguments by specifically linking their analyses to Deutsch's theory of integration; "Democracy and War: Choice, Learning and Security Communities," *Journal of Peace Research* 29, 4 (1992), 41–59.

[26] See Mearsheimer, "Back to the Future."

man, played at key moments. Although their vision would not have been sufficient if underlying conditions had not been right, nothing would have happened if there had not been people able to conceive and carry out the plans.[27] Conversely, we might have talked about the power of particular individuals to delay or divert integration schemes—for example, President Charles de Gaulle's veto of British entry into the EC, delaying British participation for nearly a decade. Governmental structures or institutions constitute important sites of communication and negotiation, whether or not supranational institutions also exist. We suggested that economies had to be capable of growth and to exhibit reasonably equitable distributions of income and wealth. Institutions for popular participation in government and self-determination are important and are not found in all states. At the levels of relations between states and the international system, we have considered many questions about supranational institutions and transnational linkages of trade and social communications.

Within societies, Deutsch's social communications model of integration starts at the level of the mass society, builds through transnational transactions between societies, and leads to interactions among governmental elites. The neo-functionalist integration model of Haas starts at the level of governmental bureaucracies and creates government-to-government ties that eventually lead to fuller societal interaction. For integration to occur, both processes must take place (and have taken place in Western Europe). Note that both processes are based on learning—learning that the interactions with other societies or governments are beneficial, creating mutual payoffs and the promise of more benefits in the future (with growing interdependence increasing the costs of stopping the integration process).

The vulnerabilities created by interdependence can very easily create conflict among states. But in stable peace, the states and peoples involved gain mutual benefits from their interconnectedness. These positive aspects outweigh the costs of vulnerability. Many international interactions—if not international relations as a whole—are ventures in which collaborative or cooperative interests outweigh competitive ones. Integration must be seen as a process for the positive management of interdependence—cooperation is the only way to manage interdependence among states without domination or constant warfare.

The Deutschian social communication model is concerned with transactions, such as the linkage between trade and democracy seen in Figure 4.2. Those transactions, however, must be at a high level relative to transactions within each state, and high relative to those states' transactions with other states. And, as noted, they must be balanced—with significant rewards for both sides and without domination by either side. The European experiment with integration has demonstrated positive effects between trade (transactions) and democracy, and negative effects between trade and conflict. From our discussions here and in Chapter 8 we also know about all the evidence for the "democratic peace" proposition—the nonoccurrence of violent conflict

---

[27] That is, for any policy to be established, in addition to the conditions of opportunity and willingness there need to be individual "entrepreneurs" who will take the lead in pushing a policy. See the model provided by John W. Kingdon, *Agendas, Alternatives and Public Policies* (New York: Harper-Collins, 1984).

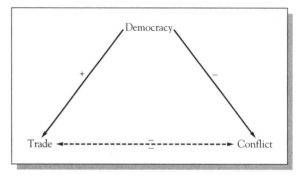

**FIGURE 14.2**   Elements of integration

between democracies. This is seen in the right-hand leg of the triangle. The effect of economic interdependence in reducing conflict is shown by the right-hand arrow along the base of the triangle. These two arrows are mutually reinforcing, as democracies usually are free-market or mixed economies open to the world economy. Another arrow goes the opposite way along the base, since countries who are fighting each other, or expect to fight each other, typically don't want to trade very much with each other. Finally, along the left-hand leg of the triangle is an arrow from democracy to trade, in line with our point about democracies typically carrying on high levels of free trade with one another.

We now can speculate on whether the experience of the OECD countries gives us any basis to hope that a stable peace based on something more than simply dominance or mutual deterrence can be achieved in other parts of the world or by the OECD countries with other states. In doing so, we break the bonds of realist assumptions about the inevitability of the pursuit of power leading to violent conflict. We are thinking like idealists and transnationalists in the search for hints of what an alternative world might look like, yet thinking "realistically" in the sense of asking whether conditions that *already exist* in part of the world might be extended further. Indeed, several scholars have looked at the positive interdependence process of integration and explicitly noted that integration provided an alternative to the realist notions of international "anarchy." By showing that states could collaborate on important issues that extended beyond traditional notions of security, that economic ties of corporations and classes across national boundaries were important, and that states could create supranational organizations that constrained them but helped them collaborate (and by explaining how such behavior could take place), integration scholars directly challenged the assumptions of realism. In the words of one such scholar, integration studies have revealed patterns of behavior that were "not supposed to happen or were not supposed to be very consequential if and when they did."[28]

---

[28] See Donald J. Puchala, "Integration Theory and the Study of International Relations," in Richard Merritt and Bruce M. Russett, eds., *From National Development to Global Community* (London: Allen & Unwin, 1981), p. 147.

Many countries that had formerly been dictatorships—both communist countries and military regimes—have moved partially or almost entirely toward free democratic governments. The shift has been dramatic and almost worldwide. A key question is whether relations in all of Europe, including the former communist countries, can be those of a security community. Liberalization and glasnost began in the 1980s. By 1991 several Eastern European countries were fully democratic, and all had progressed far in that direction. That bodes well for a peaceful future. In none of these states, however, is democracy secure. If perceptions of the other as a democratic state are important to peace, an aspect of that must be perception of the other as dependably, stably democratic. That is much less certain. Few Eastern European countries have an experience of stable democratic practices and institutions (none, except for the former Czechoslovakia, had more than ten years of multiparty democracy in this century prior to 1990). They are beset by ethnic and nationalist rivalries, as seen within Russia (for instance, the major conflict in Chechnya) and especially in the former Yugoslavia. Such forces also led to the (peaceful) separation of Slovakia from the Czech Republic. Democracy does not automatically cure these ills; by relieving the dictatorial controls that previously suppressed the expression of nationalism, it may even make things worse.

A second problem, related to the first, is the difficult economic situation of these states. All of them have experienced abrupt drops in their national incomes, as they have lost their former assured markets and supplies in other communist countries (previously joined economically in COMECON) and, especially, as they move painfully from socialist command economies to free-market ones. Already poor by Western European standards, if these states' economies do not begin to grow, and are not given full access to markets in the rich democracies, they will have economic conditions just opposite to those that promote peace (Hypotheses 3 and 4). Moreover, the people may not indefinitely support democratic governments that cannot deliver the economic goods; we have already seen the reelection of former communist leaders in several places. Some former Soviet republics such as Azerbaijan, Turkmenistan, and Uzbekistan have already been downgraded from "partially free" to "not free" by analysts (see Appendix B). These countries are not yet the dependably stable democratic regimes that most strongly promote the "democracies-almost-never-fight-each-other" condition.

The prospects are especially worrisome for Russia, partly because it is by far the biggest of the former communist countries and still a nuclear superpower. In addition, democratization and the creation of a market economy have further to go there, with a lower level of previous achievement, than in almost any other European country. Finally, nationalism is an especially serious problem there. Whether Russia can both remain somewhat united and become fully democratic remains to be seen. One, or both, of those goals may have to yield.

We are saying, then, that even if stable and established democracies are generally at peace with one another, one cannot so readily say that the *process of democratization* is necessarily a peaceful one. A brand-new democracy may be unstable and may face fierce problems of restructuring its economy and satisfying diverse interests and ethnic groups. Under these perhaps temporary circumstances, nationalism and pressures to divert attention from domestic problems to foreign antagonists may lead to conflicts with neighboring states.[29] Or authoritarian neighbors may see a new and not yet consolidated democracy as weak and a suitable target for aggression. (Transitions of democracies to authoritarian regimes are equally dangerous, however. Political instability in general, not just democratization, is the problem.)

Similarly, the requirements for economic growth and the equality of economic distribution worldwide are very demanding, given the experience of the LDCs over the past few decades. Economic stagnation has been the lot of many; although others have strong records of growth by conventional measures like GNP per capita, the record of equitable distribution within those countries is very mixed. Often economic inequality is maintained by authoritarian and coercive political institutions—a further departure from the conditions that obtain in the industrialized countries. On this basis, although it is possible to imagine stable peace arising in a few areas of the developing world where conditions are favorable, it is much harder to imagine its achievement worldwide. There is the intriguing but daunting possibility that stable peace, economic equality, decent living conditions, and political liberties may be bound together in an inseparable package; thus to strive for one requires us to strive for them all.

Some theories, especially radical ones, about the causes of underdevelopment and authoritarianism in the developing world lay much of the blame on poor countries' dependence on and penetration by the rich, industrialized countries. Such theories allege that growth, relative equality, and political peace within rich countries are obtained only by exploiting the working classes of the poor countries through multinational corporations and other means. If these theories are correct, stable peace within the industrialized countries is impossible without such exploitation. We shall discuss this issue in the next chapter.

---

[29] Edward Mansfield and Jack Snyder, "Democratization and War," *International Security* 20,1 (Summer 1995), 5–38.

## ECONOMICS AND POLITICS: INTERDEPENDENCE, DEMOCRACY, AND DEVELOPMENT

**W**e have seen that interdependence binds the units within systems and that managing interdependence is a way of dealing with present and future world problems. But interdependence has two aspects. The security dilemma, arms races, and nuclear strategy illustrate possible *negative aspects* of interdependence, from the management of interdependence based on threats to the use of military instruments of influence. The models and reality of integration demonstrate the *positive aspect* of interdependence. Looking at developed Western democracies, we have seen how the various bonds of economic transactions can be productively and positively managed through cooperation, learning how to coordinate and comply with others to the mutual benefit of all. In the previous chapter we saw that Hypothesis 4, on economic benefits, depends on economic growth and joint economic reward. The relationships highlighted in the discussion of the political economy of developed democracies were based on open markets and democratic forms of governance. Coercive dominance is missing from relationships based on integration.

But do these same relationships obtain between developed and developing countries? Among less developed countries (LDCs)? We may think of some dependence relationships between developed and developing countries as *pathologies* of interdependence. Asymmetric or one-sided relationships of sensitivity and vulnerability create an incomplete set of interdependent relationships and thus produce yet another set of problems that need to be managed.

## DEVELOPMENT AND DEMOCRACY: COMPLEMENTARY, CONTRADICTORY, OR IRRELEVANT?

From the mid-1970s to the mid-1990s, the number of countries that could be considered free rose from the low 40s to around 75, accounting for about 40 percent of the states in the international system; free and partially free states make up three-quarters of the system.[1] Some parts of the developing world, East Asia in particular, have demonstrated impressive economic growth. However, for large portions of the world's poor, development and democracy remain ever-retreating mirages. Reality is a parched existence in the midst of physical misery and political oppression. Three-fifths of the 5.5 billion people on earth live in low-income countries. Although the privileged classes in those countries live very well indeed, the average person must survive on a per capita GNP of less than $380 (in 1993 dollars, according to the World Bank). Another billion people live in lower-middle-income countries with an average per capita GNP of $1,490. This is compared to 39 countries in the high-income group, whose 800 million people have an average per capita GNP of $23,150. Moreover, a person in a poor country does not live as long; the average life expectancy for a newborn child across all developing countries is 63 years (50 years in the least developed countries) compared with 75 years in the developed countries.

Just as the lack of economic rights is the normal state of affairs in poor countries, so, too, has been the lack of political rights. Since decolonization resulted in independence for many developing countries in the 1960s, liberal democratic governments have been the exception, authoritarian regimes the rule. Poverty remains a major characteristic of nonfree countries, especially those that have tasted some measure of freedom and then returned to nondemocratic rule. Government coercion and repression—state terrorism—are part of daily life, especially for anyone who dares to challenge the existing distribution of power and wealth.

---

[1] These figures are based on the authors' revisions and modifications of the data presented in Freedom House's *Freedom Review* 25:1 (1994).

Most Western social scientists, particularly North Americans, did not expect the persistence of poverty and repression in LDCs. It was clear 30 years ago that economic development in poor countries would be slow and difficult, the result of a long process of accumulating capital investments and human skills. But most analysts did not expect the gap between the rich and the poor in these countries to be so great.

Most observers knew that the acquisition of political power by the world's poor also would be difficult. According to the accepted wisdom of political science, political development is the establishment of stable democratic regimes, possible only if certain prerequisites of democracy are met. These prerequisites are enough income and wealth to create a literate population, informed by newspapers, radio and television, and other mass media. They also include an economy healthy enough to ensure that, through industry, commerce, agriculture, or intellectual activity, a reasonable position in life can be attained—that is, there are sources of wealth and power other than simply controlling the government and looting the public treasury. Such private sources of power provide checks on authoritarian government and provide respectable sources of employment and status for defeated politicians, thereby making it possible for them to accept electoral defeat with reasonably good grace. Economic development is thus not only a way to escape the misery of poverty; it is also a way to promote political liberties.[2]

In comparing countries in the world, the strength of the theory of the economic prerequisites of democracy lies in the fact that high-income industrial countries are, without exception, political democracies. Among them, those with the most recent history of nondemocratic rule—Greece, Portugal, Spain, and Turkey—have the lowest incomes within the OECD. A few of the oil-rich Arab OPEC states—which are not democracies—have very high per capita incomes, but typically this new wealth has not been reflected in high rates of literacy or markedly improved living conditions for the whole populace. Some of the worst records in regard to democracy can be found among the nearly 30 very poor states (per capita GNP less than $380). Very few, perhaps only India and The Gambia, have operated as relatively stable democracies.

Some analysts have taken the argument a step further, contending that short-term political repression may have to be tolerated for the sake of immediate economic development and therefore the chance to establish the prerequisites for democracy. This "authoritarian-modernizing sequence," in Robert Dahl's terms, has been argued by some to be the basis of the economic development found in China as well as the Asian "Tigers" (the *newly industrializing countries*—or **NICs**—such as South Korea, Taiwan, and Singapore).[3]

---

[2] For an example of critical reviews and citation of North American development theories, see J. Samuel Valenzuela and Arturo Valenzuela, "Modernization and Dependency: Alternative Perspectives in the Study of Latin American Underdevelopment," *Comparative Politics* 10, 4 (July 1978), 553–557.

[3] See, for example, William H. Overholt, *The Rise of China* (New York: Norton, 1993).

Weak government, it is claimed, cannot satisfy the needs of a population that makes major demands on it. Trouble arises from rapid social change and the participation of new groups and classes in politics, coupled with the slower development of political institutions. LDCs typically have large urban populations, especially in the capital city (up to a quarter of the population in some capitals). Whereas LDCs had 48 large cities in 1960, there were 173 in 1990. Many of these people come in from the countryside looking for work, only to remain unemployed or underemployed, living a marginal existence. Nevertheless, in the city they are exposed to the mass media and see people in the rich sectors of the city living very well. Their expectations rise but are not fulfilled. Because they are in the capital, they can participate in political activity— street demonstrations, riots, and general strikes. The demands of these people, who can be mobilized by activists for political participation, may be nearly impossible for a weak government to meet or repress.

A stable government, it is contended, requires a strong administrative capacity and political institutions capable of channeling or, if necessary, repressing these popular demands (including organizations capable of enforcing authoritarian rule—an efficient police force and army). The institutions of authority might take the form of a mass political party like the Congress party of India, founded in 1885, and the highly capable and well-organized Indian civil service. More commonly, they would be institutions not so clearly associated with democratic rule; instead, they would more nearly resemble the authoritarian structure of the Ba'ath party in Iraq or a Communist party. One scholar puts the argument in these terms:

> The primary problem is not liberty but the creation of a legitimate public order. Men may, of course, have order without liberty, but they cannot have liberty without order. Authority has to exist before it can be limited, and it is authority that is in scarce supply in those modernizing countries where government is at the mercy of alienated intellectuals, rambunctious colonels, and rioting students.[4]

It is not a long step from such an analysis to the argument that traditional Western ideas of political rights and liberties must be put aside in the interest of economic development. Development cannot occur without order. Furthermore, development requires large-scale sacrifice on the part of the masses; without massive foreign assistance, the resources for that investment can be obtained only by reducing consumption. High incomes, however, must be available as a reward, and an incentive, to rich people who may make big investments in the country. In a very poor country with widespread misery, "forced-draft" modernization and widespread income inequalities require government action to repress discontent. Agricultural prices (and thus farmers' incomes) have to be kept low, and urban people, where they cannot be satisfied, must feel the arm of the state in discouraging protest.

---

[4] Samuel P. Huntington, *Political Order in Changing Societies* (New Haven, Conn.: Yale University Press, 1968), p. 78.

By such arguments, people in poor countries essentially must choose between political liberty and decent material conditions; they cannot have both, and it is a parochial Western prejudice to insist on traditional Western concepts of political rights. However, we think these arguments are profoundly wrong. As indicated in the previous chapter, we shall argue that good things can go together—economic development, democracy, and peace. Indeed, while state capacity is important, for a government to be effective it must be able to generate compliance from its people without the threat of coercion—that is, it must have legitimacy. "Many have exaggerated the part of force and minimized the role of legitimacy."[5]

## THE RECORD

The trouble with the economic-prerequisites argument is that it only partially fits the facts of recent experience in LDCs. In Latin America and parts of East Asia over the past decade or two, quite a number of democratic governments have emerged, but usually (as in South American countries) as the result of military dictatorships' *failure* to improve their people's living conditions rather than as a result of achieving the alleged economic prerequisites. In other areas there has been only a weaker and later trend toward an increase in political liberties. Almost all the former British and French colonies entered their era of independence with governments that were chosen by reasonably free elections and had the forms of parliamentary democracy; today, far fewer of them have free competitive elections or the institutions of free speech and free assembly. Some have had stagnant economies, others very dynamic and fast-growing ones. In many of these countries, however, income has typically been skewed sharply in favor of the rich and has had no discernible effect in promoting political liberty. In some countries the suppression of political liberty has brought economic growth, but in many others it has not.

Even more devastating for theories of political development is a pattern in some of the more prosperous LDCs that culminated in the early 1970s, when a turn away from democratic government to state terrorism was especially vicious. Uruguay and Chile in the 1960s were relatively rich and had long histories of a stable democracy. (Chile had had uninterrupted democratic government since 1927, and Uruguay since the 1930s. Along with Argentina and Venezuela, these countries were the most prosperous of the 20 Latin American countries.) The Philippines were fairly prosperous compared with other Asian countries and had a high literacy rate. For several decades the Philippines had developed the institutions and practices of political democracy with free elections, first under American colonial rule and then as an independent state after 1946. By the theory, all these countries should have been able to maintain and deepen their democratic patterns. They were not. Their democratic governments

---

[5] Robert W. Jackman, *Power Without Force* (Ann Arbor: University of Michigan Press, 1993), p. 36.

were overthrown (in 1973 in Chile and Uruguay and in 1972 in the Philippines) and replaced by repressive, coercive regimes. Argentina, with a highly sophisticated, literate population and sporadic periods of democratic government, similarly slipped back into authoritarian military rule for almost a decade.

Other theories note that Argentina, Chile, and Uruguay, though prosperous by LDC standards, nevertheless were economically stagnant by the standard of their own historical experience. They had passed through more than a decade of little or even negative growth in GNP per capita and were wracked by inflation rates sometimes exceeding 100 percent a year. This economic "stagflation" put enormous strains on social and political systems, bringing economic gains to a few and widespread deprivation and poverty to many who had once been prosperous. However, like other economic-prerequisite theories, this view focuses too much on domestic causes of development (or nondevelopment) and excludes international forces. Without careful attention to the fact that virtually all developing states are now deeply affected by external influences, one cannot really understand economic or political development in those states. Some theories have paid attention to the role of these external forces in affecting internal development, as we shall see later in the chapter. For now, it may be enough to emphasize the great diversity of experience among LDCs. Some countries have experienced rapid economic growth; some, little or none. Some have had democratic governments; others—the majority—various kinds of rightist or leftist authoritarian regimes.

Within the developing world there is only a very limited relationship between the type of political system and the level of economic activity. Only a very few really poor states are democracies, but among the middle-income LDCs there is really no relationship between income and type of political system. Nor is there much systematic relationship between the political system and the rate of growth in economic activity.

Table 15.1 shows several economic and political characteristics for some LDCs in the years 1985–93: the rate of growth in per capita gross national product, a rough political classification, and an estimate of how equally or unequally income is distributed. Among less developed countries in general, a distribution in which the richest 20 percent of households receive less than 10 times the income of the poorest 20 percent of households can be considered relatively egalitarian, and one in which the richest 20 percent receive more than 15 times that of the poorest 20 percent is inegalitarian.

The experiences of different countries vary enough to make it clear that simple explanations for the data will not do. Yet, if anything, the evidence comes in *against* the argument that rapid growth requires the toleration of huge economic inequalities and political repression. Of the ten countries with per capita growth rates over 5 percent for the 1985–93 period, six were classified as free, three as partly free, and *only one* as not free. The pattern is almost exactly reversed for those countries with negative growth rates worse than –3 percent: five were classified not free, four as partly free, and *only one* as free. This last country, Mali, was categorized as not free until changes occurred in 1991 and 1992.

The countries with rapid growth rates varied in their internal political and economic arrangements. China, the only nonfree country on the list and still politically a communist dictatorship, pursued growth from the early 1980s onward by introducing

**TABLE 15.1** Economic Growth, Political System, and Income Distribution in Some LDCs, 1985–1993

| Country | GNP per Capita Growth Rate | Political Freedom | Income Distribution |
|---|---|---|---|
| Highest-Growth Economies | | | |
| Thailand | 8.4 | PF | O |
| South Korea | 8.1 | F | E |
| China | 6.5 | NF | E |
| Singapore | 6.1 | PF | O |
| Chile | 6.1 | F | I |
| Mauritius | 5.8 | F | |
| Malaysia | 5.7 | PF | O |
| Belize | 5.7 | F | |
| Botswana | 5.7 | F | I |
| St.Kitts–Nevis | 5.2 | F | |
| | | | |
| Lowest-Growth (Stagnant or Declining) Economies | | | |
| Central African Rep. | −3.0 | PF | |
| Togo | −3.4 | NF | |
| Haiti | −3.4 | NF | I |
| Peru | −3.5 | PF | O |
| Rwanda | −3.5 | NF | E |
| Mali | −4.3 | F | |
| Ivory Coast | −5.2 | NF | E |
| Jordan | −5.9 | PF | |
| Nicaragua | −6.2 | PF | |
| Cameroon | −7.3 | NF | |

Political freedom: F = Free, PF = Partly Free, NF = Not Free.

Income distribution: E = egalitarian, I = inegalitarian, O = position between E and I. Blanks where reliable income distribution data are not available.

*Sources:* GNP per capita growth from *The World Bank Atlas 1995* (Washington, DC: The World Bank, 1994); freedom scores from authors' revisions of Freedom House data; income inequality from World Bank, *World Development Report 1994* (New York: Oxford University Press, 1994), pp. 164–65; scores for Haiti and South Korea are authors' estimates.

free-market reforms and reducing centralized economic controls. The partly free countries—Thailand, Singapore, and Malaysia—differ in the degree and nature of their somewhat authoritarian regimes and in the degree of state management of the economy.

Although many LDC governments have followed inegalitarian income policies, some states have succeeded in achieving growth while maintaining relative equality. The governments have not necessarily been democratic but have nevertheless allowed, and to some degree even encouraged, a pattern of rewards that has benefited many sectors of the populace. Both South Korea and Taiwan vigorously pursued rural development following earlier land-reform programs, thus permitting the rise of a substantial landowning, prosperous rural peasantry.

## What Goes with What, in General?

Some generalizations underlie this mixed collection of examples.

**1.** *Economic development and democracy are strongly correlated. The causal relationship seems to be from development to democracy, rather than in the other direction.* Human-rights abuse and state terrorism (imprisonment, torture, and killing of political opponents) characterize dictatorships far more than democracies. These abuses are somewhat more common in poor countries. A high level of development makes it easier to sustain democracy. Rich countries tend to be democratic. In many countries, such as Taiwan and South Korea, greater political liberalization and the relaxation of governmental repression have followed substantial economic growth. But there are exceptions. Some quite rich countries, like Singapore, are still not very democratic, and rapid economic growth in China has not yet produced notable political liberalization or greater respect for political liberties. And democracy is rare, but not unknown, in some very poor countries. Even in many countries that are not democratic in the Western sense there are different means and different degrees of enabling the majority of the populace to have some control over their government, at least at the local level. The cases of real democracy in very poor countries show that, in the right social, economic, and cultural circumstances, mass poverty need not prevent the establishment of democracy.

**2.** *There is little evidence that democracy plays a strong causal role—either positive or negative—in economic development.* For every authoritarian government that represses political opposition while promoting growth, there are several dictatorial "kleptocracies," that is, governments run by a tiny elite far more interested in stealing from the people than in stimulating general economic development. (President Mobuto made himself a multibillionaire while impoverishing the rest of Zaire.) The notion that political opposition *must* be repressed in the interest of development is, as a generalization, a lie. An excellent review of the scientific literature on political and economic development summarizes the situation well:

> There is no evidence that, on average, a democracy with civil liberties is costly in terms of economic development. If anything it may be the other way around, that a democracy with civil liberties promotes economic development. But establishing democratic

institutions is not the "deus ex machina" that resolves all the problems of development. A sound and stable political-economic development is essential.[6]

**3.** *A vicious cycle operates from political instability to low economic growth and back again.* Poor countries are often socially and politically unstable, with serious ethnic conflicts and weak or arbitrary governments that do not protect property rights. Instability reduces the incentives to save and invest, thereby reducing the capacities for economic growth. Low growth then reinforces the instabilities. Transitions from dictatorial regimes to democratic ones may produce periods of slow economic growth, ultimately endangering the new and fragile democracy. Wise policies and external assistance can help to ease and shorten the economic pain of transition. A "civic tradition" of respect and tolerance—an underpinning of democracy—encourages political stability and, in turn, enhances the prospects for economic growth.

**4.** *Economic inequality often makes political instability worse.* It frequently leads to mass violence and illegal seizures of power.

**5.** *Gross economic inequality between classes is more likely to damage economic growth than to promote it.* Human capital—good health, literacy, and education—is a great asset for economic development. The high level of economic equality that has characterized the countries of East Asia may be much more responsible for their rapid economic growth than is the dictatorial nature of many of their governments.

We shall continue exploration of these principles, with greater attention to the role of economic inequality, throughout this chapter.

## Several Developing Worlds

Looking back over the record of development, we find a mixed picture, but one that allows us to be cautiously optimistic. The last half-century has witnessed a remarkable differentiation among countries and regions of the developing world. There are areas

---

[6] Alberto Allesina and Roberto Perotti, "The Political Economy of Growth: A Critical Survey of the Recent Literature," *World Bank Economic Review* 8,3 (September 1994), pp. 35–371. This review also provides evidence for all the other numbered points. Other good pieces on one or more of these points include Ross Burkhart and Michael Lewis-Beck, "Comparative Democracy: The Economic Development Thesis," *American Political Science Review* 88,4 (December 1994), pp. 903–910; Adam Przeworski and Fernando Limongi, "Political Regimes and Economic Growth," *Journal of Economic Perspectives* 7,3 (Summer 1993), pp. 51–70; John F. Helliwell, "Empirical Linkages Between Democracy and Economic Growth," *British Journal of Political Science* 24 (1994), pp. 175–98; Robert Putnam, *Making Democracy Work: Civic Traditions in Modern Italy* (Princeton, N.J.: Princeton University Press, 1993); Zara Arat, *Democracy and Human Rights in Developing Countries* (Boulder, Colo.: Rienner, 1991); and Mansoor Moaddel, "Political Conflict in the World Economy: A Cross-National Analysis of Modernization and World System Theories," *American Sociological Review* 59 (1994), pp. 276–303.

of growing wealth and development, such as the oil-rich states or the NICs of the Pacific Rim, and also areas caught in stagnation, such as sub-Saharan Africa. This can be seen even from a quick look at Table 15.1. Half of the highest-growth economies are in East Asia but only one is in Africa; six of the lowest-growth economies are in Africa, with none in the Pacific Rim.

Clearly East Asian growth rates are strong, with many development successes achieved without massive foreign assistance. While Latin American countries appear on both lists in Table 15.1, many of those economies have turned around, gradually getting control over their problems with foreign debt and attracting foreign investment. The overall trend in both areas has also been toward liberalization of governments and the growth of democracy. Africa is quite a different story—negative growth; failure to attract foreign investment; crumbling economic and social infrastructures with significant health-care problems, including AIDS; and a breakdown in civil order in a number of countries (in both East and West Africa).

In Chapter 6 we introduced the Human Development Index (HDI) developed by the United Nations Development Programme (UNDP). Based on three elements—longevity, knowledge, and standard of living—the HDI was a reaction to the conceptualization of development on economic grounds alone. The UNDP position is that while economic growth is of great importance to development, by itself it is not a sufficient basis for thinking about and measuring human development. It is possible to find countries with approximately similar levels of GNP per capita but divergent HDI scores. For example, while both countries had per capita GNP of about $500, Sri Lanka had a 1992 HDI of 0.665, ranking 90th among the world's countries, while Guinea had an HDI of 0.191, ranking 173rd or last. Looking at Figure 15.1, we can see that HDI, too, differs across regions. Combining both social and economic development, HDI also indicates the superior performance of Latin America and East Asia and the problems facing sub-Saharan Africa.

Some gaps between the rich and poor continue to widen—especially the differences in wealth and income. While per capita wealth in OECD countries more than tripled from 1960 to 1991, in the least developed countries it was only one and one-half times as much. Income indicators have shown a steady decline in Africa since the mid-1970s; Latin American income fell steadily before a rebound in the 1990s. However, as with HDI, many social indicators have improved (or not become worse). World Bank statistics on indicators such as life expectancy, infant mortality, and illiteracy rates across the developing world show improvements such as the following: the infant mortality rate per 1,000 births has dropped by almost half in 30 years; average life expectancy has increased by 12 years in even the poorest regions; today there are 100 million more children in school than 15 years ago; during the 1980s safe water was provided to over 1.5 billion new people.[7] What was known as the "Third World" is now several worlds, with different problems and records of performance.

---

[7] See Ruth Leger Sivard, *World Military and Social Expenditures 1993* (Washington, DC: World Priorities, 1993), p. 9, and United Nations Development Programme, *Human Development Report 1994* (New York: Oxford University Press, 1994), pp. 136–137, Table 4, "Trends in Human Development."

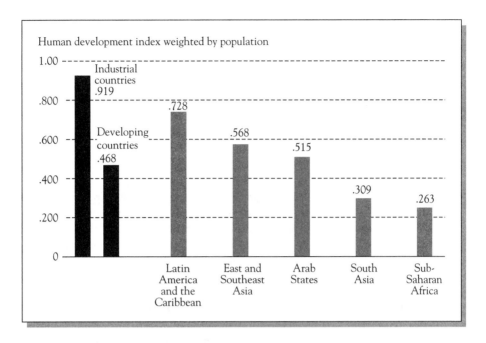

**FIGURE 15.1** Human development by region. [*Source:* United Nations Development Programme, *Human Development Report 1993* (New York: Oxford University Press, 1993), p. 15.]

## HISTORICAL VIEW OF DEPENDENCE

To some observers, the failure of Western theories of economic and political development to anticipate economic stagnation and political repression in much of the developing world was not surprising. Theorists from Latin America, Africa, and other parts of the world took a view of development that was much more attentive to international and systemic influences on development than was most Western theory. For these people, a crucial flaw in Western theory was its treatment of political and economic development as essentially determined by domestic forces. They thought that political and economic structures within LDCs were primarily determined by the role LDCs played in the world market. Even with the new theoretical and empirical attention to the important role of *inequality within countries*, it is necessary to know the impact of external economic forces. Without understanding the effect of foreign penetration of LDC economies and polities and how that penetration helped shape relations between social classes in those countries, one could understand little.

Some of these theories take a historical perspective that extends back to the establishment of a **world system** in the sixteenth century. The colonial "center" powers—Spain and Portugal, and later Britain, Holland, and France—had created a world division of labor between themselves and the territories of the "periphery." Commerce and manufacturing were established largely in the center, and the colonies of the periphery provided food and minerals for the world market. The populations of the periphery were often subjugated and made into landless peasants working on big farms or as slavelike labor in the mines. In some areas, especially in the Caribbean, the original populations were largely exterminated and replaced by slave labor imported from Africa. Governmental control was exercised from the center or, more commonly in those days of slow communication, by the big landowners and urban merchants who sold their products to the world market. Most of the colonial world was thus established as a producer of raw materials for the European center and was ruled by an upper class that imported its manufactured goods from Europe. The ruling elites had neither the power to resist European penetration and this global division of labor nor an interest in doing so.[8]

When the peripheral countries became politically sovereign in the nineteenth and twentieth centuries, their ruling elites maintained close economic links with the world market. In some instances their interests coincided closely with those of European capitalists who came to invest in the periphery, and they prospered by providing services and local expertise to the Europeans. In other instances their interests diverged, but still the peripheral states lacked strong central governments that could effectively resist or control European penetration. There were sometimes deep and violent conflicts between landowners and urban entrepreneurs, between domestic and foreign capitalists. Nevertheless, the masses of people in the countryside usually remained poor and powerless. Sharp inequalities in income distribution meant that, except in a few big countries (Argentina, Mexico, Brazil, and much later India), there could be no large mass market for domestically manufactured goods. The result was economic stagnation and relegation to the role of primary producer for the world economy.

In some areas where significant local industry had existed before the colonial era, that industry was stifled. The most famous instance is nineteenth-century India. The British colonial government deliberately destroyed the Indian textile industry; it built a railway system through India with the express purpose of opening up the country so that the textile manufactures of Lancashire could be sold to the Indian population. Another well-known case is that of the Belgian Congo in the late nineteenth century, where the colonial rulers wanted to use the local population as a labor force in the mines. Streams were poisoned, so that the Africans could not live from fishing. They were then required to pay taxes in money, and they could earn money to pay taxes only by working—for very low wages.

---

[8] See Immanuel Wallerstein, *The Modern World System* (New York: Academic Press, 1974), and Eric Hobsbawm, *The Age of Empire, 1875–1914* (New York: Pantheon, 1988).

There are important differences of interpretation about the colonial era. In discussing imperialism, we found that although there are conflicting theories about just *how* important economic motives were in promoting imperialism and precisely *what* economic mechanisms were involved (a search for markets, for raw materials, or for outlets for surplus capital), economic motives in general were a major influence. A world division of labor between an industrial center and a periphery producing primary goods (with some states in a "semiperipheral" status) did arise. Associated with this division of labor were powerful groups and classes in all parts of the world with a great stake in maintaining the basic structure. But what these historical facts mean for patterns of development in the twentieth century, what the significance is of some of the exceptions to the general picture that did exist, and what the prospects are for LDC development in the late twentieth century are issues involving much more controversy.

## CONTEMPORARY DEPENDENCE

In the view of some theorists, less developed countries dependent on the world market face great obstacles in developing advanced, diverse economies. Economies dependent upon exports of agricultural and mineral raw materials were subject to forces that maintained low wage rates, persistent inflation, low but variable prices for raw materials, and political institutions too weak to deal with these conditions.

Figure 15.2 shows the fluctuation and deterioration in the terms of trade for some principal commodity exports of LDCs. By *terms of trade* we mean essentially what can be obtained for one's exports. If the relative terms of trade improve for an LDC, it can obtain a greater volume or value of manufactured imports in exchange for a given amount of the primary commodity it exports. The graph in Figure 15.2 shows the relative value of all primary commodities other than oil (that is, minerals and agricultural products) as compared with the UN index for the value of manufactures exported by developed countries from 1957 to 1990. On a pretty steady decline since the 1970s, the terms of trade dropped even more in the late 1980s, to a new low, only 70 percent of what it had been 10 years earlier. (Of course, the value of specific products can change by more or less than the value of the index: for example, in 1955 it took 6.3 bags of coffee or 7.9 tons of tea to buy 100 tons of steel from the United States or Britain; by 1972 it took 12.1 bags of coffee or 14.1 tons of tea.)

Drops of 25 percent or more from one year to the next for cocoa, rubber, sugar, copper, lead, and zinc have been common. With prices fluctuating like that, producers have a very hard time planning future production and sales. Bad weather may reduce the volume of exports but drive up the price of what is left. Producers who increase their acreage or mining capacity to take advantage of higher prices in future years may go too far, creating an excess supply that lowers prices and earnings instead of raising them. Countries that depend heavily on earnings from commodity exports to provide foreign exchange for development can be hit hard. If export earnings fall, key development plans may have to be eliminated or postponed or loans may have to be obtained. For example, the International Monetary Fund estimated that simply

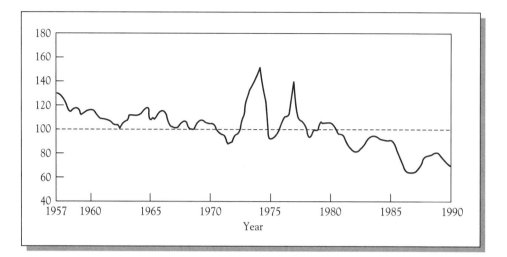

**FIGURE 15.2** Value of nonoil primary commodities imported as a percentage of the value of manufactured goods exported by developed countries. [*Source:* International Monetary Fund, *World Economic Outlook, 1983, 1991* (Washington, D.C.: International Monetary Fund, 1983, 1991).]

because of the fall in commodity prices between 1980 and 1982, the non-oil-exporting developing countries' trade deficit was 50 percent higher than it otherwise would have been.

Most big, populous countries can have reasonably diversified economies and therefore are not too vulnerable to fluctuations in commodity prices. Also, a number of big and middle-sized LDCs (the NICs) have become fairly industrialized; South Korea, Taiwan, Mexico, and Brazil are examples of industrializing states that are no longer very dependent on commodity exports. But some middle-sized countries and many small ones have been very dependent on commodity prices, and often on a single commodity. In the early 1970s, for example, Zaire derived 68 percent of all its export earnings from copper, and 47 percent of Egypt's earnings came from cotton. Other countries with similar problems were Cuba (84 percent from sugar), Ghana (62 percent from cocoa), Sri Lanka (60 percent from tea), Panama (56 percent from bananas), and Bolivia (52 percent from tin). World Bank figures for 1991 indicate that low- and middle-income countries were clearly more dependent on primary commodity exports than developed-market economies: 52 percent of all low- and middle income country exports (which totaled $686 million) were primary commodities, as against 18 percent for the OECD countries (of the total exports worth $2,441 million).

To eliminate excessive reliance on commodity exports, many countries adopted a development strategy of promoting industrialization that would substitute domestic manufactures for imported ones. For the larger countries with a reasonably big domestic market, this worked for a while. But the limits to this effort soon became apparent: these still were relatively poor countries, with an income distribution heavily favoring the rich and therefore without a really big mass market for consumer goods. Even the reasonably big domestic markets were, because of their poverty and inequality, much smaller than in European countries of comparable populations. UN figures indicate that during the period from 1980 to 1990, more than 30 percent of the population of the developing countries lived in "absolute poverty"—and as many as 64 percent for the least developed countries. In the OECD countries, the income share for the top 20 percent of the population was about 7 times the income share of the lowest 20 percent. For a number of developing countries the income share of the top 20 percent was 20 to 30 times that of the lowest 20 percent; in Botswana (for 1980–91), the richest 20 percent earned 47 times as much as the poorest 20 percent. Income inequality means that broad segments of the working class and the middle class are not rewarded, not "co-opted" into the system, as were the working and middle classes in the advanced industrial market economies. If the loyalty of these classes cannot be ensured by a wide distribution of economic and political benefits, then the state is condemned to securing grudging acquiescence through political coercion. Ultimately, the state becomes both economically active and politically repressive.

Import substitution policies also often meant subsidizing and protecting the new industry and/or required foreign loans and direct investment by multinational corporations. With the expansion of regional trading arrangements (of which the U.S. government counted 73 worldwide in 1992) and free-trade agreements such as NAFTA (the North American Free Trade Agreement), developing countries find themselves attracting large-scale foreign investment in low-wage manufacturing industries. These industries produce both for the LDC market and for export back to developed-country trading partners. Investments of this type bring their own ties of dependence. The LDC governments are urged to "get the prices right" by moving toward greater utilization of the free market, selling off state-owned industries, and cutting subsidies to inefficient industry. They also are urged toward greater governmental openness and accountability in order to reduce corruption (the World Bank's way of saying something like "democracy"). All of this may shift levels of wealth and power in their economic and social systems, raising the possibility of serious political conflict.

## Distorted Development

The Latin American and African writers who have analyzed these problems are often referred to as **dependence** theorists. Important differences exist among them. Some see LDCs as doomed to stagnation; others see possibilities of "dependent development" that could make possible rapid growth in GNP per capita, albeit in economies that are fundamentally distorted and highly inegalitarian. Writers differ on the relative importance of domestic class relations as contrasted with external forces. While all would qualify as radical theorists, their theories derive from varying mixtures of liberal Keynesian economics and Marxist analysis.[9] Yet despite their differences, all dependence theorists agree that economic, social, and political conditions in peripheral societies are inextricably linked and that realist emphasis on the nation-state level of analysis often ignores penetration by transnational and international actors in the global system. Poor countries are dependent on rich countries when the two-way aspects of interdependence are minimal. They are *unequally vulnerable;* there is only a very lopsided interdependence. Acts by the governments of developed center countries or by MNCs based in those countries affect what happens in peripheral countries much more than almost any action in a peripheral country (especially a small, poor one) can affect what happens in a rich industrialized country. Poor countries are dependent, penetrated, and vulnerable—hardly the unitary, independent actors of some realist theorists.

Nearly all developing countries are now deeply penetrated by, and in important ways dependent on, the industrial world and especially the world economy. Penetration can occur in a variety of economic, political, and cultural modes and at different periods in a country's development.

Economic penetration can be accomplished by financial or technological means. MNCs often establish subsidiaries involved in mining (Kennecott Copper in Chile, British Petroleum in Iran), agriculture (United Fruit in Guatemala, Firestone Rubber in Liberia), manufacturing (Volkswagen in Brazil), or commerce (Sears, Roebuck and Coca-Cola in Korea—and almost everywhere else). Subsidiaries of MNCs typically use technology developed in the industrial economies, often after some delay as part of a "product cycle." Previous production processes are transferred to the periphery, where labor is cheaper, after a new process is introduced in the world center. MNC subsidiaries, therefore, are likely to import capital equipment (computers, transport vehicles, and other machinery) from the advanced countries. Local manufacturing facilities are likely to use the processes developed in the center, which thus carry foreign patents, licenses, copyrights, and trademarks.

Political and cultural influences may come in material or symbolic "packages"—in books, television programs (reruns or news via satellite), newspapers and magazines, and motion pictures. They may come more abstractly, through people who become "carriers" of foreign cultures. Young people are sent to foreign educational institutions and return having adopted important elements of Western industrial culture: ways of thinking and behaving, ideologies, values, and appreciation of Western consumer goods. Tourists coming into the peripheral countries also bring their cultural values. Students may dislike many aspects of the countries in which they study, and tourists may inspire hatred as well as envy or emulation, yet exposure to the cultures of advanced countries deeply shapes and often overwhelms local cultural values. People may come to want consumer goods that are readily available in advanced industrial economies but affordable to only a small minority in poor countries: private automobiles, refrigerators and air conditioners, and color television sets and VCRs.

---

[9] A good collection of later dependence theory and related perspectives is Samir Amin, Giovanni Arrighi, et al., eds., *Dynamics of Global Crisis* (New York: Monthly Review Press, 1982).

Manufacturing enterprises in LDCs may thus turn toward this small market of upper-middle-class Westernized consumers, producing familiar products with well-established technologies, rather than aiming for a working-class market with many potential consumers but little purchasing power. This means, in effect, that industrial and commercial interests support a distribution of income that favors the well-to-do classes rather than an egalitarian distribution of income that would produce a mass market for basic consumer goods (bread rather than beef, mass transit rather than private cars, and village doctors rather than urban medical specialists).

Governments as well as private organizations and individuals import political and cultural products that shape the way they perform their tasks and how they define their tasks—importing, for example, advanced military armaments, police training programs, and computers. By all these means, peripheral countries' values regarding consumption and production become deeply conditioned by penetration from the center.

## Debt

Foreign capital tends to flow primarily to the dynamic sectors of a peripheral country's economy, thus spurring uneven development by reinforcing those sectors while ignoring backward sectors and increasing the wages of only a small but skilled part of the labor force. The effects of penetration and dependence are complex, are often indirect, and vary greatly in different kinds of countries. A country's previous colonial history, its size, its relative level of wealth, and its natural resources all influence the results. In the short run, foreign investment and foreign aid usually stimulate growth, but growth will be hindered if foreign corporations ultimately send much of the profits back to the countries where MNCs have their headquarters. Growth is also reduced through repayment of debts to foreign governments and banks. Thus, in the long run, repatriation of profits by MNCs and the effects of large-scale public debts can sharply reduce growth.

By the end of 1993 the foreign debt of all LDCs, and the cost of servicing that debt, had risen to almost $1,800 billion. That represented almost half of the entire gross domestic product (GDP) of those countries (with GDP representing GNP excluding the difference between imports and exports; see Figure 15.3). Servicing the external debt takes four times as much as health care, about twice as much as education. About 20 percent of all their export earnings went just to pay the interest on their foreign debt. The situation was especially bad for most countries of Africa. On that continent, foreign debt amounted to over 100 percent of all domestic product. Debt interest and repayment represented 25 percent of the value of African exports.[10] Many less developed countries, in fact, simply could not meet their interest payments; like Brazil, as recounted in Chapter 1, to avoid default they had to negotiate a rescheduling of their payments with the international agencies and especially the commercial banks that

---

[10] See Lester Brown, Hal Kane and David Malin Roodman, *Vital Signs 1994* (New York: Norton, 1994), pp. 74–75, "Third World Debt Still Rising."

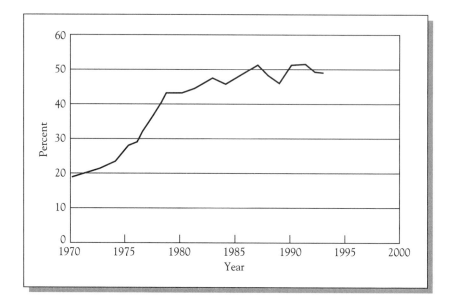

**FIGURE 15.3** Third World debt as a share of gross domestic product, 1970–1993. [*Source:* Lester Brown et al., *Vital Signs 1994* (New York: Norton, 1994), p. 75, using World Bank and IMF data.]

had lent them the money. As a result of the rescheduling, the indebted governments had to carry out deflationary austerity policies and accept declining incomes.

Many analysts of different schools—not only dependence theorists but also many quite conventional economists—have recognized problems of distorted development. Dependence theorists nevertheless interpret the phenomena in distinctive ways. They compare this pattern of development with a somewhat idealized image of an economy that is growing quite slowly but in a balanced, integrated, homogeneous manner. (In fact, many of the economic distortions in current LDCs also occurred in nineteenth-century Europe.) Most important for students of international politics, they link penetration and economic distortion with additional distortions in the social and political systems. As a consequence, they believe that the economic growth of a peripheral state may lead to the establishment not of a liberal democracy but of a dictatorship. These theorists see a state bureaucracy that controls the government and perhaps substantial state economic enterprises (in transportation, public utilities, banking, and possibly manufacturing) eager to consolidate power. According to their view, this state bureaucracy, in alliance with foreign interests and some domestic capitalists, deprives most of the population of basic human rights, both economic rights to decent living conditions and political rights to representation and protest. Violence—

both direct and structural, as defined in the preceding chapter—is thus seen as being in large part a consequence of economics and politics in the periphery and the periphery's linkages with the world economy and political system.

## Development, Demographics, and Health

Such violence can be seen in the convergence of poverty, distorted development, and social trends. As we will see in Chapter 18, recent population growth is unprecedented—with over 85 percent of the 2.5 billion people added since 1960 living in the developing countries. The annual population growth rate for all developing countries between 1960 and 1992 was 2.2 percent (though it is expected to drop to about 1.9 percent for the rest of the 1990s). These averages, however, hide huge differences between various countries and regions. In East Asian LDCs, including China, the population growth rate is expected to be 1.2 percent; in Latin America and Southeast Asia together, less than 1.8 percent. In South Asia, however, the rate is expected to be about 2.0 percent; in the Arab states and sub-Saharan Africa, 2.7 and 3.4 percent, respectively. By contrast, the growth rate for the industrial countries is expected to drop to 0.6 percent from an already-low recent rate of 0.8 percent.[11]

Greater numbers of people place greater demands on governments for food, housing, health care, and jobs. A basic rule of thumb is that an economy must grow at least as fast as the population just to forestall a degradation in economic and social well-being. Economic growth must clearly exceed population growth for conditions to improve. Economic growth rates for the least developed countries fall drastically short of even matching population growth. The low-growth countries listed in Table 15.1 saw their GDP per capita *shrink* from −3.0 to −7.0 percent during the 1985–93 period; all these countries (except Haiti) also had population growth rates over 2.5 percent from 1960 to 1992; the Ivory Coast population grew at nearly 4.0 percent (a doubling time of just 18 years!).

The drag of population is, and will continue to be, a significant obstacle to development in many LDCs. Add the issue of debt and debt servicing, and the obstacles loom even larger. Add additional problems of health care, particularly AIDS, and the task magnifies to daunting proportions. Currently 12 to 13 million people are HIV-positive, with 80 percent of the cases in the LDCs. By the year 2000 this number is expected to rise to 25 to 30 million, with 95 percent of the total in the LDCs. Sub-Saharan Africa has been particularly hard hit. According to the World Bank, the infection rate in sub-Saharan Africa is one out of every forty adults; one-third of Uganda's population will be infected by 2015 according to projections. Economic and social strains are already evident in Africa, with the costs of health care, lost work days by both AIDS vicitims and caregivers, and the fact that AIDS kills adults during their most productive years. The majority of Africa's new infections have occurred in the 15–24 age group.

---

[11] UN Development Programme, *Human Development Report 1994*, p. 211.

AIDS is truly a case of the poor getting poorer. Robert Kaplan, in a controversially pessimistic portrait of crumbling order in Africa, sees the continent being isolated by a "wall of disease" that includes AIDS, hepatitis B, tuberculosis, and malaria. Kaplan sees West African poverty inextricably linked with "disease, overpopulation, unprovoked crime, scarcity of resources, refugee migrations . . . private armies . . . and international drug cartels."[12] Indeed, one of the major areas resistant to the global trend toward democracy has been West Africa. We have tried to demonstrate that an idea of human development includes both economic and social dimensions. If good things can go together, then trends in Africa indicate that bad things also go together. One argument of dependency theory is that we should not be surprised that such a convergence is one result of distorted development.

## POLITICAL CONFLICT AND REPRESSION

Let us look at another example. Capital-intensive investment reduces the need for large numbers of workers. By limiting employment to a small force of skilled workers, even an expanded industrial sector may employ no more industrial laborers than before expansion. Other workers are left unemployed, only partially employed, or working full-time at unskilled jobs for wages that give them a marginal existence. The larger this reserve army of the unemployed, the greater the downward pressure on wage rates for workers in general (workers who demand too much can readily be replaced). In many instances, MNCs will pay relatively high wages, but high wages in MNC subsidiaries may contribute to increasing income inequalities within the working class.

These inequalities, as well as enormous inequalities elsewhere in the economy— between the cities and the countryside, between businesspeople or professionals and the unemployed, between large landowners and peasants—lead to increasing government intervention in the economy. If the government is directly dominated by either foreign or domestic investors, it will reflect their interests in stabilizing costs by keeping wages down and thereby maximizing profits. Whether the state is dominated by capitalists or begins to take on its own major economic role in the public sector, its actions are likely to intensify economic inequalities in the society.

We have already encountered the theory that relative deprivation fosters conflict. Unequal distributions of the national pie tend to induce conflict, as some groups or classes see others moving ahead rapidly while they themselves gain little or in some instances even slip backward. In highly inegalitarian societies, any appreciable change (either positive or negative) in overall national income will stimulate greater conflict over how the expanded or contracted pie should be divided, but there will be most

---

[12] Robert D. Kaplan, "The Coming Anarchy," *The Atlantic Monthly*, February 1994, pp. 44–76.

conflict during periods of economic decline.[13] Reductions in overall income clearly promote conflict. One of the most vivid examples here is Uruguay, which until 1973 was a relatively wealthy egalitarian welfare state. But decades of stagnation and economic decline brought severe social tensions, the rise of radical urban guerrilla groups, and ultimately a right-wing military coup to "impose order."

Under President Salvador Allende, a Marxist, Chile experienced economic stagnation and declines in real income in the early 1970s because of mismanagement by Allende's government and economic sabotage by Allende's domestic and foreign (especially U.S.) enemies, who wanted to see him fail. When Allende tried to pursue policies of redistributing income at a time of overall decline in growth, the result was work stoppages by key groups, riots, demonstrations, and eventually a right-wing military coup against him. The leader of that coup, General Augusto Pinochet, then instituted an extraordinarily repressive and long-lasting dictatorship. By contrast, in 1978 Iran had experienced a decade of unprecedented growth in its national income. But these economic rewards were distributed very unequally and left a variety of groups—peasants, urban workers and the urban unemployed, followers of traditional religion, and some intellectuals—very dissatisfied. Many rebelled, culminating in the shah's overthrow.

In societies marked by relative equality, economic growth is less likely to foster conflict, as seen in the apparently low levels of violent social conflict in Taiwan. Many economists now argue that the success of the Asian NICs is based in large part on policies that reduce economic inequality, raising the incomes of workers faster than those of economic elites. More generally, some have argued as we have above, that greater income equality is an important factor in economic growth (estimating that reducing the gap between the richest and poorest by a third could add almost 1 percent to the growth rate of per capita income) and the liberalization of society.[14] Here, good things do go together.

## Military Assistance and Coercion

A relatively advanced economy (like Argentina's) or one with a lot of surplus readily available to the government (like oil-rich Iraq's) may be able to develop its own coercive apparatus without too much external help. The government of a less developed state may have to depend more on purchases or gifts from abroad. The international trade in arms is important as a source of governmental coercive capacity in LDCs, and thus it is part of the distorting effects of various economic, political, and social interventions. During the 1970s and 1980s three-quarters of the world's arms trade (which peaked at $73 billion in 1984) went to the LDCs. Exports of major conventional weapons have dropped substantially (as has the entire world trade in arms) since the end of the cold war, by some measures dropping by over two-thirds. The United

[13] E. N. Muller and M. A. Seligson, "Inequality and Insurgency," *American Political Science Review* 81, 2 (June 1987), 425–452.

[14] Sylvia Nasar, "Economics of Equality: A New View," *New York Times,* January 5, 1995.

States has been the dominant supplier of arms to the developing world, as the competition for arms markets has led to the sale of the most recent and most technologically advanced weapons systems and even their production technologies. There have also been many military assistance programs for training foreign soldiers and technicians. U.S., European, Soviet, and Cuban military personnel have gone to LDCs to train local personnel while LDC military officers have often gone to the industrialized countries for intensive training programs.[15]

Remember that we are usually speaking about relatively poor, small, and penetrated societies. Foreign investors (MNCs), banks, and other financial lending institutions like the IMF may insist on "responsible" economic and political policies as a condition for making or renewing investments. They may insist, for example, that prices (and of course wages) be brought down and that wildly fluctuating inflation rates be stabilized and reduced. To do this, discipline must be enforced and sacrifices must be made. As a result, whether or not it is their intention, the demand of foreign interests for economic discipline really becomes a requirement for political discipline—that is, repression. Some observers have argued that this is exactly the mistake being made by the IMF regarding economic reform in Russia. The economic discipline–political discipline relationship is one of the mechanisms by which some theorists link economic and political conditions in the LDCs to theories of economic imperialism.

Foreign penetration (through military aid and investors' requirements for responsible economic policy) and coercive government may support each other as local governments become ever more dependent on foreign support to maintain control over the social unrest that economic developments have created. The condition of peripheral countries in the world economy thus is quite different from that experienced a century or so ago by Europe and North America or even by Japan. Today's LDCs cannot simply copy the development patterns of the OECD world. Most European countries already had a stronger tradition of representative government than exists in most LDCs, though there are exceptions. (Uruguay, for example, probably had a stronger democratic tradition than did imperial Germany.) Thus, even though most European countries experienced periods during their industrialization when income and wealth were very unequally distributed, most of them ultimately were obliged to make concessions and come to some peaceful terms with their peasants and working classes. Those who waited too long, like the czar of Russia, lost everything.

Dependence theory is not entirely correct for all countries. For many LDCs, the inflow of foreign capital may well be essential to the creation of a modern economy. Nevertheless, dependence theory shows us that the achievement of equitable economic and political development is far more complicated than merely a matter of pro-

---

[15] An interesting study reports no systematic relationship between economic dependence in general and breakdowns of democratic government but finds that military aid from the United States in the 1960s and 1970s, largely to support anticommunist regimes, was associated with breakdowns of democracy. See E. N. Muller, "Dependent Economic Development, Aid, and Dependence on the United States and Democratic Breakdown in the Third World," *International Studies Quarterly* 29, 4 (December 1985), 445–469.

moting foreign investment in LDCs. A recipe for trouble is the combination of economic penetration and military dependence (heavy arms imports). Together they tend to magnify economic inequalities, and at the same time give the state more power to repress dissent. The ultimate result may well be violent rebellion.[16]

## ALTERNATIVES TO DEPENDENCE

### *Self-Reliance*

Theorists and governments in LDCs have proposed and tried various alternative policies to avoid the worst effects of dependence. The most radical alternative is **self-reliance,** which implies shifting economic connections from the core countries, the MNCs, and Western aid-giving agencies—in other words, cutting the ties of foreign penetration and dependence. LDCs have tried to build up trade and technical exchange among themselves, especially where domestic markets are too small for economies of scale and where simple labor-intensive technologies seem appropriate for export to other LDCs. Examples include the Central American Common Market or the Caribbean Community and Common Market.

Some states took self-reliance to the extreme of a near-total withdrawal from the world market and a reduction of all exports and imports to a bare minimum. For the past three decades, the government of Burma (now Myanmar) cut most of its ties with the world economy and even sharply reduced tourism, accepting almost complete economic stagnation as the consequence. China, from its break with the Soviet Union in the late 1950s until its new openings to the West in the mid-1970s, also cut foreign economic and cultural contacts to a minimum. China, however, had some economic advantages in its vast population and the diversity of its natural resources. If self-sufficiency was to work anywhere and to allow economic growth to continue, China offered the best opportunity.

Other countries pursued less extreme versions of self-reliance, attempting to reduce, restructure, and control their contacts with the industrial world rather than cut them sharply or entirely. What all these countries had in common, however, was a desire not to emulate the development of the industrial West or of that large majority of countries closely linked with the world capitalist economy. Self-reliance was imposed on the populace by radical socialist leaders, often trying to emulate Soviet development policy during the Stalinist era. Incomes of workers and peasants were kept low to provide a surplus for the government to invest in industry. Being cut off from foreign technology meant backwardness, and being cut off from the competition of the world economy meant inefficiency. Ultimately self-reliance was a complete economic and political disaster. China's experience was the most disappointing for self-

[16] Terry Boswell and William J. Dixon, "Dependency and Rebellion: A Cross-National Analysis," *American Sociological Review* 55 (August 1990), 540–549.

reliance advocates. After running its economy with a minimum of ties to the world market—and experiencing only modest economic growth—China opened up rapidly, inviting foreign trade and investment, and sought ties to the West—especially the United States—as protection against the Soviet Union. The impressive economic growth that followed this opening has led some to project China as a possible fourth economic pole, along with the United States, the EU, and Japan. Chinese economic reform, however, was accompanied by only a limited and temporary relaxation of authoritarian political control. When in 1989 people demanded real democracy, the state showed its violent side in Tiananmen Square.

## A Basic-Needs Strategy

The sometimes extreme and angry words of many LDC representatives as they demand help and concessions from the rich nations frequently offend residents of developed countries, who often respond that they must take care of their own poor citizens before they make giveaways to foreigners. (They could possibly do both; they may in fact do neither.) Yet it is important to be aware that the content of these LDC demands is usually not radical, but reformist. That is, they still take for granted the existence of an integrated world economy and do not challenge its most fundamental hierarchical characteristics. They wish to reduce their dependence somewhat and to obtain better terms of trade for their products. But they are not seeking to overthrow the existing system of international trade and finance, nor are they seeking to withdraw from that system.

Some countries have industrialized successfully, in ways not anticipated by dependence theory. The East Asian NICs are the best examples. South Korea and Taiwan have been able to do so in a quite egalitarian manner. Both countries implemented vast land-reform programs immediately after World War II—Korea under the American occupation, and Taiwan when Chiang Kai-shek, after losing all of mainland China to the communists, fled with his army to the offshore island. In these countries, war and foreign occupation had broken down the traditional sources of resistance to economic growth and equity. Agrarian reforms and redistribution to the poor provided new incentives and a domestic market for simple manufactured goods. Rapid and sustained economic growth followed. Reducing the power of agricultural interests can also lay the basis for independent labor movements and open the possibility of legitimate political challenge to established power, as it did in much of Europe a century ago.[17]

Korea and Taiwan, of course, were not democracies during most of this period of growth. Other countries, like Malaysia, have been able to achieve moderate equality,

---

[17] See Steve Chan, "Growth with Equity: A Test of Olson's Theory for the Asian Pacific-Rim Countries," *Journal of Peace Research* 24, 2 (June 1987), 135–149; M. S. Ahluwalia, G. N. Carter, and Hollis Chenery, "Growth and Poverty in Developing Countries," World Bank Staff Working Paper 309 (Washington, D.C.: World Bank, July 1987); Dieter Senghaas, *The European Experience: A Historical Critique of Development Theory* (Shakopee, Minn.: Berg, 1982).

decent growth, and partially democratic governments. The choice is made to see that, along with economic incentives to entrepreneurs, certain essentials are provided for the mass of the population. Typically this means subsidized rice, health care, education, and transportation. Economists sometimes refer to this as a **basic-needs strategy** of development.

A basic-needs strategy is directed toward raising the living standards of the poorest parts of the population. It is not generally concerned with providing consumer goods for immediate use, which might divert scarce resources from investment and leave everyone no better off when the immediate input of consumer goods has been exhausted. Rather, it tries to build human capital that will eventually provide the basis for economic growth. Economists currently studying the impact of equality on growth have shown that investments in such human capital may be as important as investment in industrial facilities. In the Asian NICs, governments have attempted to give poor people both the incentives and capability to improve earnings through land reform, health measures, and, especially, access to high school education. Amartya Sen, one of the economists pioneering in the study of inequality, has stressed the need for enough income to buy food and has helped shift the focus of governments to improving earning power rather than simply food distribution. He has also pointed out glaring inequalities between men and women in the LDCs.[18] Increasing the equality of social and economic benefits across gender, including higher levels of education and political participation for women, helps reduce rates of population growth (see below) and thus has a positive impact on economic development. Gender equality is not only a human-rights issue but also an important element of development.[19]

An important starting point for a basic-needs strategy, therefore, is to expand primary and then secondary education, with the expectation that a literate population will be able to acquire the skills needed to operate modern industrial equipment and to employ modern agricultural methods. A second aspect is trying to improve health conditions: bringing doctors or nurses to rural villages rather than allowing medical specialists to concentrate on ministering to the rich in the cities, helping villages obtain clean drinking water and build sanitation systems, and instituting programs of mass inoculation and insect control so that major killer diseases can be nearly eliminated at a very low per capita cost.

Economists have shown that countries with basic-needs policies do not necessarily have lower growth rates even at first, and they usually show fast growth rates later on, when education and better health begin to have positive effects on productivity. People who are healthy work better than people who are sick. Children who are well fed do not have their brain development stunted by malnutrition. Moreover, as adults see their own living conditions improve, they become more confident in the future.

---

[18] See Amartya Sen, *Poverty and Famine* (New York: Oxford University Press, 1981). Sen also demonstrates that girls and women get lower levels of nutrition and health care in LDCs, estimating that as many as 100 million women have been the casualties of such structural violence.

[19] See, for instance, V. Spike Peterson and Anne Sisson Runyan, *Global Gender Issues* (Boulder, Colo.: Westview, 1993).

They become more willing to have their children educated (even at the cost of losing them as productive hands on the farm), and they become more willing to save, to the extent they are able, for the future.[20] See Figure 15.4 for an overview of development processes and basic needs.

## Basic Needs and Population Growth

One very important consequence of a basic-needs policy seems to be a greater readiness to adopt contraceptive methods and to limit the size of families. Some observers of development had feared that improving poor people's health would worsen the world population problem: the consequence of prolonging people's lives, and especially of reducing infant mortality, would simply be more mouths to feed. However, longer lives and the better chance that children will live to adulthood make a difference in how people behave. Where children are likely to die before reaching adulthood, a prudent couple who want to be reasonably sure of having heirs, or offspring to care for them in their old age, will produce many children. If, on the other hand, most children can be expected to survive, the need for large families is decreased. Instead, it makes better sense to have fewer children and to invest in those few children by seeing that they are well educated.

To make a major impact, the information and material on birth control must be supplemented either by coercion—forcing people to accept contraception or sterilization, as has been done in China—or by incentives. For a noncoercive policy of limiting population growth, people must be given reasons, principally better health and educational conditions for their offspring. Countries identified as having relatively equal distributions of income and with a strong basic-needs component in their development strategy—such as China, South Korea, and Taiwan—also show low birth rates per 1,000 and rates of population increase of well under 2 percent. These rates are substantially more favorable than those of most other low-income countries. Filling basic needs thus seems to offer the incentive as well as the means for controlling population.

Few other countries have pursued a basic-needs strategy intensively. A basic-needs strategy is not easily compatible with a development program that emphasizes urban development and heavy industry, low wage rates to ensure cheap labor, and foreign investment geared to capital-intensive technology and the production of expensive consumer goods. A revolutionary communist government, as in Cuba or China, may be able to follow a basic-needs strategy because it has expropriated the assets of large landowners and private industrialists. With power concentrated in the party and government bureaucracy rather than in private foreign or domestic interests, major obstacles are removed. Such countries nevertheless pay a heavy price in terms of bureaucratization and suppression of political liberties. As we saw, in South

---

[20] For evidence, see Hollis Chenery et al., *Redistribution with Growth* (London: Oxford University Press, 1974), and Norman L. Hicks, "Growth vs. Basic Needs: Is There a Trade-Off?" *World Development*, 7, 11–12 (1979), 985–994.

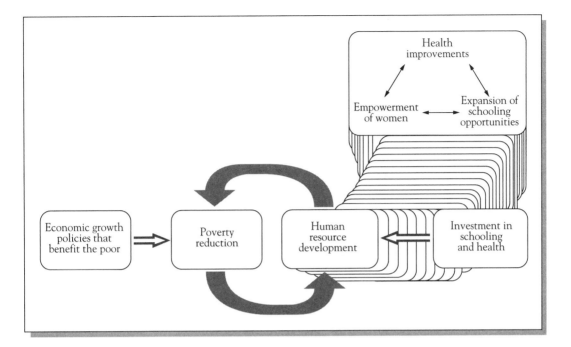

**FIGURE 15.4** Basic needs and development. [*Source:* World Bank, *World Development Report 1993* (New York: Oxford University Press, 1993), p. 37.]

Korea and Taiwan policy was aided by wars that greatly weakened the power bases of previous ruling groups.

The World Bank and some private international development–oriented agencies have encouraged the adoption of basic-needs strategies. Aid-giving institutions have partially shifted from promoting industrial development to improving agricultural productivity, especially for small and medium-sized farms, somewhat improving equity within LDCs. These agencies have also concentrated on training people for individual self-help and collective decision making at the local level. They give particular attention to helping women, who are often especially oppressed in traditional societies, to gain greater control over their own fates.

## A New International Economic Order?

At the level of international action, the LDCs, especially in the 1970s, attempted to create a program of collective international action to lessen their dependence. Demands for restructuring world trade and industry in favor of the LDCs became identified with demands for a **new international economic order** (**NIEO**). These demands included (1) change in the marketing conditions of the world trade in primary commodities,

(2) promotion of industrialization in the LDCs, and (3) increased developmental assistance and debt relief.

## Reform of Commodity Markets

The LDCs have tried to raise and to stabilize the widely fluctuating prices for their exports of agricultural products and minerals. At meetings of the UN Commission on Trade and Development (UNCTAD), which began in 1964 in Geneva (UNCTAD VIII met in Cartegena in 1992), the LDCs pushed for an integrated program for commodities. This program was advocated by a diverse and sometimes very shaky coalition of LDCs known as the Group of 77 (which has in fact grown to include about 150 members). It called for price and production agreements among producers, the creation of international buffer stocks of commodities financed by a common fund, multilateral long-term supply contracts, and other measures to reduce fluctuations in the price of commodity exports.

Some members also called for indexing the price of commodities so that their price would automatically rise with any increase in the price of manufactured goods (much as wages are often tied to the consumer price index in the United States). This last proposal was opposed, however, by many poor countries that were also major commodity importers and by developed countries (which are obviously reluctant to pay higher prices). Although the developed countries have been more open-minded about schemes for stabilizing prices, they have vigorously resisted anything that hinted of indexing. Price changes are necessary for conveying information about changes in market supply and demand. Indexing would be inefficient, encouraging surplus production (as it has for many agricultural commodities like grain and dairy products in the European Community).

Nevertheless, to argue for maintaining current market conditions purely in the name of free competition is very misleading. Most international markets are, to one degree or another, already quite removed from the economist's model of perfect competition. In the words of a prominent international trade theorist:

> Market rules of the game, and the determination of which markets are allowed to operate, are essentially political decisions. Power, whether military or corporate, abhors an uncontrolled and truly competitive market. It would be an extraordinary world in which asymmetries in military and economic power were not reflected in asymmetries in economic relations.[21]

The clearest example is OPEC, which for a while took control of the world oil market and changed the terms of trade markedly in favor of the oil exporters. But many industrial products from the developed countries are also sold in markets that are far from competitive. This is especially the case where a developed country re-

---

[21] Carlos Diaz Alejandro, "North-South Relations," *International Organization* 29, 1 (Winter 1975), 218.

ceives preferential status for its exports to a former colony. Preferential treatment may result from official government agreements or, more likely, informal arrangements that have solidified over the years. This preferential status especially hurts small LDCs (which means most of them) because their domestic markets are not big enough to attract many competitors. In addition, some of the most important primary commodities in world trade, like wheat and corn, originate in the developed countries. Arrangements among national producers and marketers create not a situation of free competition, but one in which there are only a few sellers—oligopolists—who can largely control price and quantity, at least in the short run. Finally, many products sold by LDCs are not sold in a market that is either freely competitive or dominated by the sellers. Rather, the market is often dominated by a few buyers—oligopsonists. Indeed, in most extractive industries, MNCs have the technical expertise to process the material and the marketing organization to sell it. It would be very difficult for the government of an LDC to take over the industry completely and to process and market the material itself. Given the existing market structure, an MNC must do the job. Since there are so few MNCs in most of these industries, the MNC, as buyer from the LDC and seller on the world market, has a great deal of control over price.

Relations between MNCs and LDC governments are, however, neither the same for all countries and industries nor static. Small and poor countries, as well as being weak in the traditional bases of power, also typically lack negotiating experience and skills. Hence, when they have to bargain with MNCs or with developed countries over international marketing agreements, they often do not get very favorable agreements. One study quoted a standard economic text on the topic and added a comment:

> "In a typical situation, a company earns more abroad than the minimum it would accept and a country's net social benefits from the company's presence are greater than the minimum it would accept . . . with a wide gap between the maximum and minimum demands by the two parties." Thus viewed, the outside limits of acceptability could be located by means of economic theory but the precise terms of the investment would be a function of the relative bargaining strengths of the two parties. . . . Equilibrium analysis would give way to power analysis, economics to political science.[22]

A study of long-term negotiations between the Chilean government and multinational copper corporations found that in the early years—when the companies as yet had little invested, the scope of Chilean resources was unknown, and the Chilean government was both very anxious to have the foreign investment and inexperienced in negotiation—the agreements heavily favored the MNCs. But over the years, as the MNCs accumulated huge investments (and thus had a lot to lose if the Chilean government nationalized the foreign-owned enterprises) and the Chileans gained experience, the balance of power and hence the distribution of benefits in subsequent

---

[22] Douglas C. Bennett and Kenneth E. Sharpe, *The Transnational Corporation Versus the State: The Political Economy of the Mexican Auto Industry* (Princeton, N.J.: Princeton University Press, 1985), p. 80. The sentence they quote is from Charles Kindleberger and Bruce Herrick, *Economic Development*, 3rd ed. (New York: McGraw-Hill, 1977), p. 320.

agreements shifted in favor of the Chileans.[23] The power of MNCs has thus led states in LDCs to try to control those MNCs. LDC governments have frequently taken over, or nationalized, MNCs, especially in the economically stronger LDCs where the government has some sophisticated administrative capacity and where the export sector's economic performance has been poor.

After the success of OPEC in revolutionizing the world oil market, both LDCs and developed countries expected similar arrangements to arise for other commodities, as the sellers followed OPEC's example to band together in international commodity cartels. But that did not happen, chiefly because the conditions that favored OPEC largely applied to petroleum products alone. These conditions were:

**1.** Previous cultural and political ties among the Arab members of OPEC (however, this factor should not be exaggerated).

**2.** The lack of ready substitutes for oil, making it very difficult for buyers to refuse to pay higher prices.

**3.** Temporary market conditions of high demand and little excess supply

**4.** The dominant position of Saudi Arabia, and for a while Iran, among oil exporters. If these two could agree on price and quantity, they could bring along the rest of the suppliers; even if one or two small exporters did offer cheaper terms, it did not fundamentally upset the imposed price structure.

No other major commodity cartel has emerged with anything like OPEC's *initial* success. Some effort was made in the bauxite industry (bauxite is the principal ore from which aluminum is refined), but all of the above conditions were lacking. Most important, other aluminum-bearing ores exist in many of the developed countries and would be brought into production if the price of bauxite were raised too high. Another complication for many commodities is the existence of stockpiles in the developed countries. It is not enough for an LDC to have a large share of a commodity's production; to control the world price, it must control the market. That is, it must be able to control the MNCs and the market in substitutes for its commodity as well.

## Industrialization in the Developing World

Even if LDCs could create many new OPEC-like cartels, such cartels might not be fully in their interests. They would still be specializing in primary commodities and thus denied the potential benefits of stimulating development that could come from a shift to manufacturing. At the least, most LDCs want to move into a stage of refining and processing the raw materials they produce. Otherwise, when a nonrenewable resource like a mineral has been extracted, the country is left with little more than a hole in the ground (and perhaps roads and pipelines leading to the hole). However, if the country takes a share in processing or in further manufactures from the raw mate-

---

[23] Theodore H. Moran, *Multinational Corporations and the Politics of Dependence* (Princeton, N.J.: Princeton University Press, 1975).

rial, it can benefit from spin-offs like technical expertise, an infrastructure of communications and transportation, and physical plants and equipment that can be adapted to many uses. The persistent wealth of most developed countries today is based on industry. Processing and diversification seem essential to balanced development, especially in a world where so many natural materials have given way to synthetics.

Exports of technologically advanced manufactured products from industrialized countries are typically subjected to low tariffs by other industrialized countries. This is a result of many years of negotiation and the mutual exchange of preferences, chiefly under the General Agreement on Tariffs and Trade (GATT). GATT is the principal mechanism for ordering the post–World War II system of international trade, created to promote open trade, reduce tariffs and protectionism, and assure access to markets. By the "most favored nation" (MFN) clause, once preferences are given to any country, they must be applied equally to all other countries with whom a state has such an agreement. MFN principles apply throughout most of the world now that restrictions on trade with most communist or former communist countries have been relaxed. The eighth round of GATT—the Uruguay Round—lasted from 1986 to 1994. It continued to reduce tariffs and to deal with such areas as nontariff barriers (NTBs), agriculture, intellectual property, and services. It continued to increase access to markets and trade for both large and small economies. The agreement also replaced GATT with the World Trade Organization, starting in January 1995.

But a general reduction of tariffs on imports of, say, automobiles is helpful only to exporters of automobiles. Most LDCs produce simpler manufactures and thus do not benefit. Many LDCs, by contrast, export refined or processed raw materials or relatively simple and labor-intensive manufactures like textiles. On such goods, tariffs and other restrictions on imports into the industrialized countries are often very high. LDCs can thus be effectively shut out of the world market for those exports. Therefore, they lose the revenue from value added by manufacturing and lose the spin-offs for stimulating development.

In negotiations with the developed countries, LDCs have consistently sought to restructure preferences so they could export more simple manufactures to industrial countries. Some improvements have been made. Members of the European Community in 1975 signed the Lomé Convention with most of their former colonies, and the United States instituted a Generalized Scheme of Preferences favoring some simple manufactures from LDCs. Regional free trade areas, such as NAFTA, may also become important. By 1985 developing countries accounted for 17.4 percent of world exports of manufactured goods. But less than 10 percent of the manufactured goods imported into the OECD came from NICs, and only 12 percent of all manufactured goods consumed in the OECD come from LDCs. Many potential LDC exports are in industries that are declining in developed countries, usually because they are low-technology goods requiring labor-intensive production (labor costs are high in the developed countries). The apparel industry, for instance, is endangered in most European countries, as well as in the United States and Japan. In times of recession, when unemployment and the number of business bankruptcies are high, resistance to granting preferences to exports from LDCs is especially great. For this reason, many economists say that an essential requirement for rising prosperity in LDCs is continued prosperity in the developed countries that serve as their markets.

Developed countries are often willing to see one kind of industry transferred or exported to the LDCs: highly polluting industries. In developed countries, some industries have come under severe governmental regulations to limit their damage to the environment or to workers' health. A good example is the asbestos-processing industry; in the OECD states, it came under such severe regulation to control its cancer-inducing potential that its costs become prohibitively high. As a result, asbestos-processing MNCs moved their operations to LDCs, which were glad to have the new industry. Labor unions are weak in most LDCs and are unable to protect their workers' health effectively, and the workers may be very glad to have good industrial jobs. A job now may mean not starving now; cancer is many years in the future.

Countries following an outward-oriented development strategy (South Korea, Singapore, Thailand) had faster growth rates than did inward-oriented LDCs (Argentina, Ghana, India, and Tanzania). As changes in exchange rates began to price some Japanese goods out of the world market, goods from the NICs replaced them—often spurred by Japanese capital. The industrial countries have been able to absorb the new manufactured goods exported by the NICs. The NICs' governments have targeted certain industries (in South Korea, steel and the automobile industry) for special government assistance, often with great success. Governments and businesspeople have devised some very clever strategies to get around developed countries' nontariff barriers to their trade. Yet there remains a question as to whether there is room for many more countries to follow in their path. Could world markets absorb enough manufactures from such vast countries as China and India to make much difference in those countries' levels of poverty? At the meeting of the UN Industrial Development Organization (UNIDO) in Lima in 1975, the Group of 77 set themselves a target of accounting for 25 percent of world industrial output by the year 2000. At that time their share was 7 percent. By the mid-1980s it had become 10 percent, but there is almost no prospect of the group's reaching its ambitious target.

As an alternative or supplement to export-led development, some countries are still pursuing policies of substituting domestic manufactures for imported ones. For some of the larger LDCs, like Brazil, Mexico, India, and Nigeria, this approach has some promise. Their governments have instituted various requirements for *indigenization* by MNCs; for instance, products must be composed of a certain percentage of locally manufactured components and the firms must have a certain percentage of local ownership or management.

Indigenization requirements, however, do not address questions of whether Western high-technology goods and production processes are appropriate to LDCs. Nor can they do much for small or poor countries that cannot offer large markets for import-substituting manufactures. Efforts at regional economic integration to create larger markets have had mixed results—for instance, ASEAN (Association of South East Asian Nations) has had positive results, but the Latin American Free Trade Area was not successful. MNCs have found ingenious ways to evade indigenization regulations or to persuade LDCs to admit more manufacturers than would be optimal for their small markets. For example, when the Mexican government was making plans to license a small number of automobile manufacturers to operate in Mexico, some American and Japanese MNCs feared they would be shut out. They persuaded their governments to pressure the Mexican government to include them. In the end, 10 automobile manufacturers were permitted—far too many for the fairly small Mexican market.[24] In some of the worst cases—tractor factories in Russia, shoe companies in Tanzania, shipyards in Poland—state-owned or state-protected industries have been so inefficient that the products were worth less than the raw materials from which they were made.

Economic reforms at home are a key part of recent LDC development strategies. Protective tariffs and quotas for domestic industry are being dismantled, subjecting local industry to the competitive pressures of the world market. Some such industries prove too inefficient to survive competition with imports; others, like the Chilean steel industry, thrive and become efficient exporters of specialty goods. Governments are reducing subsidies to private industry, dismantling some of the maze of government regulations, and selling off government-owned corporations. In 1991 the new government of India announced that it would reduce government regulation and encourage private investment, reversing its longstanding preferences for central planning and government ownership. Between 1982 and 1990 the Mexican government sold to the private sector 875 of 1,155 government-owned companies, including the national telephone company and airline. Private investors came in from abroad, and Mexicans who had taken their money overseas have been bringing it back—about $10 billion of it.

## Debt Relief and Developmental Assistance

Many LDCs have called for relief from or rescheduling of their foreign debts. For countries facing international bankruptcy, relief is essential. The U.S. government's own budget and trade deficits magnify the problem. Many LDCs may never repay the principal on their loans; some cannot even afford to keep up payments on the interest. Some countries that essentially solved their problems of trade dependence through industrialization have fallen back into another form of dependence—debt. Foreign debts have had the effect of severely handicapping the efforts of countries like the Philippines and many Latin American states to stabilize their economies and reinstitute democracy. If big countries like Mexico or Brazil should default on their payments, big banks in the developed countries, which have lent large sums to LDCs, could go bankrupt. The developed countries thus have a direct interest in keeping the LDCs afloat financially. As the immediate debt crisis is surmounted, the needs for long-term development financing reappear. Whereas foreign economic aid amounted to 0.51 percent of the OECD countries' GNP in 1960, it fell to about 0.35 percent in the 1980s, and only rebounded to about 0.4 percent in 1991. This occurred despite an earlier agreement by the developed countries to accept a target of raising economic assistance to 0.7 percent of their GNP. There is no indication of a general, systematic upswing in aid from the industrialized countries. Between 1970 and 1992, significant increases of aid as a percentage of GNP occurred in the Scandinavian countries,

---

[24] Bennett and Sharpe, *The Transnational Corporation Versus the State*, pp. 57–59. See also Thomas J. Biersteker, *Multinationals, the State, and Control of the Nigerian Economy* (Princeton, N.J.: Princeton University Press, 1987).

Switzerland, Italy, and the Netherlands; the percentage dropped for the United States and Britain. The absolute amount of Japanese aid also rose substantially.

The problem of maintaining LDCs' development will require creative problem solving by the industrial countries as well as by the LDCs themselves. The situation for LDCs has been exacerbated by the end of the cold war. Whatever advantage some LDCs had in the cold war competition for friends and allies—and thus in extracting aid from both the United States and Soviet Union—is gone. Instead, LDCs now find themselves in competition with the Eastern European and FSU countries for Western aid. The geographic proximity of the former communist areas make them more important to the EU and OECD countries, especially in the movement for European unity and stability. Germany's experience with the ongoing integration of the former East Germany has indicated the scope of the effort needed. Not only do some of the FSU states have significant economic problems—with negative GNP per capita growth rates (for example, for 1985–1993: Georgia, –16.4 percent; Armenia, –11.7 percent; Moldova, –5.4 percent)—they are also states that have moved away from liberalization and democracy. Some developed states are also in competition with the LDCs: the U.S. trade deficit continues to draw in huge amounts of foreign investment capital that might otherwise go into LDCs.

## THINGS THAT GO TOGETHER

Economic stagnation is both a consequence of the debt crisis (export earnings must be used to keep running in place on debt payments) and a cause of it (the debt is a bigger brake on growth for a stagnant economy in a stagnant world market). It is the combination of debt and stagnation that brought about the collapse of many authoritarian governments during the past decade. They came to power to get the economy moving, and they failed. With the economic failure, their peoples would no longer put up with governments that were politically repressive and could not deliver the material goods. Throughout the world, authoritarian regimes have been discredited. Communist and right-wing military dictatorships have shared that fate. The result gives democracy a chance. But if less developed countries cannot solve their economic problems—the need for growth, with equity—their democratic governments are not likely to be tolerated indefinitely; as noted, this reaction can already be seen in some FSU states. Without a better life, their people will lose faith in democratic government, just as they did in dictatorships. The prospects for growth, equity, and liberty in the LDCs are thus thoroughly intertwined.

The developing world is enormously diverse in many ways: in culture, in degree and kind of ties to the rest of the world, in political systems, in resources, and in levels of economic activity. Theories of development and of dependence are important but partial tools for trying to understand what is happening there. The phenomena are so complex that they defy easy generalization. LDC governments are concerned not only with gaining a higher standard of living for their people, but also with enhancing their own state power. Some of the demands for assistance simply reflect this desire to strengthen the instruments of central governmental authority.[25] Any theory has to address the effects of different developmental contexts and experiences. World resources and social conditions are changing rapidly. The menu of choice presented to leaders of LDCs is constrained by the hierarchical nature of the international political and economic system, by numerous transnational linkages (political, financial, commercial, and cultural), and by the relative strength of various groups and social classes within those countries.

The body of tested theory to support reliable policy recommendations for the LDCs is very small. The lives of billions of people—their hopes for relief from the physical misery of poverty and for the implementation of political liberties—are at stake. A responsible analyst, therefore, must tread a treacherous line between irresponsibly ignoring the desperate problems of these people and irresponsibly offering ill-conceived "solutions" that others (not the analysts) will have to live with. A responsible social scientist in a rich industrialized country cannot become, in the words of the West Indian novelist V. S. Naipaul,

> one of those who continue to simplify the world and reduce other men to a cause, the people who substitute doctrine for knowledge and irritation for concern, the revolutionaries who visit centres of revolution with return air tickets . . . the people who wish themselves on societies more fragile than their own, all those people who in the end do no more than celebrate their own security.[26]

---

[25] Stephen Krasner, *Structural Conflict: The Third World Against Global Liberalism* (Berkeley: University of California Press, 1985).
[26] "The Killings in Trinidad: Part Two," Sunday *Times* (London), May 19, 1974, p. 41.

# 16

## PROBLEMS OF ORDER AND INTERDEPENDENCE IN THE WORLD SYSTEM

## ORDER AND ANARCHY

So far we have presented several central problems that have developed since the end of World War II and that characterize international relations today. The changing menu and states' attempts to adapt to that menu have generated the political, economic, and military conflicts that shape those problems.

But as new states and other international actors have come into being and as new technologies and ideologies have altered the international environment, the practices of states and other international actors have adapted to these changes to maintain order within the international system. Although there is formal anarchy—the absence of a central authority with coercive power—within that system, we have seen that there is actually also much order, cooperation, coordination, and collaboration in international relations. There is, as Hedley Bull calls it, an "anarchical society." Bull argues that such a society exists because there is *order*. Patterns of behavior that are more or less *predictable* both produce and conform to the *expectations* of the actors in the international system.[1]

This is a crucial point: it means that order can exist without formal rules or with only a primitive system of rules. Order is difficult enough to obtain within societies that have central governmental authorities; the environment of world politics creates even more problems. The ability to create order and the frequency and virulence of conflicts depend largely on the relationships among international actors. One feature of systems and the relationships among the components of those systems is *interdependence*. Interdependence both contributes to the problems of creating order and creates the conditions necessary for attaining order. In this chapter we shall look at interdependence and its effects on order in world politics; in the following one we shall outline the ways in which international actors attempt to overcome the problems of cooperation and coordination in an anarchic but interdependent world system.

## INTERDEPENDENCE AND THE WORLD SYSTEM

We have stated that interdependence is a quality of all systems and that we can think of world politics as a system. Instead of looking at one state and the foreign policy processes that go on within it, we can look at the system of states and other international actors and the various networks of relationships among them. Systems thinking emphasizes wholeness, the larger picture; looking at the international system means looking at the patterns of interactions among the actors. Interdependence emphasizes the links or interconnectedness among the units of a system. Interdependence is one form of constraint that the system places on the state and other actors in terms of opportunities or possibilities and on decision makers in terms of willingness. What is on one actor's menu depends very much on how that menu is connected to the menus of other actors.

### Interdependence: Conflict and Harmony

How might interdependence constrain the menu? By our definition of interdependence, changes or events in any single part of a system will produce some reaction from or have some significant consequence to other actors of the system *whether they like it or not*. The images of the global village, the spaceship earth, and the shrinking planet are all derived from this idea of interdependence. One view of interdependence

---

[1] See Hedley Bull, *The Anarchical Society* (New York: Columbia University Press, 1977), chap. 1.

is positive and optimistic, seeing interdependence as leading toward more and more cooperation among states as they are brought together. The models of integration discussed in Chapter 14 were based on increasing the linkages of interdependence through functional integration (as in the movement for European unity) or through social, economic, and political integration based on transactions. Some integration models go so far as to predict that the outcomes of these integration processes will eventually lead to world community or a world state.

Another view, however, points to interdependence as a constraint on states and therefore as a potentially very important source of conflict. Interdependences (especially if, as pointed out in Chapter 15, they are lopsided, making one party much more dependent than the other) can also generate frustration and anger, as states hopelessly wish for past times when they were not inextricably linked with others and when they had greater freedom of action. Mutual dependence need not mean mutual reward (as is required in integration). One scholar simply notes that "the growth of interdependence increases the capacity of all relevant actors to injure each other."[2]

Interdependence and the idea of sovereignty, which carries the formal and legal assumption of autonomy and equality among states, *do not mix well*. Look again at the Peace of Westphalia. The statesmen and leaders who fashioned this settlement were creating agreements that met the needs of that time. Very clear *trade-offs* were made between autonomy and self-control on the one hand and the lack of order inherent in the anarchic international system on the other: princes who were striving for independence of action from the control of religious or imperial authority (the Pope and the Holy Roman Emperor) were willing to create a system of states that had no formal source of authority or higher order. This trade-off, sensible at the time, has fostered a set of contemporary problems arising from growth in the levels and scope of interdependence. The **Westphalian trade-off** stressed independence and autonomy; interdependence stresses collective problems and solutions. The balance has been changing, especially in the decades since World War II; the trade-off has come to stress the need to reduce the formal anarchy of the system in order to solve the problems of interdependence.

International law, created as a way to provide some degree of order among states, recognized that sovereignty was based on the autonomy of those states. International law, therefore, attempted to create order among states through the idea of *consent,* or self-constraint. How does interdependence produce constraints without consent? The answer derives from the elements of sensitivity and vulnerability, which make up interdependence. Interdependence can cause conflict if a sensitive state does not wish to be sensitive; for example, many trading countries were greatly affected in 1971, when the United States surprised the world by devaluing the dollar. A sensitive state need not be a vulnerable one, however: larger, wealthier, more powerful states may be able to deal with their sensitivities. Vulnerability can cause military conflict if a state finds it impossible to prevent others from imposing costs on it: U.S. interests in assur-

---

[2] Oran Young, "International Regimes: Problems of Concept Formation," *World Politics* 32 (April 1980), 331–356.

ing relatively cheap oil, for example, contributed to American use of the military to oppose Iraq. Population growth in one part of the world or greater demand in another can also affect others by the consumption of nonrenewable resources. The consumption of food that others need or the production of pollution that fouls air or kills fish in the waters of other states will affect vulnerable states whether they want to be affected or not.

## A "New" Interdependence?

Some analysts focus on the extensive new webs of interdependence that are creating a truly global system for the first time. Through technology and the dismantling of colonial empires, there is much that is new; however, much of what is being seen as interdependence is not new but is just being recognized for the first time. Thus we can talk about both the *conditions* of interdependence (the existence of linkages that hold the system together) and the *cognitions* of interdependence (people seeing or perceiving that interdependence exists).

Many of today's conditions are indeed quite new, especially in that some states are much more sensitive and vulnerable than ever before. We have discussed states that are small and poor and have only a token degree of autonomy; many of these states are constantly buffeted by systemic economic, monetary, and political forces and are far more sensitive and vulnerable than most states in the past have been. They, and all international actors, are more interdependent because of the increasing opportunities for interaction that have been provided by technological advances in communication and transportation—the increasing ability to send words and things farther, faster, and at less cost (the "microelectronic revolution"). Increasing linkages have occurred not only between governmental elites, but also through and across all segments of the population of a state, often facilitated by the activities of nongovernmental organizations (NGOs) like multinational corporations. In today's world some of these linkages can occur with incredible speed.

Technology has expanded not only the physical capabilities of people to interact with each other, but also consciousness of that interaction. A major consequence of the microelectronic revolution is the rapid spread throughout the world of analytic capabilities to individual citizens. These capabilities come from increased computer usage and the ability to communicate through telephone networks, electronic mail and fax facilities, and radio and television. The number of television transmitters in the world increased more than sevenfold from 1965 to 1985 (from 8,500 to more than 60,000); television sets worldwide rose from 186 million in 1965 to 661 million in 1985.[3] Thus the "new" interdependence is based to a large degree on new patterns of human attention. Individuals can see things that are happening in faraway places, anywhere on the planet. The democratic revolutions across Eastern Europe have been called the

---

[3] The microelectronic revolution is one of the major themes of Rosenau's sweeping look at change in the contemporary system, *Turbulence in World Politics* (Princeton, N.J.: Princeton University Press, 1990); see especially chaps. 12 and 13.

"television revolutions," as people in each country watched and then emulated what had just happened somewhere else in the region.

The microelectronic revolution highlights the psychological dimension of interdependence. This psychological aspect means not only that people are aware that activities are taking place elsewhere, but they are aware that they are aware. They understand that they belong to some sort of global village, to use Marshall McLuhan's famous term, and that they exist in some larger world system. Television and radio have brought foreign events—"live and in color"—into homes all around the world: "For Shakespeare it was a metaphor, but for our generation it has become a reality: the world is now literally a stage, as its actors dance across the TV screen."[4]

Interdependence increases as states become more vulnerable to penetration of various kinds. Interdependence can occur only when the hard shell of the state—its sovereignty—is cracked. Because of both increased interdependence and increased awareness of interdependence, governmental decision makers have to think about and take into account the effects their internal policies have on foreign relations with other states—for example, U.S. economic choices dealing with the size of its national debt and governmental deficit, South African treatment of the black population, Israeli treatment of Arab citizens of Israel. The remarkable changes in South African politics, and the progress toward peace by Israel and its neighbors, were clearly impelled by interdependence in a post–cold war period. Whether or not actions, events, or policies were meant to cross state boundaries or to affect the peoples and governments of other states, they do. This, in a nutshell, is interdependence.

## TRANSNATIONAL RELATIONS AND INTERDEPENDENCE

National boundaries have become less and less relevant. Many scholars, writers, and even statesmen feel that continuing to view the world in terms of the traditional Westphalian logic is not very useful and may be downright harmful, given the nature of contemporary interdependences. These observers are implicitly calling for a reversal of the Westphalian trade-off; they feel that if governments continue to look at the world in terms of old images (including that of sovereign nation-states concerned with independent behavior and military power), such views will lead to wrong-headed policies that may be disastrous for humankind. This view has been most extensively expressed by political scientists who see the world in terms of **transnational relations** rather than international relations.

Transnationalism has been described as the movement of goods, information, and ideas across national boundaries *without* significant, direct participation or control by high-level governmental actors. These patterns of penetration and linkage involve heavy participation by various kinds of nonstate actors, particularly NGOs. This

---

[4] Rosenau, *Turbulence in World Politics*, p. 344.

transnational view clearly reduces the importance of the ideas of sovereignty, national boundaries, and the interaction of governments in the world system. Because each state has become so permeable, so open to outside influences, domestic and international politics have become indistinguishable. These transnational patterns can be seen more clearly in Figure 16.1, which contrasts the state-centered view of international politics and the transnational view of world politics.[5]

The main point to note is the multiplicity of interactions that bypass the governments of states and act directly on their domestic environments. In the transnational view, nonstate actors (NGOs in particular) are much more important actors than previously thought, as are the interest groups or subnational actors that exist within states. We have discussed the influence of tribal, ethnic, or separatist groups within states, as well as that of economic interests, MNCs, and parts of the governmental bureaucracy. These last, acting in accordance with the organizational process model, often interact directly with comparable parts of other states' bureaucracies, many times without the knowledge of the top decision makers of the states involved.[6] Both the NGOs and the subnational actors are distinct from state actors and can act independently from states. Some observers even argue that there is no neat hierarchical pattern of influence and authority; in other words, states are not necessarily the most powerful actors, nor subnational actors the least powerful. As we have already seen when discussing power in different issue areas, it is impossible to rank states above MNCs or other groups all the time in all circumstances.

These transnational actors make up Rosenau's multicentric world—the groups of many thousands of diverse actors (individuals, groups, organizations, movements) that seek autonomy of action from states. In the multicentric world of non-sovereignty-bound, nonstate (and nonterritorial) actors, the key issue is the "autonomy dilemma" of freedom of action rather than the "security dilemma" of states. The transnational view holds that nonstate actors can affect nation-states. The different needs and vulnerabilities of states, intergovernmental organizations (IGOs), and NGOs provide all actors with some levers of influence. This is especially important to the transnational view, because it holds that the issues that have been central to international interaction are changing and that military-security issues are no longer the primary ones. Indeed, interdependence generates a new set of problems and demands on those in authority. The power of states has been based largely on military capability. But we have shown that military capability is not easily convertible across issue areas and situations, so that states are not necessarily well equipped to handle these demands (what Rosenau has called "the narrowing competence of governments").

The Westphalian, state-centered view focuses on power and security and is, in essence, the realist view of international politics. In the transnational view, such matters are no longer central but are replaced by economic, cultural, social, and other concerns. As with the phenomenon of integration, a transnational perspective presents us

---

[5] The seminal work in transnational relations is Robert Keohane and Joseph S. Nye, eds., *Transnational Relations and World Politics* (Cambridge, Mass.: Harvard University Press, 1972).
[6] See Samuel Huntington, "Transnational Organizations and World Politics," *World Politics* 25 (1973), 333–368.

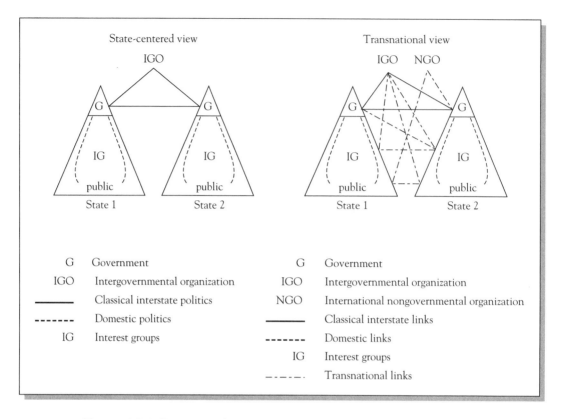

State-centered view

| | |
|---|---|
| G | Government |
| IGO | Intergovernmental organization |
| ——— | Classical interstate politics |
| - - - - - | Domestic politics |
| IG | Interest groups |

Transnational view

| | |
|---|---|
| G | Government |
| IGO | Intergovernmental organization |
| NGO | International nongovernmental organization |
| ——— | Classical interstate links |
| - - - - - | Domestic links |
| IG | Interest groups |
| – – – – – | Transnational links |

**FIGURE 16.1** Comparing the state-centered and transnational views of world politics. [*Source:* Raymond Hopkins and Richard Mansbach, *Structure and Process in International Politics* (New York: Harper & Row, 1973), p. 134. Adapted from Robert O. Keohane and Joseph S. Nye, "Transnational Relations and World Politics: An Introduction," *International Organization* 25 (Summer 1971), 332–334.]

with a multitude of anomalies, things that we should not expect to happen (or to be important) if the realist view held.

> For every quintessential "realist" happening—such as the Soviet invasion of Afghanistan or the U.S. intervention in Central America—innumerable events occur for which realism has, at best, a strained and insufficient explanation. A private group, the Natural Resources Defense Council (NRDC), negotiates with the superpower governments to monitor nuclear test-ban agreements; a representative of the Church of England serves as a link between terrorists and governments in the Middle East; a variety of organizations make decisions to invest or disinvest in an effort to alter the social policies of the South African government; the IMF instructs national governments on their economic policies; . . . Poles in the United States are given the franchise in the 1989 Polish elections, and their ballots are believed to be decisive in one Warsaw district; . . . a novel published in England leads to the withdrawal of ambassadors from Iran and to an assassination in Belgium; two poisoned grapes from Chile disrupt

world markets, provoke actions by several governments, lead to labor tensions in the docks of Philadelphia, and foster disarray in Chile itself.[7]

Clearly, removing military issues from the center of the issue agenda is based on the increasing sensitivity and vulnerability of states and nonstate actors to *economic* interdependences. International economic relationships are becoming more and more sensitive to domestic economic factors such as taxation, inflation, and monetary policy. The reverse is also true. U.S. relations with European allies, the strength of the dollar on world money markets, and thus the economic standing of the United States—as well as its trade policies regarding arms, technology, and food—are all related to domestic policies on deficits and a balanced budget. Advocates of the transnational view want to highlight the relationships between international politics and international economics, illustrated in Figure 16.2. According to a transnational view, what is new in this diagram are the diagonal dashed lines. They indicate that domestic politics can influence international economics directly, and vice versa, and that domestic economics can affect international politics directly, and vice versa.

One of the main instruments by which economic interdependences have increased is the MNC. As noted in Chapter 3, MNCs are just one of the postwar challenges to the nation-state. We have discussed several ways in which MNCs rival states. The global "megacorporation" is transforming the world political economy through its increasing control over three fundamental resources of economic life: the technology of production, finance capital, and marketing. Industry is no longer constrained by geography, since production makes national boundaries irrelevant. Transnational production also makes loyalty to any one state irrelevant. As examples of Rosenau's non-sovereignty-bound actors, such corporations have become "less and less accountable." Although loyalty is the basis of nationalism, MNCs are careful not to favor any country in which they do business over any other such country:

> "For business purposes," says the president of the IBM World Trade Corporation, "the boundaries that separate one nation from another are no more real than the equator. They are merely convenient demarcations of ethnic, linguistic, and cultural entities. They do not define business requirements or consumer trends. Once management understands and accepts this world economy, its view of the marketplace—and its planning—necessarily expand. The world outside the home country is no longer viewed as series of disconnected customers and prospects for its products, but as an extension of a single market."[8]

---

[7] Rosenau, *Turbulence in World Politics*, pp. 93–94. Rosenau provides a wide variety of examples of the spiraling growth of transnational interactions—how they characterize the multicentric system as well as impact on the state-centric system.

[8] See Richard Barnet and John Cavanaugh, *Global Dreams: Imperial Corporations and the New World Order* (New York: Simon & Schuster, 1994); the quotation is from the earlier work by Barnet and Ronald E. Muller, *Global Reach* (New York: Simon & Schuster, 1974), pp. 14–15. Also, Rosenau notes: "A particularly incisive indicator of the autonomy that has accrued to actors in the multi-centric world is the readiness of U.S. companies to abandon their national identity and proclaim themselves global enterprises whose well-being is no longer dependent on the American economy," *Turbulence in World Politics*, p. 255.

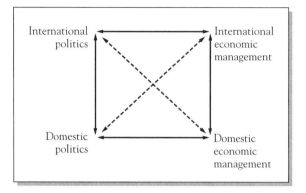

**FIGURE 16.2** Transnational linkages—politics and economics. [*Source:* Susan Strange, "The Dollar Crisis, 1971," *International Affairs* 48 (April 1972), 197.]

Although economically oriented, transnationalism does include nonstate transnational actors that are concerned with military activity. Both guerrilla movements and terrorist groups may be seen as transnational actors, penetrating the state's hard shell. Revolutionary nongovernmental groups move across national boundaries for sanctuary and aid in order to make violent attacks on people in power whom they identify as enemies. Terrorist groups may be factions of nationalist or separatist groups, or they may be ideological sects, such as the German Red Army faction or the Japanese United Red Army, or they may be transnational gangs that recruit from many countries. They may also collaborate with each other:

> In May 1970 three members of the Japanese United Red Army opened fire at the Lod Airport terminal near Tel Aviv, killing 27 and injuring 69. Many of the victims were Puerto Ricans visiting the Holy Land, prompting one survivor to ask, "What are Japanese doing killing Puerto Ricans in Israel?" The answer to this puzzled inquiry appears to be that the Japanese radicals were recruited for this mission by the Palestinian group Black September.[9]

Such groups produce several forms of interdependence. First, modern communications techniques make it possible for them to be aware of and then to copy the tactics of other terrorist groups. Thus it is not uncommon to find a rash of kidnappings or airplane hijackings occurring around the world after a major successful use of the technique. Communications, especially the microelectronic revolution, are crucial to the whole concept of terrorism. The contemporary terrorist has a global audience that can be affected in many ways by a lone act that is geographically distant in the system but that is made psychologically near through communications technology.

---

[9] Peter Sederberg, *Terrorist Myths* (Englewood Cliffs, N.J.: Prentice-Hall, 1989), p. 114.

Terrorist and guerrilla activity may also lead to governmental interactions and thus to more interdependence in the system. Governments have acted together to train antiguerrilla and antiterrorist units. Governments have also acted through IGOs, such as the United Nations or the Organization of American States, to outlaw or provide for cooperation against certain acts (for example, by treaties prohibiting offenses against diplomats). National police forces have been coordinated through Interpol to combat terrorism as well as the growing phenomenon of transnational criminal organizations.[10] Transnational terrorist activities have even prompted countermeasures from purely transnational NGOs, such as the international airline pilots unions, which brought direct pressure against governments and IGOs to institute measures against hijackings.

The growth of transnational interactions and interdependences in the post–World War II era has helped produce new problems and new challenges to the state. They mirror the transnationalist perspective's challenge to realism. This challenge, as outlined above, can be summarized in the three elements of Keohane and Nye's concept of **"complex interdependence"**: (1) complex interdependence refutes the notion that only states count, and argues that there are numerous other consequential actors and interactions; (2) complex interdependence argues that there no longer exists a set hierarchy of issues dominated by the concerns of military security; and (3) the arguments of complex interdependence preclude the use of military force among a number of states.[11]

The freedom and independence promised by sovereignty have been buffeted and challenged by technology, economics, and nonstate actors that regularly penetrate the state's hard shell. This has been a period of turbulence, characterized both by high levels of complexity and by high degrees of change. Rosenau calls this period of transition, when long-term patterns of behavior are in flux, "postinternational politics." This is another way of indicating a shift in the Westphalian trade-off, as states seek to adapt to a changing environment. These changes are outlined in Figure 16.3, which adds a dynamic dimension to the scheme presented in Figure 16.1. It shows the development of the multicentric world since 1945.

## INDIVIDUALS, GROUPS, AND INTERDEPENDENCE

States act to achieve their goals and interests both singly and in groups. As the world has become more tightly linked through various interdependences, states have found themselves grouped together in international organizations and regional groupings or

---

[10] Some have identified transnational criminal organizations as an important element of global disorder and a growing threat to national and international security. See Phil Williams, "Transnational Criminal Organizations and International Security," *Survival* 36 (Spring 1994), 96–113.

[11] Robert O. Keohane and Joseph S. Nye, *Power and Interdependence*, 2nd ed. (Boston: Scott, Foresman, 1989).

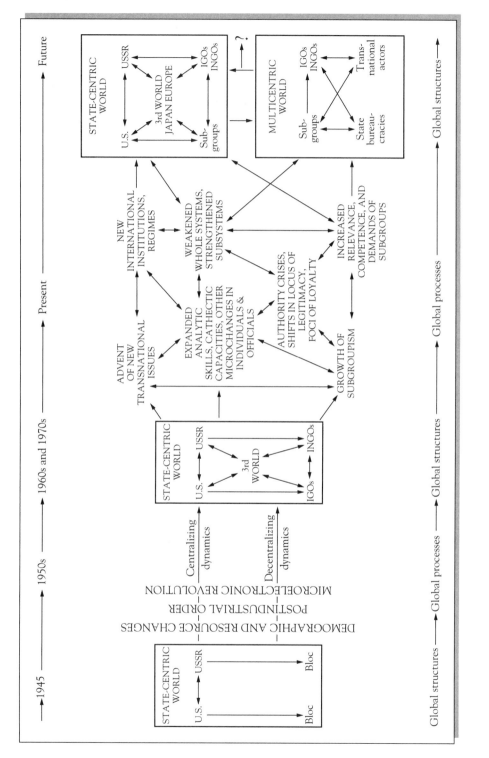

**FIGURE 16.3** Development of the multicentric world since 1945. [*Source:* James N. Rosenau, *Turbulence in World Politics* (Princeton, N.J.: Princeton University Press, 1990), p. 14.]

subsystems that are economic, political, and military in nature. States also belong to a world system. We may think of each state (as well as the other international actors) as a member of a group (or system) that includes the entire globe. Being a member of a group complicates what any individual member can achieve and how the member achieves it because of the influence of the sensitivity and vulnerability of interdependence. Clearly, interdependence affects how individual interests relate to group interests. Sometimes leaders of states think they are acting in their own interests when they are not. This is yet another argument for transnationalism; it points out that the traditional notion of individual states seeking their own special or national interests is now counterproductive in a world where states are enmeshed in many different kinds of groups.

How can we not act in our own best interest? The important point is to see *how individual interests relate to group interests*. This relationship is clearly illustrated in *Catch-22*, Joseph Heller's novel about World War II. Yossarian, a bombardier in the U.S. Army Air Force in Italy, refuses to fly any more missions. Major Major, a superior officer, in trying to persuade Yossarian to fly, asks, "Would you like to see our country lose?" Yossarian replies, "We won't lose. We've got more men, more money and more material. There are ten million men in uniform getting killed and a lot more are making money and having fun. Let somebody else get killed." Major Major replies, "But suppose everybody on our side felt that way." Yossarian's answer is devastatingly to the point: "Then I'd certainly be a damn fool to feel any other way. Wouldn't I?"[12]

This episode raises the central dilemma of the individual and the group: the interdependence of units within a system. If all the other fliers are willing to fly their missions, then Yossarian would be a fool to go along, because with 10 million men in the war, his individual presence will not make a difference. On the other hand, if none of the others wishes to fly either, then his response, "I'd be a damned fool to feel any other way," is a *rational* answer. His presence would again make no difference. However, if all the other fliers were to take the same position, then the following dilemma develops: despite the fact that missions have to be flown, it is not rational for any single individual to participate. (This dilemma is similar to the problem of cooperation in the prisoners' dilemma.) For the collective—a group of individuals—the goal of winning the war can be achieved only through group action. Yet such group action consists of the activities of individuals, and Yossarian makes it clear that it does not seem rational for any single individual to perform the actions needed to achieve the group's goal. So, how do groups of supposedly rational actors ever accomplish group or collective goals? Why, for example, should any single state stop hunting whales, stop polluting the oceans or the air, stop increasing population, stop increasing its use of oil, obey international law, or participate in arms control?

The dilemma rests in large part in the nature of the *goods* being provided. A "good"—the word is used here as economists use it—is simply the consequence of an activity. If such outcomes, consequences, or payoffs are tangible things that can be possessed as property by a single person, they are what economists call **private goods**.

---

[12] Joseph Heller, *Catch-22* (New York: Dell, 1961), p. 107.

A private good is fully or perfectly divisible, and it is "appropriable"—that is, it can be split up, and parts can be used or consumed by individual members of a group. The consumption of a private good by one person reduces the amount of that good left for any other individual. A steak one person eats cannot be eaten by another; a haircut is a good given to one individual; a pair of shoes one person wears cannot be worn by another at the same time. Land that one person (or one state) owns cannot be owned by another person (or state).

Private goods form the basis of most of the analysis involved in the study of economics. Economists have been concerned with how private goods are distributed, or allocated, among people. The allocation of private goods involves questions of costs, of how people value things. Costs are determined by supply and demand: how much of the good is available and how much people want. Economists study how supply and demand, influenced by the market mechanism, determine the prices of things and their distribution. Under ideal conditions, private goods and the market solve the individual/group problem pointed out by Yossarian: each individual, seeking to maximize his or her own interests, buys and sells as desired, affected only by supply and demand. If each individual seeks to do this in an economic system where only private goods exist, the whole group will benefit if each person follows individual interests, as we shall see below.

Suppose people were interested only in private goods, not in winning a war or preserving democracy. Then they would fly only if they would receive something that they could possess as a private good, like money. Pilots would fly if someone paid them enough, and the market mechanism would work to get some people to fly. If an insufficient number of pilots came forward, the pay for flying would go up, and more people would be willing to fly. But as the supply of fliers increased, the pay would go down, and fewer people would come forward; eventually there would be a fairly stable number of pilots willing to fly bombers. The whole group benefits from this situation.

But the world doesn't work exactly this way. The market mechanism based on supply and demand does not, in fact, work perfectly; it works poorly for many goods and not at all for others. For many goods a person's choices—costs and benefits—derive from considerations other than supply and demand. Many goods have properties and characteristics that make them different from private goods. These are goods that have "externalities." **Externalities** affect people's choices, costs, and benefits through factors other than supply and demand. Without externalities, one's costs and benefits derive from one's own values and desires, and the cost of goods is determined by the producer (according to his or her own costs, profit margin, and so on). If externalities are present, however, the activities of other consumers and producers can affect both one's benefits and the producer's costs. For example, Jones buys a cat for the private good of killing the mice on her property. However, those mice also bothered Smith's property, so that, by eating the mice, Jones's cat has produced benefits for Smith: an externality. During the nineteenth century, to protect its private good of security for its colonial possessions and its profitable trade, the British navy policed the sea lanes of the Western Hemisphere and prevented possible intervention by other European major powers. Like Jones's cat, the British navy provided externalities to the young United States, which also benefited from the conditions for secure trade.

Externalities can also increase costs. Jones's new car, while a private good in the sense that it belongs to her and only she can ride in it, is also bright red. Smith, whose front window looks directly on Jones's driveway, becomes sick at the sight of bright red. Smith thus incurs costs from Jones's car: he can look out his window and get sick or keep the curtains drawn and not be able to see outside—and have to use more electricity for lighting instead of natural light. The Soviet Union makes a private decision to provide its own electricity through nuclear power. In 1986 one of its "private" nuclear plants at Chernobyl has an accident, and all its European neighbors to the west must incur costs in being exposed to radiation and in cleaning up that radiation.

As you can see, the consequences of externalities can be any combination of positive and negative effects. Externalities involve the spillover of effects to other members of the group or system, and changes or activities in one unit produce effects in others—interdependences. Just as with interdependence, sovereignty does not mix well with externalities and may result in conflict if the effects are negative: "The principle of sovereignty in effect establishes rules of liability that put the burden of externalities on those who *suffer from them*."[13]

## Characteristics of Collective Goods

**Collective goods** are goods with certain kinds of externality properties. Here the externalities are found in their most extreme form. Collective goods possess two special characteristics, the first a prerequisite for the second. More important, these two characteristics describe a "pure" collective good, something rarely found in the real world. For that reason we should think of goods as being more or less characterized by collective-good properties.

The first special characteristic, perhaps the key one, is *jointness of supply*. If a good is supplied to any member of a group, then it is supplied to all members of that group. Jointness of supply also means that if new members are added to the group, the other members who also consume the good will not receive a diminished amount. Thus, in clear distinction to private goods, collective goods are *indivisible*. If a lighthouse is built and shines its light to guide one ship, then all other ships in that area (the group) can also use the lighthouse. Additional ships, moreover, will not diminish the amount of the good provided (so long as one ship does not physically impede another). When a government provides deterrence for its population, that deterrence is jointly supplied. When Washington threatened Moscow with retaliation for an attack on the United States, it provided deterrence for every individual in the United States. Once one person is protected by the deterrent threat, all are protected; once California is protected, so are Montana and Delaware. An increase in population does not reduce the deterrence provided to all the rest. The addition of Alaska and Hawaii to the Union in 1959 did not diminish the deterrence already being provided to the other 48 states.

---

[13] Robert O. Keohane, *After Hegemony* (Princeton, N.J.: Princeton University Press, 1984), p. 88 (emphasis added).

A factory that produces pollution in an area is producing a jointly supplied "good." The pollution that any one individual breathes can be consumed by all other individuals in an area. Again, more people in the area will not decrease the pollution available to the others. Any form of air or water pollution, then, is a jointly supplied good. Similarly, clean air provided by pollution controls and government programs is also a jointly supplied good, whether in the domestic or the international arena.

The second characteristic of an ideal collective good is called *nonexclusiveness*. A jointly supplied good may be either excludable or nonexcludable; that is, even though it is jointly supplied, it can be withheld from nonmembers. Cable television is a good example of a jointly supplied good that is excludable. Once the cable signal is supplied to any one cable subscriber, the addition of new subscribers does not reduce the supply of the good. However, it is excludable: those who do not pay for the service are not hooked up to the cable and thus cannot receive the service. Jointly supplied goods, then, can be perfectly excludable. The beam of light from a lighthouse, on the other hand, is a nonexcludable, jointly supplied good. If that lighthouse is altered to use a radar signal rather than a light, however, then the use of the lighthouse can be regulated. All those who do not buy the equipment to receive radar signals would be excluded. The *pure collective good*, then, is jointly supplied and cannot be controlled for exclusion. If the United States is deterring a nuclear attack on its own territory, it cannot exclude any specific group of persons—foreign diplomats or foreign tourists, prisoners, or citizens who do not pay taxes. Any people in the territory of the United States are part of the group included in nuclear deterrence and cannot be excluded from it.

A third important aspect of collective goods concerns not whether the group providing the good can exclude others, but whether some individual can choose whether or not to consume or be affected by the good. We are back to the idea of vulnerability in interdependence and the ways conflict may arise from interdependence. Although someone can choose whether to use a toll road (a jointly supplied good, for the most part) or subscribe to cable TV, he or she cannot choose whether to be affected by pollution or an epidemic, or even the military draft or taxes (both somewhat imperfect means of providing collective goods). One group of scholars calls this the "forced-rider" problem: individuals being forced to consume the collective good, whether they want to or not and whether or not it has negative effects (externalities) on them.[14] The negative effects of collective goods will generate conflict. International actors are thus faced with managing interdependence and the conflict interdependence can generate through collective goods. This is especially true if we understand that the greater the degree of interdependence in a system, the higher will be the proportion of activities characterized by collective goods.

---

[14] See, for example, Todd Sandler, *Collective Action: Theory and Applications* (Ann Arbor: University of Michigan Press, 1992).

## The Free-Rider Dilemma

These properties of collective goods have important implications for how individuals behave in groups. Winning a war may be seen as a good that has some collective properties. If the war is won, all citizens of the country that wins will have won: some of the benefits—political freedom and ideological victory—will go to all if they go to one. It is also difficult to exclude citizens from this good of winning. Because of this, individuals are faced with the **"free-rider"** decision: to help in achieving the good or to be a free rider on the efforts of others. This is exactly the logic that Yossarian used and the dilemma posed by that logic: if everyone wants to be a free rider, the collective good may never be achieved.

In the ideal case, then, where only private goods exist, an economic mechanism—the free market—can allocate goods within a group or society. This mechanism does not work well for the allocation of collective goods because of their indivisibility and nonexcludability. If individuals are strictly rational in the economic sense of desiring to maximize benefits and minimize costs, a collective good may never be provided, even if all members of a group desire that good. This dilemma arises from the clash between individual interests and benefits and group interests and benefits. If the good is a collective good (and thus jointly supplied), the group member will receive its benefits whether that member pays for it or not (gets a free ride). The rational individual will not have to pay (incur costs) for a benefit that he or she will gain anyway if others pay. The rational individual thus will not pay and will wait for someone else to pay. In addition, one does not want to be the sucker or patsy and buy the good that others will enjoy at no cost. This is why Yossarian did not want to be one of those getting killed while others were making money and having fun—not when there were 10 million other men in uniform. Economic mechanisms alone will not work to solve the free-rider problem. The political nature of collective goods is inseparable from their economic nature.

This dilemma is interesting because it shows the extreme interdependence of group members involved with collective goods. If everyone takes a free ride, an important good may not be produced; there can be no arms stability if everyone decides to cheat on arms control. If many decide to take a free ride, a good may be only partially provided, as, for example, when some states refuse to pay dues to international organizations that for various reasons do not wish to throw nonpayers out of the organization. This has happened with the United States and France in the United Nations. If member states refuse to contribute to the military capabilities of their alliance, alliance security will be underprovided. One major area of research has focused on the extent to which the security (deterrence as opposed to actual defense) provided by an alliance is a collective good. Because alliances can provide some amount of deterrence that has collective-good properties for alliance members (although much less so than in the case of deterrence covering a single country, as noted above), alliance burden-sharing has been studied in terms of free riding.[15]

---

[15] For an overview, see Todd Sandler, "The Economic Theory of Alliances," *Journal of Conflict Resolution* 37 (September 1993), 446–483. The pioneering work is Mancur Olson and Richard Zeckhauser, "An Economic Theory of Alliances," *Review of Economics and Statistics* 46 (1966), 266–279.

In the contemporary world system, more and more objectives of states require group action because of interdependence: monetary policy, trade, alliances, or other aspects of security, such as nonproliferation of nuclear weapons. Even the idea of order in the international system may be seen as having collective-good properties. If there is some stability, predictability, and regularity in international affairs, adding new actors may not diminish it, and it is difficult (although not impossible) to exclude actors from the benefits of international order and coordination.[16] It is possible to interpret the post–Gulf War "new international order" as something from which all members of the group—the world—might benefit, the increase or decrease of which will affect all players, and as a warning that the superpower-led United Nations will not tolerate free riders. Part of the strong reaction to the Iraqi invasion of Kuwait may have stemmed from the perception that it threatened a new chance at order presented by the end of the cold war and that Iraq's behavior adversely affected not just Kuwait but the collective good of order for the whole system.

The desire to develop economically can also be implemented only through group action, such as aid or special trade policies. Many areas of international political economy have been studied using collective-goods concepts, including international common property resources like the high seas, international trade, international monetary policy, the creation of international law, and international organizations. The desire to clean up an international body of water like the Rhine or the Mediterranean or to clean up the air can also be achieved only through group action. Although a free-rider state might appear to be following its own interests, in the long run it is acting against them because the good desired—for example, a clean river—may never be achieved. If a river that flows through many countries requires cleaning up, it may never be cleaned if all the countries wait for the others to do it, hoping to reap the benefits without paying. Because the condition of the river is jointly supplied and nonexcludable, anyone on the river will benefit from clean water (just as all will be harmed by polluted water because of the action of one or more countries). Here, free riding will stop the good of clean water from being achieved, cause it to take much longer to achieve, or cause it to be only partially achieved.

## The Tragedy of the Commons

As far back as Aristotle it was understood that pressures existed for people to take advantage of collective goods: "What is common to the greatest number has the least care bestowed upon it. Everyone thinks chiefly of his own, hardly at all of the common interest."[17] The best example of this variation of the free rider is what Garrett Hardin has called the **"tragedy of the commons."** Hardin describes a pasture, the commons, that belongs to all the members of a group:

---

[16] See Duncan Snidal, "Coordination versus Prisoners' Dilemma: Implications for International Cooperation and Regimes," *American Political Science Review* 79 (December 1985), 923–942.
[17] Aristotle, *Politics*, 11, 3.

The tragedy of the commons develops in this way. Picture a pasture open to all. It is to be expected that each herdsman will try to keep as many cattle as possible on the commons. Such an arrangement may work reasonably satisfactorily for centuries because tribal wars, poaching, and disease keep the numbers of both man and beast well below the carrying capacity of the land. Finally, however, comes the day of reckoning, that is, the day when the long-desired goal of social stability becomes a reality. At this point, the inherent logic of the commons remorselessly generates tragedy.

As a rational being, each herdsman seeks to maximize his gain. Explicitly or implicitly, more or less consciously, he asks, "What is the utility to me of adding one more animal to my herd?" This utility has one negative and one positive component.

1. The positive component is a function of the increment of one animal. Since the herdsman receives all the proceeds from the sale of the additional animal, the positive utility is nearly +1.

2. The negative component is a function of the additional overgrazing created by one more animal. Since, however, the effects of overgrazing are shared by all the herdsmen, the negative utility for any particular decision-making herdsman is only a fraction of 1.

Adding together the component partial utilities, the rational herdsman concludes that the only sensible course for him to pursue is to add another animal to his herd. And another; and another. . . . But this is the conclusion reached by each and every rational herdsman sharing a commons. Therein is the tragedy. Each man is locked into a system that compels him to increase his herd without limiting—in a world that is limited. Ruin is the destination toward which all men rush, each pursuing his own best interest in a society that believes in the freedom of the commons. Freedom in a commons brings ruin to all.[18]

By Hardin's definition, the commons is a jointly supplied and nonexcludable collective good. The tragedy of the commons is the other side of the free-rider problem. When there are free riders, some collective good is not provided. In the tragedy of the commons, although individuals follow the logic of rational self-interest, the result is the destruction of a collective good that already exists. The commons can be seen as a collective good as long as usage levels remain low, when the use by an additional member does not reduce the use of others. The tragedy occurs when usage increases so that the good is still nonexcludable (by definition it is held in common) but now it is no longer indivisible, and people do not see or understand the change. Some may see the problem but, as Aristotle noted, do not feel responsible for their own behavior as part of the problem—Yossarian didn't. Hardin has pointed out that a commons often leads people to ignore their responsibilities (but not their rights to use or exploit the

---

[18] Garrett Hardin, "The Tragedy of the Commons," *Science* 162 (1968), 1244 (Copyright © 1968 by the American Association for the Advancement of Science). See also Garrett Hardin and John Baden, eds., *Managing the Commons* (San Francisco: Freeman, 1977).

commons); thus we have tax evaders and people who feel it is not wrong to shoplift from large retail merchandisers or to rip-off large insurance companies. The goods *appear* to be indivisible (and infinite), but there are costs, and everyone else has to pay them.

The types of goods most often involved in commons situations are called **common-pool resources.** These are natural resources that do not belong to any specific state, that do not fall under a state's sovereignty or jurisdiction. They include the deep seabed, the high seas, and their fisheries; outer space; the atmosphere, including the ozone layer; the carbon dioxide balance; and the electromagnetic frequency spectrum for broadcasting. Many people see the natural resources that exist on earth, even those within national boundaries (such as the Amazonian rainforests), as a "global commons." There are many such examples, including all of the nonrenewable energy resources like oil, natural gas, and coal. But who owns or has jurisdiction over such resources? Who should? By custom and law they are in fact usually privately owned. Thus one major way to look at common-pool resources (and at any good with externalities, such as collective goods) involves *property rights.* The property rights of common-pool resources cannot be defined and enforced by economic means. We must return again to social and political mechanisms.

All the world's resources are finite: they can be used up. The limits-to-growth issues to be discussed in Chapter 18 are related to the tragedy of the commons. Factors such as population and technology are bases for the demands on the world's natural resources: water, air, arable land, and energy resources such as petroleum, coal, natural gas, and wood. They are also the bases for the pollution of air and water as well as the destruction of common-pool resources such as the ozone layer in the atmosphere, animal and fish species, forests, and topsoil. The world can and should be seen as a global commons. All the states in it, like the individuals Hardin describes, can through self-interest destroy a commons that already exists. This situation exposes another side of the metaphor of spaceship earth: a single, finite environment whose supplies can be consumed.

As we saw earlier, development is a major issue between the rich and the poor. The powerful states must continue to industrialize and produce to stay powerful. Similarly, leaders in the LDCs often must put economic development and industrialization at the top of their list of objectives. Thus all countries desire resources, and the desire becomes increasingly greater, not smaller. These resources, however, have to come from the global commons. A major issue addressed in Chapter 18 is the consumption of finite resources at exponential growth rates, leaving the resource cupboard bare. Such processes have been in full swing in the destruction of whales and some fish stocks in the oceans (especially by Japan and Russia). As recently as the mid-twentieth century blue whales, right whales, and bowhead whales numbered in the hundreds of thousands—since the late 1980s these numbers have dropped to under 8,000. In the 1940s the global fish catch was 20 million tons; by the 1970s it had risen to 70 million tons. During this period, the world's fishing fleets quadrupled in size. But many species of fish have become scarce as a result of overfishing, many parts of the ocean have become so polluted that fish can no longer live, and fish and seafood are threatened by local pollution disasters such as spills from oil tankers. The fishing problem is a striking example of the tragedy-of-the-commons process at work.

# COLLECTIVE GOODS AND THE PRISONERS' DILEMMA

Again, we have the long-term interests of the group (and the individual as well) in opposition to the short-term interests of individuals. Why are problems like the free rider and the tragedy of the commons so prevalent in the international arena? One answer is simply the nature of that arena to the extent that it is based on the Westphalian system of states, each with sovereignty and no higher authority to tell it what to do. In this anarchic system, lack of trust is built into the relations among the international actors. Lack of trust gives each individual actor the dilemma of choosing between individual and collective welfare, creating the possibility of trusting others and then being taken advantage of by them. This situation is another version of the prisoners' dilemma.

The prisoners' dilemma occurs when actors pursue individual gain and benefit over collective interest, just as with the free rider and the tragedy of the commons. Without a basis for trust, an actor in a prisoners' dilemma situation pursues individual benefits to avoid being caught as the sucker. In an arms race, the sucker does not acquire more arms, while his opponent surges ahead; in an alliance, a major power spends large amounts on defense, while smaller allies pay little and take a free ride on alliance security; in a common-pool-resource situation, the sucker stops hunting whales to give them time to repopulate, but others (such as Japan in past years or Norway since 1993) continue hunting at such a pace that the whales will be hunted into extinction anyway, while the sucker fails to receive any of the profits in the process. The formally anarchic nature of international relations in general exemplifies a prisoners' dilemma with many players. The prisoners' dilemma is a pervasive social situation or structure of payoffs affecting choice (opportunity affecting willingness through incentive structures). Indeed, one scholar has defined politics as "the study of ways of transcending the Prisoners' Dilemma."[19]

But to deal with the problems of interdependent externalities, the free rider, and the tragedy of the commons, we must look across all the levels of analysis presented in Part I and take into account the two-level games of domestic and international politics that policymakers must play simultaneously. We must deal with individual choice, collective choice, and "constitutional choice," or the structure of rules and organizations. Japan, for instance, is not a single-minded, monolithic actor. A process of bureaucratic politics goes on within Japan that has made it very difficult for the Japanese government to change its whaling policies. We have been talking about rational

---

[19] This definition of politics is that of Jon Elster, quoted by Arthur Stein, *Why Nations Cooperate: Circumstance and Choice in International Politics* (Ithaca, N.Y.: Cornell University Press, 1990), p. 33. For other examples and case studies of the prisoners' dilemma, see Glenn H. Snyder, "'Prisoner's Dilemma' and 'Chicken' Models in International Politics," *International Studies Quarterly* 15 (1971), 66–103, and Kenneth A. Oye, ed., *Cooperation Under Anarchy* (Princeton, N.J.: Princeton University Press, 1986).

state behavior in the short term versus rational behavior in the long term and about individual interests versus global interests. We must remember, however, that certain policies, such as killing whales, may be very rational in terms of domestic political games and the domestic political stakes involved, but they appear much less rational from a global perspective. Although outsiders see these issues as negotiable economic objectives, some Japanese interests, such as the whaling companies, see them as issues of survival. Japanese government officials must try to satisfy or compensate those interests. Such differing perceptions make difficult problems more difficult still.[20]

Thus we see that as an extreme form of interdependence and externality, collective goods create special needs for cooperation and collaboration. They can create conflict; they can prevent required actions from taking place; they can lead to the destruction of common-pool resources. These special needs, in turn, create special problems for establishing cooperation and collaboration: how to resolve the prisoners' dilemma by creating incentives for cooperation rather than noncooperation (through the temptation to defect). The next step is the development of political mechanisms to deal with these problems: international law, international organizations, and international regimes.

---

[20] This is the central concern of George Tsebelis—that the outside observer may see another's behavior as irrational because the observer is watching only one game, while the policymaker is involved in several nested games and is behaving quite purposefully in dealing with them. See *Nested Games* (Berkeley: University of California Press, 1990).

## ACHIEVING ORDER AND COLLABORATION IN THE WORLD SYSTEM

**S**till, there is order in anarchy. States and other international actors engage in many orderly interactions every day. Describing the international arena as anarchic, without a central authority, is not the same as saying that there are no organizations or rules to help organize and structure behavior. All international systems have regulator mechanisms to deal with disturbances in the system and the demands of its component units. Organizations (states, IGOs, NGOs) and rules (informal norms, formal international law, the domestic laws of states or municipal law) can restructure the payoff matrix to help avoid the various forms of the prisoners' dilemma. Reflecting the title of his book, *Cooperation Under*

*Anarchy*, Kenneth Oye asks a central question: "If international relations can approximate both a Hobbesian state of nature and a Lockean civil society, why does cooperation emerge in some cases and not in others?"[1]

## STRATEGIES FOR ACHIEVING COLLECTIVE GOODS

There are ways in which states in the current system have overcome the prisoners' dilemma pressures to defect. There must be strategies to promote the international cooperation required to solve the problems posed by free riders and exploiters of the commons. Collective goods present situations where the strictly economic forces of the marketplace cannot bring about solutions and where political and social action must be taken either to achieve desired collective outcomes or to prevent the destruction of common-pool resources (CPRs). Six broad strategies for achieving collective goods will be presented, all of which in some way increase the costs of defecting or increase the payoffs of cooperation.

**1.** An individual's preferences, or calculations of costs and benefits, can be changed, as pointed out in Chapter 6, through punishment or reward. One way to get individuals to cooperate is through coercion. Yossarian, for example, was in the army because it was against the law to refuse to be drafted. While he was in the army, the army could threaten imprisonment, even execution, if he refused to fight. Within states, tax systems are backed up by threats of punishment for nonpayment (that is, for free riding). When a union achieves a union shop, it forces all workers to join the union, eliminating the free rider who would not join but would still enjoy most of the benefits, like safe working conditions, obtained by the union from management.

This type of coercion is difficult in international relations. The power to tax is not readily given to IGOs because it is a threat to sovereignty (note, however, that the EU has such authority in a number of areas). Sometimes individual states, such as the United States as a dominant alliance leader, attempted to coerce its cold war allies to pay their share in an alliance like NATO by threatening to pull U.S. troops out of Europe; coercion was an important element in the Soviet Union's management of burden-sharing in the Warsaw Pact.

Many analysts feel that coercion can occur only with a central authority given enforcement powers and that this is the only way to solve collective-goods problems. Calls for some form of world government have been made on this basis. While such calls may be extreme, many issues can be handled by creating organizations that have

---

[1] Kenneth A. Oye, "Explaining Cooperation Under Anarchy: Hypotheses and Strategies," in Oye, ed., *Cooperation Under Anarchy* (Princeton, N.J.: Princeton University Press, 1986), p. 1. For the concept of system regulators, see Richard Rosecrance's classic study of the international system, *Action and Reaction in World Politics* (Boston: Little, Brown, 1963). To keep any system stable, the regulators must be capable of dealing with the levels of disturbance in the system.

been given authority by their constituent states, as in the creation of regimes. For example, according to the 1982 Law of the Sea Treaty, the common-pool resources of the deep seabed, such as the metal-rich manganese or nickel nodules, were to be "owned" by the newly created International Seabed Authority.

It has also been argued that if a group is small, a free-riding member is more easily identified. If this can be done, then social pressure can be applied to encourage the member's cooperation. A government and its leaders may lose prestige if other governments feel that that they are not pulling their weight or cooperating. NATO's annual review to identify and spotlight slackers has been used in this way. Such pressure was put on states that bore low costs during the Gulf War or that dragged their feet in paying their share.

**2.** Positive strategies based on rewards of some kind seem to be more useful than negative ones in the international sphere. Members of a group will be more likely to act to obtain a collective good if they can receive private goods as side payments. States may join alliances and provide a share of the defense burden if they receive new and sophisticated weapons in return. States may refrain from exploiting a common-pool resource if offered other goods, profits, or a technology that can substitute for the resource. We noted Hardin's argument that the commons brings about irresponsible behavior in those who use it. People have a right to the commons but rarely exercise responsibility in its use because it is large and impersonal and belongs to everyone.[2]

One way to foster responsibility is to convert parts of the commons into enclosed areas for which individual members are responsible—a process of privatization directed at removing the jointness of supply. Recipients must treat these enclosures with care, or else they will destroy their own property. It may be possible to save a common-pool resource by converting at least part of it into private goods by assigning property rights. For example, one outcome of the UN Law of the Sea Conference was the general acceptance of 200-mile-limit exclusive economic zones (EEZs), which extended coastal jurisdiction to 200 miles for economic purposes. The aim was to evade the prisoners' dilemma by firmly assigning responsibility. In this way, a large part of the continental shelf and seabed and over 40 percent of the high seas have been put under regulation and restriction. Just as some analysts feel that the best way to solve collective-goods problems is through coercion, others feel that privatization of some sort—creating private goods for the market to handle—is the best way to deal with collective goods, particularly the commons.

**3.** Sometimes the collective good is provided as a by-product of policies aimed at private goods. For example, if the states now controlling large EEZs take care of their own fisheries (for purely private reasons), they will, as a by-product, preserve the global fishery commons. Or a state might create a large army for internal control or solely for its individual deterrence or defense. If it then joins an alliance, the alliance is provided with some forces that contribute to the collective good of a strong deterrent, even though that was not the first state's intention.

---

[2] Garrett Hardin, "An Operational Analysis of 'Responsibility'," in Hardin and John Baden, eds., *Managing the Commons* (New York: Freeman, 1977).

**4.** Another noncoercive strategy is education to increase individual perceptions of the self-interest to be gained from group and long-term interests. For example, Malta's representative to the General Assembly, Arvid Pardo, proposed in 1967 that the General Assembly deal with ways to extract the resources of the seabed in the interests of humanity as a whole, calling the seabed resources the "common heritage of mankind." Much of this educational task has been performed by experts, acting singly or collectively in NGOs and IGOs as knowledge-based communities.[3] This task has also been undertaken by academics interested in world order or the environment, such as the Club of Rome. This is a group of academics, scientists, and IGO personnel gathered to study and educate the world about the nature and consequences of global interdependences.

The intent behind this strategy is to force policymakers to confront the prisoners' dilemma and to understand what the structure of the decision situation looks like. If policymakers understand that their interests are best served in the long run, they will be better able to deal with these problems. This educational strategy is also related to the process of integration that consists of shifting loyalties to new and larger political units with broader interests. But this is a slow process, and a number of our collective-goods problems require immediate attention and quick action.

**5.** A collective good can be provided if one member of the group desires that good so much that it is willing to pay the whole cost (or most of it) by itself and does not care that other group members also receive the good. In this case, one member offers to be the sucker. Besides valuing the good highly, this member is usually richer in resources or wealthier than other members. (Thus it can provide most of the collective good at much less sacrifice than could another member.) Studies of some IGO budget assessments and burden-sharing in alliances such as NATO and the Warsaw Pact show that the larger members will pay proportionately more to get the things they want, even if others ride free. Evidence for this behavior has included the U.S. desire to provide deterrence for itself and its NATO allies, possibly the U.S. role in stabilizing international trade, and even some tragedy-of-the-commons situations. For example, the maintenance of the upper atmosphere has collective-goods properties. A very large state can be very effective in environmental control, both because it is big and rich and can therefore afford to bear the costs and because it can coerce some transnational actors to provide benefits to other countries.

An example of this kind of behavior is the U.S. government's 1978 ban on chlorofluorocarbon propellants in spray cans sold in the American market, a ban instituted to reduce depletion of the ozone layer in the world's atmosphere. That ban immediately set in motion a 50 percent reduction in world usage of such propellants (although the United States did not deal effectively with other uses of those chemicals, such as in plastic foam and in refrigerants). Moreover, some MNCs producing for many countries in the world market eliminated the propellants from their production, chiefly because it was cheaper not to use fluorocarbons at all than to make one prod-

---

[3] See, for example, Peter Haas, "Introduction: Epistemic Communities and International Policy Coordination," *International Organization* 46 (Winter 1992), 1–36.

uct for sale in the United States and another for sale in countries with less rigorous restrictions. Another example is international airline safety regulations. The Federal Aviation Administration requires that all aircraft landing in the United States have elaborate safety equipment. Thus foreign airlines contemplating U.S. flights must install the equipment no matter where their airplanes customarily land. Other countries thus get the free rider's safety benefits without having to make their own safety regulations. These are the kinds of circumstances in which it can be very helpful to have a dominant or hegemonic power in the system.

**6.** One other strategy for achieving collective goods is to create localized or regional organizations from a number of small groups of states and then to create some sort of federal structure to tie together and coordinate these groups. This approach involves the use of IGOs to address collective-goods problems, often following the neo-functionalist integration model and involving regimes (as discussed below).

These general strategies for coping with and resolving collective-goods issues involve both formal and informal mechanisms. These mechanisms help states coordinate their activities and collaborate in a positive way. Possible solutions to collective goods problems include appeals to self-limitation, mechanisms that facilitate communication and monitoring of behavior, a clear definition of the group, and mechanisms that facilitate the growth of norms for self-restraint and positive cooperation.[4] The strategies just discussed only hint at a very powerful informal process that helps to overcome the problem of the prisoners' dilemma/free rider/tragedy of the commons. The most problematic aspect of the prisoners' dilemma is trusting the other side in a specific situation; the situation of the prisoners is immediately resolved by one or both going to jail. This is a *single-play* situation. But most relationships in social life, and certainly in international relations, are *continuous.* That is, there are multiple plays in any game, and the players can learn what will happen to them if they defect in the dilemma. Earlier we discussed Robert Axelrod's research showing that in experimental games players did best following a tit-for-tat strategy: cooperating until the other player defected and then retaliating. The defecting player would then return to cooperation. If both players followed the never-defect-first principle, they could avoid the dilemma.

It thus may be possible to deal with the dilemma if there are many plays (an iterated prisoners' dilemma) and the players understand that there is an interdependent **reciprocity** in the play: you might be able to hurt the other player, but the other player can also hurt you. All plays of a game, even the prisoners' dilemma, are played under the "shadow of the future": players can learn from past plays (*history*) and should be concerned with reciprocity in plays to come (*future*). Reciprocity is even more important when we recall that there are many games being played at the same time, that states interact in many issue areas at the same time, and that these are *linked*

---

[4] For a review of conditions under which a commons can be saved or destroyed (without centralized coercion or complete privatization), see Elinor Ostrom, *Governing the Commons* (Cambridge, England: Cambridge University Press, 1990).

(especially as interdependence becomes tighter).[5] A state may defect in one game (for example, arms control), but it will have to worry about the other player's defection in another (retaliatory acts in trade, wheat sales, alliance formation, military spending). The payoff matrix of costs and benefits thus will be affected by calculations of future costs and benefits.

These ideas of reciprocity (especially as sanctions that can impose costs for defecting) are central to understanding the workings of international law and the importance of regimes—formal and informal rules and expectations—in the interdependence among international actors. Reciprocity also helps explain how we can have order and certain amounts of stability and predictability in formally anarchic situations.

## INTERNATIONAL COOPERATION: INTERNATIONAL LAW

To begin solving collective-goods problems (or other problems affecting more than one state), states need to cooperate and interact in a smooth, regularized manner. Increasingly, the transnational issues of the contemporary world—economic and ecological—require action by more than one state. States need one another's aid to solve common problems in an era of interdependence. The paradox, of course, is that although states often cooperate on the basis of self-interest, the heart of the collective goods issue is the need to see the connection between individual state interests and the longer-term collective interests of the group.

### The Nature of International Law

In earlier chapters, especially Chapter 7, we discussed how states carry on regularized relations with one another; for example, through diplomacy. Traditional bilateral diplomacy must be augmented by other mechanisms to maintain and increase regular, smooth interactions of states. International law is such a mechanism. The perspective on international law provided here falls somewhere between two extreme views: that international law has no impact on the activities of states, and that international law can solve all our global problems. Following the approach of political scientist Stanley Hoffman, we will look at international law as merely a magnifying mirror that "faithfully and cruelly" reflects the realities of world politics. International law must be seen within a political context, within the historical context of the Westphalian state system that created international law in its modern form, and within contemporary interna-

---

[5]Learning from iterated plays is elaborated at length in Robert Axelrod, *The Evolution of Cooperation* (New York: Basic Books, 1984). Linkage among different issues on different levels is treated in George Tsebelis, *Nested Games* (Berkeley: University of California Press, 1990). The concept and role of reciprocity is developed in Charles W. Kegley, "The New Global Order: The Power of Principle in a Pluralistic World," *Ethics & International Affairs* 6 (1992), 21–40.

tional politics. But this is a reciprocal interaction. Politics creates law, and law shapes the form of future politics by serving as part of the menu within which future politics must occur.

Very simply, most states usually do conform to the rules of international law. In that respect, international law acts in the same way as domestic law, as a set of rules that constrain behavior. One popular international law text defines international law simply as "the system of law which governs relations between states."[6] Other definitions stress the notion that international law is a body of rules that nation-states (and recently, other international actors) take into account, accept, and consider binding upon them in relations with other states.

These definitions, and the study of international law since the nineteenth century, reflect a **positivist view** of international law, which holds that international law is created by people and that the obligation to follow law is based on self-interest, utility, and especially consent. Law is what states agree to and is based on the behavior of states. This view helps us understand why international law works: it has been created to help states interact smoothly. This positivist view gives international law a certain degree of legitimacy. International law can regulate behavior because it is based on the self-constraint of states.

Domestic law is a set of rules typically *legislated* by a *legitimate, centralized* political authority that can *enforce* the law. In the international arena, no legitimate central authority with both legislative and enforcement power exists. However, institutions and practices do exist that *make, interpret, and execute* rules. These include IGOs, as well as the formal diplomatic interactions of states. Both the sources and functions of international law have formal and informal features. If we understand that international law has many functions, including a coordinating and facilitating function similar to civil law on the domestic level, then we can see it as "law." Compared with domestic law, international law is "relatively decentralized." Another scholar says simply, "International law should be regarded as true but imperfect law."[7] If we can understand that law is more than command backed up by force, and that the command view is only one possible aspect of law, then international law can be regarded as law.

States pay great attention to international law (for example, the legal adviser's staff at the U.S. state department reviews most of the department's work). However, if the fear of enforcement by armed agents of a central authority is not the cause of states' conforming to rules, what is? Again, remember that nothing is distributed evenly in the international system. States need all sorts of things possessed by other states and international actors. The great bulk of world politics and transnational interaction consists of the exchange of goods, services, people, and information. All states benefit from this regular and routine flow of people (including diplomats),

---

[6] See Michael Akehurst, *A Modern Introduction to International Law,* 6th ed. (London: Allen & Unwin, 1987), p. 1.
[7] See Hedley Bull, *The Anarchical Society* (New York: Columbia University Press, 1977); see also Gerhard von Glahn, *Law Among Nations,* 4th ed. (New York: Macmillan, 1981), p. 4.

goods, and information. Thus states see it as in their own self-interest to constrain their behavior according to the rules of international law, most of which eases and routinizes such interaction. Foreign policy behavior that violates international norms is less probable because of the costs entailed.

## Fear of Chaos and Reprisal

There are no centralized enforcement mechanisms in international law, but there are informal mechanisms of reciprocity—tit for tat or other forms of retaliation. States live in the shadow of the future. If each state violated international law whenever it wanted, order would soon yield to chaos; the future would be unpredictable and dangerous. Clearly, when the stakes are high and when states are in very conflictual situations, then treaties, agreements, UN resolutions, and all the rest are disregarded. But most of the time such conditions do not prevail. Like Yossarian, why should any single state obey the rules of the game if all the other actors are breaking them? Order seems to be one collective good that states do see as in their interest to provide. Chaos—a truly anything-goes system, all the time and on all issues—would be costly for all states.

For example, one traditional area of international law concerns the rules of immunity extended to diplomatic personnel. These rules were established so that diplomats could engage in intergovernmental communication without interference. Without them, the processes of bargaining and negotiation would soon give way either to more violent forms of interaction or to no interaction at all. A good deal of the very strong reaction against the Iranian government's involvement in taking U.S. diplomats hostage in 1979 derived from this fear. If all governments condoned such behavior, based on justifications like the Iranians' grievances against the deposed shah, then international diplomacy would become impossible.

Related to fear of chaos is the fear of reprisal. By breaking some rule, such as taking hostages or using chemical warfare (as Iraq did against Iran during their 1980–88 war), a state may be inviting a similar reaction from other states. Although there might be some immediate advantage to such an act, it is often outweighed by the costs imposed by other states also ignoring international law. States restrain themselves because they do not want to set a precedent for certain types of behavior. There are striking examples of the effects of international law on state behavior, based on principles that reflect the shared interests of states. One is the international law on the acquisition of territory. By "intertemporal law," territorial ownership is legal if the means used to acquire territory were legal at the time of acquisition—law cannot be applied retroactively. That is, until recently it was legal to acquire territory through war and force. Even though the UN charter states that territory cannot now be acquired by conquest, a 1970 UN resolution states that this should "not be construed as affecting titles to territory created prior to the Charter regime and valid under international law."[8] Thus Iraq had no legal claim to Kuwaiti territory, and few other states supported such

---

[8] See Akehurst, *A Modern Introduction to International Law,* pp. 152–153.

a claim. The reaction to Argentina's claim to the Falklands/Malvinas was similar. While many Third World states had supported Argentina's anticolonial rhetoric, only a very few supported its military action to acquire the territory by force.[9] The legal principle of intertemporal law reflects the interests of states; almost every state is composed of territory once claimed by some other state or group. To recognize this as an excuse for military action threatens every state—especially LDCs—as well as international order. States reacted to Argentina and Iraq through fear of the precedent of using force to retake lands based on historical claims.

The term **"reprisal"** has a specific meaning in international law. It denotes an action, normally illegal but in these circumstances permissible, that is taken in response to another illegal act; for example, if one state breaks a treaty agreement, the other party or parties to that treaty are free to do so also. It was left to an unusual and obstreperous government leader, the Ayatollah Khomeini in Iran, to set the precedent of supporting actions against diplomats. Even during the world wars and at the height of the cold war, governments still respected the rights of diplomats.

The fear of reprisal also includes the fear that states other than those immediately affected will punish a lawbreaker in some way, not necessarily by similar actions. In international law the term "retorsion" is used to describe lawful retaliation of any kind—for example, the Carter administration's decision to boycott the 1980 Moscow Olympics after the Soviet invasion of Afghanistan, or the imposition of trade sanctions on the Soviet Union, South Africa, and Iraq. If international solidarity among an offending state's adversaries is high, states that fail to apply sanctions against that offending state may themselves be punished.[10] For example, punitive actions were taken against states, such as Jordan, that appeared to be disregarding the almost unanimously UN-approved trade sanctions applied to Iraq following its conquest of Kuwait.

The other side of the coin is a state's desire to appear to be a law-abiding citizen of the international community, to be a state that others can depend upon and trust. This sort of reputation enhances a state's influence in many ways. One of these might be called the *golden rule condition:* if a state behaves correctly, it can expect to receive good behavior from others. The lack of support for Iran in its war against Iraq (which was initiated by Iraqi armed forces) and on other issues was due in part to Iran's clear disregard for the norms of international law regarding diplomats, internal interference, and shipping rights, among other offenses; Iran was an example of what some observers have called "renegade states."

In sum, contrary to an extreme realist's belief, states do acknowledge international law and are constrained by it. Leaders justify their behavior in terms of international law and in questionable cases try to indicate that their behavior conforms to international law (in the immediate case and other areas). The Reagan administration,

---

[9] For a case study of the Argentine situation, see Thomas M. Franck, "The Strategic Role of Legal Principles," in Bruce Russett, Harvey Starr, and Richard Stoll, eds., *Choices in World Politics: Sovereignty and Interdependence* (New York: Freeman, 1989), pp. 295–304.

[10] Robert Axelrod, "An Evolutionary Approach to Norms," *American Political Science Review* 80 (1986), 1095–1111.

which was accused of disregarding international law in Grenada, in the mining of Nicaraguan waters, and in the April 1986 bombing of Libya, nevertheless made a great effort to contend that such behavior was permitted within the rules of international law. The Bush administration acted similarly during the December 1989 military intervention in Panama. It justified its action by arguing that it protected U.S. citizens, protected the Canal, restored democracy to Panama, and was needed in order to arrest dictator Manuel Noriega on drug charges. This action was code named "Operation Just Cause" in an attempt to appeal to the theory of just war. States understand that breaking international law imposes costs on them. International law thus becomes a component in the incentive structures—the opportunities—of states and affects the willingness of leaders to take certain actions.

## Sources and Functions of International Law

Article 38 of the Statute of the International Court of Justice identifies three major sources of international law. These are (1) international conventions or treaties, (2) custom, and (3) the general principles of law recognized by civilized nations. Two secondary sources are the judicial decisions of international courts and the writings of "qualified publicists," or legal scholars. The primary source of international law is a formal one, deriving from treaties. But custom, or the evolution of patterns of behavior that states accept and give consent to, is the next most important source. This reinforces the positivist view of international law and shows how states shape international law and how international law can change and evolve.

The rules of international law serve a number of functions in helping states create and preserve order. One basic function is to act as a means or language of communication that conveys some sense of authoritative rules. This communication is needed to educate states and their leaders and to socialize them in the political culture of the international system. By letting international actors know what their rights and duties are, international law thus clarifies *expectations* and adds some precision to relations. All this helps promote predictability and order in world politics.[11] In this way, international law also serves management and coordination functions. That is, international law is used less to command behavior or to enforce conflict resolution than to help coordinate behavior (as in domestic traffic laws or internationally in regard to weights and measures, air traffic law, and law dealing with the high seas or outer space). This function is very important because of the problems of coordination raised by collective-goods issues. Finally, international law draws upon these two functions in its ·better-known conflict-related functions. International law has been used to regulate conflict (including the use of force), to help promote conflict resolution, and to restrain behavior considered undesirable.

These international legal functions apply to all matters involving international politics. International law deals with questions of territory and nationality: which ter-

---

[11] See Gary Goertz and Paul F. Diehl, "Toward a Theory of International Norms," *Journal of Conflict Resolution* 36 (December 1992), 634–664.

ritory and people belong to which state, what states are allowed to do on their own territory and on the territory of others, and what states can do with their own people and to aliens (nationals of other countries). International law specifies which actors are "legal persons" having the capacity to enter legal relations. This is one of the areas in which the state-centric bias of international law is most clearly demonstrated.

Recent activity in regard to **human rights** represents an expansion of the domain of international law and a real erosion of state sovereignty. Concepts of universal human rights, embodied in international declarations and treaties, deny states the prerogative to withold those rights from their own citizens; individuals are considered to be legal entities separate from their state of national origin. Individuals are thus removed from important areas of state control. Human-rights norms have increasingly become the basis for intrusion by IGOs and NGOs into the domestic affairs of states—striking at the relation of the state to its citizens, and thus at the fundamental principles of legitimacy and sovereignty. Monitoring and publicizing human-rights violations by NGOs such as Amnesty International or Human Rights Watch may be the best mechanism for deterring or restraining violators.[12]

# INTERNATIONAL COOPERATION: INTERNATIONAL ORGANIZATIONS

States engaging in diplomacy create treaties, which add considerably to the body of international law. Many of these treaties also create international organizations, so that IGOs are a product of international law. However, in yet another reciprocal relationship, the growing number of IGOs is also one of the primary *sources* of international law in the contemporary system. The charters of these organizations—their rules, agreements, resolutions, and treaties—constitute many of the bylaws of everyday international interaction. Some IGOS, such as the UN (through the International Law Commission), have helped to codify, collect, and apply international law derived not only from IGOs but from treaties, custom, and the work of international courts. IGOs have been useful in applying international law, in helping to coordinate states' compliance, in organizing states around their common interests, and in pointing out the benefits of cooperation. Large regional organizations such as the European Union have worked extensively to promote economic cooperation. Others, such as the Organization of American States and the Organization of African Unity, have worked to control and manage conflict in their regions.

Realists usually see IGOs as of little importance; transnationalists see them as more useful, if not now then in the future. In thinking about IGOs in relation to international order, we need to stress their formal nature: they are created by two or more

---

[12] See Jack Donnelly, *International Human Rights* (Boulder, Colo.: Westview, 1993).

states (and possibly other IGOs or NGOs) by a formal constitution or instrument that establishes some form of continuous administrative structure. This formal structure then seeks to pursue the common interests of the members in ways that reflect the above strategies to deal with collective-goods issues.

First, and very important, an IGO provides a forum where states can interact with each other diplomatically at a permanent site. It also aids cooperation by providing a permanent mechanism for addressing policy issues. States expect the IGO to help with certain problems, for example, the World Health Organization with disease control, or UNESCO with education. An IGO often collects and makes available a great deal of information on specific problems and on its member states. UN publications, for instance, provide voluminous data on a wide variety of economic, demographic, social, cultural, and political matters. This information may be crucial in complex coordination or problem-solving situations. Finally, IGOs also perform regulative and distributive functions. IGOs make and administer rules on how states should behave in certain areas—from the IMF in monetary policy to the UN in regard to the use of force or the treatment of political prisoners to the EU on almost every area of economic interaction of its members. IGOs can distribute things, such as billions of dollars in loans from the World Bank or court decisions from the International Court of Justice.

States also use IGOs and international law as *instruments* to further their own foreign policy interests. States use international law and IGOs to legitimize or justify their behavior (the United States used the Organization of American States to justify U.S. intervention in the Dominican Republic in 1965). States use international law and IGOs as ways to pursue diplomacy and to increase their individual influence as well. International law, IGOS, and the United Nations are only as successful as the *member states want them to be*. They are only as successful as they are perceived to be. This is the essence of Hoffmann's "mirror" metaphor, and it is a result of the positivist basis of international law. International law is one of the main mechanisms by which the state attained its central place as an international actor; international law legalized the very existence of states. In essence, it created the rules and conditions that permit the individual state, as well as the international system, to survive.

## The United Nations System

Besides being a major source of international law and the most extensive system of international organization in the contemporary world (in both the extent of its membership and the broad scope of its aims and activities), the United Nations is also one of the most faithful of the mirrors that reflect the nature of international politics.

In the aftermath of World War II, the United Nations reflected the desire of the victorious states to maintain world peace and to attack the conditions that appeared to foster war: colonialism, poverty, inequality, and ignorance. The Charter of the United Nations, drawn up and signed in San Francisco in 1945, was largely the product of American, British, and Soviet negotiations. Much of this bargaining was done at the Dumbarton Oaks Conference, held in Washington, D.C., in 1944.

The founders of the United Nations were realists enough to recognize that the organization was to be composed of sovereign states; they did not see the United Nations as a device to take away or undercut their sovereignty, although some later observers have felt that this *should* be the UN role. On the other hand, since the international system was composed of sovereign states and lacked a central authority, one strategy for promoting international cooperation was the creation of a universal IGO. Their realism was tempered by enough idealist vision to seek new international institutions and procedures to promote common interests and manage conflict. Mechanisms to coordinate behavior and promote cooperation became even more crucial as international interdependences multiplied and as collective-goods issues became prominent. Perhaps one reason for the remarkable survival of the United Nations and its celebration of its 50th anniversary has been its utility in an era when environmental, economic, and ethical issues have become central in a system with many new international actors and a more sensitive and vulnerable set of international interdependences.

The Security Council, the General Assembly, the Secretariat (the international civil service bureaucracy headed by the secretary-general), the International Court of Justice, the Trusteeship Council, and the Economic and Social Council constitute the six agencies identified in the Charter as the principal organs of the UN. Today's UN system of some 30 multilateral institutions has been built incrementally over the years to promote cooperation in response to new international problems.[13]

This UN structure reflects the system within which it was created. The Security Council is the primary organ of action, and as such it reflects the unequal distribution of power in the system. Designation as one of five permanent members (the United States, Britain, France, the Soviet Union/Russia, and China), all of whom have vetoes over the actions of the Security Council, gives each of the states that was a great power at the end of World War II control over the issues of political and military security in the United Nations. In this way, the Charter sought to save the United Nations from a major weakness of its predecessor, the League of Nations: all during the League's existence, at least one of the great powers was a nonmember.

The Security Council reflects the special role that the great powers must play in the world body. The veto permits each power to protect its interests by remaining in the organization. The heavy use of the Soviet veto during the early years of the United Nations (114 times from 1945 to 1975) reflected U.S. dominance of the General Assembly. Figure 17.1 shows that in 1946 states from the Americas and Western Europe dominated UN membership with over 60 percent of the membership. Although the General Assembly had been set up as a world parliament on the basis of one-state, one-vote sovereign equality (Article 2 of the Charter), it too was dominated by the great powers in the early days of the United Nations. Not only did cold war or East–West issues dominate the agenda (with about 30 percent of the membership coming from Europe), but the United States could and did dominate voting in the General Assembly. For a long period, many small and non-Western countries were dissatisfied with the UN system because of this great-power dominance. (The United Nations was

---

[13] These institutions include some organizations that predate the UN itself—such as the International Labor Organization or the Universal Postal Union. See Roger A. Coate, "Increasing the Effectiveness of the UN System," in Coate, ed., *U.S. Policy and the Future of the United Nations* (New York: Twentieth Century Fund, 1994), p.44.

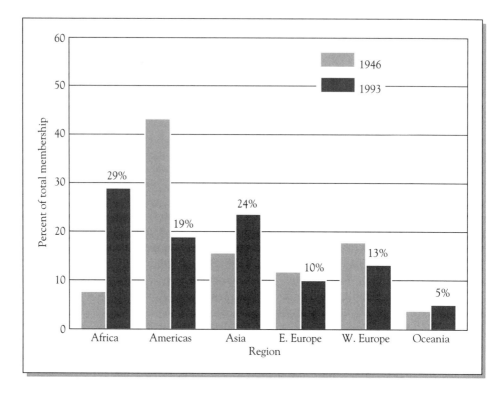

**FIGURE 17.1** UN membership by region, 1946 and August 1993.

and continues to be financially dependent on the larger states as well, particularly on the United States, although today only a little over 20 percent of the member states are in Europe.)

During the 1970s and 1980s the group most dissatisfied with the United Nations was the industrialized North. The United Nations, by welcoming all states, has grown through the addition of non-Western states created by the process of decolonization. Figure 17.1 shows the dramatic increase in African and Asian membership from 1946 to 1993. With this change, which began in earnest in 1960, came a shift in emphasis from East–West to North–South issues of the sort discussed in Chapter 15. Economic issues, and particularly issues of equity, have come to dominate many areas of the United Nations. The UN membership has powerfully affected the objectives, processes, and success of the organization, especially as they have organized into "groups" whose purpose is to foster the common interests of the members. These groups, and how they overlap in membership, are shown in Figure 17.2. The anticolonial stance of the newer

**FIGURE 17.2** (*Facing page*) UN groups and their overlapping membership [*Source: Robert E. Riggs and Jack C. Plano, The United Nations, 2nd ed. (Belmont, Calif.: Wadsworth, 1994), p. 62.*]

**1** Romania

**2**
| | |
|---|---|
| Antigua and Barbuda | Haiti |
| Argentina | Honduras |
| Brazil | Mexico |
| Costa Rica | Paraguay |
| Dominica | St. Kitts and |
| Dominican | Nevis |
| Republic | St. Vincent |
| El Salvador | Uruguay |

**3**
| | |
|---|---|
| Albania | Kyrgyzstan |
| Armenia | Latvia |
| Azerbaijan | Lithuania |
| Bosnia and | Moldova |
| Herzegovina | Poland |
| Belarus | Russian |
| Bulgaria | Federation |
| Croatia | Slovak Republic |
| Czech Republic | Slovenia |
| Estonia | Tajikistan |
| Georgia | Turkmenistan |
| Hungary | Ukraine |
| Kazakhstan | Uzbekistan |

**4** Yugoslavia

| | | |
|---|---|---|
| Bahamas | Ecuador | St. Lucia |
| Barbados | Grenada | Suriname |
| Belize | Guatemala | Trinidad and |
| Bolivia | Guyana | Tobago |
| Chile | Jamaica | Venezuela |
| Colombia | Nicaragua | |
| Cuba | Panama | |
| | Peru | |

**Key to group numbering**

1. Group of 77
2. Latin America and Caribbean group
*3. Eastern European group
4. Non-aligned movement
5. African group
6. Islamic conference
7. Arab group
8. Asian group
9. Western Europe and other states
10. European Community
11. Nordic group

**5**
| | | | |
|---|---|---|---|
| Angola | Cote d'Ivoire | Madagascar | Seychelles |
| Benin | Equatorial | Malawi | Swaziland |
| Botswana | Guinea | Mauritius | Tanzania |
| Burundi | Ethiopia | Mozambique | Togo |
| Cape Verde | Ghana | Namibia | Zaire |
| Central African | Kenya | Nigeria | Zambia |
| Republic | Lesotho | Rwanda | Zimbabwe |
| Congo | Liberia | Sao Tome | |

**6**
| | |
|---|---|
| Burkina Faso | Guinea Bissau |
| Cameroon | Mali |
| Chad | Niger |
| Comoros | Senegal |
| Gabon | Sierra Leone |
| Gambia | Uganda |
| Guinea | |

**7**
| | |
|---|---|
| Algeria | Morocco |
| Djibouti | Somalia |
| Egypt | Sudan |
| Libya | Tunisia |
| Mauritania | |

**8** China Japan

| | | | |
|---|---|---|---|
| Bangladesh | Malaysia | Bahrain | Qatar |
| Brunei | Maldives | Iraq | Saudi Arabia |
| Indonesia | Pakistan | Jordan | Syria |
| Iran | | Kuwait | United Arab |
| | | Lebanon | Emirates |
| | | Oman | Yemen |

**9**
Australia
Austria
Canada
Liechtenstein
New Zealand
San Marino

Turkey

| | |
|---|---|
| Afghanistan | Mongolia |
| Bhutan | Nepal |
| Cambodia | Papua New Guinea |
| Cyprus | Singapore |
| India | Sri Lanka |
| Korea, D.R. | Vanuatu |
| Laos | Viet Nam |

Fiji
Korea, Republic of
Marshall Islands
Myanmar
Philippines
Samoa
Solomons
Thailand

Malta

**10**
| | |
|---|---|
| Belgium | Netherlands |
| France | Luxembourg |
| Germany | Portugal |
| Greece | Spain |
| Ireland | United Kingdom |
| Italy | |

**11** Denmark

Finland
Iceland
Norway
Sweden

Member of no group
Israel
South Africa
United States

*As of January 1993, all of the former Soviet Republics were technically still members of the Eastern European group, although several of them are in Asia. A possible realignment of regional groups was under consideration.

members was often supported by the anti-Western communist states. After 1970 the United States found itself unable to command a majority in the General Assembly (as reflected in 60 vetoes the United States exercised in the Security Council between 1976 and 1990, against only 7 by the Soviet Union). This state of affairs was strikingly evident when, against U.S. opposition, the People's Republic of China was admitted to membership in 1971 and Nationalist China—Taiwan—was expelled.

The changing nature of the United Nations has been influenced by the nature of its new members. Many of these newer UN members are independent in part because of the work of the Trusteeship Council, which was established to bring an end to colonialism and to guide the former colonial areas to independence as peacefully as possible. Most observers agree that the Trusteeship Council fulfilled its purpose well. The Economic and Social Council is assigned the task of dealing with international economic, social, educational, and health matters. It is supposed to improve the world's living standards by attacking poverty, ignorance, and inequality as causes of war. Many health matters have been successfully dealt with; many educational and cultural dissemination programs have also had positive results.

A newly developed superpower cooperation once again changed the international environment:

> There have always been connections between the general climate of world politics and the functioning of the United Nations, but the usual impacts have been negative. During the cold war years, and during times of North–South confrontation, political conflict in the world was registered as political stalemate in the United Nations. Now, political settlement in the world is being registered as political cooperation among the major powers in the United Nations. The results of this cooperation are manifest in a re-invigoration of the United Nations Security Council, a new and mutually supportive relationship between the Secretary-General and the permanent members of the Security Council, and, most dramatically, the initiation of several new UN peacekeeping operations. . . . It is unlikely that any of these UN steps could have been taken unless the world political climate changed in the way it did.[14]

## The Settlement of Disputes in the United Nations

The Charter identified international peace and security as the UN's first goal, with economic and social cooperation and human rights as other objectives. Thus the various organs of the United Nations, in accordance with the UN charter, play many roles in promoting international coordination, cooperation, and the settlement of disputes.

The United Nations acts as a forum for diplomacy and facilitates communication among states. Activities directly related to the settlement of disputes are listed in Arti-

[14] Donald Puchala and Roger A. Coate, *The Challenge of Relevance: The United Nations in a Changing World Environment* (New York: Academic Council on the United Nations System, 1989), p. 100. For proposed UN reforms, see J. Martin Rochester, *Waiting for the Millennium: The United Nations and the Future of World Order* (Columbia: University of South Carolina Press, 1993), and Paul Kennedy and Bruce Russett, "Reforming the United Nations: Problems and Possibilities," *Foreign Affairs* 74 (1995), 56–71

cle 33 of the Charter. One not specifically listed is "good offices," whereby a third party provides a place for negotiations or helps to ease the communication needed for negotiations. This mechanism is built into the structure of the United Nations. Other mechanisms are negotiations, inquiry (a neutral investigating body provides information relevant to the dispute), mediation (a third party becomes an active participant in negotiations, helping the states in conflict to find acceptable terms), conciliation (the third party is an IGO, commission, or other body asked to act as a mediator), and arbitration (the parties involved agree beforehand to be bound by the decision of the group acting as an arbitrator). The last mechanism mentioned in Article 33 is adjudication, or judicial settlement, in which a dispute is brought before an international court.

The International Court of Justice (ICJ) is the judicial organ of the United Nations. Although the record is quite mixed, the ICJ has proven useful in a number of cases. The ICJ has judged cases whose issues have ranged from fisheries to frontier disputes to nuclear testing. A number of cases are submitted to the Court but then removed from the ICJ by the parties. Some are settled out of court; the rest are removed because one party refuses to accept the ICJ's jurisdiction in the dispute. Indeed, distrust of the ICJ and unwillingness to let an outside party determine a state's interests are the main reasons that many issues are not brought before it. States use the ICJ when they feel it would be a useful tool of their foreign policy (contrast the U.S. use of the ICJ in the case of the Iranian seizure of American diplomats with its refusal to accept the judgment of the ICJ in the dispute over U.S. mining of Nicaraguan waters).

In 1945 the founders of the United Nations envisaged a large role for the organization in collective security. Chapter VII, Articles 39–46 of the UN Charter call on all members to make available to the Security Council, by special agreements, armed forces and facilities "for the purposes of maintaining international peace and security." These forces were to provide the basis for UN-authorized military actions against aggressor states. Almost immediately, however, the cold war began. Soviet–U.S. hostility made it impossible for the permanent members of the Security Council to concur on the terms for a UN military force, and no agreements with individual states were ever reached. In its first 45 years the UN only once designated a state as an aggressor; that was North Korea, in 1950, and the designation was made while the Soviet representative was boycotting the Security Council.

Not until 1990, after the Iraqi occupation of Kuwait, was collective security again invoked. Then the United States and the Soviet Union were in substantial agreement, and careful negotiations between them, and with other major powers, made possible the UN-authorized military actions against Iraq. There was, of course, no standing UN military force for those operations. Rather, a multinational coalition was assembled on an ad hoc basis. In practice, the United States dominated the coalition and substantially controlled military and political strategy; the UN exercised only very general supervision. It remains to be seen whether that experience will serve as a precedent for similar peace-enforcement operations in the future, or even serve to stimulate creation of some sort of UN permanent military capability that might also act as a deterrent to aggression. A "new world order" built around the concept of collective security might well be grounded in a renewed and expanded role for the UN.

The other kind of operation in which the UN can employ military force is **peacekeeping**. Peacekeeping is very different from military enforcement: its purpose is conflict management or settlement, and it does not involve assigning guilt or identifying an aggressor. Rather, it involves recognition that a violent conflict or threat to peace is at hand. Here the role of the UN is to stop fighting already under way, separate the warring parties, and create conditions for them to negotiate instead of fight. During the cold war the UN had little success with conflicts involving both superpowers because each could veto any proposed UN action. It was often more successful, however, in dealing with medium and minor powers in situations where the superpowers were not strongly involved on opposite sides. Beginning with the Suez crisis in 1956, it dispatched lightly armed peacekeeping forces of varying magnitude to many trouble spots (with the 20,000 troops sent in 1960 to the Congo—subsequently Zaire—being the largest). These operations are carried out only with the consent of the conflicting parties; when the UN takes sides in a civil war, as in Somalia, it is less successful.

Other UN peacekeeping operations were mounted in the Middle East (including the Golan Heights and Lebanon), Indonesia, India–Pakistan, and more recently Afghanistan and in 1988 the Persian Gulf (the Iran–Iraq war). The key to many of these operations was the use of UN forces to separate the armies of the warring parties and to maintain a cease-fire. The importance of such activities was made painfully clear in 1967, when Secretary-General U Thant acceded to the request by Egypt's President Nasser to remove the UN forces that had been stationed on the Sinai border between Israel and Egypt (but in Egyptian territory) since the Suez war. Israel's decision to launch the "preemptive" strike of the 1967 Six-Day War was strongly influenced by the absence of a UN barrier to a possible Egyptian attack, which the Israelis believed to be imminent. The UN's original peacekeeping role—standing between hostile forces—has been expanded to include maintaining security or stability within a wide area (as in southern Lebanon), providing humanitarian assistance (Cyprus), disarming insurgents (Nicaragua), and monitoring elections (Namibia, Nicaragua, and Haiti). Gradually, therefore, the UN has become important in managing conflicts within a single country rather than purely between countries and has taken on a role in helping to secure peaceful transitions of government. It (and some regional international organizations, notably the Organization of American States) is increasingly helpful in aiding the establishment of democratic governments when the parties involved want such help.[15]

## Summary: The "Three United Nations"

For all its failures and limitations, the United Nations has become a powerful instrument for achieving **human security** in its broadest sense. Its founders established it

---

[15] See Bruce Russett and James S. Sutterlin, "The U.N. in a New World Order," *Foreign Affairs* 70 (1991), 69–83, for a review of the most legitimate and efficient ways for the UN to engage in peace enforcement. For a discussion of the broadened concept of peacekeeping since the end of the cold war, see Alvaro de Soto and Graciana del Castillo, "Obstacles to Peacebuilding," *Foreign Policy* 94 (Spring 1994), 69–83. Lester Brown, Hal Kane, and David Malin Roodman, in *Vital Signs 1994* (New York: Norton, 1994), p. 21, also note the improving ratio of government expenditures on UN peacekeeping to the amount spent on national military establishments: only a few years ago this ratio was about 2,000 to 1; today it is closer to 250 to 1.

with a broad vision of peace and security, and the UN continues to evolve within a changing global context. While it has not satisfied all high hopes at the end of the cold war, it has accomplished far more than its detractors recognize—and more than many of its member governments. The UN consists of organs devoted to three broad, different purposes—but organs that, as in a human body, complement each other and cannot be effective alone.

The most obvious UN is the UN of security against violence. This is the UN of the Security Council, with its powers of peacekeeping, of applying economic sanctions, and of carrying out collective security operations against aggressors like Iraq. This UN also includes the secretary-general, with his powers to promote peaceful settlement of disputes through good offices, negotiation, and mediation.

The second UN—of economic security and the provision of basic human needs—is less obvious. This is the UN of the specialized agencies and much of the Secretariat. It is the UN of emergency humanitarian assistance, of the Food and Agriculture Organization (FAO), the World Health Organization (WHO), and the United Nations Development Programme; it is also the UN of the IMF and the World Bank, affiliated organizations disposing of enormous capital resources.

Least visible, but equally important, is the UN of security of human rights. This is the UN that oversaw the treatment and ultimately the transition of Trusteeships like Namibia. It is the UN of the International Court of Justice, of the Electoral Assistance Unit of the Secretariat, of the Commissioner of Human Rights, of the High Commissioner for Refugees, and of the Universal Declaration of Human Rights.

In all three of its aspects, the UN has achieved successes as well as failures. Against the tragedy of Bosnia are substantial peacekeeping and peace-building successes, in places such as Cambodia, El Salvador, and Namibia. WHO eradicated smallpox worldwide. The economies of the LDCs have benefited from UN development assistance. The Electoral Assistance Unit has helped conduct democratic elections in more than 40 countries. UN rhetoric of human rights, while often ignored, has become embodied in international conventions and declarations that now take the form of domestic law in many states, binding governments to observe their normative principles.[16]

The United Nations in its varied guises has attempted to deal with serious environmental, economic, and political problems, which may ultimately be the most crucial the world faces because of the interdependences of the world system. The UN has held special conferences in all these areas to bring states together to air their differences, to propose various policies, and to work out agreements. The three UNs have a synergy; they reinforce and build on each other. There can be little economic security if there is no security against violence, within countries as well as between them. Peace-building, in the wake of conflict, requires reestablishing economic security and protection of human rights for the vanquished, for minorities, and for majorities that govern democratically.

---

[16] Resolutions of the General Assembly are not considered international law (as are treaties). They are, however, part of the behavioral norms that can lead to international law through custom.

## REGIMES AND INTERNATIONAL ORDER

If states and other international actors are to cooperate and deal with the prisoners' dilemma posed by collective goods, how should they organize themselves? There are, as we have seen, a number of strategies for achieving collective goods. One method, in the words of one analyst, is to "bind the members of the international community to rules of conduct, to which they agree, and which will restrain each member from free riding, and allocate burdens equitably, as a matter of international legal commitment."[17]

International law can do this, but the rules of conduct that affect international behavior go beyond those of international law. International law does not exist by itself; neither does international organization. Some groups of states, and groups of activities, exhibit strong elements of international order. Scholars have used the term **regime** to identify the complete set of *rules* that relate to some specified area of international relations. This concept helps us understand the full array of constraints imposed by international society. Regimes have been defined as networks of "rules, norms and procedures that regularize behavior and control its effects . . . sets of governing arrangements [and] principles, norms, rules, and decision making procedures around which actor expectations converge in a given issue area."[18] The regularization of behavior means the creation of patterns—patterns of procedures, patterns of compliance to norms and rules, and most especially, patterns of expectations: "What these arrangements have in common is that they are designed not to implement centralized enforcement of agreements, but to establish stable mutual expectations about others' patterns of behavior."[19]

What do these arrangements consist of, and where do these common understandings come from? There are formal components and informal components; there are national components, transnational components, and international components. The set of governing arrangements consists of national rules (the domestic laws of states), international rules (international law, the charters of IGOs, and the regulations, resolutions, and practices of IGOs), and private rules (the practices of MNCs and other NGOs, the charters of MNCs, and other formal regulations). These are the formal products of governments, IGOs, and NGOs. Regimes also include the norms and principles that reflect patterns of behavior not yet formally codified in law or organization. The development of international law through custom—the actual practice of states that is accepted as law—is an important example of informal norms that act as rules to constrain behavior. Norms, principles, and customary law all have a major psychological component in that the policymakers of states feel they *should* act in certain ways

---

[17] See Charles P. Kindleberger, "Dominance and Leadership in the International Economy," *International Studies Quarterly* 25 (1981), 252.

[18] See Robert Keohane and Joseph S. Nye, *Power and Interdependence,* 2nd ed. (Boston: Little, Brown, 1989), p. 19, and Stephen Krasner, ed., *International Regimes* (Ithaca, N.Y.: Cornell University Press, 1983).

[19] Robert Keohane, *After Hegemony* (Princeton, N.J.: Princeton University Press, 1984), p. 89.

because they are expected to (and expect others to), whether or not a rule has been formalized by treaty.

Thus we have sets of governing arrangements relating to various issue areas in international relations. Issue areas may be functional and thus be very wide or very narrow, paralleling the structure of functional IGOs. One scholar notes, "We live in a world of international regimes." Their concerns range from monetary issues, to trade issues, to the management of natural resources, to the control of armaments, to the management of power, to the management of outer space and the seabed.[20] Regimes may also be geographic, covering problems that arise within a specific area; Antarctica presents such an example. Just as with IGOs, some regimes have only a few members, like that overseeing North Pacific fisheries, while some are very large, such as the UN conflict-management regime.

Much of the regime literature looks at economic and/or ecological issues. We need to recognize, however, that regimes apply to *any* set of rules, norms, expectations, and organizations that deal with a common issue or problem. One example of a regime, created to deal with ecological problems, is the one concerned with the pollution of the Rhine. To identify the problems, causes, and possible remedies of pollution, in 1963 the affected states of West Germany, France, Luxembourg, the Netherlands, and Switzerland established the International Commission for the Protection of the Rhine Against Pollution. The political bargaining on this issue, however, took place within the context of studies, conventions, and sets of principles set out by the European Parliament, the Council of Europe, and the OECD, as well as the relevant areas of international law dealing with rivers. Related cases have been handled by the European Court of Human Rights and the European Court of Justice. Over the years, of necessity, the European Community became increasingly involved, to the point that the EC itself became a member of the International Commission.[21]

Regimes are also created to help manage common-pool resources. International management regimes act to create order in areas of market failure—where a market mechanism cannot work by itself and the tragedy of the commons is a potential threat. Many, such as those dealing with the seas and its fisheries, are about property rights. They involve such issues as *who* is in the group and thus is allowed to use some resource, how much of some resource is available ("harvesting capacity") and the rate at which it can be used, and how the benefits of some resource are to be distributed among the participants. One example of all three in action involves the North Pacific Fur Seal regime, based around a 1957 convention negotiated by the United States, the Soviet Union, Japan, and Canada. To prevent extinction of the seals, the agreement banned open-sea hunting, limited hunting to certain islands, and set quotas for yearly harvests—with a North Pacific Fur Seal Commission determining what the maximum

---

[20] See Oran Young, "International Regimes: Problems of Concept Formation," *World Politics* 32 (1980), 331–356. For a discussion of the role of IGOs in the governance activities of regimes, see Friedrich Kratochwil and John Ruggie, "International Organization: A State of the Art on an Art of the State," *International Organization* 40 (Autumn 1986), 753–775.

[21] See Karen A. Mingst, "The Functionalist and Regime Perspectives: The Case of Rhine River Cooperation," *Journal of Common Market Studies* 20 (1981), 161–173.

yearly harvest would be. More interesting, Japan and Canada agreed to abstain from hunting seals, in return being given a share of the profits by the United States and Russia.[22]

Both of these examples indicate the interaction of rules, law, IGOS, and states. If issue areas are characterized by interdependence, sets of governing arrangements will help the actors to collaborate and coordinate their actions. "Coordination" is the process of developing policy to avoid some outcome; for example, the rules of the International Civil Aviation Organization are designed to prevent air accidents. "Collaboration" is defined as agreements designed to avoid the choice of temptation ($T$) in the prisoners' dilemma and to help the actors choose the second-best strategy, the rewards from mutual cooperation ($R$). Regimes can do this by changing the structure of payoffs, making cooperation more beneficial and defection more costly. Regimes can make side payments (as in sharing the fur seal profits with nonharvesters) easier and reduce transaction costs: "International regimes do not substitute for reciprocity; rather they reinforce and institutionalize it . . . delegitimizing defection and thereby making it more costly."[23]

# REGIMES AND ECONOMIC INTERDEPENDENCE IN THE POSTWAR WORLD

Some of the most extensive analysis of regimes has focused on the post–World War II economic relations of the Western industrialized countries. In the post–World War II system, the victorious industrialized countries consciously sought to create an international economic order—or regime—that would tie the states of the world together in order to promote economic growth and peace. The 1920s and 1930s were periods when economic isolationism, protectionism, and conflict helped lead the world into war. After World War II, the United States used its Marshall Plan aid to encourage European coordination, management, and growth of economic interdependences in areas like international monetary policy and trade. But interdependence involves vulnerability and sensitivity. In the late 1960s and 1970s, when the spectacular economic growth of the postwar era slowed for a number of reasons, economic interdependence began to be increasingly costly as well as beneficial. The question, again, is: How to manage interdependence? How to build new arrangements and institutions to solve the problems posed by economic interdependence and to manage the conflict generated by it in a peaceful manner?

---

[22] See Per Magnus Wijkman, "Managing the Global Commons," *International Organization* 36 (Summer 1982), 511–536. Wijkman notes that this exemplifies a management regime for a CPR: "an efficient allocation and enforcement of harvesting rights, an acceptable distribution of the resource rents among the interested parties, and a scientifically determined harvesting quota" (p. 526).

[23] See, first, Arthur A. Stein, "Coordination and Collaboration: Regimes in an Anarchic World," in Krasner, ed., *International Regimes*; then Robert Axelrod and Robert Keohane, "Achieving Cooperation Under Anarchy: Strategies and Limitations," in Oye, ed., *Cooperation Under Anarchy*, p. 250.

## Hegemony and Regimes

At the end of World War II, the Western powers were agreed in their basic views of the international economy. The cornerstone of their vision was a liberal system, one without the economic barriers that had been set up in the 1930s. This was to be a relatively unhampered economic system based on capitalism, the free market, and minimal barriers to trade. To make the system work, states had to cooperate. Establishing this system was seen as a major step toward creating peace and order in the world, particularly within the group of OECD states. Free trade, free movement of capital, and stable monetary relations all depended on an orderly world. Thus there was also an interdependence between military and economic factors. The area had to be militarily secure from outside threats as well as internally peaceful. The same state that could provide military order—the United States—was also the only state economically strong enough to provide order in the economic system. As the source of economic growth, the United States was the "engine" of global economic development.

In this international system based on U.S. military and economic predominance, the United States followed a policy of leadership, or, as some observers describe it, **hegemony**. In a hegemonic system, "one state is able and willing to determine and maintain the essential rules by which relations among states are governed. The hegemonial state not only can abrogate existing rules or prevent the adoption of rules it opposes but can also play the dominant role in constructing new rules."[24] Under U.S. leadership, the major economic features of the postwar period were "rapidly expanding and generally non-discriminatory trade, large-scale and rapid movements of funds from one center to another under fixed exchange rates, and the rapid growth of huge multinational enterprises."[25]

Hegemony can be a useful, if not a necessary, mechanism for helping a group to achieve collective goods—this is the fifth strategy discussed at the beginning of the chapter. Mancur Olson has said that a large group member can create what he calls a "privileged" group, whereby this large member provides the collective good for the whole group. Similarly, Charles Kindleberger argues that a stable world economy needs a "stabilizer." Other scholars suggest that a group needs an "entrepreneur" to provide the political leadership necessary to help the group achieve the collective goods it desires. In sum, these views argue that whether or not a collective good is supplied, the effectiveness and the stability of the group are affected by the presence or absence of a hegemonic power. This complements the view that much regime change is related to the appearance or disappearance of a hegemonic power.[26]

---

[24] C. Fred Bergsten, Robert Keohane, and Joseph Nye, "International Economics and International Politics: A Framework for Analysis," *International Organization* 29 (1975), 14.

[25] Keohane and Nye, *Power and Interdependence*, p. 19.

[26] See Mancur Olson, *The Logic of Collective Action* (Cambridge, Mass.: Harvard University Press, 1971); Kindleberger, "Dominance and Leadership," p. 252; Norman Froelich, Joe Oppenheimer, and Oran Young, *Political Leadership and Collective Goods* (Princeton, N.J.: Princeton University Press, 1971). For a skeptical view of the hegemonic power argument, see Bruce Russett, "The Mysterious Case of Vanishing Hegemony; or, Is Mark Twain Really Dead?" *International Organization* 39 (1985), 207–231.

A related perspective on hegemony was provided by Karl Deutsch. Deutsch suggested that one helpful condition for a security community is a strong "core area" with "the capacity to act—a function of size, power, economic strength, and administrative efficiencies." It is doubtful that the existence of a large core area is essential to the kind of security community that exists among OECD countries, which have an even more stable condition of peace among themselves now, when the United States is much less predominant, than just after World War II. Nevertheless, earlier U.S. predominance may have been very important in setting in motion the economic prosperity and interdependence that now underlie that peace. In this sense there is some virtue in having one big power in the international system: if it chooses, it can not only bully others but also make short-term sacrifices that will in the long run benefit all members, not just itself. The real problem in the identification and existence of a hegemon, however, has been pointed out by Kindleberger: distinguishing between leadership and domination. The utility and desirability of having a hegemon may very well depend upon where states sit in the international economic system. As noted in Chapter 15, LDCs that are dependent upon that hegemony and that see it as domination will have views very different from those of developed, industrialized states, which see it as leadership.

Some analysts claim the problem today is that interdependence has grown and is outpacing the ability of states to manage it, and that this is due in large part to the decline of the United States as the protector. Partly because of governmental deficit and international debt, the United States *has* lost control over the international monetary system. It is clear that the United States has been constrained by its own economy in its ability to respond to the needs of the newly democratized countries in Eastern Europe, to many LDCs with debt problems, or even to the financing of the Gulf War (American diplomacy focused on raising funds from its wealthy allies and regional oil producers). Does this mean that the United States can no longer function as a system leader? The question really is that raised in Chapter 6: How do we define power? While U.S. *control over resources* is relatively less, the Gulf War indicated that the United States still wields greater military capabilities than any other country. A lessening of control over resources does not necessarily mean less *control over actors;* lower levels of tangible capabilities do not mean less influence. The United States still has a leading position and can exercise leadership (if not domination) in global relations.

## *Monetary Policy and the Bretton Woods System*

As a result of agreement in values and outlook, a small number of industrialized states led by the United States created the basis for a liberal international economic order for the developed, noncommunist states. One aspect of this order had to do with the international monetary regime. International monetary policy deals with the exchange rates between currencies, the nature of the reserve assets used as a common medium of exchange (gold, British pounds, or U.S. dollars, for example), and the degree of control over the movement of international capital.

In July 1944, 44 states met at Bretton Woods, New Hampshire, intent on creating an international monetary order that would promote economic and political stability.

This order was to be based on two international organizations that were to manage the system: the International Monetary Fund (IMF) and the International Bank for Reconstruction and Development (IBRD), or World Bank. The IMF was to keep a watch on exchange rates, which were to be fixed, based on gold, and to permit only slight shifts. Voting in the IMF was weighted to match countries' contributions to the IMF fund. In 1946 the United States contributed one-third and thus had 33 percent of the vote. Although its contribution share has declined over the years, the United States has always retained control over important IMF decisions. The World Bank was established to make loans to help postwar economic development. Despite these agreements, by 1947 it was clear that the Bretton Woods system was not working as designed. The United States, in effect, took over. The world's monetary system went on the dollar standard, managed by the United States.

The dollar became the primary reserve asset in the noncommunist economic system, just as gold had been used in the nineteenth century and the British pound in combination with gold at the end of the nineteenth and beginning of the twentieth centuries. In 1947 only the dollar was strong enough to serve this purpose. It was fixed at $35 per ounce of gold, and the firm commitment of the U.S. government to convert dollars into gold "made the dollar as good as gold. In fact, the dollar was better than gold; it earned interest and was more flexible."[27] Indeed, because of the way the dollar was being used and the need of other countries to have dollars in order to buy from the United States and to back their own currencies, the United States ran a balance-of-payments deficit and so permitted an outflow of dollars from 1947 until 1958.

Exchange rates, the type of reserve asset, and the degree of control over capital all fundamentally affect the states being linked. They help determine how rich or poor a state may be, what trade advantages it has (cheap or expensive goods), how much and with whom it trades, and how easily it can or cannot expand trade. All of these factors are significant economic constraints on a state, and they affect military and security capabilities as well. These relationships expand or reduce a state's menu. In the pre–World War I period, Britain, because of the importance of the pound, could do things both economically and politically that most states could not do; the United States was in a similar position in 1947. In 1980, by comparison, with the dollar floating against gold (at a level of $600 per ounce of gold), the rise of gold prices, and the decline of the dollar against such strong currencies as the Japanese yen and the West German Deutschmark, the United States had a much more restricted menu.

The Bretton Woods system ended in August 1971, when the Nixon administration suspended the convertibility of the dollar to gold at $35 an ounce and added a 10 percent surcharge on import duties, hoping to cut down on imported goods and the outflow of dollars. Several factors led to this situation. First, there were pressures from outside the OECD system, from the growing number of LDCs who were dissatisfied

[27] Joan Spero, *The Politics of International Economic Relations*, 3rd ed. (New York: St. Martin's, 1985). Many of the points made in this section are developed at length by Spero.

with Bretton Woods and challenged the system. More important were changes within the OECD system itself. The rate of growth in productivity of American workers lagged behind that of most European and Japanese competitors (and most recently of the NICs of the Pacific Rim). The economic growth of the West European countries and the combined strength of the EC and especially Japan created new centers of economic power and new challenges to American leadership. With these new centers came changes in monetary interdependence. MNCs from the United States, Europe, and Japan came to control vast amounts of capital. The amount of dollars held and traded abroad—Eurodollars—grew tremendously. And in the United States, the Vietnam War and President Johnson's Great Society programs to reduce poverty created pressures for inflation.

All this left the exchange rate of the U.S. dollar fixed at too high a level. For most countries the obvious solution would have been devaluation. But the United States was the protector of the system and the provider of the major reserve currency. When nothing else worked and when other countries either could not or would not cooperate, the United States finally took the major steps of August 1971. During the 1980s the debt crisis facing many LDCs produced an additional strain on the IMF system and world monetary stability, by raising the specter of many states defaulting on the loans received through various international channels. The huge twin deficits of the United States—that of the federal government's budget and, because of foreign trade, the debt to foreign countries—led to a sharp, steep devaluation of the dollar (a cut in half against the yen between January 1985 and January 1988). Some states continue to devalue their currencies competitively, trying to improve their balance of payments. The EU, as part of the Maastricht process toward a unified European economy and a single currency, has attempted a concerted, if regional, response. The European monetary system (EMS) had set up rules for controlling exchange rates within the EC countries. The exchange rate mechanism (ERM) tries to keep European Union currency values within a narrow range of exchange rates vis-à-vis one another, while letting them change value in world markets. In sum, however, a multilateral monetary system presents the existing regime with problems that will not be solved quickly or easily.

## *International Trade*

As with monetary policy, the United States was the primary organizer and support behind the postwar system of liberal international trade. The view of a nondiscriminatory, multilateral, and market-based system was shared by the industrialized Western powers, in part as a reaction to the protectionism of the 1930s. Cooperation, not protectionism, was the liberal view of trade.

Although the United States was willing to lead in this area also, the issues were much more complex because of the effects of trade on internal political issues. Although discussions on trade policy and arrangements began in 1943, the first element of the international trading order to take hold was the General Agreement on Tariffs and Trade (GATT) in 1947. Reflecting the liberal consensus, GATT was based on free trade and nondiscriminatory policies, with the members agreeing to the most-favored-nation principle. Furthermore, GATT established rules aimed at reducing trade barriers and mediating trade disputes.[28] GATT became institutionalized as an IGO, with a secretariat, a director general, and staff to handle the work relating to trade negotiations. Consequently, GATT was the central feature of the noncommunist world trade regime, which worked very well for the developed countries as quotas and other trade barriers were removed and trade was encouraged. Much of the postwar prosperity derived from this increase in trade. The high point of trade cooperation through GATT came in the tariff reductions during the Kennedy Round of negotiations (named after President Kennedy, during whose term the talks began), which was concluded in 1967. After this point, however, all the factors that caused problems in the monetary area also brought trouble to trade.

Inflation and the increased interdependence of trade caused political discontent in economic sectors within countries that were being hurt by the competition of foreign goods. Within each country there were political pressures from segments of the economy seeking protection from foreign competition. The problems in the monetary system also became trade problems, especially as European and Japanese goods came to rival U.S. goods and helped lead to U.S. balance-of-trade deficits (the United States went from a very small balance-of-payments surplus in 1968 to a deficit of $24 billion by 1971). The United States no longer was able or willing to protect the system. Some European actions in particular were highly preferential or protectionist, especially in the EC's Common Agricultural Policy. Japanese restrictions on imports of U.S. agricultural products and U.S. restrictions on imports of Japanese textiles and electronics became continuing irritants.

Finally, until the recently completed Uruguay Round, GATT (now WTO) did not adequately address nontariff barriers (NTBs). These are barriers to trade based on regulations that can be used to discriminate against imports, such as health and safety standards, pollution and environmental standards, technical regulations, and customs valuations and procedures.

From 1967 onward, pressures for trade protection and discrimination increased in the United States, Europe, and Japan, with the loss of cheap oil as an energy source and, with wage increases, a loss of cheap labor for much of the OECD area. As part of the August 1971 economic shock, the Nixon administration began what was to be a continuing American demand for changes in European and Japanese trade restrictions. By 1973 it was clear that a new international trading order had to be established. In September 1973 representatives of about 100 states met in Tokyo to tackle the complex issues of international trade. The Tokyo Round was essentially completed by early 1979. It brought about some reduction of tariff and nontariff barriers, including import licensing codes and customs valuations. These efforts were continued by the

---

[28] In addition to the IMF and the World Bank, there was to have been a third institution, the International Trade Organization (ITO), to reduce tariffs and some nontariff barriers and so promote competitive international trade. Because of reservations by the United States, the ITO was never established, but GATT took its place for manufactured goods. No comparable institution, however, was established for trade in raw material commodities, a reflection of the fact that the advanced economies exported chiefly manufactures while at least half of world commodity exports were from LDCs.

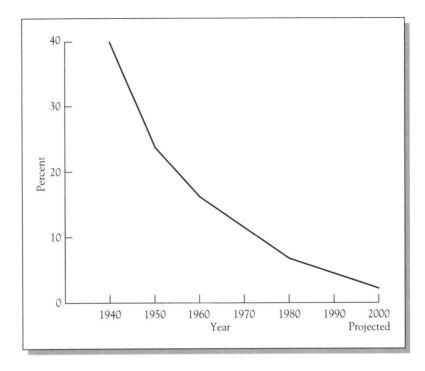

**FIGURE 17.3** Average tariffs of industrial countries. [*Source:* United States Government, Office of the U.S. Trade Representative.]

Uruguay Round of trade talks, begun in 1986, which also introduced new issues, such as North–South trade. By exceeding its goals of cutting tariffs by one-third, the Uruguay Round continued the downward spiral of average tariffs generated by GATT; see Figure 17.3.

Both the monetary and trade regimes have been complicated by the European and Japanese economic recovery and growth since the devastation of World War II. Japan has become America's largest creditor, and the trade disputes between the two countries have become major issues of contention that will not be solved easily or soon. In 1991, for instance, Japanese cars (imports or from Japanese factories in the United States) accounted for 30 percent of the North American market.

The Japanese economic miracle was only one part of an economic resurgence and growth along the whole Pacific Rim, especially in the NICs (Taiwan, South Korea, Singapore, and Hong Kong). During the 1980s the Pacific Rim countries replaced Western Europe as the major trading partners of the United States—and mostly with trade surpluses. The Asian NICs' currencies depreciated almost as fast as the dollar, maintaining these countries' competitiveness and allowing them to export twice as much to the United States as they imported from it. Meanwhile, rapid increases in Japanese productivity, and continuing Japanese informal as well as official restrictions on imports of goods and services, enabled Japan to export three times as much to the United

States as it imported from it. The Pacific Rim countries of Brunei, Indonesia, Malaysia, the Philippines, Singapore, Thailand, and now Vietnam are members of the Association of South East Asian Nations (ASEAN), which has facilitated economic cooperation and growth among them. ASEAN represents yet another source of economic growth in the Pacific Rim.[29]

More recently, the rise of China as a major economic power has complicated matters further. Chinese controls on imports and foreign investment are far more restrictive than Japan's. In 1993, Chinese exports to the United States amounted to nearly $34 billion, as against less than $9 billion in imports from the United States. This was not absolutely as big a trade gap as that between Japan and the United States, but it was by far the biggest proportional difference (exports nearly four times imports) between the United States and any of its major trading partners. Moreover, many Chinese firms "pirated" computer software, recordings, and high-tech goods protected by copyrights and patents in the West—virtually eliminating Chinese importation of these goods and even allowing the Chinese firms to compete sharply with the original producers in Asian export markets. After very hard bargaining, in February 1995 China agreed to stop these abuses—but whether the agreement will be effective remains to be seen.

The shift in world trade patterns has meant more trouble for the "hegemon." The American dependence on Japanese purchases of corporate securities and U.S. government debt restricts the freedom of the U.S. government to set domestic economic policy. If it looks as though the federal deficit will continue to grow or inflation will continue to rise, foreign investors will find U.S. securities less attractive. They will pay less for them and demand higher interest to compensate for the expected inflation and the further devaluation of the dollar against their own currencies.

As the United States's ability to lead or dominate the world economy wanes, it looks for its major partners (the EU and Japan) to carry more of the burdens, both in maintaining the trading system and in contributing to the costs of military security (as in the Gulf War). None is willing or able to do the job alone, and it is not clear even what a "fair share" would be. The Japanese, for example, resist spending more directly on defense; they insist that by their capital investment in LDCs and by their investments in the United States, in effect subsidizing the federal budget while the United States spent so much on defense, they are doing their share. As American ability to lead or dominate the world economy declines, so does the ability to maintain the established international regimes. If U.S. allies are to share in that effort, they will do so increasingly on their own terms and in their own ways.[30]

---

[29] See Steve Chan, *East Asian Dynamism: Growth, Order, and Security in the Pacific Region,* 2nd ed. (Boulder, Colo.: Westview, 1993).

[30] See Robert Gilpin, *The Political Economy of International Relations* (Princeton, N.J.: Princeton University Press, 1987); Martin Tolchin and Susan Tolchin, *Buying into America: How Foreign Money Is Changing the Face of Our Nation* (New York: New York Times Books, 1988); and Takashi Inoguchi and Daniel Okimoto, eds., *The Political Economy of Japan: Vol 2. The Changing International Context* (Stanford, Calif.: Stanford University Press, 1988). For a long-term perspective, see Paul Kennedy, *The Rise and Fall of the Great Powers* (New York: Random House, 1988).

The United States must also learn new patterns of economic diplomacy, because the Pacific countries have a state-centered capitalism different from that of the United States or even from that of Western Europe. Their domestic markets, investment efforts, and export practices are characterized by a partnership between their state bureaucracies and private corporations. "Managed trade" is as typical there as the American ideal of free-market competition, and states bargain with each other over tariffs, quotas, and NTBs to advance and protect the interests of their producers. The Asian countries and those of continental Western Europe traditionally have been more comfortable with protectionism than have the British and Americans. It is not at all clear whether most of the structures of international free trade can be retained or whether barriers will increasingly restrict trade, to the detriment of countries (like the United States) that try to hold to the former, more open practices. The risk is both of lopsided costs to some countries, such as the United States, and of a general slide to slower economic growth for all in a less open world system. The probability that the world may split into competing protectionist blocs (a German-led Europe, a Japan-led Asian group, and a United States–led Western Hemisphere grouping) also cannot be ignored.

In our earlier discussion of the OECD countries, we reviewed various theories of political integration to understand the peaceful relations among them. Integration was seen as both a process and a result of cooperation. Scholars who take a functional view of integration in particular look to the formation of new and bigger states as the result of integration. This has not happened; however, the logic of the functionalist approach still leads us to expect the development of functional cooperative structures among states. Regimes like those that have developed among the OECD countries are informal structures. Rather than the formal creation of new states, the creation of new international organizations, new patterns of interaction among state and nonstate actors, and formal and informal rules and norms that govern behavior may all be seen as the results of integrative processes.

In general, the complex set of arrangements found in regimes may be the most promising way to achieve coordination and collaboration in an interdependent world system. Those arrangements are easiest to establish when one dominant state (a hegemon) can set forth the basic principles and enforce them. When hegemony wanes, the arrangements become fragile and harder to hold in place among competing interests. With waning hegemony, it becomes even harder to replace the old arrangements (regimes) with new and more suitable ones—but that is precisely the challenge facing the world in the twenty-first century.

# Confronting Ecological Challenges to the World System: Which Global Future?

## World Order and World Futures

Through interdependence in its various forms, we are confronted by a set of important problems in the global system that constrain all international and transnational actors. We have come full circle, from consideration of the world system in Chapters 4 and 5 to the discussion here on the ecological limits of that system. The earlier chapters discussed how the global political structure affects states; this chapter looks specifically at ecological linkages and constraints in the contemporary world. We have also come full circle in thinking about what we mean by "security," "power," and "interests." The earlier chapters on systemic effects were concerned with military capabilities and the autonomy of states in the

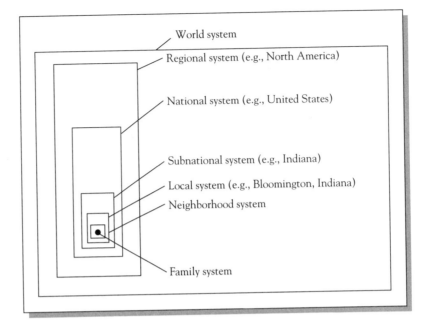

**FIGURE 18.1** A world of systems. [*Source:* Modified from Ervin Laszlo, *A Strategy for the Future* (New York: Braziller, 1974).]

Westphalian system. Our discussions of interdependence, common-pool resources, the tragedy of the commons, and other collective-goods issues indicated that we must rethink and broaden the notion of security. Human well-being, individual or collective, can be threatened in many ways that have nothing to do with the acquisition, threat, or use of military capabilities. A central theme of the United Nations Development Programme is that, "the search for human security lies in development, not in arms."[1] In this chapter we shall discuss ecological problems with collective goods characteristics that flow from global interdependences. We are again confronted by the question of how to manage interdependence, by the need for institutions and mechanisms that can handle such issues.

Scholars interested in world order, peace research, international systems, and alternative world futures try to teach us why we should be aware of and interested in the international and transnational problems of interdependence. To appreciate such concern, we need to see where we fit in the global system. Figure 18.1 presents the

---

[1] United Nations Development Programme, *Human Development Report 1994* (New York: Oxford University Press, 1994), p. 1. The need for broadening the concept of security to include ecological and economic dimensions has become widespread; see, for example, Jim MacNeill et al., *Beyond Interdependence: The Meshing of the World's Economy and the Earth's Ecology* (New York: Oxford University Press, 1991); Gareth Porter and Janet Welsh Brown, *Global Environmental Politics* (Boulder, Colo.: Westview, 1991); and The World Resources Institute, *World Resources 1992–93* (New York: Oxford University Press, 1992).

world system as a set of systems. Individuals tend to give most of their attention to immediate, personal concerns (their families, neighborhoods, and local systems); our typical area of awareness is really quite limited. However, to become aware of and concerned with, and then to solve, the sort of issues discussed in this chapter, we must expand our perspectives both in space (to the world system) and in time (to at least the next 50 to 100 years). Over 25 years ago Ervin Laszlo, a futurist and student of world order, observed, "World order reform starts at home: with the ideas and values we entertain, the objectives we pursue, the leaders we elect, and the way we talk with and influence those around us."[2]

This observation is even more relevant today with the microelectronic revolution and the technologically driven growth of both interdependence and the perceptions of interdependence. With the increased attention to transnational relations and regimes in the study of world politics, the decreasing concern about East–West security issues, and the growing importance of economic and ecological issues, the interconnectedness of systems and issues has become central. The Club of Rome has called this interconnectedness of issues and consequences the *problematique,* or "predicament." With the persistence of ecological threats and their appearance in newer and more dangerous forms—acid rain, ozone holes, atmospheric warming through the greenhouse effect, increased soil erosion and degradation, and continued deforestation of the planet—interest in the ecological problematique became revitalized in the late 1980s and early 1990s.

## THE IMPACT OF CHANGE

We face serious dangers from the demands of the world's population, which generates pollution, consumes the earth's natural resources, and puts pressure on the world's food supply. These problems are worsened by being part of an era of rapid change, what Alvin Toffler called "future shock." Things have changed so rapidly in so many areas that the consequences of those changes have become challenges to the quality of humanity's existence.

The revolutions in industrial production technology, along with the medical and hygienic advances responsible for much of the increase in population, have combined to increase human demands and the attendant problems of pollution and resource depletion. Statistics abound on the consumption of natural resources (especially nonrenewable resources) and the production of pollution. Why have these revolutions brought about world problems today? One answer is related to the important phenomenon of **exponential growth,** which is very much responsible for the "now you don't see it, now you do" nature of these problems. Exponential growth occurs when some quantity continuously increases by a constant percentage over a given period of time—when, for example, a population grows by 2 percent every year. This is the

---

[2] Ervin Laszlo, *A Strategy for the Future* (New York: Braziller, 1974), p. 79.

**TABLE 18.1**    Doubling Time

| Growth Rate (Percent per Year) | Doubling Time (Years) |
|---|---|
| 0.1 | 700 |
| 0.5 | 140 |
| 1.0 | 70 |
| 2.0 | 35 |
| 4.0 | 18 |
| 5.0 | 14 |
| 7.0 | 10 |
| 10.0 | 7 |

principle at work when we deposit money in a savings account so that it will grow through compound interest. It is also a very common process in all sorts of natural biological systems. Figure 18.2 contrasts exponential growth to other common patterns of growth.

Common as it is, exponential growth can provide very surprising results; we do not think a problem exists until it hits us between the eyes. Two stories presented in the Club of Rome's initial major study, *The Limits to Growth*, illustrate these observations.[3] Exponential growth can generate large numbers very quickly. A Persian legend tells of the courtier who presented a beautiful chessboard to the king. In return, the courtier requested one grain of rice for the first square, two grains for the second square, four grains for the third square, eight grains for the fourth square, and so on (a constant increase of 100 percent). By the fifteenth square, the amount was 16,384 grains; by the twenty-first square, over 1 million grains; and by the sixty-fourth square, about 18 quintillion grains. The other story also illustrates the suddenness and surprise of exponential growth. A French riddle supposes that you own a pond. The pond has a water lily that doubles in size every day (again, 100 percent growth). If left unattended, the lily will cover the pond in 30 days. However, the lily seems very small, so you should not worry about cutting it back until it covers one-half of the pond. When will that be? The answer, of course, is the twenty-ninth day; you will have one day to save the pond. Statements about the current global plight are similar to this second story; there is only a short time left to save the pond.

These stories also illustrate the value in thinking of exponential growth in terms of doubling time (see Table 18.1). Even low rates of yearly growth, such as 2 percent,

---

[3] See Donella Meadows et al., *The Limits to Growth*, 2nd ed. (New York: New American Library, 1974), pp. 36–37.

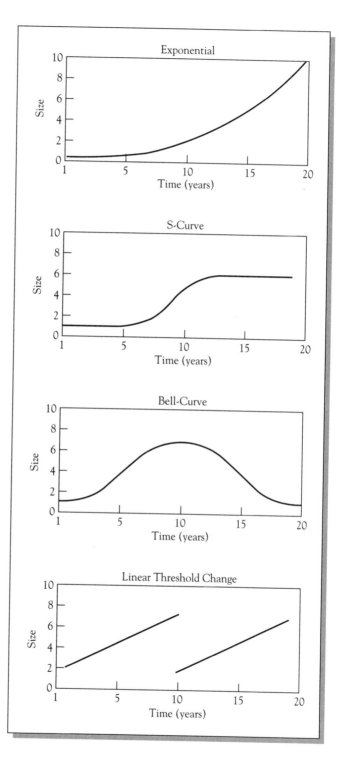

**FIGURE 18.2** Different patterns of growth. [*Source:* Barry B. Hughes, *International Futures* (Boulder, Colo.: Westview), p. 13.]

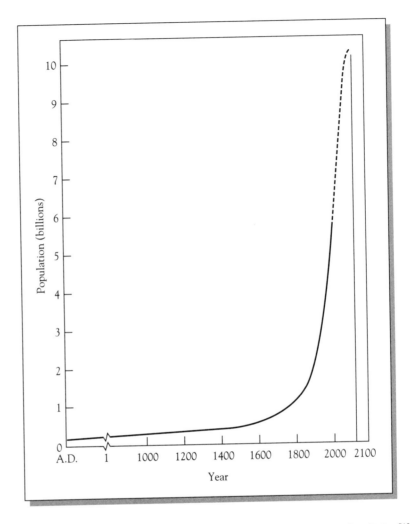

**FIGURE 18.3** The growth in world population. [*Source:* World Resource Institute, *World Resources, 1986* (New York: Basic Books, 1986), p. 10, using 1984 World Bank data.]

can double the size of something in only 35 years. When considering population growth, we can understand how it has jumped so relatively suddenly (Figure 18.3). In Barry Hughes's terms, global population has grown "superexponentially." In 1650 the population of the world was half a billion people, and the growth rate was 0.3 percent—a doubling time of 250 years. In 1987, however, the globe's population was 5 billion. Because of advances in medicine, hygiene, and nutrition, the world's population growth rate was 1.7 percent—a doubling time of less than 40 years! (From 1970 to 1975 the growth rate was over 2.0 percent.) If we think we have political, social, and economic problems with the present population, imagine the problems with a population twice that size 40 years or so from now. In the early 1980s the UN projected that global population would stabilize at 10.2 billion around the year 2100. The newest UN estimate is that population will continue to grow to over 11.5 billion and not stabilize until 2200.[4] As the economist Kenneth Boulding observed, "Anyone who believes that exponential growth can continue indefinitely in a finite world is either a madman or an economist." How long do we have to save the pond?

In the discussion in Chapter 15, we saw that dependence was based in good measure on economic and resource differences. Given the differences that already exist among countries in a measure such as GNP per capita, only small differences in exponential growth rates can make large absolute differences in population and economic performance. Figure 18.4 compares GNP per capita over time for seven countries. Differences in exponential growth rates are widening the economic gap between developed and most developing states. Thus exponential growth is a powerful factor affecting the menus of states, limiting economic growth through the exponential growth of, among other things, population, pollution, and energy requirements.

# THE PROBLEMATIQUE OF SUSTAINABLE DEVELOPMENT

We now face ecological and environmental problems very different from those in the past. The exponential growth of population and economic activity has alerted people to the fact that the earth is finite and that the limits of its *carrying capacity* can be reached—the key condition in creating the tragedy of the commons. Resources that were adequate at lower absolute levels of demand are inadequate at higher levels. Exponential growth sharpens the interdependence of problems that characterize the "problematique." It challenges our ability to provide a balance between human economic and social needs and environmental quality in both the short term and the long term, that is, **sustainable development**.

> The last third of the twentieth century has become increasingly characterized as the age of critical revolution and discontinuity. . . . Our present waves of change differ not only in their quantitative aspects from those of the recent past, but also in the quality and degree of their interrelationships. While previously we might have dealt with relatively separate change factors within local and limited contexts, our present changes are now global in their spatial and quantitative dimensions. They are no longer isolatable sequences of events separated in time, in numbers of people affected, and in the social and physical processes which are perturbed.[5]

---

[4] See Aaron Sachs, "Population Increase Drops Slightly," in Lester R. Brown et al., eds.,*Vital Signs 1994* (New York: Norton, 1994), pp. 98–99.

[5] John McHale, "World Facts and Trends," *Futures* 3 (1971), 216–301.

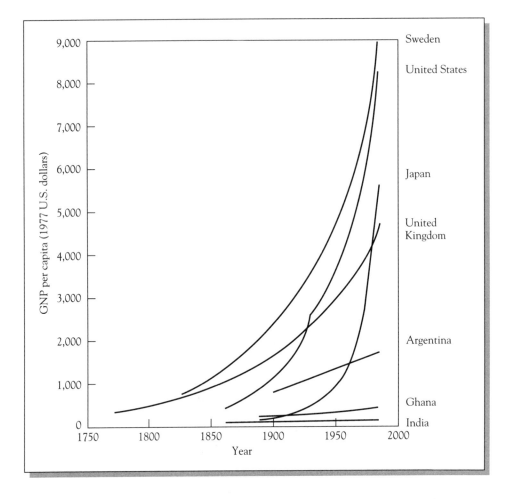

**FIGURE 18.4** Long-term economic growth rates since 1775; the widening gap between rich and poor countries. [*Source:* Simon Kuznets, *Economic Growth of Nations* (Cambridge, Mass.: Harvard University Press, 1971); World Bank, *World Development Report, 1979* (Washington, D.C.: World Bank, 1979), pp. 126–127.]

It is also possible that the earth's carrying capacity is being reduced through the disruption of natural ecosystems that have either been destroyed or are only slowly regenerating; examples include overfarming in many areas, the southward spread of the Sahara Desert, and the destruction of the Amazon rainforest. In the past, when a tribe exhausted the productive capacity of an area, it simply moved on or died off. Today, the threatened ecosystem is not local but global. If our ecosystem is damaged or destroyed, there is nowhere else to go.[6] As both a concept and policy guide, sustainable development has achieved wide popularity. As a result it means many different things to different actors, groups, and interests. At its core it permits us to address environmental concerns simultaneously with more traditional concerns of economic growth. It carries the basic message that environmental resources *are* finite and that ecosystems will collapse if resource utilization and destruction exceed regenerative capacity.[7]

Most of the major issues identified with the problem of sustainable development were introduced by the Club of Rome in the early 1970s in the limits-to-growth perspective. This often controversial series of books provided an outline of the ecological problematique: (1) the exponential nature of the growth of population and human demands on the environment; (2) the finite limits to ecological resources (energy sources such as oil or coal, arable land, the ability to absorb pollutants)—even if we cannot agree exactly on what those limits are; (3) the intricate interdependence among population, capital investment, and the factors that influence growth—such as food, resources, and pollution—which means that working to solve one problem may very well create others; (4) the long delays in the feedback processes, that is, the long time lag between the release of pollutants or creation of other ecological damage and our realization that damage has been done.

The limits to growth, and thus sustainable development, can be addressed in two ways: remove or expand the limits, or weaken the forces of growth. The first has been the traditional political and social response, the latter the view of environmentalists. As Barry Hughes points out, there are distinct worldviews on these problems, structured along two very different dimensions. The *neotraditional view* of ecological issues (e.g., the Club of Rome) is a pessimistic one, holding that the ecosystem is fragile and thus difficult to control and manage, that it has been damaged when we have tried to control it, and that technology will not solve our problems. Neotraditionalists are "inclusionist" in looking at humankind as an important and integral part of the interdependent global ecology system. In distinction, the *modernist* view is an optimistic one, holding that ecological problems are solvable through technological innovation and application—the "technological fix." This view is "exclusionist" in that humans are seen as outside of the global ecostructure but able to manipulate it through technology.[8]

In addition, Hughes points out a *political economy* dimension with three broad categories: classical liberal, internationalist, and radical. These correspond, respectively, to the realist, transnational, and radical worldviews we have been using. Both classical

---

[6] See Sandra Postel, "Carrying Capacity: Earth's Bottom Line," in Lester R. Brown et al., *State of the World 1994* (New York: Norton, 1994), pp. 3–21.

[7] Lester Brown sees the following as examples of the principles of sustainability: "Over the long term, species extinction cannot exceed species evolution; soil erosion cannot exceed soil formation; forest destruction cannot exceed forest regeneration . . . and human births cannot exceed human deaths." See "Overview: Charting a Sustainable Future," in Brown et al., eds., *Vital Signs 1994*, p. 15.

[8] Barry B. Hughes, *World Futures: A Critical Analysis of Alternatives* (Baltimore: Johns Hopkins University Press, 1985), chap. 3. Neotraditionalists have also been termed "neo-Malthusians," while modernists have been called "cornucopians"; see Thomas F. Homer-Dixon, "On the Threshold: Environmental Changes as Causes of Acute Conflict," *International Security* 16, 2 (1991), 99–100.

liberal (or realist) and radical views of political economy are modernist—they see the world as manipulable through technology by human beings, especially if their ideology is the "correct" one. Some neotraditionalists do not approve of any of these economic views. Thus modernists, from both the left and the right, may disagree with the assumptions of neotraditionalists who argue for limits to growth. Modernists argue that technological change has been continuous (and perhaps even exponential), able to keep up with any challenge.

Neotraditionalists face the dilemma of dealing with ecological issues and still addressing the need for economic growth. In Chapter 14 we identified moderate economic growth as a condition that seemed to be necessary for the existence of peaceful security communities. From the point of view of an LDC, this dilemma is even more pronounced. And it is this dilemma that helps to explain the broad acceptance of the need for some form of sustainable development. Most countries, developed or developing, have come to recognize the interdependence of economics and ecology and the need to pay attention to both. This was clearly seen in the deliberations of government representatives, NGO advocacy groups, and private citizens at the 1992 United Nations Conference on Environment and Development (UNCED) held in Rio de Janeiro and the fifth International Conference on Population and Development held in Cairo in 1994. While a general notion of sustainable development could be agreed upon, exactly what it means and how to achieve it is still subject to intense debate. Thus perceptions of ecological problems and how to deal with them will depend, as do most issues raised in this volume, on one's worldview and its assumptions about human nature, human control over fate or the environment, and which values should be maximized.

## POPULATION

Many people feel that at the heart of all ecological issues is the question of population, which has three central dimensions. The first is the *Malthusian dimension,* which relates population to world food supplies. The possibility of starvation is not the only Malthusian outcome. If population growth strains food resources, then malnutrition will continue to limit the mental and physical development of children and the energies and abilities of adults—in other words, the quality of the population.

The second dimension is what we may call the *deprivation dimension.* This is the political, economic, and social dimension of the population problem. It pertains to the discontent produced among people by the lack of food or its inequitable distribution—and the political consequences of the development of radical political forces. Discontent caused by relative deprivation drives various ideological and political movements, especially those seeking revolutionary change. The uneven distribution of population growth in LDCs, especially the tremendous growth of urban populations (and attendant air- and water-pollution problems), exacerbates this trend.

The *ecological dimension* is often the most emphasized aspect of the population problem and is currently seen as the most dangerous: increases in population

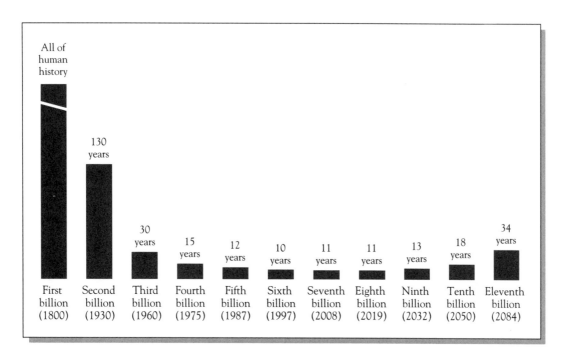

**FIGURE 18.5**   Rate of global population increase across history. [*Source: A Citizen's Guide to the International Conference on Population and Development* (1994), p. 14.]

inevitably increase the demands on the ecological system for natural resources and goods and services, thus generating ever greater pollution.

The current global population is around 5.5 billion. It took from 1825 to 1930 to add a billion people to the world's population; the most recent billion was added in a little more than a decade. The present burst in population growth is due mostly to the drastic reduction in death rates caused by the public health improvements made in the past 200 years (see Figures 18.5, 18.6, and 18.7). Populations tend to level off after upsurges; eventually birth rates fall, as they have done in the Western industrialized states, where birth and death rates nearly balance each other. (In some European countries in recent years, notably Germany, the population growth rate has actually been negative.) Most of the LDCs are experiencing rapid population growth because of greatly reduced death rates. Some, like China and Taiwan, have managed to reduce birth rates sharply, but many others, such as India and Mexico, have yet to do so. Birth rates tend to fall when there is widespread distribution of information about contraception and when people begin to feel that their basic needs are being met. Social and economic changes are thus essential if population growth in LDCs is to be slowed; it is not just a matter of finding a "technological fix."

Even so, the uneven distribution of population will worsen for several decades. It is a mistake to look only at the crude birth and death rates. To get a true picture of

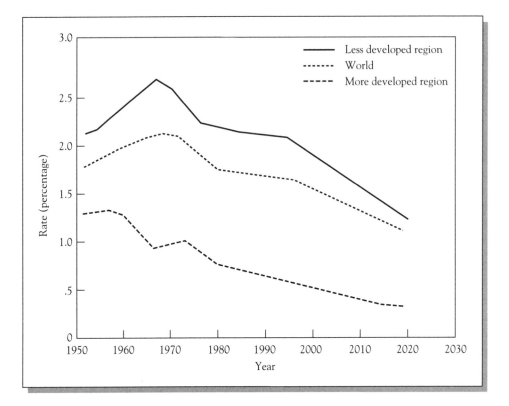

**FIGURE 18.6** Overall population growth rates, developed and developing countries, 1950–2020. [*Source:* World Resources Institute, *World Resources 1988–89* (New York Basic Books, 1990), p. 17]

population growth, we have to look at the *population structure* of a country; that is, the numbers of people in different age groups and the fertility rates for those categories. As child and infant mortality rates fall, a country's population becomes younger and a greater proportion of women will be of childbearing age. Figure 18.8 shows the different population structures for developed and developing countries. The developing countries, with a large bulge representing the population under 20, will have much greater population growth in the future. Proportionately many more women have yet to reach childbearing age in the LDCs, and a much larger portion of the populace will be reproducing: the larger group now at childbearing age and those who have yet to reach that age. For example, data from the late 1980s indicated the existence of more than 40 countries where 45 percent or more of the population were *under 15 years of age*. Even if future parents should merely replace themselves with two children, so that the death rate would eventually equal the birth rate, so many people have yet to do this that the population of the LDCs will continue to grow for some time.

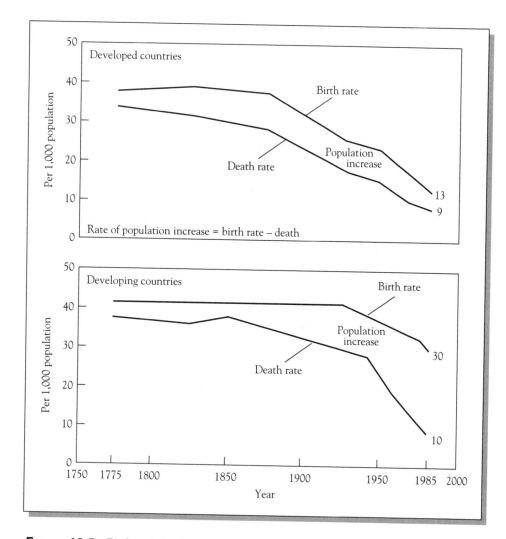

**FIGURE 18.7** Birth and death rates, developed and developing countries since 1775. [Courtesy of the Population Reference Bureau, Inc., Washington, D.C.]

This is an important aspect of the idea of "deadly delays." We need to look at least 50 years ahead. The longer population control is delayed, the more people of child-bearing age will enter the population. When population growth is indeed level—that is, there is no growth—the absolute level of population will be much higher. That means that the absolute number of people will continue to grow for decades after a population control policy is initiated. The uneven rate of population growth is a major factor in the food trade patterns of North America and Latin America. In 1950 both

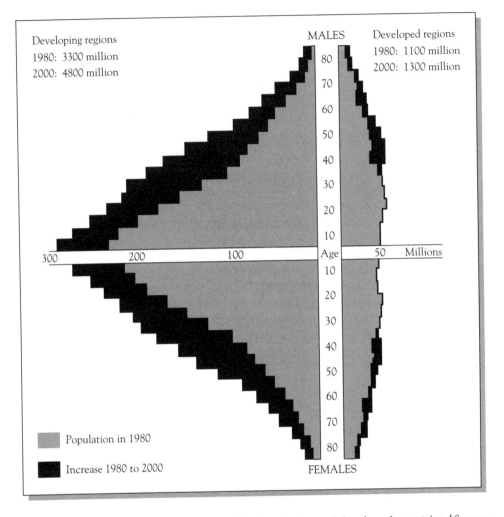

**Figure 18.8** Population age structure for developing and developed countries. [*Source: Jerusalem Post*, May 11, 1989.]

regions had approximately the same population, 163 and 168 million, respectively. But the rapid increase in the Latin American population and the emphasis in commercial agriculture on exports have forced Latin America to become a net importer of basic foodstuffs, while North America exports food. Had North America's population since 1960 grown at the same 2.5 percent rate as did Latin America's, then instead of about 270 million people in 1987, it would have had 390 million.

Increased population also includes a deprivation dimension that involves political, social, and economic consequences of ecology issues. As politics is the process by which it is decided who gets what, when, and how, anything that creates even more resource scarcities and complicates resource distribution will increase political conflict both *within and across* societal boundaries. Such conflict may be handled peacefully within stable societies or relatively stable international systems. But as population pressures lead to scarcities, there will be deprivation and unmet demands. A struggle for resources will frequently cause instability and political violence within new, poor, and politically underdeveloped states or in international systems where common interests go unrecognized, regulator mechanisms are underdeveloped, and levels of community feeling are low.

## DEPLETION OF NATURAL RESOURCES

Population growth, combined with the demands for maintaining high standards of living in the rich countries and demands for development and industrialization in the poor ones, has put great pressures on the world's supply of natural resources. These pressures belong to both the deprivation and ecological dimensions of the population problem. They are important to our conception of the world as a global commons. Many studies indicate that the use of the world's resources is growing exponentially and that in many areas and for many resources it is growing at a rate faster than the growth in population. For example, while world population has increased three and a half times since 1890, industrial energy use per capita has increased over seven times and total world energy use has grown almost *fourteen* times.[9]

Thus every additional human being and every additional demand for every new item produced place demands on the earth's mineral and energy resources. Figures on known reserves of minerals and other nonrenewable resources are deceptive. Many parts of the world are not yet fully explored, so new reserves of many minerals will undoubtedly be found. (Geologists sometimes make estimates of these "probable" and "possible" reserves.) Known bodies of resources may be too difficult or too expensive to tap into, given current knowledge and prices. New technology may be developed for extracting the materials, and a rise in prices may make it profitable to exploit deposits that previously were too costly to mine. Thus known reserves can be greatly expanded even without any exploration. This has happened with some petroleum deposits in the United States, where oil fields that were no longer profitable could once again yield valuable supplies when prices rose.

Still, there are limits. A 1985 U.S. government study projected that with 1985 rates of usage and even assuming *five times* the amount of known reserves, there were only 53 years of tin reserves, 72 years for lead, and 149 years for iron ore. World energy consumption has been projected to rise over 50 percent within the next 20 years, assuming no substantial change in the types of fuels used. Analyses using the ratio of proven world reserves to the 1992 production rate have projected only 45 years of remaining

---

[9] See the special issue of *Scientific American*, September 1990, on "Energy for Planet Earth," especially John P. Holdren, "Energy in Transition," pp. 156–163.

petroleum production. Clearly, at some point the world's petroleum really will be exhausted; long before that happens, it will become too expensive to use except for very special purposes for which there are no acceptable substitutes. If the world expands its reserves of minerals chiefly by making them very expensive, it will have made a very dubious bargain.

It is important to understand that industrialized countries use far more resources than do the overpopulated LDCs. Thus a cutback in resource consumption by the industrialized countries could reduce the projected usage rates of nonrenewable resources and increase the years of remaining reserves. The United States, with about 5 percent of the world's population, has accounted for about 60 percent of the world's consumption of natural gas, 40 percent of coal and aluminum, and 30 percent of nickel, copper, and petroleum. It accounts for a quarter of the world's total energy consumption (as well as about a quarter of the world's air pollution). India, with 16 percent of the world's population, accounts for about 3 percent of its energy usage and 3 percent of global air poluution. If the world energy-usage rate was the same as that of the United States, the total consumption in 1990 would have been four times larger than it was. Figure 18.9 provides one example of the great differences in energy consumption across countries, especially between some industrialized countries and some LDCs. Note that the yearly per capita average of energy usage for the United States and Canada is the equivalent of over 40 barrels of oil; Nigeria and India average about 2 barrels of oil per person.

Another resource, often neglected because it is not strictly nonrenewable, is water. Only about 2 to 3 percent of the world's water is fresh water, and most of that is in the icecaps. Less than 1 percent of the world's water is fresh water that we can work with in the ecosphere: rivers, lakes, water in soil and plants, and vapor in the atmosphere. Though water is a scarce resource, usage is rapidly increasing to meet human consumption and food-production demands. Water must not only be available but also be of sufficiently high quality for drinking, washing, and growing food. While desalination of seawater has become more widespread among countries that can afford it, the quality of fresh water is being threatened by a wide range of human-generated pollutants, from sewage to industrial waste to chemical outputs from mining and agriculture.

Vast quantities of water are needed for opening up new farmland, reclaiming old land, maintaining the land in use, and maintaining the ongoing "green revolution" in overpopulated areas. To produce one pound of grain requires 60 to 225 gallons of water, and the production of one pound of beef requires 2,500 to 6,000 gallons. Industrial activities also require great quantities of water: one ton of steel requires 65,000 gallons, and one automobile requires 100,000 gallons. Water usage grows faster than population. It is estimated that water usage triples as population doubles. Demand will rise most quickly in the industrialized areas.

We began by examining population growth, but many analysts begin with and stress energy consumption, calling energy "the master resource." With enough energy, other resources can be mined or otherwise acquired, processed, substituted for, or recycled. In other words, the limits to these resources can be relaxed. Increasing food production or cleaning up polluted air and water also requires expending large amounts of energy. Economic development and growth in national wealth correlate

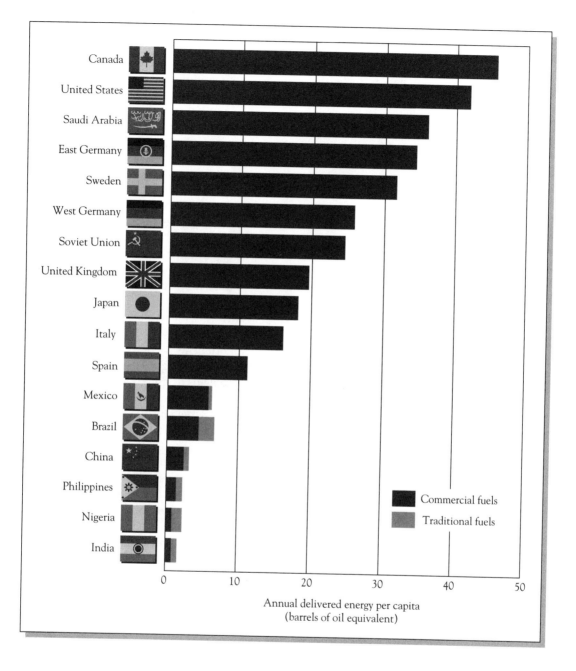

**FIGURE 18.9** Disparities in energy usage: 1988 use per capita for selected countries. [*Source: Scientific American,* September 1990, p. 57.]

with the use of energy; consequently, poor countries will require more energy to develop. A vicious cycle emerges here: birth rates tend to drop and stabilize as countries develop economically, but for this to happen, more energy is needed. Meanwhile, the added population creates demands that devour additional energy and wealth just to maintain the current level of usage. This means that very large amounts of energy must be devoted to the less developed areas.

Energy consumption did drop slightly in the early 1980s, in part because of effective conservation (especially in Europe and Japan) and in part because of the worldwide recession. The latter is not a viable long-term strategy. Given the possibility of a new "oilshock" in terms of rising prices and declining supply, new sources of energy and new ways to conserve must be found.

The drain on the global commons is highly uneven. While population increases in the developing world drive resource consumption, by far the greatest drain occurs in the developed states. Strategies should therefore include changes in lifestyles, as well as changes in the structure of the manufacturing economy: eliminating planned obsolescence, designing longer-lasting and more easily repaired products, recycling, and ceasing to produce products that wind up in rubbish mountains. The current pattern of production and distribution in the industrialized countries probably cannot be maintained even there; an attempt to imitate it worldwide would cause ecological disaster.

Individual actions and attitudes can be important, as we first noted in Chapter 16. Some people in the developed countries are slowly changing their habits to reduce consumption and to conserve energy. Yet the problems of collective goods continue to hamper those efforts when people (as most people do most of the time) emphasize their own self-interest and do not see how it can be served by making sacrifices: "Why should I turn off the lights to save electricity? It's priced cheaply enough and it's such a tiny contribution." Altruism alone cannot produce the necessary sacrifices; we still need a combination of raised costs (money and otherwise) and a heightened awareness of the effects of our actions. Short- and medium-term strategies, including resource substitution, can allow the development not only of new lifestyles but also of whole processes, technologies, and synthetic materials. Short- and medium-term strategies must therefore bring the world through a difficult period of transition to a longer run. Very basic changes must be made in resource usage, population growth, and substitutes for exhausted resources. Changes in behavior must occur across all levels of analysis: individual, group, economic enterprise, society, region, and the world system as a whole.

## POLLUTION

The interdependent relationship among population, economic growth, energy consumption, and pollution pointed out by early neotraditionalists produces a dilemma that is again coming to the forefront of attention. One way to control population growth is through economic development; yet to maintain developed economies or to continue development in LDCs means higher energy usage and the creation of ever higher levels of pollution. For example, production of carbon dioxide contributes to global warming. In 1950 only 10 percent of global $CO_2$ emissions came from the developing countries; in 1985 it was 16 percent; and by 2020 it is projected to be a full 50 percent. The Worldwatch Institute points to the "frustrating paradox" of sustainable development: "Efforts to improve living standards are themselves beginning to threaten the health of the global economy. The very notion of progress begs for redefinition in light of the intolerable consequences as a result of its pursuit."[10]

The increasing use of nonrenewable fuels, as well as the manufacture of chemicals and other industrial products, is producing rising levels of pollution worldwide. Burning fossil fuels produces carbon dioxide, carbon monoxide, sulfur oxides, nitrogen oxides, hydrocarbons, and solid particles. These are emitted into the air and water of our planet. Some of these emissions produce acid rain. They settle into or are washed into the soil and into the plants and animals that live in polluted areas. Water is also damaged by thermal pollution: heat from industrial processes and nuclear energy reactors disrupts the ecological balance of rivers, streams, and lakes. In addition, nuclear power produces radioactive wastes, which could become the most dangerous pollutants of all. Some of the most difficult, controversial, and critical issues involved with nuclear power concern accidents—Chernobyl is the most striking example—which produce radiation leaks into the ecosystem around the nuclear power plant. Equally difficult is the problem of disposing of the highly radioactive wastes that nuclear power plants produce. Many countries simply have no safe disposal site or viable disposal policy. Hence, this is a problem demanding international cooperation.

Pollution can be anything from a bother or an inconvenience to an immediate danger to animal, plant, and human life. It can destroy precious food and water resources and make many of the limited resources of the earth unusable. *The Limits to Growth* made four main points about pollution:

**1.** The few kinds of pollution that have been measured over time seem to be increasing exponentially and even faster than population growth.

**2.** We have almost no knowledge about what the upper limits to these pollution growth curves are.

**3.** The presence of natural delays in ecological processes increases the probability of underestimating the control measures necessary and therefore of inadvertently reaching those upper limits.

**4.** Many pollutants are globally distributed; their harmful effects appear long distances away from their point of generation.[11]

---

[10] *State of the World, 1987* (Washington, D.C.: Worldwatch Institute, 1987).
[11] Meadows et al., *The Limits to Growth*, p. 78.

The spread of pollutants throughout the ecosystem is one of the major indications of global interdependence. For example, lead emitted into the air by the industrial countries has been found in the Greenland icecap. Large DDT deposits have been found in the bodies of whales that have lived almost entirely in the Antarctic region. Increases in the carbon dioxide content of the atmosphere (resulting especially from the burning of fossil fuels) create a greenhouse warming effect, which traps heat inside the atmosphere. The result will be to raise world temperatures by between 1.5 and 4.5 degrees Celsius (2.7 and 8.1 degrees Fahrenheit) over the next 50 years. The effect will be concentrated in the upper latitudes (perhaps an increase of 1 degree Celsius per decade there) rather than in the tropics. Climate will change in erratic and unpredictable ways: forests will move poleward; arid zones in the middle of continents will grow and make grain cultivation uneconomical; the icecaps will melt and the sea level will rise, drowning low-lying coastal areas. Harmful effects will be greater in some areas of the world (such as North America) than in others (such as Russia). Scientists agree on the general outlines, though not the details, of what will happen, but they disagree as to what should be done about it. Energy conservation and, perhaps ironically, greater emphasis on nuclear energy will be required.

Pollutants are also responsible for punching the holes that have appeared in the earth's atmospheric ozone layer over Antarctica. Partly they are the result of the use of chlorofluorocarbons (CFCs), now mostly banned from spray cans but still widely used in plastics and refrigeration. In 1987, 31 major producing countries signed the Montreal Protocol to cut worldwide production of these chemicals by 50 percent by the year 2000. It was a fairly impressive agreement, given the difficulties: delay caused by vested economic interests, uncertainty about the scientific evidence, and the reluctance of LDCs to pay for more expensive substitutes. In 1990 in London, 93 countries agreed to accelerate the ban, agreeing to end production of chemicals that destroy the ozone layer by the year 2000; the 1992 Copenhagen amendment moved this date up to 1996. The London agreement came about only through compromise, which included the industrial countries setting up a fund to help developing countries pay for the phasing in of CFC substitutes.

The ozone problem is compounded by another contributory factor to global warming, the destruction of the Amazon rainforest. Large areas of the forest have been and are being cleared in the interests of commercial development and of settling new farmers pushed out of their former homes by the South American population explosion. Tropical forests, once estimated to have covered 16 percent of the world's terrestrial surface, now cover only 7 percent. Such a loss represents a reduction in the global biomass (total amount of living things), in biological diversity (the variety of living things), and in the overall ecological community.[12] When the jungle is cleared for farming, plant life undergoes two damaging changes. Trees that absorbed carbon dioxide are cut down, and the new plants emit some compounds that may worsen the ozone problem. This is a situation in which *national* decisions cause *global* problems,

---

[12] Porter and Brown, *Global Environmental Politics*, p. 14. Regarding biological diversity, perhaps as many as 1 million species have disappeared from the world's rainforests over the past two decades.

and the problems cannot be dealt with only by restraint at the national level. They require agreement among nations and changes by international development agencies like the World Bank in the kind of projects they support and encourage. Time for effective action is short.

To prevent even further destruction of tropical rainforests, programs of "debt-for-nature" swaps have been worked out. Governments of developed countries and international organizations forgive a large portion of some LDCs' foreign debts in return for agreement by the LDCs to give permanent legal protection to large tracts of forest. As with developed countries paying for CFC substitutes, agreements for debt relief, trade, and aid to save tropical forests are an example of using side payments for private goods to get actors to cooperate in a tragedy-of-the-commons situation. Such actions come none too soon. Costa Rica illustrates some of the problems. For its size, it has the largest system of protected land and national parks in the world, with 12 percent of its land area in the national parks. Yet it also has had one of the highest rates of deforestation in the world; in essence, everything not protected is being cut at breathtaking speed.

Banana growing vividly illustrates the dilemmas of Costa Rican development. The country has long been a big banana producer, and the government hopes to make it the region's foremost banana exporter. Multinational corporations are powerful actors in the domestic politics of this small and not wealthy country. Great plantations provide jobs at good wages, but the environmental effects of clear-cutting forests for cultivation, subsequent exhaustion of the land, and widespread pollution are immense. Bananas are no free lunch.

Tourism is Costa Rica's third largest industry, thanks to the country's political stability, its great and varied natural beauty, and the park system. Yet its ecological assets are being endangered. The same coral reef that begins far north in Mexico's Yucatan peninsula extends all the way down Costa Rica's east coast and had been a major tourist attraction. But most of the reef in Costa Rica is now dead, a sad remnant of what still remains in the Yucatan and Belize. The runoff of silt and pesticides from coastal banana plantations has killed it.

Tourism can be a mixed blessing. Costa Rica is not yet plagued by wall-to-wall high-rise hotels, but they may soon come. Some Costa Ricans are trying to promote "ecotourism" as an alternative. By that term they mean building small-scale units that blend with rather than dominate the natural environment, employing residents as managers and as guides who can interpret local culture and ecology, and promoting direct and relatively close contact with the indigenous people—by, perhaps, meals in private homes rather than restaurants. A central aim is the education of tourists about ecological problems and possibilities. Tourism of this form is not for everyone, either tourists or hosts. It cannot provide anything like the number of jobs that mass tourism provides, and visitors' contacts with the local culture will remain fairly superficial. But perhaps ecotourism can interact with Costa Rica's efforts to preserve large segments of its natural environment.

Pollution, then, is a clear example of a collective "bad": a jointly supplied externality generated by interdependence. Individual states cannot avoid taking in others' pollution; individual state action cannot provide the collective good of a clean environment. Collective action is required. Starting in the late 1980s, some impressive movement toward action on ecological issues has taken place, led by IGOs (the United Nations Environment Program, the World Bank's Environment Department, and the European Community), NGOS, and various transnational environmental groups. "Green" groups have proliferated around the globe, creating the core of a growing environmental regime. This, of course, is what is needed to deal with a transnational, interdependent, collective goods problem. A primary dilemma, however, is sustainable development—containing pollution must somehow be reconciled with the need for greater global equity and the need to improve living conditions in the LDCs.

# FOOD

As much as 40 percent of the world population suffers from some form of undernourishment. The UN Food and Agricultural Organization (FAO) has noted that the populations of most LDCs suffer calorie-intake shortages and that malnourishment because of insufficient protein—which is vital to mental development—is especially serious.

By one estimate, about half of the arable land in the world today is being cultivated, but the other half would be very costly to prepare for growing food. In fact, every year much arable land is lost to cultivation, perhaps permanently, through the expansion of roads and urban areas and, increasingly, through deforestation and pollution. People in poor countries cut down trees for firewood because they cannot afford commercial cooking fuels; forests are lost and deserts spread. As noted above, this is also related to global warming, which has been found to have some negative impact on world grain production. The increase in prices due to such effects would not hurt the developed countries much but could have a deleterious effect on LDCs. The World Resources Institute has identified soil degradation (soil erosion, loss of soil fertility, silting, flooding, and acid rain) as one of the key resource issues we face today. Agricultural scientists try to keep up with population growth and loss of arable land by introducing new seeds, fertilizers, and pesticides to raise the productivity of existing land. Nevertheless, it is a hard race, and the new technologies consume a great deal of energy and cause new pollution problems as well.

Estimates of how many people the world could feed diverge widely and are part of a major debate. Some argue that there is enough potential capacity for food production to feed the developing countries as they move through the period of rapid population growth. Estimates range from the very optimistic one (based on Japanese standards of farming and nutrition) that the world could support 95 billion people, to another (based on Dutch standards) of around 30 billion. The Committee on Resources and Man of the National Academy of Sciences has argued that a much more realistic number is about 10 billion, and the number should be lower if people are to be more than merely adequately nourished.[13]

---

[13] Richard Falk, *This Endangered Planet* (New York: Random House, 1971), p. 134.

Part of the problem lies in the definition of "adequate nourishment." Obviously, "adequate" means a certain minimum intake of calories, protein, vitamins, and minerals. It does not, however, require that everyone adopt the dietary habits of people living in the industrial countries, where diets are heavy in meat and other animal products (a steer must take in six to eight pounds of grain to produce one pound of beef). Thus we see the virtue of development programs that stress meeting the basic needs of everyone and avoiding a distribution of income and consumption skewed heavily in favor of people in the rich countries or the rich people in poor countries.

A global food paradox has also appeared. By the mid-1980s world food production had reached record levels; indeed, because so much food was produced, prices fell, leading to ever higher subsidies from governments to farmers in the United States, Europe, and even the then-Soviet Union. During this same period China became self-sufficient in grain (exporting corn to Japan) and India found itself with a grain surplus. Through improved biotechnology food production was increased dramatically: American farmers get five times the yield of 50 years ago. Because of new frost-resistant breeds of corn, the corn belt in the United States now extends 250 miles farther north than it did in the mid-1970s. The development of aquaculture—the use of fish farms—has been particularly important in China and India. Nevertheless, the steadily rising production of grain, fish, beef, and mutton that characterized the period from 1950 to the mid- to late-1980s has now leveled off and has even begun to decline, while population continues to grow.[14]

The four decades of increases in food production have also not eliminated the problems of malnourishment or even starvation. One study estimates that over 1 billion people in the LDCs do not have the money to buy the food that exists in the world market. In the short term, yearly harvest fluctuations cause food crises in particular areas. Weather conditions make the world grain crop volatile, and, as seen in 1993, in any one year the grain harvest can drop as much as 5 percent. Still, the larger problem is getting the financial resources needed to produce the food, to pay for the energy needed to produce the food, and to buy the food that is available. The amount of food on the world market may even depress local prices, reducing the money and food available in local areas (as local producers stop producing). Situations of starvation derive primarily from *political* factors that affect the distribution of food: civil war and insurgency (as in Africa) preventing food from getting to certain areas, government decisions to reward and punish certain regions or groups within the state, or urban demands for cheap food (and potential urban support of antigovernment forces).

More generally, in many LDCs food-distribution facilities are terribly inadequate. Food may rot on the piers of a port city or be eaten by pests on the farms. International food assistance is sometimes diverted by corrupt officials who sell the food for profit. Further, development patterns oriented toward the export market—big commercial crops like cotton, coffee, sugar, fruit, and flowers—may bring in foreign exchange, enabling the rich to buy luxuries or giving LDC governments the finances needed for industrial development. However, when subsistence farms are converted into big

---

[14] See Lester R. Brown, "Facing Food Insecurity," in Brown et al., *State of the World 1994*, pp. 177–197.

commercial establishments raising cash crops, an immediate food deficit is created. Laborers who used to raise their own food must now use part of their earnings to buy food. Part of this problem could be eased by development programs aimed at strengthening small farmers, who could raise some crops for sale but keep a part of their land for raising their own food.

Land reform and technical assistance to small farmers are receiving increasing attention by international lending organizations like the World Bank, but political and economic resistance to a major reorientation of agricultural development is nevertheless very great. International cooperation has also been channeled through the FAO and other agencies. Agencies such as the World Food Council help keep track of and aid in the deliveries of food, and the Agricultural Development Fund helps developing countries increase production. Yet such activity (a world "food regime") only begins to meet the problems—problems requiring a global approach along with investment and food aid, an effective population policy, and balanced economic development within and among the regions of the world.

## INTERDEPENDENCE, EQUITY, AND SUSTAINABLE DEVELOPMENT

People in sovereign states must stop thinking solely in terms of short-term, domestic policy when dealing with resource consumption, population, and pollution. Long-term, collective ways must be devised to cooperate in protecting the global commons and achieving various collective goods. This requires the complex bargaining that goes into the formation and maintenance of regimes that can help provide governance over specific issue areas.[15] One of the major difficulties, however, remains the division of the world into haves and have-nots. The developed and the developing countries have tended in the past to approach these issues from very different perspectives, making cooperation even more difficult and complex. One good example is the negotiation of the UN Law of the Sea Convention.

The Third UN Law of the Sea Conference (UNCLOS III) met from 1973 to 1982 to settle unresolved issues caused by technology and collective-goods problems. Two major strategies were used. First, coastal states were given, with certain limitations, exclusive use of 200-mile economic zones off their coasts. In these zones (including the continental shelf), states would have the rights of exploration and exploitation of mineral and animal resources. This part of the oceans regime is an international equivalent of the English enclosure movement of the early nineteenth century, which similarly eliminated the remaining commons pastureland.

A second matter addressed by UNCLOS III was the attempt to create an International Seabed Authority to manage the resources beyond the 200-mile limit in the

---

[15] See Robert O. Keohane and Joseph S. Nye, *Power and Interdependence,* 2nd ed. (Boston: Scott, Foresman, 1989); see also Porter and Brown, *Global Environmental Politics,* chap. 3.

interests of the "common heritage of mankind." Here was a second mechanism: developing supranational institutions for the oceans regime that were centralized to manage seabed resources jointly for all states. Here, however, the LDCs and the developed states held two different views on how the seabed commons should be regulated. LDCs wanted the International Seabed Authority (and its operational arm, the Enterprise) to control all exploitation of the seabed. Developed states, the Reagan administration in the forefront, desired national control. With their own sophisticated mining industries, the United States, Britain, West Germany, and others wanted free access and less control by the Authority. Because of the control by the Authority, the United States did not sign the draft treaty in 1982, although 130 other states did. With hard bargaining, the Clinton administration renegotiated the terms, but it is still unlikely that the U.S. Senate will ratify the treaty.

The Law of the Sea process illustrates several previously discussed topics. As we saw in Chapter 15, differences in wealth and development, past colonial relationships, and dominance or dependence complicate the uneven distribution of resources and the use of those resources around the world. To develop, the LDCs need vast amounts of resources, energy, capital, and aid. In the process of developing they will consume nonrenewable resources and will also generate a great deal of pollution. Their view is generally that the developed states are trying to keep them in an underdeveloped, neocolonial, and subordinate position, as evidenced by Western opposition to the mining and wealth-sharing provisions of the Law of the Sea. This view is strengthened when ecologically minded people (neotraditionalists or "greens") tell them that they should not aim for similar levels of development as the rich countries. So we have a tragedy-of-the-commons situation worsened and complicated by a history of colonialism and exploitation.

Many analysts have emphasized the need to stabilize the demand for resources, to keep the demand from growing and even to reduce demand in some cases. This is important and can happen, as seen by the results of conservation efforts to date (for example, in CFC emissions). Not only do neotraditionalists and modernists argue over the best ways to reduce demand, but this issue is at the core of many differences among classical liberals (realists), internationalists (transnationalists), and radicals. Some argue that demand is mostly generated by overpopulation, others that demand is a function of more intense usage. Garrett Hardin, with his position on **"lifeboat ethics,"** is the best example of the analysts who blame the pressures on the world's natural and food resources on population growth in the developing countries. Others have rejected Hardin's metaphor of the "lifeboat," or at least the implication that some people will have to be "thrown overboard" if the rest want to survive.[16] Instead, we might think of the lifeboat as filled with many people, including quite a few first-class passengers with all their luggage. The need may be to throw overboard some golf clubs and guns rather than people.

---

[16] See Garrett Hardin, "Lifeboat Ethics: The Case Against Helping the Poor," *Psychology Today* 8 (1974), 38–43, 124–126. For a response and critique, see Marvin Soroos, "The Commons and Lifeboat as Guides for International Ecological Policy," *International Studies Quarterly* 21 (1977), 647–674.

Development strategies based on more equality within nations and across the entire globe could greatly improve the living conditions of the world's poor. This improvement could be bought at a relatively modest cost. The graph in Figure 18.10 shows the relation between per capita income and life expectancy in LDCs. Per capita income is shown on the horizontal axis and the average life expectancy at birth on the vertical axis. The lower curve shows the typical relationship between income and life expectancy in 1972, and the upper one the relationship in 1982 after improvements in health care had raised life expectancy almost everywhere.

There is a fair amount of scatter among points; nonetheless, it is clear that at 1982 income levels under $2,000 per capita—typical of most of Africa and much of Asia and Latin America—life expectancy varies between about 40 and 65 years, with most of the poorest countries showing the lower life expectancies. At the low end of the graph (under $1,000) the curve that best fits the relationship indicates that life expectancy goes up about a year for every $50 increase in income per capita. Toward the right side of the graph, from about $3,000 upward, the slope becomes quite flat, requiring an increment of almost $1,000 to show an increase of a year in life expectancy. Beyond $6,000 for the developed industrial countries (not shown here), the slope becomes really flat, demonstrating almost no relationship between income and life expectancy at the high levels.

This pattern implies that major improvements in health and living conditions for the poor could be bought at a price not requiring major sacrifices by people in the rich countries. A transfer of income from the rich countries to the poor need not hurt very much and could have an enormous impact. For a transfer of resources to one person in a poor country, the benefits would be almost 100 times greater than the cost in life expectancy to the person in a rich country from whom the transfer came. By giving up increased luxuries—or through cuts in military budgets with the demise of the cold war—the cost could be made nearly painless.[17] In a poor country, $2 may cover the cost of an inoculation against some killer disease; in an industrialized country, $2 might buy you a minute with a psychiatrist.

It is worthwhile to notice the implications of great inequalities within countries. The countries found below the line, such as some of the newly prosperous OPEC states like Algeria and Iraq, have quite unequal internal distributions of income. Shifts to greater equality within those states would markedly improve the living conditions of their many poor citizens. Countries such as China, Sri Lanka, and Costa Rica, while hardly rich in per capita terms, show the benefits to their citizens of a more egalitarian distribution of income. Large numbers of developing countries could also cut the resources that they devote to the military, on which they spend many times more than on health and education. In the mid-1980s, Iraq spent more than 700 times as much on the military as on health and education; Pakistan spent almost 300 times as much.

Of course, the calculation of costs and benefits for transferring income or wealth from rich to poor is much more complicated than this simple illustration suggests.

---

[17] See Alex Mintz and Chi Huang, "Defense Expenditures, Economic Growth and the 'Peace Dividend,'" *American Political Science Review* 84 (1990), 1283–1293, on the long-run diminution of investment by defense spending.

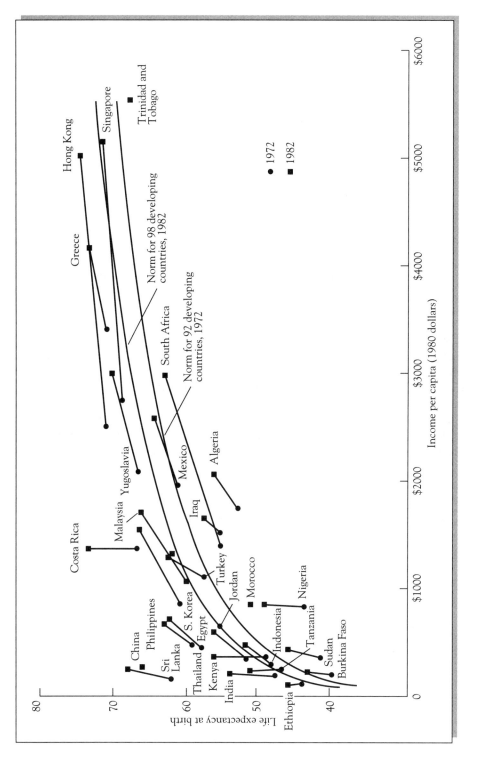

**Figure 18.10** Life expectancy in relation to income in less developed countries, 1972 and 1982. [*Source:* World Bank data.]

Nonetheless, a goal of a life expectancy of about 65 years for people in the poor countries could be achieved by the year 2000. Its cost would not much exceed a doubling of current nonmilitary international development assistance. It would require some sacrifices, and it would have to be carefully targeted to meet public health, sanitation, and nutrition needs. But it could be done.

This issue raises old and ever-present ethical questions about what responsibility each of us owes others. We typically feel the greatest responsibility for those in our immediate systems (see Figure 18.1). Our families and close friends get the highest priority; our fellow nationals may occupy some sort of middle ground; and inhabitants farther away, about whom we know little, receive the lowest priority. Yet, given such enormous differences in well-being, to what degree is it just to ignore what could be done? Efforts to promote growth in the LDCs, while essential, should not be pursued to the exclusion of growth in the industrialized world. On the contrary, some continued growth in the industrialized countries seems necessary to provide markets for LDC exports and an increased supply of financial resource transfers—private investment and foreign aid—from rich to poor countries.

Trust, cooperation, and common interest—necessary ingredients for the bargaining, agreements, and IGOs needed for creating the regimes to solve prisoners' dilemma problems—will not come easily. How difficult the process will be is a matter of debate between optimists and pessimists and among those holding different worldviews. Lester Brown has observed: "The widening gap between the rich countries and poor is more than just a quantitative economic difference. It is increasingly a gap in values, in social organization, in contrasting life styles, in perceptions of the world in which we live and, ominously, a gap over which it may be increasingly difficult to communicate effectively."[18] On the other hand, signs of positive cooperation across states have been shown through activities such as the UN Environment Program (UNEP) established by the General Assembly and at a series of UN-sponsored environmental conferences such as the 1992 UNCED held in Rio de Janeiro. Awareness of the impact of interdependence and the need for global cooperation, however, was clearly evident even in the early 1970s, when a UN Conference on Human Environment held in Stockholm was praised as a conference at which people of all states began to come to some consensus:

> The Third World countries understood that, far from being an exclusive problem of the industrialized world, environmental degradation and overtaxing of nature formed very much a part of their predicament. On the other hand, the industrialized countries abandoned their initial narrow technocratic view of environment and ended by admitting that patterns of resource use and maldistribution were an important aspect. . . . Both sides really grasped that they were living on only one earth and that the existence of international commons . . . as well as the finiteness of spaceship earth, were binding them into a pattern of real interdependence.[19]

---

[18] Lester Brown, *World Without Borders* (New York: Random House, 1972), p. 44.
[19] Jan Tinbergen, ed., *Rio: Reshaping the International Order* (New York: Dutton, 1976), p. 284.

## ENVIRONMENT, SECURITY, AND CONFLICT: THE WAR PROBLEM AGAIN

Ecological problems interact with concepts of security, conflict, and the risk of escalation to war. With conflicting claims to scarce resources like energy and possible conflicts generated by the vulnerabilities and sensitivities of interdependence, political pressures could lead to a major war long before the ecological system has a chance to collapse; predictions about the Gulf War anticipated a much more extensive conflict, and the ecological consequences of even that limited action were serious.

We have several times discussed Choucri and North's analysis of World War I. Look again at Figure 12.3. In the years leading up to 1914, population growth and economic development led to competition for natural resources, manifested in competition for colonial areas and spheres of influence. This competition helped cause and was heightened by the expansion of military expenditures by the competing states; that is, by the arms race, itself driven in part by domestic and bureaucratic pressures. The arms race and the intensity of competition for spheres of influence in turn led to an increasingly rigid system of international alliances. Ultimately, the system blew up in the most devastating war ever experienced to that time.

Some of the parallels between 1914 and the present are unsettling. We are again in a period of growing resource shortages and increasing fears of the political and economic effects of those shortages. Modern industrial economies require assured access to vital raw materials like oil. Scarcity (which also includes such resources as fresh water and the effects of upstream pollution) could be one important source of international conflict. However, conflict might also be generated by the movement of refugees, displaced by overpopulation or environmental disaster. Or, as environmental disruption wreaks particular havoc on the LDCs, these countries may confront the developed world for their share of the remaining wealth.[20] Or, as noted previously, states may suffer environmental damage generated by other states (or at least *see* others as being responsible) and resort to violent conflict to "solve" their problems.

## A VISION OF A PEACEFUL WORLD: DEMOCRACY, DEVELOPMENT, AND PEACE

Lynn Miller's book, *Global Order,* begins by quoting the famous opening lines of Charles Dickens's *A Tale of Two Cities*:

It was the best of times, it was the worst of times, it was the age of wisdom, it was the age of foolishness, it was the epoch of belief, it was the epoch of incredulity, it was the

---

[20] See Homer-Dixon, "On the Threshold."

season of Light, it was the season of Darkness, it was the spring of hope, it was the winter of despair, we had everything before us, we had nothing before us.

These lines are just as appropriate for our conclusion. They refer to a period of change and transition; a period fraught with problems and the dangers they pose, but also the opportunities for significant progress if those problems could be solved. We, too, live in a period of change. We have seen a series of challenges to peace, democracy, and development in an increasingly interdependent world, a world in the midst of a shift in the Westphalian trade-off. The challenges are daunting, the possibilities enormous.

The Universal Declaration of Human Rights, adopted by the General Assembly in 1948, incorporates economic, social, and political components. Included are rights "to own property," "to protection against unemployment," "to remuneration insuring . . . an existence worthy of human dignity," and "to a standard of living adequate for . . . health and well-being"; "to freedom of thought, conscience, and religion" and "to economic, social, and cultural rights"; "to seek, receive, and impart information and ideas," "to freedom of peaceful assembly," "to take part in the government . . . directly or through freely chosen representatives . . . in periodic and genuine elections which shall be by universal and free suffrage and shall be held by secret vote," and "to a social and international order." In this book we, too, have focused on the foremost desires of all humanity: political liberty and material well-being. We have found that in order for these to be achieved, we must combine some degree of economic growth with some degree of equality in the distribution of material goods. People vary in their relative evaluation of growth and equality. Some prefer great equality of condition, others prefer a distribution that heavily rewards great contributions to society. Compounding the differences in values are different theories about economic reality, about the necessary trade-offs between equality and efficiency. Too great an equality of reward might destroy incentives and hence stifle growth. There is no easy resolution of the value differences or easy testing of the theories about how reality works. Most people would not accept a total concentration on either equality or growth; thus most people, while disagreeing about necessary or desirable trade-offs, want a condition of well-being derived from some degree of equality and growth.

Stable peace, as we used the phrase in Chapter 14, means security in the enjoyment of well-being under liberty; that is, order without dominance. Some of us would accept political repression in return for a decent material living standard; others say, "Give me liberty or give me death." All of us have some sense of the kind of trade-off we would accept, how much liberty for how much creature comfort. As with economic theories about equality versus growth, we also have varying ideas of how much trade-off is actually necessary. An often-malicious piece of mythology used to be that peace, democracy (the widespread achievement of political rights), and development (broadly distributed achievement of a better standard of living) could not be pursued equally or simultaneously. Development might require state control of the economy, the repression of political opposition, and enforcement of heavy sacrifices on the current generation so as to benefit later generations. War might be necessary to achieve or acquire a desirable political system, or to acquire resources needed for development.

Development may enhance the prospects for democracy, and democracy may avoid the kinds of economic distortions derived from central planning; peace makes possible the growth and consolidation of democracy, and democracies rarely fight each other; broadbased economic development promotes social and political harmony, and peaceful relations facilitate the devotion of economic resources to development. The relationships among these "good things" are complex and contingent on circumstances; surely they are not always positive. But they can support each other. Peace, political justice, and economic justice, as Immanuel Kant suggested in his vision of "perpetual peace," are interwined. Together they form the elements of a broad vision of human security.

Growth can be achieved without much equality: the history of the industrialized countries in the nineteenth century and the present conditions of many LDCs and of the globe as a whole attest to that. Some material equality can be achieved without political liberty, as is evidenced in some LDCs and possibly some communist states. But material equality not based on a reasonable equality of political power must be precarious in the modern world, where the state is so powerful. We can conceive of this three-way tension among growth, equality, and liberty in the way pictured in Figure 18.11. Stable peace within a nation-state probably requires a combination of all three. The shaded area toward the top of the pyramid suggests that there is some choice about the precise combination of the three values. Equality is possibly more important than growth (at least in rich countries), and so we have drawn one line for the lower bound of stable peace sloping somewhat toward the right. In a poor country, one might tip the line back toward a horizontal position, like the lower line.

Within the OECD countries, domestic peace has been achieved by a combination of growth, equality, and liberty. This same combination has produced the condition of international peace between these rich and democratic states. In Eastern Europe, the combination of economic stagnation and political repression proved politically explosive and helped destroy the communist regimes. In the LDCs, many repressive governments that magnified economic inequalities and failed to produce growth have also been overthrown in the growing global movement toward free government.

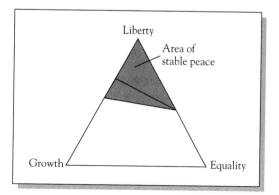

**FIGURE 18.11** Trade-offs among growth, equality, and liberty.

These same trade-offs apply in the world at large. Demands for material well-being can be satisfied peacefully only by some concessions to equality, both within and between countries. Attempts to improve well-being solely through growth will surely require severe repression. Similarly, and despite the global problems of resource availability and pollution, it is almost impossible to imagine the imposition of a no-growth policy worldwide. With so many desperately poor LDCs, some real growth in the world economy, as well as greater equality within and between countries, seems unavoidable. If global no-growth could be achieved in the near future, it would be only under conditions of catastrophe—ecological collapse or thermonuclear war—or global repression. If by repression, it could be achieved only if the world's poor were brutally suppressed by oligarchies within their countries and from outside by the rich and powerful states. It is possible to imagine circumstances in which neither growth nor equality nor liberty was common in the world; in that case, the shaded area of the triangle in Figure 18.11 could shrink drastically.

A failure to pursue both equality and some growth at the global level is therefore a sure recipe for repression; if war could be avoided, it would be only by the unstable mechanisms of deterrence and domination. Surely it will not be easy to achieve growth and equality in the global economy, especially given the ecological problems that exist today. There is no guarantee that peace can truly be achieved.

We can see, however, that material well-being, political liberty, and stable peace really are interconnected. The exclusive pursuit of material well-being can end in war and material destruction. The failure to maintain decent living conditions can result in the loss of liberty in industrialized countries—as happened when Hitler rose to power as Germany suffered from a worldwide depression; as has happened in some LDCs. United Nations Secretary-General Boutros Boutros-Ghali has presented his vision of interdependence among good things:

> Peace is a prerequisite to development; democracy is essential if development is to succeed over the long term. The real development of a State must be based on the participation of its population; that requires human rights and democracy. . . . Without peace, there can be no development and there can be no democracy. Without development, the basis for democracy will be lacking and societies will tend to fall into conflict. And without democracy, no sustainable development can occur; without such development, peace cannot long be maintained. And so it has become evident that three great concepts and priorities are interlinked, and they must be addressed at every level of human society.[21]

Although we may differ about the kind and degree of trade-offs necessary or desirable, it is nevertheless apparent that none can be pursued to the complete exclusion of all others. In relating the ecological problems facing the world to the ever-present possibility of armed conflict, relating our limited capabilities for dealing with

---

[21] Boutros Boutros-Ghali, *Report on the Work of the Organization from the Forty-seventh to the Forty-eighth Session of the General Assembly* (New York: United Nations, 1993), paragraphs 9–12.

collective problems to the conflicts that they engender, we raise a very basic question: Can an anarchic international system cope with the demands of the future? We have outlined a truly daunting range of problems, but we have also indicated how international actors have brought order to this anarchy and the alternatives available for regulating conflict.

## A Final Word

We have discussed levels of analysis and the interactions and interdependences of the world system. We have spoken about individual states and the consequences of their following narrow self-interests. These interests are derived from the politics of the various governments and societies: bureaucratic politics, the politics of interest groups like the oil industry and military contractors, and public opinion in general. The outcomes of these political processes help determine whether states will "defect"— exploit the commons—or take a free ride on international efforts at cooperation, allowing individual citizens within the individual states to use environmentally damaging chemicals, to hunt whales, to use as much gasoline as they like, to disregard birth control. The security dilemma may mean that we are damned if we do and damned if we don't. Weakness can invite attack, but too much strength can threaten others and also invite attack. There is no better way to illustrate how the various levels of analysis can be linked, constraining the menu of choice for everyone.

The three worldviews—realist, transnationalist, and radical—are not merely philosophical points of view possessed by distant observers; they are representative of the policies pursued by states and their leaders. These policies not only vary among different states, but are held variously by each of the same states over time. Some periods of history are marked by greater realist competition: alliance formation, arms races, frequent crises and wars to challenge or maintain the balance of power. Other periods, often following wars, show great transnational or radical creativity for changing the international system, limiting the frequency and intensity of war, and creating new international organizations, regimes, and norms to guide behavior.[22] We may not be fully trapped forever in the realist's assumptions; the challenge is to modify them now, at the end of the cold war and before the occurrence of ecological disaster or nuclear war.

Although the state system is vast and nation-states continue to play on center stage, the actions of individuals also have an impact on the future. Changes in our own conceptions of our interest and inclusion of others in a larger or long-term way will make a difference, as will changes in the demands we make on our governments. New social and political structures can be created to channel individual self-interests into collective benefits. We hope you will come away from this book with a deeper

---

[22] See Peter Wallensteen, "Universalism vs. Particularism: On the Limits of Major Power Order," *Journal of Peace Research* 21 (1984), 243–257, and John Vasquez, *The War Puzzle* (Cambridge, England: Cambridge University Press, 1993), especially chap. 8.

understanding of what the world looks like and how it works, as well as with a concern to make it work better.

> The creative personality is one that always looks on the world as fit for change and on himself as an instrument for change. . . . If the world is perfectly all right the way it is, you have no place in it.[23]

---

[23] Jacob Bronowski, *The Origins of Knowledge and Imagination* (New Haven, Conn.: Yale University Press, 1978), p. 123.

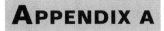

# APPENDIX A

## CHRONOLOGY OF INTERNATIONAL EVENTS

| | |
|---|---|
| 1804 | Napoleon becomes emperor of France. |
| 1812 | Napoleon invades Russia: disastrous campaign ultimately leads to French defeat. |
| 1814–1815 | Congress of Vienna: victorious powers reconstitute European order. |
| 1823 | Monroe Doctrine: President James Monroe declares the Western Hemisphere "off limits" to European interference. |
| 1846 | Mexican war: the United States defeats Mexico, annexes New Mexico and California (war ends February 1848). |
| 1848 | *Communist Manifesto* published by Karl Marx and Friedrich Engels. Antimonarchical liberal revolutions in France, Prussia, Austria-Hungary, and the Italian states. |
| 1852 | Napoleon III establishes the Second French Empire. |
| 1853 | Japan opened to West by American Commodore Matthew Perry. |
| 1854–1856 | Crimean War: France and Britain ally with Turkey against Russia. |
| 1857–1858 | Sepoy rebellion: Indian soldiers revolt against British rule in India. |
| 1859 | Construction begins on Suez Canal (completed in 1869). |
| 1861 | Kingdom of Italy established after process of unification led by Sardinia; emancipation of serfs in Russia; U.S. Civil War (1861–1865). |
| 1864 | First International organized by Marx in London. |
| 1864–1870 | Lopez War: Argentina, Brazil, and Uruguay virtually destroy Paraguay. |
| 1867 | British North America Act creates Canada as a confederation; Marx publishes *Capital*. United States purchases Alaska from Russia. |
| 1870–1871 | Franco-Prussian war: German states, led by Prussia, invade and defeat France (completing a process of German unification that included the 1864 Second Schleswig–Holstein War against Denmark and the 1866 Seven Weeks' War against Austria). |
| 1871 | German empire established under leadership of Prussia; Wilhelm I becomes kaiser. |
| 1878 | Congress of Berlin: European powers meet to thwart Russia and carve up Ottoman Empire. |
| 1882 | Triple Alliance is formed by Germany, Austria-Hungary, and Italy. |
| 1894–1895 | Sino-Japanese War: Japan defeats China and becomes an imperial power with acquisition of Taiwan. |
| 1898 | Spanish-American War: the United States defeats Spain, acquires the Philippines, and becomes a great power. |
| 1899 | "Open Door" policy forced on China by the Western powers. Boer War (1899–1902) between British and Dutch settlers begins in South Africa. |

| | |
|---|---|
| 1900 | Boxer rebellion: forces of the European powers, Japan, and the United States sent to China to put down revolt against foreign penetration. |
| 1904–1907 | Entente Cordiale signed between France and England. (1907: Russia joins and Triple Entente is formed.) Russo-Japanese War: Japan defeats Russia, becomes great power (1904–1905). |
| 1911 | Chinese Revolution led by Sun Yat-sen removes emperor and establishes a republic. |
| 1912–1913 | First and Second Balkan wars drive Turkey from Europe. |
| 1914 | June: Assassination of Archduke Franz Ferdinand of Austria-Hungary. August: World War I breaks out between Triple Entente and Central Powers; Panama Canal opens. |
| 1917 | April: United States enters World War I on the side of the Allies. November: Bolshevik Revolution in Russia, led by Vladimir Ilyich Lenin. |
| 1918 | March: Treaty of Brest-Litovsk: Bolshevik government of Russia signs separate peace with Germany. November: Armistice signed; World War I ends. |
| 1919 | Treaty of Versailles negotiated by victors of World War I (signed by Germans in June). |
| 1920 | January: League of Nations, created by Treaty of Versailles, established in Geneva; United States does not join. |
| 1922 | October: Benito Mussolini and Fascist party come to power in Italy. December: Union of Soviet Socialist Republics is officially created, the first communist state. |
| 1923 | October: Kemal Ataturk's westernized Turkish Republic officially proclaimed. |
| 1924 | January: Lenin dies; Joseph Stalin emerges as Soviet leader. |
| 1929 | October: Great Depression begins with the collapse of the New York stock market. |
| 1931 | September: Japan occupies Manchuria. |
| 1933 | January: Adolph Hitler comes to power in Germany. |
| 1934–1935 | Mao Zedong leads the Red Army on the Long March in China. |
| 1936 | July: Spanish Civil War begins; clash between fascists and communists is a precursor of World War II (Spanish Civil War ends January 1939 with fascist Francisco Franco as ruler of Spain). November: Rome-Berlin-Tokyo Axis formed (formalized in 1937 treaty). |
| 1938 | September: Munich agreement—French and British appease Germany over claims to Czechoslovakia. |
| 1939 | August: Germany and the Soviet Union sign a nonaggression pact. September: Germany invades Poland, World War II begins. |
| 1941 | December: Japan attacks Pearl Harbor, United States enters World War II. |
| 1944 | July: Bretton Woods meeting establishes postwar economic system. |
| 1945 | February: Yalta Conference—Churchill, Roosevelt, and Stalin plan postwar Europe. March: Arab League established. May 8: V-E (Victory in Europe) Day marking German surrender. June: United Nations charter signed in San Francisco. August: Hiroshima destroyed by first atomic bomb used in war; August 15, V-J (Victory in Japan) Day, Japanese surrender. |
| 1947 | June: Marshall Plan for economic recovery of Europe proposed. August: British leave Indian subcontinent; India and Pakistan separate and become independent. |
| 1948 | February—Communists seize power in Czechoslovakia. May: Israel established as an independent state; first Arab–Israeli war (ends January 1949); Organization of American States (OAS) established. June: Berlin blockade; Soviets bar Western access to Berlin (Allies supply city by airlift, blockade ends May 1949). |

1949 April: North Atlantic Treaty Organization (NATO) established. August: Soviet Union explodes its first atomic weapon. October: People's Republic of China proclaimed.

1950 June: North Korea invades the South; Korean War begins. October: Communist China enters Korean War.

1951 March: European Coal and Steel Community formed (forerunner of European Economic Community).

1952 November: United States explodes the first hydrogen (thermonuclear) bomb.

1953 March: Stalin dies. July: Korean armistice signed.

1954 July: Geneva settlement ends French rule in Indochina; Vietnam divided into North and South. September: Southeast Asia Treaty Organization (SEATO) formed.

1955 May: West Germany joins NATO; Warsaw Treaty Organization (Warsaw Pact) established.

1956 July: Gamal Abdal Nasser nationalizes Suez Canal. October: Hungarian revolt against communist rule crushed by Soviet troops. October–November: Britain, France, and Israel invade Egypt (Suez War).

1957 March: European Economic Community (Common Market) established by the Treaty of Rome. October: Soviet Union launches Sputnik, first artificial satellite.

1958 June: Charles de Gaulle takes over leadership of France (elected president in January 1959). July: United States sends troops to Lebanon, Britain sends troops to Jordan to forestall radical takeovers.

1959 January: Fidel Castro leads the overthrow of President Fulgencio Batista in Cuba.

1960 February: France explodes an atomic weapon. July: The Republic of the Congo becomes independent; civil war begins.

1961 April: United States sponsors unsuccessful Bay of Pigs invasion of Cuba. August: East Germany builds the Berlin Wall.

1962 October: Cuban missile crisis. October–November: China and India fight border war.

1963 November: President John F. Kennedy assassinated in Dallas.

1964 October: Nikita Khrushchev deposed by Leonid Brezhnev and Aleksei Kosygin; China explodes its first atomic bomb.

1965 April: United States sends troops to Dominican Republic to prevent radical takeover. July: President Lyndon B. Johnson announces major U.S. buildup of 125,000 troops in Vietnam. September: War between India and Pakistan over Kashmir begins. November: White-dominated government of Rhodesia unilaterally declares independence from Britain; United Nations imposes economic sanctions.

1966 April: Mao-inspired Cultural Revolution begins in China.

1967 May: Biafran civil war begins; Nigerian government ultimately defeats attempt at secession (ends January 1970). June: Six-Day War between Israel and Egypt, Jordan, and Syria.

1968 July: Nonproliferation treaty signed by United States, the Soviet Union, and Britain. September: Soviet and Warsaw Pact troops invade Czechoslovakia.

1969 March: Soviet-Chinese conflict erupts into border fighting at the Ussuri River. July: American Neil Armstrong is first human being to walk on the moon.

1970 September: Marxist Salvador Allende elected president of Chile (killed during a coup to overthrow his government in September 1973).

1971 October: People's Republic of China admitted to United Nations. December: Bangladesh established by breakaway of East Pakistan after civil war and India-Pakistan War.

1972    January: Britain, the Republic of Ireland, and Denmark join European Economic Community. February: U.S. President Richard Nixon visits People's Republic of China. May: United States and the Soviet Union sign strategic arms limitation treaty (SALT I).

1973    June: East and West Germany establish diplomatic relations. October: Yom Kippur War between Israel and Egypt and Syria (ends in November). November: Arab members of OPEC embargo oil to United States, Japan, and Western Europe and begin series of price hikes.

1974    May: India explodes nuclear device. August: Nixon resigns as president of United States after Watergate affair.

1975    April: Serious fighting begins in civil war in Lebanon; Saigon taken by communist forces, and Indochina War ends with collapse of U.S.–backed South Vietnam and Cambodia. June: Indira Gandhi imposes emergency rule in India and arrests opposition. August: European Agreement on Security and Cooperation signed in Helsinki. November: Angola becomes independent from Portugal after long guerrilla war; struggle between liberation movements supported by different countries (including Cuban troops).

1976    September: Mao Zedong dies.

1977    March: Gandhi allows free elections in India; opposition wins. August: United States and Panama sign treaty to cede Panama Canal to Panama (ratified March 1978). November: Egyptian president Anwar Sadat makes dramatic trip to Israel.

1978    August: China and Japan sign treaty of peace and friendship. December: United States and People's Republic of China establish full diplomatic relations.

1979    January: Shah resigns in Iran; Ayatollah Khomeini forms revolutionary government in February. February: War breaks out between two communist states as China invades Vietnam. March: Egyptian–Israeli peace treaty signed at Camp David. June: President Jimmy Carter and Brezhnev sign SALT II in Vienna. July: Sandinista rebels overthrow dictator Anastasio Somoza in Nicaragua. November: Iranian "students" and government seize U.S. embassy personnel as hostages. December: Soviet troops invade Afghanistan. Agreement reached on independence for Zimbabwe (Rhodesia) under black government; UN-imposed economic sanctions lifted.

1980    September: Iraq attacks Iran. October: Strikes by Polish workers' union (Solidarity) force extensive concessions from government. November: "Gang of Four" put on trial in China amid criticism of Mao Zedong; Ronald Reagan elected president, says United States will observe but not ratify SALT II.

1981    January: Greece joins European Economic Community. October: Sadat assassinated by Moslem extremists; succeeded by Vice President Hosni Mubarak. December: General Wojciech Jaruzelski declares martial law in Poland and arrests Solidarity members; United States imposes economic sanctions on Poland and the Soviet Union.

1982    April: Argentina seizes Falkland Islands; British naval and air force retakes them by June. May: Spain becomes sixteenth member of NATO. November: Brazil holds free congressional elections; Brezhnev dies, is succeeded by Yuri Andropov, in turn by Konstantin Chernenko (February 1984). December: Final act of the Law of the Sea Convention signed by 117 states, not including the United States.

1983    September: Korean Airlines civilian passenger plane shot down by the Soviet Union over Soviet territory. October: Nearly 300 French and U.S. troops of peacekeeping force killed by terrorist bombs in Lebanon; United States invades Grenada to overthrow Marxist government. December: Brazil reaches agreement to reschedule debt.

1984    October: Prime Minister Indira Gandhi assassinated.

1985    March: Chernenko dies, is succeeded by Mikhail Gorbachev; civilian government restored in Brazil.

1986    January: Spain and Portugal join European Community; U.S. space shuttle *Challenger* explodes. May: Nuclear accident at Chernobyl power station in the Soviet Union.

1987    January: Gorbachev calls for glasnost and political reforms; United States and the Soviet Union sign INF Treaty to eliminate intermediate range missiles in December. September: Treaty to protect the ozone layer is approved.

1988    May: Soviet troops begin withdrawal from Afghanistan. August: Iran and Iraq agree to cease-fire.

1989    April: Chinese students rally in Beijing, marking onset of democracy movement (in June pro-democracy movement is crushed as troops kill thousands). November: Berlin Wall falls; subsequently, barriers to the West are thrown open thoughout Eastern Europe.

1990    February: South African government legalizes the African National Congress and Nelson Mandela is freed from jail. March: Communist party loses its monopoly in the Soviet Union; Namibia becomes independent. August: Iraq invades Kuwait; UN votes a trade embargo against Iraq. October: East and West Germany unite. November: The UN authorizes the use of force against Iraq; CSCE summit meeting ends the cold war with conventional arms agreement (Warsaw Pact dissolves in July 1991).

1991    January: UN coalition, led by the United States, launches air war against Iraq; retakes Kuwait in four-day ground campaign in February. June: South Africa repeals land laws that are central to apartheid; fighting erupts in Yugoslavia over Slovenian and Croatian secession; Boris Yeltsin elected president of the Russian Republic. August: Attempted KGB/military coup to oust Gorbachev fails. December: European Community leaders agree to closer integration. Union of Soviet Socialist Republics dissolved.

1992    March: Referendum among South African whites endorses new consititution and end to minority rule. June: Earth Summit held in Rio de Janiero, Brazil. December: First U.S. troops in Operation Restore Hope arrive in Somalia; United States, Canada and Mexico sign NAFTA treaty.

1993:   January: United States and Russia sign START II nuclear arms agreement. September: Israeli Prime Minister Rabin and PLO Chairman Arafat agree to framework for interim Palestinian self-rule. November: European Community's Maastricht Treaty goes into effect. December: The Uruguay Round of GATT officially concludes; a joint Irish-British framework for peace in Northern Ireland is issued. IRA announces cease-fire in August 1994

1994:   January: NATO endorses "partnership for peace" plan, which would include former Warsaw Pact members. March: United States ends peace-keeping mission in Somalia. April: Civil war and massive ethnic violence breaks out in Rwanda. May: Nelson Mandela and ANC emerge victorious in South Africa's first universal suffrage elections; PLO asssumes self-rule in Gaza and parts of the West Bank. July: Israel and Jordan formally end state of war; UN Security Council approves U.S.–led invasion of Haiti to restore democracy (Aristide reinstated as president in October). December: Russian army invades breakaway republic of Chechnya.

1995:   January: The World Trade Organization (WTO) begins its work as successor to GATT; Austria, Finland, and Sweden officially enter the European Union, bringing EU membership to 15. February: The United Kingdom and Ireland agree on a peace framework for Northern Ireland. May: Representatives of over 170 countries approve the indefinite extension of the Nonproliferation Treaty. July: The United States opens full diplomatic relations with Vietnam. August: Croatian armed forces reoccupy Serbian controlled regions; 200,000 Serb refugees flee. September: The United Nations General Assembly commemorates its 50th Anniversary.

# APPENDIX B

## CHARACTERISTICS OF STATES IN THE CONTEMPORARY INTERNATIONAL SYSTEM

Appendix B lists all of the independent states in the international system as of January 1995. Unless noted otherwise, data are from World Bank, *The World Bank Atlas, 1995* (Washington, DC: The World Bank, 1994). Some figures are estimates calculated from data of previous years.

**1.** *Date of independence.* The date of independence is provided for all states that became independent after 1816 (the conclusion of the Napoleonic Wars). If no date is provided, that state was independent before 1816. Most data are from Bruce Russett, J. David Singer, and Melvin Small, "National Political Units in the Twentieth Century: A Standardized List," *American Political Science Review* 62, 4 (1968), 932–951; some data are from *Information Please Almanac* (Boston: Houghton Mifflin, 1991) and the Central Intelligence Agency, *The World Factbook, 1994–95* (Washington: Brassey's, 1994).

**2.** *Population.* The figures are in millions for 1993.

**3.** *Area.* The figures are for thousands of square kilometers. One square kilometer equals 0.386 square mile. Some data are from the CIA, *The World Factbook, 1994–95.*

**4.** *Density.* Number of people per square kilometer of area.

**5.** *GNP.* The figures are in millions of international dollars, calculated from World Bank 1993 PPP (purchasing power parity) per capita data.

**6.** *GNP/capita.* GNP divided by population (GNP per capita), using World Bank PPP international dollars.

**7.** *Military expenditures.* This figure shows how much a state spent on its military establishment (in millions of U.S. dollars). Data are for 1991, from U.S. Arms Control and Disarmament Agency, *World Military Expenditures and Arms Transfers 1991–92* (Washington, DC: ACDA, 1994).

**8.** *Armed forces.* Number of people on active duty in the armed forces (in thousands). Data are for 1991, from U.S. Arms Control and Disarmament Agency, *World Military Expenditures and Arms Transfers, 1991–92.*

**9.** *Literacy rate.* Percentages of population over age 15 able to read and write (1990 data).

**10.** *Infant mortality.* Number of deaths of infants (under 1 year of age) per 1,000 live births. Data are for 1992.

**11.** *Life expectancy.* Expected life span at birth. Data are for 1992.

**12.** *Status of political freedom.* According to a number of indicators of political rights and civil liberties, states are labeled free (F), partly free (PF), or not free (NF). Data are from Freedom House as modified by the authors; ratings are for 1993.

A dash indicates that data is not available.

| Country | Date of independence | Population (millions) | Area (1,000 km²) | Population density | GNP (millions of PPP dollars) | GNP/capita (PPP dollars) | Military expenditure | Armed forces (thousands) | Literacy rate | Infant mortality | Life expectancy | Status of freedom |
|---|---|---|---|---|---|---|---|---|---|---|---|---|
| Afghanistan | — | 22.1 | 648 | 34 | — | — | — | 55 | 29 | 162 | 43 | NF |
| Albania | 1912 | 3.4 | 29 | 118 | — | — | — | 48 | 72 | 32 | 73 | PF |
| Algeria | 1962 | 26.9 | 2,382 | 11 | 118,012 | 4,390 | .52 | 126 | 57 | 55 | 67 | NF |
| Andorra | — | .06 | 0.5 | 126 | — | — | — | — | — | 11 | 78 | F |
| Angola | 1975 | 10.0 | 1,247 | 8 | — | — | — | 150 | 42 | 124 | 46 | NF |
| Antigua & Barbuda | 1981 | .07 | 0.4 | 168 | — | — | — | — | 89 | 20 | 74 | PF |
| Argentina | 1816 | 33.5 | 2,767 | 12 | 305,700 | 9,130 | 3.77 | 70 | 95 | 29 | 71 | F |
| Armenia | 1991 | 3.7 | 30 | 124 | 7,760 | 2,080 | — | — | 100 | 21 | 70 | PF |
| Australia | 1920 | 17.7 | 7,687 | 2 | 327,402 | 18,490 | 7.20 | 67 | 100 | 7 | 77 | F |
| Austria | 1918 | 7.9 | 84 | 94 | 149,216 | 18,800 | 1.64 | 44 | 99 | 7 | 77 | F |
| Azerbaijan | 1991 | 7.4 | 87 | 85 | 16,580 | 2,230 | — | — | 100 | 32 | 71 | NF |
| Bahamas | 1973 | .3 | 14 | 19 | 4,474 | 16,820 | — | — | 90 | 25 | 72 | F |
| Bahrain | 1971 | .5 | 1 | 544 | 7,333 | 13,480 | — | 8 | 77 | 21 | 70 | PF |
| Bangladesh | 1972 | 116.7 | 144 | 810 | 150,545 | 1,290 | .33 | 102 | 35 | 91 | 55 | PF |
| Barbados | 1966 | .3 | 0.4 | 650 | 2,844 | 10,940 | — | 0 | 99 | 10 | 75 | F |
| Belarus | 1991 | 10.3 | 208 | 50 | 65,628 | 6,360 | — | — | 100 | 15 | 71 | PF |
| Belgium | 1830 | 10.1 | 31 | 325 | 186,028 | 18,490 | 4.53 | 101 | 99 | 9 | 76 | F |
| Belize | 1981 | .21 | 23 | 9 | — | — | — | — | 91 | 41 | 69 | F |
| Benin | 1960 | 5.2 | 113 | 46 | 8,466 | 1,630 | .04 | 7 | 23 | 110 | 51 | F |
| Bhutan | 1949 | 1.5 | 47 | 33 | — | — | — | — | 38 | 129 | 48 | NF |
| Bolivia | 1825 | 7.1 | 1,099 | 6 | 16,954 | 2,400 | .15 | 33 | 77 | 82 | 59 | F |
| Bosnia/Herzegovena | 1992 | 4.4 | 51 | 86 | — | — | — | — | — | 19 | 71 | NF |
| Botswana | 1966 | 1.4 | 600 | 2 | 6,519 | 4,650 | .09 | 6 | 74 | 35 | 68 | F |
| Brazil | 1822 | 156.4 | 8,512 | 18 | 855,540 | 5,470 | 7.04 | 295 | 81 | 58 | 66 | PF |

| | 1984 | .28 | 6 | 47 | — | — | — | — | 77 | 7 | 74 | NF |
|---|---|---|---|---|---|---|---|---|---|---|---|---|
| Brunei | 1984 | .28 | 6 | 47 | — | — | — | — | 77 | 7 | 74 | NF |
| Bulgaria | 1908 | 8.5 | 111 | 76 | 31,552 | 3,730 | .22 | 107 | 93 | 16 | 71 | F |
| Burkina Faso | 1960 | 9.8 | 274 | 36 | 7,864 | 800 | .07 | 10 | 18 | 132 | 48 | PF |
| Burundi | 1962 | 6.0 | 28 | 213 | 3,943 | 660 | .02 | 12 | 50 | 106 | 48 | NF |
| Cambodia | 1953 | 9.6 | 181 | 53 | — | — | — | 99 | 35 | 116 | 51 | PF |
| Cameroon | 1960 | 12.6 | 475 | 27 | 25,979 | 2,060 | .25 | 24 | 54 | 61 | 56 | NF |
| Canada | 1920 | 27.8 | 9,976 | 3 | 567,704 | 20,410 | 10.22 | 86 | 99 | 7 | 78 | F |
| Cape Verde | 1975 | .40 | 4 | 100 | 728 | 1,830 | — | 1 | 66 | 40 | 68 | F |
| Central African Rep. | 1960 | 3.2 | 623 | 5 | 3,444 | 1,060 | .02 | 4 | 38 | 105 | 47 | PF |
| Chad | 1960 | 6.1 | 1,284 | 4 | 4,353 | 710 | .06 | 50 | 30 | 122 | 47 | NF |
| Chile | 1818 | 13.8 | 757 | 18 | 115,753 | 8,380 | 1.50 | 90 | 93 | 17 | 72 | F |
| China | — | 1,175.4 | 9,561 | 123 | 2,491,761 | 2,120 | 18.49 | 3200 | 73 | 31 | 69 | NF |
| Colombia | 1818 | 35.7 | 1,139 | 31 | 200,890 | 5,630 | 1.13 | 110 | 87 | 21 | 69 | PF |
| Comoros | 1975 | .53 | 2 | 264 | 697 | 1,320 | — | — | 48 | 89 | 56 | PF |
| Congo | 1960 | 2.5 | 342 | 7 | 6,094 | 2,430 | .09 | 9 | 57 | 114 | 51 | PF |
| Costa Rica | 1820 | 3.3 | 51 | 64 | 18,230 | 5,580 | .03 | 8 | 93 | 14 | 76 | F |
| Croatia | 1991 | 4.8 | 56 | 86 | — | — | — | — | — | 12 | 73 | PF |
| Cuba | 1902 | 10.9 | 115 | 95 | — | — | — | 297 | 94 | 10 | 76 | NF |
| Cyprus | 1960 | .7 | 9 | 81 | 11,231 | 15,470 | — | 10 | 94 | 11 | 77 | F |
| Czech Republic | 1918 | 10.3 | 128 | 81 | 79,487 | 7,700 | .53 | — | — | 10 | 72 | F |
| Denmark | — | 5.2 | 43 | 121 | 98,318 | 18,940 | 2.35 | 30 | 99 | 7 | 75 | F |
| Djibouti | 1977 | .57 | 23 | 25 | — | — | — | — | 48 | 115 | 49 | NF |
| Dominica | 1978 | .07 | 1 | 72 | — | — | — | — | 94 | 18 | 72 | F |
| Dominican Republic | 1844 | 7.4 | 49 | 152 | 24,128 | 3,240 | .06 | 21 | 93 | 41 | 68 | PF |
| Ecuador | 1830 | 11.3 | 284 | 40 | 47,959 | 4,260 | .16 | 53 | 96 | 45 | 67 | F |
| Egypt | 1922 | 55.7 | 1,001 | 56 | 196,780 | 3,530 | 1.21 | 434 | 48 | 57 | 62 | NF |
| El Salvador | 1821 | 5.5 | 21 | 261 | 12,930 | 2,360 | .17 | 60 | 73 | 40 | 66 | PF |
| Equatorial Guinea | 1968 | .45 | 2 | 224 | — | — | — | 1 | 50 | 117 | 48 | NF |

| Country | Date of independence | Population (millions) | Area (1,000 km²) | Population density | GNP (millions of PPPdollars) | GNP/capita (PPP dollars) | Military expenditure | Armed forces (thousands) | Literacy rate | Infant mortality | Life expectancy | Status of freedom |
|---|---|---|---|---|---|---|---|---|---|---|---|---|
| Eritrea | 1993 | — | 121 | 0 | — | — | — | — | — | — | — | NF |
| Estonia | 1991 | 1.5 | 45 | 34 | 10,606 | 6,860 | — | — | 100 | 13 | 70 | F |
| Ethiopia | — | 53.3 | 1,222 | 43 | 20,253 | 380 | .81 | 120 | 62 | 122 | 49 | NF |
| Fiji | 1971 | .76 | 18 | 42 | 3,962 | 5,220 | — | 5 | 85 | 23 | 72 | PF |
| Finland | 1919 | 5.1 | 337 | 15 | 77,247 | 15,230 | 2.09 | 32 | 100 | 6 | 75 | F |
| France | — | 57.7 | 547 | 105 | 1,120,716 | 19,440 | 42.00 | 542 | 99 | 7 | 77 | F |
| Gabon | 1960 | 1.2 | 268 | 5 | — | — | .22 | 10 | 61 | 94 | 54 | PF |
| Gambia | 1965 | 1.0 | 11 | 93 | 1,304 | 1,280 | — | 2 | 27 | 132 | 45 | F |
| Georgia | 1991 | 5.5 | 69 | 79 | 7,693 | 1,410 | — | — | 100 | 19 | 72 | PF |
| Germany | 1871 | 80.8 | 357 | 226 | 1,694,534 | 20,980 | 43.96 | 457 | 99 | 6 | 76 | F |
| Ghana | 1957 | 16.3 | 239 | 68 | 35,124 | 2,160 | .04 | 9 | 60 | 81 | 56 | PF |
| Greece | 1828 | 10.4 | 132 | 79 | 86,743 | 8,360 | 3.19 | 205 | 93 | 8 | 77 | F |
| Grenada | 1974 | .06 | 0.3 | 190 | — | — | — | — | 98 | 29 | 71 | F |
| Guatemala | 1839 | 10.0 | 109 | 92 | 33,971 | 3,390 | .10 | 43 | 55 | 62 | 65 | PF |
| Guinea | 1958 | 6.3 | 246 | 25 | — | — | .04 | 15 | 24 | 133 | 44 | PF |
| Guinea-Bissau | 1974 | 1.0 | 37 | 28 | 824 | 790 | — | 12 | 36 | 140 | 39 | PF |
| Guyana | 1966 | .8 | 215 | 4 | 1,389 | 1,710 | — | 3 | 96 | 48 | 65 | F |
| Haiti | — | 6.8 | 28 | 244 | — | — | .04 | 8 | 53 | 93 | 55 | NF |
| Honduras | 1821 | 5.6 | 112 | 50 | 10,548 | 1,890 | .19 | 17 | 73 | 49 | 66 | F |
| Hungary | 1918 | 10.3 | 93 | 111 | 64,353 | 6,260 | .62 | 87 | 99 | 15 | 69 | F |
| Iceland | 1944 | .26 | 103 | 3 | 4,530 | 17,160 | — | 0 | 100 | 6 | 78 | F |
| India | 1947 | 900.5 | 3,288 | 274 | 1,125,679 | 1,250 | 6.88 | 1200 | 48 | 79 | 61 | PF |
| Indonesia | 1949 | 187.6 | 2,027 | 92 | 587,654 | 3,140 | 1.98 | 285 | 77 | 66 | 60 | PF |
| Iran | — | 61.4 | 1,648 | 37 | — | — | 2.04 | 465 | 54 | 65 | 65 | NF |

| | | | | | | | | | | | |
|---|---|---|---|---|---|---|---|---|---|---|---|
| Iraq | 1932 | 19.8 | 435 | 45 | — | — | — | 475 | 60 | 58 | 64 | NF |
| Ireland | 1922 | 3.6 | 70 | 51 | 42,293 | 11,850 | .55 | 13 | 98 | 5 | 75 | F |
| Israel | 1948 | 5.3 | 21 | 251 | 78,634 | 14,890 | 5.42 | 190 | 95 | 9 | 76 | F |
| Italy | 1861 | 57.8 | 301 | 192 | 1,045,169 | 18,070 | 24.15 | 473 | 97 | 8 | 77 | F |
| Ivory Coast | 1960 | 13.4 | 322 | 41 | 18,968 | 1,420 | .09 | 15 | 54 | 91 | 56 | NF |
| Jamaica | 1962 | 2.4 | 11 | 220 | 7,245 | 3,000 | .02 | 3 | 98 | 14 | 74 | F |
| Japan | — | 124.8 | 372 | 336 | 2,632,981 | 21,090 | 33.60 | 250 | 99 | 5 | 79 | F |
| Jordan | 1946 | 4.1 | 98 | 42 | 16,449 | 4,010 | .37 | 100 | 80 | 28 | 70 | PF |
| Kazakhstan | 1991 | 17.2 | 2,717 | 6 | 64,727 | 3,770 | — | — | 100 | 31 | 68 | PF |
| Kenya | 1963 | 25.4 | 583 | 44 | 33,243 | 1,310 | .16 | 20 | 69 | 61 | 59 | NF |
| Kiribati | 1979 | .08 | 1 | 76 | — | — | — | — | — | 60 | 58 | F |
| North Korea | 1948 | 23.1 | 121 | 191 | — | — | — | 1,200 | 99 | 24 | 71 | NF |
| South Korea | 1948 | 44.1 | 98 | 450 | 432,189 | 9,810 | 10.75 | 750 | 96 | 13 | 71 | F |
| Kuwait | 1961 | 1.5 | 18 | 81 | — | — | — | 10 | 73 | 14 | 75 | PF |
| Kyrgyzstan | 1991 | 4.5 | 199 | 23 | 10,919 | 2,420 | — | — | 100 | 37 | 66 | PF |
| Laos | 1949 | 4.5 | 237 | 19 | — | — | — | 55 | 44 | 97 | 51 | NF |
| Latvia | 1991 | 2.6 | 64 | 40 | 13,380 | 5,170 | — | — | 100 | 17 | 69 | PF |
| Lebanon | 1946 | 3.9 | 10 | 386 | — | — | — | 36 | 80 | 34 | 66 | PF |
| Lesotho | 1966 | 1.9 | 30 | 63 | 3,418 | 1,800 | — | 2 | 74 | 46 | 60 | PF |
| Liberia | 1822 | 2.4 | 111 | 21 | — | — | — | 5 | 39 | 142 | 53 | NF |
| Libya | 1952 | 5.0 | 1,760 | 3 | — | — | — | 86 | 64 | 68 | 63 | NF |
| Liechtenstein | — | .03 | .02 | 150 | — | — | — | — | 100 | 5 | 77 | F |
| Lithuania | 1991 | 3.7 | 65 | 58 | 11,841 | 3,160 | — | — | 100 | 16 | 71 | F |
| Luxembourg | — | .40 | 0.3 | 1,323 | 11,715 | 29,510 | — | 1 | 100 | 9 | 76 | F |
| Macedonia | 1991 | 2.2 | 25 | 88 | — | — | — | — | — | 29 | 72 | PF |
| Madagascar | 1960 | 12.7 | 587 | 22 | 8,910 | 700 | .04 | 21 | 80 | 93 | 51 | PF |
| Malawi | 1964 | 9.3 | 118 | 79 | 7,256 | 780 | .03 | 8 | 41 | 134 | 44 | NF |
| Malaysia | 1957 | 19.0 | 330 | 58 | 164,246 | 8,630 | 1.46 | 114 | 78 | 14 | 71 | PF |

| Country | Date of independence | Population (millions) | Area (1,000 km²) | Population density | GNP (millions of PPP dollars) | GNP/capita (PPP dollars) | Military expenditure | Armed forces (thousands) | Literacy rate | Infant mortality | Life expectancy | Status of freedom |
|---|---|---|---|---|---|---|---|---|---|---|---|---|
| Maldives | 1965 | .24 | 0.3 | 787 | — | — | — | — | 92 | 55 | 62 | NF |
| Mali | 1960 | 9.2 | 1,240 | 7 | 4,894 | 530 | .08 | 13 | 32 | 130 | 48 | F |
| Malta | 1964 | .36 | 0.3 | 1,207 | — | — | — | 2 | 84 | 9 | 76 | F |
| Marshall Islands | 1986 | .05 | 0.2 | 265 | — | — | — | — | 93 | 50 | 63 | F |
| Mauritania | 1960 | 2.1 | 1,031 | 2 | 3,398 | 1,590 | .04 | 17 | 34 | 117 | 48 | NF |
| Mauritius | 1968 | 1.1 | 2 | 556 | 13,832 | 12,450 | .005 | 1 | 83 | 18 | 70 | F |
| Mexico | 1821 | 86.7 | 1,973 | 44 | 615,655 | 7,100 | .85 | 175 | 87 | 35 | 70 | PF |
| Micronesia | 1986 | .11 | 0.7 | 157 | — | — | — | — | 90 | 36 | 63 | F |
| Moldova | 1991 | 4.4 | 34 | 128 | 13,983 | 3,210 | — | — | 100 | 23 | 68 | PF |
| Monaco | — | .03 | 0.002 | 15,500 | — | — | — | — | — | 7 | 78 | F |
| Mongolia | 1921 | 2.4 | 1,565 | 2 | — | — | — | 31 | — | 60 | 64 | F |
| Morocco | 1956 | 26.7 | 447 | 60 | 87,378 | 3,270 | 1.27 | 195 | 49 | 57 | 63 | PF |
| Mozambique | 1975 | 16.9 | 802 | 21 | 6,428 | 380 | .16 | 65 | 33 | 162 | 44 | NF |
| Myanmar | 1948 | 44.7 | 677 | 66 | — | — | — | 200 | 81 | 72 | 60 | NF |
| Namibia | 1990 | 1.6 | 824 | 2 | 6,150 | 3,930 | .04 | — | 38 | 57 | 59 | F |
| Nauru | 1968 | .01 | 0.02 | 450 | — | — | — | — | — | 41 | 67 | F |
| Nepal | — | 20.4 | 141 | 145 | 23,449 | 1,150 | .05 | 35 | 36 | 99 | 54 | PF |
| Netherlands | — | 15.3 | 41 | 373 | 275,750 | 18,050 | 7.28 | 104 | 99 | 6 | 77 | F |
| New Zealand | 1920 | 3.5 | 269 | 13 | 53,280 | 15,390 | .82 | 11 | 99 | 7 | 76 | F |
| Nicaragua | 1821 | 4.0 | 130 | 31 | 8,243 | 2,070 | .63 | 20 | 57 | 56 | 67 | PF |
| Niger | 1960 | 8.4 | 1,267 | 7 | 6,836 | 810 | .02 | 5 | 28 | 123 | 46 | PF |
| Nigeria | 1960 | 104.9 | 924 | 114 | 155,242 | 1,480 | .31 | 94 | 51 | 84 | 52 | NF |
| Norway | 1905 | 4.3 | 324 | 13 | 82,450 | 19,130 | 3.29 | 41 | 99 | 6 | 77 | F |

| Country | | | | | | | | | | | |
|---|---|---|---|---|---|---|---|---|---|---|---|
| Oman | 1970 | 1.7 | 300 | 6 | 18,428 | 10,720 | 1.67 | 29 | — | 20 | 70 | PF |
| Pakistan | 1947 | 122.8 | 804 | 153 | 259,169 | 2,110 | 2.61 | 803 | 35 | 95 | 59 | PF |
| Panama | 1903 | 2.6 | 77 | 33 | 15,224 | 5,940 | .14 | 12 | 88 | 21 | 73 | PF |
| Papua/New Guinea | 1975 | 4.1 | 462 | 9 | 10,246 | 2,470 | .11 | 4 | 52 | 54 | 56 | PF |
| Paraguay | — | 4.7 | 407 | 11 | 16,232 | 3,490 | .06 | 16 | 90 | 36 | 67 | PF |
| Peru | 1824 | 22.8 | 1,285 | 18 | 71,367 | 3,130 | 1.02 | 123 | 85 | 52 | 65 | PF |
| Philippines | 1946 | 65.8 | 300 | 219 | 174,961 | 2,660 | .72 | 112 | 90 | 40 | 65 | PF |
| Poland | 1919 | 38.4 | 313 | 123 | 192,614 | 5,010 | 2.11 | 305 | 98 | 14 | 70 | F |
| Portugal | — | 9.8 | 92 | 107 | 97,397 | 9,890 | 1.92 | 86 | 85 | 9 | 74 | F |
| Qatar | 1971 | .5 | 1 | 520 | 11,913 | 22,910 | — | 11 | 76 | 26 | 71 | NF |
| Romania | 1878 | 22.8 | 238 | 96 | 66,235 | 2,910 | .39 | 201 | 98 | 23 | 70 | PF |
| Russia | — | 148.5 | 17,075 | 9 | 778,334 | 5,240 | — | — | 98 | 20 | 69 | PF |
| Rwanda | 1962 | 7.5 | 26 | 288 | 4,794 | 640 | .02 | 30 | 50 | 117 | 46 | NF |
| St. Kitts & Nevis | 1983 | .04 | 0.3 | 137 | — | — | — | — | 98 | 34 | 68 | F |
| St. Lucia | 1979 | .16 | 1 | 158 | — | — | — | — | 67 | 19 | 70 | F |
| St. Vincent & Grenadines | 1979 | .11 | 0.4 | 275 | — | — | — | — | 96 | 20 | 71 | F |
| San Marino | — | .02 | 0.06 | 400 | — | — | — | — | 96 | 6 | 81 | F |
| Sao Tome & Principe | 1975 | .13 | 1 | 125 | — | — | — | 1 | 57 | 65 | 68 | F |
| Saudi Arabia | 1902 | 17.4 | 2,150 | 8 | — | — | 15.20 | 191 | 62 | 28 | 69 | NF |
| Senegal | 1960 | 8.1 | 196 | 41 | 13,209 | 1,640 | .12 | 18 | 38 | 68 | 49 | PF |
| Seychelles | 1976 | .07 | 0.4 | 175 | — | — | — | — | 58 | 16 | 71 | PF |
| Sierra Leone | 1961 | 4.5 | 72 | 62 | 3,440 | 770 | .005 | 5 | 21 | 143 | 43 | NF |
| Singapore | 1965 | 2.9 | 1 | 2,867 | 58,687 | 20,470 | 2.32 | 55 | 86 | 5 | 75 | PF |
| Slovak Rep. | 1993 | 5.3 | 49 | 109 | 34,475 | 6,450 | — | — | — | 13 | 71 | PF |
| Slovenia | 1991 | 2.0 | 20 | 100 | — | — | — | — | — | 8 | 73 | F |
| Solomon Islands | 1978 | .35 | 30 | 12 | — | — | — | — | — | 44 | 62 | F |
| Somalia | 1960 | 8.5 | 638 | 13 | — | — | — | — | 24 | 132 | 49 | NF |
| South Africa | 1920 | 40.7 | 1,221 | 33 | — | — | 3.19 | 80 | 76 | 53 | 63 | PF |

| Country | Date of independence | Population (millions) | Area (1,000 km²) | Population density | GNP (millions of PPP dollars) | GNP/capita (PPP dollars) | Military expenditure | Armed forces (thousands) | Literacy rate | Infant mortality | Life expectancy | Status of freedom |
|---|---|---|---|---|---|---|---|---|---|---|---|---|
| Spain | — | 39.1 | 505 | 77 | 520,754 | 13,310 | 8.96 | 246 | 95 | 8 | 77 | F |
| Sri Lanka | 1948 | 17.6 | 66 | 267 | 53,395 | 3,030 | .39 | 88 | 88 | 18 | 72 | PF |
| Sudan | 1956 | 27.3 | 2,506 | 11 | — | — | — | 65 | 27 | 99 | 52 | NF |
| Suriname | 1975 | .41 | 163 | 2 | 1,486 | 3,670 | — | 4 | 95 | 37 | 69 | PF |
| Swaziland | 1968 | .89 | 17 | 52 | 1,501 | 1,690 | — | 3 | 68 | 108 | 57 | PF |
| Sweden | — | 8.7 | 450 | 19 | 152,983 | 17,560 | 4.74 | 63 | 99 | 5 | 78 | F |
| Switzerland | — | 7.0 | 41 | 170 | 164,797 | 23,620 | 3.48 | 22 | 99 | 6 | 78 | F |
| Syria | 1944 | 13.4 | 185 | 72 | — | — | 2.89 | 408 | 64 | 36 | 67 | NF |
| Tajikistan | 1991 | 5.7 | 143 | 40 | 8,128 | 1,430 | — | — | 100 | 49 | 69 | NF |
| Taiwan | 1949 | 21.1 | 36 | 586 | — | — | — | 424 | 86 | 6 | 75 | PF |
| Tanzania | 1964 | 26.7 | 945 | 28 | — | — | .15 | 40 | 46 | 92 | 51 | PF |
| Thailand | — | 58.8 | 514 | 114 | 375,885 | 6,390 | 3.27 | 283 | 93 | 26 | 69 | PF |
| Togo | 1960 | 4.0 | 57 | 71 | 4,187 | 1,040 | .05 | 8 | 43 | 85 | 55 | NF |
| Tonga | 1970 | .09 | 1 | 93 | — | — | — | — | 57 | 21 | 68 | PF |
| Trinidad & Tobago | 1962 | 1.3 | 5 | 256 | 11,346 | 8,850 | .30 | 2 | 96 | 15 | 71 | F |
| Tunisia | 1956 | 8.6 | 164 | 52 | 43,648 | 5,070 | .34 | 35 | 65 | 48 | 68 | PF |
| Turkey | — | 59.5 | 781 | 76 | 330,009 | 5,550 | 3.83 | 804 | 81 | 54 | 67 | PF |
| Turkmenistan | 1991 | 3.9 | 488 | 8 | — | — | — | — | 100 | 54 | 66 | NF |
| Tuvalu | 1978 | .01 | 0.03 | 300 | — | — | — | — | — | 27 | 63 | F |
| Uganda | 1962 | 18.0 | 236 | 76 | 15,142 | 840 | .02 | 60 | 48 | 122 | 43 | NF |
| Ukraine | 1991 | 52.1 | 604 | 86 | 210,128 | 4,030 | — | — | 100 | 18 | 70 | PF |
| United Arab Emirates | 1971 | 1.7 | 84 | 21 | 40,301 | 23,390 | — | 66 | 68 | 20 | 72 | PF |
| United Kingdom | — | 58.0 | 244 | 238 | 1,030,210 | 17,750 | 36.83 | 301 | 99 | 7 | 76 | F |
| United States | — | 258.1 | 9,363 | 28 | 6,387,059 | 24,750 | 286.11 | 2115 | 98 | 9 | 77 | F |

| | | | | | | | | | | | |
|---|---|---|---|---|---|---|---|---|---|---|---|
| Uruguay | 1825 | 3.1 | 176 | 18 | 19,983 | 6,350 | .20 | 25 | 96 | 20 | 72 | F |
| Uzbekistan | 1991 | 22.0 | 447 | 49 | 56,680 | 2,580 | — | — | 100 | 42 | 69 | NF |
| Vanuatu | 1980 | .16 | 12 | 13 | — | — | — | — | 47 | 45 | 63 | F |
| Venezuela | 1821 | 20.8 | 912 | 23 | 168,941 | 8,130 | 1.07 | 73 | 92 | 33 | 70 | PF |
| Vietnam | 1954 | 70.9 | 330 | 215 | 73,716 | 1,040 | — | 1000 | 88 | 36 | 67 | NF |
| Western Samoa | 1962 | .16 | 3 | 54 | — | — | — | — | 97 | 25 | 65 | F |
| Yemen | 1990 | 13.4 | 528 | 25 | — | — | 1.08 | 127 | 38 | 106 | 53 | PF |
| Yugoslavia | 1878 | 10.7 | 256 | 42 | — | — | — | 169 | 93 | 28 | 72 | NF |
| Zaire | 1960 | 41.0 | 2,345 | 17 | — | — | — | 60 | 72 | 91 | 52 | NF |
| Zambia | 1964 | 8.5 | 753 | 11 | 9,977 | 1,170 | .12 | 16 | 73 | 107 | 48 | PF |
| Zimbabwe | 1980 | 10.6 | 391 | 27 | 20,212 | 1,900 | .50 | 45 | 67 | 47 | 60 | PF |

# INDEX

Note: Page numbers in *italics* indicate figures; those in **boldface** indicate definitions; those followed by t indicate tables; and those followed by n indicate footnotes.